# Authorizations Made Easy

# Evaluation Form

**Your feedback on the *Authorizations Made Easy* guidebook is important to us.**

**Please complete and return this evaluation form as soon as possible. Thanks for your help!**

D1918842

**Please send to:**

**Mail:** SAP Labs, Inc.
R/3 Simplification Group
3475 Deer Creek Road
Palo Alto, CA 94304 (USA)

**Fax:** **(650) 849-4004**

**Email:** **simplify-r3@sap.com**

## General Impression

| On a scale of 1 to 10 (10 being most satisfactory), please rate the items listed to the right by circling a number. | | Poor ◂ | | | | | | | | | ▸ Very good |
|---|---|---|---|---|---|---|---|---|---|---|---|
| | Relevance of topics | 1 | 2 | 3 | 4 | 5 | 6 | 7 | 8 | 9 | 10 |
| | Ease of use | 1 | 2 | 3 | 4 | 5 | 6 | 7 | 8 | 9 | 10 |
| | Overall quality | 1 | 2 | 3 | 4 | 5 | 6 | 7 | 8 | 9 | 10 |
| | Organization | 1 | 2 | 3 | 4 | 5 | 6 | 7 | 8 | 9 | 10 |
| | Accuracy of information | 1 | 2 | 3 | 4 | 5 | 6 | 7 | 8 | 9 | 10 |
| | Overall usefulness | 1 | 2 | 3 | 4 | 5 | 6 | 7 | 8 | 9 | 10 |

## Questions

1. Would you recommend this guidebook? ☐ Yes ☐ No

2. Approximately how many person-days did you save by using this guidebook?
   - Consultant person days: ☐ 0-5 days ☐ 6-10 days ☐ 11-20 days ☐ 20+ days
   - Customer person days: ☐ 0-5 days ☐ 6-10 days ☐ 11-20 days ☐ 20+ days

3. What amount (in U.S. dollars) do you estimate you or the customer saved by using these guidebooks? Include consulting days saved in this dollar amount.
   ☐ $0-10,000 ☐ $10-15,000 ☐ $15-20,000 ☐ $20-30,000 ☐ $30,000+

4. By how many project days (estimated) were you able to cut your implementation time in this area?
   ☐ 0-5 days ☐ 6-10 days ☐ 11-20 days ☐ 20+ days

5. How did you use this guide (for example, as a tutorial and/or a reference guide)?
   ☐ Step-by-step tutorial ☐ General reference ☐ Refresher ☐ Training material
   Comments:

6. What did you like about this guidebook? Check all that apply.
   ☐ Ease of use ☐ Screenshots ☐ Step-by-step procedures
   ☐ Business examples ☐ Templates ☐ Explanations
   ☐ Learn a new way to use existing tools ☐ List of user role templates ☐ Other ____________

**Please fax your completed evaluation to (650) 849-4004**

AMEZ form version 1 01/20/00

| | |
|---|---|
| 7 | If there was anything you did **not** like about this guidebook, please explain: |
| | Comments: |
| | |
| | |
| 8 | If there is anything you feel would improve the overall usability of this book, what would it be? |
| | Comments: |
| | |
| | |
| 9 | What have been the most difficult areas in authorizations for you? How did the *Authorizations Made Easy* guidebook help you with those difficult areas? Please explain. |
| | Comments: |
| | |
| | |
| 10 | What additional authorizations-related topics should have been included in this guidebook? |
| | Comments: |
| | |
| | |
| 11 | Are there any other R/3 topics you would like to recommend for future Made Easy guidebooks? |
| | ☐ Archiving ☐ HR ☐ Plant Maintenance ☐ Asset Management |
| | ☐ User Exits ☐ EDI ☐ Other ____________ |
| | Comments: |
| 12 | What other areas of R/3 simplification do you feel SAP should address? |
| | Comments: |
| | |
| | |

## About Yourself

| | | | | |
|---|---|---|---|---|
| Name | | Job title | | |
| Company | | Check one | ☐ Consultant ☐ Customer ☐ Other | |
| Address (street, city, zip, country) | | R/3 Experience | Years | |
| | | Email | | |
| | | Phone | | |
| | | May we contact you? | ☐ Phone | ☐ Email |
| Would you like to join the authorizations focus group? | | ☐ Yes | ☐ No | |
| How did you find out about this guidebook? | ☐ AcceleratedSAP ☐ SAPNet | ☐ Simplification Group's web site ☐ Events (please explain) ____________ | ☐ Other ____________ | |

**Please fax your completed evaluation to (650) 849-4004**

AMEZ form version 1 01/20/00

# Authorizations Made Easy

## *User Role Templates and Generating Authorization Profiles*

Release 4.6A/B

SAP Labs, Inc.

Palo Alto, California

## Copyright



## Trademarks



Simplification Group
SAP Labs, Inc.
3475 Deer Creek Road
Palo Alto, CA 94304

*www.saplabs.com/simple*
*simplify-r3@sap.com*

Printed in the United States of America.
ISBN 1-893570-24-X

This book uses EcoFLEX™ lay-flat binding. With this lay-flat feature—developed by and exclusively available at Johnson Printing Service (JPS)—you can open this book and keep it open without it snapping shut on you. You need not worry about breaking the spine. EcoFLEX makes books like this one easier to use.

# Contents at a Glance

# Detailed Table of Contents

# Acknowledgments

I wish to express appreciation to the following individuals who provided time, material, expertise, and resources to help make this guidebook possible (in alphabetical order):

| | |
|---|---|
| **SAP AG:** | Norman De Leeuw, Mathias Kinzler, Erwin Rojewski, Markus Schmidt, Heiko Stock, Sven Schwerin-Wenzel, Thorsten Vieth |
| **SAP America:** | Maria Gregg, "Casper" Wai-Fu Kan, Daniel-Benjamin Fig Zaidspiner |
| **SAP Labs:** | Anil Jain, John Kanclier, Oliver Mainka, Gary Nakayama, Kurt Wolf |

Nihad Al-Ftayeh
SAP Labs, Inc., 2000

# Introduction

## Contents

# What Is this Book About?

This guidebook is designed to help you set up the authorization environment in the customer system using the Profile Generator (PG). It explains what you need to know to perform this task and helps you use the standard tools provided with your system.

This book does not cover authorizations for add-on components or New Dimension products. It also does not cover Internet-related authorizations (encryption, authentication, and credit card security).

This guide refers to Release 4.6A/B of the SAP R/3 System. All screenshots are from Release 4.6A unless otherwise noted.

The structure of this guidebook matches the setup of the authorization concept, progressing from a new R/3 installation all the way to an upgrade. If you upgrade from an older release see chapter 14, *Upgrade,* for more information.

The graphic below provides an rough overview about the R/3 authorization cycle. For a more detailed information on the authorization cycle and the tools used see chapter 1, *R/3 System Security and the Authorization Concept*.

This guide provides you with the following:

- The big picture (security and the authorization concept in R/3)
- Tasks you need to perform during and after installation of R/3 to facilitate the use of the PG
- Tasks you need to perform after an upgrade of the R/3 System
- All the essential steps for security implementation using the PG and Central User Administration
- Tasks to prepare for going live
- Appendixes with the most important SAPNet – R/3 Frontend notes for authorizations and the most frequently asked questions.

# Who Should Read this Book?

This guide was designed for the following people using the PG either in an implementation project or as an ongoing reference:

- **Basis Consultants** who install R/3 and set up the security at customer sites

- **Application Consultants** who want to start using the PG as the basis for their customer security implementation
- **Customer IT and help desk personnel**

## How to Use this Guide

Depending on your general SAP and authorization-specific knowledge, start with the following sections:

- If you have little or no knowledge concerning security and the authorization concept in R/3, start with chapter 1, *R/3 System Security and the Authorization Concept.*
- Everyone, even the experts, should read chapter 3, *Setting Up the Profile Generator.* Familiarity with this chapter ensures a complete setup before you actually start working with the PG.
- If you have already used the PG in Release 3.0F/3.1G/3.1H/4.0A/4.0B/4.5A or 4.5B we strongly recommend that you read the chapter *What's New in Release 4.6* and the appropriate section in chapter 14, *Upgrade.* In this chapter, we discuss the steps to be performed before you continue working with the PG after an R/3 System upgrade. We provide information for a smooth transition to your next release.
- Read chapters 1–9 at least once for information related to the implementation of security and using the Profile Generator. After that, you can browse the chapters on performing specific tasks.
- Before transporting activity groups, read chapter 7, *Preparing the R/3 Environment for Go-Live* carefully.
- Chapter 12, *Tips and Troubleshooting* helps solve ongoing authorization problems once you go live.

Certain terminology, user information, and special icons are used throughout this guide. The following sections explain how to identify and use these helpful features.

## Conventions

In the table below, you will find some of the text conventions used throughout this guide.

| Column Title | Column Title |
|---|---|
| *Sans-serif italic* | Screen names or on-screen objects (buttons, fields, screen text, etc.) |
| `Monospace` | User input (text the user types verbatim) |
| *Name1* → *Name2* | Menu selection *Name1* is the menu name, and *Name2* is the item on the menu |

### Sample R/3 Release 4.6 Screen

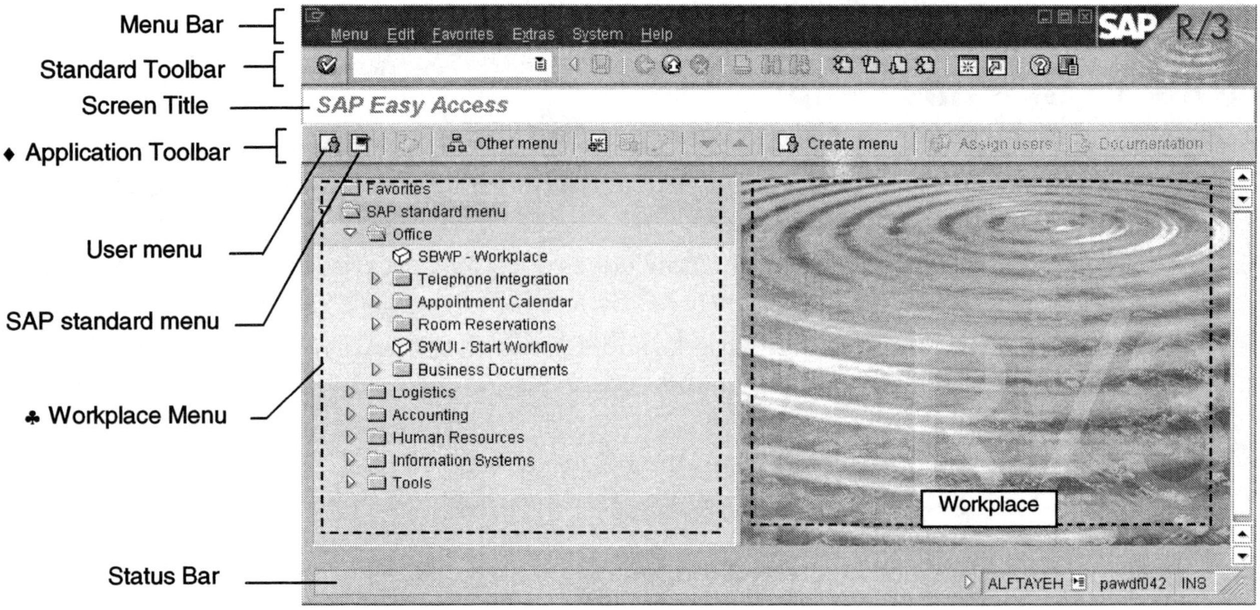


♦ **Application toolbar:**

The screenshots shown in this guide are based on full user authorization (SAP_ALL). Depending on your authorizations, some of the buttons on your application toolbar may not be available.

♣ **Workplace menu:**

Depending on your authorizations, your workplace menu may look different from screenshots in this guide which are based on SAP_ALL. The *User menu* and *SAP standard menu* buttons provide different views of the workplace menu.

In this guidebook you learn how to build user menus.

**Note:** In this guidebook, we show the technical names of each transaction. To match our settings, choose *Extras* → *Settings* and select *Show technical names*.

### Special Icons

Throughout this guide special icons indicate important messages. Below are brief explanations of each icon:

Exercise caution when performing this task or step. An explanation of why you should be careful is included.

This information helps you understand the topic in greater detail. It is not necessary to know this information to perform the task.

These messages provide helpful hints and shortcuts to make your work faster and easier.

# What's New in Release 4.6

## Contents

# Overview

This chapter provides a brief description of the new functionality in authorization-related topics in the R/3 Release 4.6.

For step-by-step procedures and detailed information on specific topics, please see the appropriate chapters, as referenced.

Tips & Tricks

For the latest information, you should always check the release notes for Release 4.6.

# User Role Templates

With Release 4.6A SAP delivers over 100 user role templates. The user role templates are predefined activity groups consisting of transactions, reports, and web addresses. You have three methods to work with user role templates:

- Use as delivered
- Copy and change them to suit your needs
- Create your own activity groups from scratch

Once users are assigned to one or more activity groups and log onto the system, they see their user menu. As shown in the graphic on the next page, this user menu contains only those items, such as transactions, reports, and web addresses, they need to perform their daily tasks. Users can also add their most frequently used transactions to a Favorites menu for quicker access.

# Flexible User Menus

As of Release 4.6A, the system displays a specific user menu in the form of a tree after users log on to the system (see graphic on next page). This user menu is based on the user role template or activity group the user is assigned to. Users no longer have to navigate through unnecessary R/3 functions for which they have no authorization. The company menu is no longer available as of Release 4.6A.

When a function is selected, it starts in the same session, replacing the user menu with the executed function. When a user exits a transaction or starts a new session, the specific user menu automatically reappears.

Along with the user menus, you can display a complete view of all functions delivered by SAP using the SAP standard menu. This complete view displays automatically if no user menus have been defined or if the administrator has chosen this option when defining new user menus.

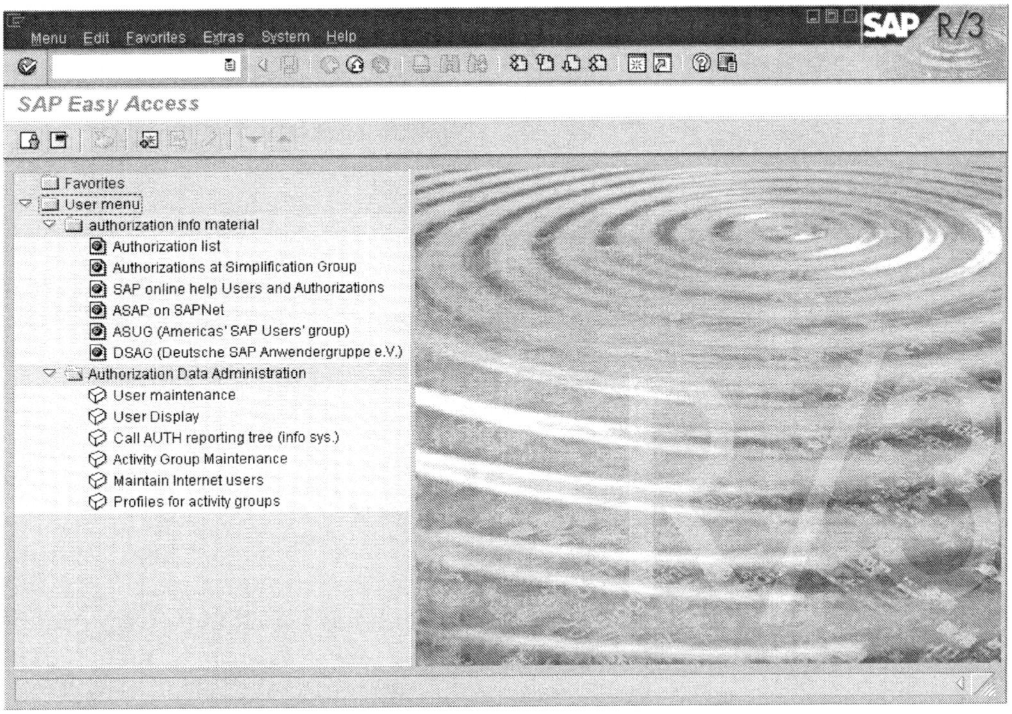


**User Menu Example**

Here are some examples of delivered activity groups:

| **Basis** | **Miscellaneous** |
|---|---|
| Authorization data administrator | CO: Sales manager |
| Authorization profile administrator | CO: Head of controlling |
| User administrator | FI: Accounts payable accountant |
| System administrator | FI: Accounts receivable accountant |
| Background administrator | LO Production planning: Worker |
| Database administrator | LO Production planning: Operator |
| Customizing project member | MM: Accounts payable clerk |

# Composite Activity Groups

As of Release 4.6A it is possible to create an activity group that contains a collection of other activity groups. This activity group is called a composite activity group. Composite activity groups contain only other activity groups and no authorization data.

# User Groups

Instead of using user groups to only distribute user maintenance among several administrators, you can now assign users to one or more user groups. The category *User group* can be used as a basis for better distribution of user data, increasing the speed of Central User Administration.

# Central User Administration

If a system group consists of different R/3 Systems with multiple clients, then the same users are created several times in every client and assigned to activity groups. Central User Administration is designed to carry out these tasks in a central system and then distribute this data to all systems in the system group.

The Global User Manager provides the system administrator with an overview of the users, existing user groups, the systems in the system group, and the activity groups. By simply using drag-and-drop, the system administrator can make changes in the overview. These changes take effect after distribution to dependent systems.

# Chapter 1: R/3 System Security and the Authorization Concept

## Contents

# Overview

In this chapter we explain the setup and maintenance of the R/3 authorization concept through the complete R/3 lifecycle.

The graphic below illustrates the R/3 authorization cycle and the tools used in various stages of the implementation.

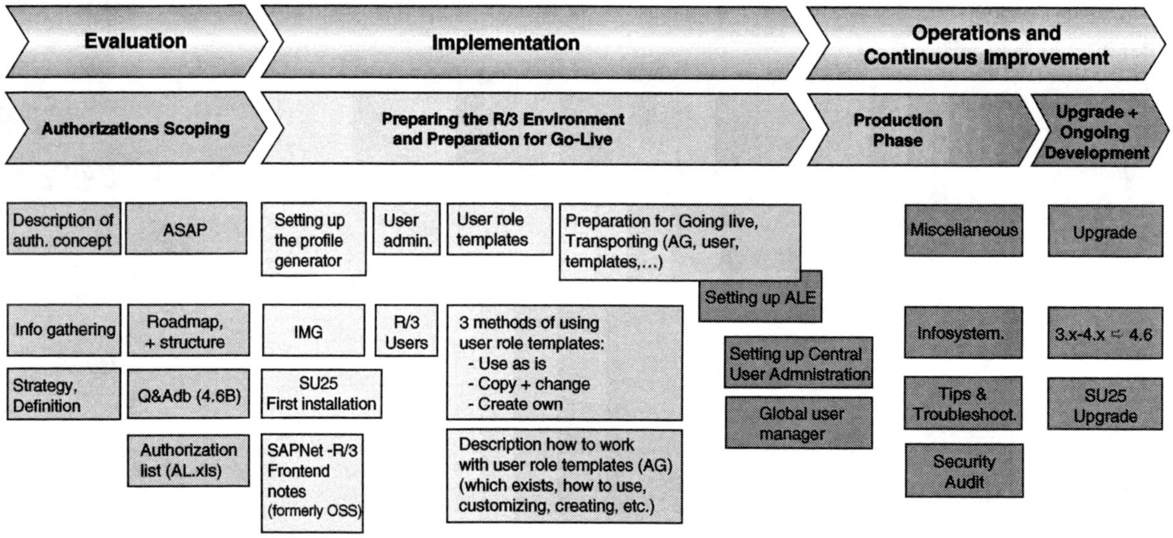


**Tools to Support the R/3 Authorization Cycle**

The guidebook is divided into four separate phases:

- *Authorization Scoping* (chapter 1, 2)
- *Preparing the R/3 Environment and Preparation for Go Live* (chapter 3, 4, 5, 6, 7, 8, 9, 10, 11)
- *Production Phase* (chapter 10, 11, 12, 13)
- *Upgrade and Ongoing Development* (chapter 14)

We begin with the R/3 authorization concept and the authorization design so you can meet requirements such as maximum security, easy user maintenance, and sufficient privileges for end users to fulfill their job duties. The authorization concept defines the functions to be carried out in various organizational units by people in specific positions. The concept also extends the R/3 online documentation on authorizations and profiles required for the various enterprise areas.

Implementing a multilevel client/server environment on WANs provides great flexibility. But, in this environment, highly sensitive data and programs are at a greater risk of being lost, manipulated, and spied upon than in a conventional mainframe environment. Even with local operation, this risk applies to all three layers (Presentation, Application, and Database) and becomes even more acute than WANs.

The following graphic shows how R/3 covers the aspects of data protection and security:

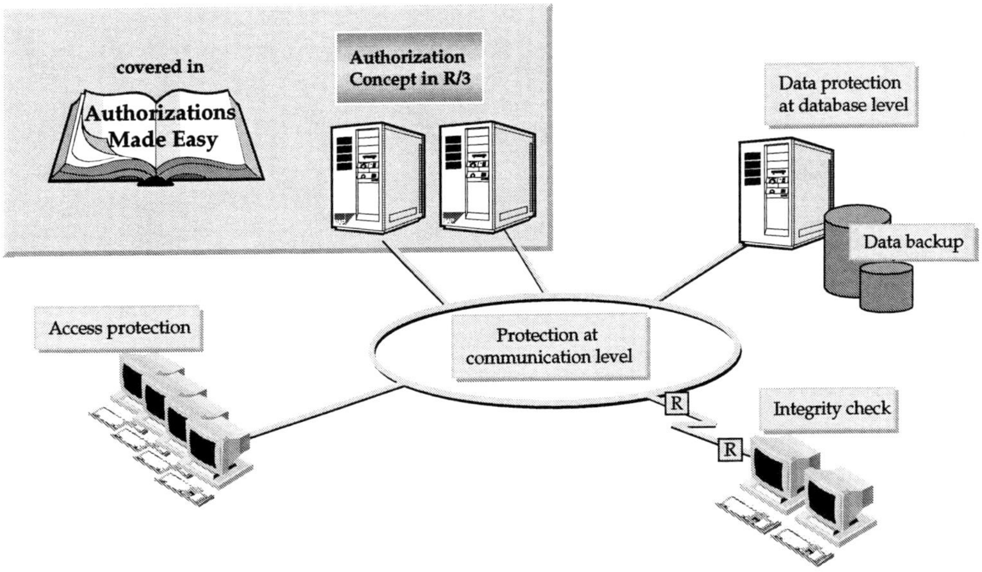


### Data Protection and Security

To meet the high demands of data protection and security, SAP provides the following R/3 security mechanisms:

- Authorization concept (this guidebook discusses an authorization design using the Profile Generator)
- Access protection and authentication outside of R/3, including authorizations between Web-based applications and R/3 (not discussed in this guide)
- Protection at network communication level (not discussed in this guide)
- Data protection at database level (not discussed in the guide)

# The Authorization Concept

The concept of authorizations in the R/3 System includes the following:

- Profile Generator
- Locking and unlocking transactions
- Locked records
- Structural authorizations (Not discussed in this version, see *Authorizations Made Easy* guidebook 4.5 A/B for information.)
- Data encryption (not discussed in this book)
- Locking system for changes

The R/3 authorization concept permits the assignment of general and/or finely detailed user authorizations. These assignments can reach down to the transaction, field, and field value level. These authorizations are centrally administered in user master records and most allow the handling of certain R/3 components applicable to specific operations. Actions by a user may require several authorizations. For example, to change a material master record, authorizations are required for the:

- Transaction "change"
- Specific material
- General authorization to work within the company code

The resulting relationships can become very complex. To meet these requirements, the R/3 authorization concept has been implemented as a form of pseudo-object-oriented concept with complete **authorization objects**. Each authorization object is a combination of authorization fields. An authorization always refers to an authorization object and can contain intervals for the field values. **Authorization checks** protect the functions or objects you choose. Standard-delivered R/3 has authorization checks embedded in the program logic. Programmers have to decide which aspects of their programmed functionality should be checked and how the check should be conducted.

Authorization administrators create authorizations that are assigned to users in collections called **profiles**. The **Profile Generator (PG)** usually generates authorizations and authorization profiles, although authorizations can also be manually inserted into a profile.

The following graphic shows the authorization components and explains their relationship.

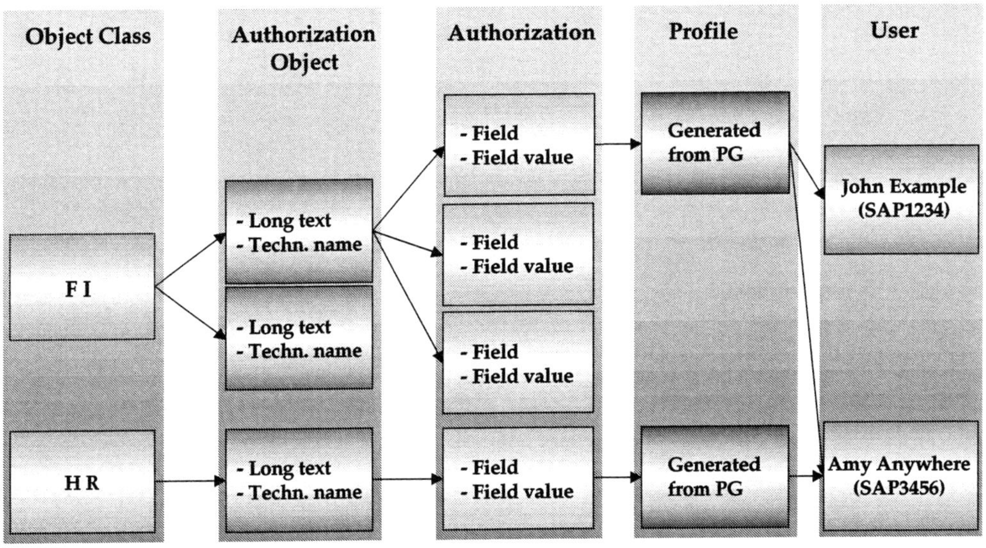


**SAP Authorization Concept**

## Authorization Object

As shown in the graphic "SAP Authorization Concept" above, objects allow complex user authorization checks. An authorization object works as a template for a to-be-defined authorization and contains a maximum of ten fields per object. Users may only conduct an activity if they satisfy the authorization check for each field in the authorization defined on a specific authorization object.

Authorization objects are grouped in an object class, such as Financial Accounting or Human Resources. Authorization objects can be created manually by choosing *Tools → ABAP Workbench → Development → Other Tools → Authorization Objects → Objects.* Because authorization objects are client-independent and defined in the ABAP Workbench, developers and programmers are generally responsible for creating new authorization objects.

Changes are necessary only if you "modify" your system and want to include AUTHORITY-CHECK calls or new authorization objects. You can only change or delete authorization objects added by your company. R/3 authorization objects may not be deleted or changed. To change an object, you must first delete all authorizations with which it is associated.

TechTalk

An AUTHORITY-CHECK is an ABAP command.

## Authorization Object Fields

Authorization fields for an object can be created manually by choosing *Tools → ABAP Development Workbench → Development → Other Tools → Authorization Objects → Fields.*

The fields in an authorization object are linked to data elements in the SAP ABAP Dictionary. The permissible values constitute an authorization. When an authorization check takes place, the system checks the values you have specified in an authorization against those required to carry out the action. Users may only carry out the action if they satisfy the conditions for every field defined for a specific authorization object.

Using the authorization maintenance functions, define all authorization fields in the system development environment. Changes are necessary only if you "modify" your system and the new system elements are subjected to authorization checks.

## Authorizations

An authorization allows you to carry out an R/3 task based on a set of field values in an authorization object. Each authorization refers to exactly one authorization object and defines the permitted value range for each authorization field of this authorization object. Authorizations are used in the user master record as profiles.

**By themselves, authorizations do not exist. They only have meaning inside a profile.**

| Field | Value |
|---|---|
| Customer type (CUSTTYPE) | * |
| Activity (ACTVT) | 02 |

Explanation: * = all possible values; 02 = display

Authorizations are used to specify permitted values for the fields in an authorization object. There may be one or more values for each field. Authorizations allow you to determine the number of specific values or value ranges for a field. All values or empty fields can be permissible values. Changes affect all users whose authorization profile contains that authorization. The R/3 authorization administrator can maintain authorizations automatically, using the PG, or manually. Once the authorization is activated, changes affect all users which contain the profile with the activated authorization.

Caution

Once generated, authorizations and profiles created with the PG are automatically activated. If you manually create and maintain authorizations and profiles, you must also manually activate them. Generated profiles and authorizations cannot be maintained manually with the conventional maintenance transactions *SU02* and *SU03*. However, we do not recommend the use of these transactions for profile and user administration anymore. You should use the Profile Generator instead.

## Authorization Profiles

User authorizations are not directly assigned with the PG to the user master records. Instead, these authorizations are assigned as authorization profiles. The authorization administrator can create authorization profiles manually or automatically.

Changes affect all users to whom this profile is assigned and take effect only when the user logs on. Users who are logged on when the change takes place remain unaffected during their current session, but when they log on again, their profile changes accordingly. A user's authorizations are loaded into the user buffer only when they log on.

Caution

> You cannot use the authorization profile maintenance transaction *SU02* to manually manipulate the PG-created authorization profiles. Although technically possible, never create a profile that contains both manually and automatically generated authorizations or profiles. We no longer recommend the use of transaction *SU02* for profile and user administration. You should use the Profile Generator instead.

### Naming Convention for Authorization Profiles

Caution

> Authorization profiles beginning with a *T* may contain critical *(S_USER*)* authorization objects. Also, use the PG to exclude further authorization objects (for example, HR data) from the profile.
>
> Note that we are talking about authorization profiles not activity groups.

TechTalk

> When you first save the authorization profiles, you are prompted to enter a profile name. The system proposes a name for the profile; however, only the first 10 characters (the profile torso) can be freely assigned. The number of profiles generated depends on the number of authorizations in each activity group. A maximum of 150 authorizations fit into a profile. If there are more than 150 authorizations, an additional profile is generated. It has the same 10-character torso as the profile name, and the last two digits (positions 11 and 12) are used as a counter.
>
> To avoid conflicts between customer-defined profiles and those profiles supplied by SAP, you should not use any name that has an underscore in the second position. SAP places no other restrictions on the naming of authorization profiles (refer to note *16466*). Therefore, if your company has its own naming conventions, you are allowed to overwrite the proposed name.
>
> The names of the authorizations are also derived from the profile torso. When more than one authorization is required for an object, the last two places are used as a counter. Based on the name for the authorization profile, the technical names for the authorizations to be created start with a *T* and comprise the internal number of the activity group and two end digits in the range 00–99. (*T-5000031800* is a sample authorization name.)

## User Master Records

Master records enable the user to log on to the R/3 System and allow limited access to the functions and objects. The user administrator maintains user master records by choosing *Tools → Administration → User maintenance → Users.*

## Authorization Checks

To conduct an authorization check, this check must be included in the transaction's source code. During the check, the system compares authorization profile values (assigned by the authorization administrator) to the values needed to carry out a program-specified action. A user may only carry out the action if the authorization check is successful for every field in the authorization object.

Authorization checks are triggered by the ABAP *AUTHORITY-CHECK* statement. The programmer specifies an authorization object and the required values for each authorization field. The *AUTHORITY-CHECK* then verifies if a user has authorization and if this authorization is from the user master record. The check is successful if an authorization is found that contains the values specified in the *AUTHORITY-CHECK*.

When R/3 transactions are executed, since the transaction calls other work areas in the background, many authorization objects are often checked. For these checks to be successful, the user must have the appropriate authorizations. Authorization checks can be disabled by setting check indicators in transaction *SU24* or by switching off objects globally.

### Activating and Deactivating Authorization Checks in Transactions

It is possible that users receive more authorizations than necessary, leading to an increased maintenance load. Authorization checks are conducted wherever they are written into a transaction's source code. Only by using the PG can check indicators be set to exclude:

- Certain authorization objects from authority checks
- Specific authorization checks in specific transactions
- An authorization object from being checked

All of these adjustments are possible without altering the program code. Prior to automatically generating the authorization profile, use the check indicators to control which objects appear in the PG and which field values are displayed. SAP delivers a default check indicator setting with R/3. For more information refer to chapter 12, *Tips and Troubleshooting*, the section *Reducing the Scope of Authorization Checks*.

# SAP* and DDIC Users

During your R/3 installation, clients *000, 001,* and *066* are created. In clients *000* and *001,* two special users are defined, but no special user is created in client *066*. Since these users have standard names and passwords, you need to secure these users from unauthorized usage (the EarlyWatch and CPIC users are not covered in this book).

The two special R/3 users are:

- *SAP**

  Defined as the standard R/3 superuser, *SAP** does not require a user master record. Rather, it:

- Is defined in the system code
- Has a default password (**PASS**)
- Has unlimited system access authorizations

When you install R/3, a user master record is defined in clients *000* and *001* with the initial password **06071992**. *SAP** user master record deactivates *SAP*'s* special properties. To prevent *SAP** misuse, change the password. We recommend, however, that you deactivate *SAP** and define your own superuser.

- *DDIC*

This user is the maintenance user for the ABAP Dictionary and software logistics. The user master record for *DDIC* is automatically created in clients *000* and *001* and has the default password **19920706**. System code testing allows *DDIC* special privileges for certain operations. For example, *DDIC* is the only user that can log on during an upgrade. To prevent *DDIC* misuse, change the password.

TechTalk

Use report *RSUSR003* to check whether the standard *SAP** and *DDIC* passwords have been changed. This report is restricted to users who belong to the user group *SUPER* with activity 02 and client administration.

# What Is the Profile Generator?

SAP's Profile Generator (PG) helps the authorization administrator create, generate, and assign authorization profiles. First released with 3.1G, the PG accelerates R/3 implementation by simplifying the task of setting up the authorization environment. The administrator only needs to configure the customer-specific settings; the PG manages other tasks, such as selecting the relevant authorization objects for consideration. The PG is fully integrated with R/3 and is available on all R/3-supported platforms. The PG represents yet another improvement of SAP's tool-based support and a reduction in R/3 implementation time.

The PG is an approach to defining the authorization environment. The administrator no longer uses the authorization objects to define the authorizations for various user groups; instead, authorization profiles are built around the functions to be performed in R/3. Based on the functions selected, the PG picks the relevant authorization objects and groups them in a new authorization profile.

Using functions to define authorization profiles:

- Speeds up the process
- Defines authorization profiles
- Simplifies administrator/user communication, allowing both the administrator and users to use the same R/3 function terminology

To use the PG, you first have to set it up. The one time set up involves the following steps:

1. Check if the SAP R/3 System parameter is set correctly to active.

2. Use *SU25* to initialize the tables *USOBT_C* and *USOBX_C* (and then customize them if desired).

For detailed information, please read chapter 3, *Setting Up the Profile Generator*.

Once the PG is set up, you can work with it. Before working with with the PG, it is useful to understand its components.

## Components of the Profile Generator

The PG has the following components:

### Activity Groups

An activity group is a collection of R/3 transactions, authorizations, and additional objects. You can assign an activity group to as many users as you want. You can create, display, change, copy, and transport activity groups.

### Composite Activity Groups

Composite activity groups are made up of a collection of activity groups. The users assigned to a composite activity group are automatically added to the activity groups during a comparison. Composite activity groups themselves do not contain any authorization data. Instead of having to assign each user to each activity group, you can set up a composite activity group and then assign the users to this group.

### Derived Activity Groups

You can use an existing activity group as a reference when creating a new one. The system transfers the transactions in one activity group to a new activity group—one that remains dependent on the first. You can display the hierarchy of the activity groups that inherit transactions from each other by choosing *Activity group → Where-used list*.

With an activity group derived from a different activity group, you cannot enter transactions directly. You cannot reset the definition of the initial activity group from which the derived activity group inherited its transactions. Passing on transactions only refers to the menu selection and not to the authorizations. You must maintain authorizations separately in each activity group; these are not passed on. It is also possible to transfer the authorization data of the previous activity group to the derived activity group as a copy.

### User Assignment

Users can be assigned to single activity groups or to composite activity groups which mostly represent job roles. Users that you assign to an activity group may execute the transactions, reports, or any other task in the activity group with the corresponding authorizations.

## Generating the Profiles

The administrator chooses the specific menu paths and functions for each user group. This selection determines the R/3 activities that users in each user group are authorized to perform.

Using the selected transaction codes, the PG determines the affected authorization objects. To simplify the creation of subsequent individual authorization profiles, R/3 contains default values for many authorization fields in specific authorization objects. For example, one possible access restriction might be the default value *Display*, limiting the user to display mode on certain transactions.

Additionally, the PG identifies the organizational levels that play a role in the extracted authorization objects and clearly displays these levels for the administrator. The authorization administrator may have to intervene and manually define the levels to which the users need access (for example, the company code).

The PG then places the specified levels in the authorization objects. At this point, a lot of authorization object fields for the new authorization profile have been filled, however there are still fields that need to be maintained. The authorization objects are displayed hierarchically in a special maintenance transaction. The administrator may adjust the remaining values, such as material type, order type, etc.

Within this maintenance transaction, the administrator can easily navigate from the overview screen to the lowest display level (the authorizations and their fields) and directly assign the values. Generally, permissible values can also be assigned at higher levels. The following utilities to specify the values are available at every level of the hierarchical display:

- Value selection from lists
- Checkboxes for simple activity selection
- Delete and copy functions

If administrators determine that no further authorization restrictions are necessary on a certain level, by choosing a button, the PG fills in the remaining values.

Finally, another menu item in the system assigns the users to the R/3 functions. In this process, the PG automatically copies all the corresponding authorization profiles to the user master record. Of course, users can be assigned multiple selections, which means that certain general authorizations need to be maintained only once and are available for assignment to all system users.

Integrating the PG in R/3 also enables the administrator to access the documentation on every authorization object directly from the PG. Furthermore, the PG can list all R/3 functions that check a specific authorization.

Tips & Tricks

**Requirements and Availability**
The PG runs on all supported platforms and has been available since Release 3.1G for general customer use. Starting with Release 4.5, it is already activated for use.

# What Is an Activity Group?

The process of security implementation with the PG is based on the creation of activity groups or a collection of linked or associated activities, such as tasks, reports, and transactions. An activity group is a "data container" for the PG to generate authorization profiles and usually represents a job role in your company. (However, customers often define activity groups somewhat differently. As such, there is no one concrete definition of an activity group, other than it is a data container for authorizations.)

Activity groups are defined by the customer performing the implementation and allow systematic organization and efficient maintenance of system activities.

The SAP Business Workflow, Personnel Planning and Development as well as the Report Writer and other reporting tools are tightly linked with the PG. SAP Business Workflow includes workflow tasks that can be linked to an activity group. Users assigned with access to a particular activity group really come from the HR-Personnel Planning and Development functionality. Furthermore, the plan version that is used in HR-Personnel Planning and Development is the same plan version used by the PG and Workflow.

Using an activity group as an information database reduces data entry time. Select the criteria, such as access rights, and divide the activities into appropriate groups. For example, you could decide to group activities by subject matter, such as personnel, payroll, or budgeting. Or, you could group activities by job classes, such as translation activities, computer programmer activities, or secretarial activities. You could also set up a combination of subject matter and job-oriented activity groups. After setting up activity groups, you can assign them to various R/3 objects.

## Activity Group Assignments

An activity group can be assigned to many users. One user can also be assigned to many activity groups.

An activity group can be assigned to the following types of users:

### R/3 login user IDs

An R/3 user is an individual who is recognized by the R/3 System and is allowed to log on. For the system to recognize users, their names must be entered in the user master record of the Basis component.

### Jobs

A job represents a general classification of work duties, such as administrative assistant, computer programmer, instructor, etc. Many employees in your company may hold the same job classification. (For example, there might be 20 people whose job is administrative assistant.) Positions are usually based on jobs. Anyone who holds a job automatically inherits the infotype settings, attributes, and properties of that job. Unless the activity groups grants general access rights such as the rights needed to work with SAPoffice, be careful when assigning activity groups to jobs.

### Positions

A position represents an employee's unique, individual assignment within a company (for example, marketing assistant, sales manager, etc.) Positions should not be confused with jobs. You can handle authorization management in an almost completely position-oriented fashion. All the access rights are then linked to the position, so it does not matter who fills this position. Once a user changes positions, and after the user master record is updated, the authorization profile automatically changes.

### Organizational units

Organizational units represent any organizational entity that performs a specified set of functions within a company. For example, organizational units represent subsidiaries, divisions, departments, groups, special project teams, etc. Identify the organizational structure at your firm by creating organizational units and identifying the relationships among the units. Anyone who is assigned to an organizational unit automatically inherits the infotype settings, attributes, and properties of this organizational unit.

Examples of units include:

- Subsidiaries
- Divisions
- Departments
- Groups
- Special project teams

Unless the activity groups grants general access rights, such as printing, be careful when assigning activity groups to organizational units. For example, if authority profiles tend to be fairly standard for all workers in an organizational unit, it may be most effective to assign activity groups and its profiles to organizational units. When exceptions occur for jobs or positions, create additional activity groups for them. If, however, authorities vary by job or position, it may be best to assign activity groups to the jobs or positions concerned. By creating organizational units and identifying the relationships between the units, you identify your company's organizational structure.

## What Is a User Role Template?

**User role templates** are activity groups in the standard R/3 System, delivered by SAP, that already contain transactions and reports from all application areas. These user role templates are ready to use. You have the option to use a user role template as is or copy and change it to your needs. If users are assigned to a job role and they log on to the system, they only see those tasks they are allowed to perform.

# R/3 Tools for Security Implementation

| Information Source | Location |
|---|---|
| Overview of important *SAPNet – R/3 Frontend notes* (formerly *OSS*) | Appendix A |
| Frequently asked questions (FAQ) | Appendix B |
| Overview of system profile parameters | Appendix C |
| Library/Online Documentation | Choose *Help* → *R/3 library* → *Basis* → *Computer Center Management System* → *Users and Authorizations* |
| Release Information | Choose *Help* → *Release notes.* |
| R/3 Security Guide | Note 39267 |
| Report Documentation | Report documentation can be accessed from the selection screen by either choosing *Help* → *Extended Help* or *System* → *Services* → *Reporting*, entering the report name, and then selecting *Goto* → *Documentation.* |
| Training courses | See *SAPNet* for current courses, *http://www.sap.com* |
| Glossary | Choose *Help* → *R/3 library* → *Glossary* for the entire glossary or choose *Help* → *Glossary* for a context-sensitive glossary. |
| Context-Sensitive Help | Move the cursor to a field or to a system message and press *F1.* |
| Knowledge Products | Note 61675 |
| ABAP Workbench Docuset | Note 60382 |
| SAP*Net* | *SAPNet* is an internet service that brings new information and communication channels between SAP and its customers. Log on by entering *http://www.sap.com/* on an internet browser and click the *Partner Customer* button. Click *Frequent users* and enter your *SAPNet – R/3 Frontend note* (formerly *OSS*) password. |
| SAP Labs/ Simplification Group | Simplification Groups web page *http://www.saplabs.com/auth* for updates, beta releases of new guidebooks, additional information, predefined activity groups, guidebooks for previous releases, etc. |
| *Accelerated*SAP Roadmap (ASAP) | The ASAP Implementation Roadmap recommends using the PG in its authorization design proposal. You can also find links to this guidebook from different locations in the roadmap structure. Inside ASAP, choose *Implementation Roadmap* → *Phase 3: Realization* → *Establish Authorization Concept*. |

# Case Study: Security Strategy in a Three-System Environment

## Development System (DEV)

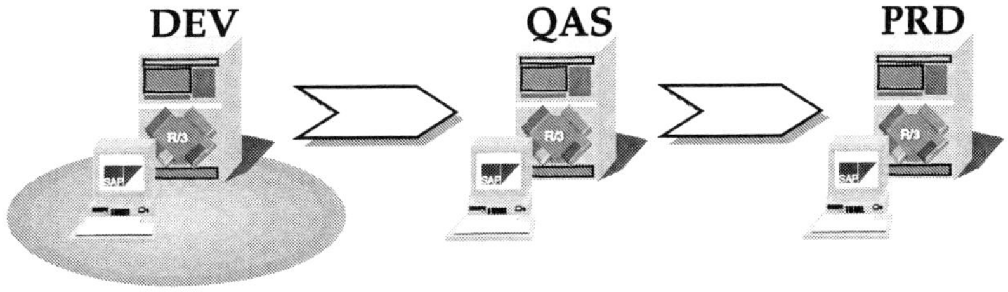


**DEV System in a Three-System Environment**

When the development system (DEV) is first installed, project members including configurators, developers, system administrators, and recent trainees comprise the bulk of R/3 users. SAP recommends the use of job-role templates. As the R/3 project progresses, the need to limit user access increases. In general, DEV system users have more access than quality assurance (QAS) or production (PRD) system users.

As configuration is done in DEV you can now use the new functionality of customizing activity groups to ensure that people are configuring only their own part of the system. (Please read chapter 6 for detailed information on customizing authorizations.)

Treat superuser accounts like "root" in UNIX. The *<YourCompany>_ALL* profile limits risk on the DEV system. System malfunctions due to excessive access can also cause project development delays.

You now control who creates and maintains:

- Users
- Profiles
- Authorizations

You also eliminate attempts to:

- Lock transactions
- Delete user sessions
- Stop work processes

This control maintains the system's integrity and stability. Using the PG, the authorization administrator develops end user profiles and authorizations in the DEV system. These profiles and authorizations will be transported to the QAS system for final testing before moving to PRD. The end user master records are usually created in PRD closer to the go-live date. The activity groups, together with the transported authorization data, are assigned to the end users as required in PRD. When you transport activity groups, this also transports the authorization profiles. These profiles do not need to be regenerated in the target system. However, you should compare the user master records when you import activity groups into the target system if users are already assigned. See chapter 7 for more information about transporting.

Maintaining documentation is also important because it:

- Helps future project rollouts proceed smoothly
- Is essential to pass security administrative functions to other project members
- Is required by auditors

The authorization administrator should work closely with the client copy administrators. When new clients are created, activity groups are not automatically copied. Since users, activity groups, authorization profiles, and authorizations are all client-dependent, the client copy administrator also needs to know which user master records to copy. See chapter 7 for more information about transporting.

The authorization administrator should also work closely with those in your company that function as change management administrators. Both administrators are important project control points. The system landscape, client landscape, and client roles should be clearly defined and presented to the project team. Development classes and authorization groups should be established for all new development. All administrators should complete appropriate SAP's training courses for the authorization environment they are trying to set up. We recommend that you attend courses and workshops immediately after the initial installation of your R/3 System.

Next, these administrators should conduct a project-specific workshop to both review the system and client landscape, and discuss the following control points:

- When development requests will move
- To which clients these requests will move
- Whose signatures will be required along the way

The authorization administrator should work closely with the developers to enforce security standards for new ABAP programs and transactions, which can be enforced through Change Management. All new customer-written codes should be assigned to an authorization group, with transaction *SE38* and *SE80,* the ABAP editor attributes screen. Unprotected customer-written programs and transactions in PRD always present problems.

The authorization administrator should involve the corporate auditors at this juncture.

Tips & Tricks

> We recommend involving the corporate auditors up front so their requirements are incorporated in the development efforts. It is always unpleasant to audit post-live projects. In the worst case scenario, projects should be halted until auditor requirements are met, and at a minimum, all of the original development work may have to be revised.

# Quality Assurance System (QAS)

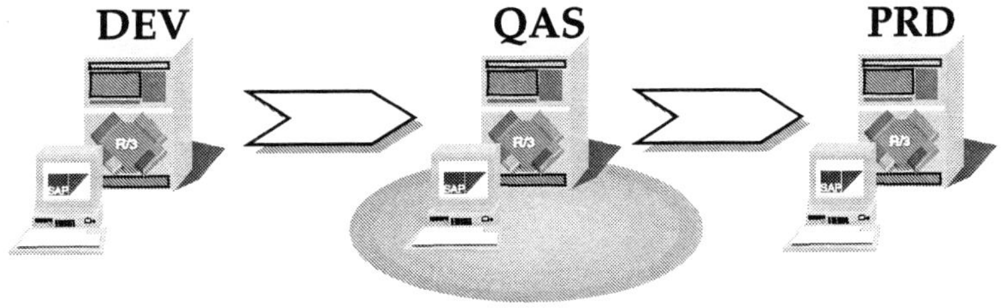


**QAS System in a Three-System Environment**

When the QAS system and client are created, the authorization administrator can start transporting the components of the authorization system (table *USOBX_C*, templates, activity groups and composites activity groups) from the DEV system to the QAS system (see chapter 7 on how to transport). Authorization profiles for imported activity groups no longer need to be regenerated, since the system can do this automatically now. Before moving the activity groups and authorization data to PRD, a final testing plan should be produced.

For example, an FI project team member may use a sample accounts payable user ID to:

- Confirm that the user has access to the specific transactions governed by each activity group to which the user is assigned.
- Ensure that these transactions match the company-defined role for accounts payable.
- Verify that the sample user ID does not have access to unauthorized transactions.

Some sites conduct a day-in-the-life test as part of their go-live plan, where end users log on to a preproduction environment and simulate real production. This process is an excellent way of testing the generated authorization profiles.

## Training Client System (TRG)

While many customers do not put their training environment on another system entirely, many do. You need to set up the appropriate authorizations for the training system as well. The appropriate authorization setup cannot be determined without first knowing from where the data that appears in the training system comes from (or how the system and training client were created.) For example, if the training system is a copy of the production environment or a copy of the client where conversions and interfaces were initially tested, it may be possible that the training system contains sensitive information such as social security numbers, converted payroll information, addresses, etc.

## Production System (PRD)

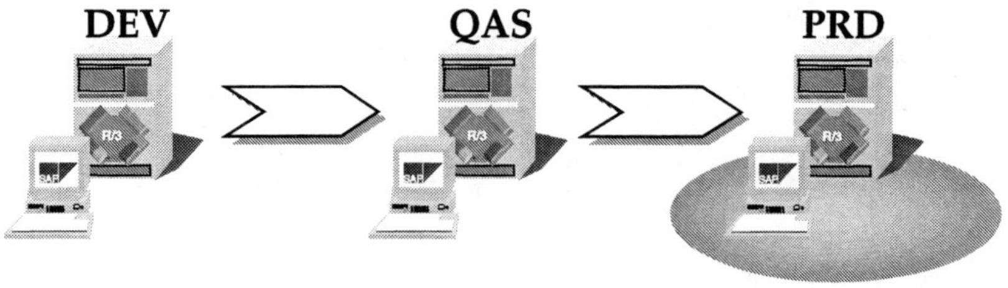


**PRD System in a Three-System Environment**

Once the activity groups and authorization profiles have been fully tested in QAS, and end user and project team approval has been provided, the components of the authorization system (table *USOBX_C*, templates, activity groups and composites activity groups) are moved to PRD (see chapter 7 on how to transport). Actual end user IDs can be created. A form that includes all of the pertinent information for user-ID creation, along with the proper signatures, is developed and distributed to the departments.

The authorization administrator should be a part of the go-live plan. The first days of going-live are hectic, and there should be a procedure to report access problems in production. The help desk is a good focal point. When users have access problems (for example, when users see the message: *No authorization for transaction XXXX*), they should execute transaction *SU53* to obtain the authorization required for this transaction. (Remember, since 3.1H, transaction *SU53* is also protected by object *S_TCODE*. See chapter 8, *Inserting Missing Authorizations,* for more details). A screen print should be sent to the help desk and the authorization administrator for evaluation. Once the application area owner approves the additional access, it is assigned to the user. Additional access means that the activity groups might be changed or that a missing authorization object may need to be manually inserted in the authorization profiles.

The authorization administrator should start planning for other project phases. This may include other rollouts to different locations, different plants, different modules, or R/3 upgrades. All of these rollouts should involve the authorization administrator.

# Setting Up the Authorization Administrators

We recommend you divide the system administration tasks, as shown in the graphic below, to ensure greater system security. For companies that have several people devoted to the authorizations component of R/3, this division makes good sense. SAP supports this approach with the user role templates for these administrators. In the standard R/3 System you can find the following templates:

| Administrator | User Role Template |
|---|---|
| Authorization Data Administrator | SAP_BC_AUTH_DATA_ADMIN_AG |
| Authorization Profile Administrator | SAP_BC_AUTH_PROFILE_ADMIN_AG |
| User Administrator | SAP_BC_USER_ADMIN_AG |

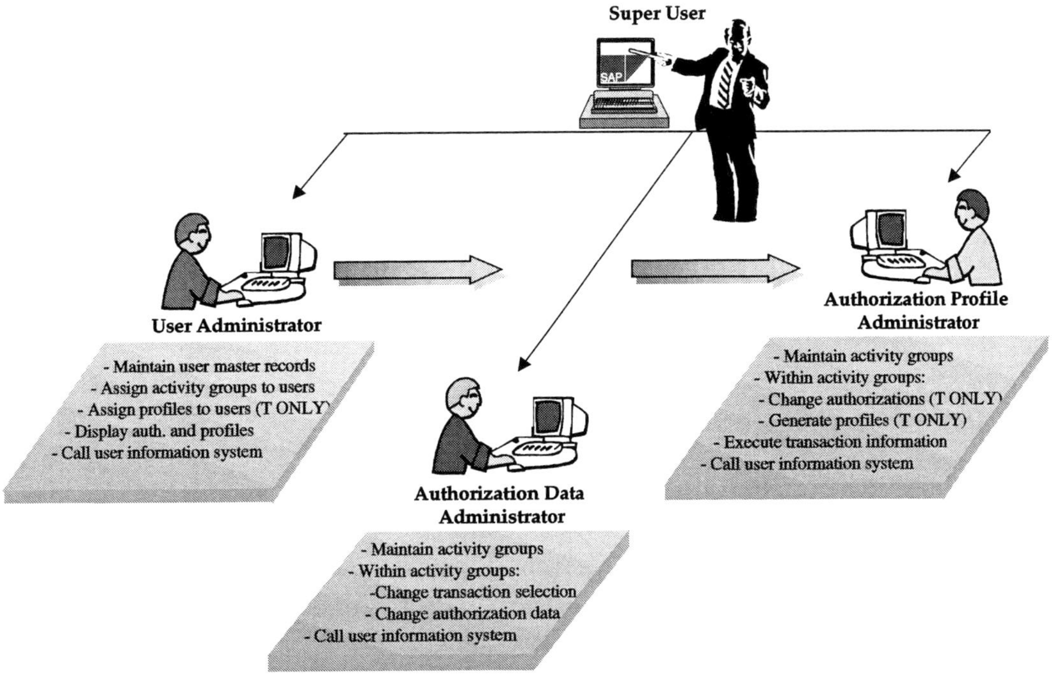


### Organizing Authorization Administration

For companies with very few people involved in setting up and maintaining authorizations, dividing up such tasks complicates the process of creating and maintaining the authorizations component. You should also decide whether maintenance of users, activity groups, authorization profile, and authorizations should be centralized or decentralized. We recommend centralizing maintenance until your go-live date and first rollout. Centralized administrators have a better understanding of what is involved in a rollout, and centralizing the administrative tasks establishes naming standards. By the first rollout, all administrative functions should be documented and can then be decentralized.

Conversely, when the administrative functions are decentralized up front, administrators use different naming standards for their activity groups, authorization profiles, and authorizations, and different approaches to implementing security. If each administrator creates his or her own standards, everything has to be renamed once the authorization implementation is standardized.

The superuser sets up user master records, profiles, and authorizations for administrators in a department, a cost center, and other organizational units. Within an area, administrative tasks are divided between the user administrator, authorization data administrator, and authorization profile administrator. The following is a list of each administrator's tasks and responsibilities:

- **User Administrator**
  - Creating and changing users
  - Assigning users to activity groups
  - Assigning profiles beginning with *T* to users (or following your own naming convention)
  - Displaying authorizations and profiles
  - Working with the user information system

  Displaying or changing activity group data and changing or generating profiles should **not** be permitted for user administrators.
- **Authorization Data Administrator**
  - Displaying users
  - Creating and changing activity groups
  - Changing the transaction selection and authorization data in activity groups
  - Displaying profiles
  - Working with the user information system

  Changing users and generating profiles should **not** be permitted for authorization data administrators.
- **Authorization Profile Administrator**
  - Displaying activity groups and their data and users
  - Generating authorizations and authorization profiles beginning with *T* based on existing activity groups (or respectively following your own naming convention)
  - Working with the user information system

  The following tasks should **not** be permitted for authorization profile administrators:
  - Changing users
  - Changing activity group data
  - Generating authorization profiles containing authorization objects beginning with S_USER

## How the Administrators Work Together

The authorization data administrator:

- Creates an activity group
- Chooses transactions
- Maintains authorization data

Without the appropriate authorization to generate the profile, the authorization data administrator saves the profile and accepts the default profile name *T*, or a name that follows your naming convention.

The authorization profile administrator:

- Calls transaction **PFCG**
- Selects the *Display mode* to check the data
- Generates the authorization profiles

Finally, the user administrator assigns the activity group to a user or a PD object, such as a position, and updates the user master record. The authorization profile is then added to the user master record.

# Policies and Procedures

The following shows a sample of policies and procedures, however for your company it might be different.

## User Administration

### Policies

- Superusers *SAP** and *DDIC*
  - There is no user *SAP** and *DDIC* in any client without a password.
  - The *SAP** user has no authorizations.
- User naming convention

  All users are assigned names identical to their employee ID numbers (personnel numbers).
- User maintenance
  - The system administration department has to receive the *User Modification Request Form*, with e-mail, signed by the user's application department manager.
  - All profiles that the user requires must be specifically listed on the request form. The form must indicate whether the user is temporary or permanent.
  - For temporary employees, an account expiration date must be included.
- User leaving the company
  1. The *User Modification Request Form* must be filled out and signed by the application department manager.
  2. A copy of this form must be sent to HR department.

3. The HR department manager must sign the request for deletion.
4. This manager sends the signed copy back to the system administration department.
5. All employee master record information, including internal post office, must be deleted.

### Procedures

- Superusers *SAP** and *DDIC*
  - *SAP** is used only for client copies.
  - Pseudo superusers are created in each client with the *SAP_ALL* profile.
  - The password is changed every month.

    This can be determined with the following system profile parameters: *login/password_expiration_time* (see appendix C for the list of system profile parameters).
  - Use report *RSUSR003* to check whether the standard passwords for *SAP** and *DDIC* have been changed from the defaults.
- User naming convention

  The application manager must contact the HR department and receive the new employee ID number. This ID number is entered into the *User Modification Request Form* where indicated.
- User maintenance

  The *User Modification Request Form* must be completed and mailed to the system administration department.
- User leaving the company

  The *User Modification Request Form* must be completed and sent to the system administration department and to the HR department manager. The HR department manager must sign the form and return the signed copy to the system administration department.

### Roles and Responsibilities

| Task | Role |
|---|---|
| Maintaining superusers | System administrator |
| Maintaining naming conventions | Application department manager/HR department |
| Maintaining users | Application department manager/system administrator |
| Maintaining users leaving company | Application department manager/system administrator/HR department |

# System Security

## Policies

- IT Manager

  The IT Manager, who is responsible for all aspects of system security, must review the security strategy every two months.

- Superusers

  For revision and security purposes, the superuser *SAP** will not be used for system maintenance. All maintenance has to be performed with newly defined superusers.

- System passwords

  System passwords (DB user *sapr3*, O.S. user *<SID>ADM, DDIC*) must be changed every four weeks. In case of an emergency, password access must be ensured.

- User passwords

  To protect the system from unauthorized access, make users change their password every four weeks. A minimum password length of six characters is required. After three unsuccessful logon attempts the account will be locked.

- SAP connection

  The connection to SAP is opened only for a service session. These connections are *SAPNet – R/3 Frontend notes* (formerly *OSS*), *Early Watch,* and *Remote Consulting.* Connection to SAP can only be opened from the customer site. Connections have to be monitored with an appropriate tool.

- SAProuter

  SAProuter, a SAP-supplied tool for securing R/3 access, is necessary for connecting to SAP systems.

- Remote connections

  For external connections (mobile end users), fixed IP addresses are assigned. One explicit entry per external connection is maintained in the permission list for SAP router.

## Procedures

- IT Manager

  Every two months, the IT manager and the system administrator should review system security.

- Superusers

  The *SAP_ALL* profile is removed from the user *SAP**, and the *SAP** user is locked. All maintenance tasks are performed using accounts with the *SAP_ALL* profile.

- System passwords

  The system administrator changes the system passwords every four weeks. The system administrator must write down the current passwords and place them in a sealed envelope, which must be stored in the data safe and be accessible in case of emergency. Use report *RSUSR003* to check if system passwords have been changed.

- User passwords

  Users must change their passwords every four weeks by setting the appropriate parameters in the *DEFAULT* profile. This step ensures that the settings are valid in the entire system. The minimum number of characters for a password is six, and the intruder-lockout count is set to three.

- SAP connection

  A connection between SAP and the customer is established by starting SAP router in the customer network and starting, for example, SAP GUI for an SAPNet – R/3 Frontend note connection.

- SAP router

  SAP router is started and stopped once a day to ensure there is no open connections.

- Remote connections

  For remote users, dedicated IP addresses are maintained. These addresses must also be maintained in the *SAPROUTTAB* to make sure that unauthorized users do not log on to R/3.

### Roles and Responsibilities

| Task | Role |
|---|---|
| Defining and maintaining *SAPROUTTAB* | System administrator |
| Monitoring open connections | Operator |
| Shutting down/restarting SAP router daily | Operator |
| Reviewing security strategy | IT manager |
| Changing system passwords | System administrator |

# Auditing Requirements

In R/3 there are several areas related to auditing:

- Process controls
- Change management
- Authorization implementation
- UNIX
- Database

Your site may have additional auditing requirements. Numerous companies have implemented excellent auditing procedures based on standard SAP tools and customer-built tools. Americas' SAP Users' Group (ASUG) Internal Controls and Security offers the best information on how other companies have handled auditing in R/3. For more information, on ASUG see *http://www.asug.com/*. For more information on auditing see chapter 13, *SAP Security Audit and Logging*.

# Chapter 2: Authorizations and ASAP

## Contents

# Overview

AcceleratedSAP (ASAP) is SAP's comprehensive implementation solution to streamline R/3 projects. ASAP integrates three components, the *ASAP Roadmap, Tools,* and *R/3 Service and Training,* which work in conjunction to support the rapid and efficient implementation of the R/3 System.

- ***AcceleratedSAP Roadmap*** delivers a process-oriented, clear and concise project plan to provide step-by-step direction throughout your implementation of R/3.
- ***Tools*** includes ASAP specific tools to support project management, questionnaires for the business process consultants and numerous technical guidebooks and checklists.
- ***R/3 Services and Training*** includes all consulting, training, and support services (for example, hotline, EarlyWatch, remote upgrades or archiving, etc.). These products help to standardize certain tasks to perform them as quickly as possible.

In respect to authorizations, ASAP describes the process to set up an authorization concept. While this guidebook helps you in the technical implementation of authorizations ASAP describes the setup of an authorization concept from a methodical and organizational view point. By following the steps of ASAP Roadmap, you can establish your authorization concept with a proven implementation process. The Knowledge Corner provides you with tools that help you to accelerate the authorization implementation.

In this chapter, we briefly discuss how to work with ASAP and what it contains in regards to authorizations. We explain how to access the ASAP components containing authorization-related resources rather than discussing the contents themselves.

# ASAP Roadmap

The ASAP Roadmap structure is divided into different levels:

- Phase
- Work package
- Activity
- Task

On the highest level, the ASAP Roadmap consists of five phases, as follows:

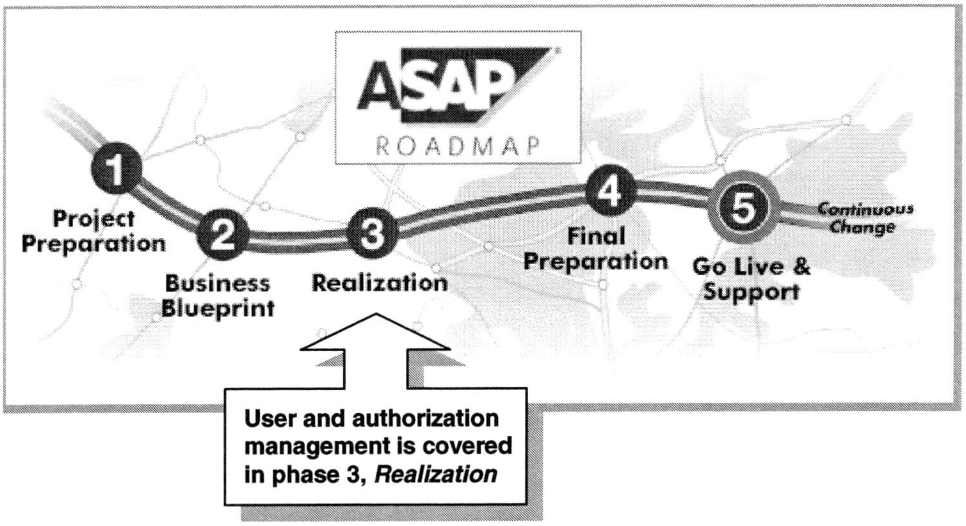


1. **Project Preparation**
   In this phase, you make sure all decision makers are on board for your R/3 implementation and gather your internal and external implementation team.

2. **Business Blueprint**
   Create the Business Blueprint documenting your company's business requirements. The Business Blueprint is a visual model of your business' future state after you've implemented the R/3 System. It allows your project team to clearly define your scope, and only focus on the R/3 processes needed to run your business.

3. **Realization**
   In this phase, your implementation team configures and fine-tunes the R/3 System.

4. **Final Preparation**
   Test all interfaces, train all end users, and migrate your business data to your R/3 System.

5. **Go Live & Support**
   In this phase, go live with R/3. You establish procedures and measurements to review the benefits of your R/3 investment on an ongoing basis. SAP support and services assure that your system continues to run smoothly, cleanly, and efficiently.

User and authorization management is covered in the *Realization* phase of the ASAP Roadmap. In the work package *Establish Authorization Concept*, you find a description of the methodology to set up an authorizations concept. Follow the steps below.

# Authorizations in the Roadmap Structure

1. Start the Implementation Assistant.
2. On the *Roadmap* tab of the *ASAP Implementation Assistant,* choose *Implementation Roadmap → 3 Realization → Establish Authorization Concept.*
3. On the right side, an explanation of the contents appears for the node selected on the left.

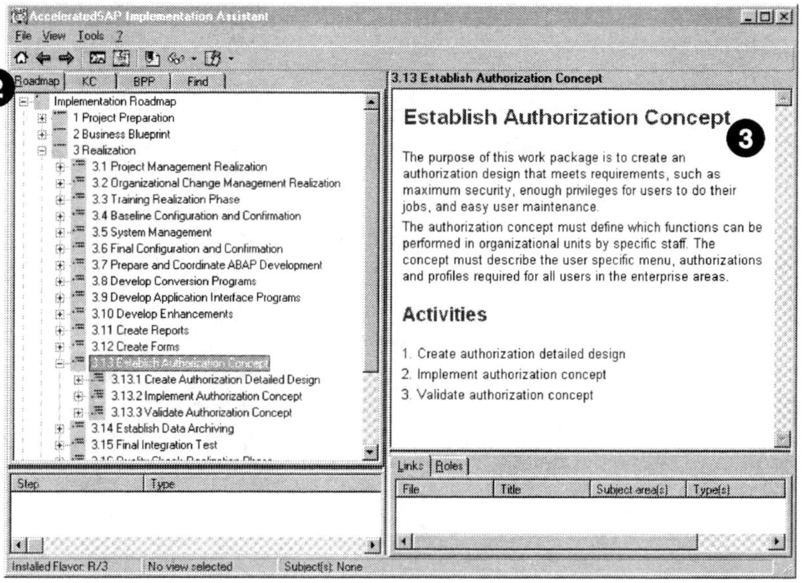


**Note:** Due to structural differences in the ASAP roadmap between ASAP Release 4.6A and 4.6B, the number of the workpackage *Establish Authorization Concept* is either 3.13 in ASAP Release 4.6A or 3.26 in ASAP Release 4.6B.

The workpackage *Establish Authorization Concept* contains three activities, which are:

1. *Create Authorization Detailed Design*
2. *Implement Authorization Concept*
3. *Validate Authorization Concept*

To access the activities belonging to the workpackage *Establish Authorization Concept* follow the steps below.

1. Choose the first activity, *Create Authorization Detailed Design,* to get an overview about the tasks this activity contains.

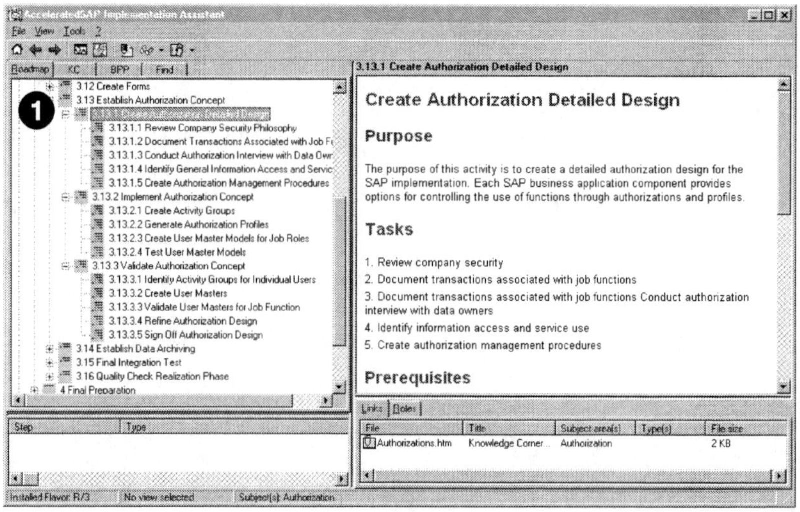

2. Work your way through the different tasks.
3. When you finish these tasks, continue with the next activity and its tasks.

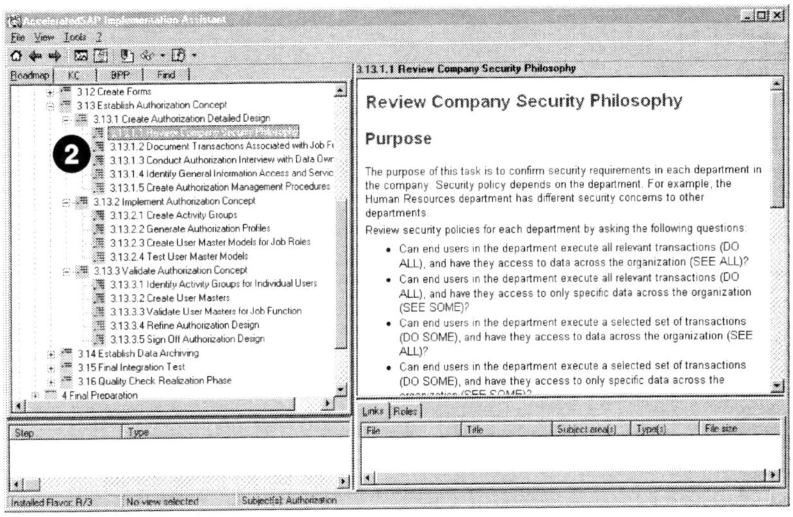


# Knowledge Corner

The Knowledge Corner (KC) is a collection of resources that helps you to accelerate the R/3 implementation. In order to access all available authorization documents and tools in the Knowledge Corner, follow the steps below.

1. Start the Implementation Assistant.
2. On the KC tab of the *ASAP Implementation Assistant*, choose *SAP Products → Cross Application → Authorizations.*
3. The upper right tile shows an explanation of the contents from the left.
4. The lower right tile shows all authorization documents and tools available in the KC.

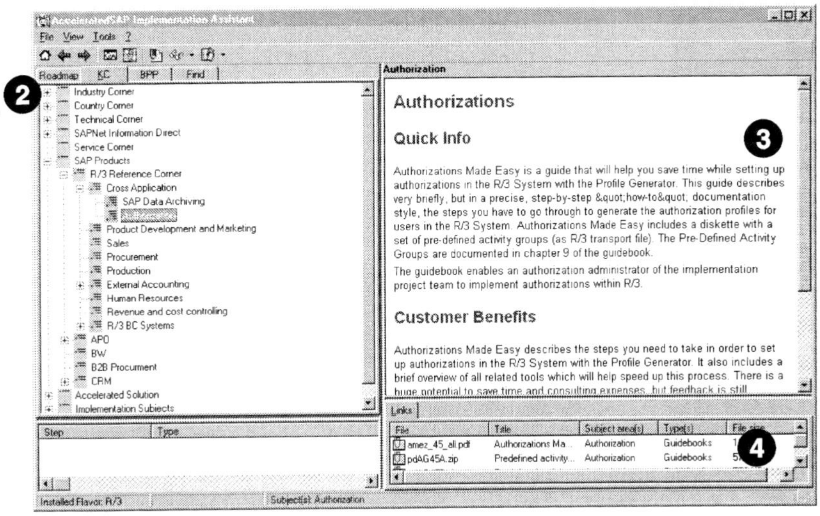

# Questions and Answers Database (Q&Adb)

## What Is the Q&Adb?

The Questions and Answers Database (Q&Adb) is a tool that helps you to analyze and determine the scale and scope of your system implementation during the Business Blueprint phase of an ASAP implementation project. In the Q&Adb, all processes that can be implemented in the R/3 System are displayed in a tree called the reference structure. While defining the Business Blueprint, you are setting the business processes in scope that you aim to implement with the R/3 System.

As of ASAP Release 4.6B, you can create user roles in the Q&Adb and assign the processes to be implemented to these roles. This information is later passed to the Authorization List where you can complete the user role definition.

## How to Work with the Q&Adb

For details on how to create and maintain user roles within the Q&Adb, see the Q&Adb online help.

## How to Generate the Authorization List from the Q&Adb

In order to refine the user roles that you have defined in the Q&Adb, you can generate the Authorization List. During the generation of the Authorization List, both the processes set in scope and the defined user roles are transferred to the Authorization List. For details on how to generate the Authorization List from the Q&Adb, see the Q&Adb online help.

# Authorization List

## What Is the Authorization List?

The Authorization List is an Excel worksheet that helps you to model your user roles prior to the implementation in the R/3 System. Using the Authorization List, you can design user roles in an early system implementation phase even without having installed R/3.

In the Authorization List, you create user roles and define the transactions associated with these roles. To model the user roles, the Authorization List provides you two different views:

- **Process view**

  The process view (*Roles Design - Q&Adb scope* tab) is generated from the Q&Adb and contains the processes that have been set in scope during the Business Blueprint phase. All processes are displayed in the same hierarchy as in the reference structure of the Q&Adb. You can define your user roles and select the processes to include them in the user roles.

- **Menu view**

  In the menu view (*Roles Design – SAP menu* tab), all transactions in the standard SAP menu are displayed. You can define your user roles and select transactions from the SAP menu to include them in your user roles.

After completing the modeling of user roles, you can generate an overview of all transactions included in each user role.

## How to Work with the Authorization List

To use the *Authorization List* for the design and implementation of your authorization concept, follow the steps below.

1. Generate authorization list from the Q&Adb
2. Define user roles
3. Generate user roles overview
4. Build user roles

### Generate Authorization List from the Q&Adb

To work with process view, you need to generate the *Authorization List* from the Q&Adb. Proceed as described in the Q&Adb online help.

Tips & Tricks

Even if you do not work with the *Q&Adb*, you can use the *Authorization List*. The template can be found in the *ASAP Knowledge Corner*. However, the process view will be empty; thus you can define your user roles only via the menu view.

## Define User Roles

To define a user role, you need to create a user role and assign processes or transactions to that user role.

1. Open the Authorization List.
2. Enter *Business Area* and *Role Name* for the user role that you want to create.
3. Mark the desired transactions.

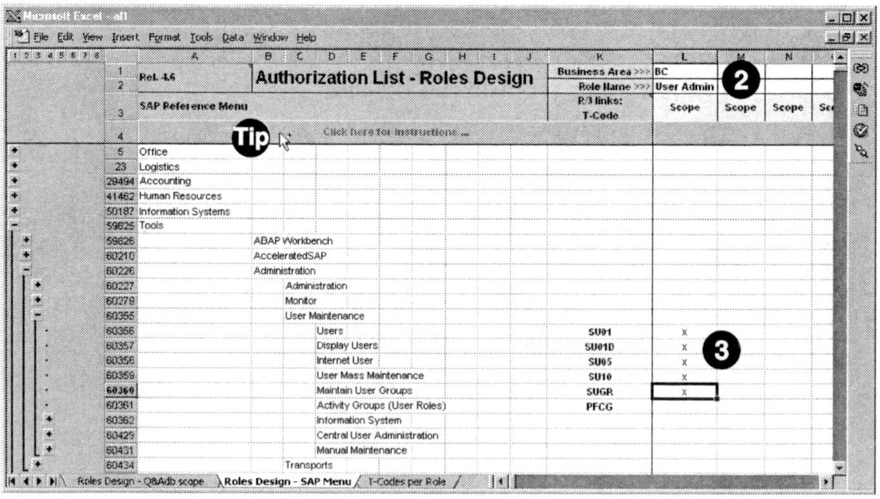


Tips & Tricks

Choose *Click here for instructions* to get an explanation on the functionality of the Authorization List.

The complete functionality of the Authorization List is described in the help window shown to the right.

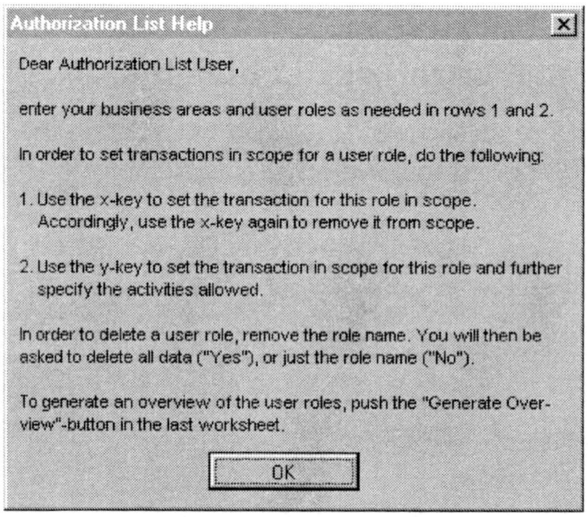

## Generate User Roles Overview

To generate the user roles overview from the Authorization List:

1. Select the *T-Codes per Role* tab.
2. Choose *Generate Overview* to create for each user role a list of transactions assigned to that role.

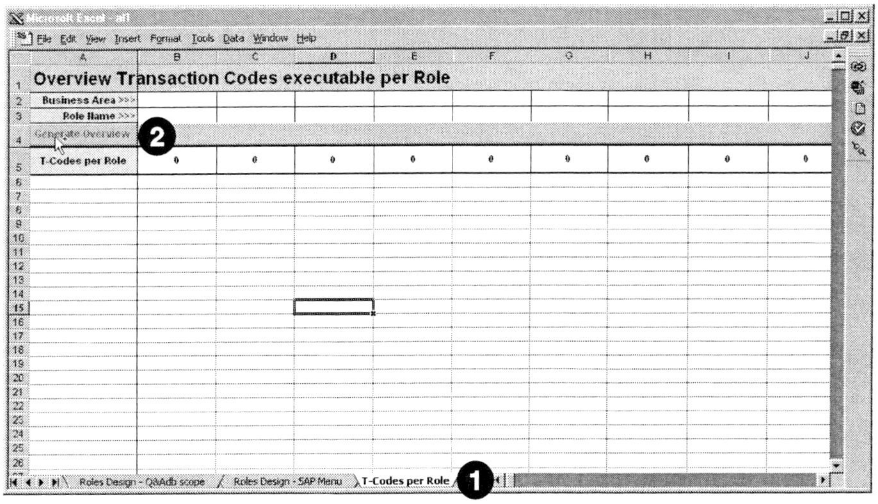


3. For all user roles, the selected transactions are summarized in the Authorization List.

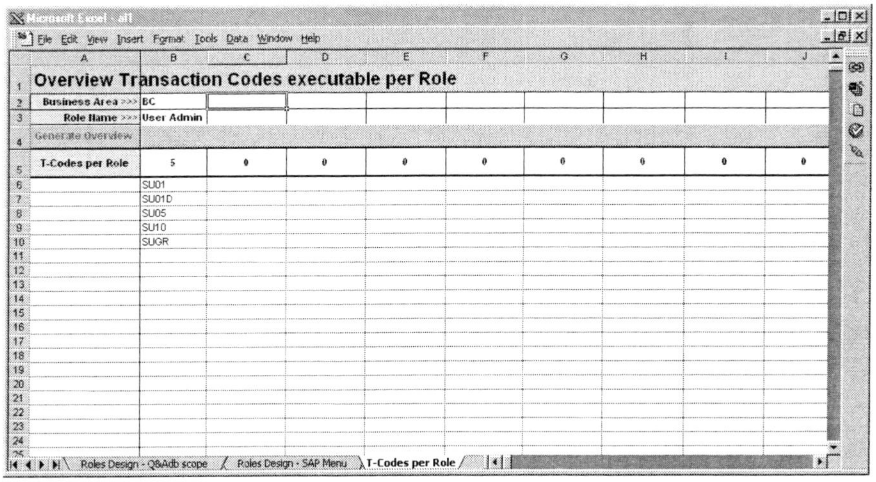


Caution

Every time you make changes to the roles or create new roles the *T-Codes per Role* overview needs to be regenerated.

## Build User Roles

Using the PG, create all the single and composite activity groups required to implement the user roles defined in the Authorization List.

# Chapter 3: Setting Up the Profile Generator

## Contents

# Overview

Using the Profile Generator (PG) in Release 4.6x makes sense for new customers just starting their R/3 project and current customers with authorization profiles created in an earlier R/3 release. Maintenance transactions *SU02* and *SU03* are no longer required, and customers who have previously been using this method should familiarize themselves with the PG. If you have already created authorization profiles without the PG, SAP offers you a way to migrate these profiles to the PG.

For information on upgrading to Release 4.6 from a previous release, see chapter 14, *Upgrade*.

Setting up the PG in 4.6x consists of two steps:

1. Confirming that the PG is active.
2. Loading the customer tables (USOBX_C and USOBT_C).

# Confirming that the Profile Generator Is Active

With R/3 Release 4.6, the PG is already activated. You do not have to set the system parameter in the R/3 instance profile if you have installed the R/3 Release 4.6 as a new system. The default value is *auth/no_check_in_some_cases = Y*.

## Checking the Required Instance Profile Parameter

If you are not sure whether the PG is activated, you can check the instance profile parameter. The following procedure shows you how to check if your profile parameter is set correctly and active. To check if the instance profile parameter is set correctly, run the report *RSPARAM* as show below.

1. In the *Command* field, enter **SA38** and choose *Enter* (or choose *System* → *Services* → *Reporting*).
2. Enter **RSPARAM** in the *Program* field.
3. Choose *Execute*.

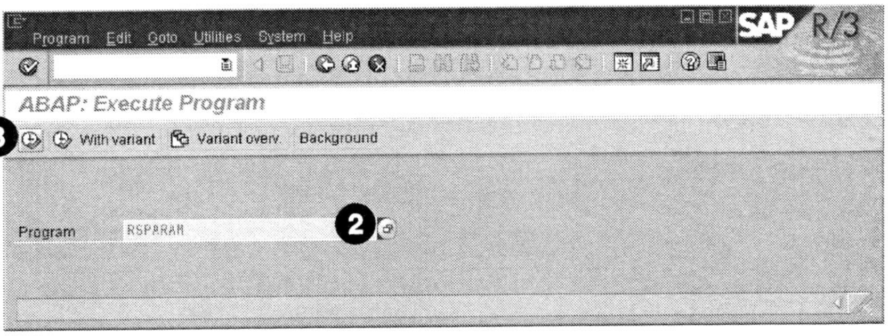


TechTalk

A list of parameter names appears with corresponding user-defined values. The parameter names are provided in variable form. At runtime, these variables are replaced with actual values. User-defined values are the actual values of the individual parameters.

4. If active, the profile parameter for the PG *auth/no_check_in_some_cases* is displayed as a *Y* in the third column.

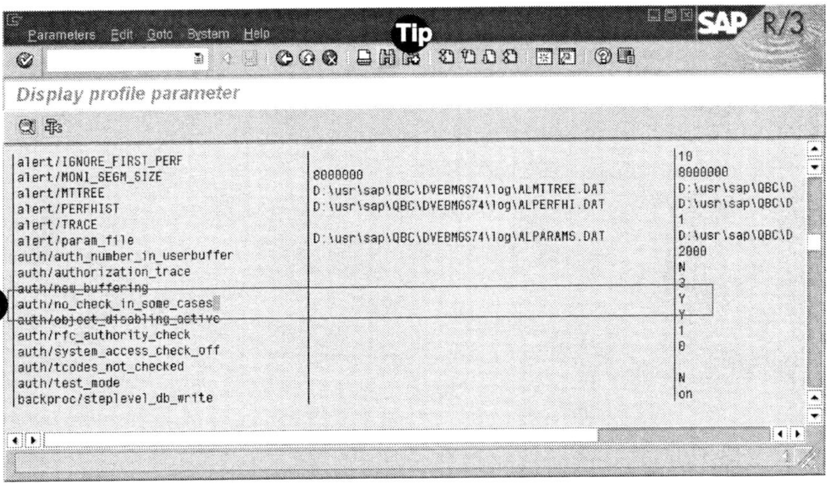


Tips & Tricks

Use the icon to search for the entry **auth/no_check_in_some_cases** in the list if you do not see it right away.

If the value *Y* for the instance profile parameter *auth/no_check_in_some_cases* is not displayed, you must first change the instance profile and then reboot the R/3 instance. For more information on how to do this, see chapter 14, *Upgrade*.

# Loading the USOBX_C and USOBT_C tables

Loading the *USOBX_C* and *USOBT_C* tables is accomplished in two steps:

1. Initial copying of SAP defaults into the customer tables
2. Transporting the defaults.

## Initial Copying of SAP Defaults into the Customer Tables (SU25)

Using transaction *SU25* (*Copy initial defaults*), copy the supplied SAP defaults, tables *USOBX* and *USOBT*. This step imports the SAP check indicator defaults for the authorization objects within a transaction and the authorization field values for the PG into customer tables *USOBX_C* and *USOBT_C*. We discuss how to edit these values using transaction *SU24* in chapter 12, *Tips & Troubleshooting*.

1. In the *Command* field, enter transaction **SPRO** and choose *Enter* (or from the *SAP standard menu* tree, choose *Tools* → *AcceleratedSAP* → *Customizing* → *Edit Project*).
2. Choose *SAP Reference IMG*.
3. In the IMG, open *Basis Components* → *System Administration* → *Users and Authorizations* → *Maintain Authorizations and Profiles Using Profile Generator* and choose next to *Work on SAP Check Indicators and Field Values*.

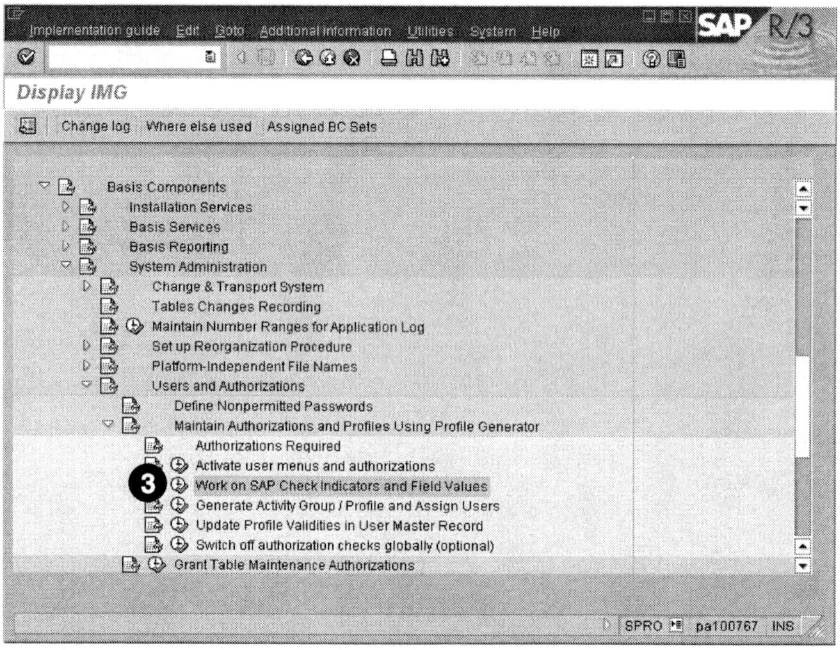


Tips & Tricks

To reach the *Profile Generator: Upgrade and First Installation* screen you may alternatively use transaction **SU25**.

4. On the next screen select *Copy SAP test statuses and field values* (this translation is incorrect; the text should read *Copy SAP check indicators and field values*).

5. Choose next to *1. Initially fill the customer tables*, if you have not previously worked with the PG or if you want to retransfer all SAP default values. This step may take several minutes.

If you have not previously worked with the PG or you want to retransfer all SAP default values, use *1. Initially fill the customer tables* function under *Installing the Profile Generator*.

If you have already worked with the PG and want to compare your data with the SAP default values, see chapter 14, *Upgrade*.

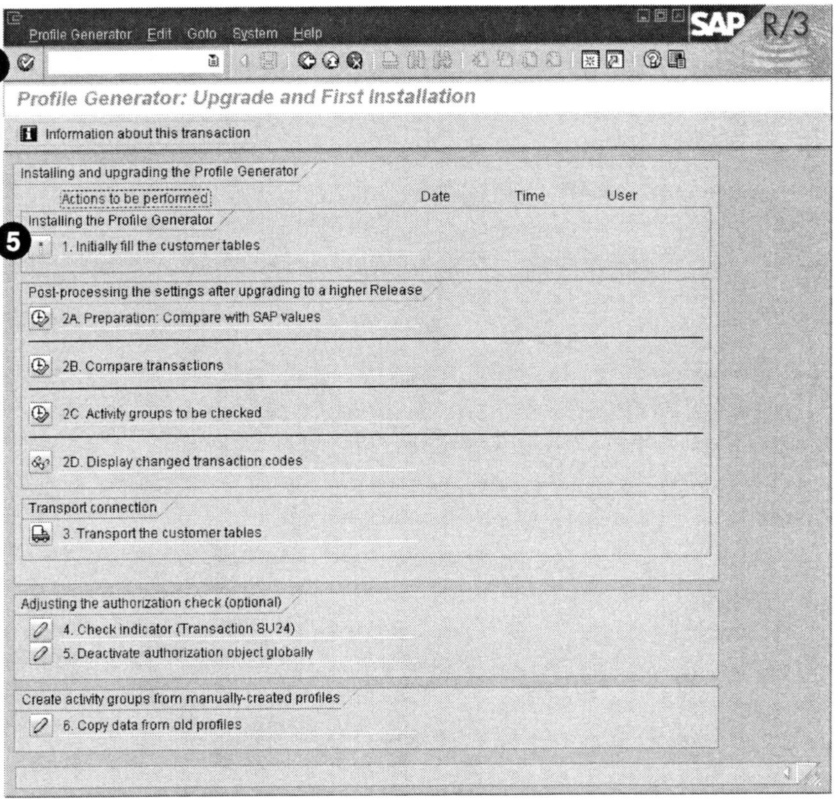


6. A warning message appears on a dialog box. Read it carefully and choose .

## Transporting the Defaults

7. Choose next to *3. Transport the customer tables* to transport the PG customer tables (*USOBX_C* and *USOBT_C*).

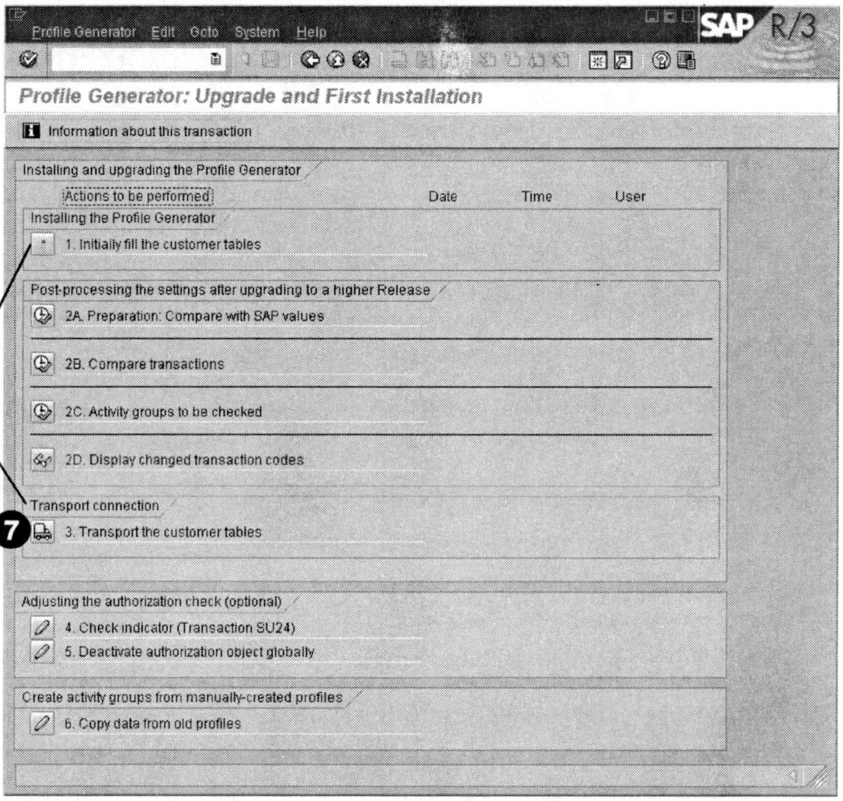


Caution

At this time perform only steps *1* and *3*. Do not run steps *2A* through *2D* yet. See chapter 14, *Upgrade* for more information.

Caution

Note that the customer tables (*USOBX_C* and *USOBT_C*) are completely transported. All changes to authorization checks that were made in this transaction or in *SU24* are also transported into the target system. This step replaces all the field value and check indicator settings in the target system.

No activity groups or authorization profiles are transported in this step. To transport newly generated activity groups, use the activity group transport connection.

8. Choose after the report is finished.
9. Choose on the following screen to finish the procedure.

# Getting Support from the SAPNet – R/3 Frontend Notes

A smooth security implementation of your project is important. The top priorities of the SAPNet – R/3 Frontend Notes (formerly OSS) are to support your work and speed up your implementation. The SAPNet – R/3 Frontend notes are an easy-to-use, direct communication link to SAP so you can quickly and efficiently obtain problem-solving information. SAPNet – R/3 Frontend notes gives you a faster response time by allowing you to bypass the SAP help desk and enter problems directly into our database.

By entering problems or inquiries directly into the SAPNet – R/3 Frontend notes, you can:

- Take advantage of R/3 services, regardless of the availability and workload of the responsible help desk personnel
- Quickly report your problems
- Directly submit your problems to first-level customer service for processing

## Accessing the Error Notes Database

SAPNet – R/3 Frontend notes actively involves you in the problem-solving process by giving you direct access to SAP's interactive Error Notes database. This database contains error listings and solutions to common system problems. With the SAPNet – R/3 Frontend notes, you can view these solutions without submitting a problem message to first-level customer service. Direct access to the Error Notes database, with the SAPNet – R/3 Frontend notes, also provides helpful tips on avoiding potential problems.

Tips & Tricks

Now is a good time to look at the SAPNet – R/3 Frontend notes listed in appendix A. These notes help you prepare for further R/3 security setup tasks.

You should also look into the SAPNet – R/3 Frontend notes if any experiences occur that are not covered by this guidebook.

Tips & Tricks

**To use SAPNet – R/3 Frontend notes:**

1. Contact your system administrator for any further information about the SAPNet – R/3 Frontend notes .
2. Find out who already has access to the SAPNet – R/3 Frontend notes in your company.
3. Make sure you have access to the SAPNet – R/3 Frontend notes .
4. Log on to the SAPNet – R/3 Frontend notes and browse through the SAPNet – R/3 Frontend notes in appendix A.

## Printing Important SAPNet – R/3 Frontend Notes

Since we refer to certain SAPNet – R/3 Frontend notes in this guidebook, please learn how to print a note properly. The print function is not supported in SAPNet – R/3 Frontend notes, so you must first download the note and print it locally. Read notes *26746* and *15641* to familiarize yourself with downloading and printing the notes. Before you continue, print out the notes in appendix A and keep them as handy reference tools.

## Applying Advance Corrections to Your R/3 System

Caution

Advance corrections should be applied only with the approval of the Basis System Administrator.

The R/3 System needs certain corrections to perform properly. To apply these corrections in advance, refer to SAPNet – R/3 Frontend note *97612* for the availability of the PG hot packages for Releases 4.6A and 4.6B.

# Chapter 4: User Administration

## Contents

# Overview

You have two options to set up your user administration:

- Central User Administration
- Client-specific user administration

In this chapter, we only describe the client-specific user administration. If you are using the Central User Administration, see chapter 11, *Setting Up Central User Administration*, for more information.

R/3 allows you to define and maintain users and user authorizations by giving you precise control over user access. The definition and validation of authorization technology is integrated into the SAP development environment and is easily added to customer modules.

Although user administration is an ongoing process, you should not administer your users in a productive environment. Perform user administration tasks in your DEV system. When you transport the activity groups, the users are also transported through the QAS to your PRD system, whenever users and authorization objects are:

- Created
- Deleted
- Changed
- Monitored

However, you might have different users in the DEV and QAS system that you do not need in your PRD system later (for example a developer). An administrator's role in this process varies depending on how user administration tasks are delegated.

Tips & Tricks

Even if you are using the HR module, user administration still needs to be set up, but maintenance in the long run includes other facets.

# System Users

In client-specific user administration, users must be separately defined for each client in your system. A user definition has many of the following components:

- Basic user data
  - Name
  - Password
  - Address
  - Company information

- User defaults
  - Logon language
  - Default printer
  - Date and decimal formats
  - Default time zone
- User profile information
  - Parts of R/3 a user can access
  - User groups
  - Active and expiration dates of a user's account

There are two ways to create users. First, from scratch, by defining the various user components; and second, by copying an existing user. When copying an existing user, you may also copy the defaults, address, and memory parameter settings.

## External R/3 Users

External users include those created for Windows NT activities (for example <SAPSID>adm, administrator, and SAPService <SAPSID>) and database connections (SAPR3, database administrator, and SQL users).

## Internal R/3 Users

Internal users are created and maintained in R/3. Each user is assigned a **user type** which controls how the user interacts with R/3.

Internal user types include:

- Dialog
- Batch Data Communication (BDC)
- Background
- CPIC

### Dialog

The dialog user type handles online transactions and applies to most users in a company. Dialog users may log on and interactively work with R/3. These users are subject to authorization checks and require authorization profiles and passwords. Although it is not required, dialog users should be assigned to a user group.

### Batch Data Communication

The batch data communication (BDC or batch input) user type is used for authorization checks when processing a batch input session. These users cannot log on or work interactively and are subject to authorization checks.

### Background

The background user type runs background jobs. These users cannot log on and work interactively. The administrator can create background users with the necessary authorizations to perform a series of tasks. To define the background jobs, change the user field to the background user name you created. All authorization checks go against the background user rather than the user creating the job. Although background users are unaffected by password control parameters (for example password expirations or character length), these users are subject to authorization checks.

### CPIC

The CPIC user is delivered in client 000 with no authorizations and logs on using the CPIC interface. This interface does not work interactively with R/3. The CPIC user receives return codes from external programs and the **statistic collectors** (refer to SAPNet – R/3 Frontend note *3310*). SAPCPIC is no longer required for the transaction *SM51*.

The CPIC user requires an authorization to perform the necessary activities in R/3 and is subject to authorization checks.

## Special R/3 Users

### SAP*

In clients 000 and 001, the R/3 System includes the default superuser *SAP**. During installation, a user master record is defined for *SAP**. However, *SAP** is programmed in R/3 and does not require a user master record. After installation, once the SAP* user master record becomes available, use the password `06071992`. If the *SAP** user master record is deleted and a user logs on again as **`SAP*`**, with the initial password **`PASS`**, then *SAP** is not subject to authorization checks and has the password **`PASS`**, which cannot be changed.

### DDIC

The DDIC user maintains the ABAP Dictionary and the software logistics. A DDIC user master record is automatically created in clients 000 and 001 when R/3 is installed and has standard password `19920706`. This is the only user that can log on to R/3 during a new release installation. Protect the DDIC user from unauthorized access by changing the initial password in clients 000 and 001. This user is required for certain installation and setup tasks, so it should not be deleted.

### EarlyWatch

The EarlyWatch user is only delivered in client 066 with the initial password **`SUPPORT`**. Access is limited to monitoring and performance data. The EarlyWatch user is used by SAP's EarlyWatch experts. This user should not be deleted, and the password should be changed. EarlyWatch should not be used for any purpose other than EarlyWatch functions.

## Creating Users

If you do **not** use the Central User Administration function, the user master records and authorization components are client-specific and must be separately defined for each system client.

Users are created either from scratch (using transaction *SU01)* or from a copy of an existing user by:

- Using transaction *SU01*
- Creating a template user
- Copying it to other similar users
- Manually entering each password

The hierarchical security effect of user groups enables the administrator to distribute user maintenance tasks and maintain high security. Within a specific group, security tasks can be distributed in such a way that three people are required to create users and manage activity groups and authorizations. Thus, user and authorization administrators can only complete certain parts of the required tasks. This process ensures that no one person can circumvent R/3's authorization scheme. If a company has a centralized organizational structure, all maintenance tasks may need to be performed by a single user, the so-called superuser.

To allow users to see their own user master records, use transaction *SU01D*.

For security reasons, the responsibility for the following maintenance tasks should be distributed among three different administrators (see chapter 1 for additional information).

# User Groups

Instead of using user groups to only distribute user maintenance among several administrators, you can now assign users to one or more user groups. Note that one group is still the primary group for the authorization check. This is the group that appears in the top field on the *Logon data* tab in the user maintenance transaction. The category *User group* can be used as a basis for better distribution of user data, thus increasing the speed of Central User Administration. You may use any naming convention.

User groups enable the administrator to provide application managers with the rights required to control their users. Thus, these managers can control all users in their user groups and users not yet assigned to a user group. However, application managers cannot change users in other user groups.

Although a user group affiliation is not required when you create users, this affiliation is necessary to delegate user maintenance tasks to application managers and staff. Later, we show how to distribute user administration tasks to the appropriate application personnel.

User groups are normally based on the requirements dictated by the different application groups. The number of users in each user group also influences these groups. Since user groups distribute user administrative tasks, your user groups will be based on the available organizational support structure. A few things to remember when working with user groups are that:

- User groups are created with transaction *SUGR* (*Tools → Administration → User Maintenance → Maintain Users Groups*).
- User groups affect nothing until you set up your group administrators within a user group.
- Each user can belong to many user groups.
- User groups can be maintained before they are assigned to users.

# Authorizations and Authorization Profiles

Authorization profiles allow you to organize access privileges by task or job function. Specifically, this profile contains the access privileges needed to perform particular jobs, such as data entry or application maintenance. To authorize a user for a job, you only need to give the user the corresponding authorization profile. The Profile Generator (PG) simplifies the task of setting up authorization profiles.

# Mass Operations

The R/3 System provides several utilities to administer all, or a selected set, of users. Changes made for one user in user administration can also be made for a large number of users all at once. You can change logon data, default values, parameters, activity groups, and profiles for a particular set of users (for example, all users of a user group).

To access the mass changes screen, enter transaction `SU01` and choose *Environment → Mass changes*.

If you are using Central User Administration (by making mass changes in the central system), the profiles and activity groups are displayed according to the relevant system.

The mass change functions on the initial screen affect the user data of all displayed users, unless you have selected specific users.

Caution

For every change on the *Address*, *Logon data*, and *Default values* tabs, you must choose *Change*. This ensures that your changes, such as deletion of field contents, take effect for the corresponding fields.

# Creating a New User (Client-Specific)

Caution

Do not create or change users in clients 000 or 066. To create other new clients, make a copy of client 000 (standard SAP client).

1. Log on to the SAP client where you wish to create a new user.
2. In the *Command* field, enter transaction **SU01** and choose *Enter* (or choose *Tools → Administration → User maintenance → Users*).
3. In the *User* field, enter the new user name.
4. Choose 🗋.

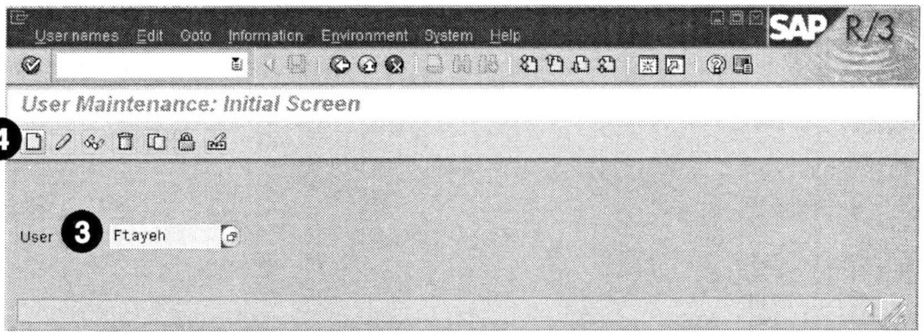


5. Enter the required data into the fields. You can always come back and change the data later.
6. Choose the *Logon data* tab.

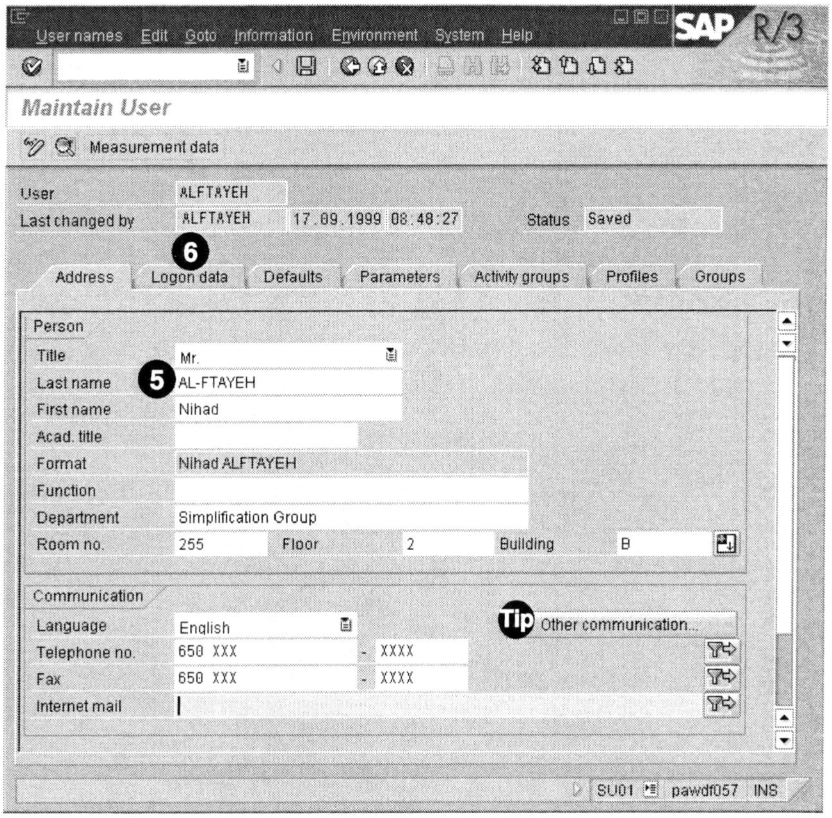


Tips & Tricks

The button *Other communication …* links you to the central address administration functionality. This functionality is not covered in this book.

7. Enter an *Initial password* (for example, `init`) which the user uses for the first log on. During that first logon, the user chooses a new password.
8. Reenter the password to verify the spelling in the field *Repeat password.*
9. You may edit other *Logon data* fields, such as *User group* or *User type* as needed (see the TechTalk below).
10. Choose the *Defaults* tab.

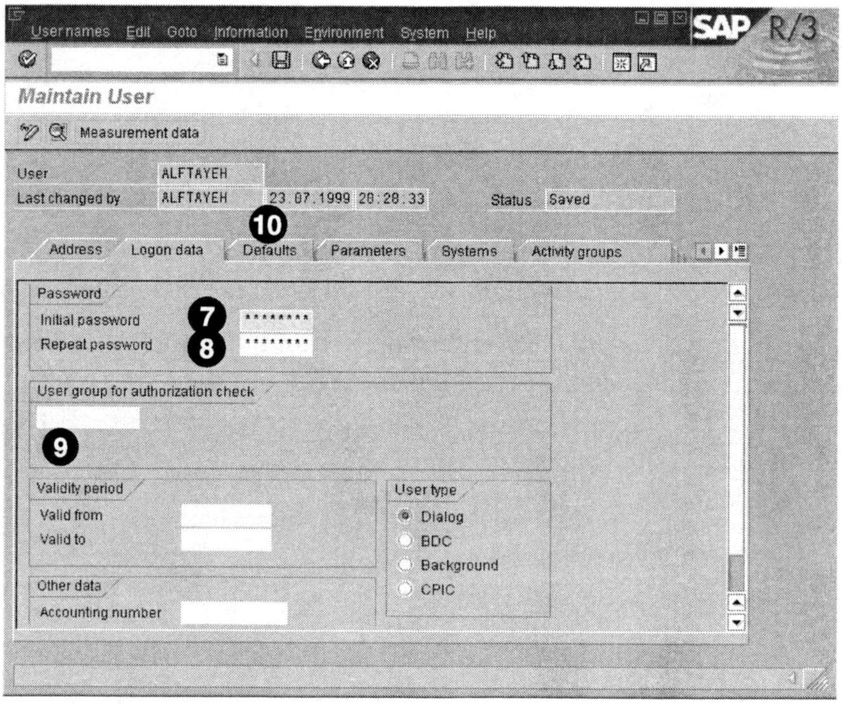


TechTalk

**Logon Data Field Definitions**

*User group for authorization check*

Assigning users to groups allows the user maintenance task to be distributed among several user administrators. You can assign users to one or more user groups.

*Valid from/Valid to*

These fields are useful if you are creating a temporary user, such as a contractor. To immediately activate the user, leave the *Valid from* field blank. For a user with no anticipated termination date, leave the *Valid to* field blank, which allows indefinite access.

*Accounting number*

This field is for a freely selectable accounting name or number. If you use the SAP accounting system, the user's system usage is assigned to this account. The accounting name or number may be unique to each user or can be shared among groups of users.

*Cost Center*

Use this field for the user's cost center number.

*Dialog*

Select this user type for normal dialog users.

*BDC*

When you process a batch input session, select this user type for users who are only used for the authorization check.

*Background*

Select this user type for users who are authorized to execute batch runs.

*CPIC*

Select this user type for users who are authorized to execute CPI-C calls.

11. You may either enter a *StartMenu* or leave the field blank.
12. Enter a language code in the *Logon language* field.
13. Enter a default *OutputDevice* (the printer or file to which the user will automatically print).
14. We recommend selecting *Output immediately* and *Delete after output*.

    *Output immediately* releases spool requests. Otherwise, spool requests stay in the spool system until manually released. The *Delete after output* option prevents spool requests from being retained after printing.
15. Select the desired *Decimal notation* and *Date format*.

17. Choose [save icon].

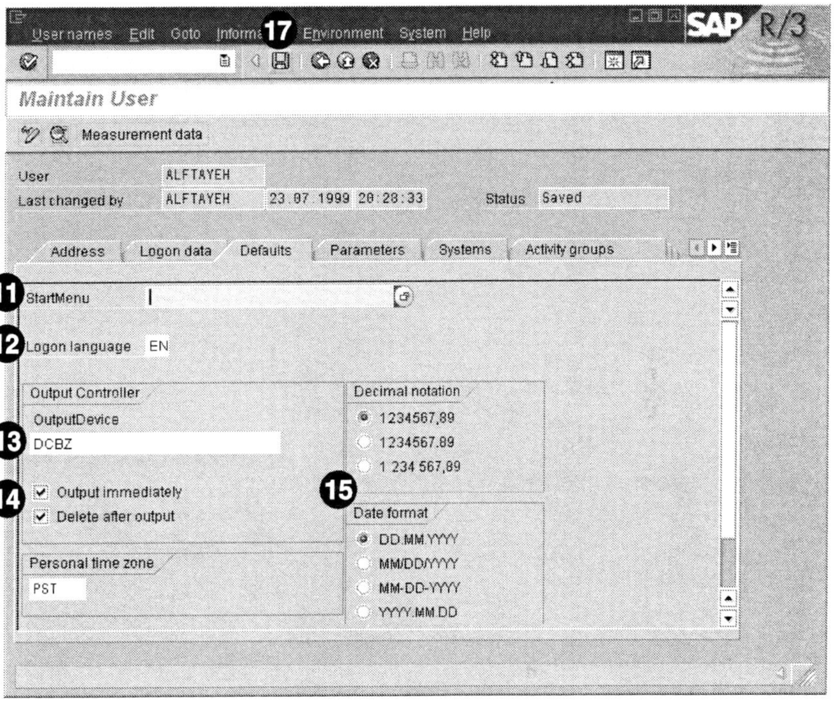


TechTalk

For each user, field defaults or **parameters** store default values for R/3 fields. When a field is displayed, the parameter's value (if any) is a default value. User parameters are optional and do not yet need to be defined.

Tips & Tricks

To assign an authorization profile to your new user master record:

1. Select a user role template or create an activity group yourself.
2. Generate authorization profiles for the activity groups.
3. Assign activity groups to new users and transfer profiles.

For more information about transporting user master records, see chapter 7 *Preparing the R/3 Environment for Go-Live*.

# Changing a User's Password

Users can change their own passwords and administrators can change any user's password. Users may only change their passwords once a day; however, an administrator can change passwords whenever required. An administrator may need to change passwords after a new installation (when the default password should be changed for security purposes), or when users lose or forget their passwords. When an administrator changes a password, the new password is only temporary. At the next logon, the user enters this password and then selects a permanent one. Refer to the table *Password Requirements* on the next page for password requirements.

Caution

If you do not use Central User Administration, the users are client-specific. Before proceeding, be sure that you are logged on to the SAP client that contains the user whose password you want to change.

1. To change a user's password, in the *Command* field, enter transaction **SU01** and choose *Enter* (or choose *Tools → Administration → User maintenance → Users*).
2. In *User*, enter the name of the user whose password you would like to change.
3. Choose the change password icon.

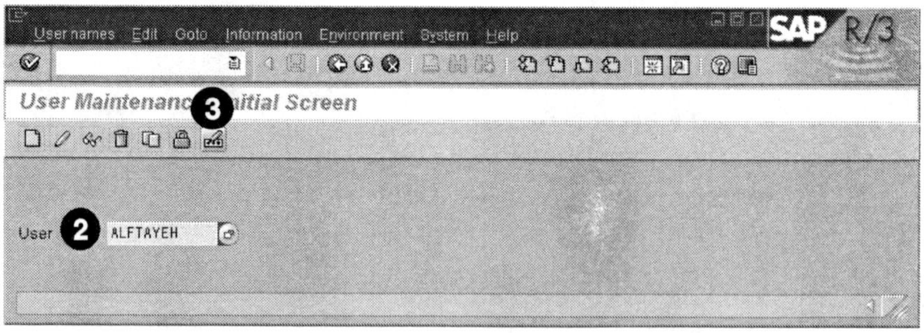


4. Enter the new initial password (for example, **init**) and reenter the password for verification in the next line.
5. Choose ✔ *Copy* to change the password.

## Password Requirements

The following table lists the password requirements. Additionally, it will help you determine if these requirements can be customized. Appendix C also lists important system profile parameters to customize password settings.

| Password Requirements | Default | Options |
|---|---|---|
| Minimum length is three characters | | Minimum length can be increased. |
| Expiration | Password must not be changed | Number of days after which a password must be changed can be set. |
| Password may not be set to any value in a lockout list | No passwords are blocked other than PASS and SAP* | Can be customized. |
| First character may not be an exclamation point (!) or question mark (?). | Fixed in the R/3 System | |
| First three characters may not appear in the same sequence in the user ID. | Fixed in the R/3 System | |
| First three characters may not be identical. | Fixed in the R/3 System | |
| Space character not allowed within first three characters. | Fixed in the R/3 System | |
| Password may not be `PASS` or `SAP*`. | Fixed in the R/3 System | |
| Any keyboard character is allowed in a password. Passwords are not case-sensitive; no distinction is made between upper- and lowercase letters. | Fixed in the R/3 System | |
| Users can change their passwords only once a day. This restriction does not apply to user administrators. | Fixed in the R/3 System | |
| A password may not be changed back to a user's previous five passwords. This restriction does not apply to user administrators. | Fixed in the R/3 System | |

# User Information System

In the *User Information System,* you have the option to run different reports to obtain information on all related data concerning users. These reports are all integrated in the menu tree and can be started directly from there.

Information is available for the following categories:

- User
- Profiles
- Authorization objects
- Authorizations
- Activity groups
- Transactions
- Comparisons
- Where-used list
- Change documents

Retrieving the information is basically the same for all categories. In the following example, we demonstrate how it works. To get information for a different category, run the corresponding report with your specific requirements.

**Example:** Find out which users are allowed to run a specific transaction.

1. In the *SAP standard menu,* choose *Tools → Administration → User maintenance → Information System.* In this menu area there are several different reports to choose from. To see which users are allowed to run a particular transaction, you may choose any transaction code you are interested in.

2. In the *Information System* menu area, double-click *By transaction authorizations.*

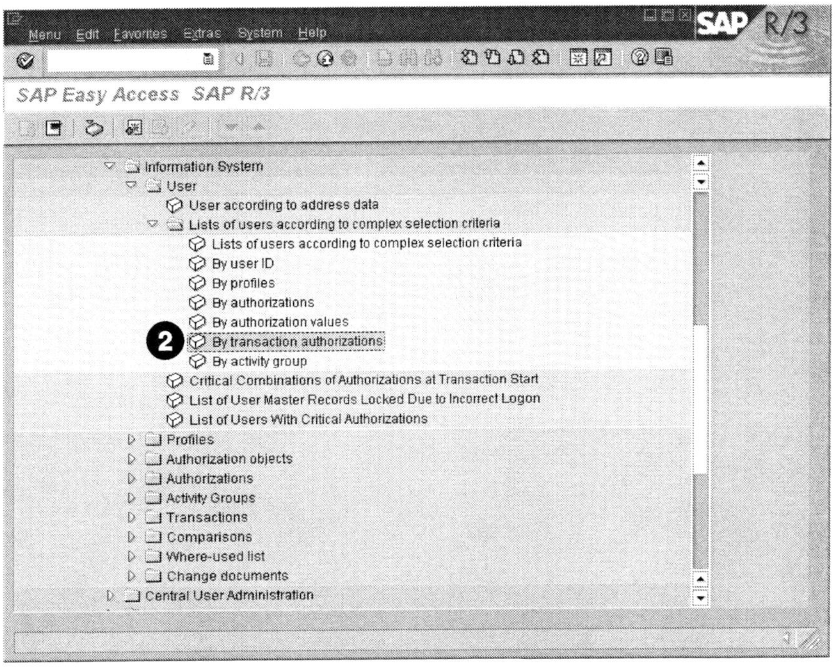


3. Enter a transaction code to determine which users have access to that transaction (for example, **`FB01`**).

4. Choose [execute icon] to start the report.

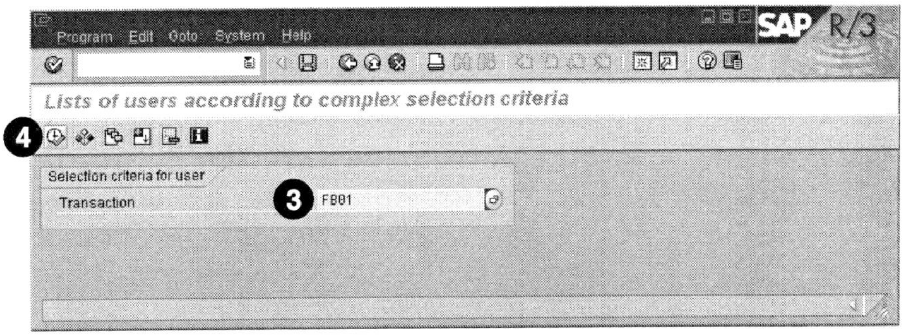


5. A table appears listing all the users allowed to run that transaction.

6. Choose [back icon] if you wish to return and review a different transaction code.

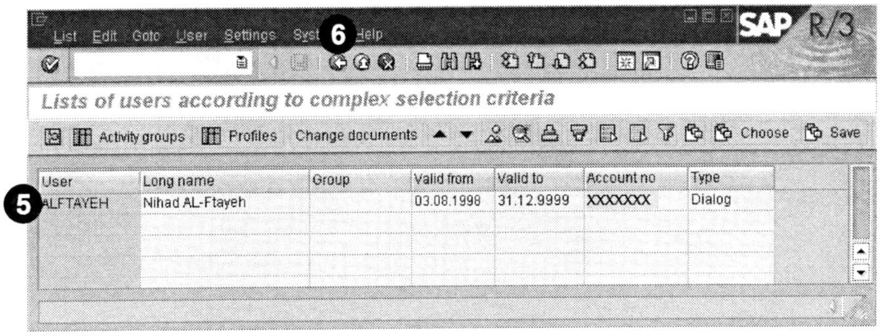

# Chapter 5: User Role Templates

## Contents

# Overview

In this chapter, we describe how to work with **user role templates** and set up your activity groups. For more information on how to work with the activity groups and user role templates with the Profile Generator (PG), see chapter 6, *Advanced Profile Generator Functionality.*

# What Are User Role Templates?

SAP delivers more than 150 user role templates (formerly known as predefined activity groups), which can be directly assigned to users. These user role templates consist of composite activity groups or single activity groups which are predefined with transactions and authorizations. These activity groups are created by application consultants in conjunction with customers to fulfill the most stringent requirements. User roles are assigned individual users. When users log on to the R/3 System they only see the part of the SAP menu which is required to fulfill their role tasks. This individual menu is called the **user menu**. Users can arrange the structure of their menu and have the option to add frequently used transactions to a personal favorites folder. They can also add web links and links to local documents, for example Microsoft Word or Excel files.

To work with these user role templates, use the transaction *PFCG* which is known as the Profile Generator (PG). The user role templates are standard delivered activity groups filled with data. All SAP-delivered user role templates start with *SAP_*.... Activity groups are used by the PG to generate authorization profiles. The first priority is to select transactions and reports. This information (transactions codes, menu paths, report names, etc.) is saved in an activity group, which serves as a database to help the PG determine the necessary authorizations and generate the profile(s).

You may set up as many activity groups as your company requires. A single activity (a transaction, report, or task) can be included in many different activity groups, and an activity group can include as many single activities as needed.

To save time, SAP provides user role templates so you do not have to create all activity groups on your own. However, you may still create your own activity groups or modify the ones SAP delivers.

# User Menu

Users only see the transactions they are allowed to execute in the system—those defined in the activity group assigned to them.

In the following example, the user menu for the user role template "Quality Manager" is shown. The *SAP Easy Access* menu serves as the individualized user menu. The menu structure is exactly what the Quality Manager sees when logged on to R/3. In our example, we have assigned only one activity group; of course you can assign many more.

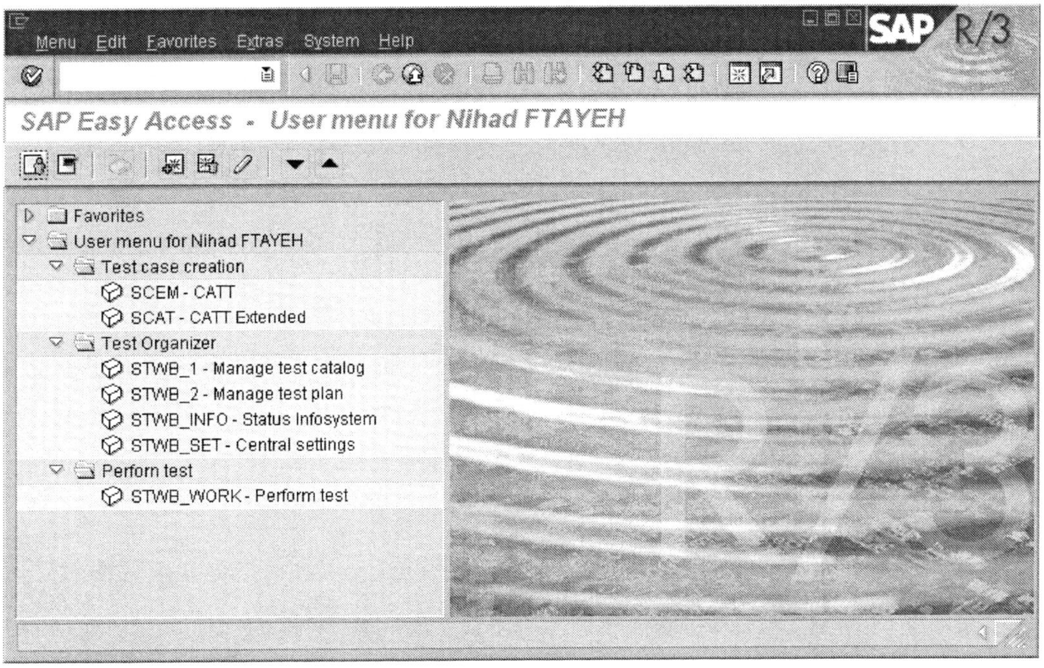


An example user menu using the user role template SAP_BC_CAT_QUALITYMANAGER_AG

You can still switch to the complete *SAP standard menu* using , though the user is not authorized to run every transaction in the standard menu. To return to the user menu, choose .

# How to Work with User Role Templates

There are different methods to work with user role templates. You may either:

- Use the SAP-provided user role templates as is
- Copy and modify the SAP-provided user role templates
- Create your own user role templates

In the following sections, we explain each option and provide the basic knowledge you need to work with user role templates. If you need more advanced information on how to work with the user role templates, refer to chapter 6, *Advanced Profile Generator Functionality*.

The tool used to work with the user role templates and activity groups respectively is the Profile Generator (PG). Use the transaction **PFCG** for the PG.

## Starting Activity Group Maintenance (PFCG)

Start the Profile Generator (PG) by one of the following methods from the *SAP Easy Access* screen:

- Choose *Create Menu*
- Enter the transaction **PFCG** in the *Command* field and choose *Enter*
- Choose *Tools → Administration → User maintenance → PFCG – Activity groups*

Then you can start working with the user role templates.

## Using the SAP-Provided User Role Templates

To use the SAP-provided user role templates just assign the user role template to a user. When that user logs on to the system, a specific user role menu appears.

To assign user role templates, you have two options:

- Use the PG, select the desired activity group, generate it, assign it to a user, and do a user compare. The following example explains how to assign a user role template using the PG.
- Use the user maintenance transaction SU01 to assign the desired user role templates to a specific user. See chapter 9, *Assigning Activity Groups*.

**Example:**

How to assign a user role template to a user, for example the Quality Manager using the Profile Generator.

1. Access the PG (transaction **PFCG**).
2. On the *Activity Group Maintenance* screen, use *possible entries* to select the desired activity group in the *Activity group* field (for example, *SAP_BC_CAT_Qualitymanager_AG*).
3. Choose *Change*.

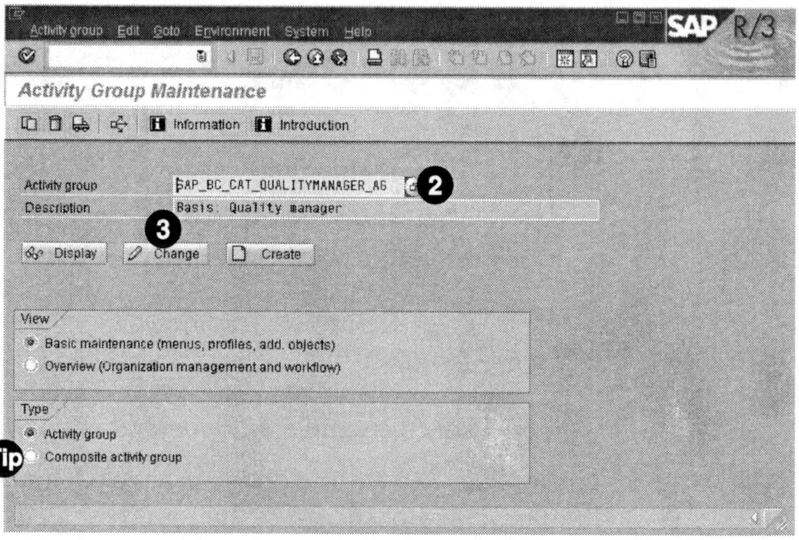


Tips & Tricks

You have the option to assign single activity groups or composite activity groups that can contain multiple activity groups.

4. Choose the *Menu* tab to review the transactions assigned to this activity group.

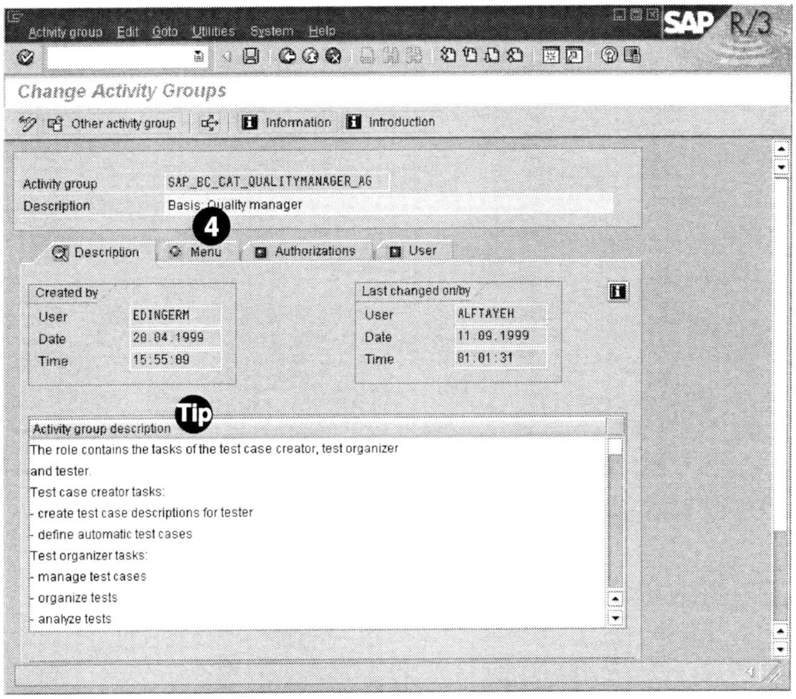


**Tips & Tricks**

In the SAP-delivered activity groups you always see an *Activity group description* of the content for the selected activity group. You can also add your own description.

5. The end user will see the folders and transactions as they appear in the *Activity group menu*.
6. You can change the order of any item by selecting it and using ▼ and ▲ to move it up and down.
7. Select the *Authorizations* tab to generate this activity group.

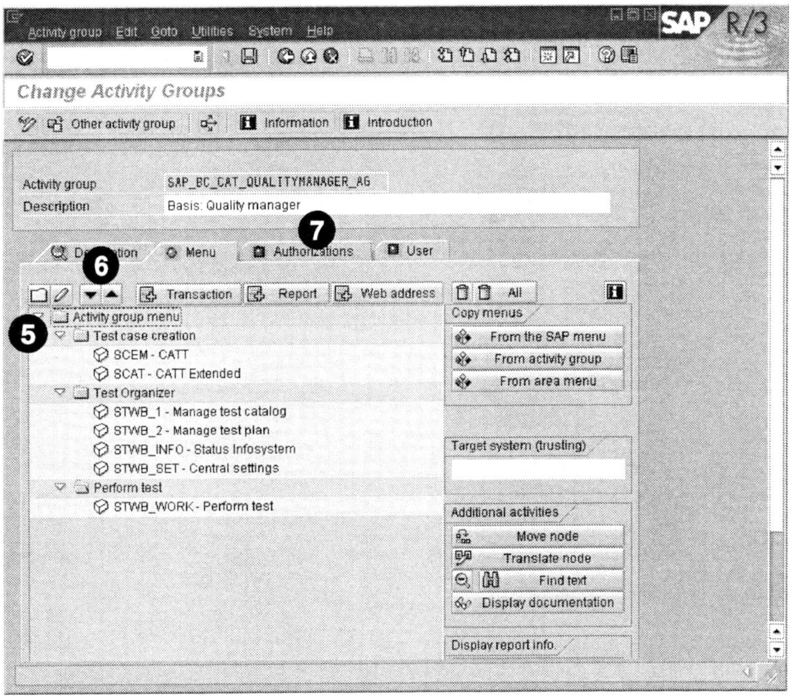


**Tips & Tricks**

The red light on the *Authorizations* tab indicates the profile is not generated yet.

8. Choose *Change authorization data.*

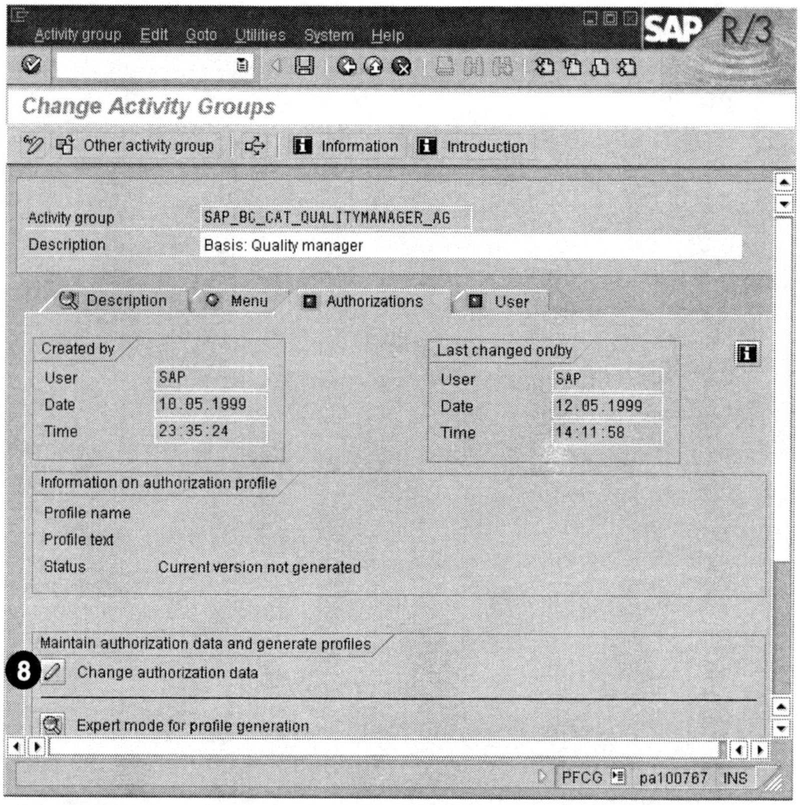


9. To generate the authorization profile, choose .
10. Choose .

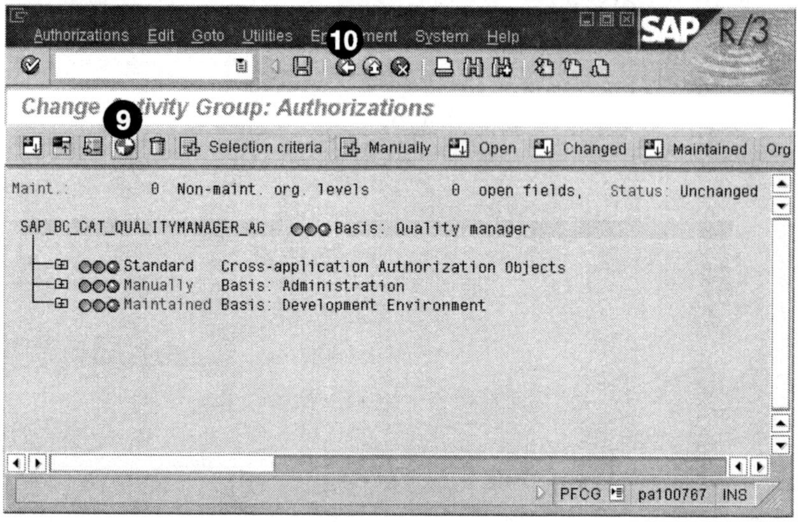

11. Choose the *User* tab to assign a user to this activity group.

Tips & Tricks

The red light on the *User* tab indicates that no user is assigned yet.

Tips & Tricks

**Status Display on the Tab**

The status display on the tab indicates if a user is already assigned to an activity group.

*User* – **Green**: At least one user is assigned to the group.
*User* – **Red**: No users are assigned.
*User* – **Yellow**: Although users have been assigned to the activity group, the user master record comparison is not current.

If the activity group is a composite activity group, the status display only indicates whether users are assigned to the activity group.

12. In the *User ID* field, select the desired user by either entering the name directly or using *possible entries*. You may select multiple entries from the list.

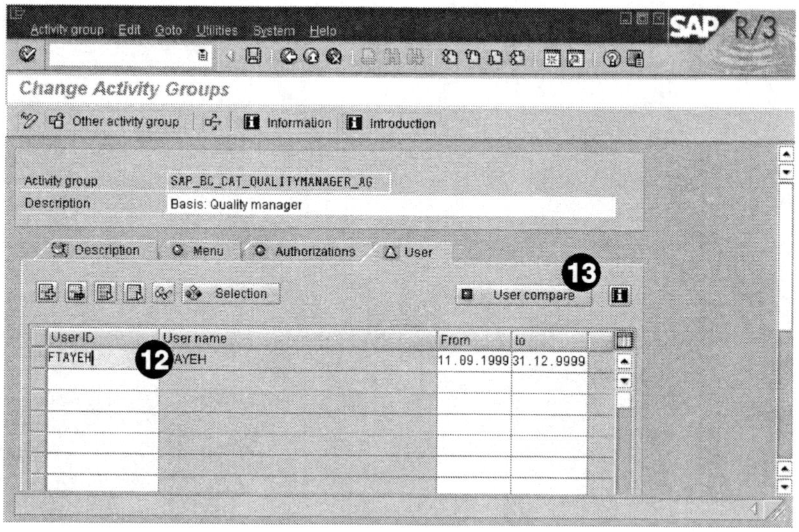


Tips & Tricks

The *User name* is automatically entered in the second column next to the user ID. In the two additional columns (*From, to*) you can specify a validity period for the assignment. You can delete the user IDs by using [icon] and insert an additional one in front of a selected user ID using [icon].

To get additional information on assigning users and time dependency, choose [icon].

13. After entering all users, select [icon] *User compare*.

Tips & Tricks

On the *Compare User Master Record of Activity Group* screen, note the status of the user master record. It says: *User master record has not yet been completely compared.* Therefore perform complete compare in step 14.

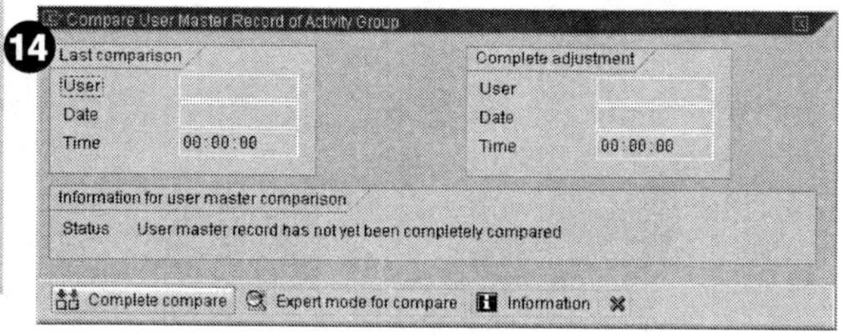


14. Choose [icon] *Complete compare*.

15. The user is now assigned to the activity group. When logging on to R/3, the user will see a specific user menu with only those transactions from the selected activity group.

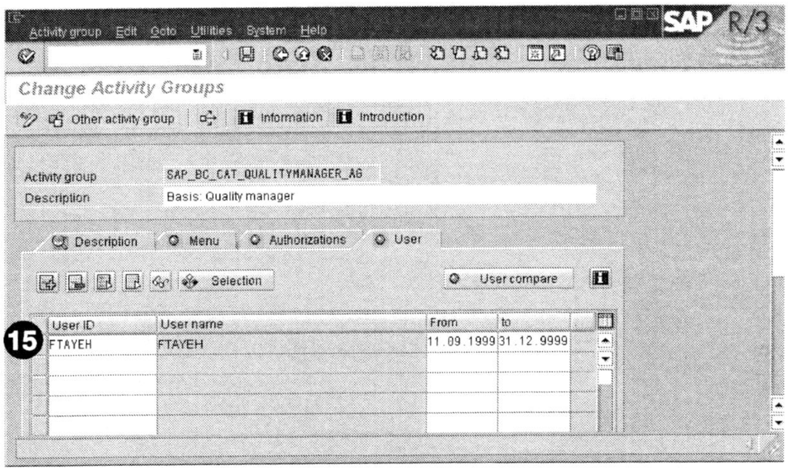


The process is now complete.

When the user *FTAYEH* logs in, the screen to the right appears after an activity group (for example, *SAP_BC_CAT_QUALITYMANAGER_AG*) has been assigned to *FTAYEH*.

As you can see, the menu is similar to the one created in the PG.

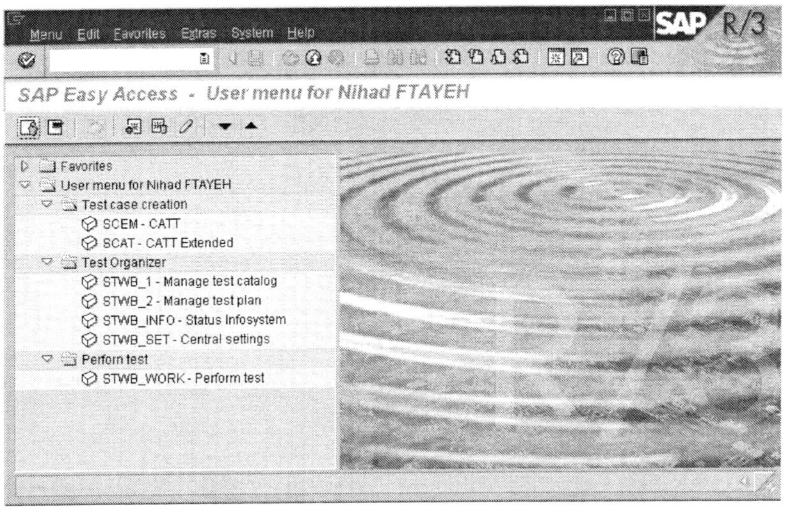

## Copying and Modifying SAP-Provided User Role Templates

If you are not completely satisfied with the content of an SAP-delivered user role template, you can modify the template. We recommend that you first copy the activity group and then make any changes to the newly created copy. Copying first ensures that you keep the original SAP template intact. Document the changes you make to the standard.

In this section, we show you how to copy an existing activity group, modify it, and assign it to a user.

If you want advanced information on how to work the complete PG functionality, see chapter 6, *Advanced Profile Generator Functionality*.

**Example:**

The following example demonstrates how to copy and rename the user role template for the Accounts Payable Accountant (we will use "Accounts Payable Accountant" variant). We assume that only one company code will be used, so we delete the folder *Cross-Company Code Transaction*, as well as *Bill of Exchange* and *Reject Parked Documents*. Furthermore, we add two transactions—*MRHR-Enter Invoice* and *MRHG-Enter Credit Memo*—into the folder Invoice/credit memo. Finally, we assign the new activity group *FI_AP_ACCOUNTANT_VARIANT_AG* to a user using the PG and demonstrate what this user is going to see when logging on to R/3.

1. Access the PG (transaction **PFCG**).
2. On the *Activity Group Maintenance* screen, use *possible entries* to select the desired activity group in the *Activity group* field (for example, *SAP_FI_AP_ACCOUNTANT _AG*).
3. Choose 🗐 to copy the activity group.

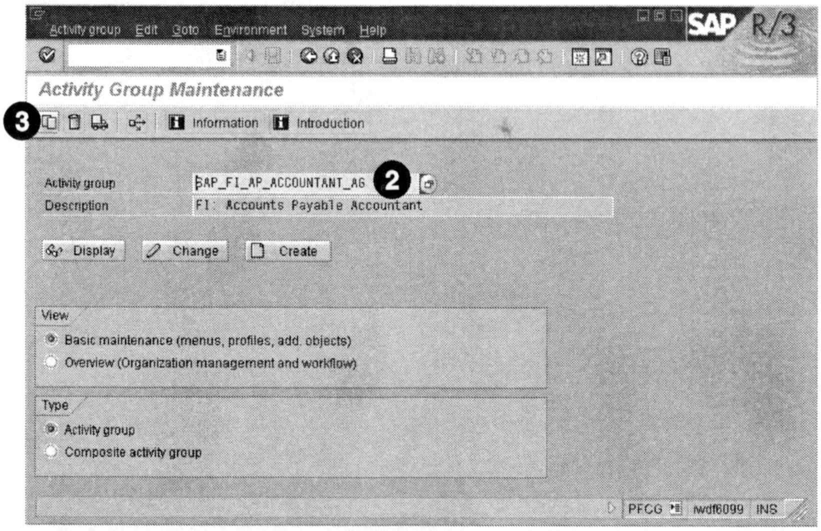


4. Enter a name for the new activity group.
5. Choose 🗐 *Copy selectively* to decide what objects you would like to copy with the activity group.

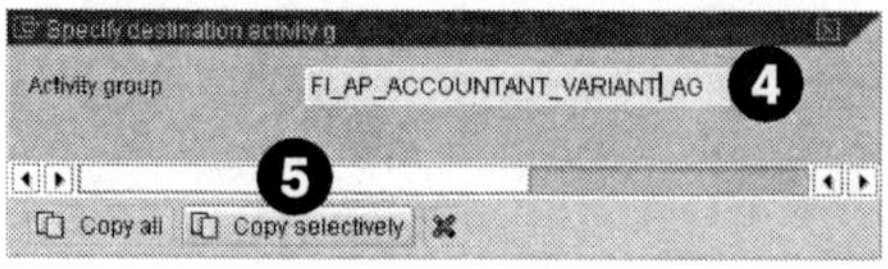

6. Choose ✔ without selecting anything. You should copy the activity group without the user assignment.

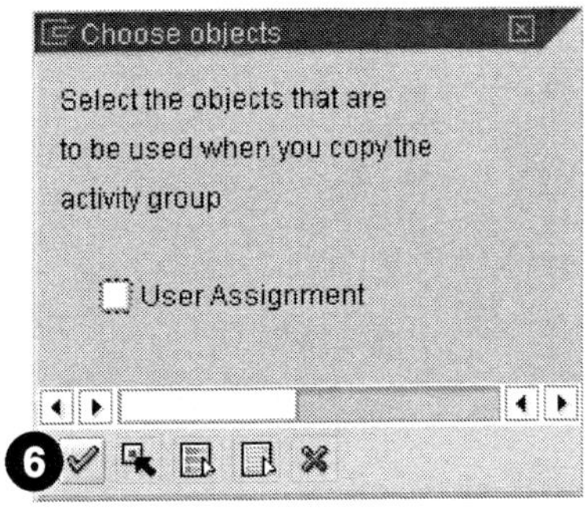


7. Choose ✎ *Change* to modify the new activity group.

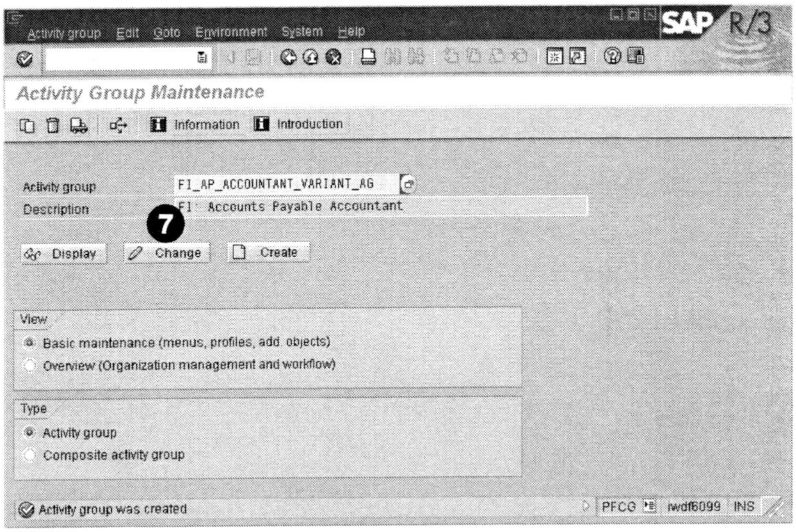


8. Enter a short description for your new activity group in the *Description* field.

9. Under *Activity group description,* enter a free text description.

10. Choose the *Menu* tab.

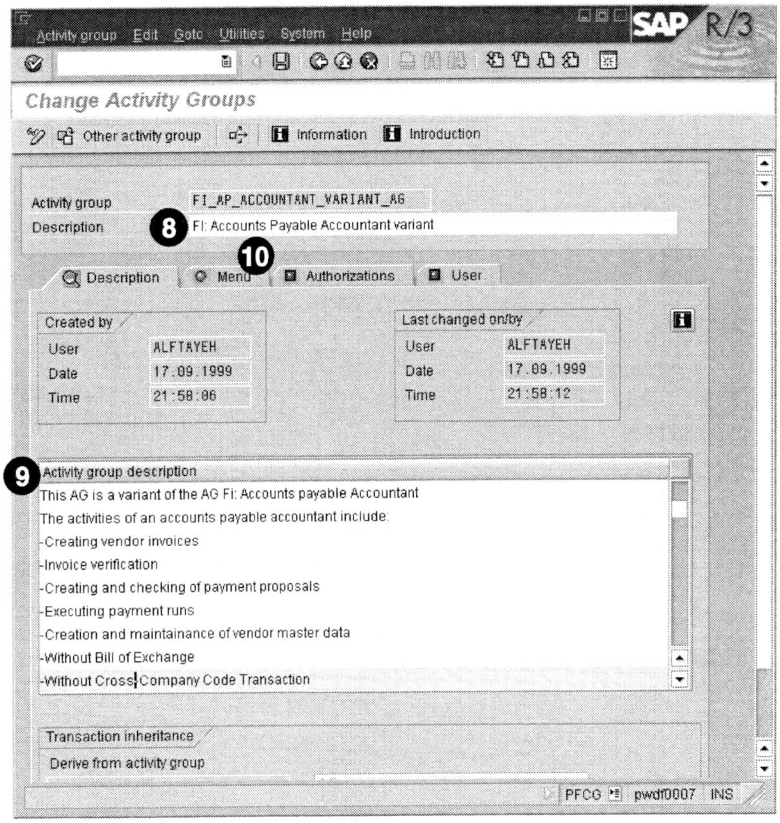

Now you see the menu of the original activity group in the new activity group. Open the desired folder where you want to modify or delete transactions. In our example, we would like to delete transaction *FBV6* and the folders *Cross-company code transaction* and *Bill of exchange* under the *Payment and clearing* node.

11. Select *FBV6 – Reject*.
12. To delete the transaction, choose 🗑.

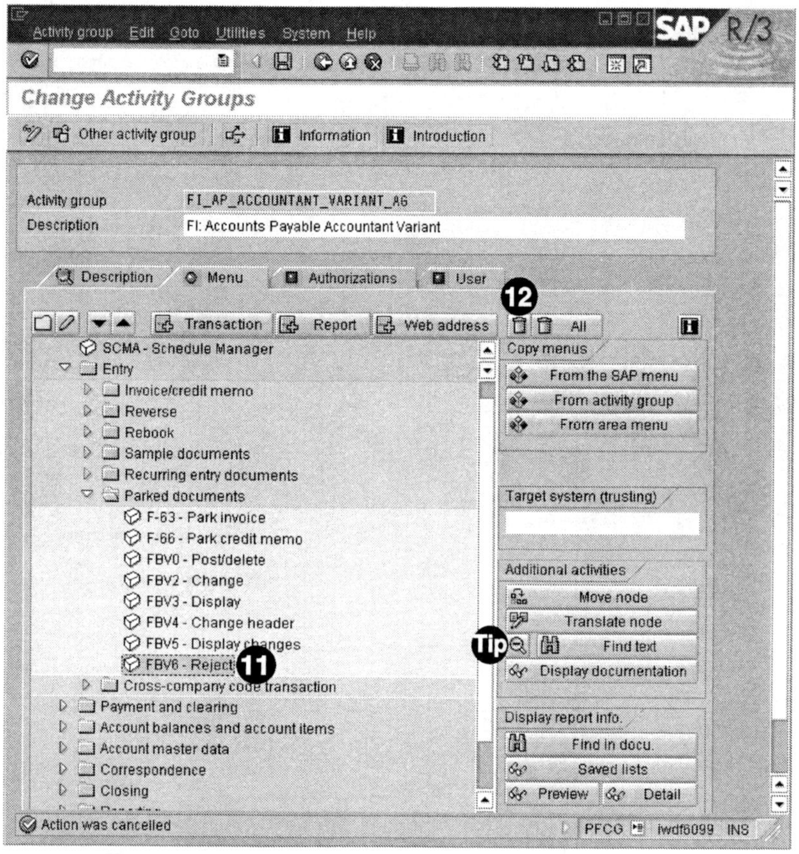

To display the transaction codes, choose 🔍+. If they are turned on, the icon changes to 🔍−.

13. Select the *Cross-company code transaction* line and choose 🗑.

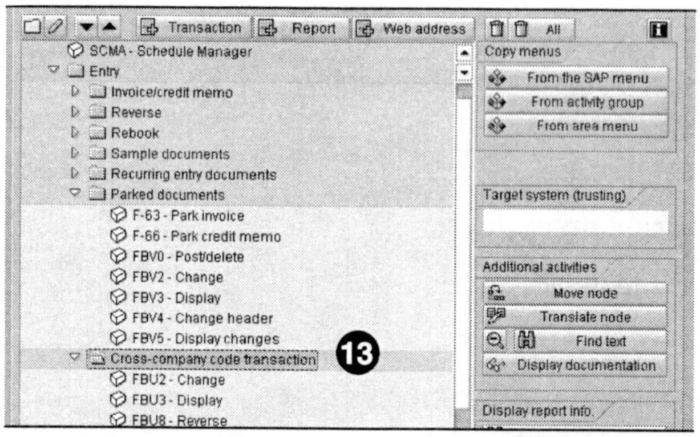


14. Select the *Bill of exchange* line and choose 🗑.

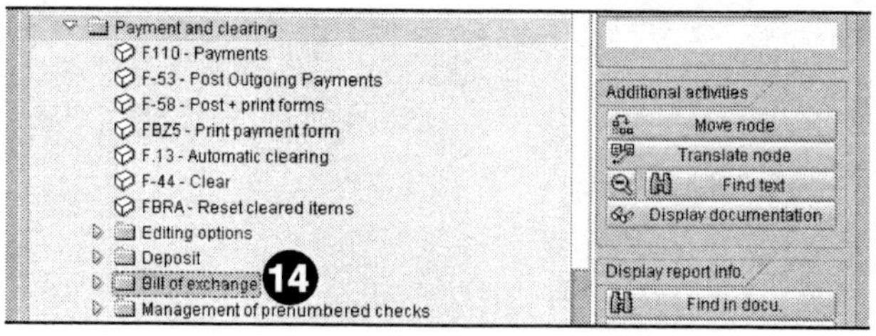

15. To insert a new transaction code manually, select the folder in which you would like that transaction to appear and choose *Transaction* (for example, we would like to enter the transaction *Enter Invoice* into the folder *Invoice/credit memo*).

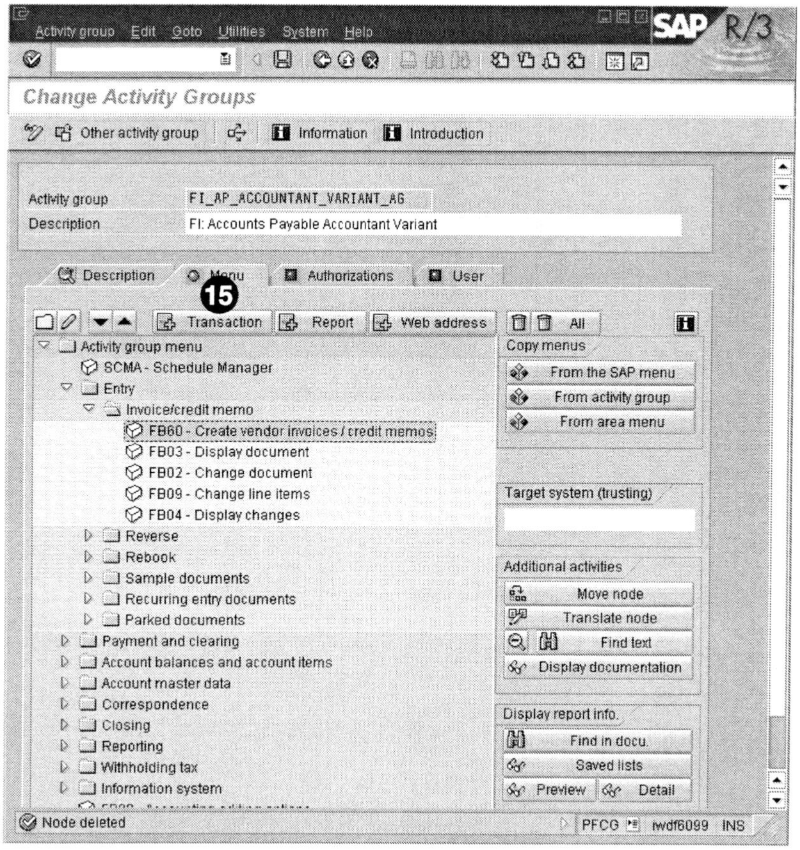


16. Enter the transaction code into the *Transaction code* field. If you press *Enter*, the text of the transaction code will appear in the *Text* column.

17. Choose *Assign transactions* to transfer the transaction into the activity group menu.

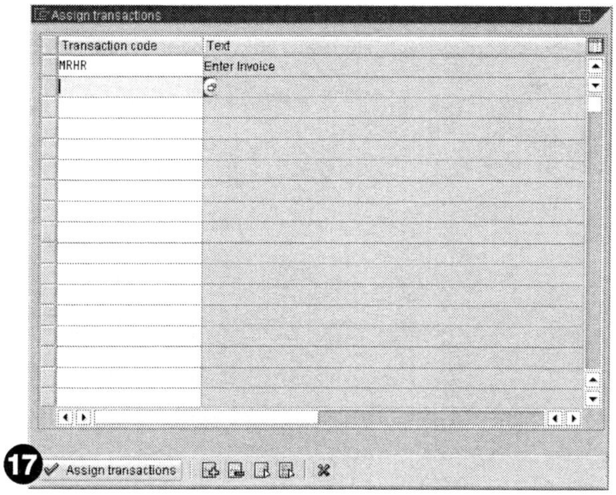

Tips & Tricks

If you would like to change the position of the transaction in the hierarchy, select the transaction and use the ▼▲ to move the transaction down or up.

18. If you do not know the transaction code and would rather select the transaction from the SAP menu, choose *From the SAP menu*.

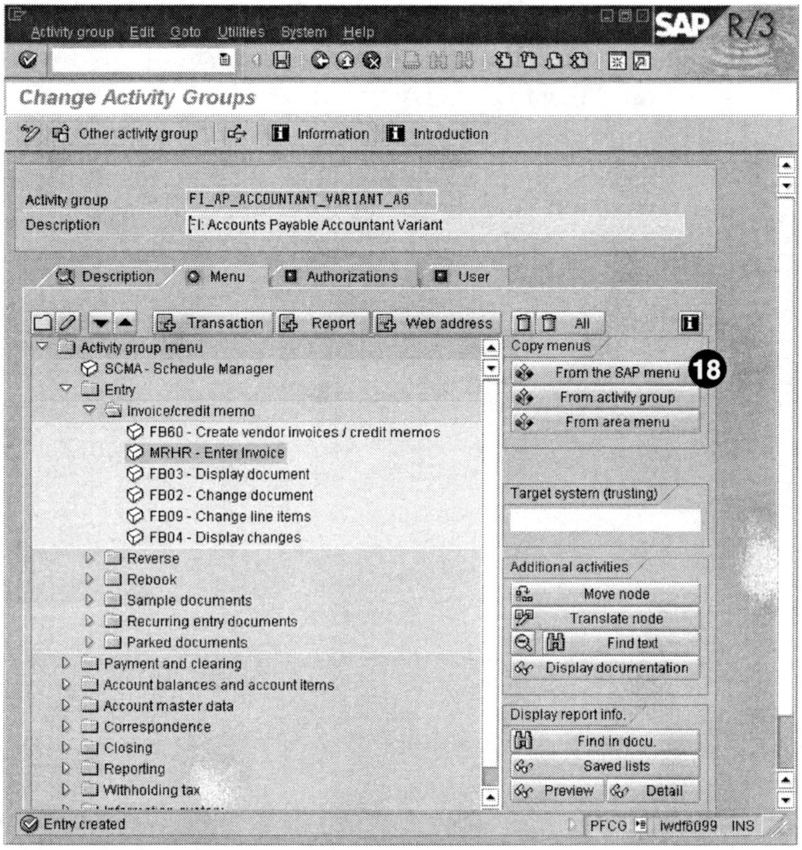


Tips & Tricks

We recommend you stay with one option: Either enter the transaction manually or enter it through one of the menus (SAP menu, activity group, or area menu). If you choose to enter from the menu, the menu path will be transferred to the activity group menu as well.

19. Select the desired transaction code (it is possible to select more than one).

20. Choose ✔ *Transfer* to transfer the transaction into activity group menu.

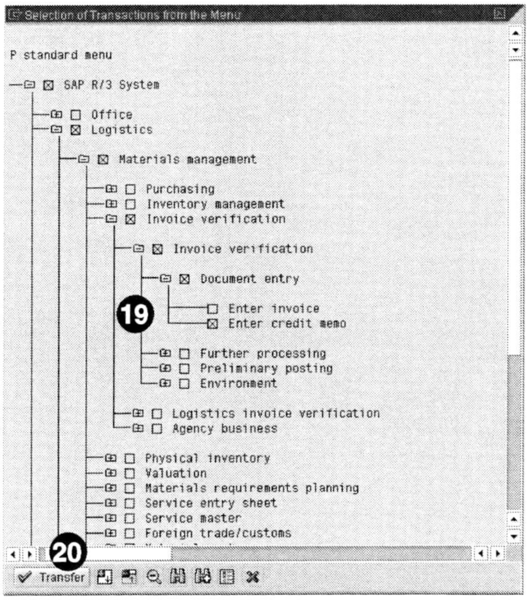

To switch the technical names on or off choose 🔍 or 🔍. If you cannot see the technical name of the transaction, scroll to the right where it is shown.

The transaction is transferred to the activity group menu and includes the complete menu path from the SAP menu.

21. Select the desired transaction and move it to the desired position by either:
    - Drag and drop
    - ▼ or ▲
    - *Move node*

    In this example, we used drag and drop.

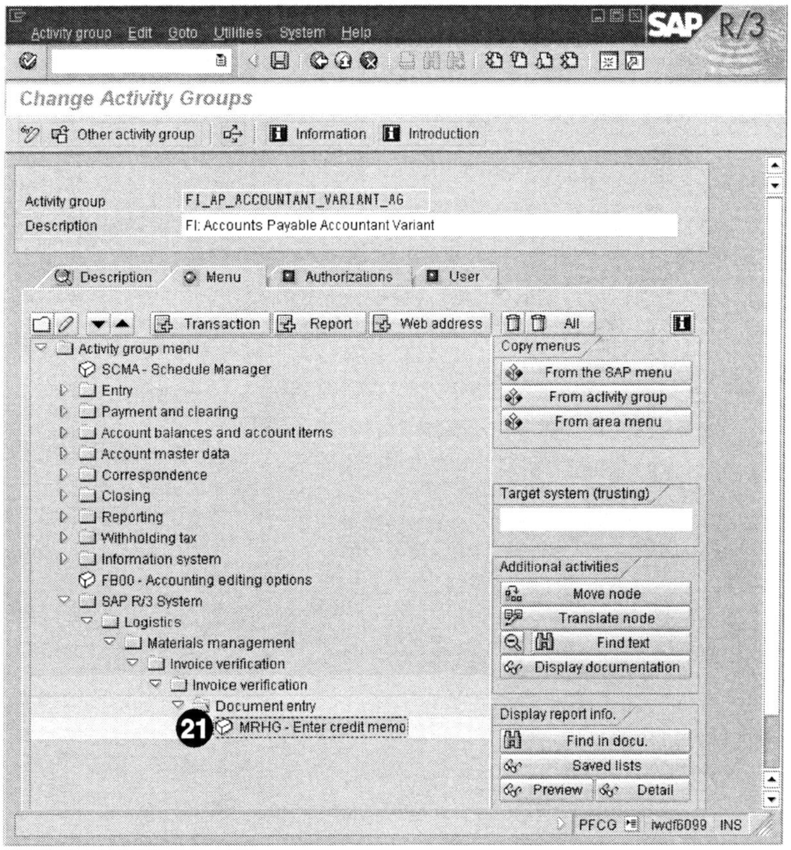

We moved the transaction into the folder *Invoice/credit memo,* below the transaction *MRHR-Enter Invoice.*

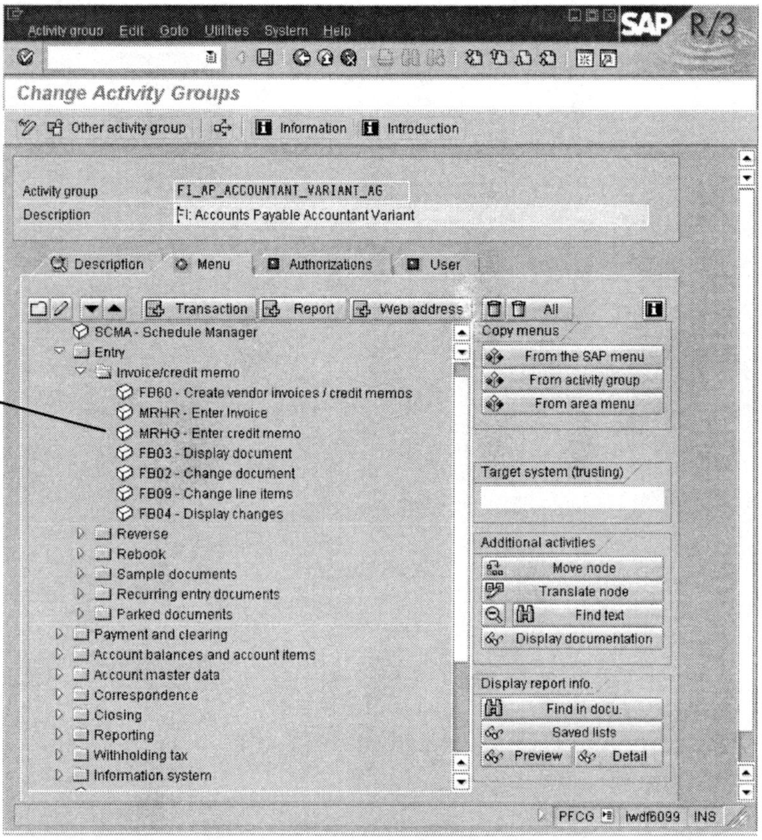


22. To delete the left menu path from the just inserted transaction, scroll down to the menu path that begins with *SAP R/3 System.*
23. Select the desired folder and choose 🗑 to delete the folder and the complete structure below it.

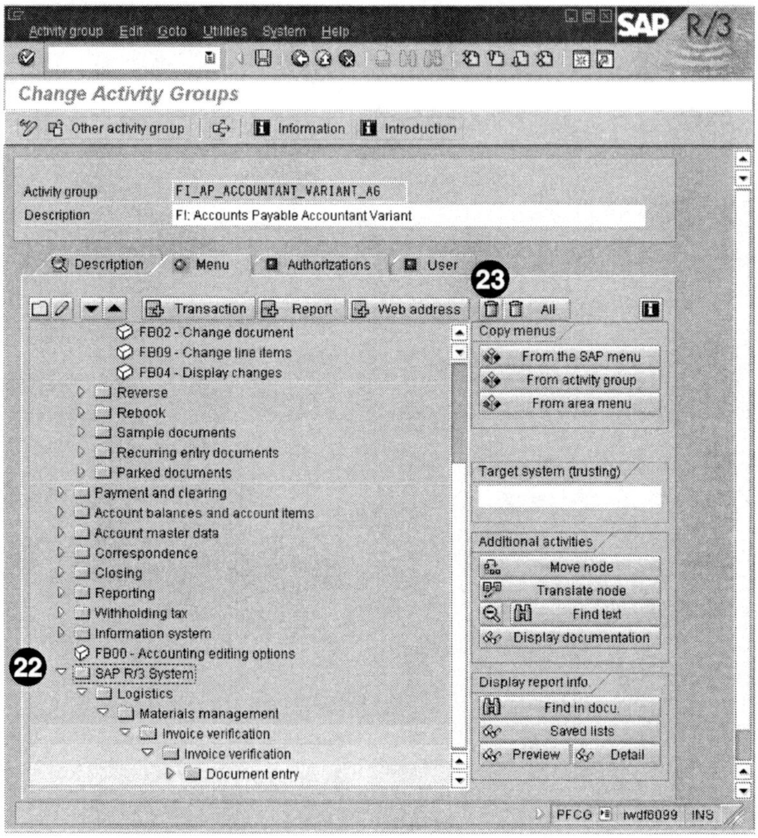

After you finish deleting and inserting transactions, maintain the authorizations for the transactions in this activity group.

24. Choose the *Authorizations* tab.

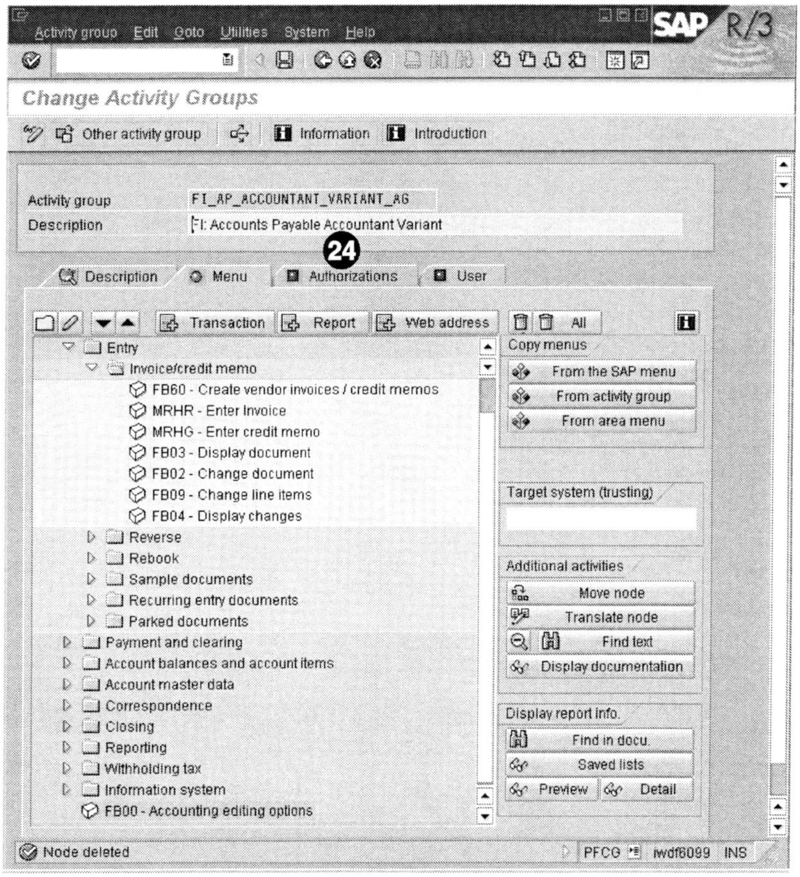


25. Choose *Change authorization data* to maintain the authorization data.

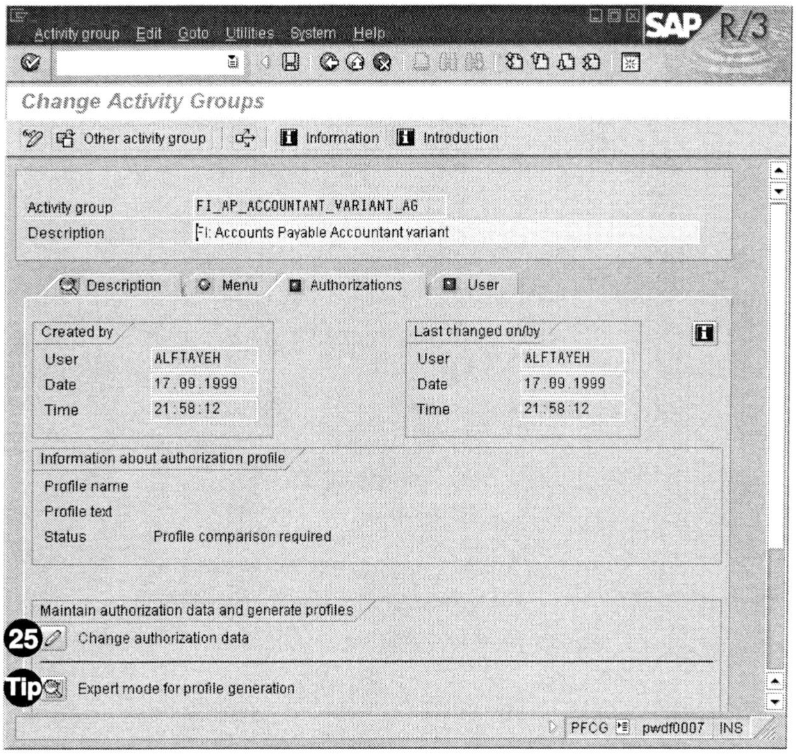


Tips & Tricks

In *Expert mode for profile generation* you can select explicitly the option with which you want to maintain authorization values. This option is automatically set correctly in normal mode.

Now adjust the authorizations to your specific needs. Open the desired folder and check or change the values.

In this example, we are not changing anything because everything from the copied activity group is correct.

For detailed information on how to work with the authorization fields, see chapter 6, *Advanced Profile Generator Functionality*.

26. To generate the profile, choose .

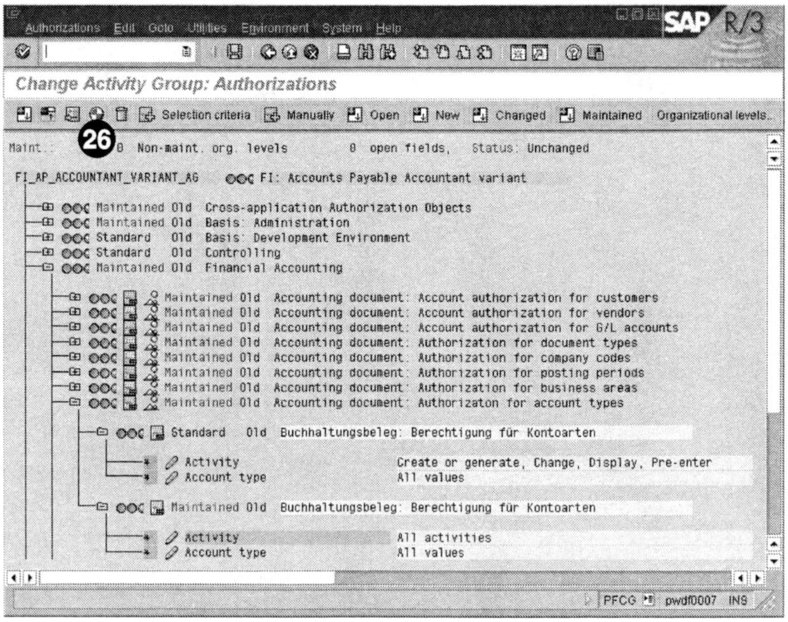


**Explanation of the Traffic Lights**

– **Green**: All authorization fields have been maintained.
– **Red**: Organizational levels are not maintained.
– **Yellow**: Open authorization fields exist without values that are not organizational levels.

27. The system suggests T-<*internal number*> as the default name. The *Profile name* cannot be changed later, however the *Text* can.

28. To continue, choose .

**Naming Conventions for Authorization Profiles and Generated Authorizations**

When you save your changes, you are prompted to enter a profile name. However, only the first 10 characters (the profile torso) can be freely assigned. The number of profiles generated depends on the number of authorizations in each activity group. A maximum of approximately 150 authorizations can fit into a profile. If there are more than 150 authorizations, an additional profile is generated. It has the same 10-character torso as the profile name, and the last two digits are used as a counter.

To avoid conflicts between customer-defined and SAP-supplied profiles, do not use any name with an underscore (_) in the second position. SAP places no other restrictions on the naming of authorization profiles (refer also to note *16466*). If your company has its own naming conventions, you may overwrite proposed names.

The names of the authorizations are also derived from the profile torso. The last two digits are used as a counter when more than one authorization is required for an object.

Depending on the authorization profile name, the technical names for authorizations are named as follows:

- Begin with a *T-*
- Comprise an internal number
- End with a two-digit number between *00* and *99*

Sample authorization name: T-5000001900.

29. Choose [icon] to return to the *Change Activity Groups* screen.

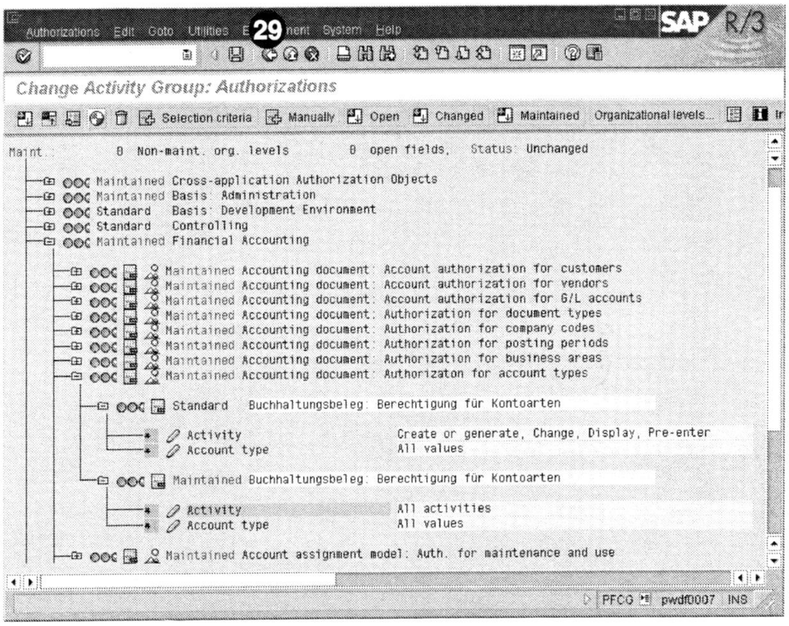


All the transactions and authorizations for the activity group have now been collected and generated. The next step is to assign a user to the activity group.

30. Choose the *User* tab to assign a user.

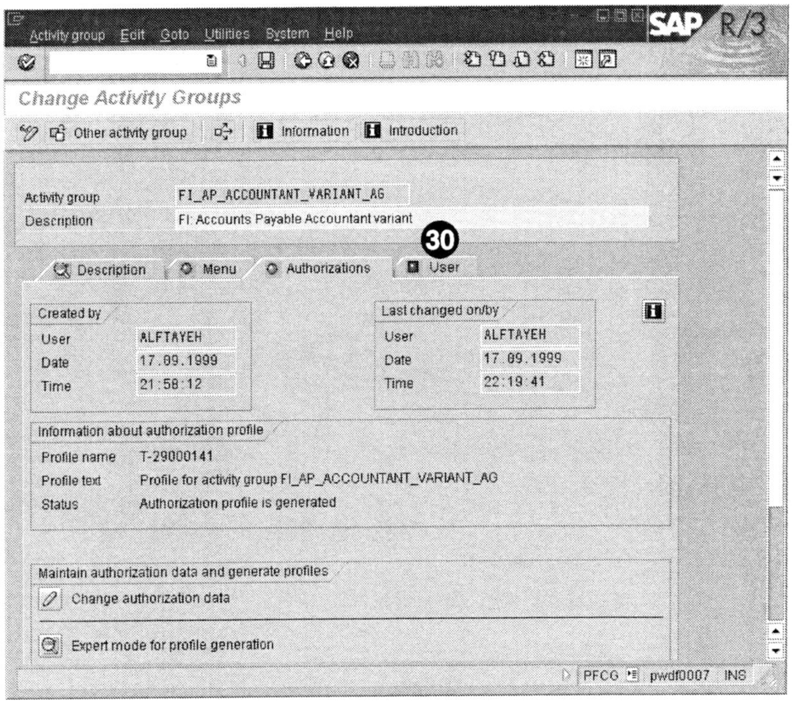


Tips & Tricks

The red light [icon] on the *User* tab indicates that no user has been assigned.

**Status Display on the Tab**

The status display on the tab indicates if a user is already assigned to an activity group.

*User* – **Green**: At least one user is assigned to the group.
*User* – **Red**: No users are assigned.
*User* – **Yellow**: Although users have been assigned to the activity group, the user master record comparison is not current.

If the activity group is a collective activity group, the status display only indicates whether users are assigned to the activity group.

31. In the *User ID* field, select the desired user by either entering the name directly or using *possible entries*. You can select multiple entries from the list at the same time.
32. In the *From* and *to,* column you can enter the date range for how long the user is assigned to the activity group.
33. After entering all users, select *User compare*.

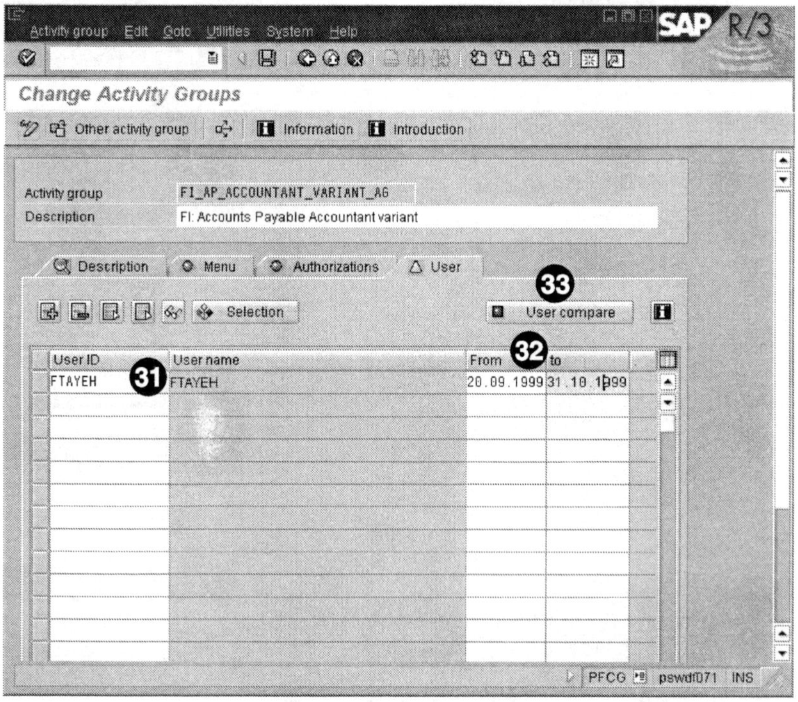


The *User name* is automatically entered in the second column next to the user ID. In the two additional columns (*From, to*) you can specify a validity period for the assignment. You can delete the user IDs by using the delete icon and insert an additional one in front of a selected user ID using the insert icon.

For additional information on assigning users and time dependency choose the information icon.

34. Choose *Complete compare.*

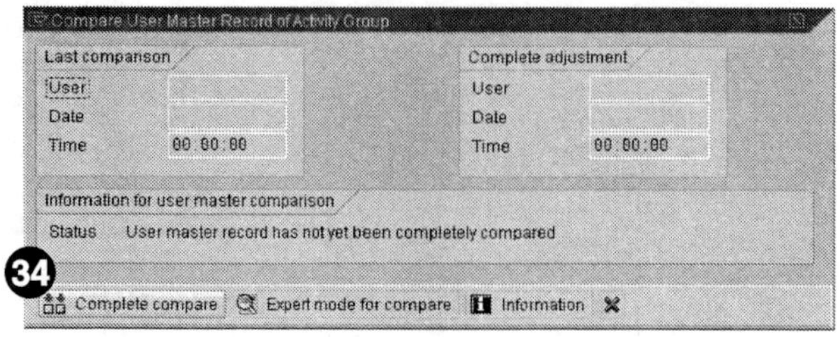

Tips & Tricks

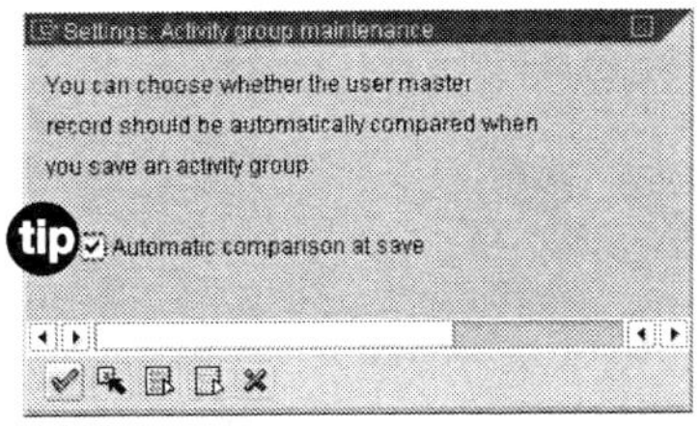


If you choose *Utilities* → *Settings* and select *Automatic comparison at save*, the user compare occurs automatically when you save the activity group.

35. The user is now assigned to the activity group.

    When logging on to R/3, the user will see a specific user menu with only those transactions from the selected activity group.

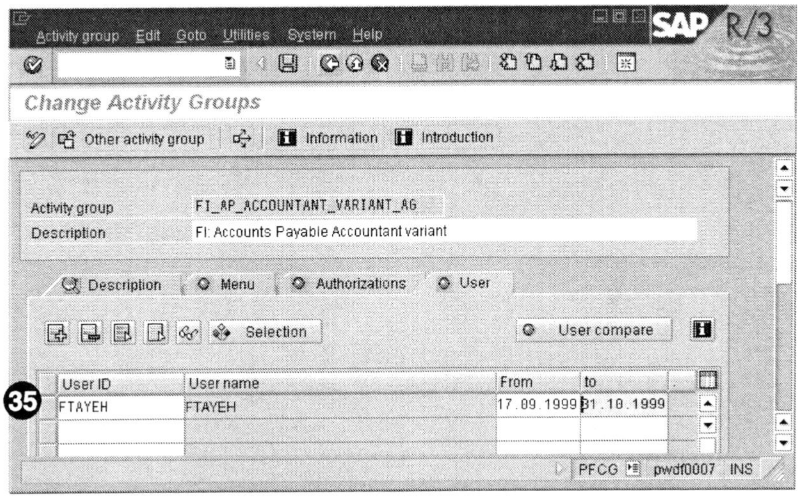


This is the screen a user sees when logging on to the system after an activity group (for example, *FI_AP_ACCOUNTANT_VARIANT_AG*) has been assigned to that user.

As you can see, the menu looks the same as that created in the PG.

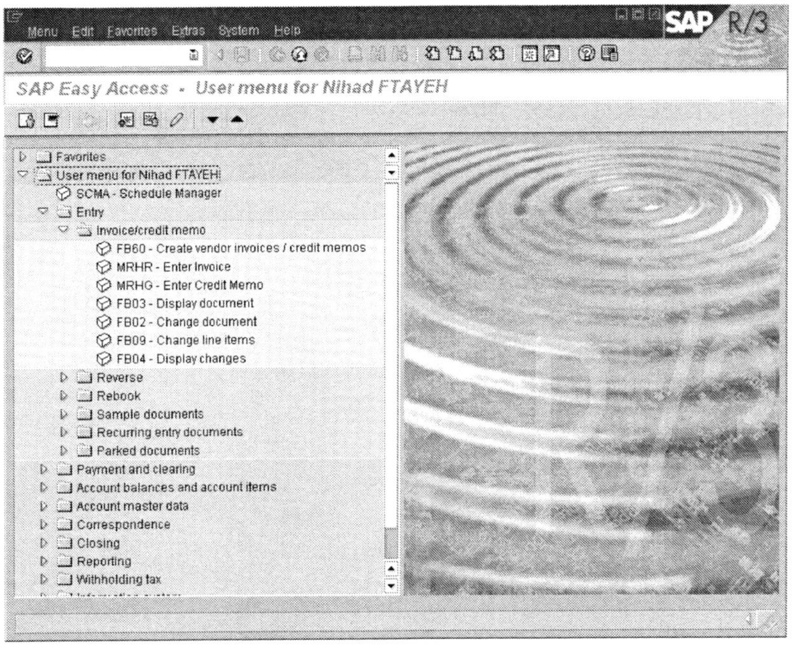

## Create your own User Role Templates

If you need user role templates in addition to the ones SAP delivers, you can create your own activity group.

In this section, we show you how to create an activity group, select transaction codes, generate the authorizations, and assign them to a user.

If you would like advanced information on how to work the complete PG functionality, see chapter 6, *Advanced Profile Generator Functionality*.

> **Example:**
>
> In the following example, we demonstrate how to create a new activity group and therefore the user role template for a data entry clerk. At the end, we assign the new activity group, which we name *FI_AP_DATA_ENTRY_CLERK_AG* to a user with the PG and demonstrate what this user is going to see when logging on to R/3.

1. Access the PG (transaction **PFCG**).
2. In the *Activity group* field, enter the name for the new activity group (for example, **FI_AP_DATA_ENTRY_CLERK**).
3. To create the new activity group, choose *Create.*

You have the option to assign single activity groups or composite activity groups which can contain multiple activity groups. See *Creating Composite Activity Groups* on page 5–32.

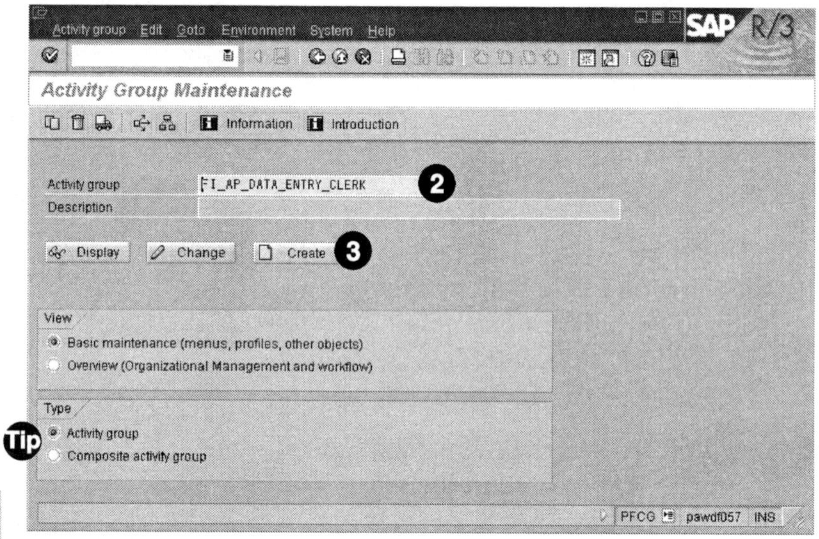

4. In *Description*, enter a short description.
5. Under *Activity group description*, enter a description of the activity group.
6. To save the activity group, choose 💾.
7. Choose the *Menu* tab to select the transactions for the activity group.

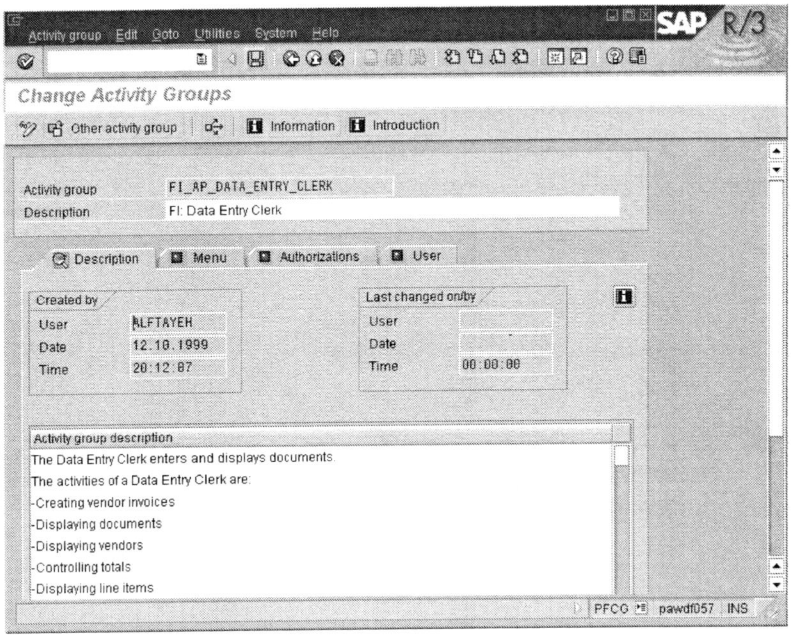


TechTalk

There are different ways to assign transactions to an activity group. You can assign a transaction by doing one of the following:

- Entering it directly (only the transaction without the menu path is added)
- Selecting it from the SAP menu (the complete menu path will be shown)
- Selecting it from an existing activity group (the complete menu path will be shown)
- Selecting it from an area menu (the complete menu path will be shown)

In this example, we demonstrate how to insert a transaction from an existing activity group and how to insert the transaction code directly. The other options work accordingly.

We would like to insert the transactions for "creating vendor invoices/credit memo" (FB60) and "displaying documents" (FB03) with the same menu path as it is in the activity group for the "accounts payable accountant" *(SAP_FI_APACCOUNT_AG).*

8. Choose *From activity group.*

Tips & Tricks

If you would like to select the transaction code from the SAP menu, choose *From the SAP menu*. Then follow the same procedure.

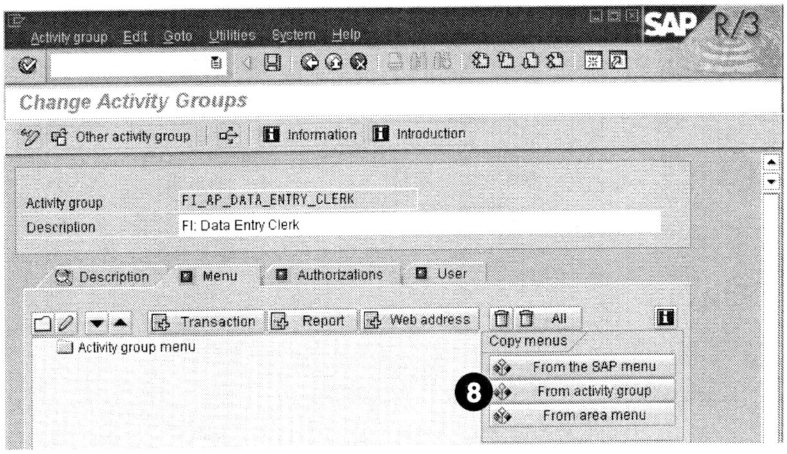


9. In the following screen, select the activity group *SAP_FI_AP_ACCOUNTANT_AG.*
10. Choose *Enter*.

11. Select the desired transactions. For example, we selected:
    - *Schedule Manager*
    - *Create vendor invoices/credit memos* (under *Entry* → *Invoice/credit memo*)
    - *Display document* (under *Entry* → *Invoice/credit memo*)
    - *Display vendor* (under *Account master data*)
12. To add the selected transactions to the activity group menu, choose *Add*.

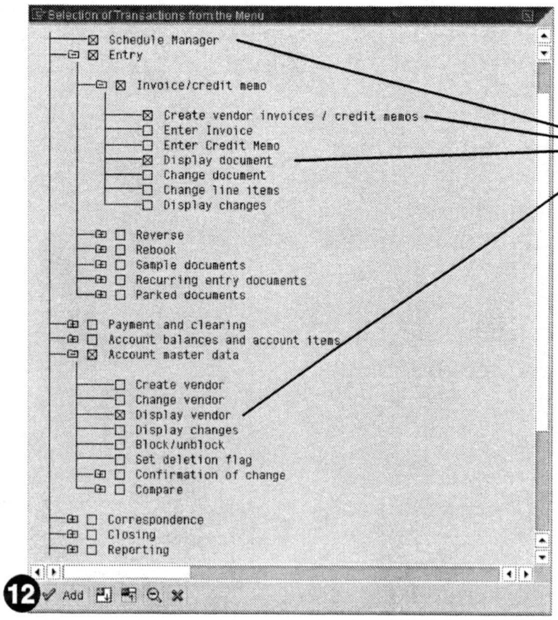


Tips & Tricks

To switch the technical names on and off, choose or . If you cannot see the technical name of the transaction, scroll farther to the right.

If you open the folders, you can see how the transactions and paths have been inserted. They appear in the *User menu* in exactly the same way as defined in the PG.

The next transactions to insert are *FB00* and *FB03*. For those transactions, we will create a new folder called *User settings*.

13. To create a new folder, choose and enter the new name for the folder (in example, *User settings*).

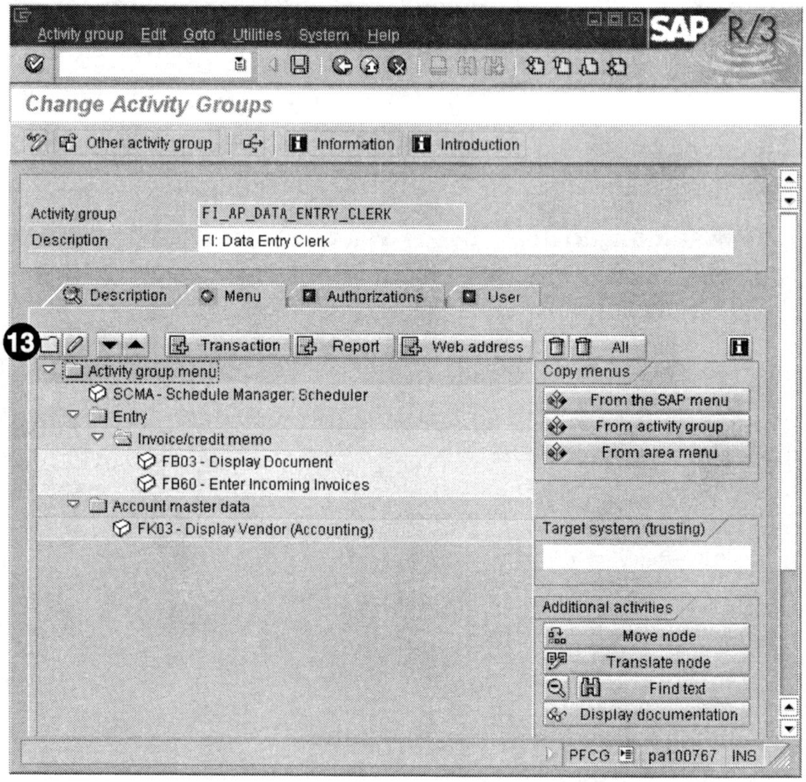


Tips & Tricks

To switch the technical names on and off choose or . The technical names appear in front of the transaction code text.

14. To move the folder to the end of the menu, highlight the folder you want to move and choose ▼ to move it down.
15. To enter the transactions, choose *Transaction.*

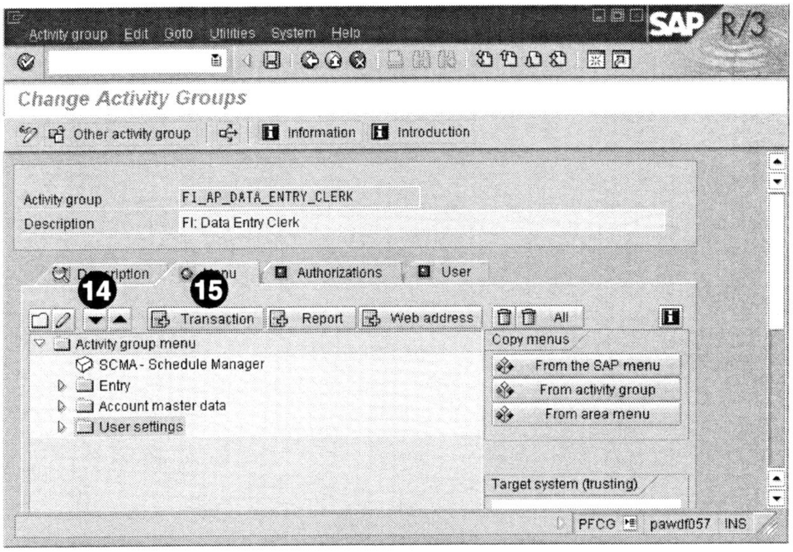


16. Enter the desired transactions (for example, **FB00** and **FB07**). The description text for the transaction code appears in right column.
17. Choose *Assign transactions.*

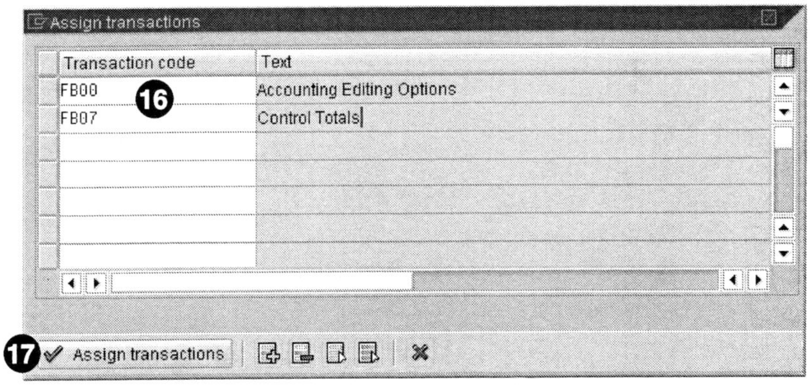


After you select all the transactions necessary (for example, for the *Data Entry Clerk*):

18. To save the activity group, choose 💾.
19. To maintain the authorization data, choose the *Authorizations* tab.

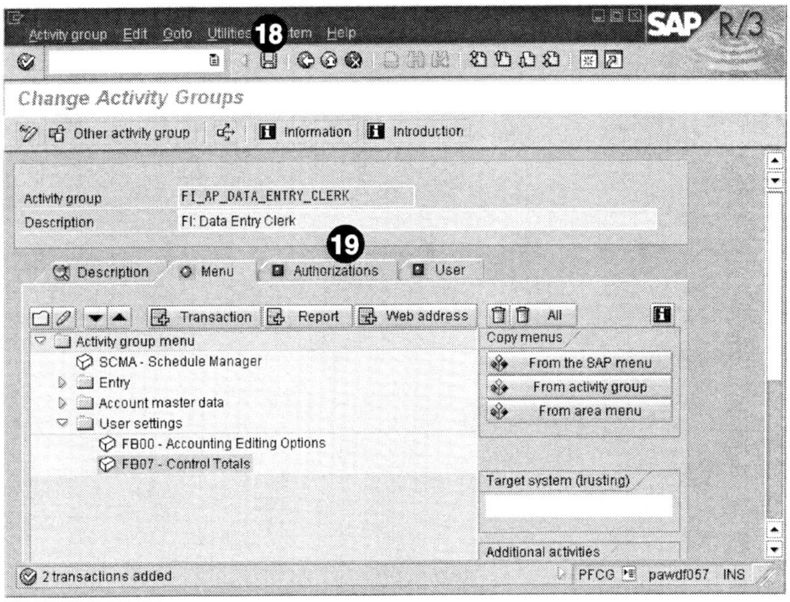

20. To maintain the authorizations data, choose *Change authorization data*.

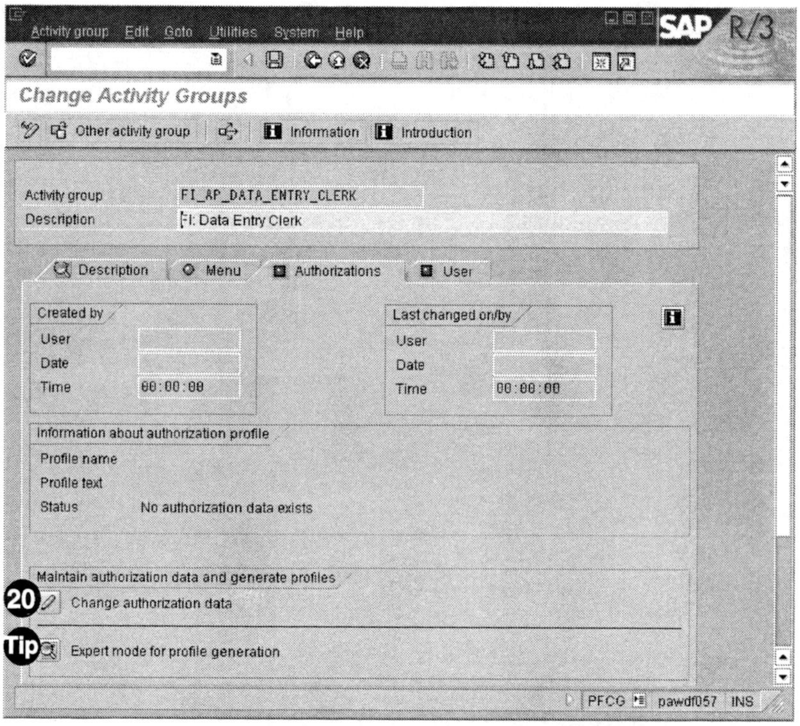


**Tips & Tricks**

In *Expert mode for profile generation* you can specifically select the option with which you want to maintain authorization values. This option is automatically set correctly in normal mode.

If necessary, the *Define Organizational Levels* dialog box appears. This screen usually pops up the first time you choose *Change authorization data*.

Use *possible entries* to select the desired values or value range.

21. In this example, we selected *Full authorization* for the organizational levels.
22. Choose *Save*.

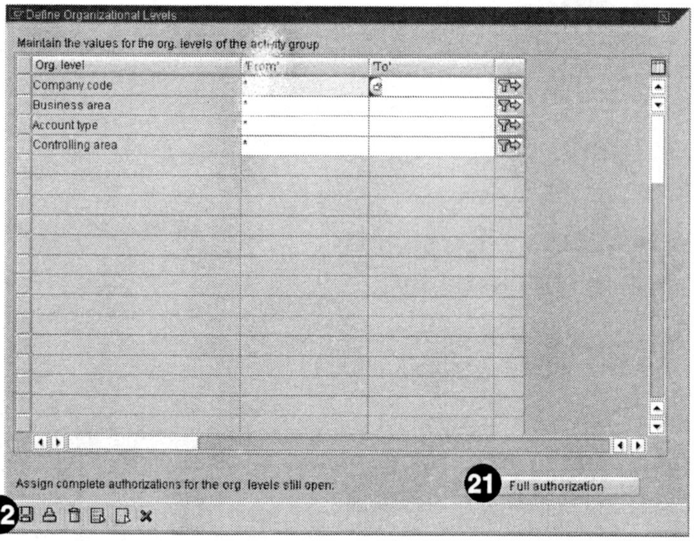


**Tips & Tricks**

Company codes, business areas, and plants are examples of organizational levels. You can display and maintain a list of existing levels with transaction *SUPO*.

On the *Change Activity Group: Authorizations* screen, the authorization data appears hierarchically.

The activity group appears at the first level (blue). Underneath you find:

- *Object classes = purple*
- *Authorization object = green*
- *Authorization = yellow*
- *Authorization fields = light blue*

23. To maintain the activity, click the *Activity* value field.

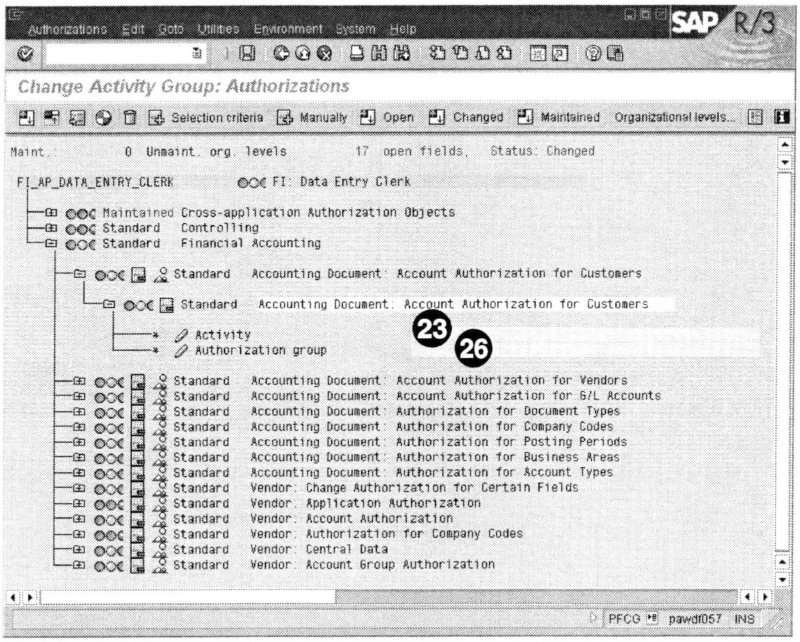


**Tips & Tricks**

**Explanation of the Traffic Lights**

– **Green:** All authorization fields have been maintained.
– **Red:** Organizational levels are not maintained.
– **Yellow:** Open authorization fields without values exist that are not organizational levels.

24. Select the desired authorization (for example, *Display*).
25. To transfer, choose 💾.

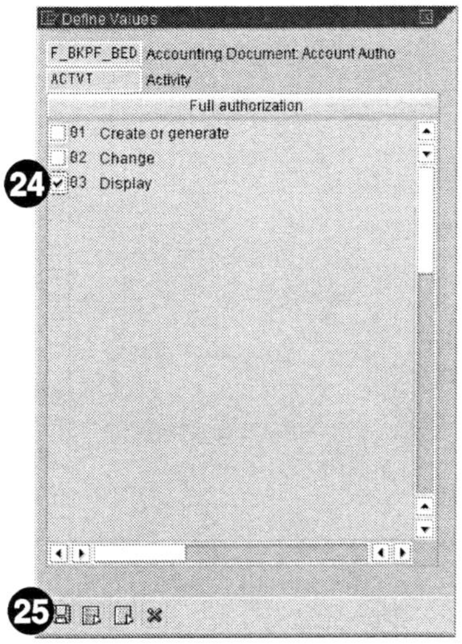


26. On the *Change Activity Group: Authorizations* screen, to maintain the *Authorization group,* click the *Authorization group* value field.

27. Enter or select the desired value (we choose *Full authorization*).
28. To transfer, choose 💾.

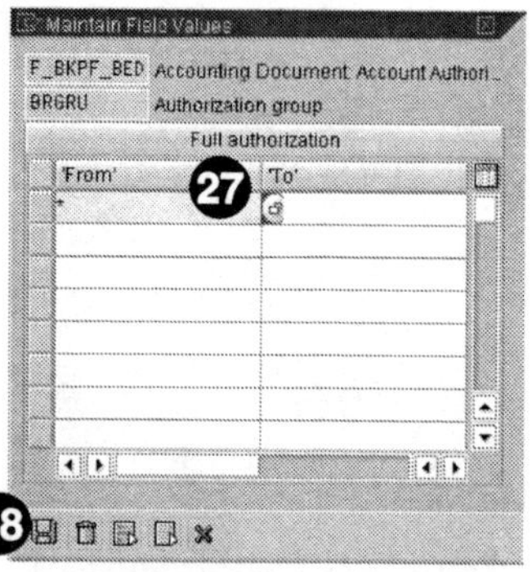


Proceed with all open fields in the same way until all lights switch to green.

29. Choose 💾.
30. To generate the profile, choose the generate icon.

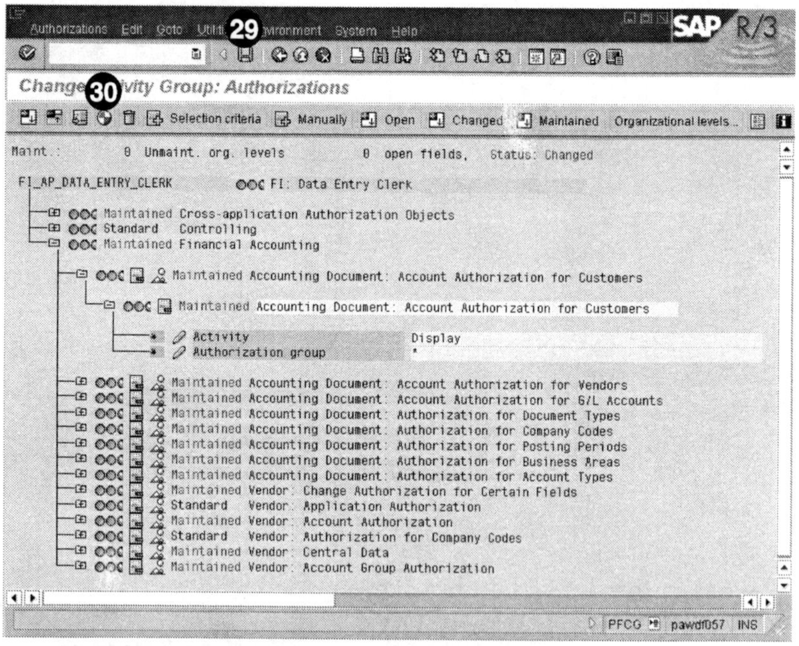


31. The system suggests T-<*internal number*> as the default name. The *Profile name* cannot be changed later, however the *Text* can.
32. To continue, choose ✔.

Tips & Tricks

**Naming Conventions for Authorization Profiles and Generated Authorizations**

When you save your changes, you are prompted to enter a profile name. However, only the first 10 characters (the profile torso) can be freely assigned. The number of profiles generated depends on the number of authorizations in each activity group. A maximum of approximately 150 authorizations can fit into a profile. If there are more than 150 authorizations, an additional profile is generated. It has the same 10-character torso as the profile name, and the last two digits are used as a counter.

To avoid conflicts between customer-defined and SAP-supplied profiles, do not use any name with an underscore (_) in the second position. SAP places no other restrictions on the naming of authorization profiles (refer also to note *16466*). If your company has its own naming conventions, you may overwrite proposed names.

The names of the authorizations are also derived from the profile torso. The last two digits are used as a counter when more than one authorization is required for an object. Depending on the authorization profile name, the technical names for authorizations are named as follows:

- Begin with a *T-*
- Comprise an internal number
- End with a two-digit number between *00* and *99*

Sample authorization name: T-5000001900.

33. Choose to return to the *Change Activity Groups* screen.

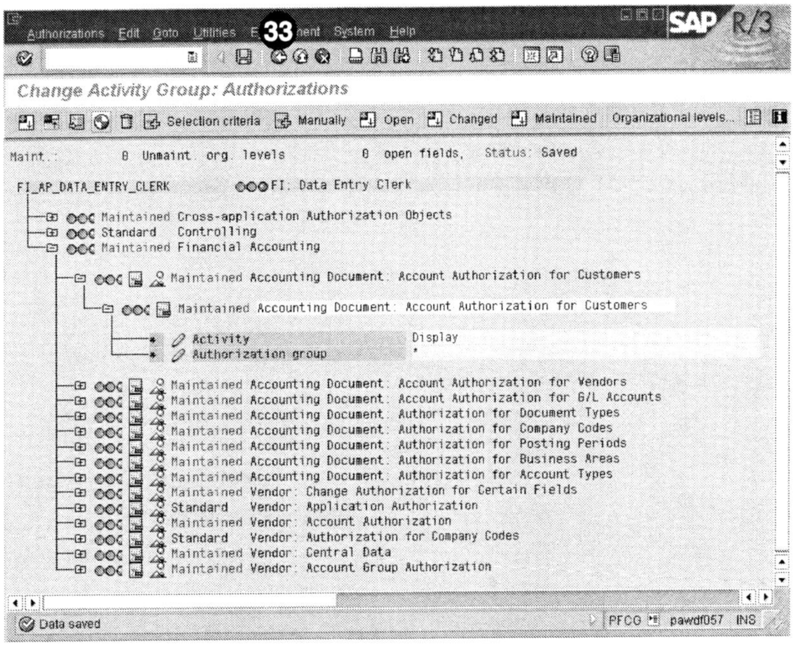


**Tips & Tricks**

If you choose and forget to generate the activity group, the system shows you the status and reminds you to generate the activity group.

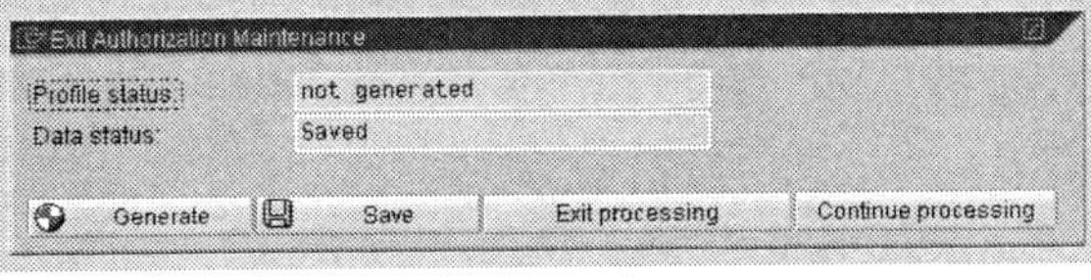

All the transactions and authorizations for the activity group have now been collected and generated. The next step is to assign a user to the activity group.

34. Choose the *User* tab to assign a user.

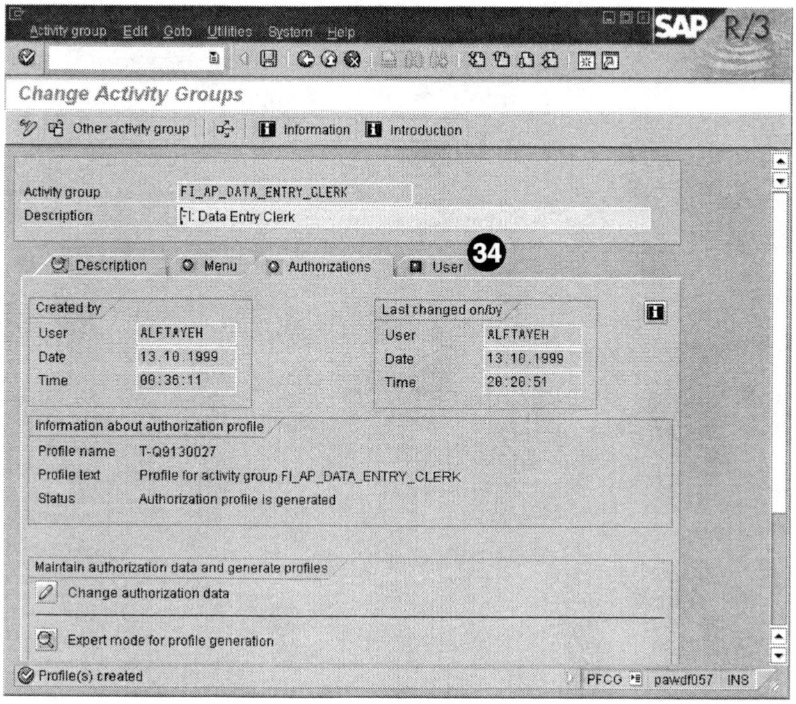


Tips & Tricks

The red light on the *User* tab indicates that no user has been assigned.

Tips & Tricks

**Status Display on the Tab**

The status display on the tab indicates if a user is already assigned to an activity group.

*User* – **Green**: At least one user is assigned to the group.
*User* – **Red**: No users are assigned.
*User* – **Yellow**: Although users have been assigned to the activity group, the user master record comparison is not current.

If the activity group is a collective activity group, the status display only indicates whether users are assigned to that activity group.

35. In the *User ID* field, select the desired user by either entering the name directly or using *possible entries*. You may select multiple entries from the list at the same time.
36. In the *From* and *to* column, enter the date range for how long the user should be assigned to the activity group.
37. After entering all users, select *User compare.*

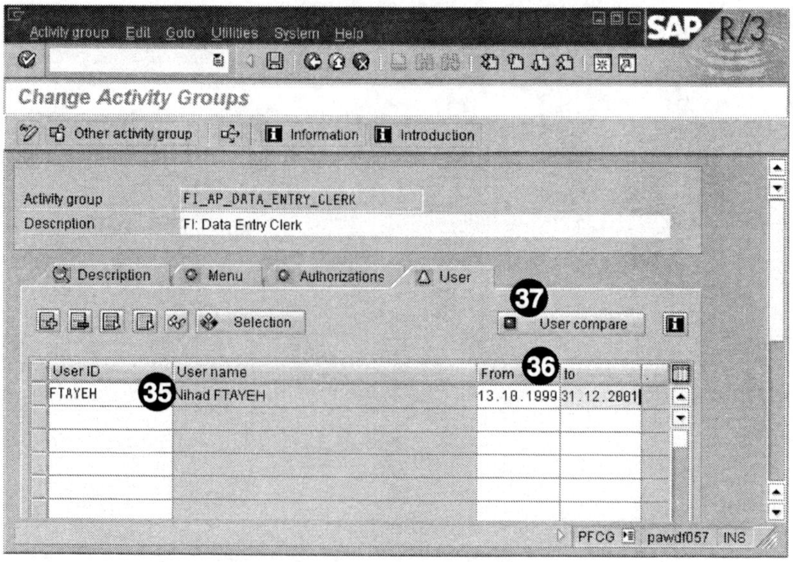

The *User name* is automatically entered in the second column next to the user ID. In the two additional columns (*From, to*) you can specify a validity period for the assignment. You can delete the user IDs by using and insert an additional one in front of a selected user ID using .

For additional information on assigning users and time dependency, choose .

38. Choose *Complete compare.*

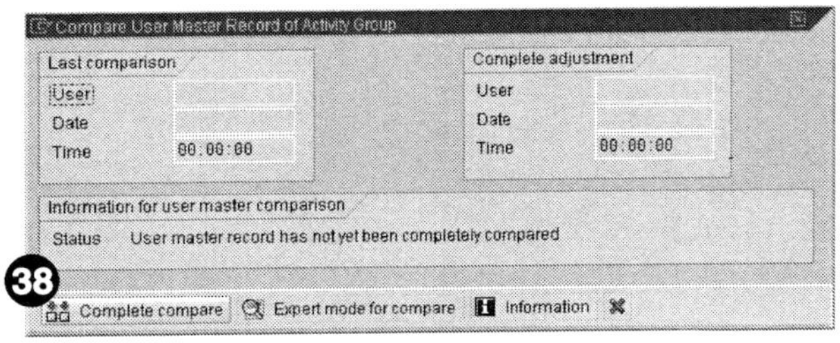


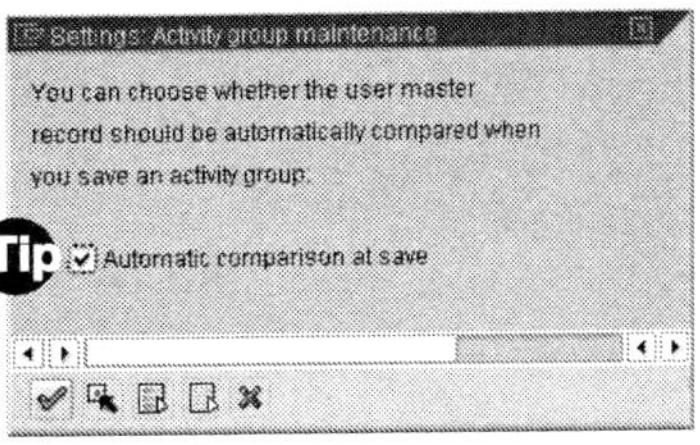


If you choose *Utilities → Settings* and select *Automatic comparison at save,* the user compare occurs automatically when you save the activity group.

39. The user is now assigned to the activity group. When logging on to R/3, the user sees a specific user menu with only those transactions for the selected activity group.

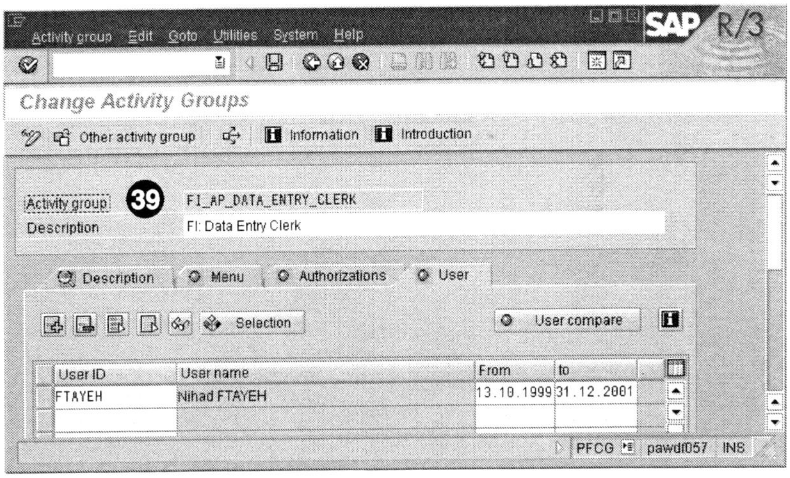

The user sees the *SAP Easy Access – User menu for <user's name>* when logging into R/3 after the assignment of the activity group (in this example, the user menu from *FI_AP_DATA_ENTRY_CLERK*).

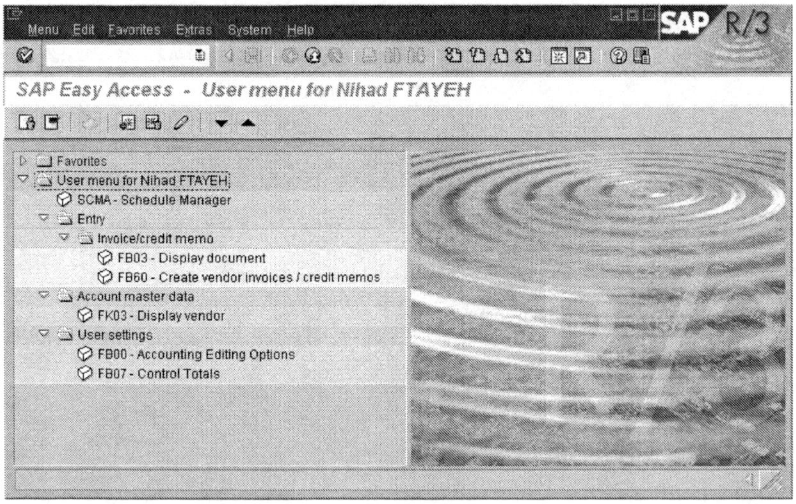


Users can maintain their own favorites and insert links to their menu. See chapter 6, *Advanced Profile Generator Functionality* for details.

## Creating Composite Activity Groups

In the previous section, we described how to create your own user role templates using single activity groups. You also have the option to create composite activity groups, which consist of multiple single activity groups. In those composite activity groups, you cannot assign transactions directly. You have to enter single transactions into separate activity groups and then assign those activity groups to composite activity group.

In the following procedure, we demonstrate how to create a composite activity group that includes three single activity groups.

1. Access the PG (transaction **PFCG**).
2. Under *Type*, select *Composite activity group*.
3. In the *Activity group* field, enter the name for the new activity group (for example, **FI_AP_DATA_MANAGER**).
4. To create the new activity group, choose *Create*.

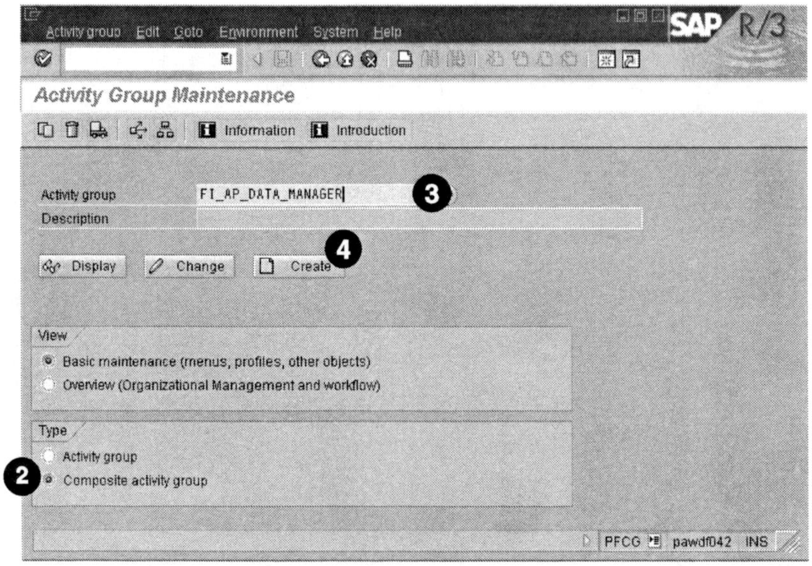

5. In *Description*, enter a short description.
6. Under *Activity group description*, enter a description of the activity group.
7. To save the activity group, choose 💾.
8. Choose the *Activity groups* tab to select the activity groups for this composite activity group.

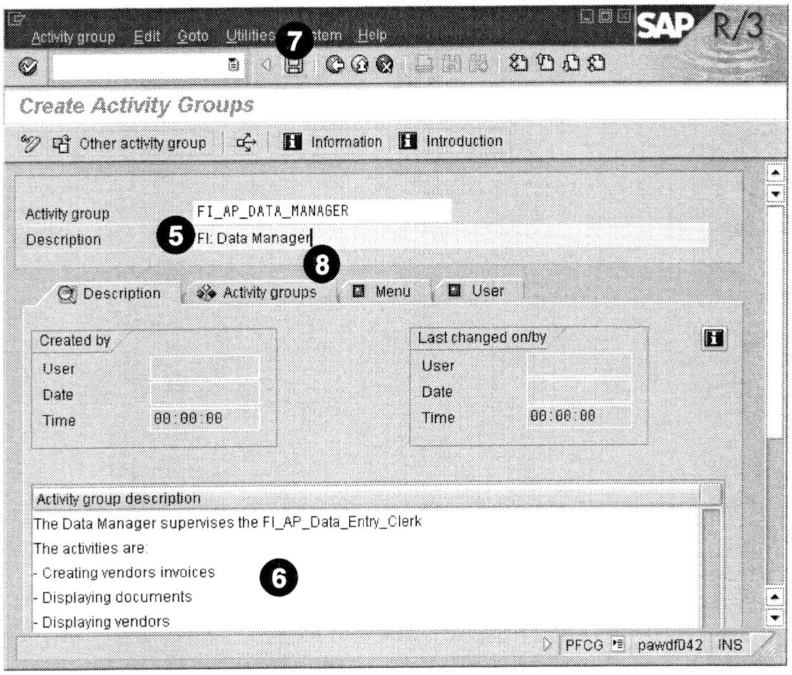


9. Select the insert icon to insert the activity groups.

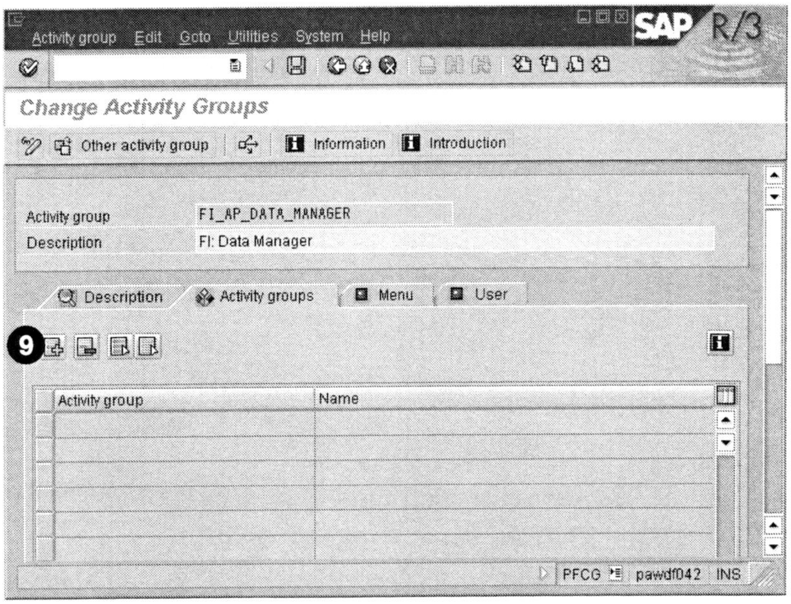


**Tips & Tricks**

You can only insert activity groups into composite activity groups. It is not possible to assign other composite activity groups or single transactions to a composite activity group.

10. Select the activity groups that you would like to include in the composite activity group.
11. Choose ✔.

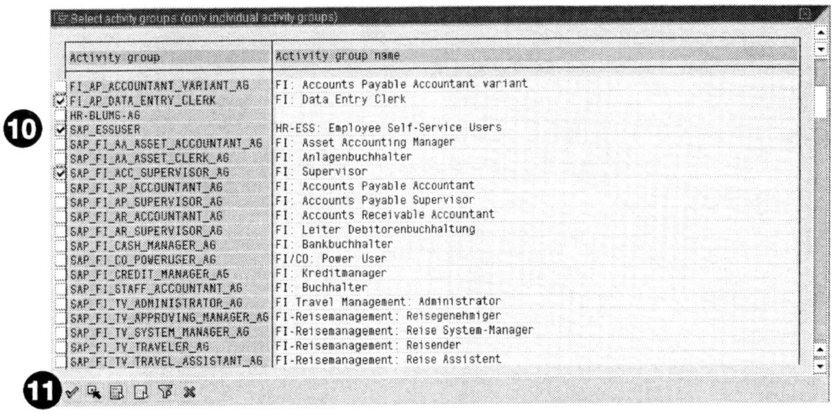

The activity groups have been inserted.

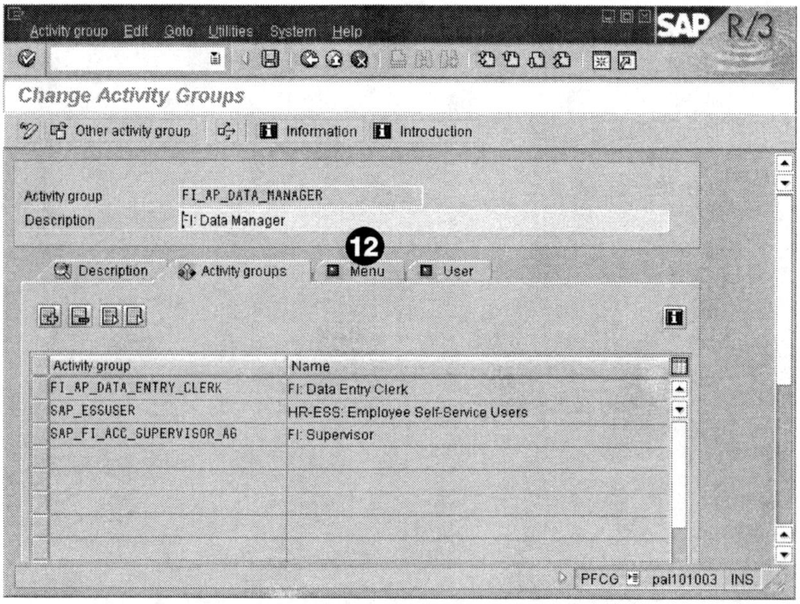


12. Choose the *Menu* tab to check that you cannot maintain the menu for the composite activity group.

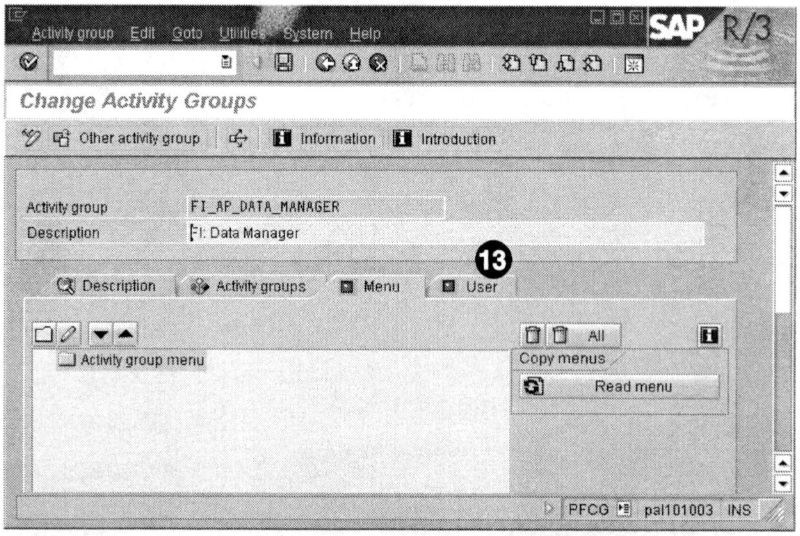


13. Choose the *User* tab to assign users.

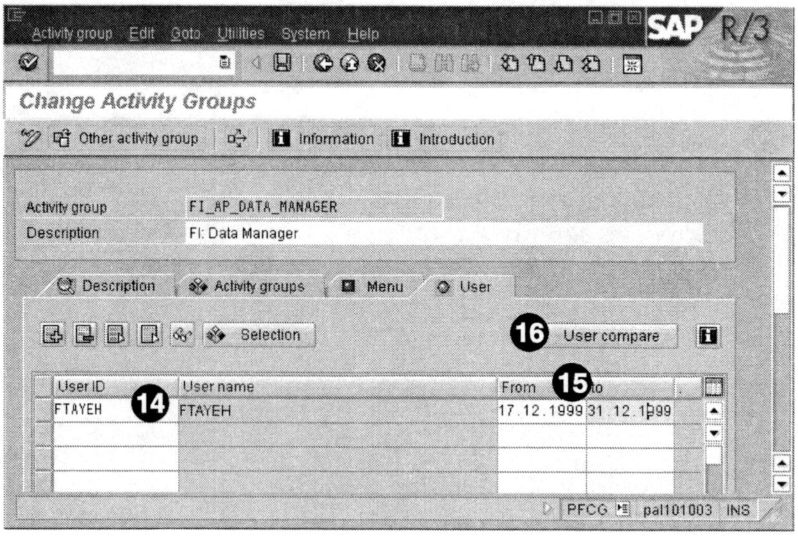


14. In the *User ID* field, select the desired user by either entering the name directly or using *possible entries*. You may select multiple entries from the list at the same time.

15. In the *From* and *to* column, enter the date range for how long the user should be assigned to the activity group.

16. After entering all users, choose *User compare.*

Tips & Tricks

The *User name* is automatically entered in the second column next to the user ID. In the two additional columns (*From, to*) you can specify a validity period for the assignment. You can delete the user IDs by using , and insert an additional one in front of a selected user ID using .

For additional information on assigning users and time dependency, choose .

You are now finished creating a composite activity group and assigning this to a user. When users log on to the R/3 System, their menu will contain the transactions of the three inserted activity groups from our example.

# Tips for an Administrator

As an administrator with special authorizations, you can have a shortcut for assigning user roles to a user without going into transaction *PFCG* or *SU01*.

To see and perform the shortcut, you need access to transaction code *PFCG*. The field values need to be set to full authorization (*) in the authorization objects *S_USER_PRO, S_USER_GRP, S_USER_AUT* as show in the table below.

| **Authorization object *S_USER_PRO*** | |
|---|---|
| Activity | * |
| Auth. profile in user master maintenance (PROFILE) | * |
| **Authorization object *S_USER_GRP*** | |
| Activity | * |
| User group in user master maintenance (CLASS) | * |
| **Authorization object *S_USER_AUT*** | |
| Activity | * |
| Authorization name in user master maintenance (AUTH) | * |
| Auth. object in user master maintenance (OBJECT) | * |

* = full authorization

In the following example, we demonstrate how to assign a user role template to a user using this shortcut.

1. On the *SAP Easy Access* screen, choose *Other menu.*

   The menu will only be displayed in this way if the settings for the authorization objects are set as described in the table on the previous page.

2. Select the user role template that you would like to assign to a user.
3. Choose ✔.

**Tips & Tricks**

Depending on your settings, the window might look different, but it provides the same functionality.

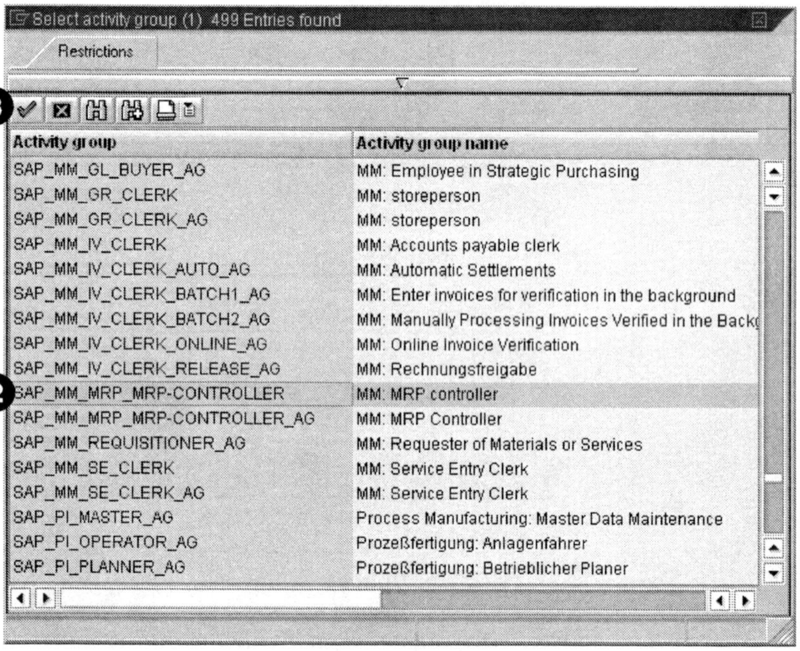

4. The structure of the user role template appears the same way an end user sees it later.
5. For an overview of what this user role template covers, choose *Documentation.*

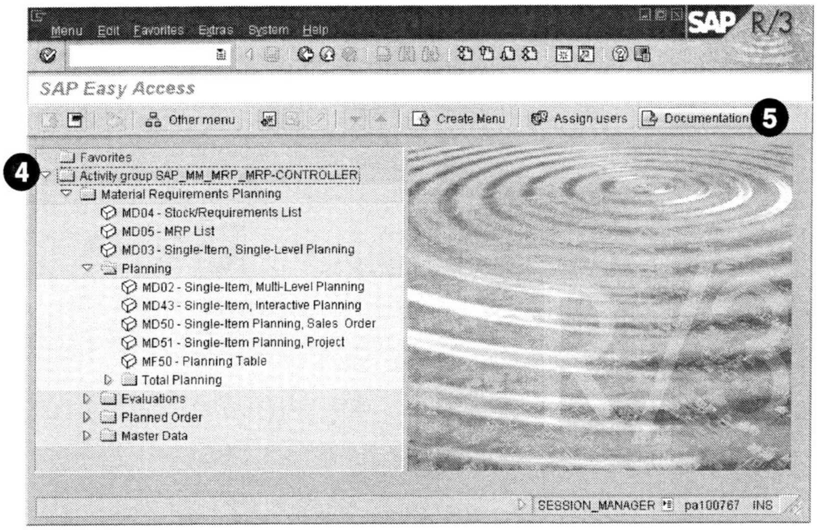


6. The description about the selected user role template is maintained in the activity group description field in the PG.
7. Choose ✔.

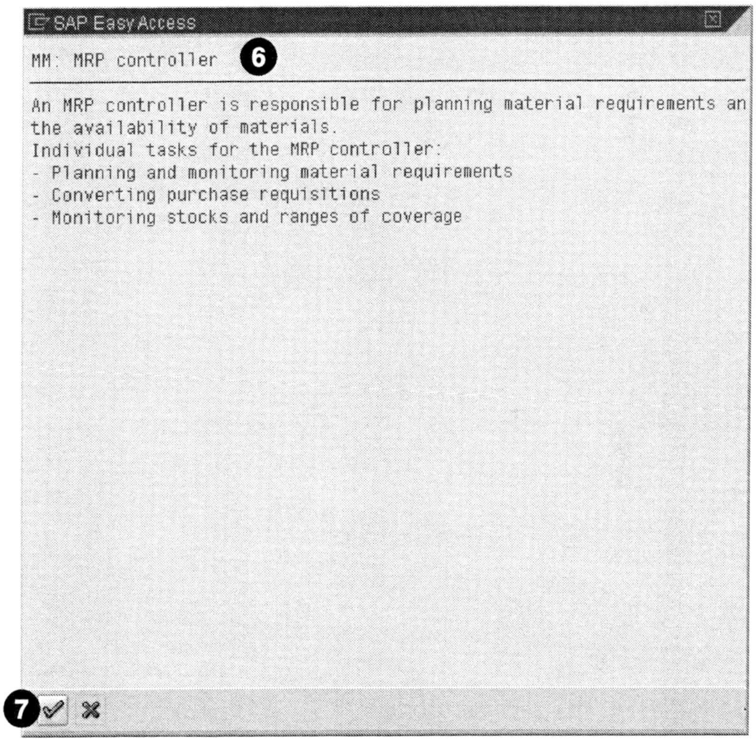

8. To assign a user to this user role template, choose *Assign users*.

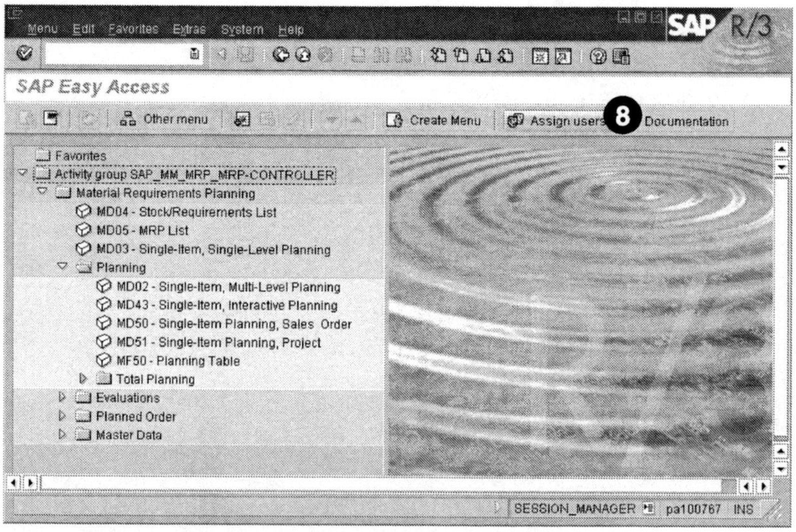


9. In the *Assign users* window, enter the users name directly or use *possible entries* to select a user from a list.
10. Choose ✔.

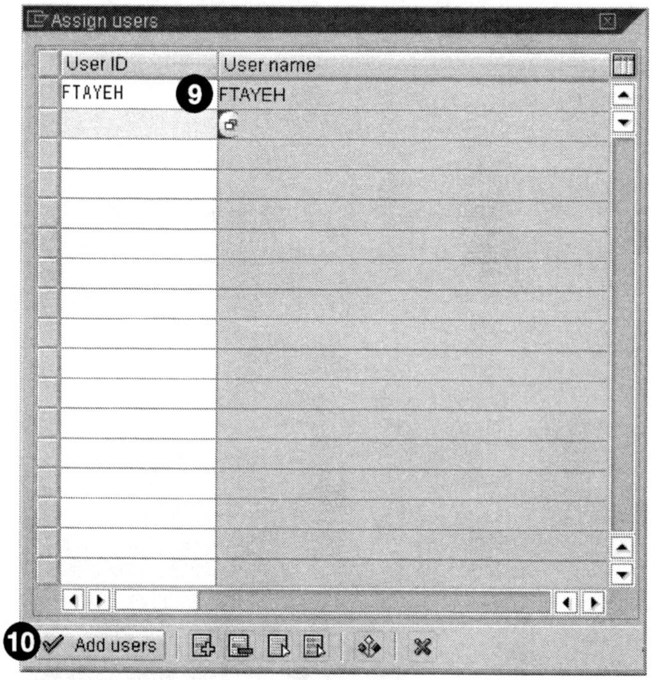


11. To generate the profile for the activity group, choose *Yes*.

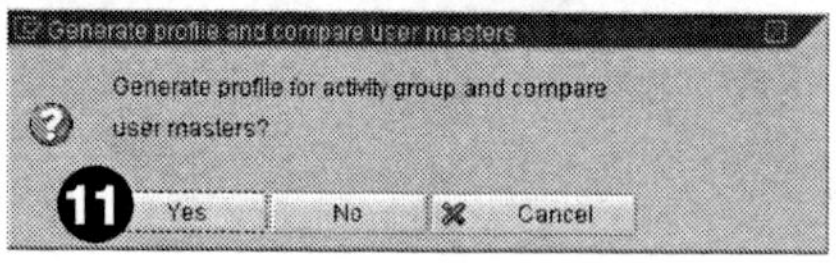

12. The selected user has been assigned to the user role template and the data was saved.
13. Choose [icon] or repeat the steps for a new assignment.

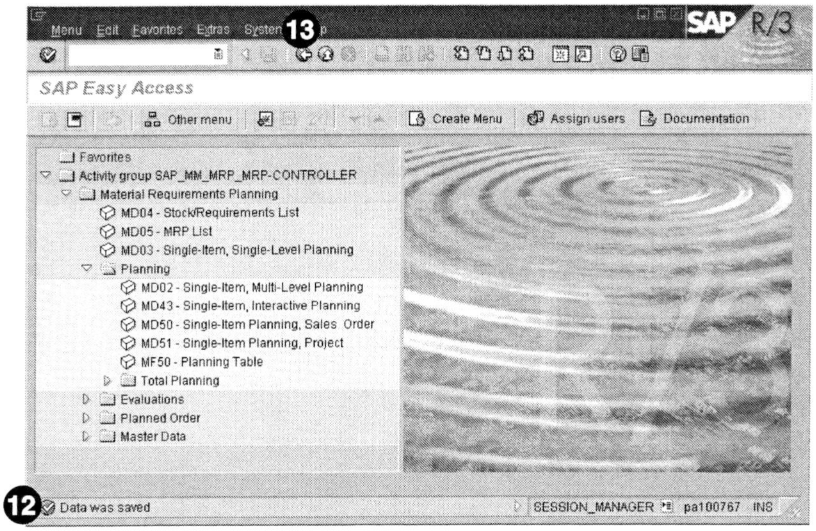

# Available User Role Templates

In the previous section, we explained how to work with the user role templates. This section provides an overview of the user role templates delivered with R/3, sorted by application area.

Each user role template contains a:

- Short definition of the role and an overview of tasks
- Role-based menu
- Completely maintained authorization profile according to the functionality accessible

## Release 4.6A

The following user role templates are available with R/3 Release 4.6A and are distributed as activity groups.

**Area Cross-Application:**

Auditor

Data Protection Auditor

Auditor HR

Auditor System

Specialist Data Transfer

**Area Materials Management/Procurement:**

Requisitioner

MRP-controller

Buyer

GR Clerk

SE Clerk

GL Buyer

IV Clerk

**Production Planning**

PP Operator

PP Product Manager

PP Supervisor

Kanban Controller

MRP Controller

Rep. Manufacturer

**Area Logistics Execution:**

Transport Cost Manager

Transport Cost Clerk

Warehouse Worker

Warehouse Manager

Warehouse Clerk

Logistics Manager

Logistics Clerk

Transport Planner

Transport Manager

Transport Clerk

Shipping Manager

Shipping Clerk

**Project Management**

Project Manager C.

Project Manager T.

Work Package Responsible

Investment Management

Investments Analyst

Investments Manager

Investments Planer (OR)

Investments Planer (PR)

Settle Specialist

**User Role Templates 4.6A (continued)**

**Basis / Development**

Authorization Data Administrator
Authorization Profile Administrator
System Administrator
Batch Administrator
Administrator
Process Controller
Workflow Developer
Workflow Process Controller
Quality Manager
Transport Manager
Customizing Project Member
Database Administrator
ABAP Developer
Development Manager
Documentation Developer
Project Manager
Enduser Profile
Every Employee
ALE Administrator
ALE Developer
Administrator Authoriz. for System Administration Assistant
Project Leader Authoriz. for System Administration Assistant
User Authoriz. for System Administration Assistant
SAPscript Power User
Spool Administrator
Archivelink Administrator
Archivelink User
Technical Engineer
User Adminstrator
Business Workplace for all Users
Administrator
Controller
Implementations Team

**Quality Management**

Certificate
Equipment Manager
Inspection Manager
Inspection Planer
Problem Author
Problem Processor
Quality Analyst
Quality Engineer
Quality Inspector
Support Line Level 1
Support Line Level 2

**Sales & Distribution**

Order Processing Clerk
Sales Representative
Sales Manager

**Controlling**

Planning Activity Coordinator
Senior Costmanager
Managerial Accountant
Sales Manager

**Finance Management**

Asset Clerk
Asset Accountant
Staff Accountant
Accounts Receivable Accountant
Accounts Receivable Supervisor
Accounts Payable Accountant
Accounts Payable Supervisor
Cash Manager
Credit Manager
Accounting Supervisor

**Profit Center Accounting**

Profit Center Controller
Profit Center Manager

**User Role Templates 4.6A (continued)**

**Travel Management**

Travel Administrator
Travel Approving manager
Travel System manager
Travel Assistant
Traveler

**Treasury**

Administrator
Credit Analyst
Department Manager Loans
Loans Officer
Rollover Officer
Staff Accountant
Backoffice Process
Cashmanager
Controller
Fund Manager
Risk Controller
Staff Accountant
Trade Controller
Trader
Treasury Manager

**Product Data Management**

Designer
Work Preparer

**Foreign Trade**

Con. Export Control Manager
Gov. Period Manager
Local Doc. Payment Manager
Preference manager
Pro. Export Manager
Pro. Import Manager
Supervisor

**Real Estate**

Controller and Manager
Rent Adjustment Clerk
SCS Clerk
Tenant Clerk
Tenant Rental Clerk

**Human Resources**

Administrative Clerk
Administrative Clerk Benefits
Administrative Clerk Compensation
Administrative Clerk Organizational Management
Benefits Specialist
Compensation Specialist
Line-Manager Benefits
Line-Manager Organizational Management
Line-Manager Personnel Cost Planning
Line-Manager Appraisal System
Line-Manager Room Reservations
HR-Manager
HR-Manager Organizational Management
HR-Manager Personnel Cost Planning
HR-Manager Appraisal System
HR-Manager Room Reservations
HR-Manager Compensation

- Administrative Clerk
- Administrative Clerk Benefits
- Administrative Clerk Compensation
- Administrative Clerk Organizational Management
- Benefits Specialist
- Compensation Specialist
- Line-Manager Benefits
- Line-Manager Organizational Management
- Line-Manager Personnel Cost Planning
- Line-Manager Appraisal System
- Line-Manager Room Reservations
- HR-Manager

**User Role Templates 4.6A (continued)**

- HR-Manager Organizational Management
- HR-Manager Personnel Cost Planning
- HR-Manager Appraisal System
- HR-Manager Room Reservations

HR-Manager Compensation

Incentive Wages Specialist

Time Recording Specialist

Specialist Operationsplanner

Payroll Clerk

- *Payroll Clerk Austria*
- *Payroll Clerk Belgium*
- *Payroll Clerk Canada*
- *Payroll Clerk Germany*
- *Payroll Clerk Spain*
- *Payroll Clerk Great Britain*
- *Payroll Clerk Indonesia*
- *Payroll Clerk Mexico*
- *Payroll Clerk Malaysia*
- *Payroll Clerk Netherlands*
- *Payroll Clerk Norway*
- *Payroll Clerk New Zealand*
- *Payroll Clerk Philippines*
- *Payroll Clerk Portugal*
- *Payroll Clerk Signapore*
- *Payroll Clerk Taiwan*
- *Payroll Clerk USA*
- *Payroll Clerk Venezuela*
- *Payroll Clerk SouthAfrica*

Payroll Specialist

- *Payroll Specialist Argentinia*
- *Payroll Specialist Austria*
- *Payroll Specialist Australia*
- *Payroll Specialist Belgien*
- *Payroll Specialist Brasil*
- *Payroll Specialist Canada*
- *Payroll Specialist Suisse*
- *Payroll Specialist Germany*
- *Payroll Specialist Danmark*
- *Payroll Specialist Spain*
- *Payroll Specialist France*
- *Payroll Specialist Great Britain*
- *Payroll Specialist Hong Kong*
- *Payroll Specialist Indonesia*
- *Payroll Specialist Ireland*
- *Payroll Specialist Japan*
- *Payroll Specialist Mexico*
- *Payroll Specialist Malaysia*
- *Payroll Specialist Netherlands*
- *Payroll Specialist Norway*
- *Payroll Specialist New Zealand*
- *Payroll Specialist Philippines*
- *Payroll Specialist Portugal*
- *Payroll Specialist Sweden*
- *Payroll Specialist Signapore*
- *Payroll Specialist Thailand*
- *Payroll Specialist Taiwan*
- *Payroll Specialist USA*
- *Payroll Specialist South Africa*

Recruiter

System Administrator

- *System Administrator Argentinia*
- *System Administrator Austria*
- *System Administrator Australia*
- *System Administrator Belgium*
- *System Administrator Brasil*
- *System Administrator Canada*
- *System Administrator Suisse*
- *System Administrator Germany*
- *System Administrator Danmark*
- *System Administrator Spain*
- *System Administrator France*
- *System Administrator Great Britain*

**User Role Templates 4.6A (continued)**

*System Administrator Hong Kong*
*System Administrator Indonesia*
*System Administrator Ireland*
*System Administrator Japan*
*System Administrator Malaysia*
*System Administrator Netherlands*
*System Administrator Norway*
*System Administrator New Zealand*
*System Administrator Philippines*
*System Administrator Portugal*
*System Administrator Sweden*
*System Administrator Signapore*
*System Administrator Thailand*
*System Administrator Taiwan*
*System Administrator USA*
*System Administrator International*
*System Administrator South Africa*

System Administrator Room Reservations
System Administrator Benefits
System Administrator Compensation
System Administrator Organizational Management
System Administrator Personnel Administration
System Administrator Personnel Cost Planning
System Administrator Personnel Development
System Administrator Appraisal System
System Administrator Training and Events
System Administrator Room Reservations
System Administrator Payroll
System Administrator Recruitment
Training and Development Clerk
Training and Development Clerk, Personnel Development
Training and Development Clerk, Appraisal System
Training and Develpm. Clerk, Training and Event Management
Training and Development Clerk, Room Reservation
Training and Development Specialist, Personnel Development
Training and Development Specialist, Appraisal System
Training and Development Specialist, Training
Training and Development Specialist, Room Reservation
Training and Development Specialist

## Release 4.6B

The following user role templates available with R/3 Release 4.6B are in addition to the existing from Release 4.6A as shown above.

**Basis**

ABAP Developer
Ale Administrator
ALE Developers
Master Data Distribution
Accounting Master Data Distribution
HR Master Data Distribution
Logistics Master Data Distribution

**Finance management**

FI: Advance Payer for Trip Advances

**Human Resources**

Incentive Wages Clerk
Incentive Wages Specialist
Time Recording Administrator
Time Recording Specialist
Shift Planning Clerk
Shift Planning Specialist

**Material Master**

Buying

**User Role Templates 4.6B (continued)**

| |
|---|
| **Retail** |
| Allocation Table |
| Assortment Management |
| Retail Stock Planner |
| Order Optimizing |
| Perishables Planning |
| Category Manager |
| Classification |
| Maintenance of Purchase Price Conditions |
| Maintenance of Sales Price Conditions |
| Goods Receipt |
| Goods Receipt Associate |
| Internal Warehouse Handling |
| Warehouse Manager |
| Shipping Associate |
| Warehouse Worker |
| Retail Buyer |
| Buying Activities |
| Gathering Information and Changing Master |
| Invoice Verification Clerk |
| Verification of Invoices |
| Archiving of Invoices |
| Functions in the Invoice Verification Environment |
| Coordination of Merchandise and Assortment |
| Execution of Merchandise and Assortment Planning |
| Merchandise Category Hierarchy Creation |
| Requirements Planning |
| Maintenance of Sales Price Calculations |
| Pricing Environment |
| Sales Price Calculations (Strategic) |
| Promotion Management |
| Store Manager |
| Triggering and Controlling Merchandise Procurement in a Store |
| Gathering Information and Changing Master |
| Store Goods Receipts/Issues and Inventory |
| Management of Instore Personnel |
| Instore Planning and Control |
| Sales Activities in a Store |
| Sales Department Manager in a Store |
| Store Associate Using SAP Retail Store |
| Settlement of Customer Arrangements |
| Maintenance of Customer Arrangements |
| Settlement of Vendor Arrangements |
| Maintenance of Vendor Arrangements |
| Transportation Manager |
| Transportation Planner |
| **Logistics Execution** |
| Shipping Clerk |
| Shipping Manager |
| **Planing Systems** |
| Display and Maintain Work Center Master Data |
| Sales Price Valuation |

# Chapter 6: Advanced Profile Generator Functionality

## Contents

# Overview

In addition to the three methods of using the user role templates, the Profile Generator (PG) provides additional optional functionality.

In this chapter, we explain more of the vast functionality of the PG. Examples show how to enhance the use of your user role templates.

# Selecting Views/Types in Activity Group Maintenance

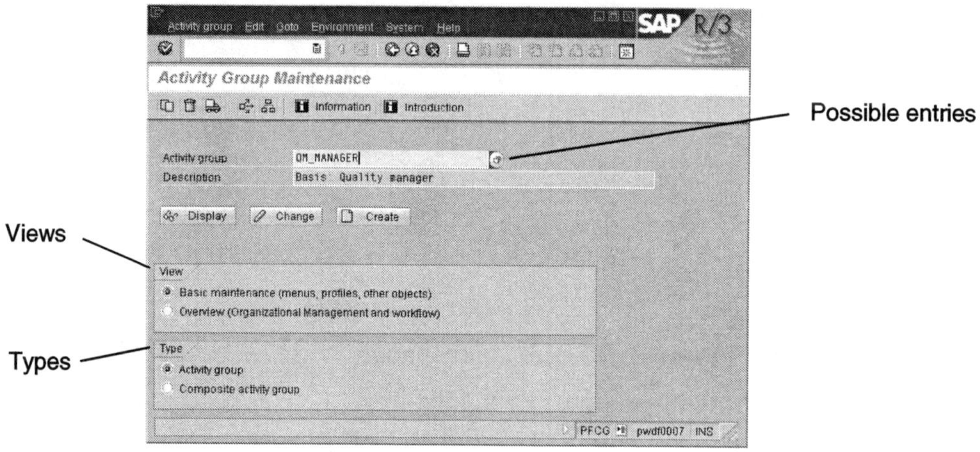


In the *Activity Group Maintenance* window (transaction *PFCG*), you can toggle between different views and types. For views you can choose:

- *Basic maintenance (menus, profiles, other objects)*
- *Overview (Organizational Management and workflow)*

For types you can choose:

- *Activity group*
- *Composite activity group*

These views and types are described in the following sections.

### Basic Maintenance

Select *Basic maintenance (menus, profiles, other objects)* to create activity groups and assign these groups to users.

### Overview (Organizational Management)

Select *Overview (Organizational Management and workflow)* to create activity groups and assign these activity groups to R/3 users or PD objects. *Overview* gives you full access to all activity group maintenance functions, including organization management and the related time dependencies. For example, when you are creating or changing an activity group, you can only link workflow tasks to an activity group in *Overview*.

### Activity Group

Select *Activity group* to display all available activity groups, including composite activity groups when you select *possible entries.*

### Composite Activity Group

Select *Composite activity groups* to display only composite activity groups when you select *possible entries.*

## Exploring Advanced Profile Generator Functionality

In chapter 5, *User Role Templates,* we described three methods to work with user role templates. You actually have more options when working with the activity groups and Profile Generator (PG). For example, there are different ways to assign objects to an activity group—you can create your own hierarchy with customized folders, names, and links for the user role templates you create.

On the *Change Activity Groups* screen (see below), a series of buttons around the assigned transactions provide different functionality.

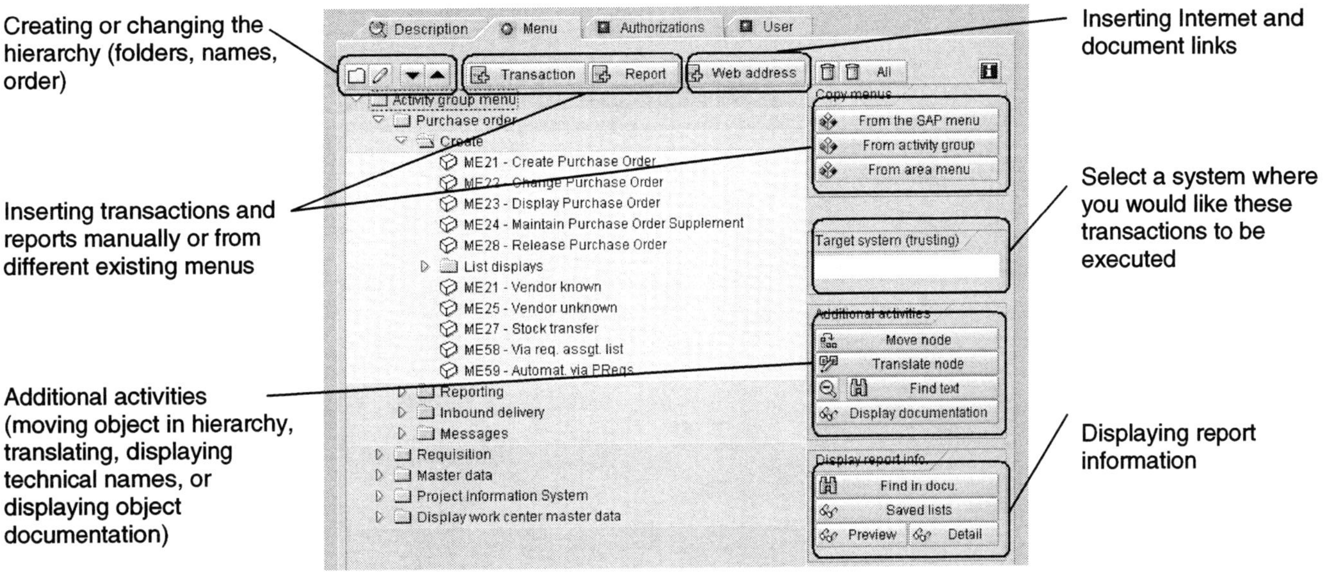

## Creating and Changing the Hierarchy

You can assign objects to an activity group by either:

- Creating your own hierarchy
- Moving objects into the existing hierarchy and renaming them to suit your needs

In the following example, we demonstrate how to insert a folder, give it a new name, and move it into the hierarchy.

We want to create a new folder and call it "Buyer" under *Master Data → Vendor* in the activity group *MM_BUYER_AG.*

1. Access the PG (transaction **PFCG**).
2. Select the desired activity group (for example, *MM_BUYER_AG*) and choose *Change.*
3. In the *Change Activity Groups* screen, select the hierarchy level under which you want to insert the folder (for example, *Vendor* in *MM_BUYER_AG).*
4. Choose .

5. Enter the name of the new folder.
6. Choose .

7. The new folder is placed one level below the selected folder in the hierarchy. To move it up or down, use the arrows ▼▲ or use drag-and-drop.

Tips & Tricks

To change the text of the node, select it and enter the new name.

Caution

You need to be certain how you change your menus, because if the original R/3 menu path changes, you might not be able to find your selected transaction in the same position as before.

## Inserting Transactions

We continue from the step above to show how to insert transactions under the newly created folder.

If you know the transaction code, you can insert it manually by choosing *Transaction* and entering the transaction code (see chapter 5, the section *Copy and Modify the SAP-provided User Role Templates* for details).

To select the transaction from a menu, choose one of the following buttons:

*From the SAP menu* (see chapter 5, the section *Copy and Modify the SAP-provided User Role Templates*)

*From activity group*

*From area menu*

1. Choose from where you would like to insert the transaction (in this example, we chose *From activity group*).

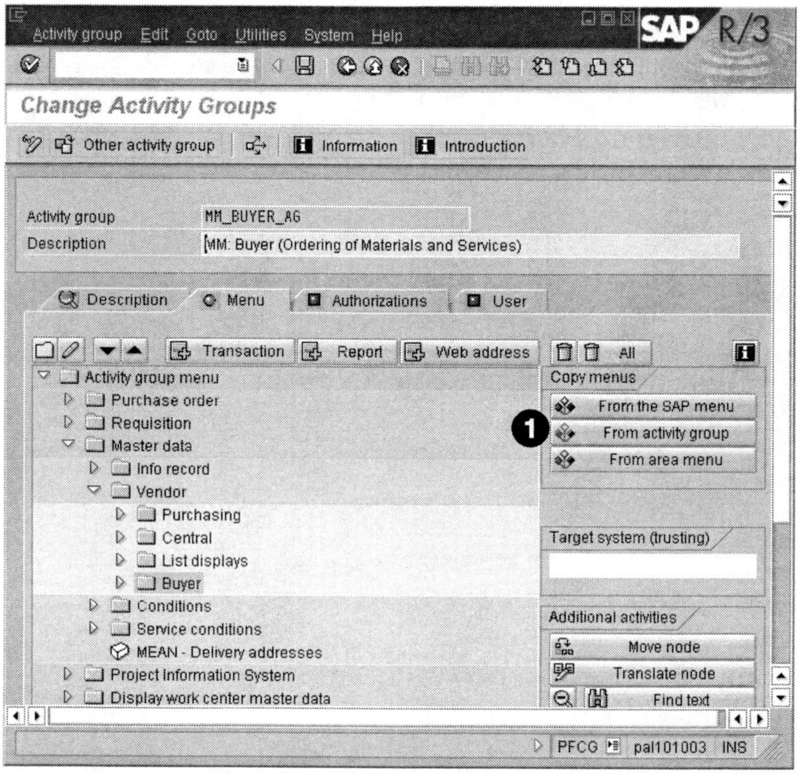


**Tips & Tricks**

If you insert transactions from a different menu, the complete menu path from that source will be added.

2. Select the activity group from where you would like to transfer the transaction code. You need to know what activity group contains this transaction. We selected *SAP_MM_GL_BUYER_AG*.
3. Choose ✔.

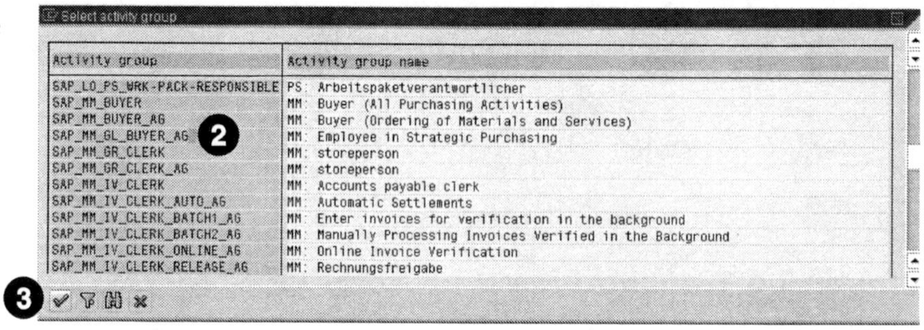

The menu structure of the selected activity group appears.

4. Open the desired hierarchy level and select the desired transaction(s).

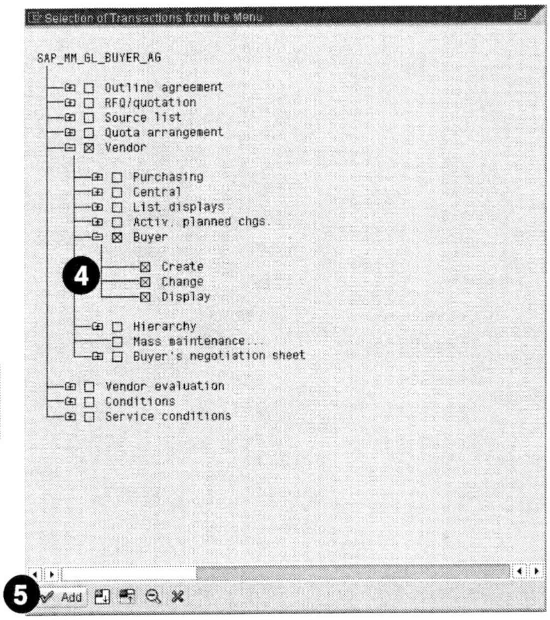


Tips & Tricks

To simplify your search, turn on the technical names by choosing 🔍.

5. Choose ✔ *Add* to transfer the transactions to your activity group. The complete menu path (in this case, *Vendor* → *Buyer* with activity groups *Create, Change,* and *Display*) is transferred.

After the complete menu path is inserted, you have the option to rename it and move the inserted transactions to the desired position using drag-and-drop or *Move node.*

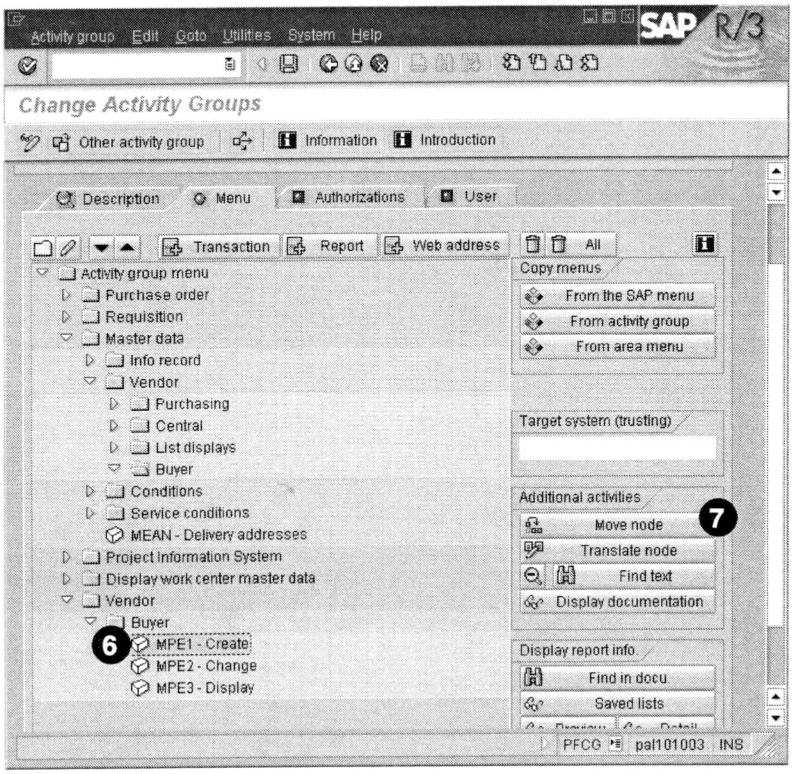


6. Select the transaction to be moved.

7. Choose *Move node* or use drag-and-drop to move it.

8. Select the desired folder (for example, *Buyer*).
9. Choose ✔.

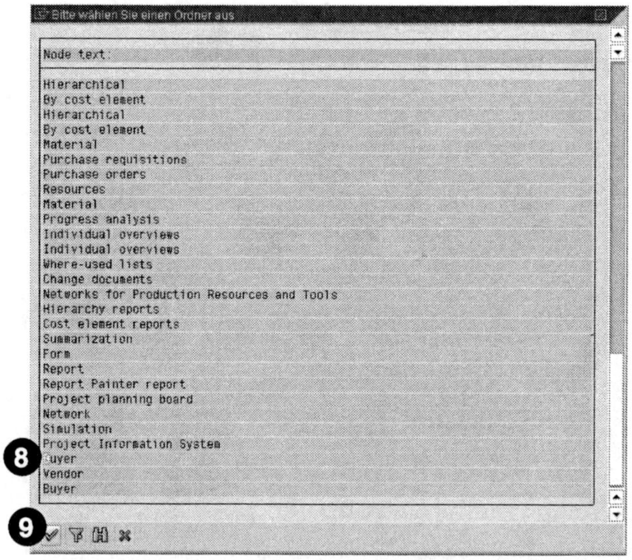


The transaction has been moved.

Do the same for the other transactions until all are in the right folder.

10. Select the menu entry that was transferred (for example, *Vendor*).
11. Choose 🗑 to delete the entry.

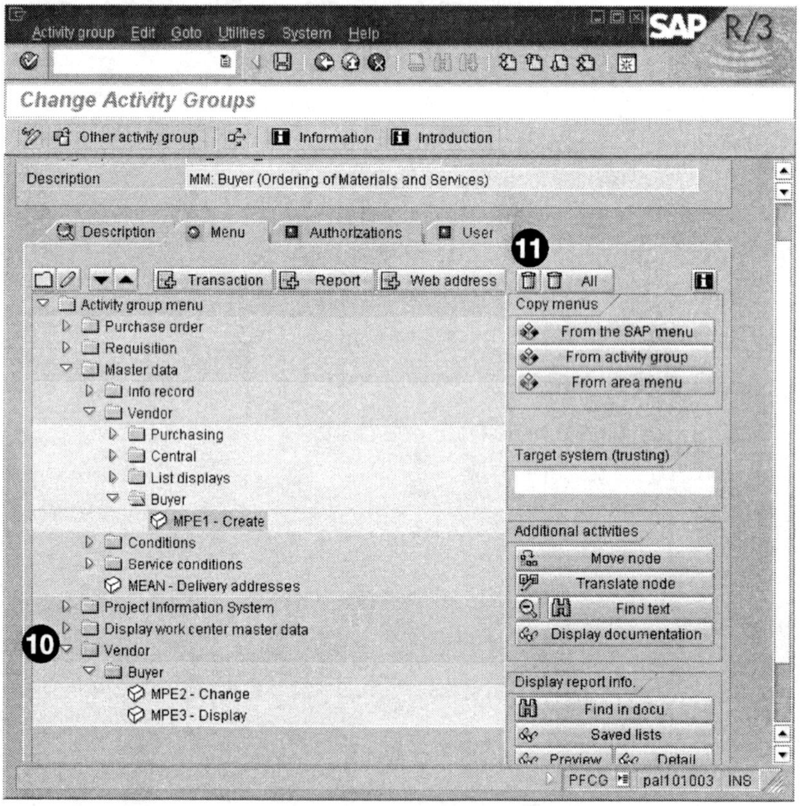

The transactions have been moved and the node has been deleted.

After inserting all the desired transactions, you have to generate the activity group and assign users.

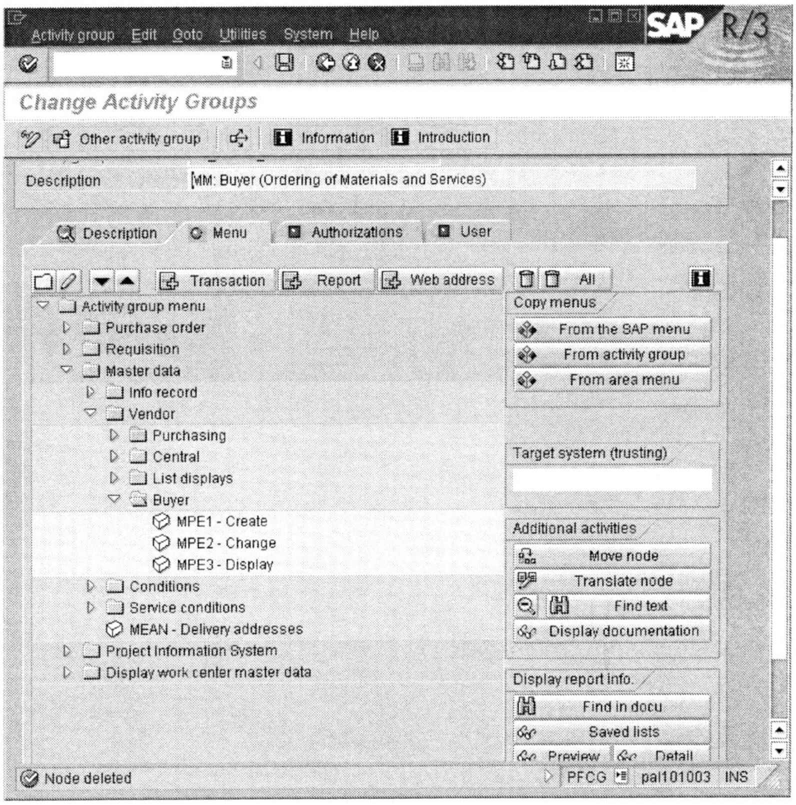

## Inserting Internet and Document Links

You have the option to assign links—for example Microsoft Word, Excel documents or Internet sites—to an activity group so that these links will be available to all end users assigned to that activity group. End users also have the option to create their own links later on their Easy Access screen. In the following example, we add a link to a local Microsoft Excel spreadsheet and a web page. We are going to use the activity group from above and will insert a folder called *Information source* as a prerequisite.

1. Access the PG (transaction **PFCG**).
2. Select the desired activity group (for example, *MM_BUYER_AG*) and choose *Change*.
3. In the *Change Activity Groups* window, select the position where you would like to insert the document link (for example, the folder *Information source*).
4. Choose *Web address*.
   **Note:** Even if you want to insert a document link, you must use the *Web address* button.

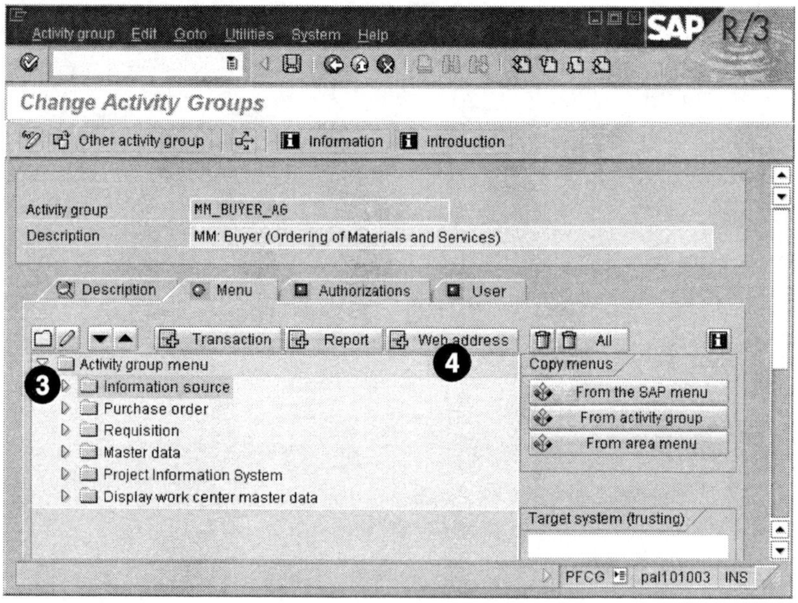


5. Enter the text for the link in the *Text* field.
6. Enter the path to the document or use *possible entries* to select it.
7. Choose ✔.

Tips & Tricks

The document can be a local document or a document from the network. Note that names for different hard drives may be different.

8. The link to the Excel spreadsheet has been inserted. The system displays an icon that represents the document type.
9. Choose *Web address* to insert the Internet link.

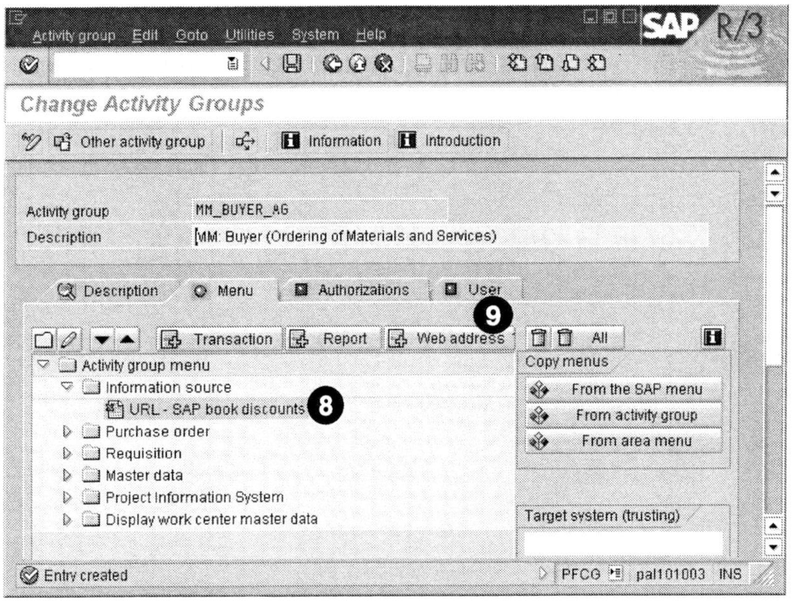


10. In *Text*, enter the text for the link.
11. In *Web address or file*, enter the URL link to the desired page or use *possible entries* to select a saved URL.
12. Choose ✔.

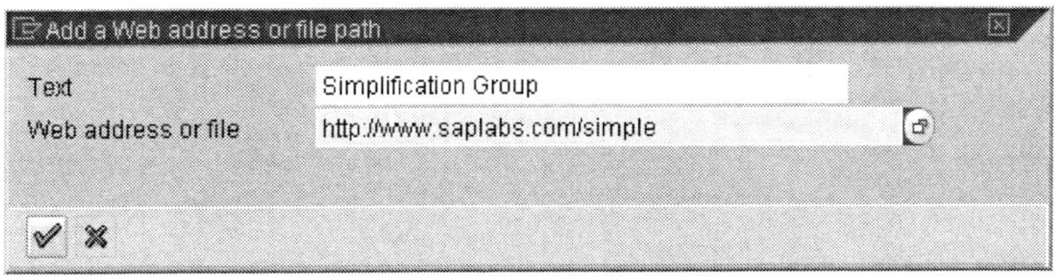


13. The link to the Internet page has been inserted. The system displays the icon for Internet links.

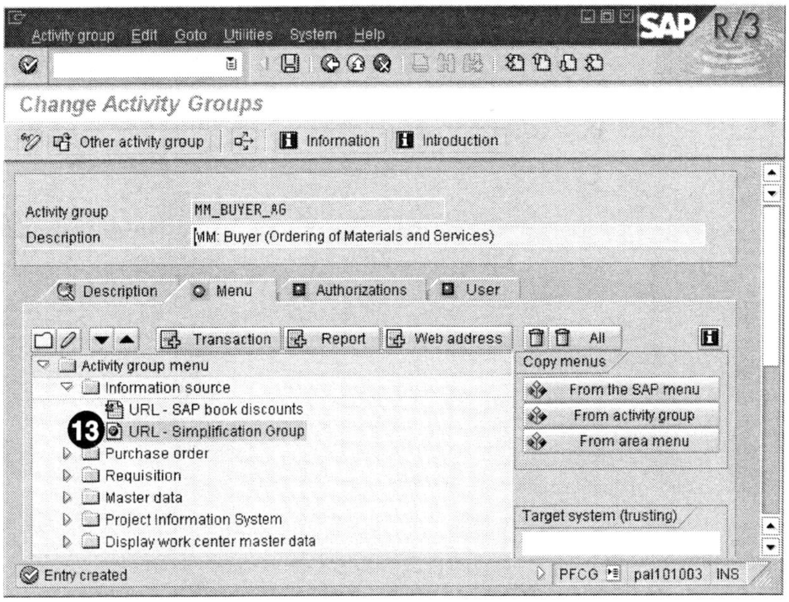

## Inserting Reports

Nearly every report in the system has a transaction assigned to it. Therefore you can select any report and authorize users just for certain reports. There are different options to assign a report to an activity group. You can select from either:

- ABAP report
- SAP query
- Transaction with variant
- ReportWriter
- Drilldown
- Rep.portfolio

Not only can you assign reports to the menu that are provided by SAP that already have a transaction, but it is also possible to assign self-developed reports with this functionality. When you assign a self-developed report, you can create a transaction code to the report when adding it to the menu.

In the following example, we demonstrate only one method (the others are similar).

**Example:**

We select the report *Due Date Analysis for Open Items* from the application class *FI: Accounts payable* and assign it to a folder called *Reports*.

1. Access the PG (transaction **PFCG**).
2. Select the desired activity group (for example, *MM_BUYER_AG*) and choose *Change*.
3. On the *Menu* tab, select the folder where you would like to insert the report.
4. Choose *Report*.

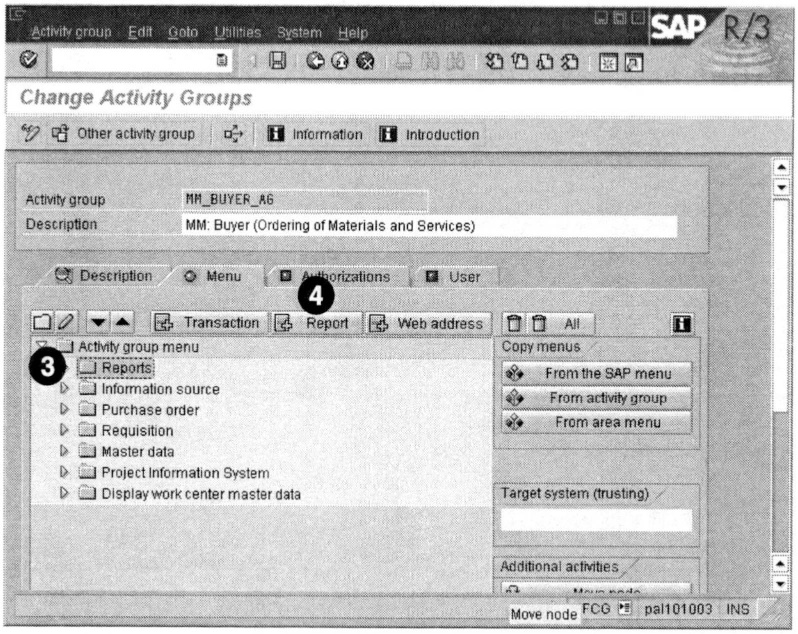

In our example, we demonstrate how to select a report from the application class.

5. Choose *Drilldown*.

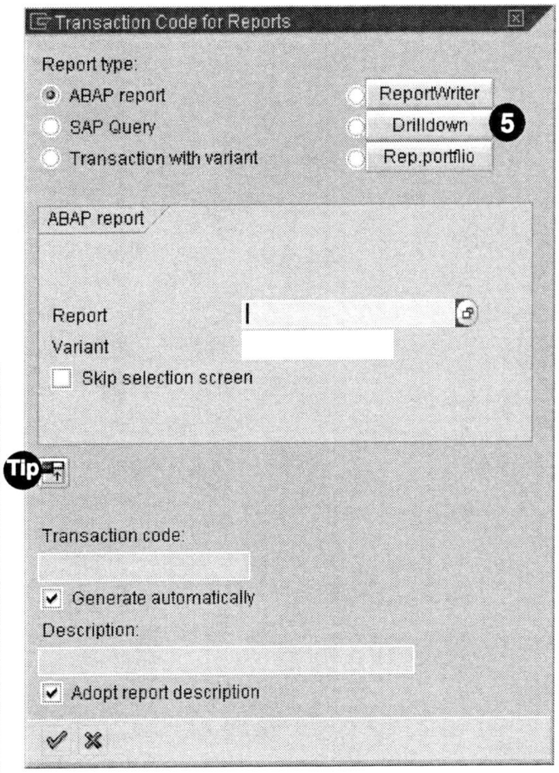


Tips & Tricks

If you expand the popup using [icon] to display other options, you can choose whether to assign your own transaction code or description to the report, or generate the transaction code automatically and adopt the report transaction.

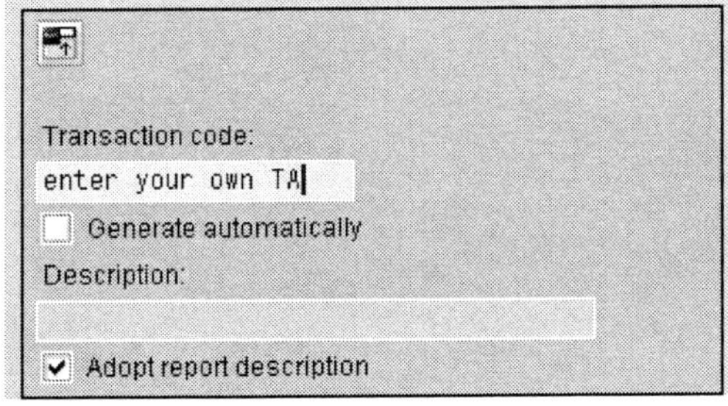


6. Select the desired class from the list.

7. Choose *Enter*.

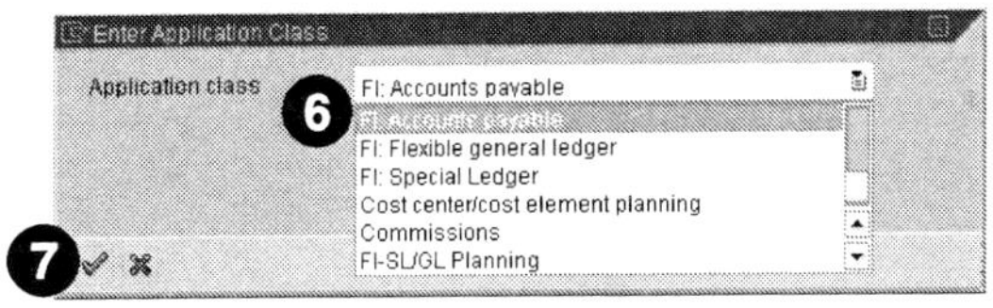


Tips & Tricks

Depending on what you selected, the following window (or windows) for steps 8–9 might differ.

8. Select the desired report type.

9. Choose ✔.

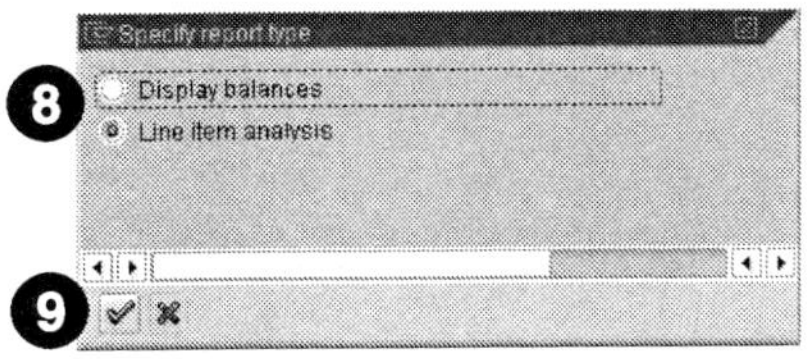


10. Choose *possible entries* to select the report.

11. Select the desired report from the hit list.
12. Choose ✔.

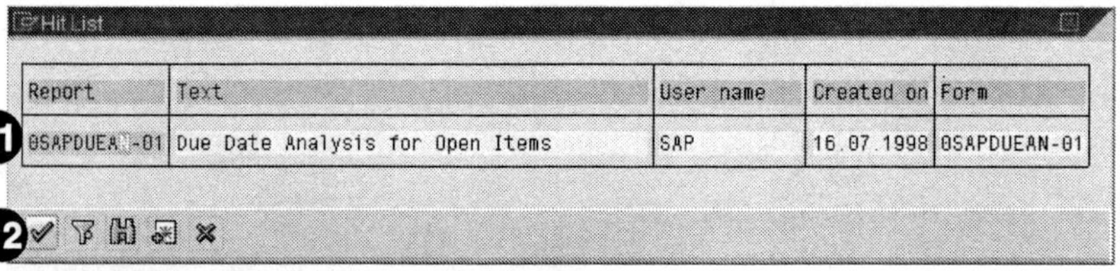


13. Choose ✔.

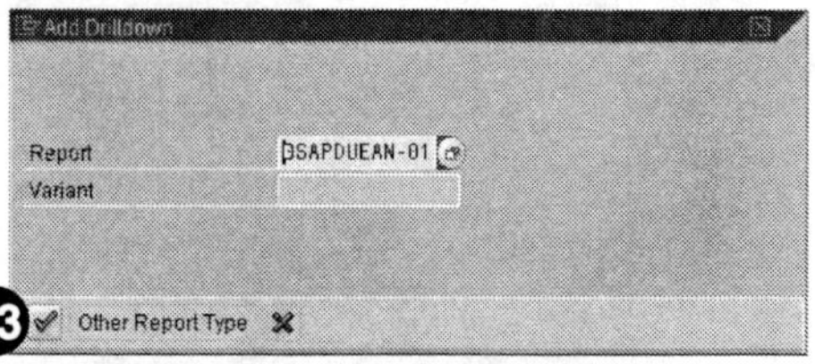


14. Choose ✔.

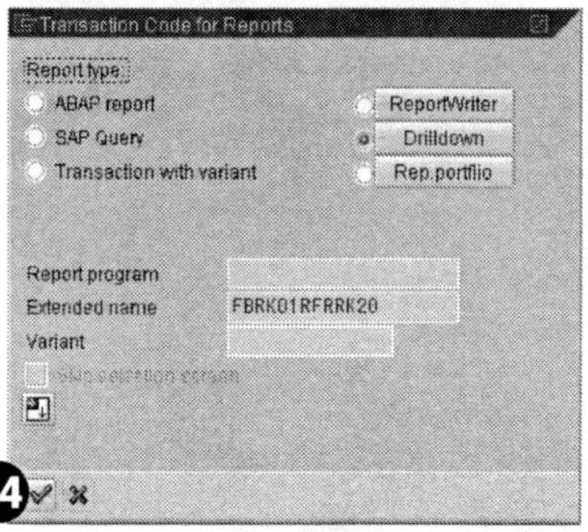


15. To save your work, choose 💾.

The report has been assigned.

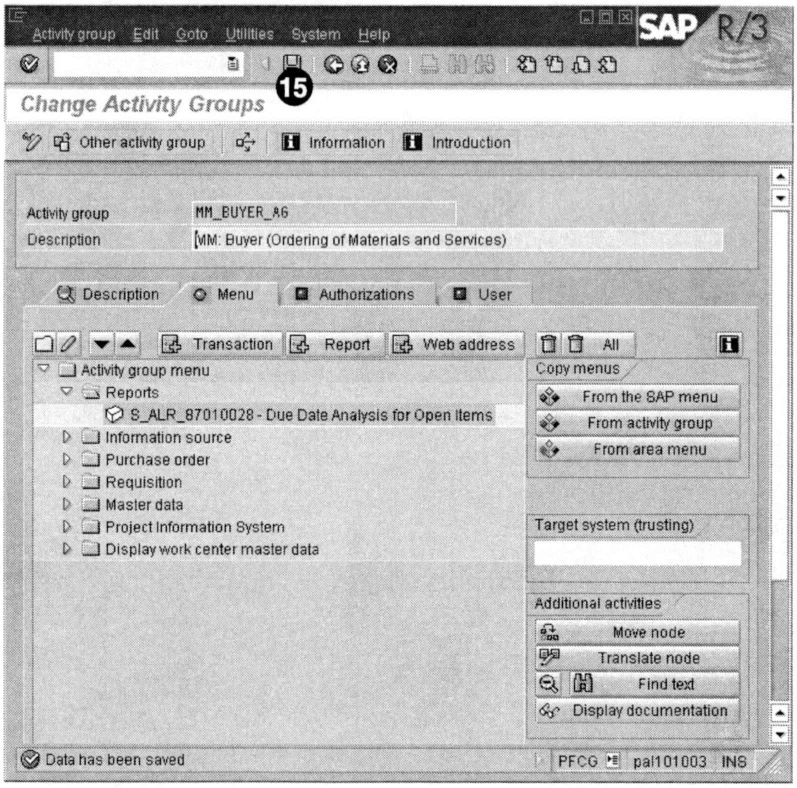


**Tips & Tricks**

If you decided to give the report a different name and description, the new information would be displayed in the menu instead.

# Displaying the Online Documentation for Activity Group Objects

You may review the online documentation for nearly every object in the activity group structure (if available). If you are not sure about a certain transaction, instead of going through the online documentation, just mark it in the structure and choose *Display documentation*. The advantage of this method is you do not need to know what area your object belongs to.

In the following example, we would like to know more about the transaction *ME21 Create purchase order*.

1. Select the object for which you want to read the documentation.
2. Choose *Display documentation*.

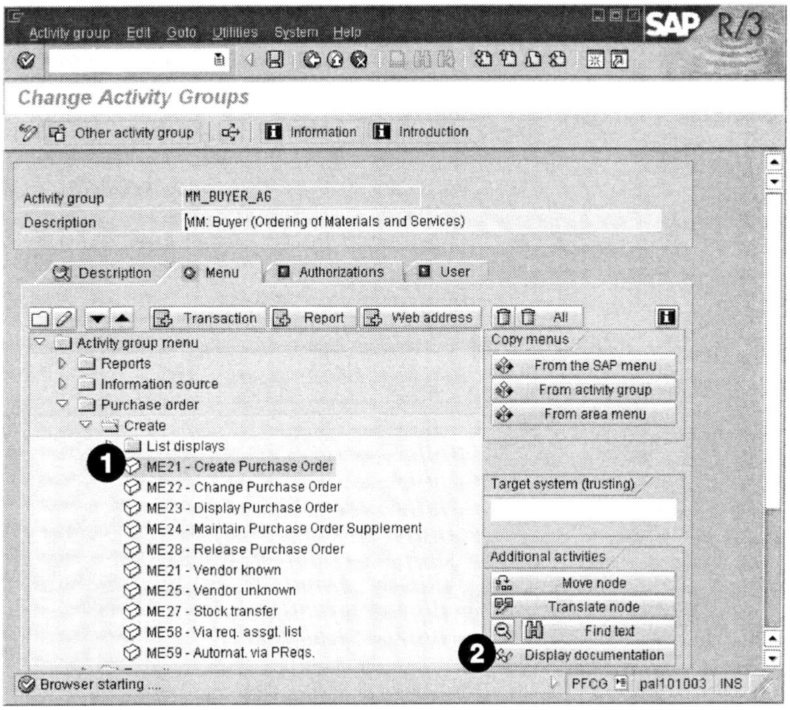


3. The documentation browser appears with the online documentation for the selected object.

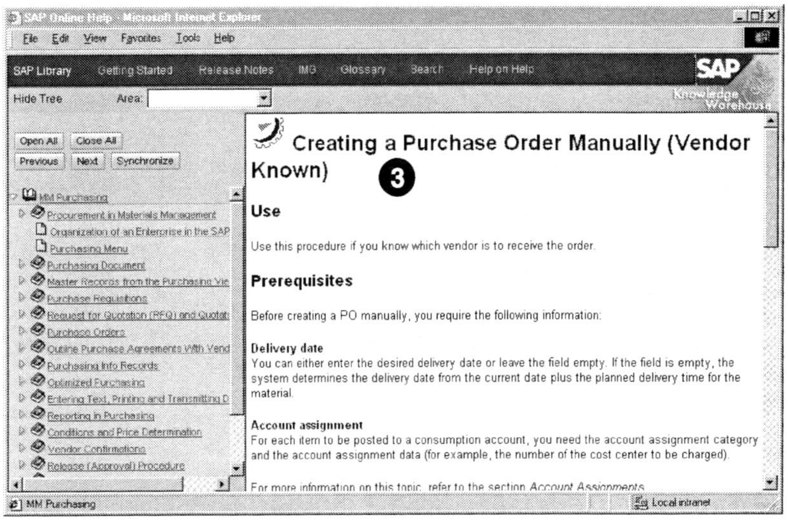


Tips & Tricks

> Depending on how you set up your online documentation, the browser might look different.

# Copying and Deriving Activity Groups

## Basics on Duplicating Activity Groups

It is acceptable to utilize only activity groups in your implementation and create them as needed. However, SAP provides two methods to make activity group maintenance easier.

These two core methods include:

- Copying activity groups
- Using derived or inherited activity groups

The diagram below provides an overview of what to expect from those options.

- The green circle indicates that maintained or assigned items exist.

- The red X indicates that **no** maintained or assigned items exist.

### Copying an activity group without a user

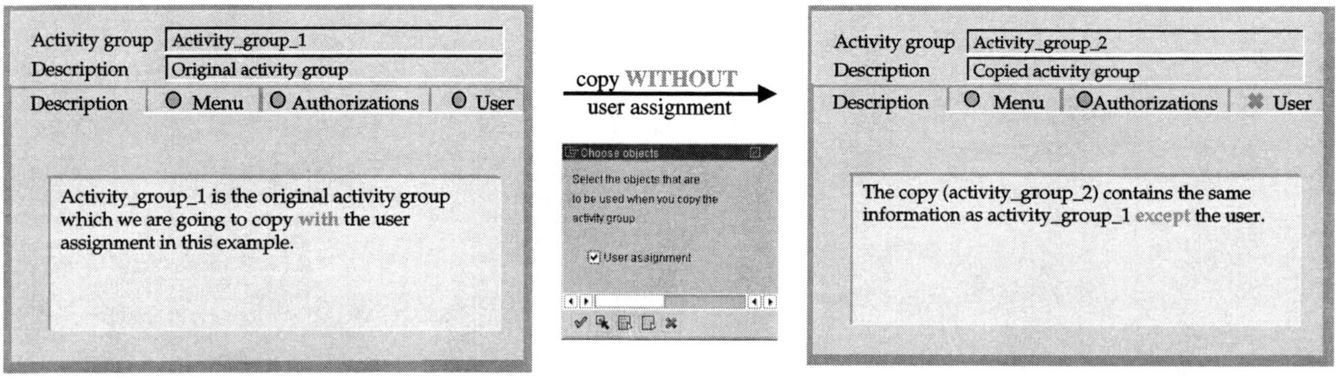


### Copying an activity group with a user

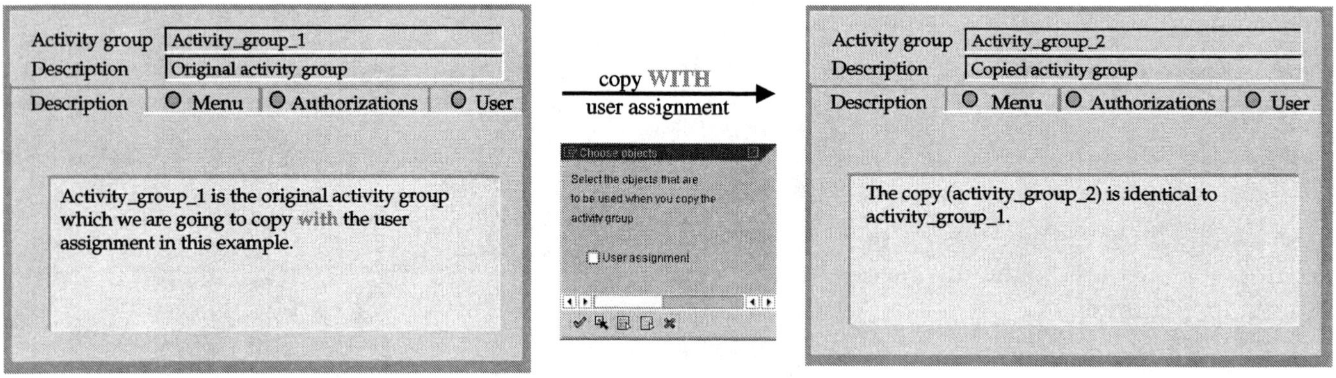


There is no linkage between *activity_group_1* and *activity_group_2* after the copy process is performed in the two cases above.

### Deriving an activity group

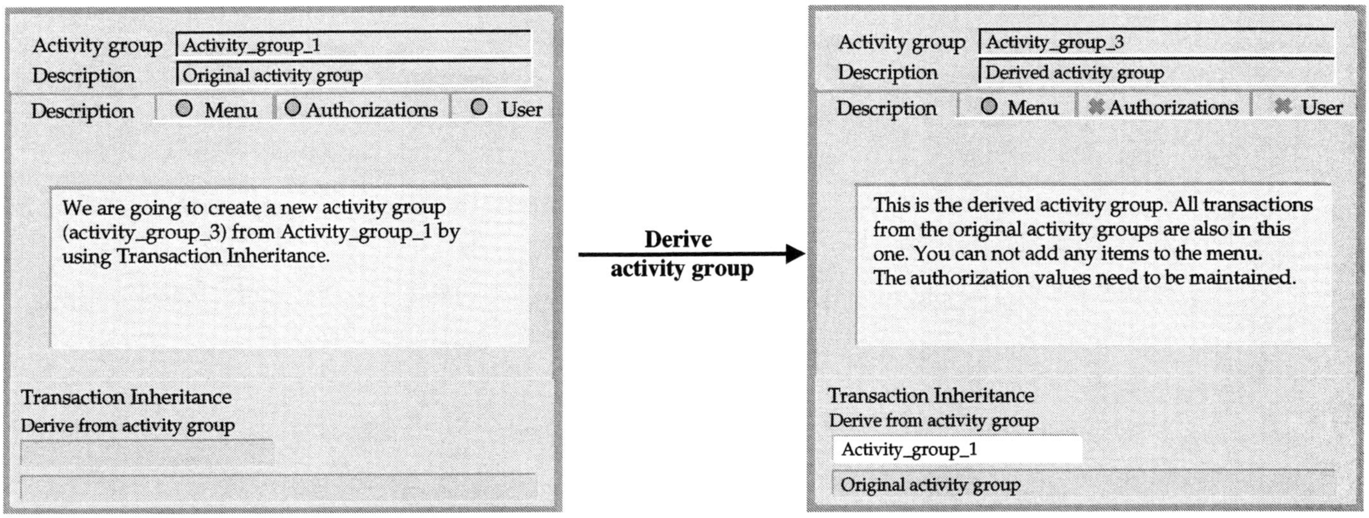


TechTalk

Adding transaction codes to *activity_group_1* after *activity_group_3* is created or generated, automatically impacts *activity_group_3*. Linkage between *activity_group_3* and *activity_group_1* is always updated automatically when *activity_group_1* has new transaction codes added to it.

## Copying Activity Groups

As shown in chapter 5, the section *Copy and Change Existing User Role Templates,* copying means that you reproduce an existing activity group. You can choose whether or not you want to copy the user assignment with this activity group.

On the *Activity Group Maintenance* screen, enter the name of the activity group which you would like to copy or select it by using possible entries. Then choose to copy it. On the following screen, enter the new name for the copied activity group. For a more detailed description, see chapter 5, the section *Copy and Change Existing User Role Templates.*

## Deriving Activity Groups

Deriving an activity group (also called transaction inheritance) means you can use an existing activity group as a reference. Essentially, the system transfers the transactions from an existing activity group. This process of deriving one activity group from another is only possible if you have not yet assigned any transactions to the new activity group. The previous activity group passes on all its transactions to the activity group dependent on it. If you use derived activity groups, it is easy to maintain consistency between access to transaction codes.

Caution

If you are going to use derived activity groups, it does not make much sense to use templates or manually inserted authorizations with the original activity group. **Only** the transaction codes are passed along to the derived activity group. The manually inserted authorizations and templates in activity group 1 will not be copied into activity group 2 (nor will the linkage be maintained if manually inserted in activity group 2).

As of Release 4.6B, it is also possible to adjust and generate the profiles for all activity groups derived from the original activity group. All the authorization data for this activity group is passed to the derived activity groups, except for the organizational levels. The organizational levels of the derived activity groups remain unchanged. The data for the corresponding organizational level is only passed if no data has been maintained for the organizational level in a derived activity group.

To execute this action, you need full authorization for the object *S_USER_VAL* as well as the authorization to change the derived activity groups.

To access this functionality, choose *Authorizations* → *Adjust derived activity groups* on the *Change Authorization Data* screen of the original activity group.

**Example: Usage of Derived Activity Groups**

A manager wants her staff to be able to access all the transactions that she can. However, her employees are **not** to have all the functionality that each transaction offers.
As such, we could create an activity group called *MANAGER-A-ACCESS* with the transaction codes. We would also maintain all the authorization field values for this activity group. Then we would create an activity group called *EMPLOYEES-MANAGER-A* and use *MANAGER-A-ACCESS* as the derived activity group (On the *EMPLOYEES-MANAGER-A* activity group's description screen of transaction *PFCG*, in the field *Divert Activity Group*, we would place *MANAGER-A-ACCESS*). Since only the transactions are copied into the "menu" (derived from *MANAGER-A-ACCESS*), we still need to maintain the authorization field values for the *EMPLOYEES-MANAGER-A* activity group.

1. Access the PG (transaction **PFCG**).
2. On the *Activity Group Maintenance* screen, enter the name for your new activity group in the *Activity group* field.
3. Choose 🗋 *Create.*

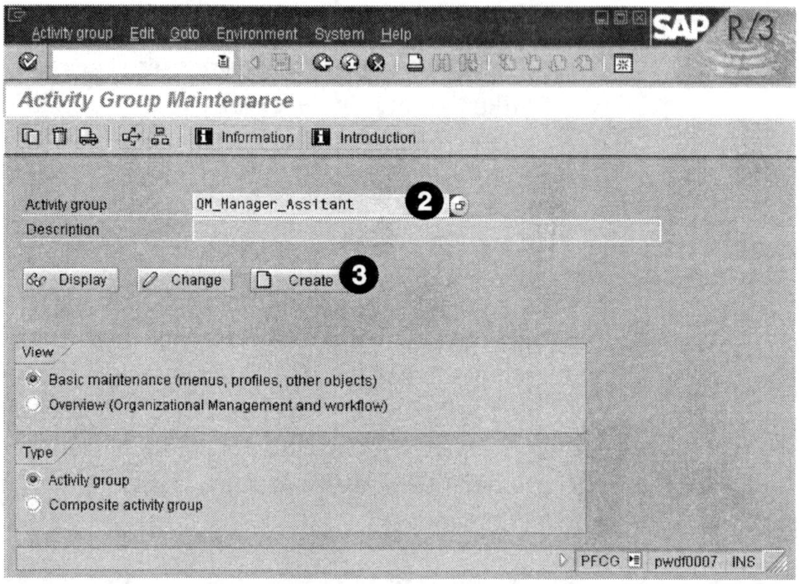

4. In *Description,* enter a short description.
5. Under *Activity group description,* enter a long description.
6. Under *Transaction inheritance,* select an activity group from which you want to inherit the transactions, by either entering the name in the *Derive from activity group* field or by using *possible entries.*

7. Choose *Yes.*

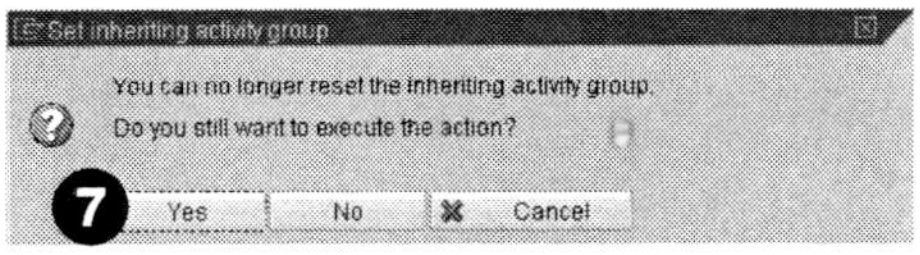

8. Choose 💾.
9. To review the inherited transactions, choose the *Menu* tab.

All the transactions from your original activity group have been inherited. The menu is going to look the same for the user as you defined it here.

Now you can maintain the authorizations for the activity group.

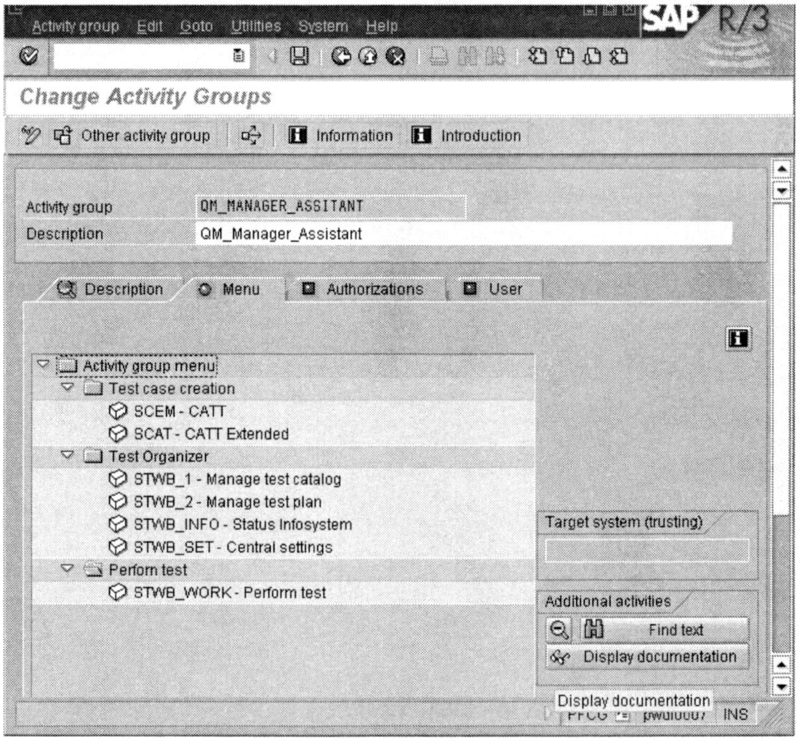

# Selecting Workflow Tasks

## What You Should Know About Workflow

This section provides a step-by-step sample *SAP Business Workflow* and an explanation of what you should know about tasks before you assign them to your activity group.

Tasks are used to expedite a business procedure. A task can be either a **single-step task** or a **multi-step task**. In the following example, creating the *Request for Leave* form and then checking this request are both single-step tasks. The procedure for processing a *Request for Leave* form is a multi-step task, consisting of several combined single-step tasks.

There are differences between the single-step standard tasks and the multi-step workflow templates. Standard tasks are the single-step tasks used in SAP's workflow templates. Many standard tasks and workflow templates are provided by SAP and should not be changed by customers. Customers can, however, copy and modify these templates to create their own standard tasks and workflow templates.

| Workflow objects that can be linked to an activity group | |
|---|---|
| Standard tasks (TS) | TS – client independent |
| Workflow templates (WS) | WS - client |

### Example: Sample Workflow for a Notification Absence

This process begins when an employee submits a completed *Request for Leave* form. This form is automatically forwarded to the employee's supervisor. If the supervisor approves the request, the employee is informed and the workflow ends. If the supervisor rejects the request, the employee must decide whether he or she should to revise the request, or withdraw it completely. If the employee decides to revise the request, the form is automatically returned to the employee's inbox, and the workflow begins again.

In the following procedure, we show how to assign the standard task *Confirmation of Leave Request* to the activity group *FI Supervisor*.

## Selecting Workflow Tasks

1. Access the PG (transaction **PFCG**).
2. On the *Activity Group Maintenance* screen, select *Overview (Organization Management and workflow)*.
3. On the *Change Activity Groups* screen, choose the *Workflow* tab.
4. Choose *Workflow tasks*.

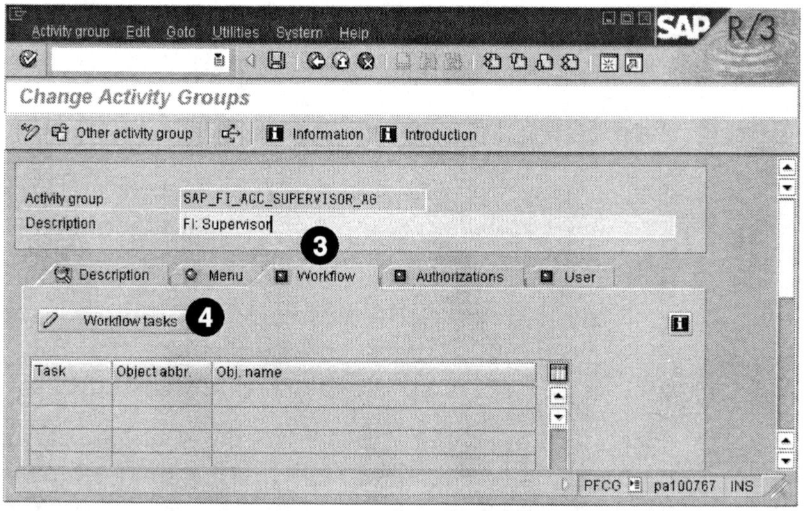


Tips & Tricks

The *Workflow* tab is only displayed if you selected *Overview (Organization Management and workflow)* at the beginning of transaction *PFCG*. If you do not see this tab, the view *Basic maintenance (menus, profiles, other objects)* was probably selected on the *Activity Group Maintenance* screen.

5. Choose to add a task.

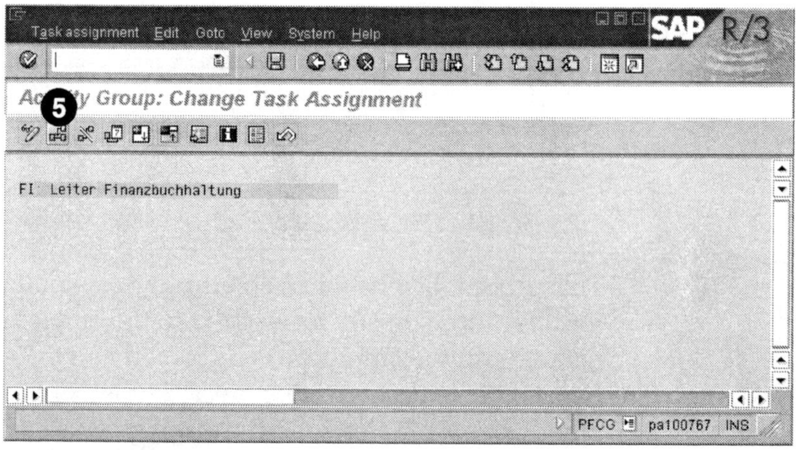


6. Select the desired task type (for example, *Standard task*).
7. Choose ✔.

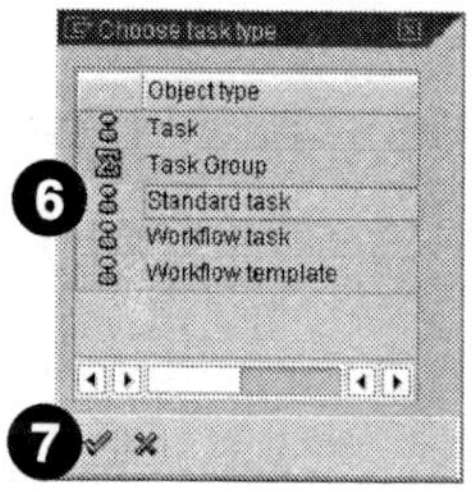


Tips & Tricks

Although the options *Workflow task* and *Task* still appear, they are no longer used or supported.

8. Choose ✔ to continue.

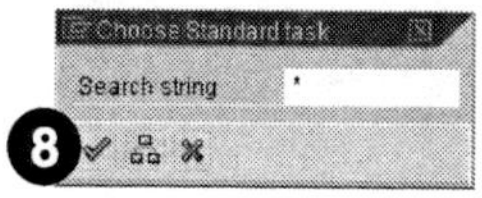

9. Select the desired item (for example, *Confirmation of Leave Request*).
10. Choose ✔.

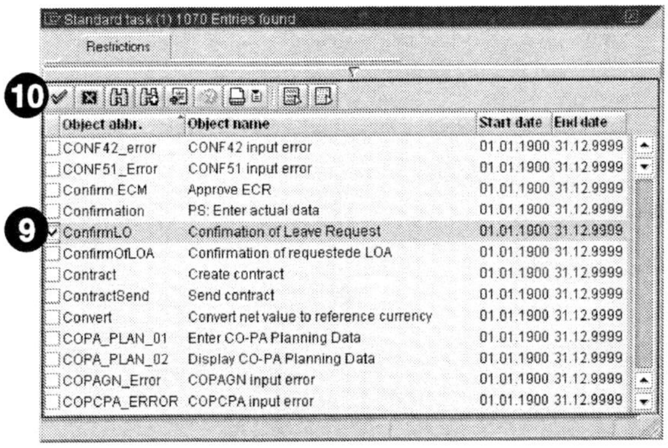


11. Choose the correct time period for the assignment.
12. Choose 🗋.

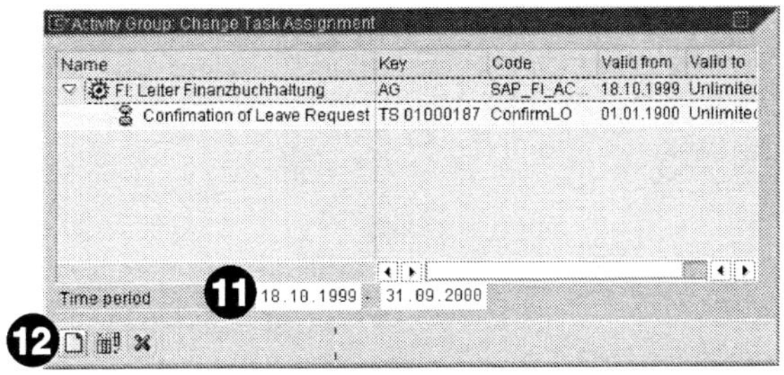


13. Choose 💾.

The selected task is now assigned to the activity group. Everyone to whom this activity group will be assigned can confirm the leave request in the defined time period.

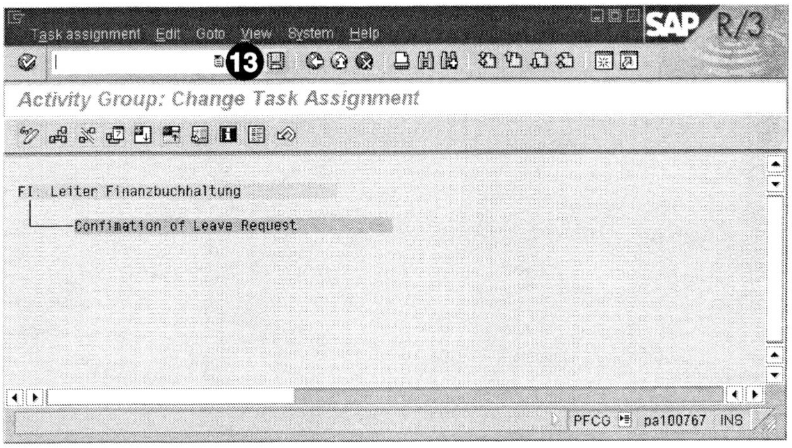

# Deleting Activity Groups

**Tips & Tricks**

When you delete an activity group, the system automatically deletes any assignments existing between the activity group and R/3 users, positions, jobs, or organizational units.

1. Access the PG (transaction **PFCG**).
2. In the *Activity Group Maintenance* screen, select the activity group you would like to delete by either entering the name in the *Activity group* field or choosing *possible entries*.
3. Choose 🗑 to delete the activity group.

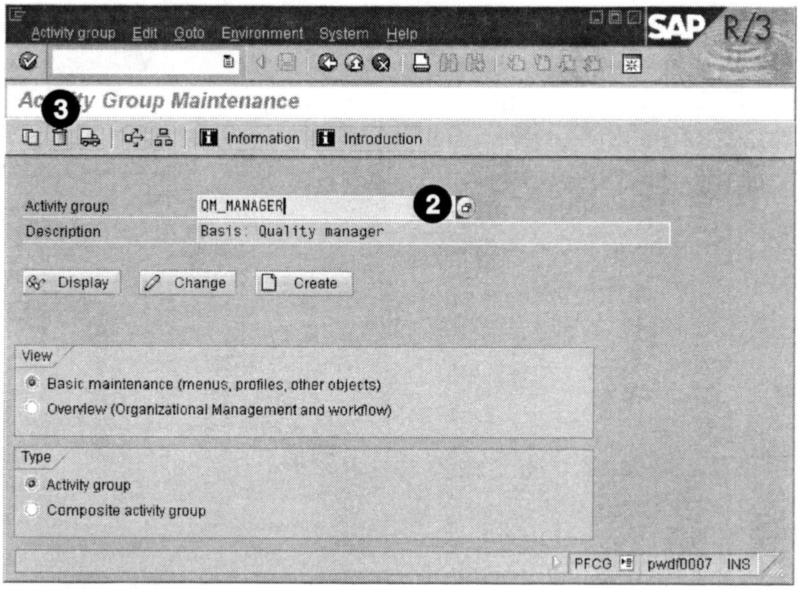


4. Choose *Yes*.

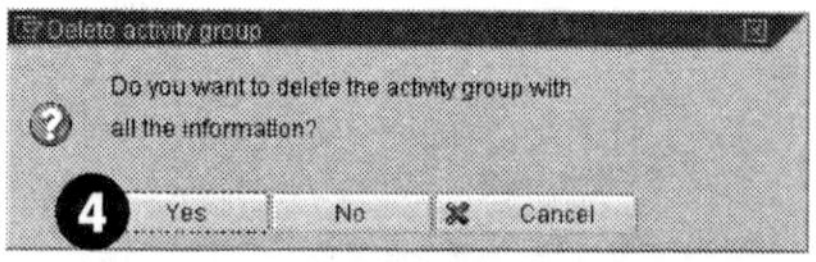


**Caution**

Verify that your activity group was actually entered in a transport request completed earlier. Otherwise the deletion cannot be transported.

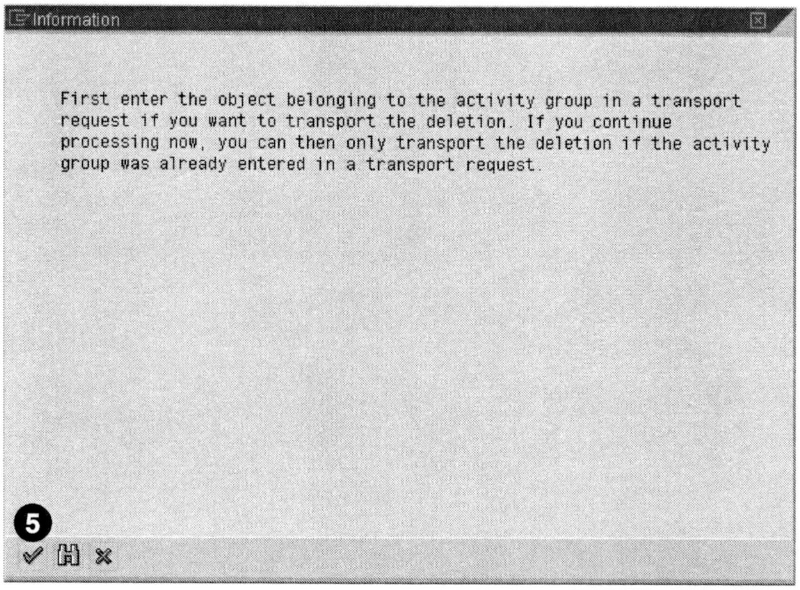


5. Choose ✔.

   The chosen activity group and all the corresponding assignments have now been deleted. The authorization profiles—including the authorizations generated for this activity group—are also deleted.

# Postmaintaining User Role Templates

To generate an authorization profile, you must first create or use an existing activity group. In chapter 5, *User Role Templates,* we demonstrated how to use the user role templates and generated the related authorizations and their profiles. In this section, we show you how to postmaintain existing activity groups in greater detail.

Once you have defined an activity group, use the Profile Generator (PG) to automatically generate an authorization profile. Authorizations automatically generated for activity groups use SAP-supplied data so that most fields are already filled with proposed values.

To generate an authorization profile:

1. Start the generation process.
2. Maintain the organizational levels.
3. Postedit the authorizations and organizational levels.

Tips & Tricks

The SAP-delivered user role templates already have some authorization data. All open authorization fields and organizational levels such as company codes, business areas, or plants have the asterisks (*), for full authorization assigned, but the profiles are not generated yet.

## Different Settings for the Maintenance View

You have different options to display several buttons in the tree structure for the maintenance process.

To access the selection screen, start the PG and go to the *Change Activity Groups* screen. On the *Authorizations* tab, choose *Change authorization data*. Choose *Utilities → Settings* to get to the *Define Settings for User* window.

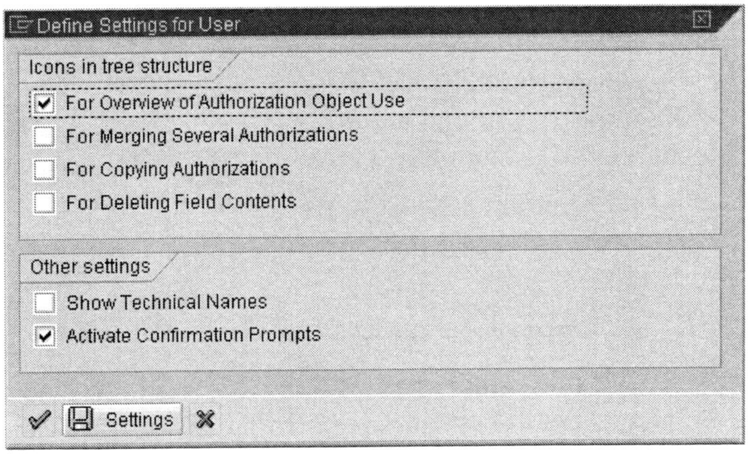


Different buttons simplify your work. In the tree structure you see:

– Overview of authorization object use

– Merging several authorizations

– Copying authorization

– Deleting field contents

The technical name is displayed at the end of the corresponding line.

Save your settings after the selection.

For further explanation of the icons, choose on the *Change Activity Groups* screen.

# Maintaining and Generating the Authorization Profiles

In this section, we assume the activity group has already been created and saved. We show how to generate the authorization profiles for the activity group.

1. Access the PG (transaction **PFCG**).
2. Select the activity group you want to maintain and choose *Change* (for example, *MM_BUYER_AG*).
3. On the *Change Activity Groups* screen, choose the *Authorizations* tab.
4. Choose *Change authorization data*.

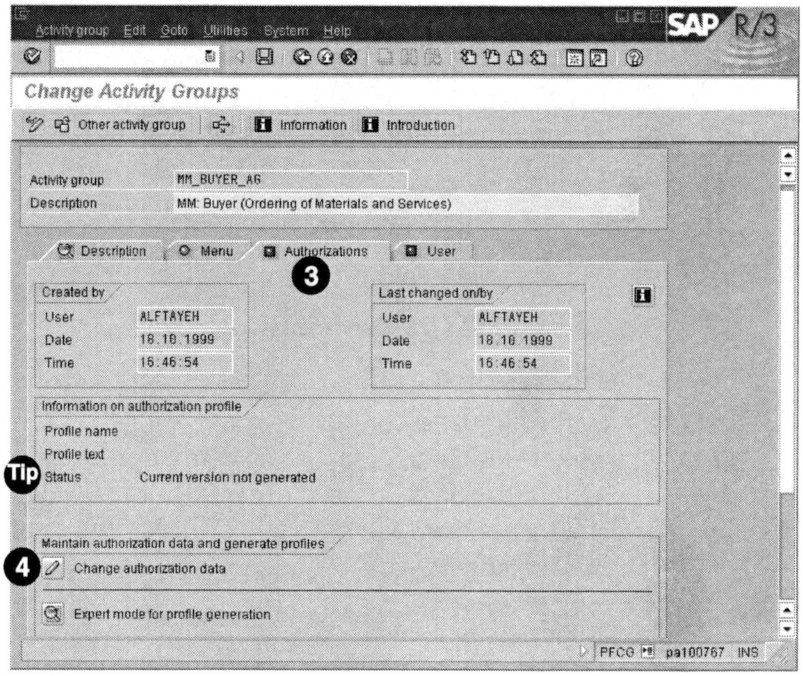

The red light on the *Authorizations* tab indicates that no authorization profiles have been generated for this activity group. You can also see the status for the authorization profile in the *Information on authorization profile* box.

On the *Change Activity Group: Authorizations* screen, the authorizations data appears hierarchically.

The activity group appears at the first level (highlighted in blue). Underneath you find lines highlighted as follows:

- *Object classes = orange*
- *Authorization object = green*
- *Authorization = yellow*
- *Authorization fields = light blue*

To view the legend for the icons and colors choose .

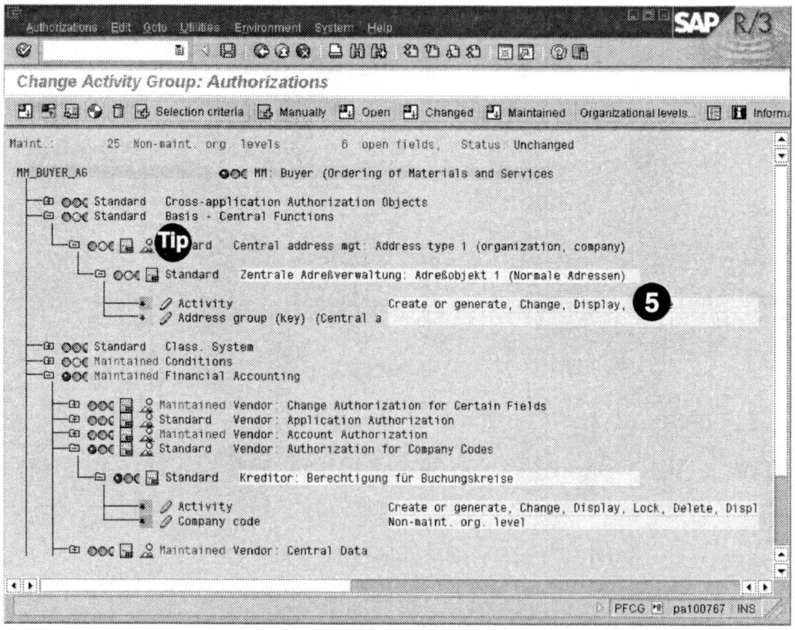


5. To maintain or change the activity, double-click on the entry next to the activity field.

Tips & Tricks

To display all selected transactions that check this authorization object for the underlying activity group, choose .

**Explanation of the lights.**

**Green**: All authorization fields have been maintained.

**Red**: Organizational levels are not maintained.

**Yellow**: Open authorization fields without values exist that are not organizational levels.

6. Select or deselect all desired values for the activity (you can use *Full authorization*).
7. To transfer your selection, choose .

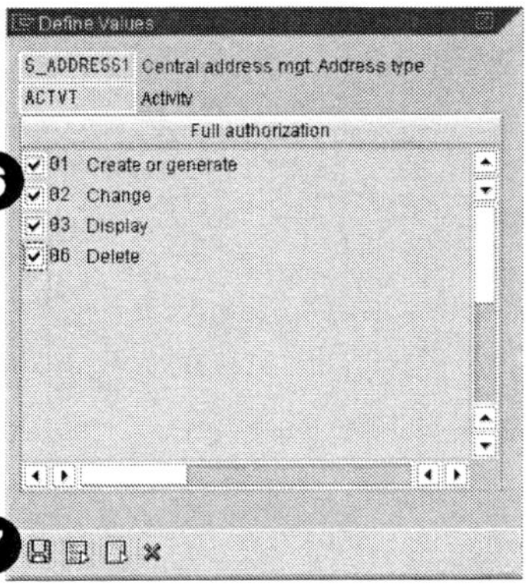


8. To maintain the values for the open authorizations, click next to the authorization field name.

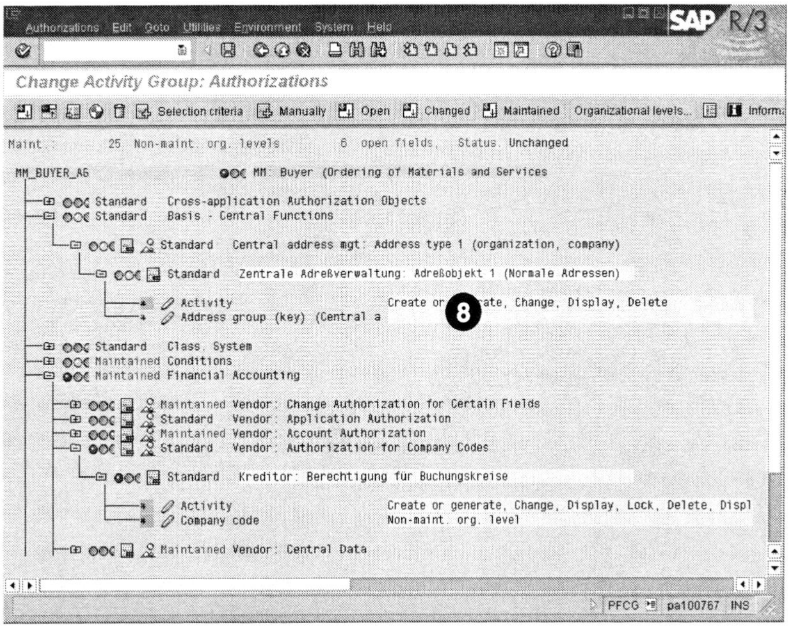


9. Enter a single value in the *From* column or a value range in the *From* and *To* columns either directly or by using *possible entries*.

   For multiple selections, fill in the rows below the entry.
10. To transfer the data, choose .

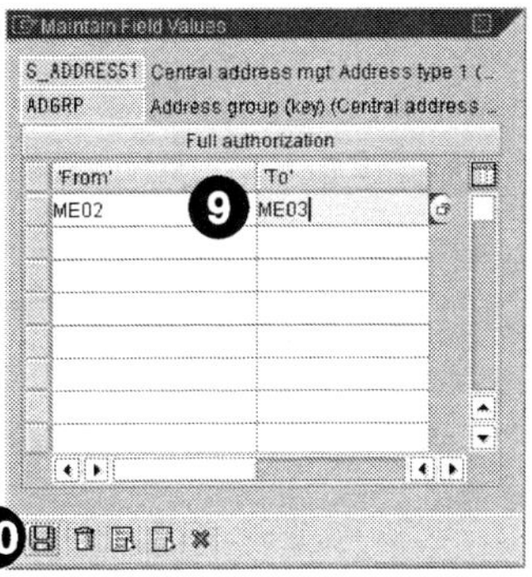

After maintaining the activity and the field values for the authorization, the light changes from yellow to green.

11. To maintain the missing organizational levels, click on the field next to the authorization field name (for example, *Company Code* under the object *Authorization for Company Codes*.)

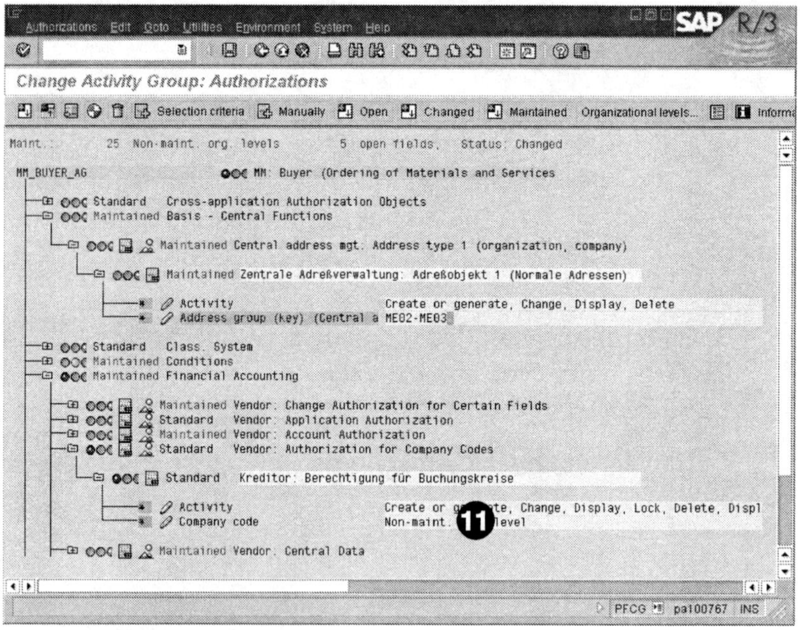


12. Enter a single value in the *From* column or a value range in the *From* and *To* columns either directly or by using *possible entries*.

    (For multiple selections, fill in the rows below the entry.)

13. To transfer the data, choose 💾.

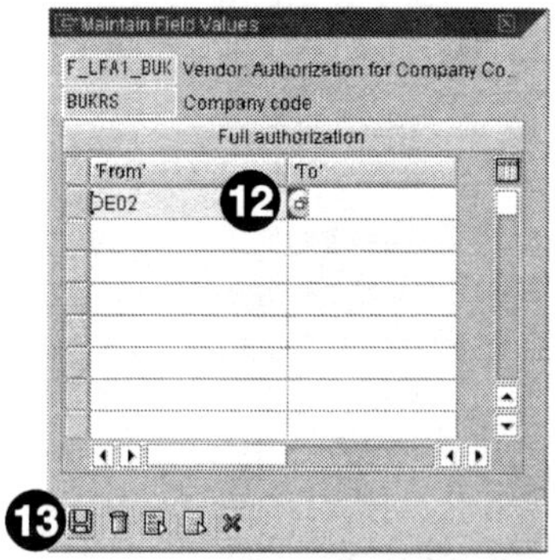


After maintaining the missing data for this organizational level, the light changes from red to green.

Proceed with the other open fields in the same way until all lights have changed to green.

14. To save your changes, choose 💾.

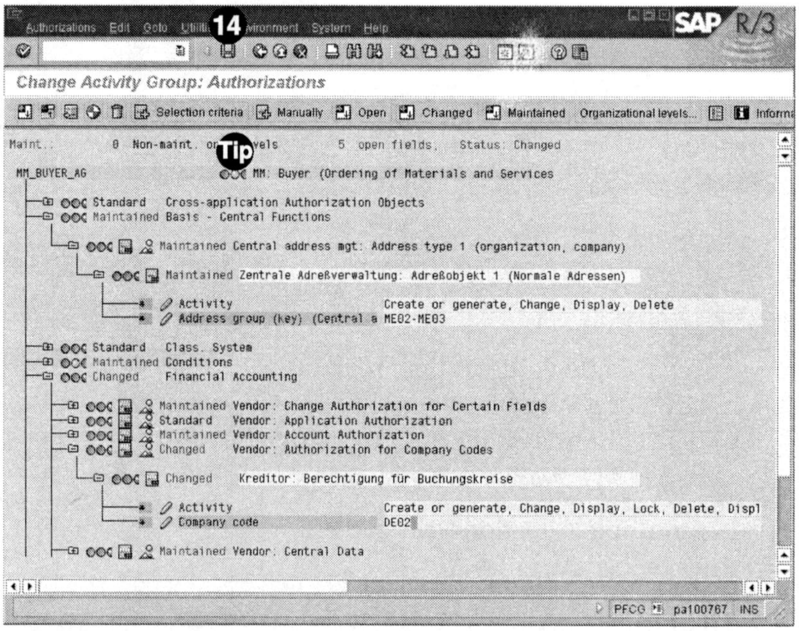

To assign full authorizations to all open fields, click on the yellow light at the top, next to the activity group.

Tips & Tricks

Remember to maintain each open authorization field with a suitable value. For some authorizations, enter a suitable value in *Authorization group*. If you are not sure of a suitable value, use the asterisk (*) to assign overall authorization for unmaintained fields. Remember that you can always change values later.

When all lights have changed to green and you have saved your changes, generate the authorization profile.

15. To generate the authorizations, choose .

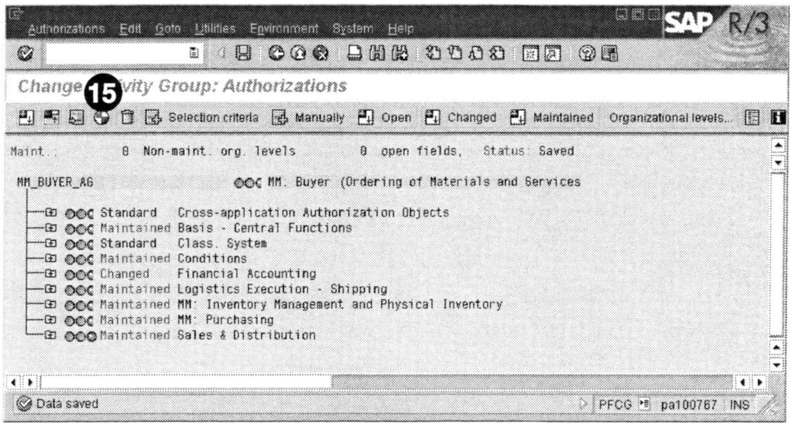


TechTalk

The system generates an authorization for each authorization in the tree and an authorization profile for the activity group that applies to the entire tree.

16. The *Assign Profile Name for Generated Authorization Profile* dialog box appears. The system suggests *T_<internal number>* as the default profile name.

17. Choose .

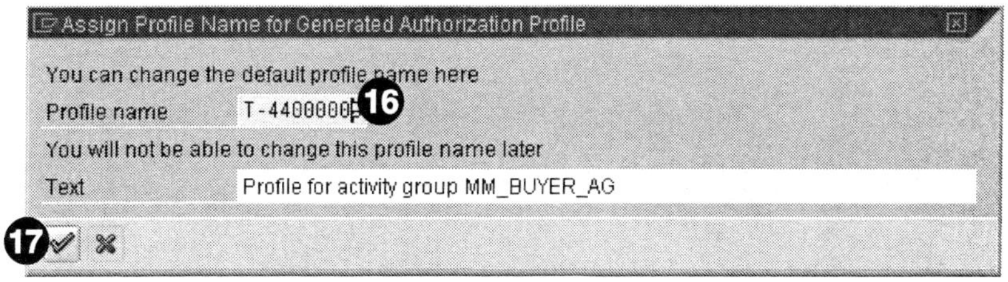


Tips & Tricks

The short profile name cannot be changed later. However, the long text for the profile can be changed at any time.

TechTalk

**Naming Conventions for Authorization Profiles and Authorizations Generated with the PG**

When you save your changes, you are prompted to enter a profile name. However, only the first 10 characters (the profile torso) can be freely assigned. The number of profiles generated depends on the number of authorizations in each activity group. A maximum of approximately 150 authorizations can fit into a profile. If there are more than 150 authorizations, an additional profile is generated. It has the same 10-character torso as the profile name, and the last two digits are used as a counter.

To avoid conflicts between customer-defined and SAP-supplied profiles, do not use any name with an underscore (_) in the second position. SAP places no other restrictions on the naming of authorization profiles (refer also to note *16466*). If your company has its own naming conventions, you may overwrite proposed names.

The names of the authorizations are also derived from the profile torso. The last two digits are used as a counter when more than one authorization is required for an object. Depending on the authorization profile name, the technical names for authorizations are then named as follows:

- Begin with a *T-*
- Comprise an internal number
- End with a two-digit number between *00* and *99*

Sample authorization name: T-4400001900.

The authorization object *S_USER_PRO* is checked during authorization maintenance. The object is defined with the following fields: *Authorization profile* and *Activity*. In *Authorization profile*, enter the authorization profiles that an authorization administrator can maintain or that user administrators can assign to their users. In *Activity*, you can limit what the administrator is allowed to do.

If you want to set up an authorization administrator who can maintain only certain profiles, set up your own naming convention.

# Displaying an Overview of Generated Profiles

After successfully generating the authorization profiles, to find out how many profiles were generated, you have to know the number of authorizations in each activity group. A maximum of approximately 150 authorizations fit into a profile. If there are more than 150 authorizations, an additional profile is generated. It has the same 10-character torso as the profile name, with the last two digits used as a counter.

If an activity group is changed so that one profile becomes two or more, the additional profiles are automatically assigned to all the original profile's users. The user master of this user is automatically updated.

In the following procedure, we demonstrate how to display the overview of the generated profiles for the activity group *SAP_ALL_DISPLAY_AG*, which contain the authorization to display "everything" except for HR.

1. Access the PG (transaction **PFCG**).
2. Select the activity group you would like to view (for example *MM_BUYER_AG*) and choose *Change*.
3. On the *Change Activity Groups* screen, choose the *Authorizations* tab.
4. Choose *Change Authorization Data*.

5. Choose *Authorizations → Profile Overview.*

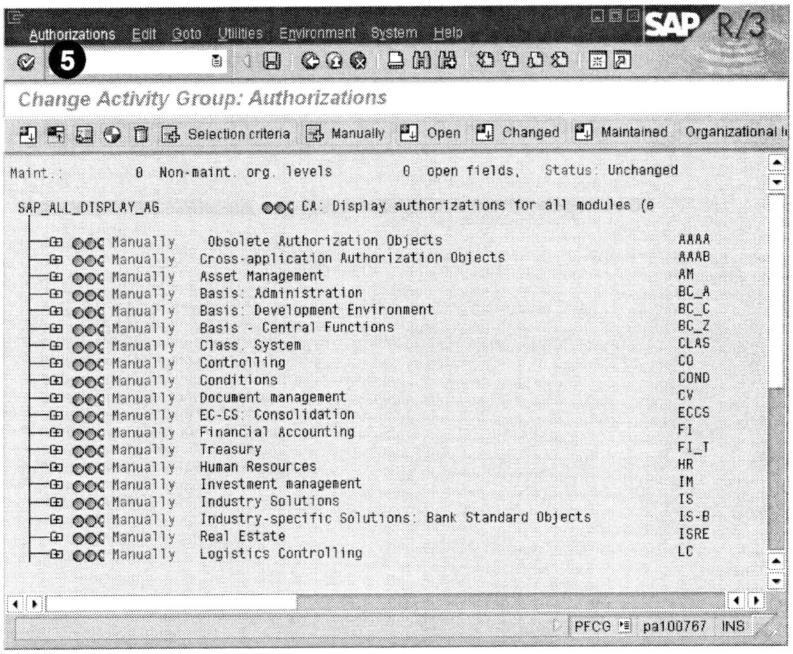


If the generated authorization profiles are already active, the dialog box provides an overview of the current profile with profile name, long text, and the status of the version.

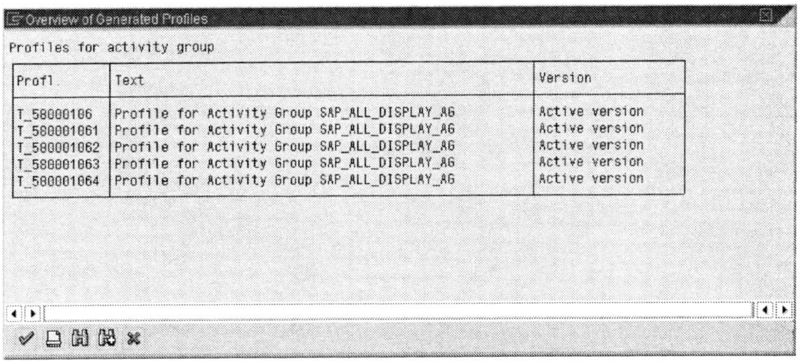

# Regenerating Authorization Profiles After Making Changes

When an activity group is changed, for example after you add transactions, regenerate its authorization profiles with transaction *PFCG*.

For the following example, we have taken the activity group *MM_BUYER_AG* added some transactions and saved the changes. Now we have some more authorizations that need to be maintained and the activity group needs to be regenerated.

TechTalk

When you change an activity group, the status on the *Authorizations* tab indicates whether a profile is current or not. If the display shows a red or yellow light, the profile is not current. The *status* text on the screen explains why the profile is not current.

- Red light and the text *Profile comparison required*

  The menu has been changed since the profile was last generated. Therefore the profile is not current and the authorization profiles needs to be regenerated. You may also have to maintain the authorization field values.

- Yellow light

  The profile has been changed and saved since it was last generated, the profile is not current anymore, and the authorization profile needs to be regenerated.

- If you are unsure whether an authorization profiles should be regenerated:

  1. Run transaction **SUPC**.
  2. Select *Also act. grps to be adjusted.*
  3. Choose to execute the transaction.

The system generates a list of all activity groups with existing authorization data in the system. Activity groups in red need to be regenerated after postmaintaining any open authorization fields. Select one of these activity groups and choose *Maintain profile*. From **SUPC**, call transaction **PFCG** and proceed as described below.

**Prerequisite:** You must make changes to an activity group and save them before you can regenerate authorization profiles.

1. Access the PG (transaction **PFCG**).
2. Select the desired activity group (for example *MM_BUYER_AG*) and choose *Change*.
3. On the *Authorizations* tab choose *Expert mode for profile generation.*

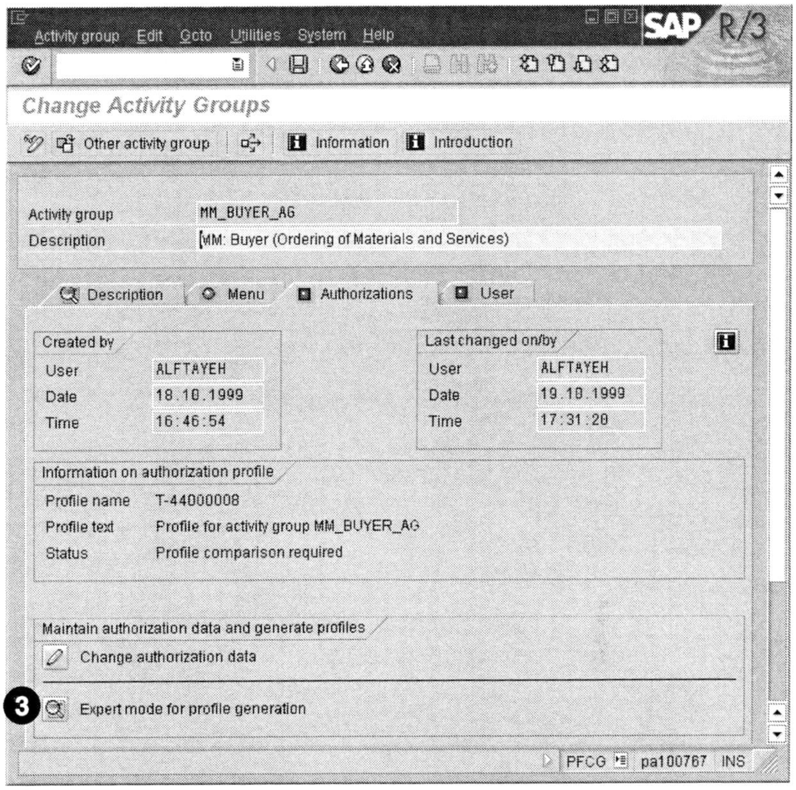


Tips & Tricks

In expert mode, you can select explicitly the option with which you want to maintain the authorization values. This option is automatically set correctly in normal mode.

4. Select *Read old status and merge with new data.*
5. Choose ✔.

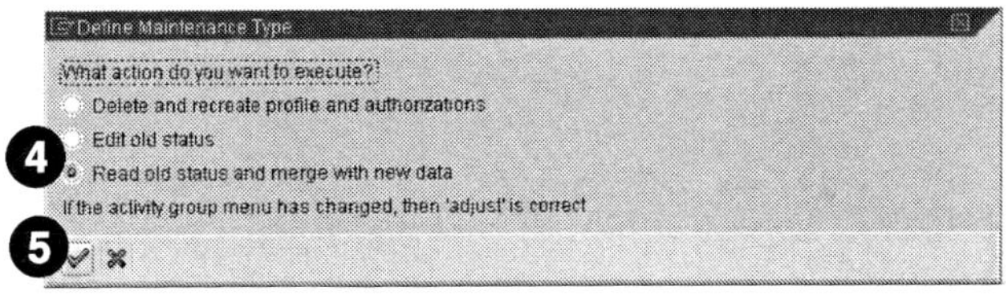


Tips & Tricks

Options on the *Define Maintenance Type* screen:

- *Delete and recreate profile and authorizations*

  All authorizations are re-created. Values that have previously been maintained, changed, or entered manually are lost. Only the maintained values for organizational levels remain.

- *Edit old status*

  You can edit the authorization profile you previously maintained with its old values. It is not worth editing if the assignment of transactions to activity groups has changed.

- *Read old status and merge with new data*

  The PG compares the old and current data from the activity group. This choice is the best option if the activity group has changed. Unchanged data is marked as *Old*, new data as *New*.

TechTalk

We added a few transactions to the activity group. The previously maintained organizational levels are kept. When new organizational levels are added, they must be maintained.

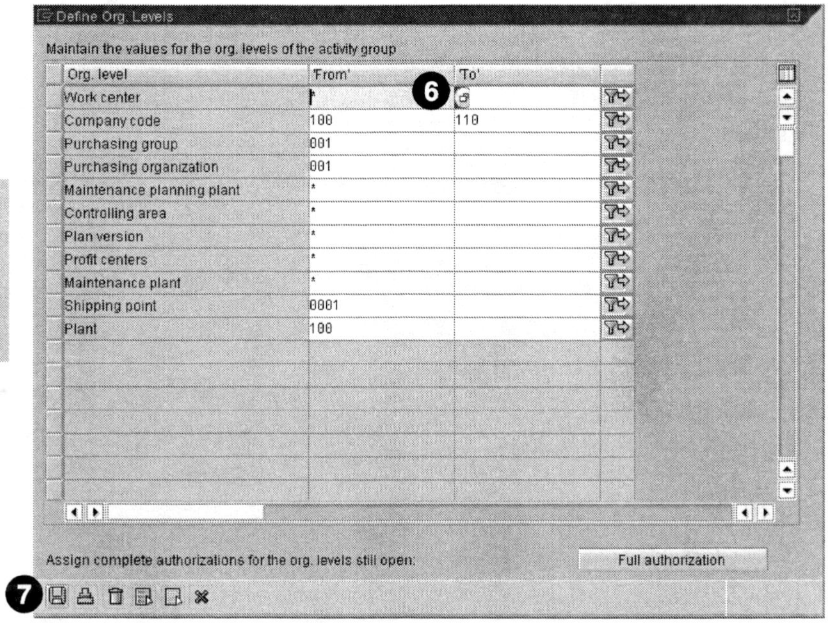


6. Maintain the organizational levels with the right values, or choose *Full authorization* to fill all blanks with asterisks (*) (We chose *Full authorization* in our example.)
7. Choose [save icon].

   Old authorizations are marked *Old*, new authorizations are marked *New*.
8. Maintain the open fields as described in *Maintaining and Generating the Authorization Profiles* on page 6–26.
9. Choose [save icon].

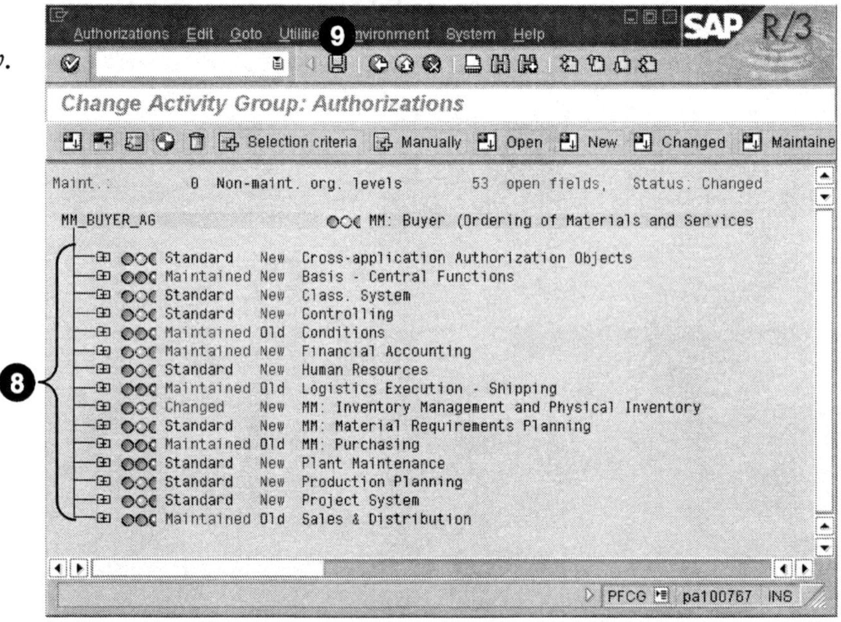

Caution

**Please keep the following in mind when making the post-change comparison:**

- Previously maintained organizational levels are kept. If new organizational levels are added, you must maintain these levels.
- If authorizations within an authorization object have changed, you need to execute the comparison manually. You must decide whether to keep the old modified data or use the current data. Delete or maintain the authorizations you no longer require.
- Maintained authorizations are configured with the values you maintained for them. For example, for authorization group *0001*, certain activities (*Insert*, *Change*, and *Display*) and maintained authorizations for the activity group transactions are required (you maintained the value for authorization group). Change the activity group so that the following activities arise: *Change*, *Display*, and *Delete*. The value *0001* is copied for the authorization group for *Change* and *Display* (these activities were already maintained). The *Insert* option disappears. For the *Delete* activity, maintain the authorization group again, since this group was not maintained in the old profile's status.
- Wherever the *New* attribute appears, check if the new authorizations make sense (you can compare them manually with the old values).
- Manually entered authorizations are not deleted.

The values for the authorization object *S_TCODE* are always automatically filled with the current transaction from the activity group, but have the attribute *Old*.

When there are only green lights in the tree, there are no more open authorization fields to maintain.

10. Choose to regenerate the existing authorization profiles.

    After the regeneration of the authorization profiles is finished, you can go back to the main screen.

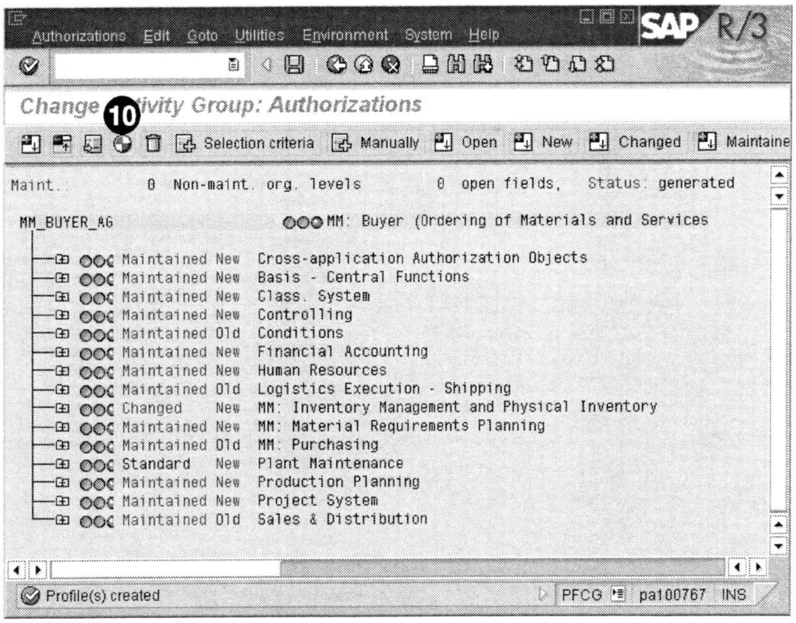

# Using Utilities to Change Generated Authorizations

There are two options to alter the automatically generated authorizations. These options are found in transaction *PFCG,* under the *Utilities* menu in the *Change Activity Group: Authorizations* screen.

## Merging Authorizations

1. Access the PG (transaction **PFCG**).
2. Select the desired activity group (for example *MM_BUYER_AG*) and choose *Change*.
3. On the *Authorizations* tab, choose *Change authorization data*.
4. Choose *Utilities → Merge authorizations.*

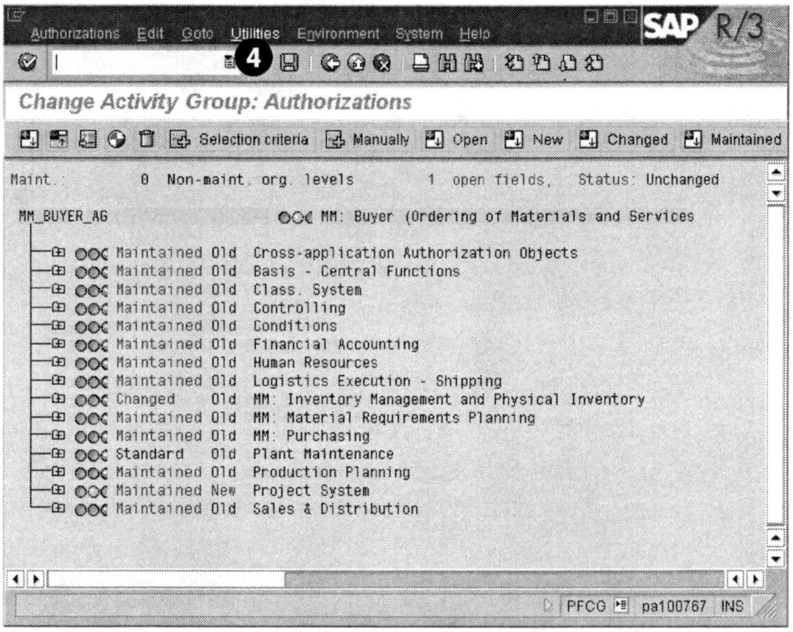

5. The system automatically summarizes all possible authorizations and the result appears in a system message.

   In our example, the status bar shows that five authorizations have combined with others.

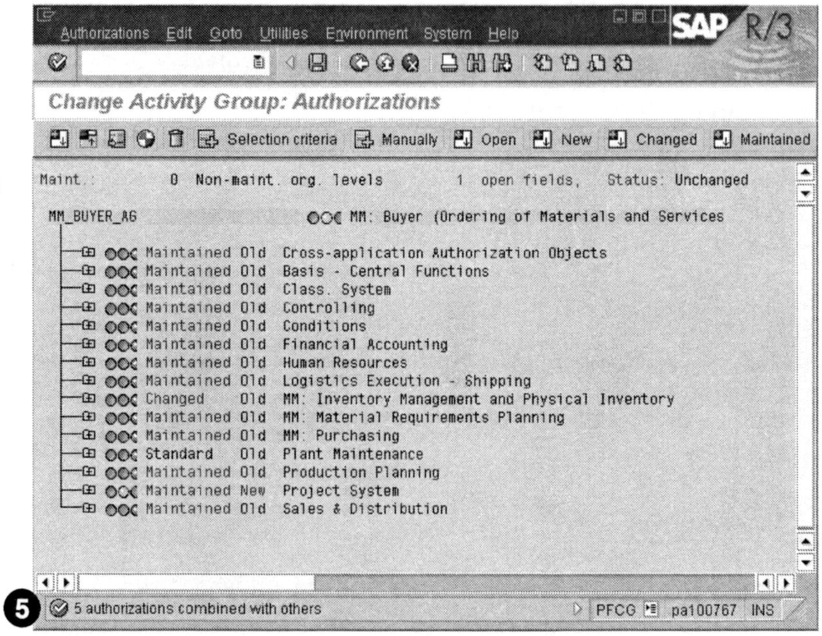

## Reorganizing Technical Names of Authorizations

The technical name of an authorization for an authorization object is the name of the activity group and a two-digit number between 00 and 99.

*T-<internal number>nn*, for example: *T-5002995604*

If the authorization profiles changed as a result of changes in the appropriate activity group, reorganize the numbers to avoid number assignment problems. The following procedure restarts the number assignment from 00. Whenever you generate a new authorization profile, this reorganization is automatically taken into account.

1. Access the PG (transaction **PFCG**).
2. Select the desired activity group (for example *MM_BUYER_AG*) and choose *Change*.
3. On the *Authorizations* tab choose *Change authorization data*.
4. Choose *Utilities → Reorganize*.

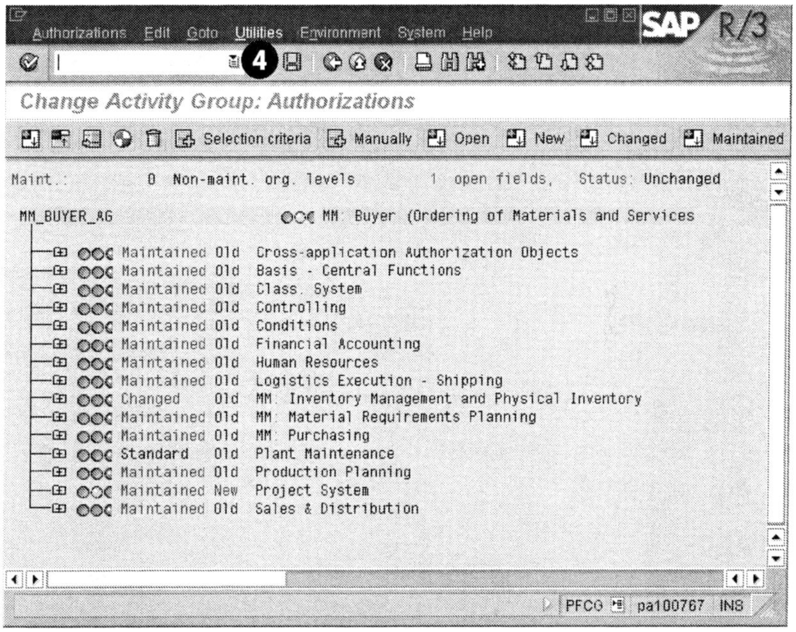


The system automatically reorganizes the final digits of the authorizations technical names and the result appears in a system message (for example, *Authorizations were reorganized*).

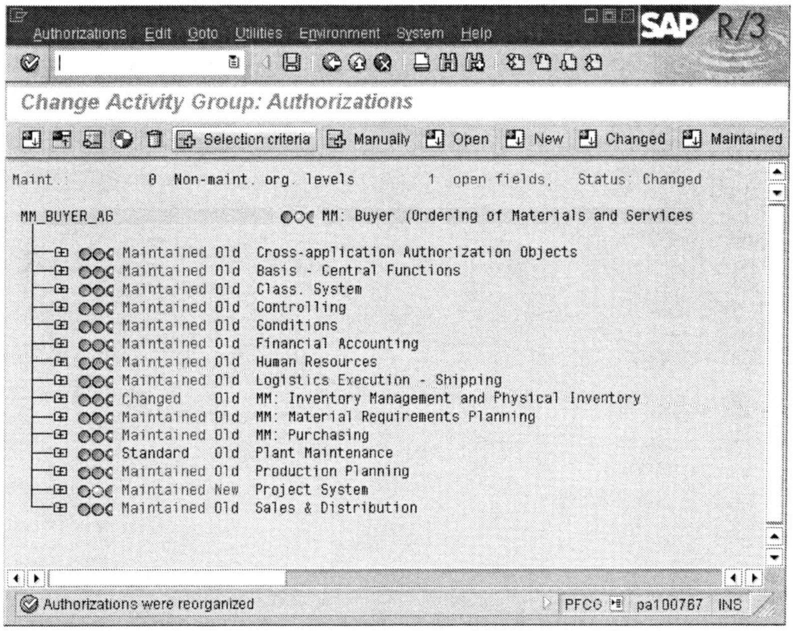

# Customizing Authorizations

SAP delivers a user role template for the Customizing Project Member, which is called *SAP_BC_CUS_CUSTOMIZER_AG*. This activity group can be assigned to any person doing customizing in R/3. In addition, you can assign projects or views of the Implementation Guide (IMG) to an activity group. The aim of this assignment is to generate authorizations for and assign users to specific IMG activities. That insures that users are only allowed to perform tasks in their customizing project and not in any other. When you generate profiles, it also generates the authorizations necessary to execute all activities in the assigned IMG projects or project views.

## Assigning IMG Projects or Project Views to Activity Groups

In the following example we demonstrate how to create a customizing activity group for a QM customizing project. Therefore, we will create a new activity group called *QM_CUSTOMIZING* and assign the QM customizing project to it. You can assign different project views if available.

1. Access the PG (transaction **PFCG**).
2. In the *Activity group* field, enter a name for your new activity group.
3. Choose *Create*.

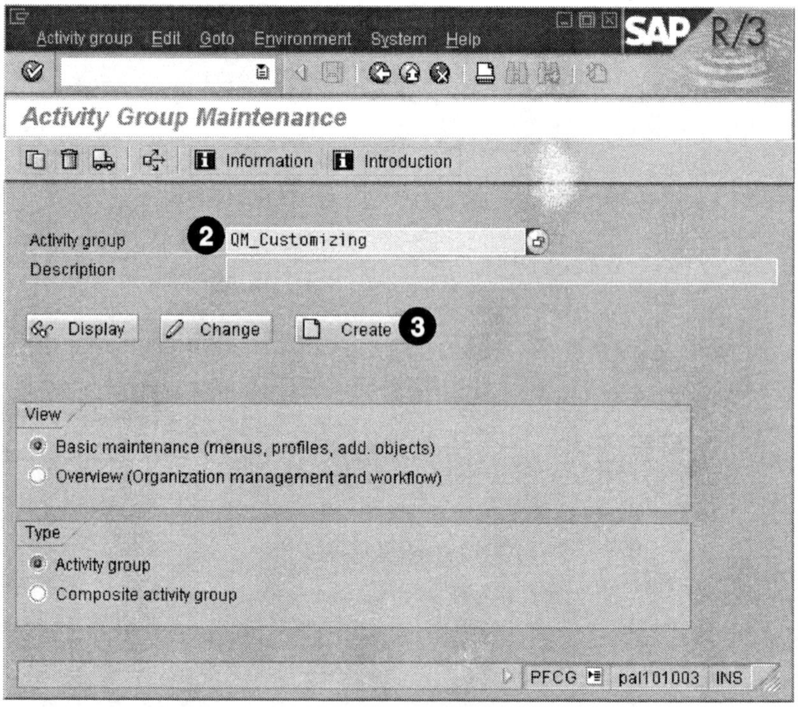

4. Enter a short description in the *Description* field.
5. Enter a long text description for the activity group (optional).
6. To save the activity group, choose 💾.
7. Choose the *Menu* tab.
8. Choose *Utilities* → *Customizing auth.*

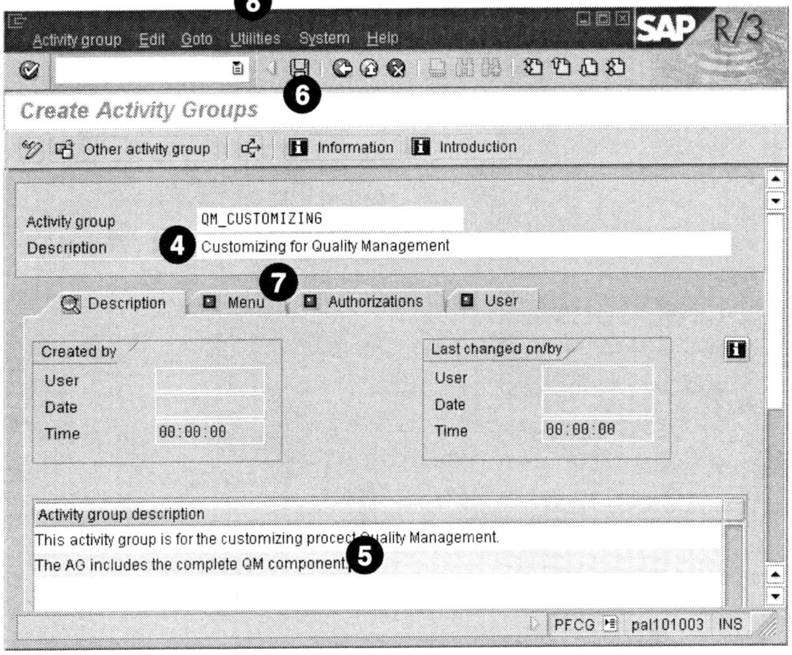


You can see the status of the activity group in the dialog box.

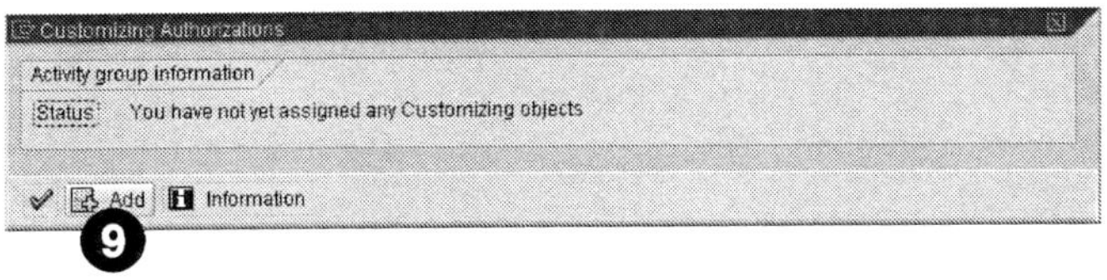


9. Choose *Add* to assign a customizing project or project view to the activity group.
10. Select *IMG project* or *IMG project view*, depending on what you would like to assign. In our example, we assigned an IMG project.
11. Choose ✔.

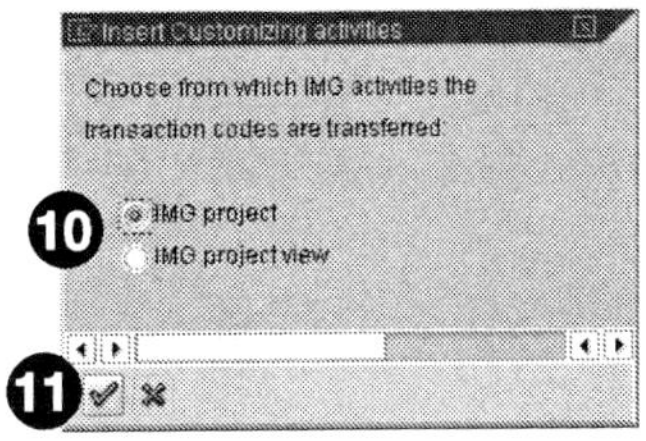


12. Select the desired project or project view (in this example, we selected the project *QM_CUSTOM*).
13. Choose ✔.

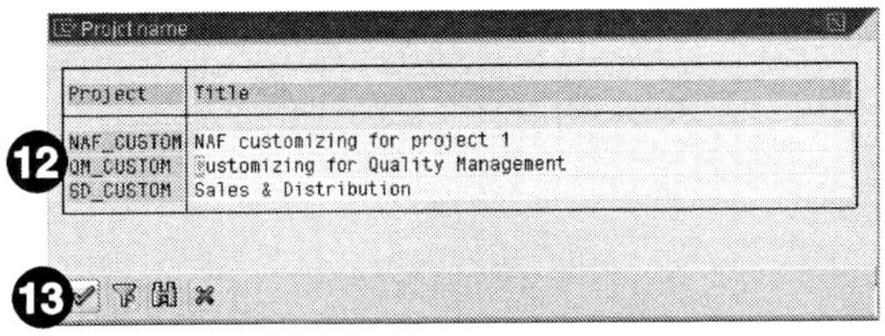


14. Choose ✔ to continue.

> **Transferring Users from an IMG Project**
>
> On the *Customizing Authorizations* screen, if there are users assigned to the IMG project that you would like to assign to this activity group, choose *User*. This action copies the users from the IMG project to the activity group.
>
> Note that you must call this function again each time changes are made in the IMG project administration.

The system automatically determines the transaction codes and additional authorization objects that are required to maintain the tables for this IMG project or project view, and imports them into the activity group.

15. To save your activity group, choose .

> You cannot manually assign transactions to this activity group nor can you select any from the SAP menu. Note that the buttons to do this have vanished.

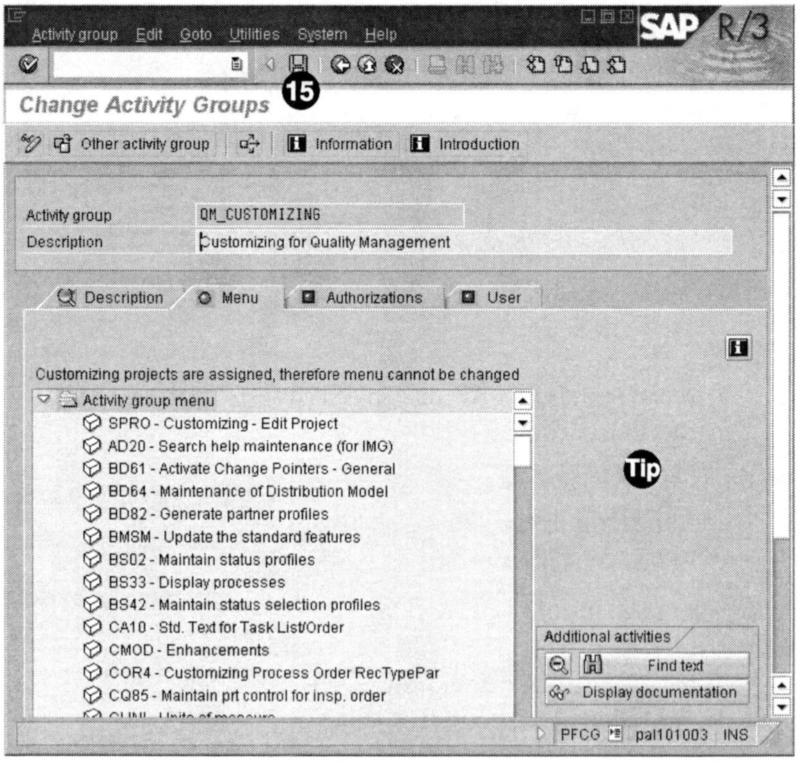

16. Choose the *Authorizations* tab to continue the generation process.
17. Choose ✏ *Change authorization data.*

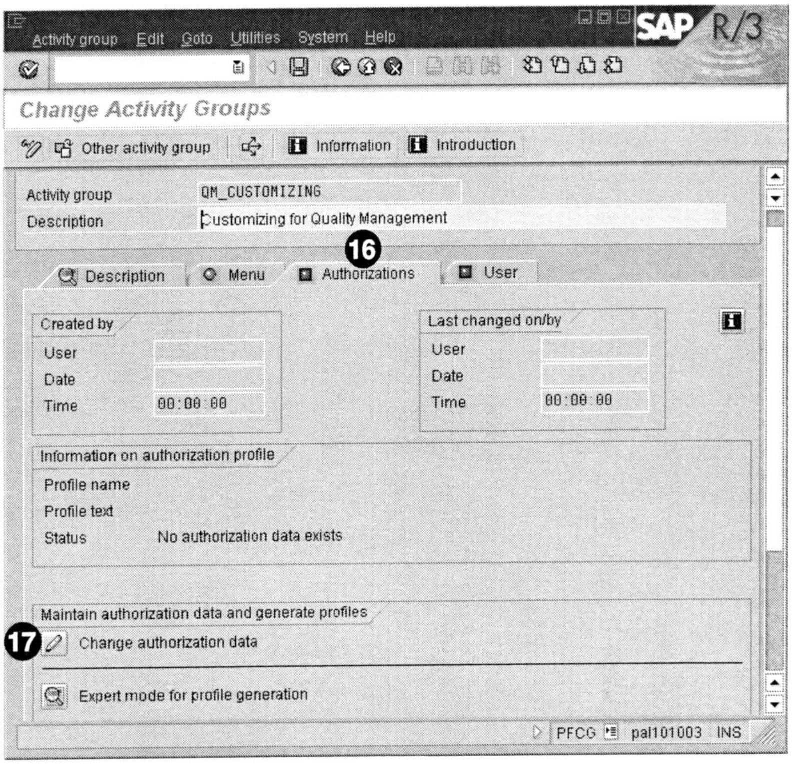


If necessary, the dialog box *Define Org. Levels* appears.

18. Enter the appropriate data. You can give full authorizations by choosing *Full authorization* in the lower right corner.
19. Choose 💾.

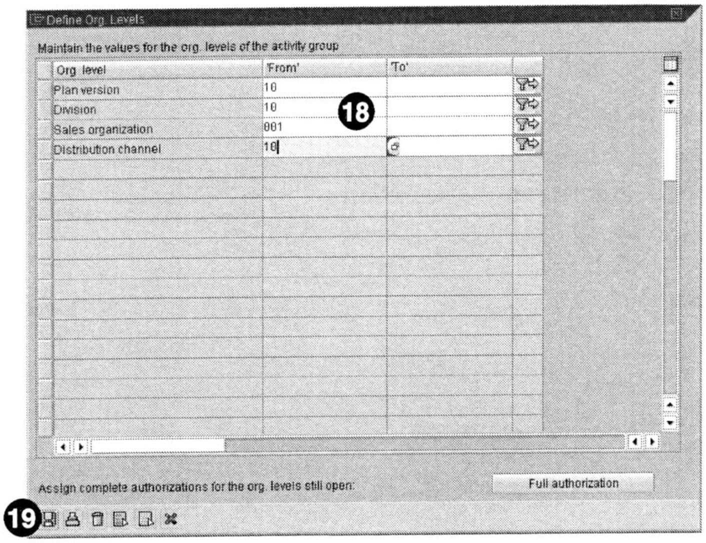

20. Maintain all open authorization fields indicated by the yellow light as described earlier in this book. In our example, we chose full authorization by clicking on the upper most yellow light.

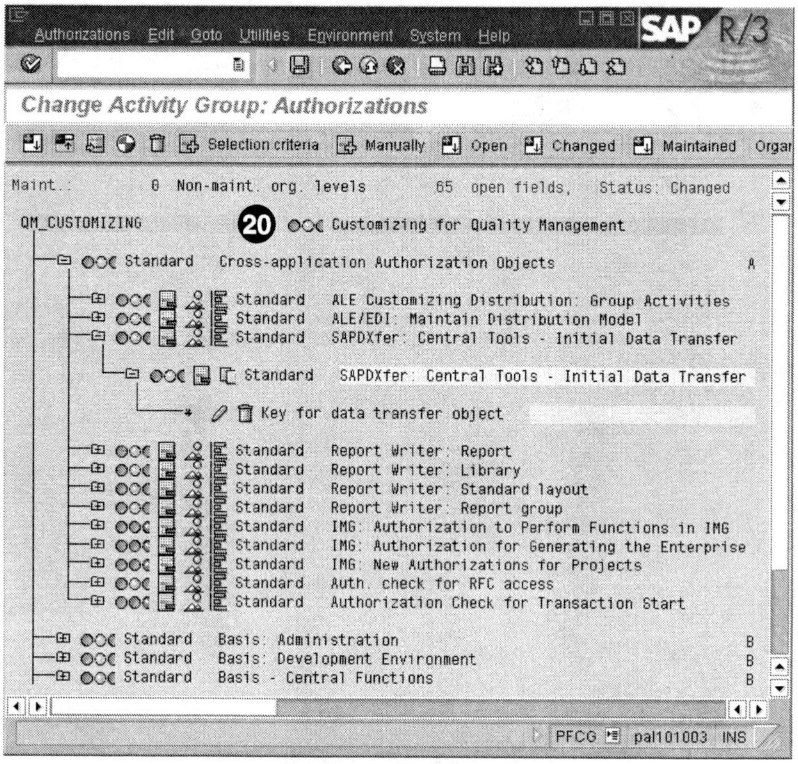


If you choose full authorizations, a confirmation screen appears.

21. Choose ✔ to continue.

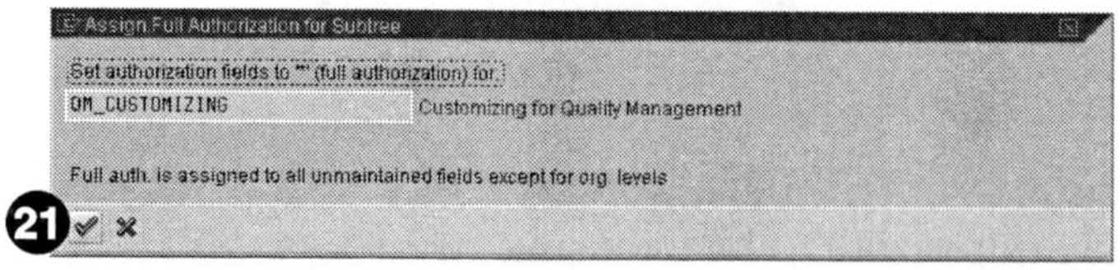


All open authorizations are filled when all the lights have changed to green.

22. Save the activity group.

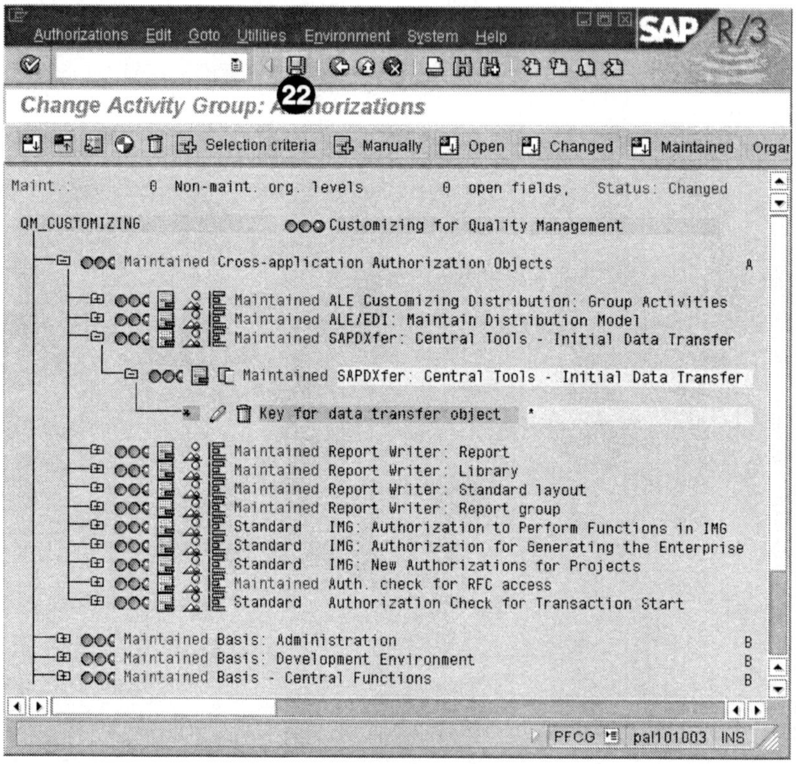

23. On the *Assign Profile Name for Generated Authorization Profile* screen, you have the option to change the *Profile name*. You will **not** be able to change it later.

24. Choose .

25. To generate the activity group, choose .

26. To go back to the main screen, choose .

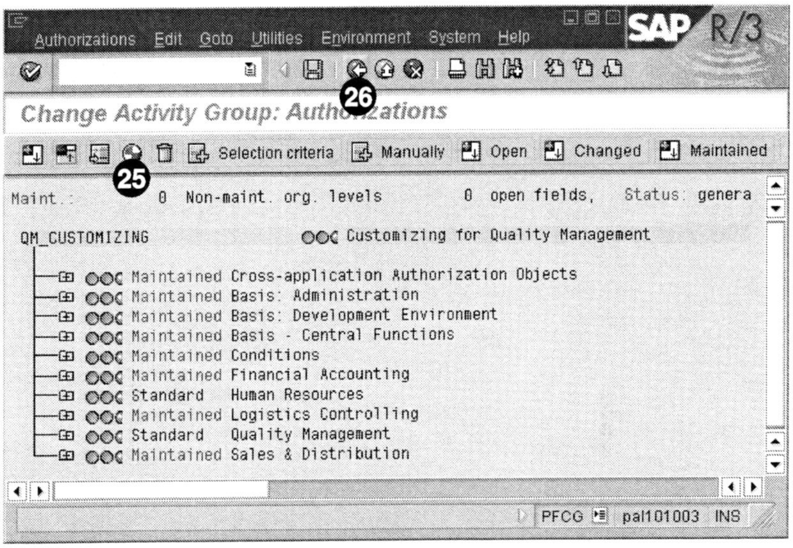


You have now created a customizing activity group and assigned authorization data to it.

If there are no users assigned to the selected IMG project or if you chose not to copy them to the activity group in an earlier step, you still have to do so. Choose the *Users* tab to assign users to the activity group, as demonstrated in chapters 5 and 8.

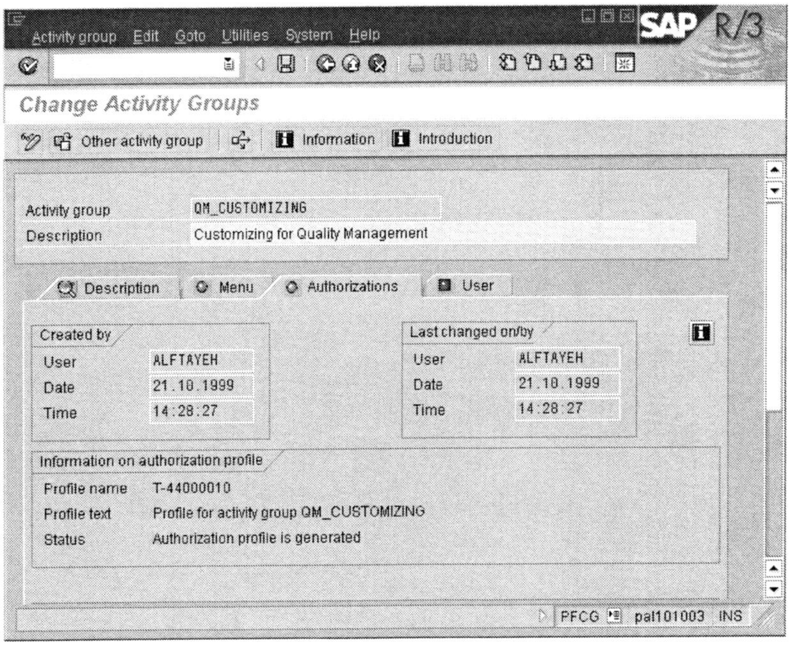

Tips & Tricks

If the IMG project has changed, you should regenerate the authorization data for this activity group. The first step is to choose *Refresh* on the *Customizing Authorizations* dialog box (see step 14 on page 6–39). This action recalculates the transaction codes. You must then regenerate the authorization profiles for the activity group.

To assign users to the customizing activity group, you can transfer the users that are already assigned to the customizing project or project view. You can also assign any other user to this customizing activity group.

You should consider using the SAP-provided user role template *SAP_BC_CUS_CUSTOMIZER_AG* for every customizing project member.

# Chapter 7: Preparing the R/3 Environment for Go-Live

## Contents

# Overview

When you finish using one of the three possible methods for working with user role templates—and you have maintained and generated all necessary authorizations—you can prepare for go-live. Preparation means that you have to transport everything you have created in your DEV system to your QAS system, and finally to your PRD system (see chapter 1 on the three-system environment).

You can transport either between clients, within an R/3 System, or between R/3 Systems. Depending on the type of transport, you can transport the following items:

- Activity groups
- Composite activity groups
- Authorization profile data
- Authorization data
- User master records

# Transports Between Clients

The items in the list above are client-dependent. Therefore, separate records, activity groups, profiles, and authorizations must be maintained for each R/3 client. Transaction *SCCL (Tools → Administration → Administration → Client Administration → Client Copy → SCCL – Local Copy)*, which must be run from the target client, transports user master records, authorization profiles, and authorizations between clients. As of Release 4.5A, activity groups are copied with Customizing.

Caution

When you carry out a transport, all user master records, profiles, and authorizations in the target system with the same names as items in the transport will be overwritten. Therefore, do not use *SCCL* if your target client contains authorizations and user master records that you want to keep. Only use *SCCL* to create a new client with the objects *SAP_CUST* (users will be kept) or *SAP_UCUS* (users come from the source client).

Tips & Tricks

Since activity groups belong to Customizing, they are copied automatically during client copy. It is also possible to copy them manually (see below).

The transaction documentation contains additional information about the necessary authorizations. Use transaction *SCC1 (Tools → Administration → Administration → Client Administration → Special Functions → SCC1 – Copy Transport Request)* to manually copy activity groups between existing clients.

To copy activity groups between clients:

1. Create a transport request with the appropriate activity groups.
2. If you use transaction *SCC1*, do not release the transport.

   Transaction *SCC1* works with released and unreleased transports.
3. Log on to the other client.
4. Run transaction *SCC1*.
5. Choose the *Source client* and *Transport request* including the *task* number.
6. Execute.

The activity group(s) should now be active in transaction *PFCG*.

Caution

When you transport using *SCC1*, the report tree inside the activity group is transported, but not the report tree itself. You have to transport the report tree beforehand. Also remember that report trees are client-dependent.

# Transports Between R/3 Systems

You can transport authorization components, activity groups, and user master records between R/3 Systems. Components may be transported independently or with all of their associated authorizations.

# Transporting Activity Groups

When you transport activity groups, this also transports the authorization profiles. The profiles no longer have to be regenerated in the target system in transaction *SUPC*. However, you should compare the user master records when you import activity groups into the target system.

Once you have entered the activity group in a transport request, you should not make any more changes to the authorization profiles of that activity group. If you change profiles or generate them for the first time, you should enter the whole activity group in a transport request again.

The activity groups entered in a transport request can be displayed with transaction *SE10*.

## Transporting Single Activity Groups Using the Activity Group Maintenance Transaction

1. Access the PG (transaction **PFCG**).
2. Enter the activity group you would like to transport or select it using *possible entries.*
3. Choose to transport the activity group.

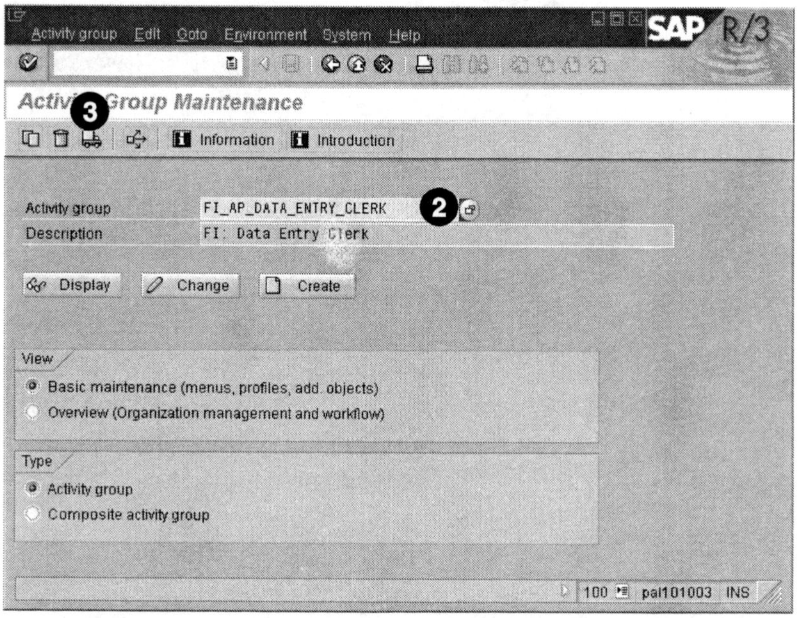


4. Choose to continue.

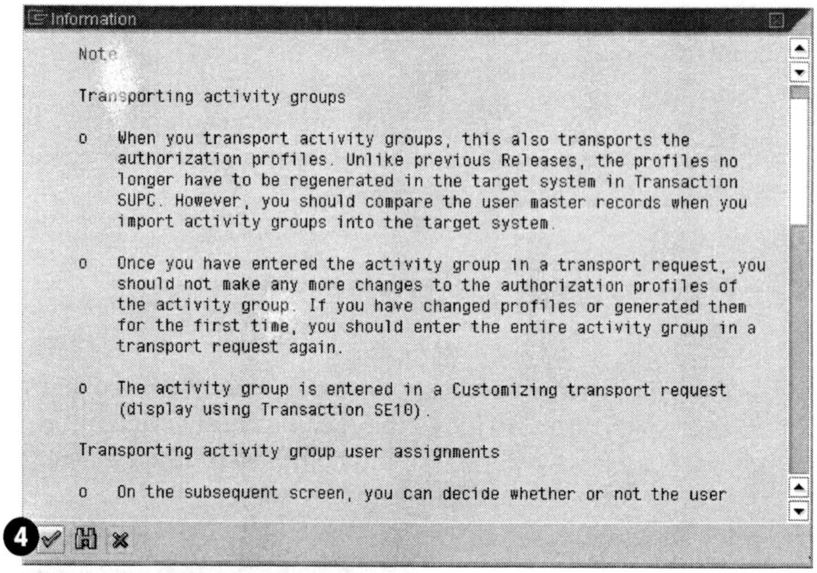


5. If you would like to transport the user assignment as well, select *User Assignment*. If you do not want to transport the user assignment with the activity group, make sure it is deselected.
6. Choose .

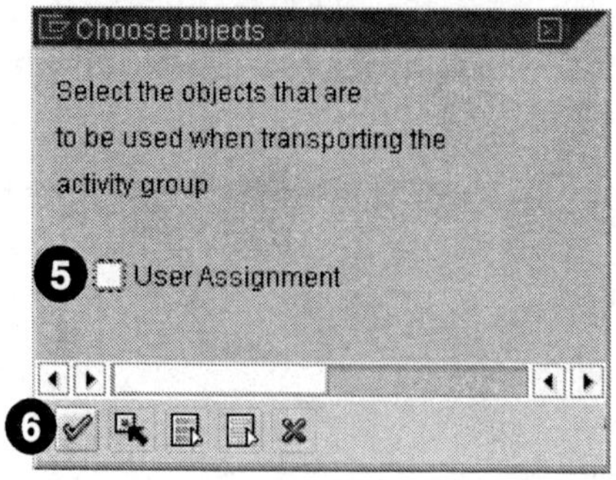

You can decide whether the user assignments should also be transported. Please note that when you transport the user assignments with the activity groups, this action replaces the activity group user assignment in the target system.

If you are using Central User Maintenance, you can only create user assignments in the central system. These user assignments can then be sent by request to the system group that you specified. If user assignments to activity groups were additionally transported, the Central User Administration display would be inconsistent. The users transported in this way would be removed at the next user distribution.

If you want to lock the system against importing user assignments from activity groups, you can specify this in the Customizing table *PRGN_CUST* (using transaction *SM30*). Enter a line with the identifier **`USER_REL_IMPORT`** and the value **`NO`**.

7. In the *Prompt for Customizing request* dialog box, enter the correct Customizing request number or use *possible entries* to select an existing one. If none exists, create a new one using 🗋.

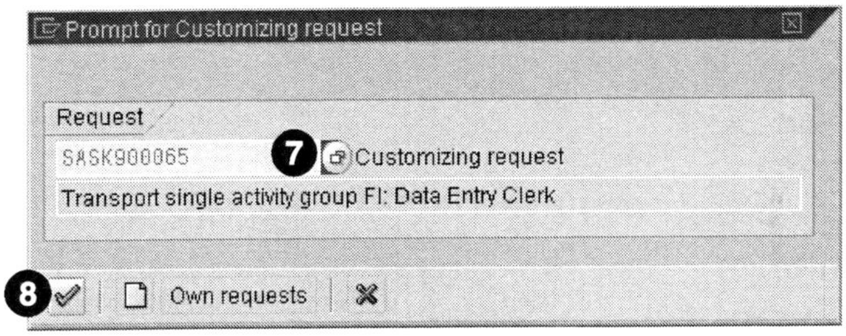


8. Choose ✔.
9. You can use transaction *SE10* to display your customizing transport requests.
10. To import the request with the data, log on to the client you would like to import the data to and execute transaction *SCC1* (see *Transport Between Clients,* steps 1–6 on page 7–3).

# Mass Transport of Activity Groups

To transport a set of activity groups all at once, use the mass transport function inside the PG.

1. Access the PG (transaction **PFCG**).
2. On the *Activity Group Maintenance* screen, choose *Environment* → *Mass transport.*

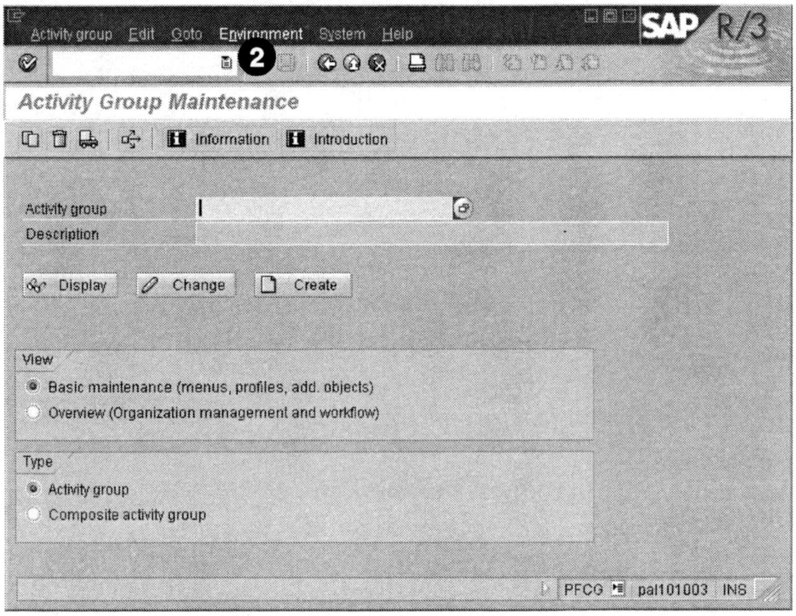


3. Enter the first and last activity group of the range that you would like to transport. You can also use *possible entries* for a list of all existing activity groups.

   In this example, we chose all activity groups from *FI_AP_Data_Entry_Clerk* to *QM_Manager_Assitant.*

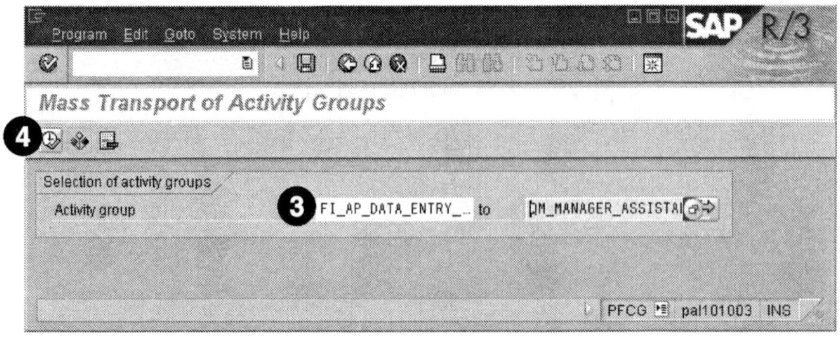


4. Choose [icon].
5. Choose ✔ to continue.

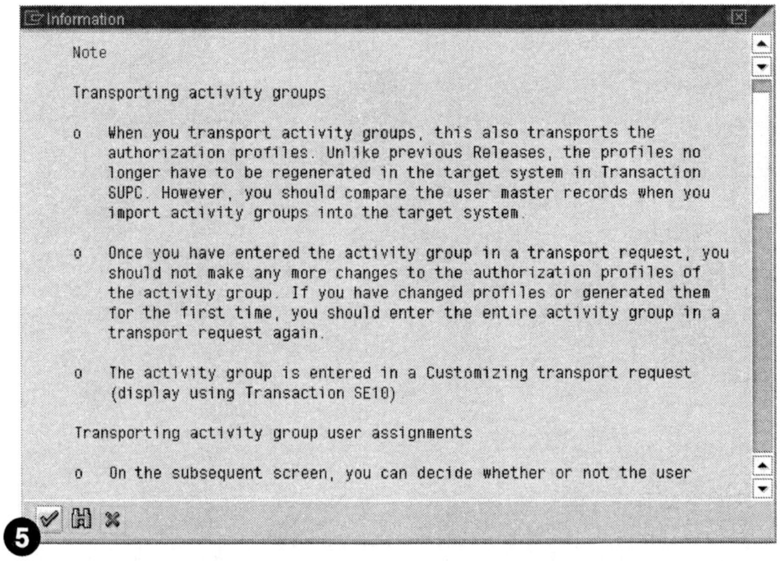

6. If you would like to transport the user assignment as well, select *User Assignment*. If you do not want to transport the user assignment with the activity group, make sure it is deselected.
7. Choose ✓.

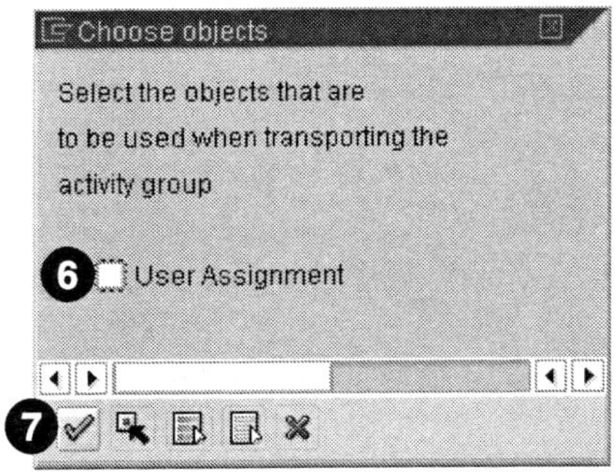


**Tips & Tricks**

You can decide whether the user assignments should also be transported. Please note that when you transport the user assignments with the activity groups, this action replaces the activity group user assignment in the target system.

If you are using Central User Maintenance, you can only create user assignments in the central system. These user assignments can then be sent by request to the system group that you specified. If user assignments to activity groups were additionally transported, the Central User Administration display would be inconsistent. The users transported in this way would be removed at the next user distribution.

**TechTalk**

If you want to lock the system against importing user assignments from activity groups, you can specify this in the Customizing table *PRGN_CUST* (using transaction *SM30*). Enter a line with the identifier `USER_REL_IMPORT` and the value `NO`.

8. In the *Prompt for Customizing request* dialog box, enter the correct Customizing request number or use *possible entries* to select an existing one. If none exist, create a new one using ☐.
9. Choose ✓.

**Tips & Tricks**

**User Master Record Comparison After Import into the Target System**

Once the activity groups have been imported into the target system, you should compare the user master records of the activity groups concerned. Execute this comparison using report *PFCG_TIME_DEPENDENCY*, which you should schedule periodically.

If you do not want to wait until that report runs and want the activity groups in the target system to be immediately consistent, compare the activity groups by choosing *Environment → Mass compare* in transaction *PFCG*. In the *Activity group* field, choose the activity groups concerned. Select *Complete compare* in the *Selection of action* field and start the report by choosing the icon. The activity groups in the target system are then made consistent.

# Transporting Check Indicators and Field Values

With transaction *SU25* you can copy the supplied SAP defaults concerning check indicators, field values, and tables *USOBX* and *USOBT*. This procedure imports both the SAP check indicator defaults for authorization objects in a transaction, and the authorization field values for the PG into the customer tables *USOBX_C* and *USOBT_C*.

Whether you run transaction *SU25* initially, or change the defaults later with transaction *SU24*, the process is recorded in the correction and transport systems. By carrying out the corresponding transport request, you distribute your check indicators in the system.

The *<Transaction name>* corresponds to normal SAP transaction names, such as *VA01*. The check indicators and field values are included in the transport. Check indicators are saved in table *USOBX_C* and field values for the PG are saved in table *USOBT_C*.

# Transporting Authorization Templates

After an upgrade, all SAP-delivered templates will be identical in all systems. You cannot change these templates; you can only copy and alter them. You can, however, create your own templates, as described earlier in this book. When you compare activity groups, unlike SAP default changes, template changes are not automatically passed on to the appropriate authorization profile(s) where the template was inserted. Once you have changed a template that was previously inserted in an authorization profile for an activity group, you must manually update that profile with the same changes that were made to the template. Changes to your own templates are recorded by the correction and transport systems. To carry out the transport request, objects in the request must contain the following syntax:

```
R3TR SUSP <Template Name>
```

# Transporting User Master Records

To transport user master records between clients, run the client copy transaction **SCCL** *(Tools → Administration → Administration → Client Administration → Client Copy → SCCL – Local Copy)* and select profile *SAP_USER*. For transporting user master records between R/3 Systems, use transaction **SCC8** *(Tools → Administration → Administration → Client Administration → Client Transport → SCC8 - Client Transport)* with profile *SAP_USER*.

# Chapter 8: Inserting Missing Authorizations

## Contents

# Manually Postmaintaining Authorizations

Although the Profile Generator (PG builds authorization profiles, it may sometimes be necessary to insert a missing authorization or to adjust a field value. The process of maintaining PG's suggested authorizations (as derived from the transactions selected for an activity group) is called **postmaintaining authorizations.** Manual postmaintenance may be necessary in the parameter and variant transactions, and during the upgrade.

## When to Insert Missing Authorizations?

Shown below are some of the typical cases where you must manually include authorizations:

### Case #1: Authorization Is Missing for Related Transactions

Although the PG assigns a particular profile to a user, it is possible that the same user may receive the error message "You are not authorized…" when attempting to use a related transaction.

To address the authorization settings for the related transaction, do the following:

1. Use transaction *SU53 (Display check values of authorization checks if: not authorized)* to see the last authorization check that failed (see chapter 12, *Tips and Troubleshooting,* to learn how to use transaction *SU53).*
2. Check the related transaction to confirm if an authorization object is checked.
3. Check the generated profile to confirm if the authorization for the related transaction is incorrectly set.
4. Use transaction *SU24* to change the check indicator for the authorization object in the desired transaction (see chapter 12, *Tips and Troubleshooting* to learn how to use transaction *SU24*).

### Case #2: The Generated Profile Does Not Assign Any General Rights to the User

Since basic authorizations are so general, it is not practical to include them in individual transactions.

To improve system performance (though unusual from an authorizations standpoint):

- R/3 does not check if an authorization is needed for an existing transaction
- New authorizations are added without checking for existing authorizations

The system provides the functionality to summarize authorizations for the same authorization object.

### Case #3: Cannot Select Transaction SU53 from the Menu in PFCG

SAP recommends including the appropriate authorizations for transaction *SU53* in each authorization profile. These authorizations guarantee that if users get an error message (for example, "You are not authorized...," "No authorization for..." or any message regarding an authorization problem), the help desk can more easily assist them. The activity group *SAP_BC_ENDUSER_AG* already contains the authorization for *SU53*. This activity group is also included in the composite activity group *SAP_BC_EVERY_EMPLOYEE*.

## How to Insert Missing Authorizations

You may insert missing authorizations:

- Manually
- From a template
- From a profile
- By inserting complete authorizations

# Manually Inserting Authorizations

Using transaction *SU53 (Display check values of authorization checks if: not authorized)*, you can find out if an authorization check for your transaction is missing. Transaction *SU53* is only one of the ways to determine missing authorizations. Sometimes, traces are more useful because they are more accurate and complete—particularly when dealing with HR authorization problems. Identify the authorization object and the missing authorization field values. Then manually insert the missing authorization.

You can use the following two options to insert authorizations:

- *Selection criteria* (choose from authorizations sorted by class)
- *Manually* (if you know the object, or can choose from an object list)

Tips & Tricks

To assign general authorizations, choose one of the following options:

- Create a separate activity group containing only general authorizations (for example, printing), and assign this activity group to all users. This method works best if users will print to particular printers. A generic printing authorization can be assigned. Generate the authorization profiles for these activity groups and assign the profiles to the users.
- Include the required objects in the activity group by using SAP templates, or your own templates by maintaining any missing field entries. This method works best if users will be assigned to specific printers.
- SAP already delivers activity groups with general authorizations, for example, *SAP_BC_EVERY_EMPLOYEE* and *SAP_BC_ENDUSER*.

# Using Selection Criteria

You can use selection criteria to insert missing authorizations.

1. Access the PG (transaction **PFCG**).
2. Select the desired activity group (for example *MM_BUYER_AG*) and choose *Change.*
3. Choose the *Authorizations* tab.
4. Choose *Change authorization data.*

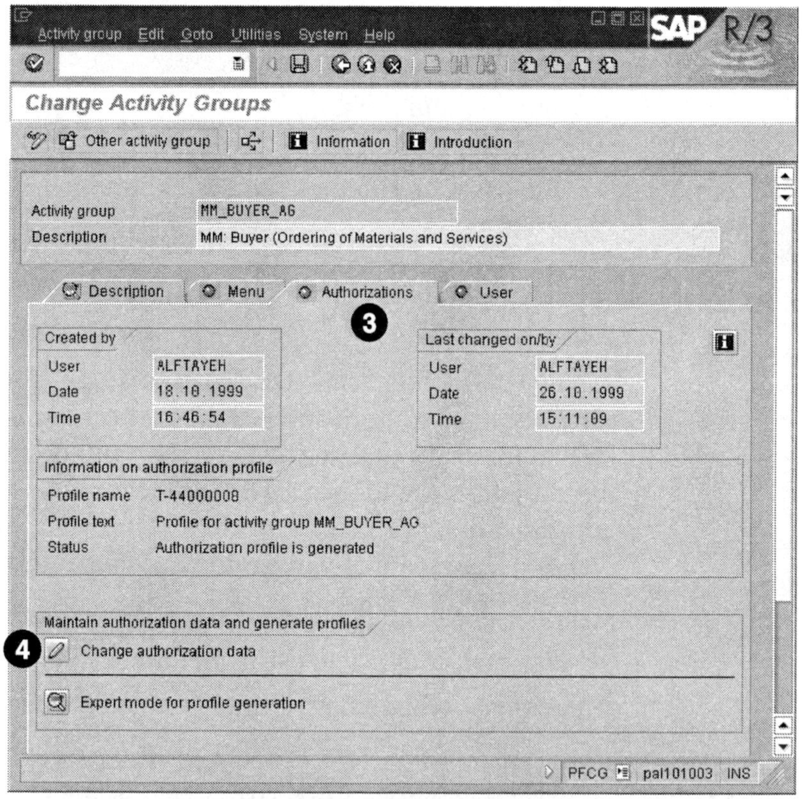


On screen, you can see the currently included authorization classes for the selected activity group.

5. Choose *Selection criteria* to select the authorization you would like to insert (sorted by class).

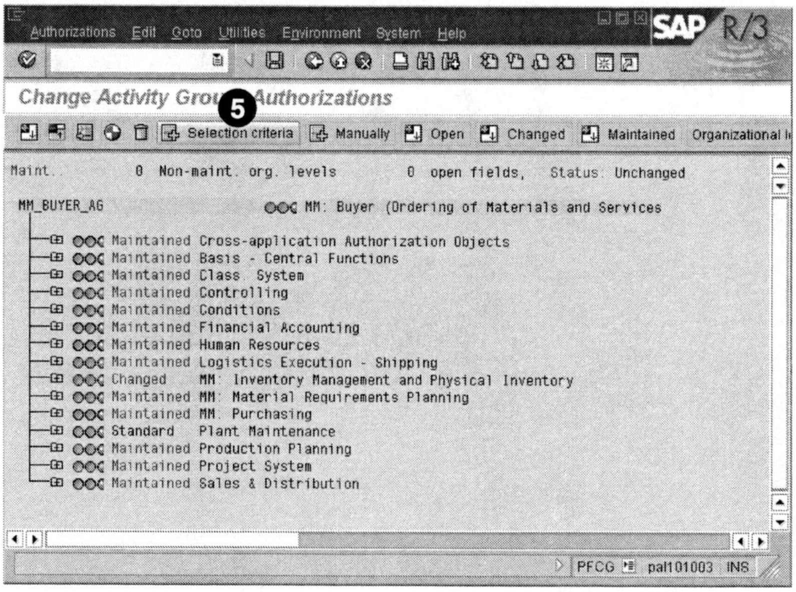

If you already know the authorization object you would like to insert manually, choose *Manually* and enter the object, or use *possible entries* and select it from a list (see example shown below).

6. Expand the object classes and choose the desired authorization object (for example, we selected *Basis: Administration* to choose the authorization objects for printing).

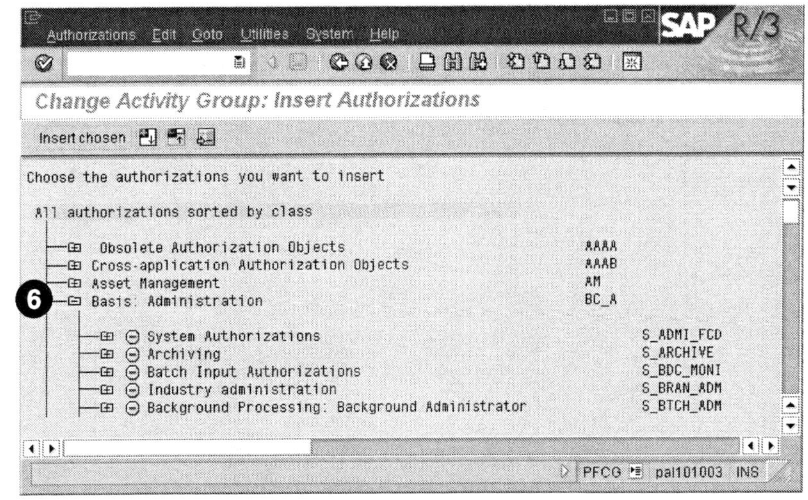


7. Scroll down until you see the desired authorization objects.
8. Select the authorization objects you want to insert by clicking the red minus (-) signs (for example, *Spool: Actions* and *Spool: Device Authorizations*). The green plus (+) signs indicate that the objects have been selected.
9. Choose *Insert chosen*.

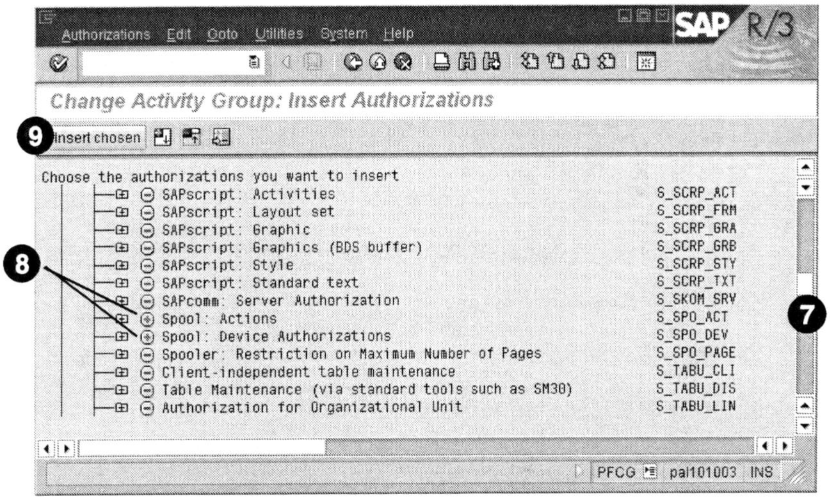


10. The selected authorization objects are transferred back to the authorization classes for the given activity group. The system creates a new authorization for each authorization object. The yellow light indicates that no authorization field values are maintained.
11. The system status is displayed as *Manually*, which means that there are manually inserted authorizations in this object class.
12. Choose Open to display all open authorization fields.

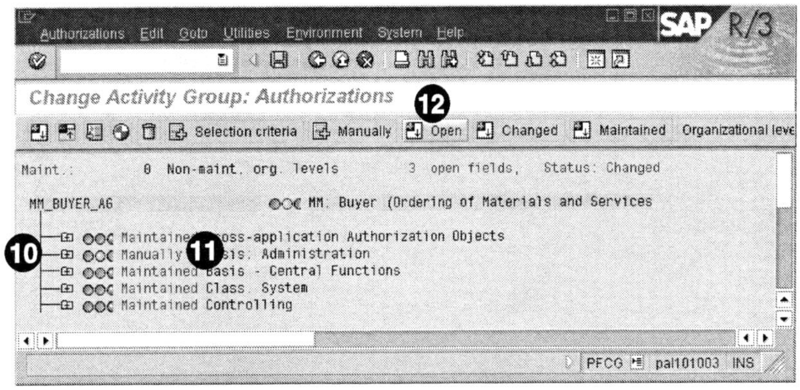

13. Maintain the appropriate values for the open authorization profiles.
14. Save and generate the activity group.

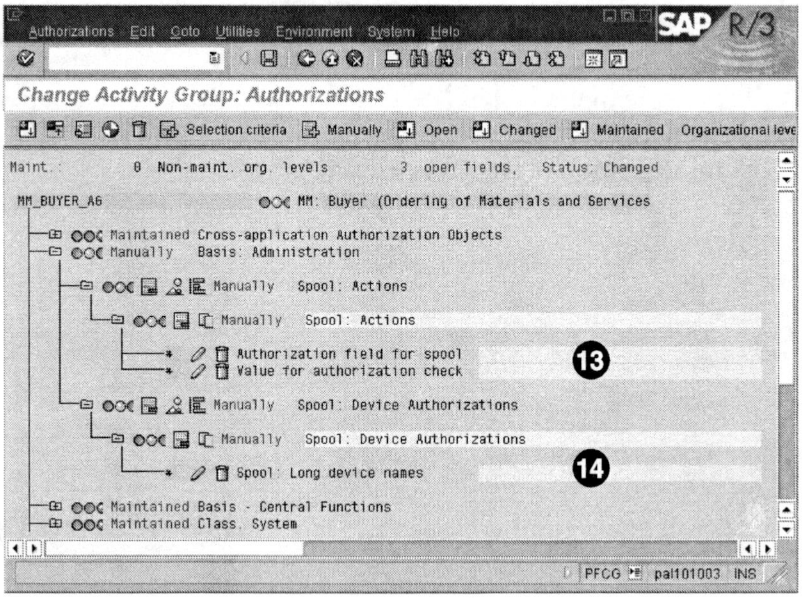


## Inserting Manually

If you know the authorization object you would like to insert, perform the following steps.

1. Access the PG (transaction **PFCG**).
2. Select the desired activity group (for example *MM_BUYER_AG*) and choose *Change*.
3. On the *Change Activity Groups* screen, choose the *Authorizations* tab.
4. Choose *Change authorization data.*
5. On the *Change Activity Group: Authorizations* screen, choose *Manually*.
6. Enter the authorization object or choose *possible entries*.
7. Choose .

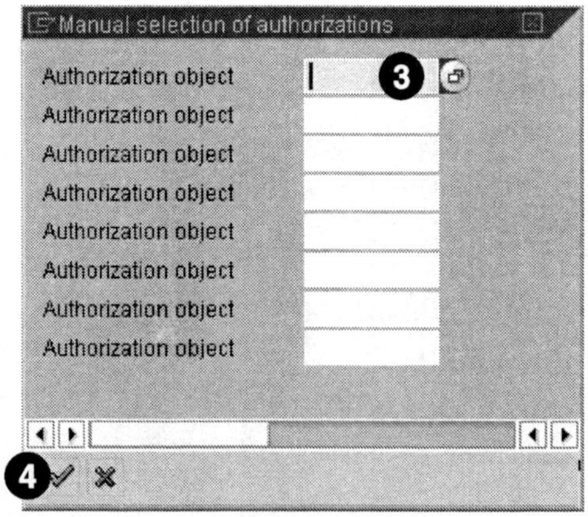

# Inserting Authorizations from Templates

Generated profiles do not automatically grant any general rights to:

- Print
- Log on to SAPNet – R/3 Frontend notes
- Use transaction *SU53*
- Debug (view only)

In the following example, we will first create a new template and then insert the template into an existing activity group.

## Creating a New Template

1. Access the PG (transaction **PFCG**).
2. On the *Activity Group Maintenance* screen, choose *Environment* → *Check indicator*.
3. Select *Edit authorization templates*.
4. Choose [icon].

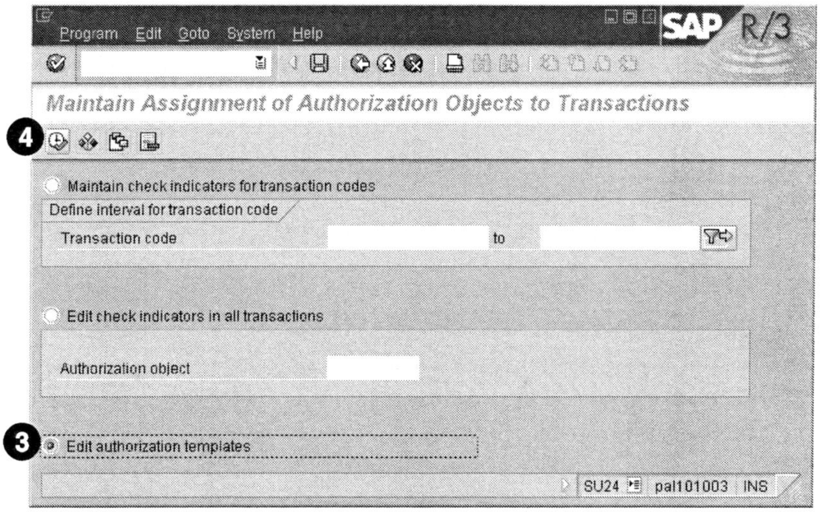


5. Choose [icon].

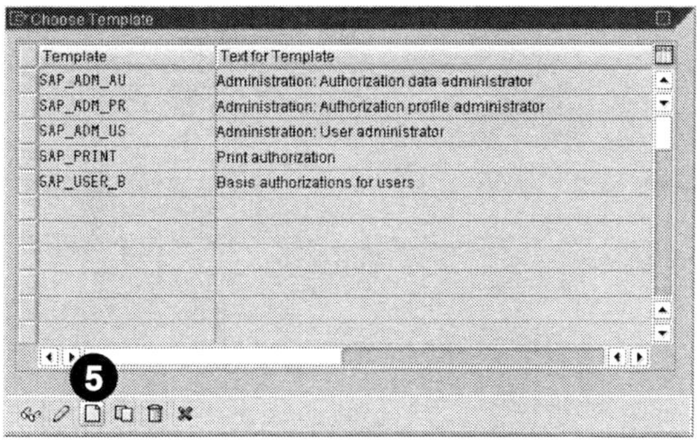


Caution

To avoid conflicts between customer-defined templates and the SAP-delivered templates, do not use names for your templates that begin with *S* or *J*. For additional information, see SAPNet – R/3 Frontend note *16466* and look for transport object *R3TR SUSP*.

Template changes are not passed on when you compare activity groups. That is, if you change a template that you already inserted into an activity group, there is no indicator in the activity group to show that the inserted template has changed.

6. Enter the template name and a short description.
7. Choose .

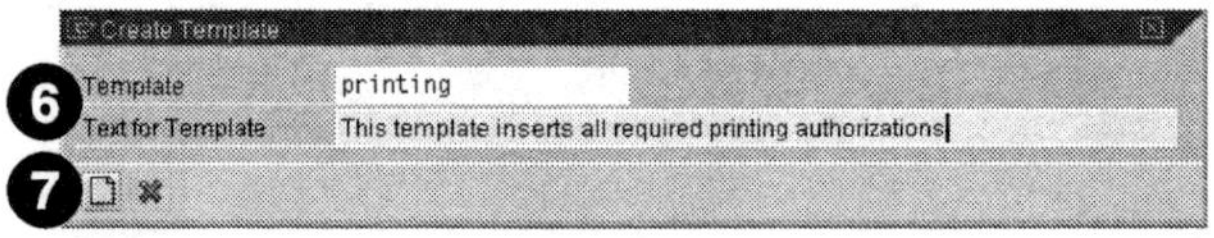


8. Choose *Selection criteria* to select the authorization you want to insert (sorted by class).

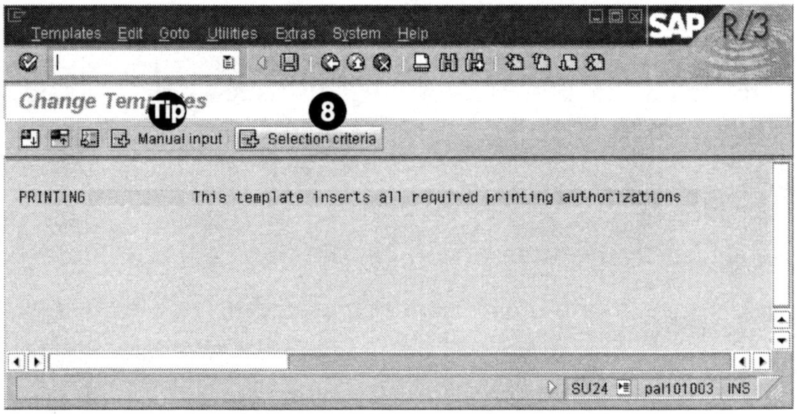


Tips & Tricks

If you already know the authorization object you want to insert manually, you can choose *Manual input* and enter the object (or use *possible entries* and select it from a list).

9. Expand the object classes to choose the desired authorization object (for example, we selected *Basis: Administration* to choose the authorization objects for printing).

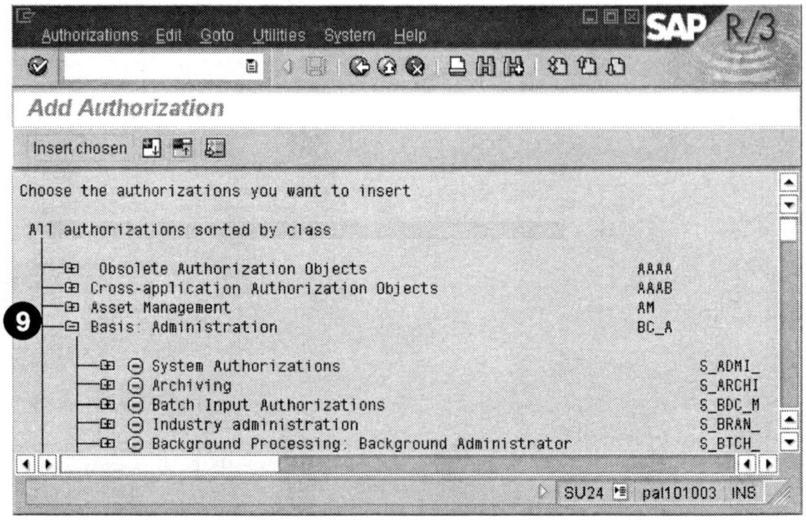

10. Scroll down until you see the authorization objects you want to insert.
11. Select the authorization objects you want to insert by clicking the red minus (-) signs (for example, *Spool: Actions* and *Spool: Device Authorizations*). The green plus (+) signs indicate that the objects have been selected.
12. Choose *Insert chosen*.

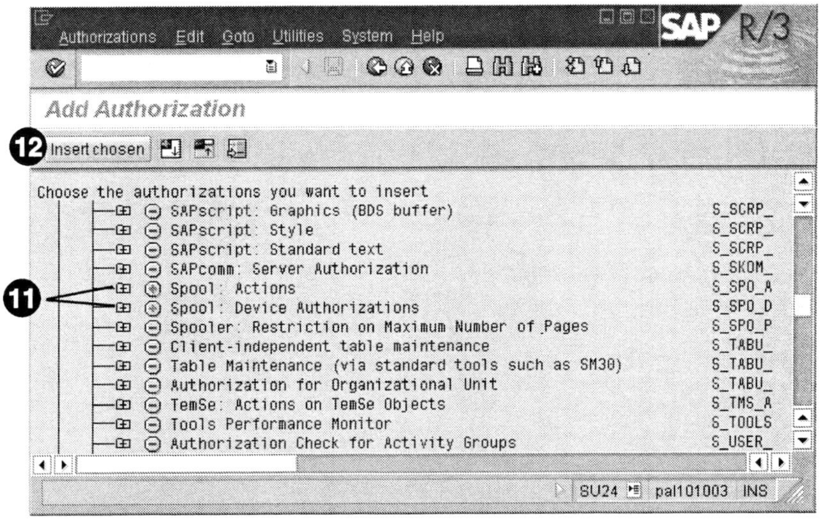

13. Maintain all the appropriate values for the authorization fields (for example, we chose *Full authorization*).
14. Choose [save icon].
15. Choose [back icon].

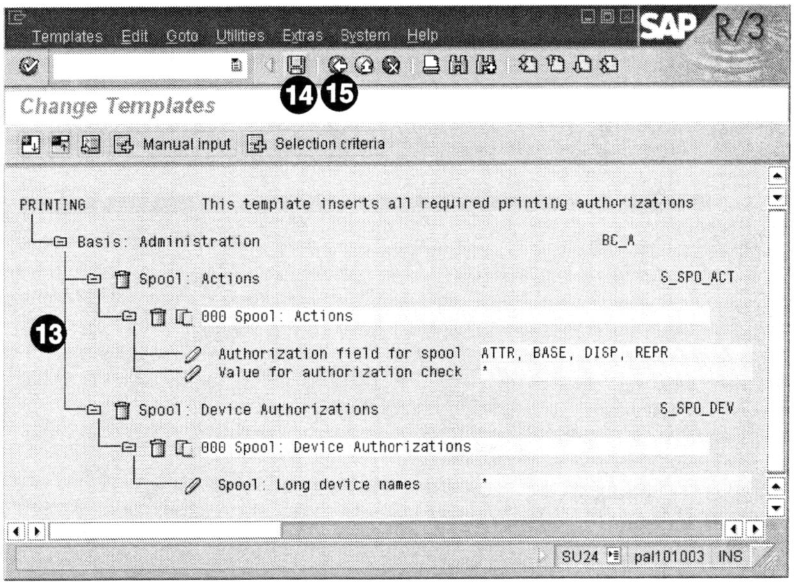

The template now appears in the template list and is ready for use.

16. Choose [cancel icon].

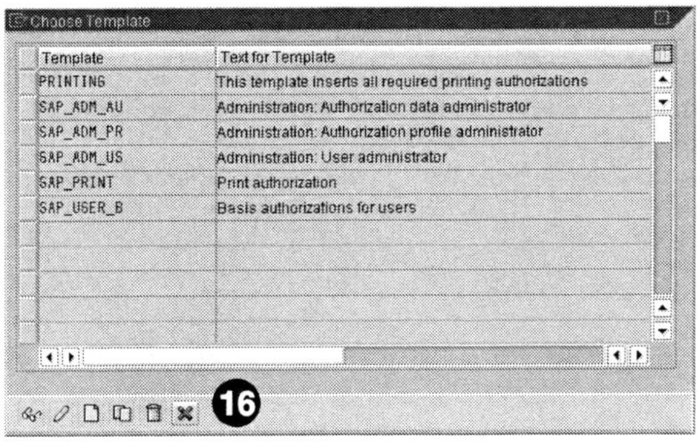

# Inserting Authorizations from a Template

1. Access the PG (transaction **PFCG**).
2. Select the desired activity group in which you would like to insert a template (for example *MM_BUYER_AG*), and choose *Change.*
3. Choose the *Authorizations* tab.
4. Choose *Change authorization data.*

5. Choose *Edit → Insert authorization(s) → From template…*

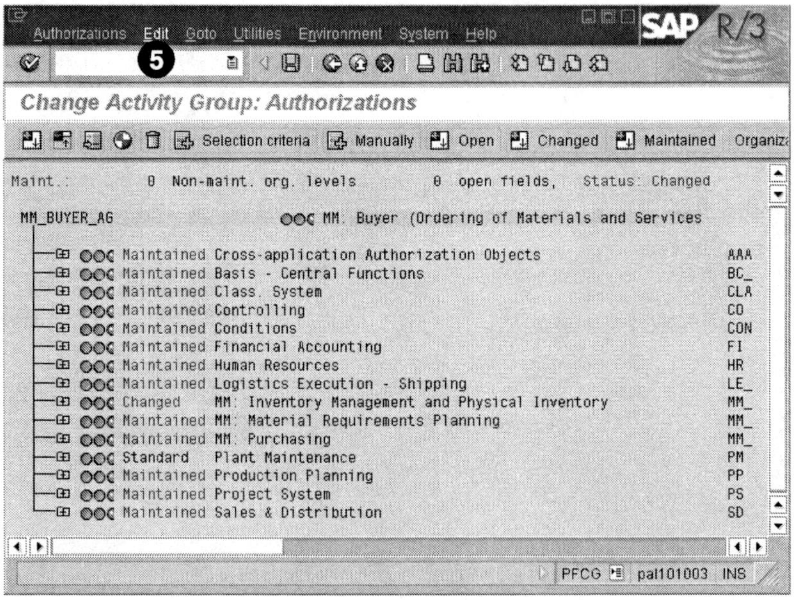

6. Select the template you want to include (for example, *PRINTING* template).

   Multiple template selections are possible.

7. Choose ✔.

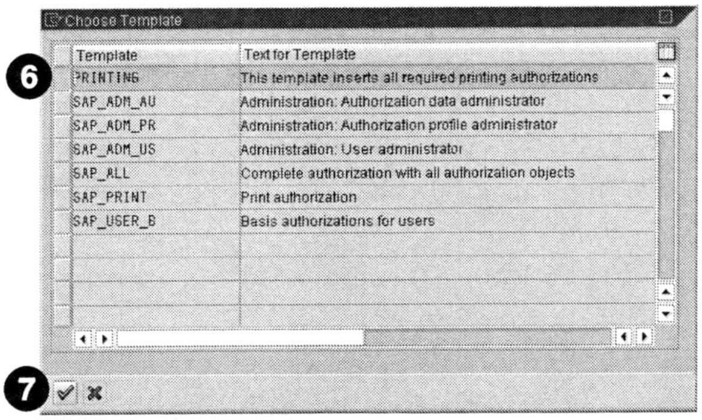


The template was inserted and marked with status *Manually*. The green light indicates that the authorization fields are maintained.

8. To regenerate the authorization profile, choose the generate icon.

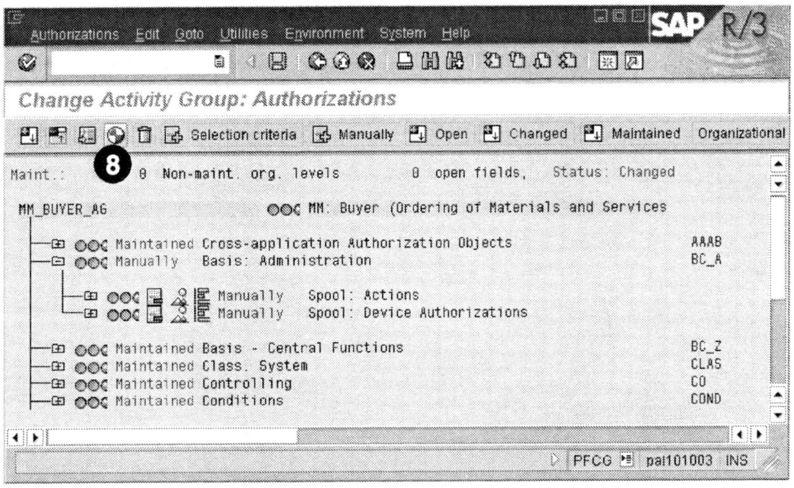


Tips & Tricks

If you inserted a template with authorization fields that are not maintained, the indicator lights appear as yellow or red for the appropriate authorizations. Before proceeding, you must first postmaintain all open fields.

# Inserting Authorizations from a Profile

If you have already created authorization profiles using transactions *SU02* and *SU03*, you can insert these authorizations profiles into the list of the authorizations for the activity group.

> **Migrating Profiles Created with Transactions *SU02* and *SU03***
> Note that **no** activity group information (such as transaction codes automatically maintained for object *S_TCODE*) can be regenerated for inserted profiles. The technique below **only** allows profiles created with transactions *SU02* and *SU03* to migrate to such profiles and later be maintained with the PG. There is no way to re-create the appropriate activity group information.
>
> This means that everything under the *Menu* tab will be unchanged if *SU02* profiles are copied into the activity group.
> However with 4.6 you have now the option to migrate profiles created with *SU02* and *SU03* into activity groups. See chapter 14, the section *Converting Previously Created SU02 Profiles into Activity Groups*.

> In certain circumstances, you may first create a template from your profile and then insert the template. Templates are reusable and easy to insert.

1. Access the PG (transaction **`PFCG`**).
2. Select the desired activity group in which you would like to insert the authorization (for example *MM_BUYER_AG*), and choose *Change*.

3. Choose the *Authorizations* tab.
4. Choose ✎ *Change authorization data.*

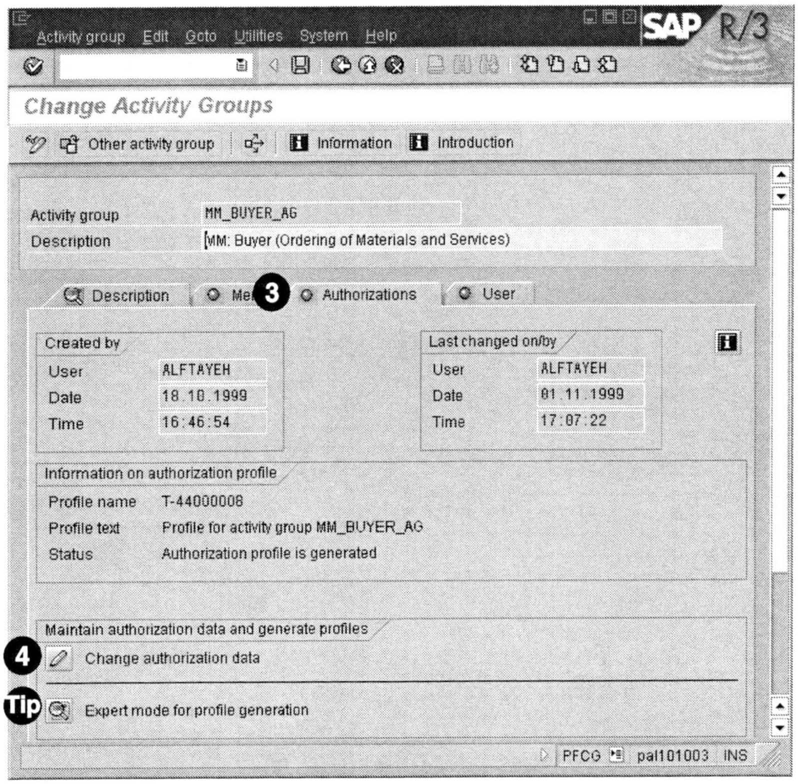


**Tips & Tricks**

In Expert mode for profile generation you can specify the option with which you want to maintain the authorization values. This option is automatically set correctly in normal mode.

5. Choose *Edit* → *Insert authorization(s)* → *From profile.*

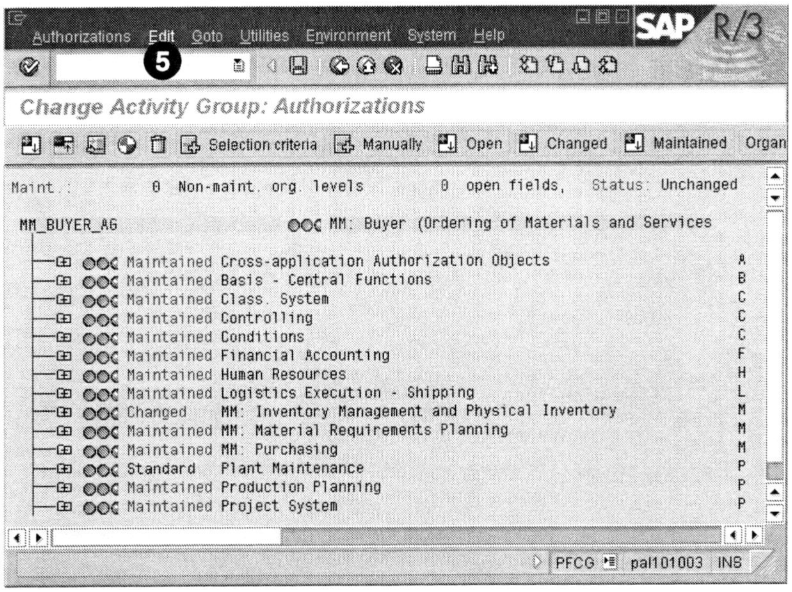


6. Enter the profile name or use *possible entries.*
7. Choose ✔.

**Caution**

If you include a profile that includes the object *S_TCODE,* it does **not** add the transaction code to the menu portion of the activity group definition.

8. Select the desired profile from the list of profiles.
9. Choose ✔.

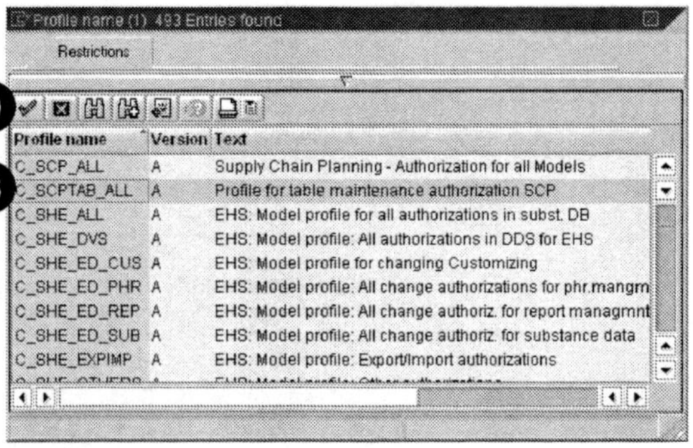

Your dialog box may look different. The appearance depends on the settings for *possible entries* under *Help → Settings → Possible entries → Settings.*

10. The selected profile is transferred.
11. Choose ✔.

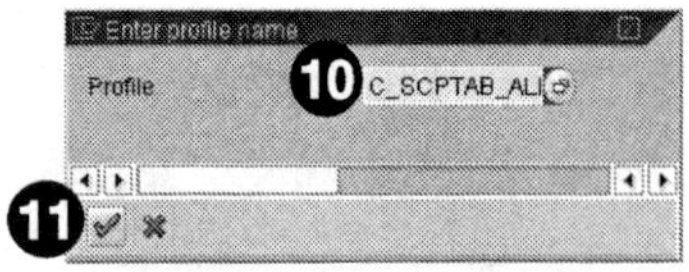


12. All the authorizations in the selected profile are transferred and marked with the status *Manually*. The green light indicates that the profile is maintained.

If you insert authorizations from a profile with nonmaintained authorization fields, the red light appears and you have to postmaintain all open fields before proceeding.

13. To regenerate the authorization profile, choose ◑.

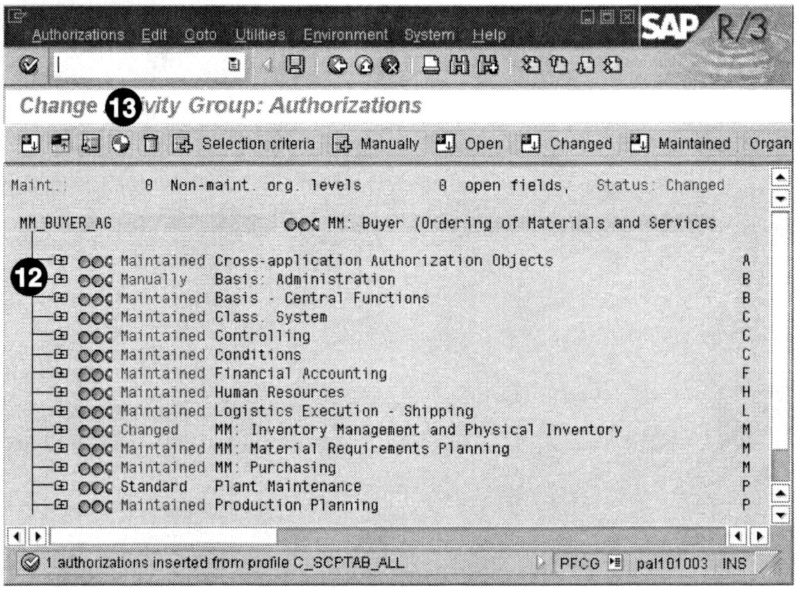

# Inserting Full Authorizations: Profile "<YourCompany>"

In the following example, you learn how to create a new profile called *COMP_ALL*, where "COMP" stands for your company name. This profile will be modeled after *SAP_ALL*, but with the superuser authorization removed. Therefore, we will create an activity group called *COMPANY_ALL* and include the profile *COMP_ALL*.

1. Access the PG (transaction **PFCG**).
2. Enter the name of the activity group you want to create (for example, **COMPANY_ALL**).
3. Choose *Create*.

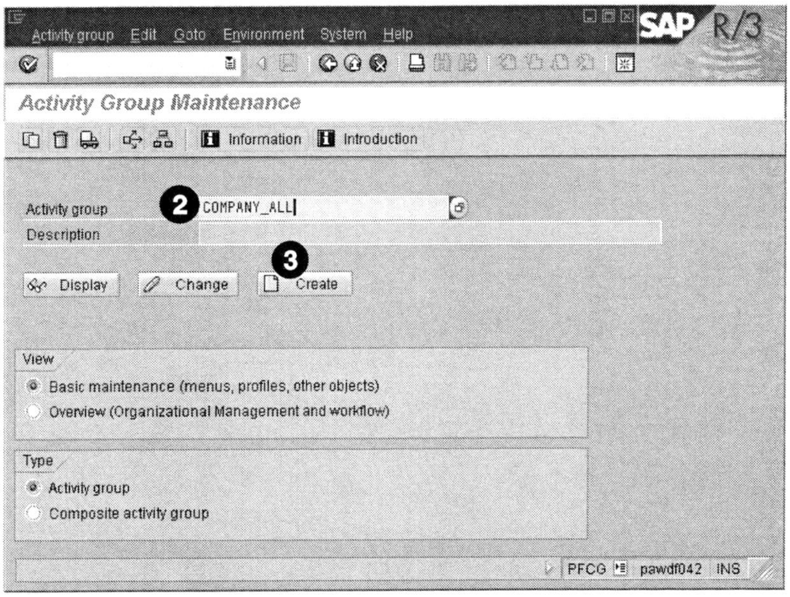


4. In the *Description* field, enter a description for the activity group.
5. Choose to save the activity group.
6. Choose the *Authorizations* tab.

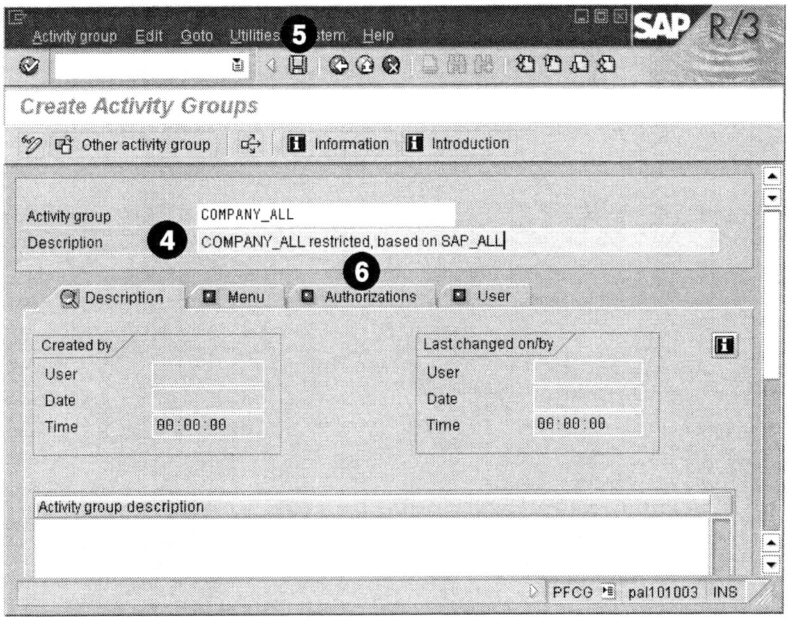

7. Choose *Change authorization data.*

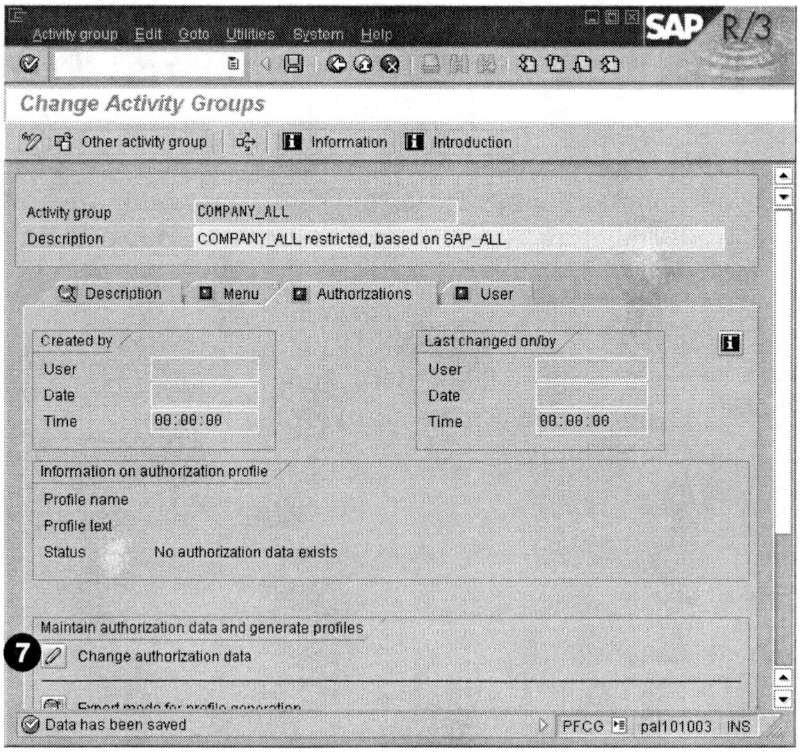


8. Choose *Do not select templates.*

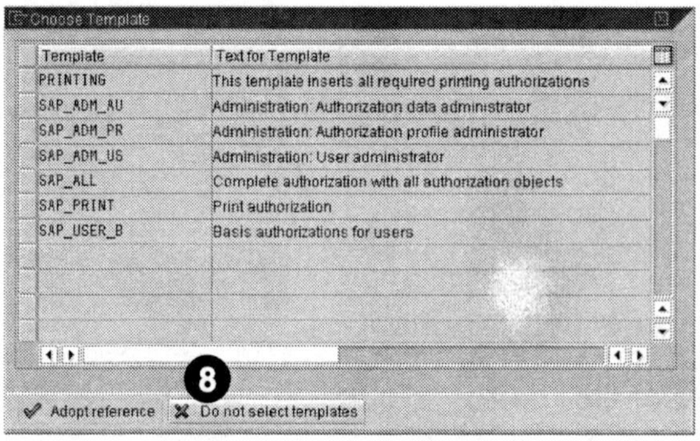

The system displays the *Choose Template* window because we chose the *Authorizations* tab without selecting any transactions.

9. Choose *Edit* → *Insert authorization(s)* → *Full authorization.*

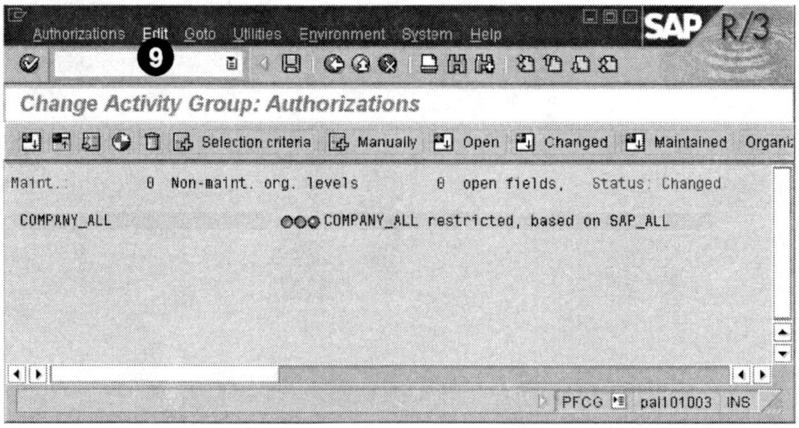

10. Choose *Yes*.

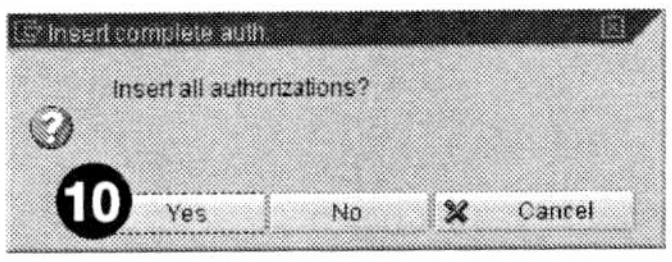


**Tips & Tricks**

The insertion does not include add-on components, except deduction management add-on components.

11. Choose ✔ to continue.

12. Click on the node for the object class *Basis: Administration* to open it.

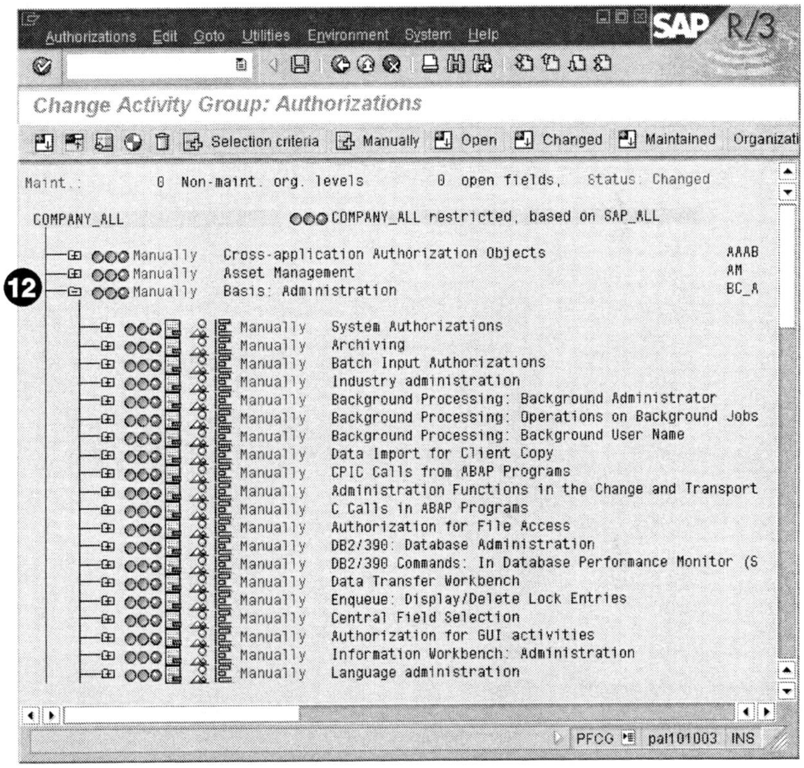

13. In the *System Authorizations* line, choose [icon] to deactivate the object. The authorization object *System Authorizations* (*S_ADMI_FCD*) is now inactive and will not be generated into the authorization profile for *COMP_ALL*.

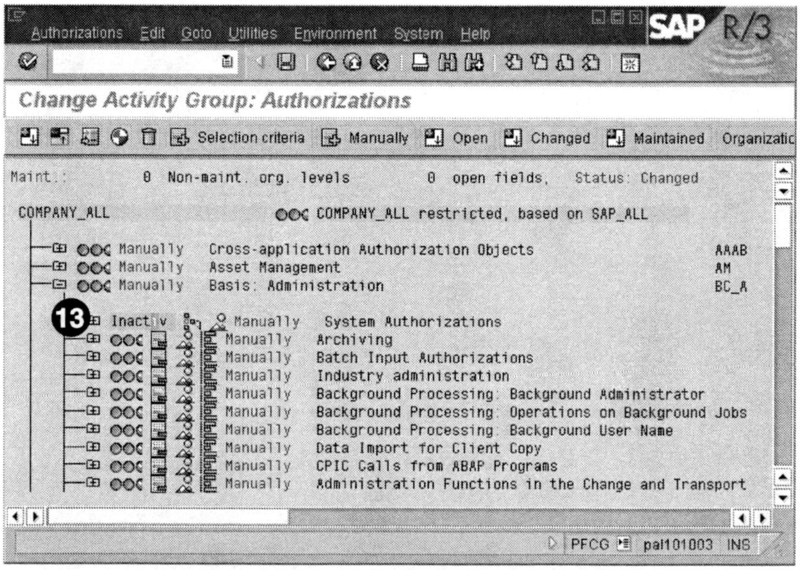


14. Scroll down until you see the authorization objects that begin with *Authorization Check for Activity Groups*.
15. Choose [icon] in front of the following authorization objects to deactivate them:
    - *Authorization Check for Activity Groups (S_USER_AGR)*
    - *User Master Maintenance: Authorizations (S_USER_AUTH)*
    - *User Master Maintenance: User Groups (S_USER_GRP)*
    - *User Master Maintenance: Authorization Profile (S_USER_PRO)*
    - *User Master Maintenance: System for Central User Maintenance (S_USER_SYS)*
    - *Transaction Assignment of Transactions to Activity Groups (S_USER_TCD)*

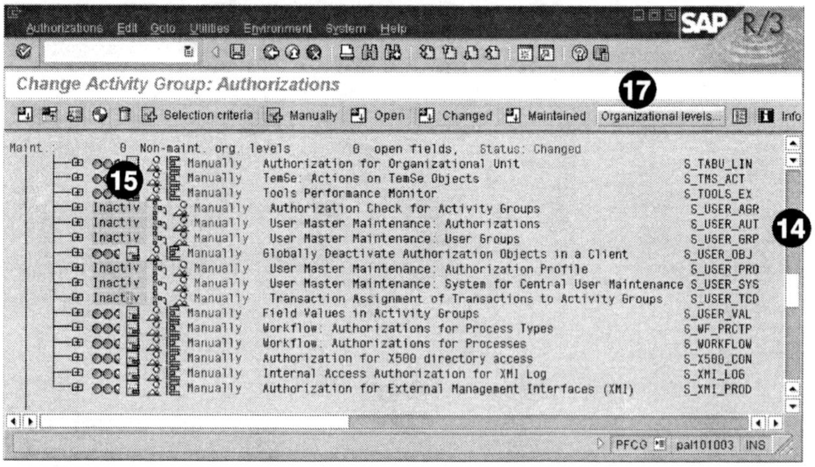


16. Once you have deactivated these critical authorization objects for your authorization profile, select and deactivate other critical authorization objects, if needed.
17. Choose *Organizational levels*.

18. Choose *Full authorization* for the organizational levels. The asterisks (*) will be inserted in all the open fields.
19. Choose 💾.

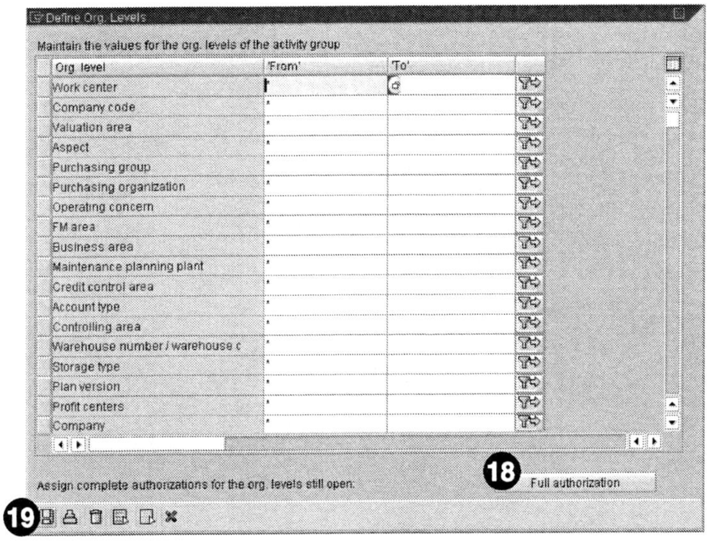


20. To generate the profile, choose ◐.

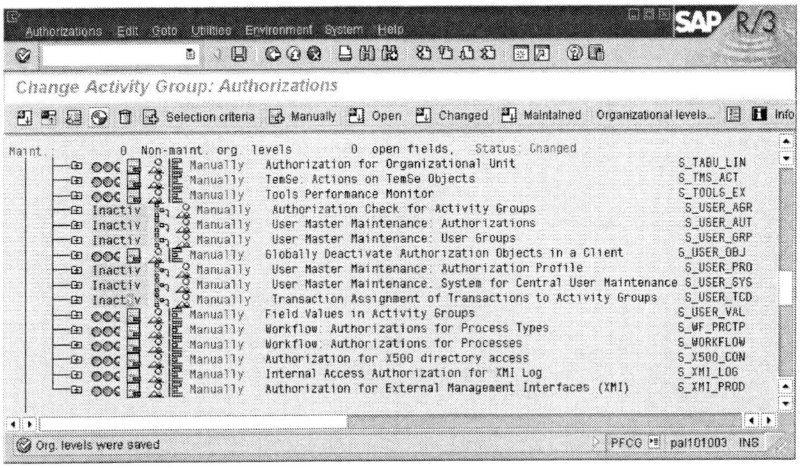


21. You can give the new profile the same name and description as the activity group (for example, **COMP_ALL**).
22. Choose ✔ to generate the authorization profile(s).

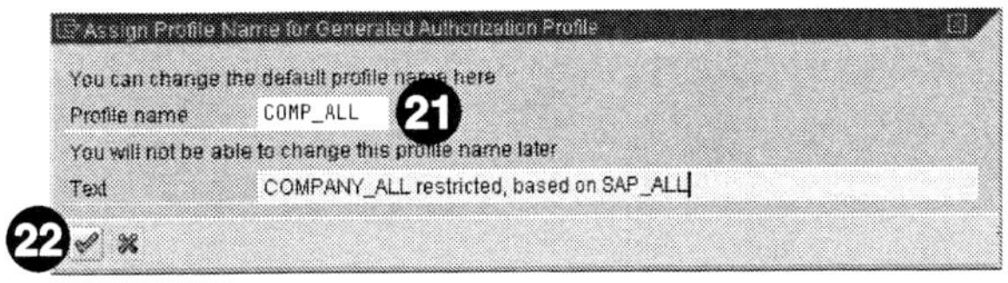

23. To view all the created profiles, choose *Authorizations → Profile overview.*

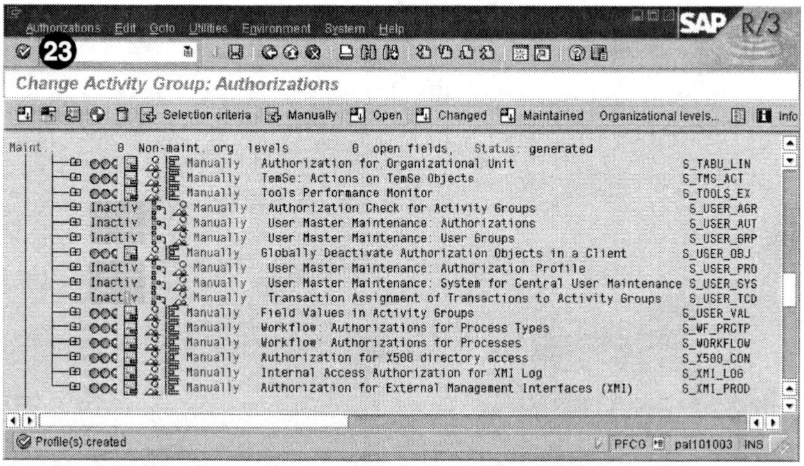


24. The *Overview of Generated Profiles* screen lists all the generated authorization profiles.

25. Choose ✔ to continue.

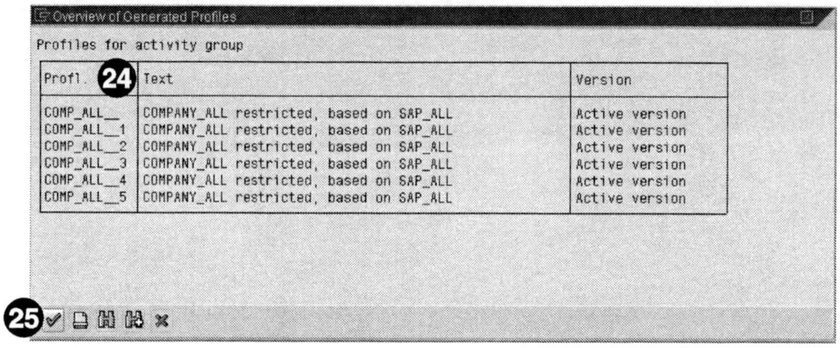

# Chapter 9: Assigning Activity Groups

## Contents

# Overview

The new **SAP Easy Access** user menu is the user-specific point of entry into the R/3 System. Depending on the assigned user role template or activity groups, the user menu looks different for each user. The user menu contains only those items—such as transactions, reports, and web addresses—that the assigned activity groups contain and therefore only those tasks needed to perform the daily work.

Depending on the area of the system you work in, assigning activity groups to R/3 objects (such as users, positions, jobs, or organizational units) affects the following areas:

- In Business Workflow, these assignments determine the system tasks a user can perform (for workflow users, it is mandatory to only include tasks in activity groups).
- In Human Resources, these assignments serve as highly detailed object descriptions (for job, position, descriptions, etc.).

The same activity group can be assigned to several different objects. A single object may also be related to several different activity groups. The different activity groups assigned to an object are together referred to as the object's activity profile. The various R/3 objects are:

- **R/3 users** – Object type *US*

  An R/3 user is an individual who is:

  - Recognized by R/3
  - Allowed to log on
  - Allowed to perform specified system activities

    For the system to recognize users, their names must be entered in the Basis component of the user master record.

- **Work center** - Object type *A*

  A work center identifies a location where work is carried out. A location can represent a geographic location, such as the Philadelphia branch office or the Singapore subsidiary, or it can be more precise. For example, it can identify a specific workstation with certain materials and equipment, on a specific floor of a specific building. Work centers can be used with jobs and tasks to create comprehensive job descriptions. The job identifies the job classification, the tasks indicate the types of duties performed, and the work center identifies where the tasks are carried out.

- **Job** - Object type *C*

  A job is a general classification of work duties, such as administrative assistant, computer programmer, or instructor. Many employees may hold the same job (for example, there might be 20 employees working as engineers). Jobs are normally used to create positions. Anyone who holds a job automatically inherits the infotype settings, attributes, and properties of the job. Unless these groups grant general access rights, such as those required to work with SAP office, use care when assigning activity groups to jobs.

- **Organizational unit** - Object type *O*

  Organizational units represent organizational entities designated to perform a specified set of functions. For example, organizational units represent subsidiaries, divisions, departments, groups, special project teams, etc. Identify the organizational structure at your firm by creating organizational units and identifying the relationships among the units. An employee assigned to an organizational unit automatically inherits the infotype settings, attributes, and properties of this unit.

  Unless these groups grant general access rights, such as printing, use care when assigning activity groups to jobs. For example, if authority profiles tend to be fairly standard for all workers in an organizational unit, it may be most effective to assign activity groups and their profiles to organizational units. If exceptions occur, create additional activity groups. If, however, authorities vary by job or position, it may be best to assign activity groups to the specific jobs or positions.

- **Person** - Object type *P*

  A person.

- **Position** - Object type *S*

  A position represents a unique individual employee assignment within a company (for example, the marketing assistant, sales manager, etc.) Positions should not be confused with jobs and are usually created based on jobs. Anyone who holds a position automatically inherits the infotype settings, attributes, and properties of the position. This process allows you to handle authorization management in almost a completely position-oriented fashion. Since all of the access rights are now linked to the position, it does not matter who fills this position. Once a user changes positions, the authorization profile automatically changes after the user master record is updated.

Caution

**Assigning Activity Groups**

Make sure you assign the activity group to the specific position that will receive an authorization profile. If you assign the activity group to a job, all of the positions created from that job will inherit the activity group and its authorization profile(s).

# Assigning Users to Activity Groups

Although we already demonstrated in chapter 5, *User Role Templates*, how to assign a user to a user role template or activity group using the PG, we will demonstrate it here in more detail.

The following method is recommended if you want to assign more users to a specific activity group.

1. Access the PG (transaction **PFCG**).
2. Select the activity group you want to assign to an employee and choose *Change*.

3. Choose the *User* tab.
4. Enter the user ID in the *User ID* field.

   You can include user IDs by one of the following methods:
   - Enter the user ID directly.
   - Make a selection from the *possible entries* list.
   - Use multiple selection from a selection list by choosing *Selection*. See the following *Tips & Tricks*.
5. To save your assignment, choose .

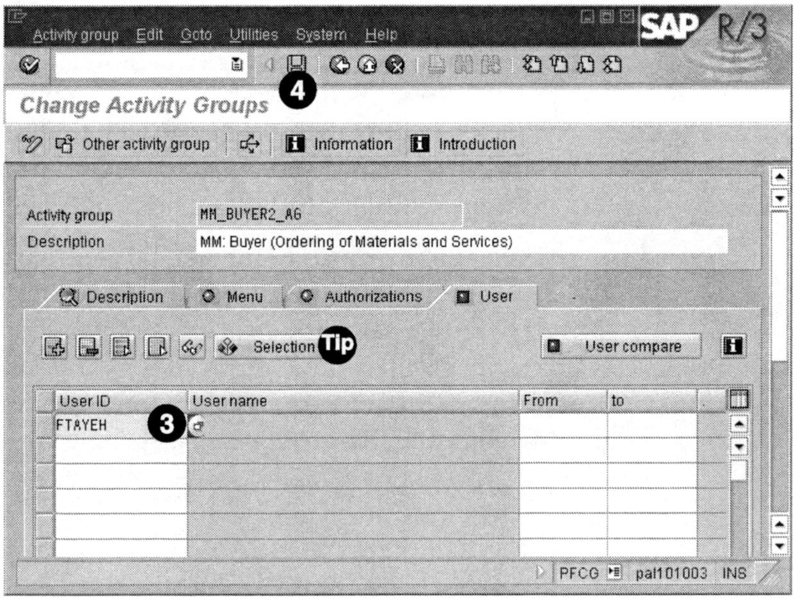


Tips & Tricks

By using the button *Selection*, you can include several users (for example, all users in a particular user group or all users in the R/3 System). Select the desired user and choose .

If you cannot find the required user or if you want to choose the user through a user group:

a. Choose .

b. On the *Execute value restriction* window, find the user by either:
   - Entering the first letter(s) of the user name and an asterisk (*) to expand selection list
   - Using the *User group* field to find the user through their user group

c. Choose .

d. Select the user.

   It is possible to select several users.

e. Choose .

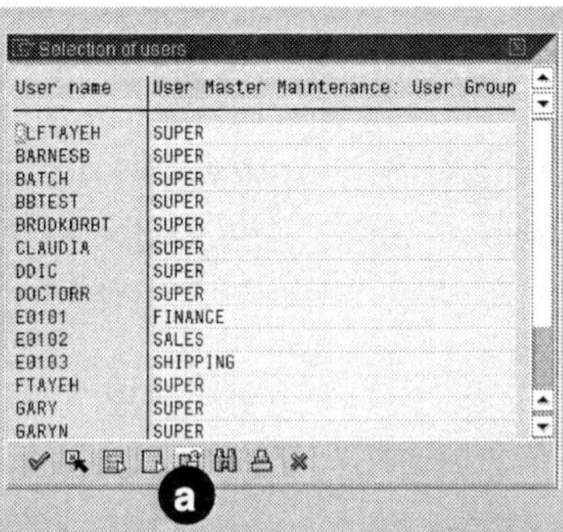

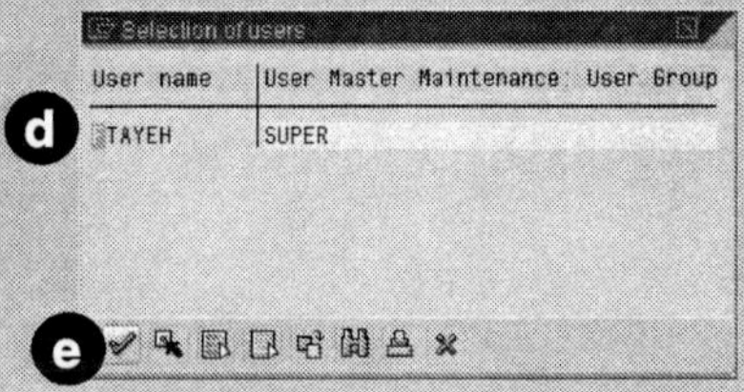

6. The chosen user(s) appear in the *User ID* and *User name* columns.
7. In the *From* and *to* columns, restrict the start and end date of the user assignment.

   The system enters by default the current date as the start date and *31.12.9999* as the end date.
8. Choose [save icon] to save your selection.
9. Choose [icon] *User compare.*

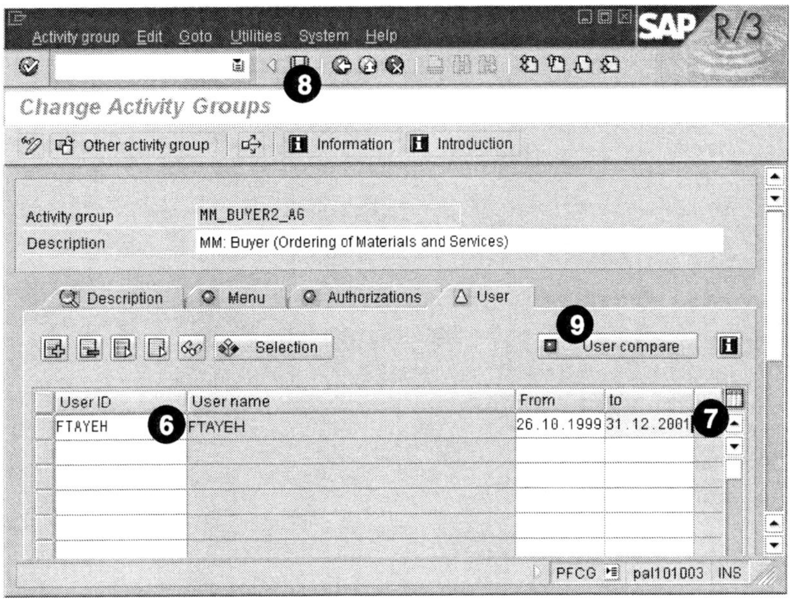


### Status Display on the Tab

The status display on the *User* tab displays whether or not users are already assigned to the activity group. If the display appears in red, no users are assigned. If green, at least one user is assigned to the group. If yellow, it means that although users have been assigned to the activity group, the user master record comparison is not current.

### Time-Dependency of User Assignment and Authorizations

If you also use the activity group to generate authorization profiles, then you should note that the generated profile is not entered in the user master record until the user master records have been compared. When you specify the users for the activity group, the system defaults to the current date as the start date of the user assignment, and *31.12.9999* as the end date. If you want to restrict the start and end dates of the assignment, for example if you want to define a temporary replacement for a user, the system automatically makes the changes to the user. This automatic adjustment of the user's authorizations is executed by report *PFCG_TIME_DEPENDENCY*. In this case, you should schedule report *PFCG_TIME_DEPENDENCY* daily, for example early in the morning, to run in the background (in transaction *SA38*, for example). This report compares the user master records for all activity groups and updates the authorizations for the user master records. The system removes authorization profiles from invalid user assignments and enters authorization profiles from valid assignments.

# Assigning Activity Groups to Users

You can also assign user role templates or activity groups to users using transaction *SU01 – Users*. If you would like to assign several activity groups to one user this is a more efficient way for the assignment.

1. In the *Command* field, enter transaction **SU01** and choose *Enter* (or in the *SAP standard menu*, choose *Tools → Administration → User maintenance → Users*).
2. Enter the name of the user to whom you would like to assign the activity group, or use *possible entries*.
3. Choose ✏.

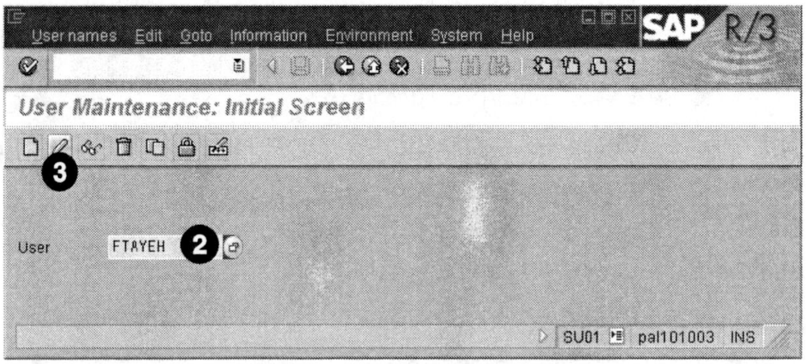


4. Select all the desired activity groups by entering the correct names, or use *possible entries.*
5. Enter the correct validity period for the assignment.
6. Choose 💾 to save your assignment.

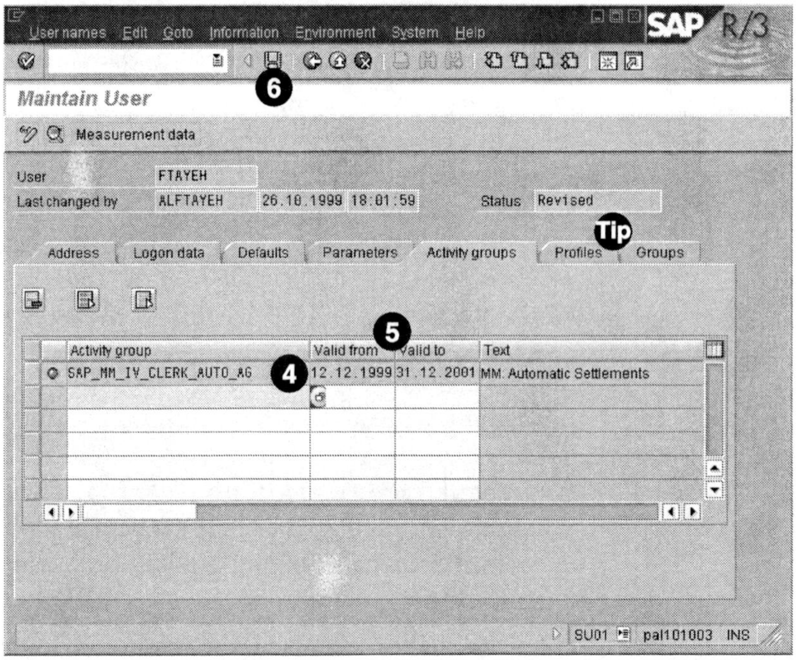


**Tips & Tricks**

To see the corresponding profiles, select the *Profiles* tab.

All changes have been saved to the user master record.

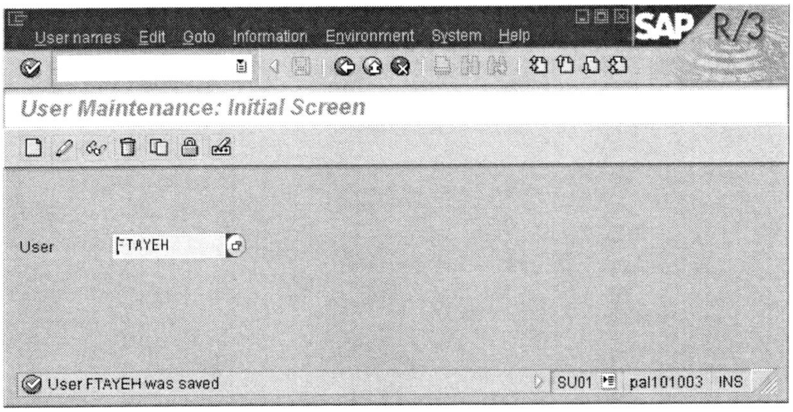


Remember, as long as an activity group is assigned to an R/3 user, you can change this activity group and the appropriate authorization profiles as often as you want **without** updating the user master record.

If an activity group is changed so that one profile becomes two or more, these profiles are automatically assigned to all the users to whom the old profile belonged. The user master of this user automatically gets updated.

# Assigning PD Objects to Activity Groups

You can assign PD objects such as positions, jobs, or organizational units to activity groups. Using transaction **PFCG**, verify that the authorization profiles have been generated (the light on the *Authorizations* tab should be green).

**Create a Sample Organizational Plan**

To assign PD objects to activity groups, your system must have an organizational plan. If you have not created one for your company but you want to test this functionality, see *Creating a Sample Organizational Plan* on page 9–21.

1. Access the PG (transaction **PFCG**).
2. Select the activity group to be assigned to a PD object.
3. Select *Overview (Organizational management and workflow).*
4. Choose *Change.*

5. On the *Change Activity Groups* screen, choose the *User* tab.
6. Choose *Organizational M....*

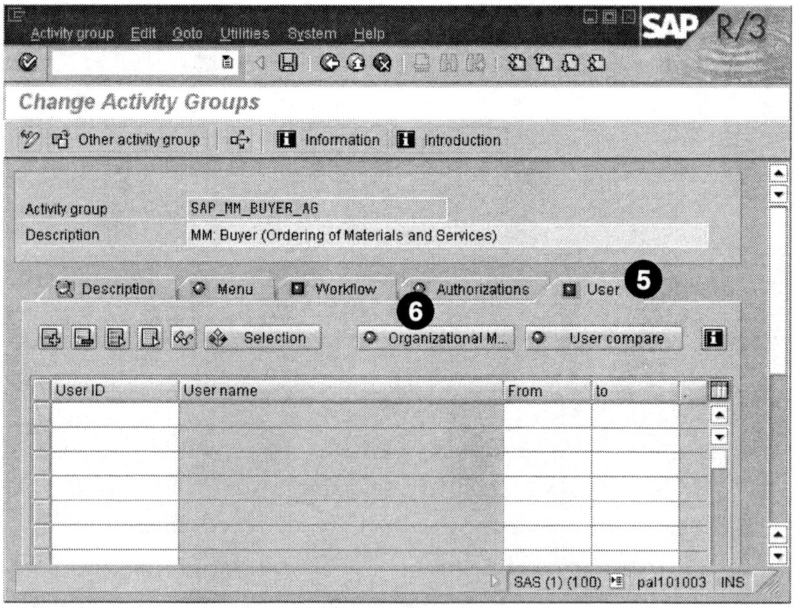


7. To create the assignment , choose .

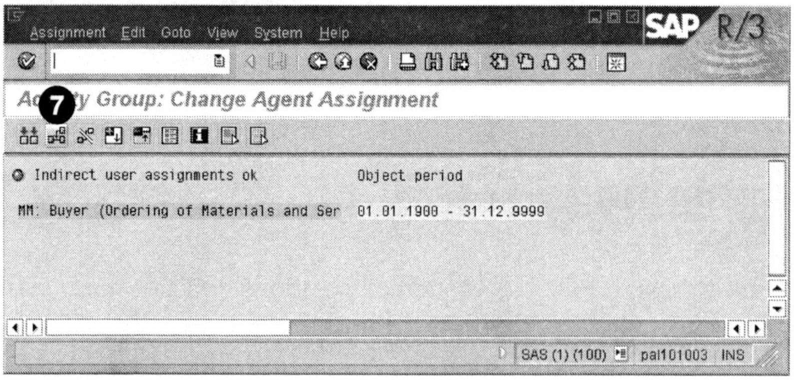


8. Select the object to be assigned (for example, *Position*).
9. Choose .

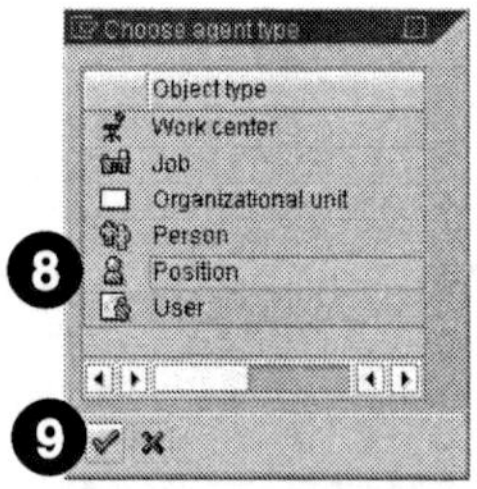


10. Choose  to get a list of positions.

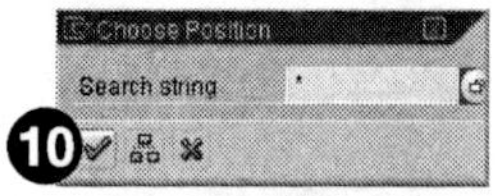


11. From the list of positions, select the position you would like to assign to the selected activity group (more than one position may be selected).
12. Choose .

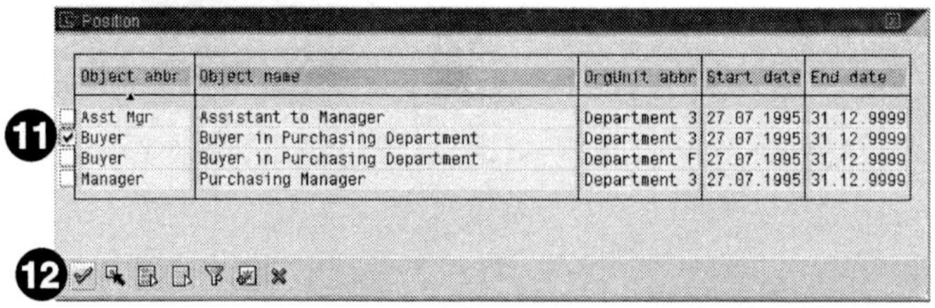

13. Enter the time period for the relationship.
14. Choose ☐ to create the relationship.

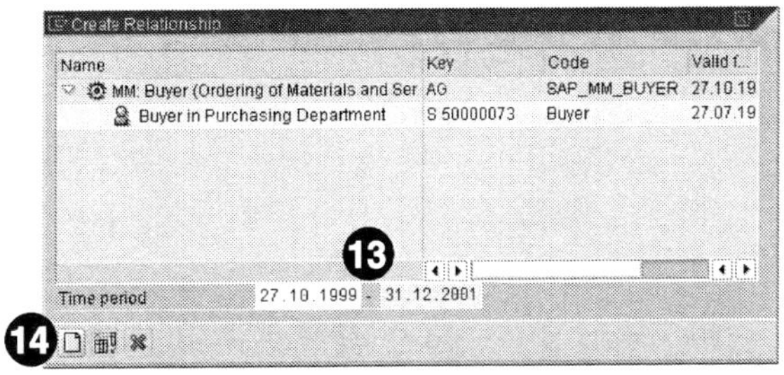


The relationship is established.

15. Under the activity group you can see the assigned position. Under the position you can see the assigned user.
16. To update the user master records so that the appropriate profiles are inserted into this record, choose ☐.

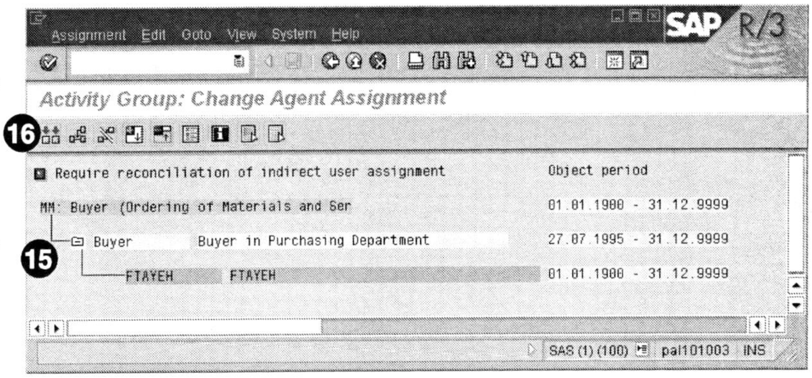


Tips & Tricks

You have the option to select between different views for the assignment. From the menu bar, choose *View* and then select any of the following menu options: *Key, Abbreviation, Object period, Relationship period, Users only.*

The assignment is saved and the user master data updated.

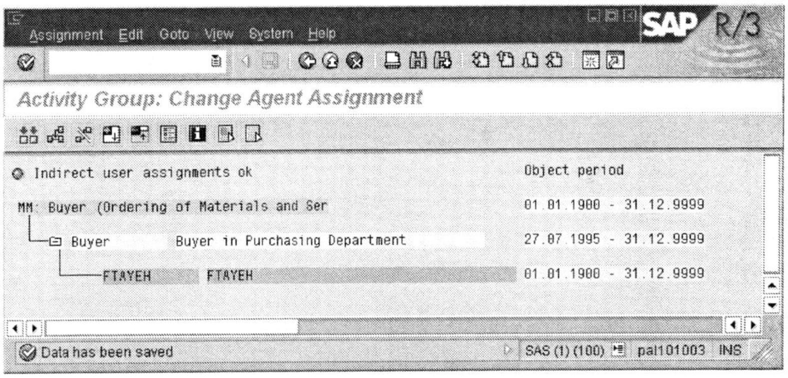

# Assigning Activity Groups to PD Objects

You can assign activity groups to PD objects. Using the PG, verify that the authorization profiles have been generated (the light on the *Authorizations* tab should be green.)

1. In the *Command* field, enter transaction **ppom_old** and choose *Enter* (or in the *SAP standard menu*, choose the *Human resources → Organizational management → Expert mode → Simple maintenance → PPOM_OLD – change*).
2. Enter the organizational unit, or use *possible entries*.

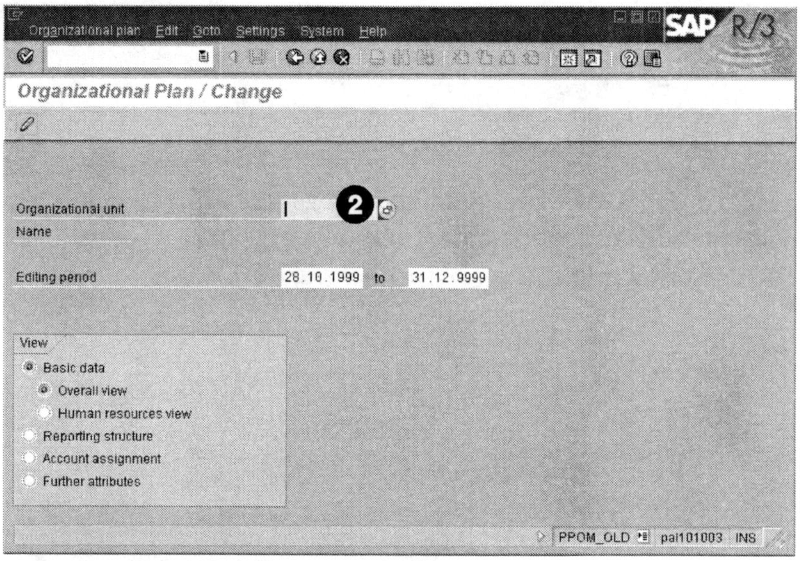


3. Choose *T. Structure Search* to select the organizational unit using a structural search.

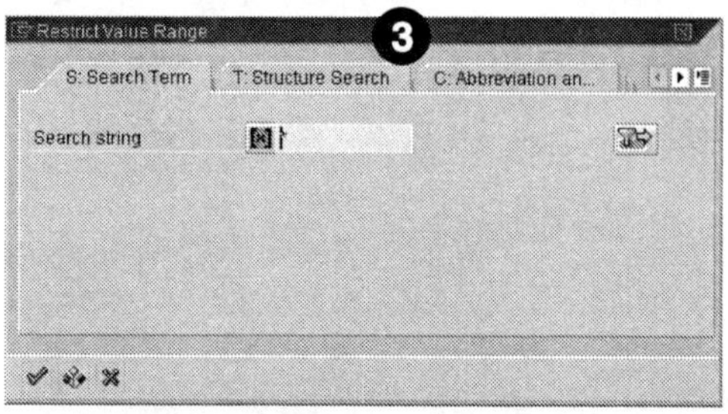


4. Select the appropriate root organizational unit. In this example, we chose the root organizational unit from the sample organizational plan.
5. Choose ✔.

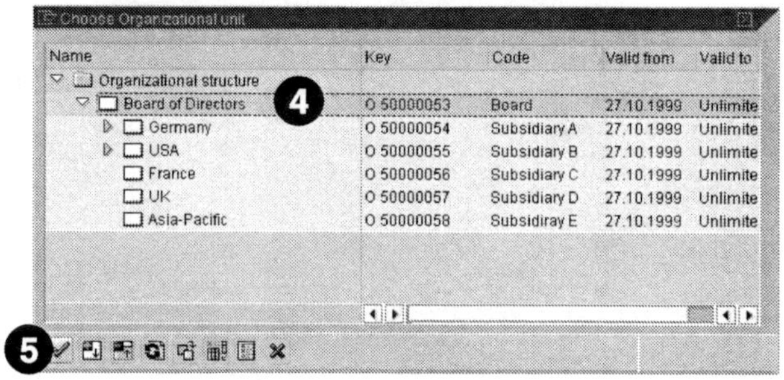

6. The selected organizational plan appears in the *Organizational unit* field.
7. Choose ✎.

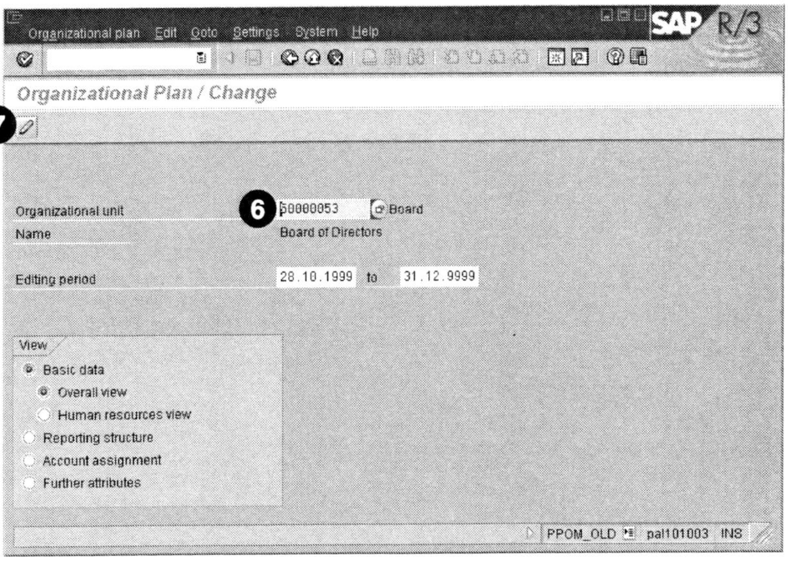


8. Choose *Staff assignments*.

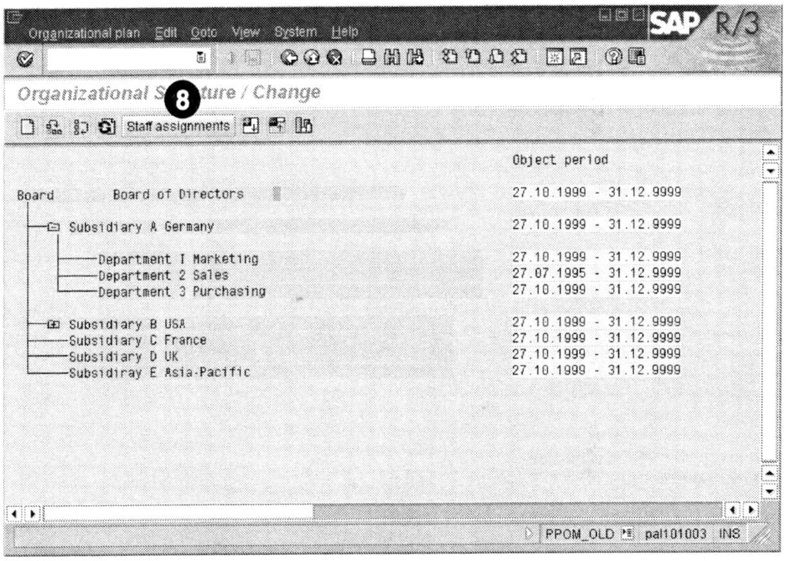


9. Expand the units and select the one to which you would like to assign the activity group (for example, *Buyer*).
10. Choose *Task profile*.

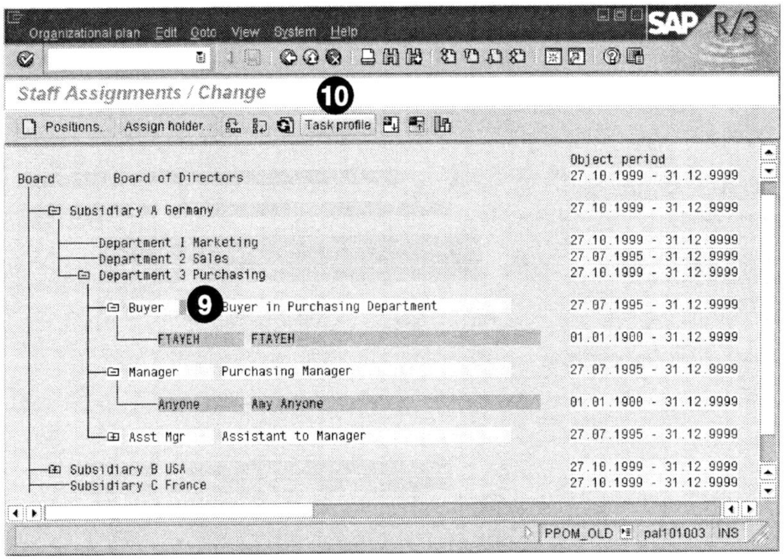

11. On the *Task Profile/Change* screen, select the position to which you would like to assign an activity group.
12. Choose *Activity group*.

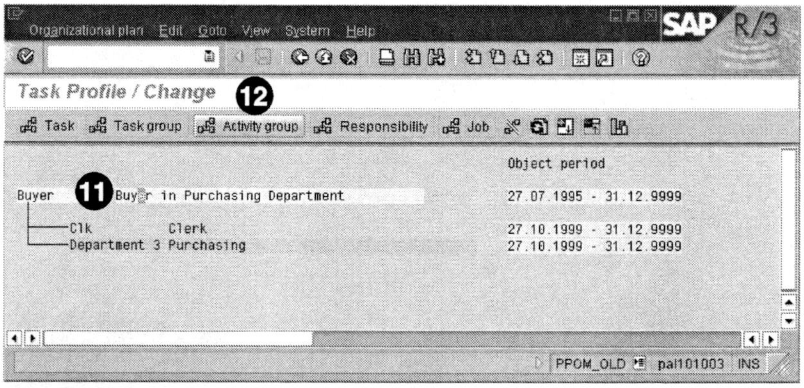


13. Enter the first letter of the activity group you would like to assign or leave the asterisks (*) in the field to get a list of all activity groups.
14. Choose ✔.

15. Select the activity group you wish to assign (multiple selections are possible).
16. Choose ✔.

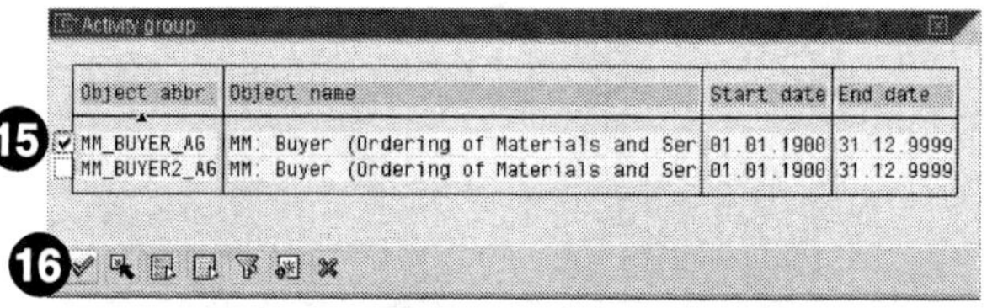


17. To verify the assignment, choose 💾.

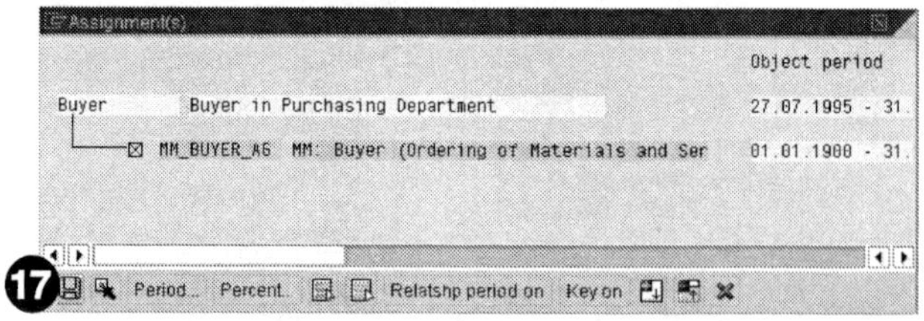


The assignment between the position and the activity group has been saved.

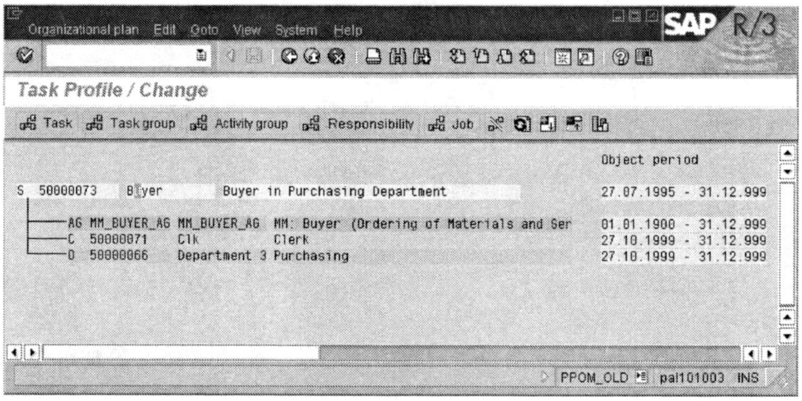


Tips & Tricks

To make changes to the assigned activity group, select the activity group and choose *Goto → Activity group*.

The next step is to update the user master records so that the appropriate profiles are inserted into the user master record and assigned to the organizational units.

# Transferring Users from an IMG Project to an Activity Group

If you assigned users (resources) to an IMG project in the project management, and did not copy the user assignment when creating the customizing authorizations, you can transfer these users to the activity group using the following procedure.

Tips & Tricks

Note that you must call this function again each time you make changes in the IMG project administration.

For the following example, we assume that:

- An IMG project with at least one assigned user exists
- You assigned an IMG project or project view to the activity group (see chapter 6, the section *Assigning IMG Projects or Project Views to Activity Groups*)
- You maintained the authorizations for the customizing activity group (see chapter 6, the section *Assigning IMG Projects or Project Views to Activity Groups*)

To transfer users from an IMG project to an activity group:

1. Access the PG (transaction **PFCG**).
2. Select the customizing activity group to which you would like to transfer the user from an IMG project (for example, *QM_CUSTOMIZING*), and choose *Change.*
3. Choose the *Menu* tab.
4. Choose *Utilities* → *Customizing auth.*

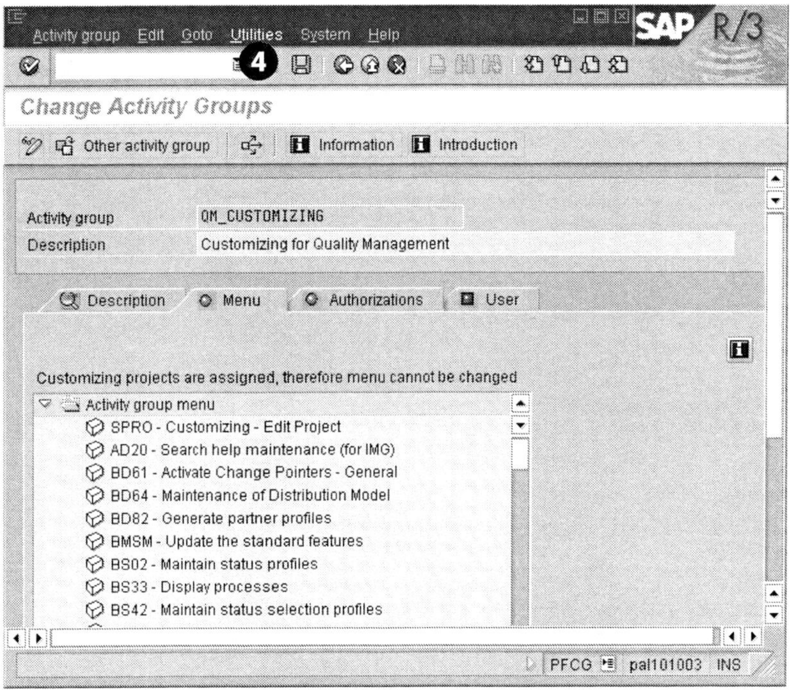

5. Choose *User*.

6. Select the users you would like to assign.
7. Choose ✔.

   All selected users will be transferred by default.

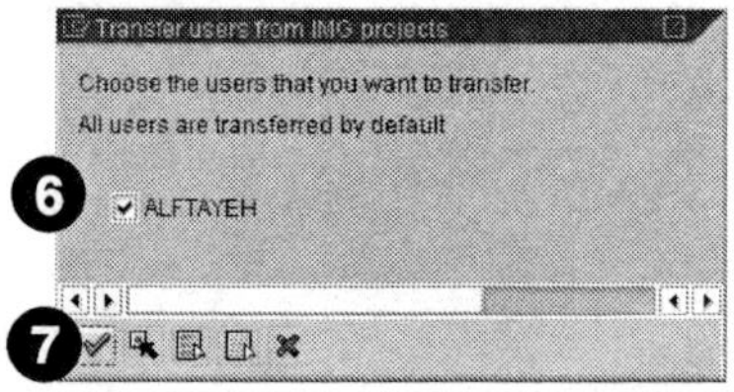


8. Choose .
9. Choose the *User* tab.
10. Choose *User compare*.

Tips & Tricks

As customizing is project-related and runs for a limited period, you should maintain the end date for the user in the user assignment. Time restrictions prevent users who are assigned to the activity group from having authorization for the assigned projects or project views after the customizing project is complete.

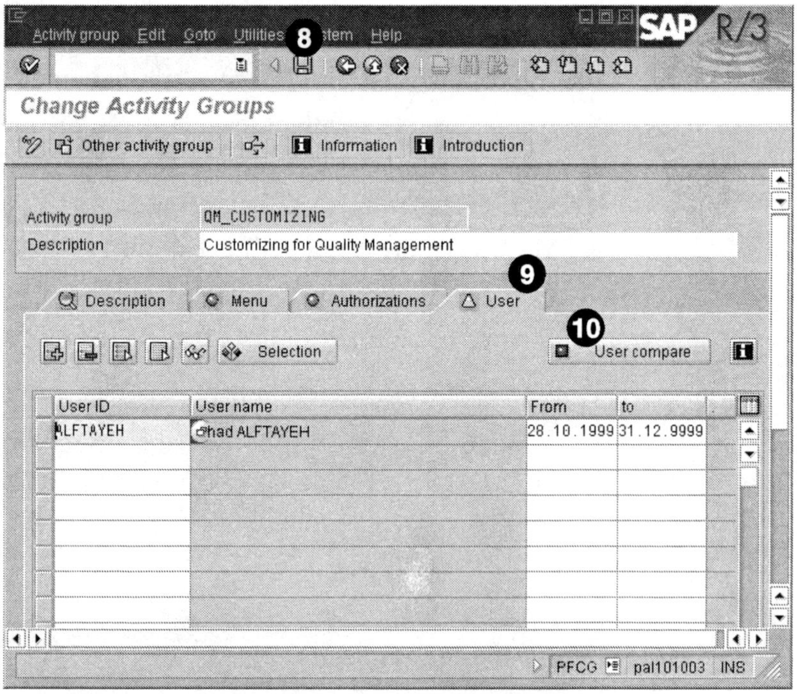


11. Choose *Complete compare*.

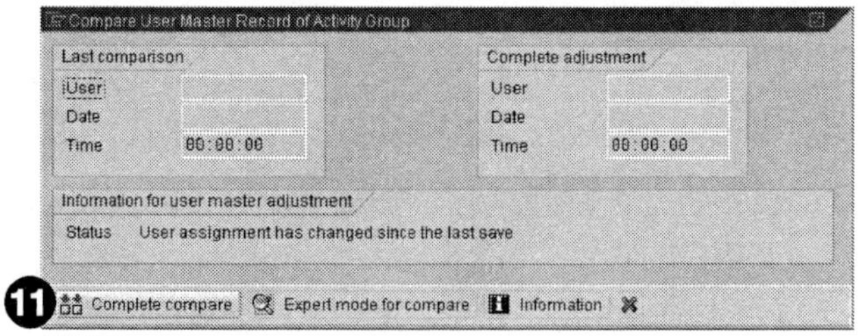

The users from the customizing project are transferred to the activity group.

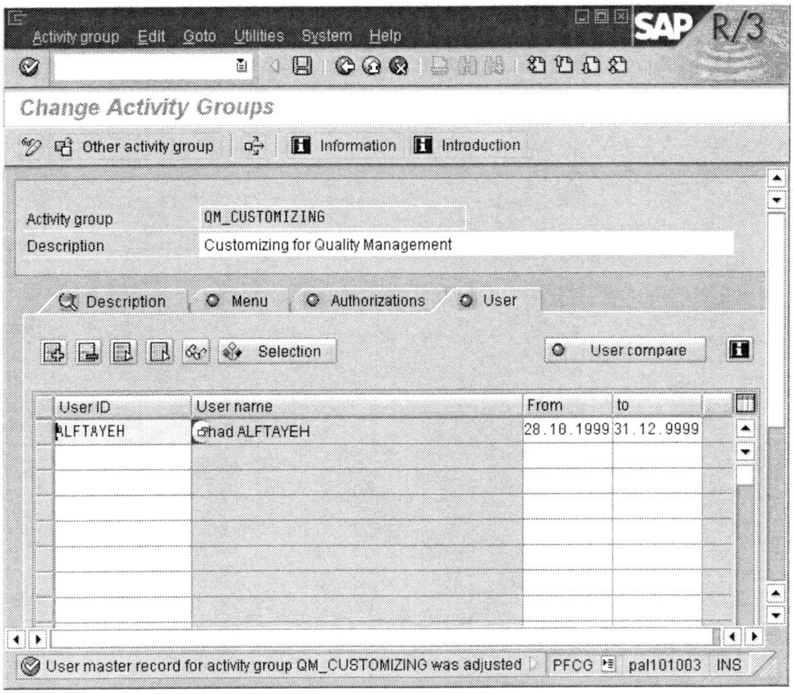


# Updating Profiles in the User Master Records

This section describes the steps involved in using report *PFCG_TIME DEPENDENCY* to update user master records. Remember that activity groups, their assignment to user master records, or PD objects can be delimited.

To ensure that only valid authorization profiles remain in the user master record each day, conduct daily profile comparisons. For the changes in the user master record to be effective, this comparison must take place before the user logs on.

To conduct a comparison, you can either:

- Compare the user master data directly from within the PG
- Use mass compare within the PG *(Environment → Mass compare)*
- Run report *PFGC_TIME_DEPENDENCY* in a background job before the start of each day

These options are discussed in the following three sections.

## Comparing User Master Data from Within Transaction PFCG

A comparison of user master data directly from within the PG immediately updates a specific user master after creating an assignment.

1. Access the PG (transaction **PFCG**).
2. Select an activity group for which you would like to update the user master data and choose *Change*.

3. On the *Change Activity Groups* screen, choose the *User* tab.
4. In the *User ID* column, enter a user ID or select it from a list using *possible entries*.
5. Enter a validity period.
6. Choose *User compare*.

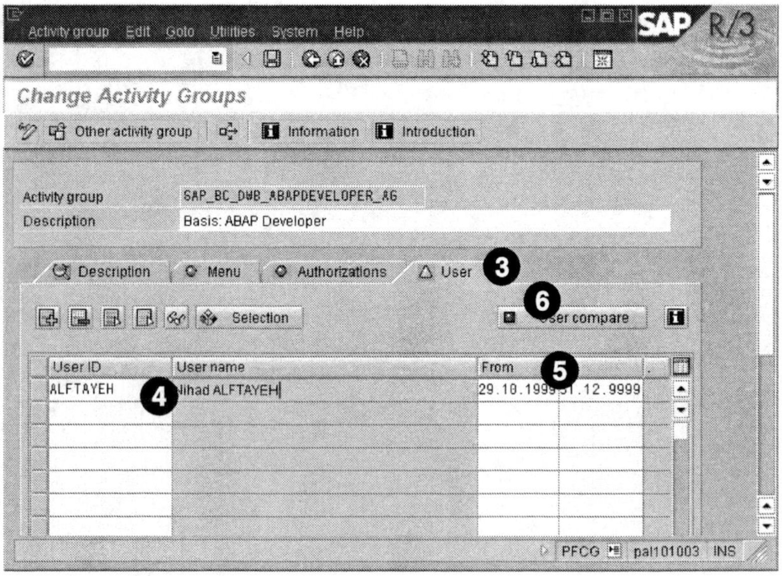


**Status Display on the User Tab**
The status display on the tab tells if a user is already assigned to an activity group. If the indicator is red, no users are assigned. If green, at least one user is assigned to the group. If yellow, this means that although users have been assigned to the activity group, the user master record comparison is not current.

7. Choose *Complete compare*.

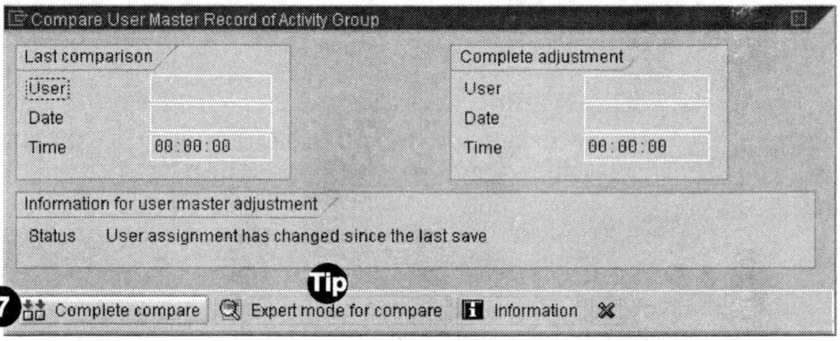


The expert mode displays exactly which profiles were inserted and removed for each user. As you have the option to restrict the selection of the profiles for processing, the status of *User compare* is not switched to green. This status is only the case if the comparison is executed by choosing *Complete compare*. If you choose *Expert mode for compare*, the status is not set to green.

8. If you have not saved the activity group yet, choose *Yes*.

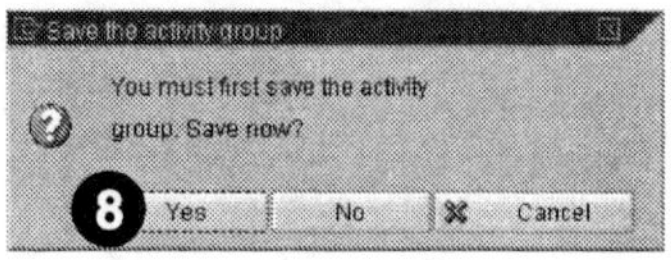

9. The green light on *User compare* indicates that the comparison is complete.

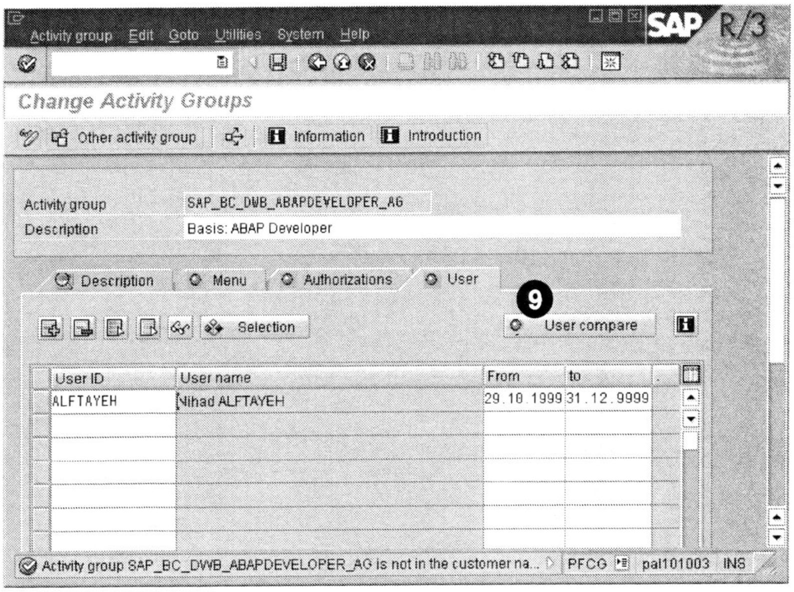


Note that changes are first active with the next user logon.

# Profile Comparisons Using Mass Compare (PFUD)

For profile comparison within the PG, you can use the mass compare function regularly to check for background job errors.

1. In the *Command* field, enter transaction **PFUD** and choose *Enter* (or access the PG and choose *Environment → Mass compare*).
2. Choose the activity groups you would like to reconcile.
3. Select one of the following actions:
   - *Schedule or check job for full reconciliation* (see the next section)
   - *Manual selection of profiles* (for selected profiles)
   - *Complete compare* (to adjust user master records for all activity groups)
4. Under *Options*, select the desired settings (we selected all).
5. If you would like to reconcile with organizational management, select *Reconcile with HR Organizational Management*.
6. Choose .

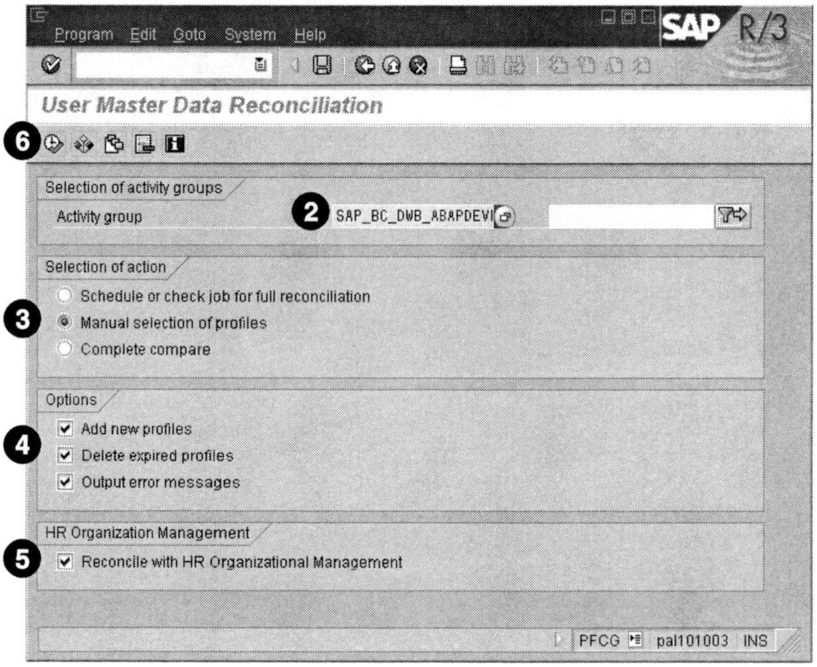


**Tips & Tricks:** The following window only appears if you select the option *Manual selection of profiles* in step 3, because the status for the complete compare has not been set. If you leave the default value, which is *Complete compare*, you will not get the following window, because the status will already be set correctly for the PG.

7. Choose .

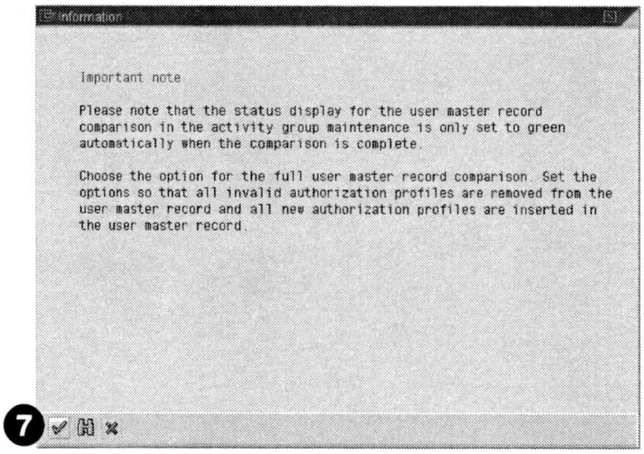

8. Choose *User master record*.

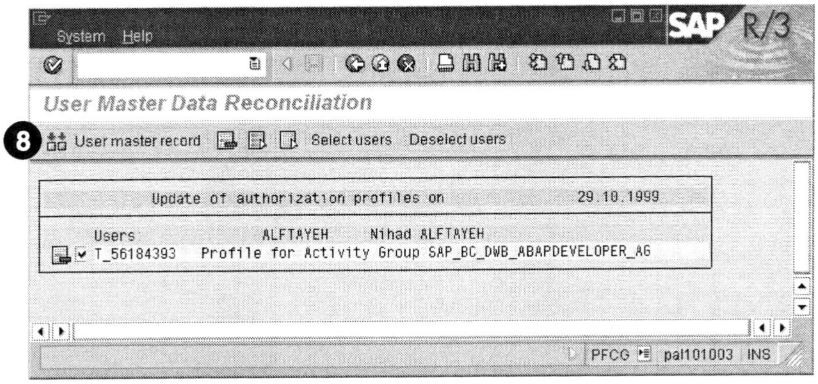


The user master records have been successfully updated.

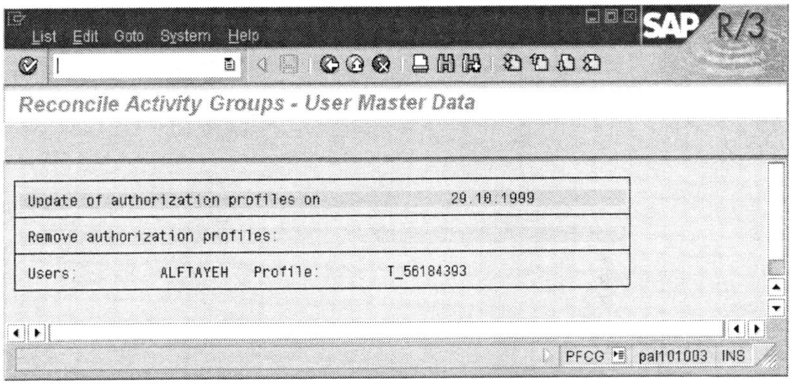


Caution

Note that changes are first active with the next user logon.

## Report PFCG_TIME_DEPENDENCY to Schedule Time Dependency

TechTalk

**Time Dependency of User Assignment and Authorizations**

When you specify the users for the activity group, the system defaults to the current date as the start date of the user assignment, and *31.12.9999* as the end date. If you want to restrict the start and end dates of the assignment, for example if you want to define a temporary replacement for a user, the system automatically makes the changes to the user. This automatic adjustment of the user's authorizations is executed by report *PFCG_TIME_DEPENDENCY*. In this case, you should schedule report *PFCG_TIME_DEPENDENCY* daily, for example early in the morning, to run in the background (in transaction *SA38*, for example). This report compares the user master records for all activity groups and updates the authorizations for the user master records. The system removes authorization profiles from invalid user assignments and enters authorization profiles from valid user assignments.

If the report *PFCG_TIME_DEPENDENCY* runs every night, the authorization profiles in the user master will be updated each morning. The best procedure is to schedule this report in a periodic background job.

1. In the *Command* field, enter transaction **PFUD** and choose *Enter* (or access the PG and choose *Environment → Mass compare*).
2. In the *Activity group* field, select the desired activity group.
3. Select *Schedule or check job for full reconciliation.*
4. Choose ⏱.

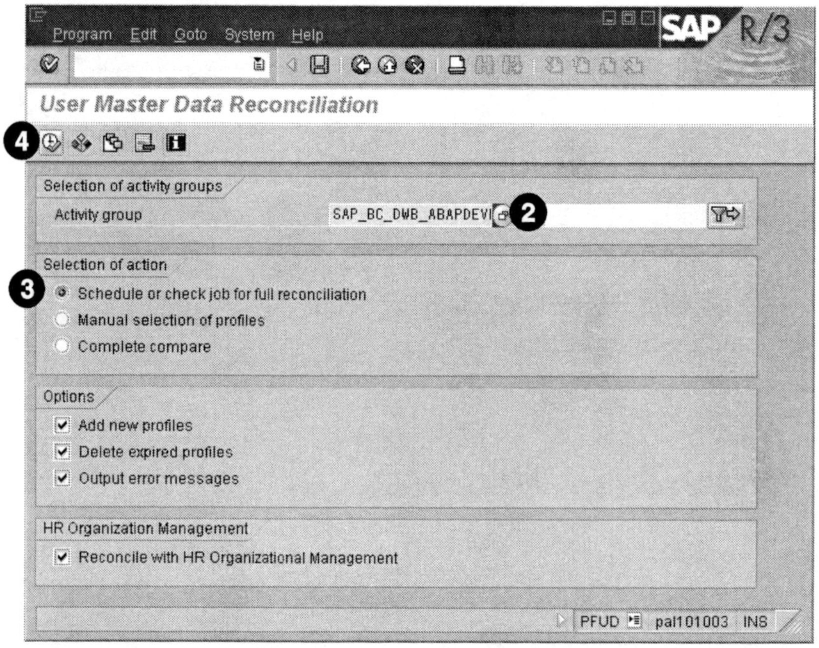


5. In *Job name*, enter a job name or leave the default.
6. Under *Start date*, select the date and time you want the report to start automatically.
7. Choose ⏱ *Execute*.

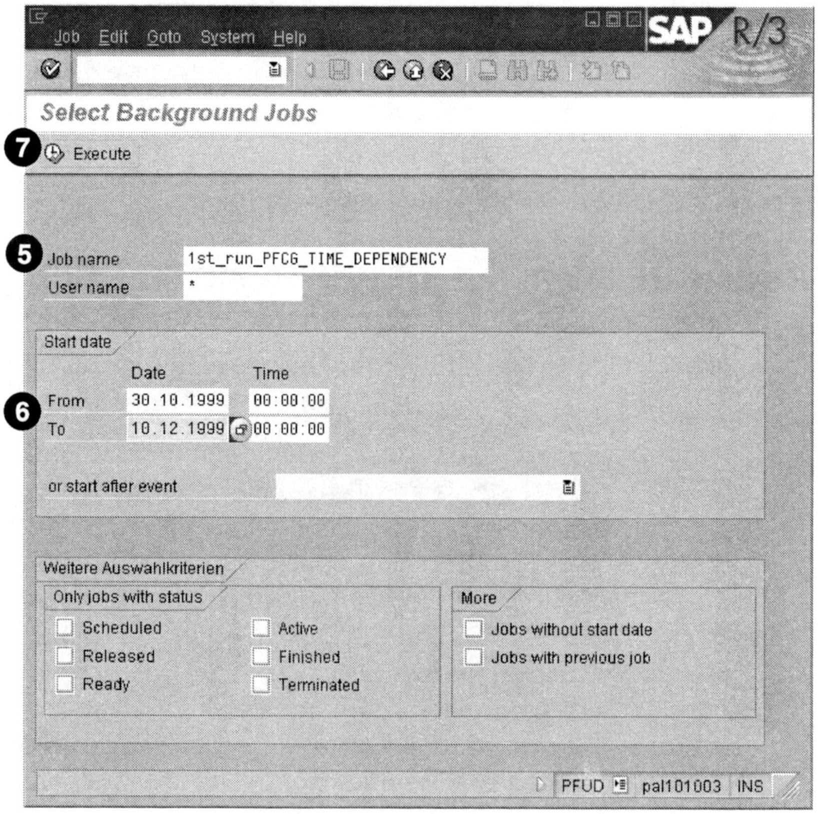

8. Choose ✔.

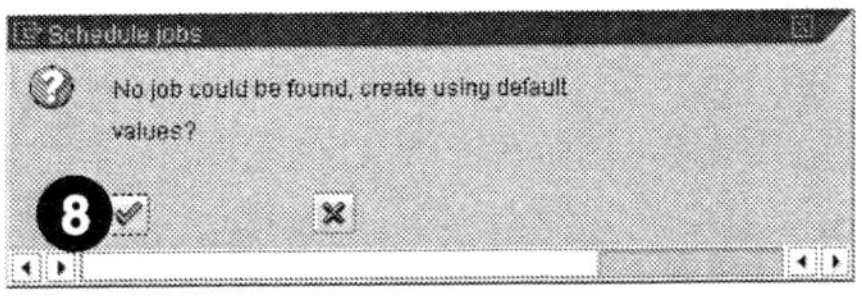


9. Enter a job name or leave the default.
10. Enter a job class (priority).
11. Choose 💾.

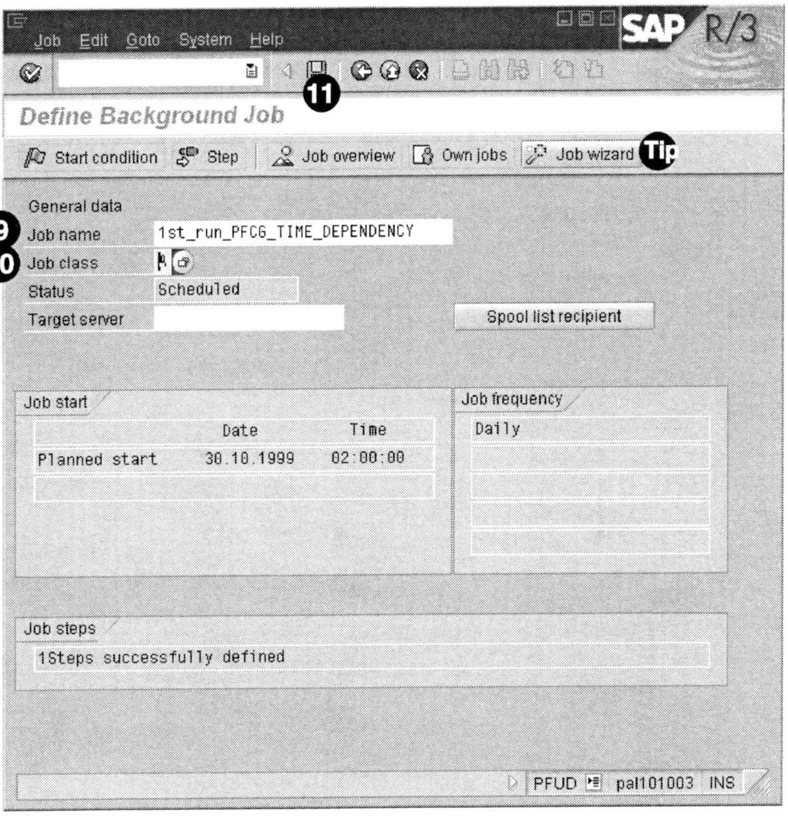


Tips & Tricks

The job wizard helps you to define a job using step-by-step dialog screens to guide you through the process. On the last screen, you see a summary of what you have defined before you save.

# Creating a Sample Organizational Plan

You have two options to create an organizational plan:

- The classic R/3 transaction (**PPOC_OLD**)
- The Enjoy transaction (**PPOCE**)

Both can be found in the *Organizational management* under *Human Resources* in the *SAP standard menu*.

In the following section, we describe the steps to create a sample organizational plan for testing. This plan is not complete, but shows the required elements.

# Using the Classic R/3 Transaction

1. In the *Command* field, enter transaction **PPOC_OLD** and choose *Enter* (or choose *Human Resources → Organizational management → Expert Mode → Simple Maintenance → PPOC_OLD Create*).

   A root organizational unit (the highest level in an organizational structure) needs to be created. Then build up the organizational structure from the root organizational unit.

2. Enter the short and long name for the root organizational unit.
3. Choose 🗋.

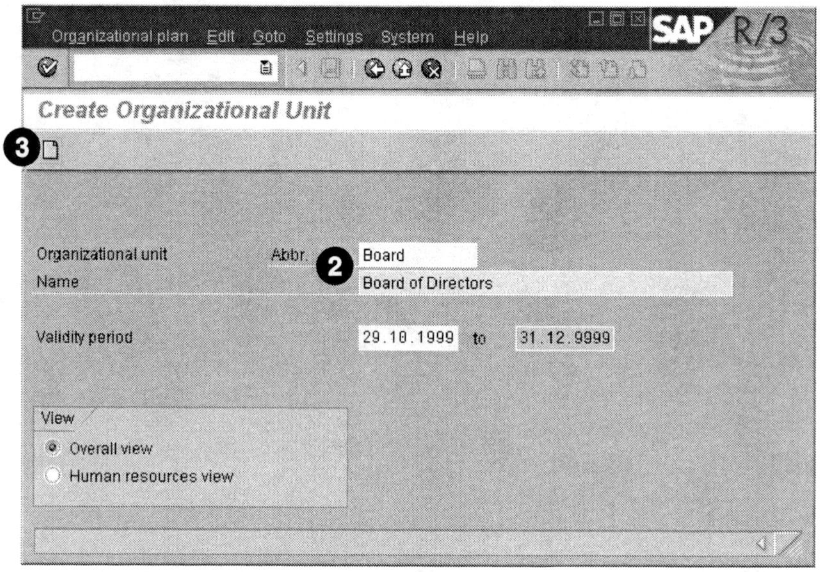


4. In the *Request* field, use *possible entries* to select a change request. If none exists yet, use 🗋 to create one.
5. Choose ✔.

   (In the following steps, we will not show this dialog box anymore. If it does appear, proceed in the same way as here.)

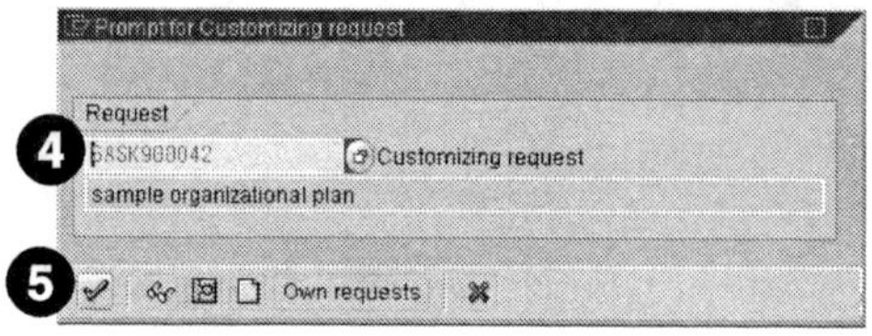


6. Choose 🗋 to create the organizational units that follow your root unit.

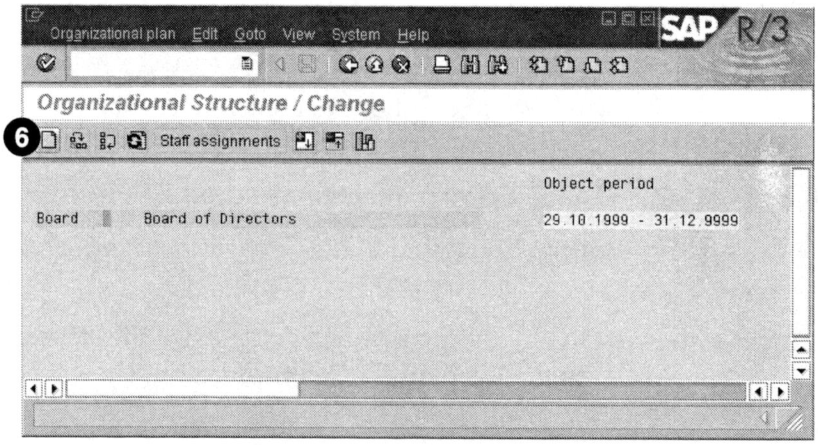

7. Enter the next organizational units under your root unit.
8. Choose .

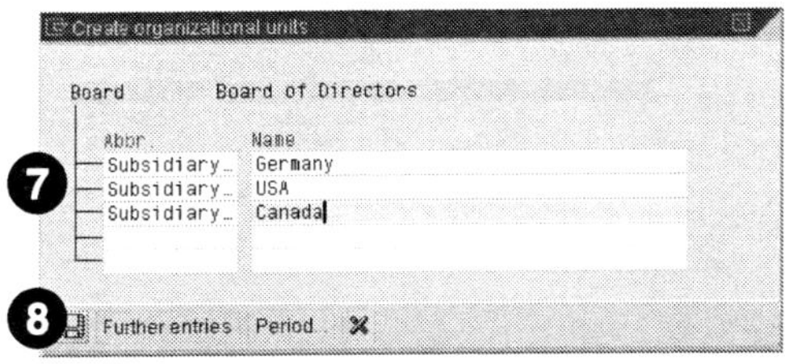


9. Select an organizational unit and choose  to enter the next level.

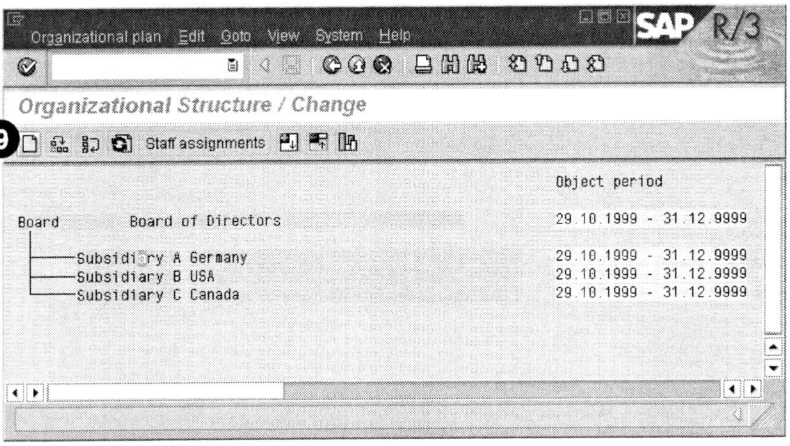


10. Enter the next organizational unit under the selected level (for example, *Subsidiary A Germany*).
11. Choose .

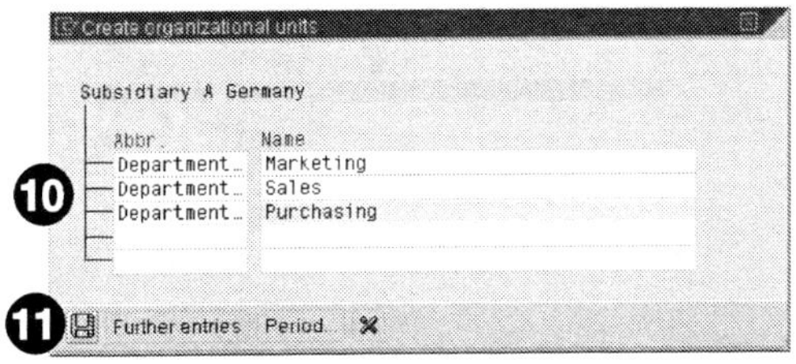


12. Choose *Staff assignment*.

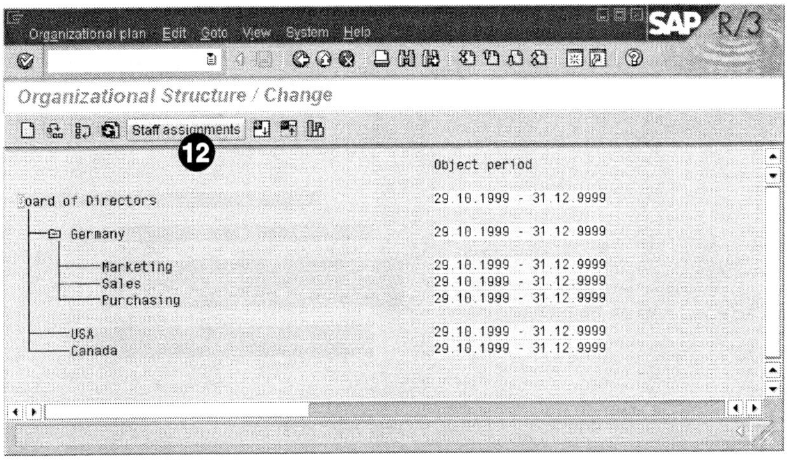

The *Staff Assignments / Change* window allows you to identify the fundamental staffing details required for an organizational plan. This step is achieved by creating jobs, and positions, and by assigning holders to positions.

13. Choose *Edit → Create → Jobs.*

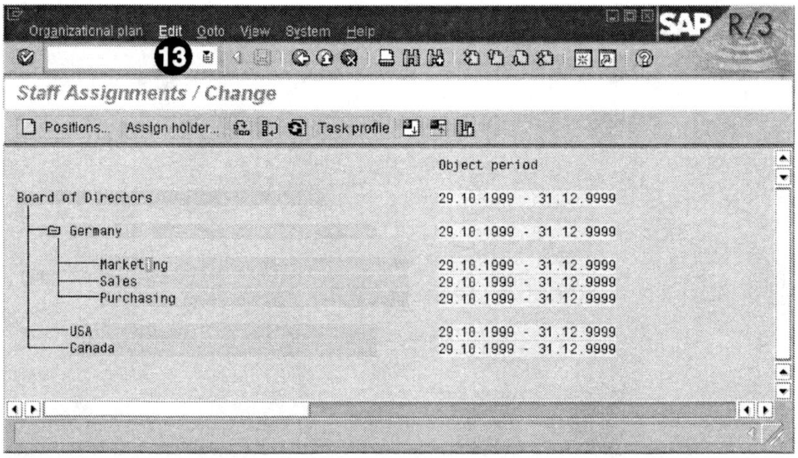


Tips & Tricks

Jobs are one of the objects that make up an organizational plan. A job is a general classification, such as administrative assistant, computer programmer, instructor, etc. You may create as many jobs as you want. Once a job is created, describe its attributes by defining infotypes. An employee automatically inherits the infotype settings, attributes, and properties of the job (positions are usually based on jobs).

14. Enter the job information.
15. Choose the Save icon.

16. Select an organizational unit, then choose *Positions.*

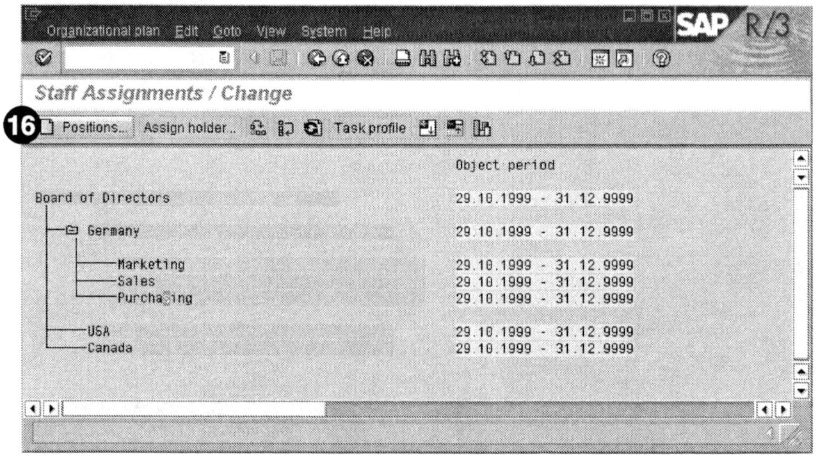

17. Choose *possible entries* for *Abbr.*

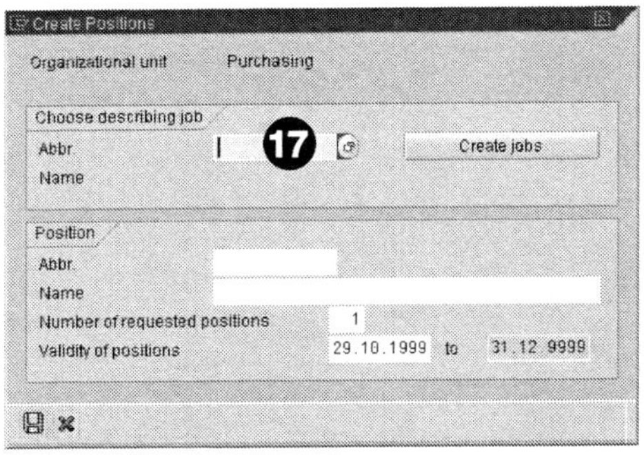


Tips & Tricks

Positions are the individual employee assignments within a company, for example:

- Sales manager
- Marketing assistant
- Junior manufacturing engineer

By creating positions and relationships among the different positions, you can identify the reporting structure at your firm. Positions are usually based on jobs.

18. Select the *Abbreviation and Name* tab.
19. Choose ✓.

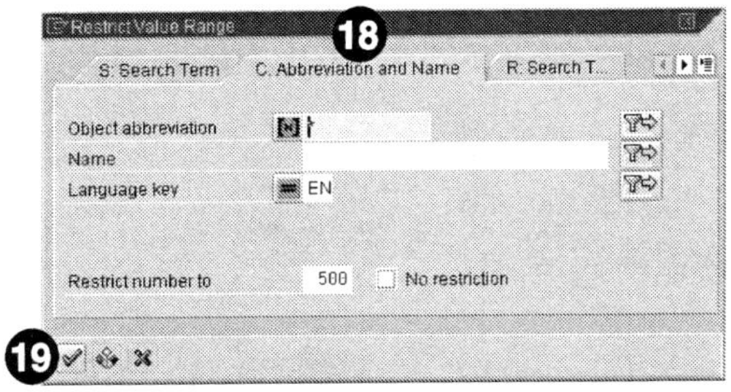


20. Select the appropriate job.
21. Choose ✓.

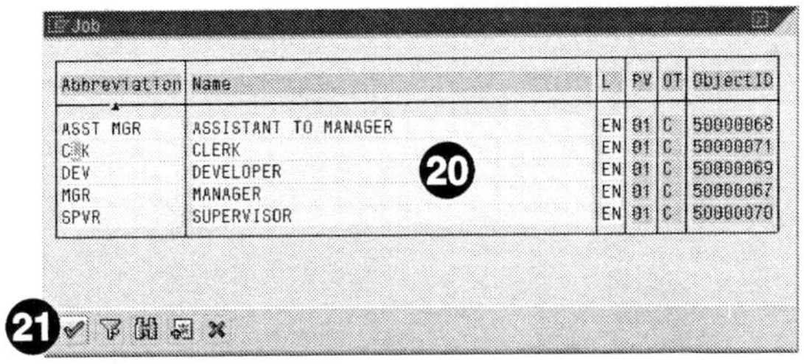


22. Under *Position,* enter a description of the position in the appropriate fields.
23. Choose 💾.

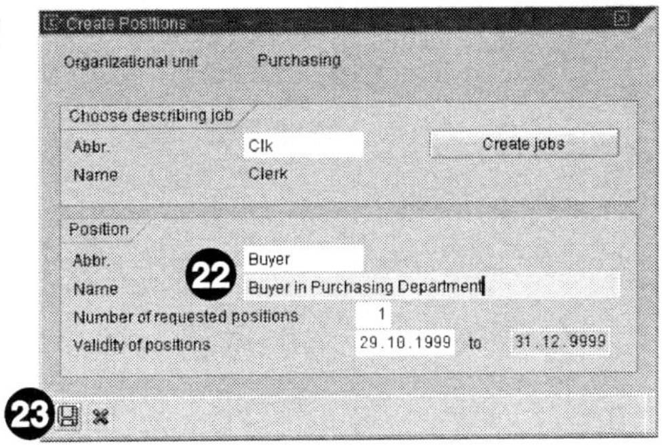

Repeat steps 16–23 to create additional positions.

24. Select a position and choose *Assign holder…*

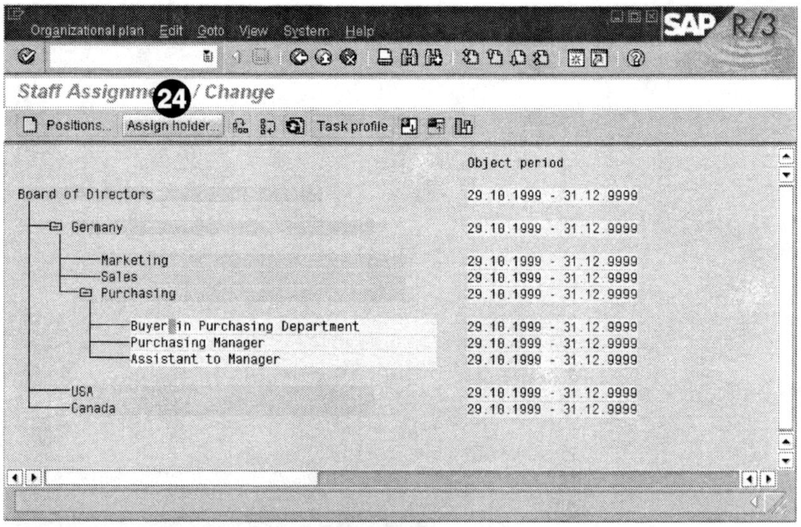


Assign holders when you want to identify who occupies, or fills, a specific position.

In *Simple Maintenance*, assign either an employee or R/3 user to a position. Workflow users assign R/3 users to positions. Personnel administration users assign employees to positions.

25. Choose *possible entries* to display the list of R/3 users already in your system.

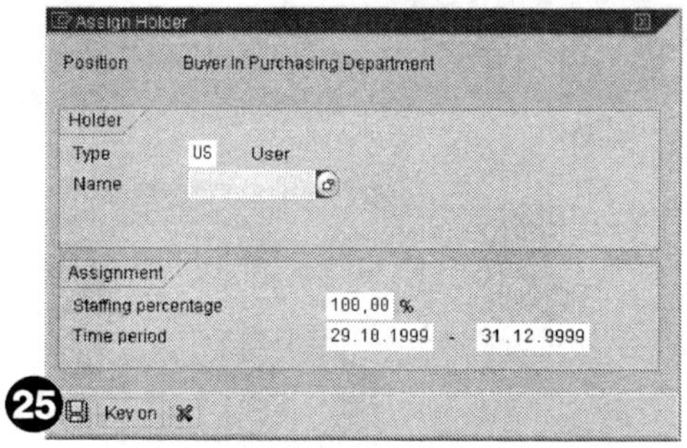


26. Select the correct user of the position from the list.

27. Choose ✔.

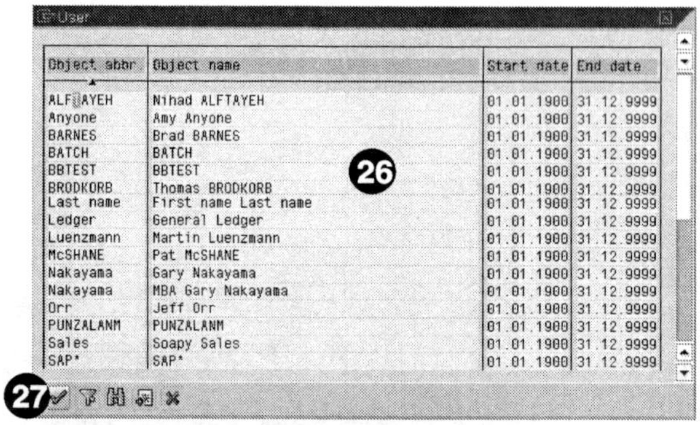


28. Enter the validity period of the assignment.

29. Choose the save icon.

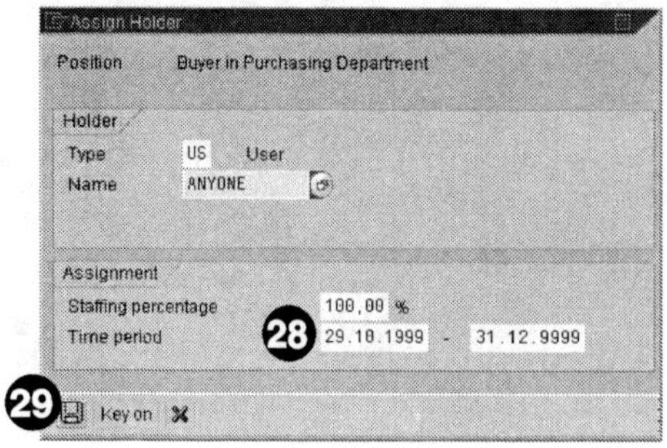

Repeat steps 24–29 to assign additional holders to positions.

The organizational plan is now created. To get a graphical overview, continue with the following steps.

30. Select the root organizational unit.
31. Choose [icon] to display the *Structural Graphics.*

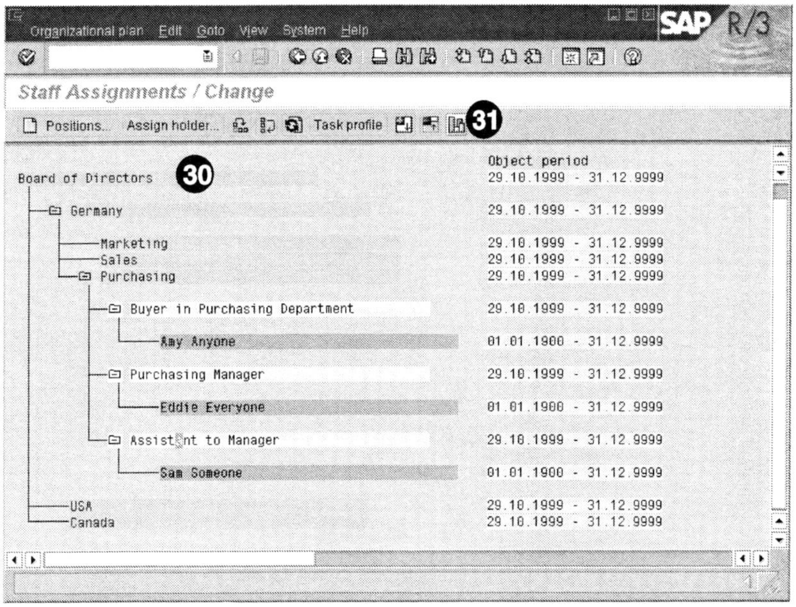


## Using the Enjoy Transaction

The procedure to create the organizational plan using the Enjoy transaction is basically the same as the common R/3 style. The only differerence is that all the procedures are displayed and performed on one screen.

At the time of this writing, the Enjoy functionality was still under development. Therefore, we only provide the screen below which you can reach the following way:

In the *Command* field, enter transaction **PPOCE** and choose *Enter* (or choose *Human Resources → Organizational management → Organizational plan → Organization and Staffing → Create*).

Here you enter the new *Organizational unit* and all the other data, as we describe using the common R/3 style.

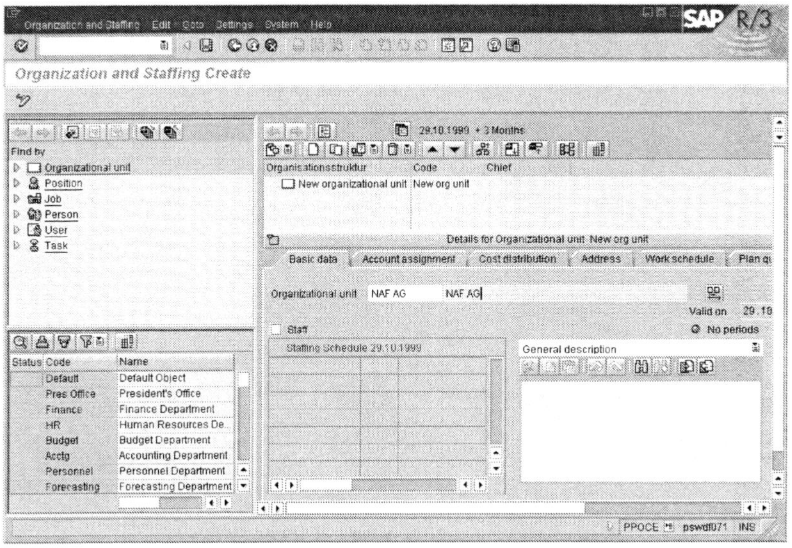

# Structural Authorizations

Structural authorizations are not covered in this guide. However, if you need information on structural authorizations, refer to the *Authorizations Made Easy* guidebook, Release 4.5 A/B, chapter 7, *Structural Authorizations*. This chapter can also be downloaded from the Simplification Groups web page at *http://www.saplabs.com/auth.*

# Chapter 10: Setting Up the ALE Environment for Central User Administration

## Contents

# Overview

**Central User Administration** is new to Release 4.6. In earlier releases user master records were created in each client and each system the user logged on to (for example, DEV, QAS, PRD, etc.). Each user master record for the same user was independent of other user master records. If a user was changed in one client, then the same user had to be changed in all other clients and systems manually. Central User Administration reduces the maintenance and synchronization issues faced by authorization administrators.

The core concept behind Central User Administration is to designate one client in one system as the repository for maintaining authorizations. This client system is designated as the sender. All other clients in other systems are designated as receivers. **Application Link Enabling (ALE)** is R/3's technology to enable data exchange between different systems. Central User Administration distributes user data between central and client systems.

This chapter discusses how to set up ALE for use with Central User Administration. The next chapter discusses the steps involved in using Central User Administration.

Caution

Setting up ALE must be done together with a system administrator or the person who first set up the clients. In setting up ALE, the entire client's definition will be changed and this must not be done without the consent of the system administrator.

During the installation of an ALE environment, you must follow every step for all client-systems to be integrated into one **user account**. This user account needs to have system administrator rights. Each client-system combination is recognized by ALE as a **logical system**.

Setting up an ALE environment allows you to distribute data between logical systems and keep this data consistent. The systems of an ALE environment are only loosely linked. The data is being exchanged asynchronously, which insures that the data will be received by the recipient system even if the receiving system is turned off at the time of sending. Synchronous connections are only being used to read data by ALE.

The graphic on the right shows an ALE environment for Central User Administration.

One system needs to be defined as the central system. The links run from the central system to the client systems where the central system serves as the hub.

The client systems are not directly linked to each other.

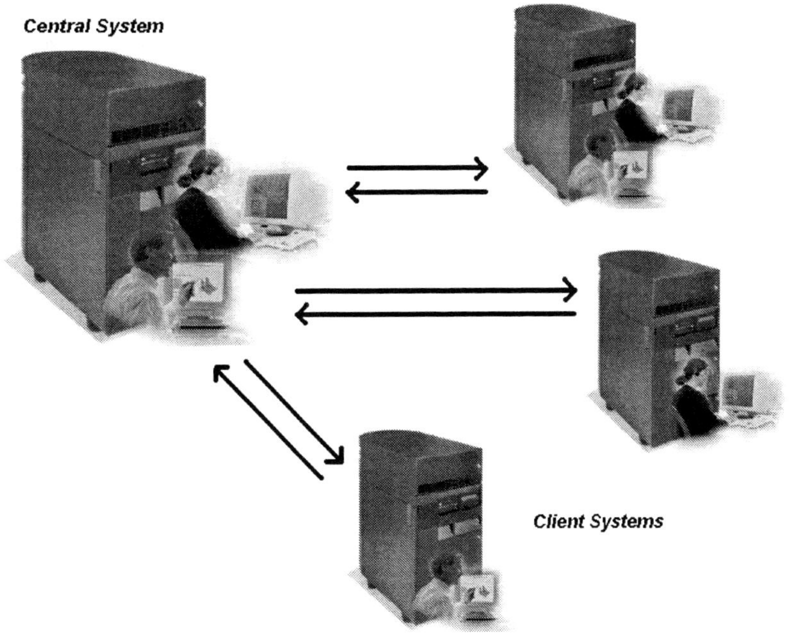


# Setting Up an ALE User

For internal communication between all systems in an ALE environment you need a user account. Used for internal communication, this user account is not used in dialog mode. The user needs to have the same user name and password for all the systems in an ALE environment.

1. In the *Command* field, enter the user maintenance transaction **SU01** and choose *Enter.*
2. In *User*, enter a user name for the internal user.
3. To create the user, choose ☐.

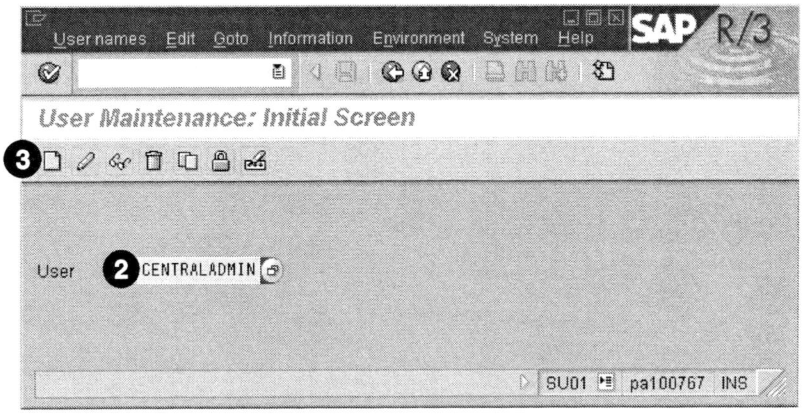

4. On the *Address* tab, specify at least the last name of the user.
5. Choose the *Logon data* tab.

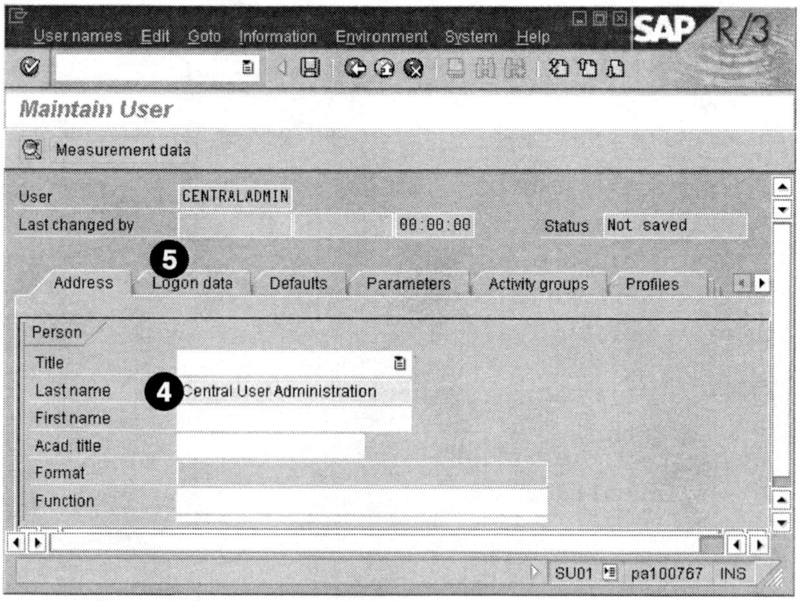


6. Under *Password*, enter an initial password.
7. Repeat the initial password.
8. Under *User type*, select *CPIC*.

Tips & Tricks

We recommend you use the user type *CPIC*, since such a system user cannot log on to R/3 using a dialog window. This user can only be used for the internal communication between systems. However, it is possible to use a dialog user for this communication.

9. Choose *Profiles tab.*

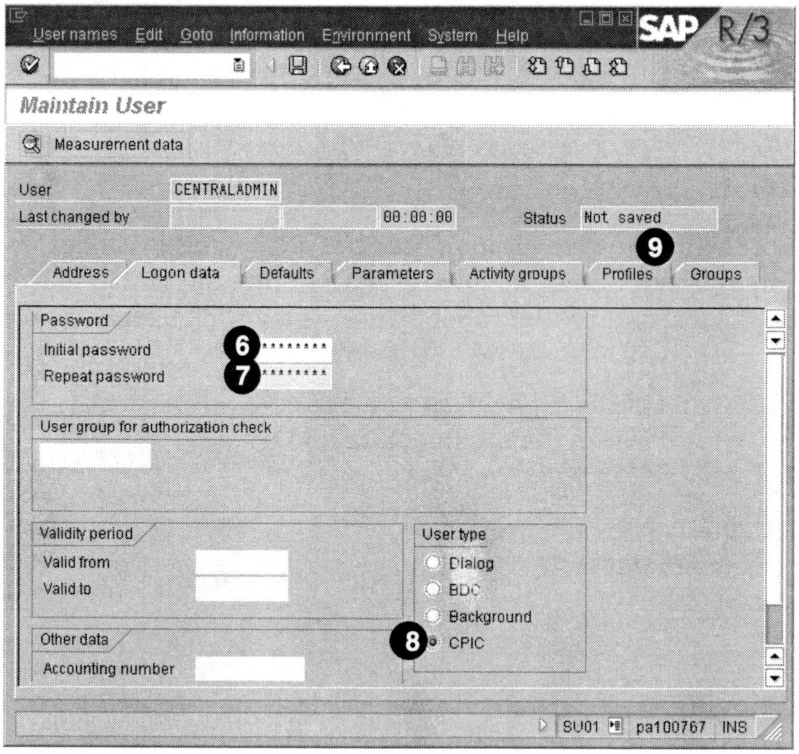

10. In the *Profl.* column, enter the profile **SAP_ALL**.
11. To save the user, choose .
12. Repeat steps 1–11 for all clients you want to set up for the ALE environment.

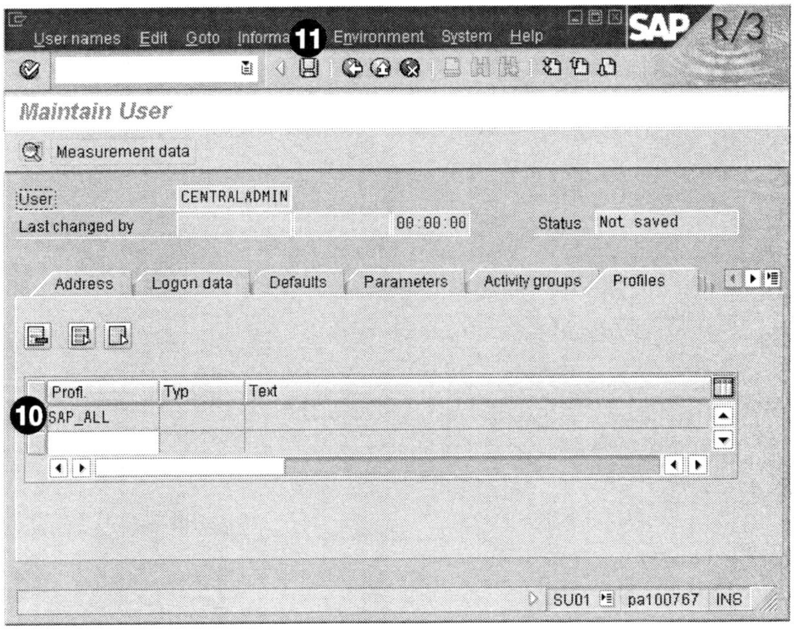


# Naming Logical Systems

1. In the *Command* field, enter transaction **SALE** and choose *Enter*.
2. Expand the nodes for *Sending and Receiving Systems* and *Logical Systems*.
3. Choose  next to the IMG activity *Name Logical System*.

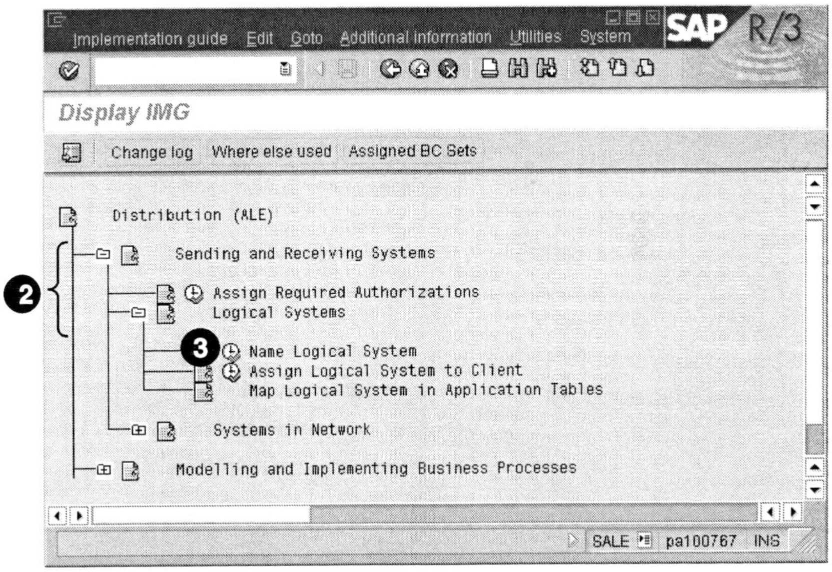


4. Note that the table is client-independent and choose .

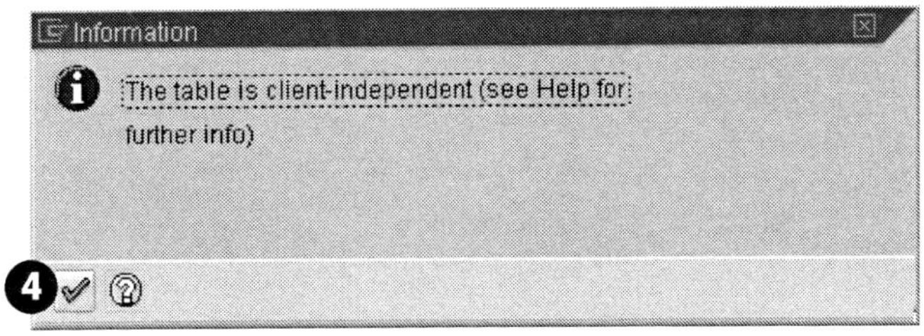

Tips & Tricks

The data for the logical systems is stored in a client-independent table. Therefore it is valid for all clients in an R/3 System. If your ALE environment consists only of logical systems in one R/3 System, you need to define the logical systems only once. If you are using multiple R/3 Systems, all logical systems need to be set up in every instance.

A table appears with all defined logical systems for the data distribution of your central R/3 system.

5. To add new logical systems into the list, choose *New entries.*

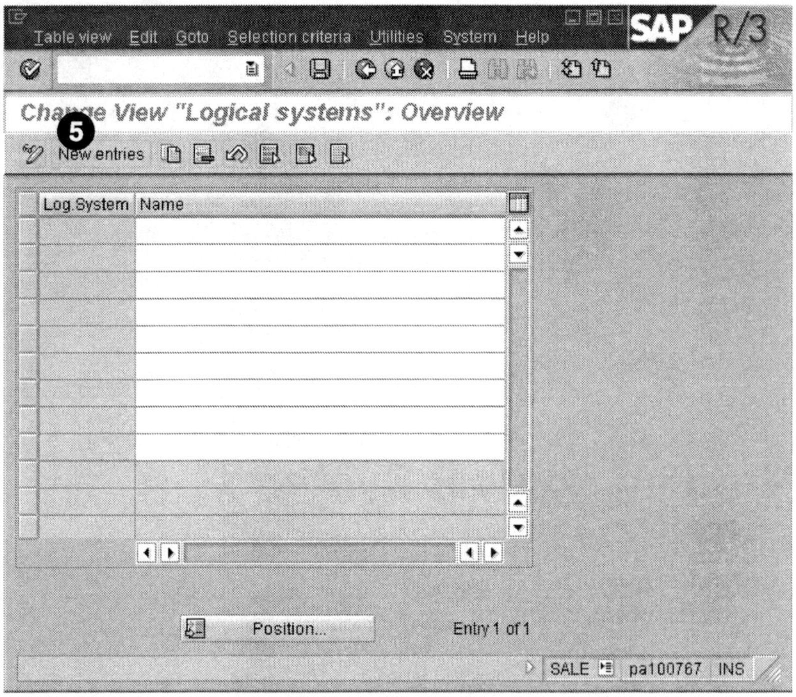


6. In the column *Log.System,* enter a short name in **capital letters** that you would like the system to be identified as in the ALE environment. Enter a clear description in the *Name* column for the logical system.
7. After entering all the logical systems, choose 💾 to save your data.

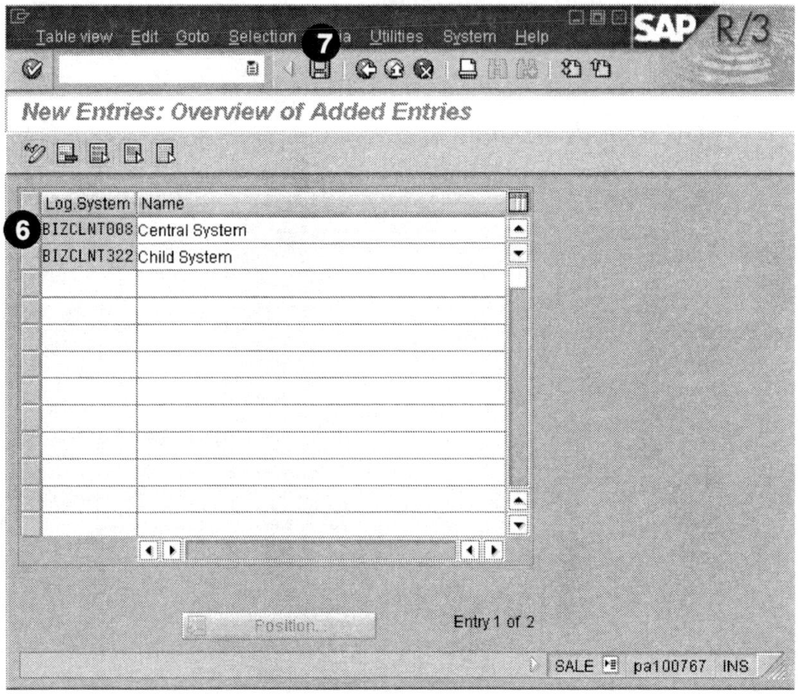


Caution

Remember to enter, if available, all logical systems that are not part of the actual R/3 Systems. All logical systems need to be defined in every R/3 System of the ALE environment.

Tips & Tricks

We recommend you name the system using a combination of the system name and client number (for example, for system BIZ with the client 008 the name *BIZCLNT008*).

Enter your transport request for the above entered data:

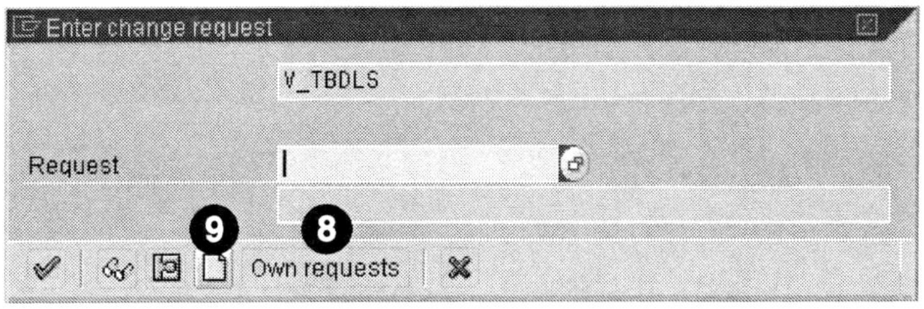


8. If you already have a transport request in this system, choose *Own request* and select it from the list and Continue with step 10.
9. If you do not have a transport request yet or would like to create a new one, choose .
   a. In *Short description*, enter a short description for the transport request.
   b. Choose .

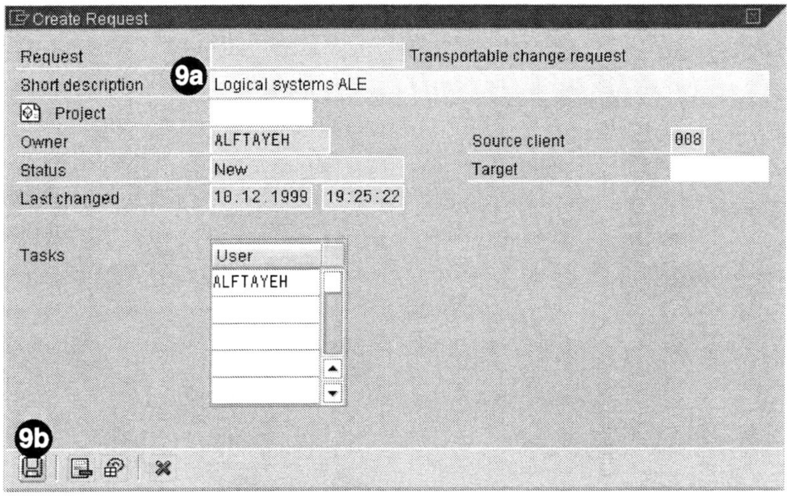


The system suggests a counting number for the request.

10. Choose ✔ to enter the transport request.

Caution

If your logical system is exclusively in one R/3 System, the naming process is now complete.

If your logical systems are in different R/3 Systems, you have to repeat steps 1–10 for each R/3 System. All logical systems need to be defined in all R/3 Systems of the ALE environment.

Tips & Tricks

Although you named the logical systems, you have not yet linked the logical systems to the existing clients in your R/3 System.

# Assigning Logical Systems to Clients

After naming the logical systems, the next step is to assign logical systems to clients. In this section, we link the newly named logical systems to the existing clients in your R/3 System.

1. From the last screen of the previous section, choose twice to return to transaction **SALE**.

2. Under the nodes *Sending and Receiving Systems* and *Logical Systems,* choose next to the IMG activity *Assign Logical System to Client*.

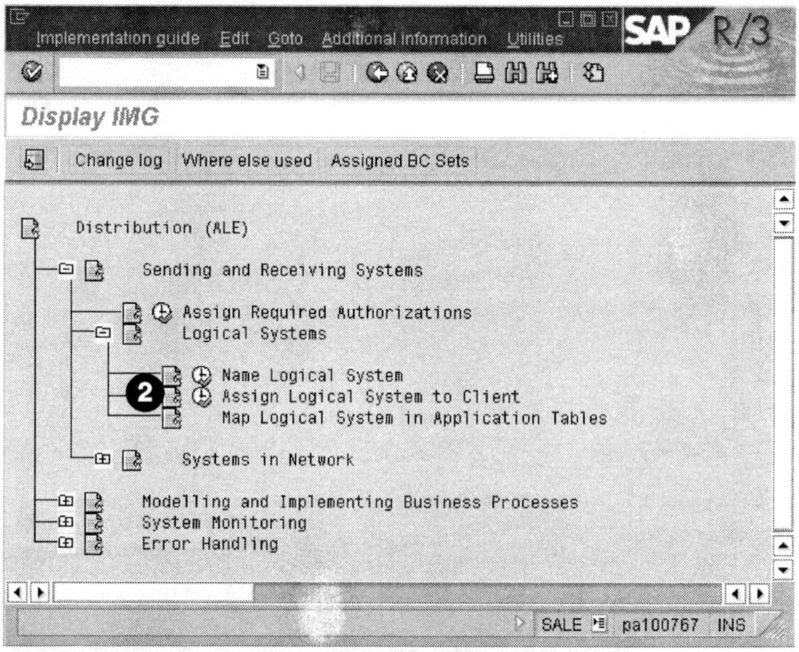


3. Note that the table is client-independent and choose to continue.

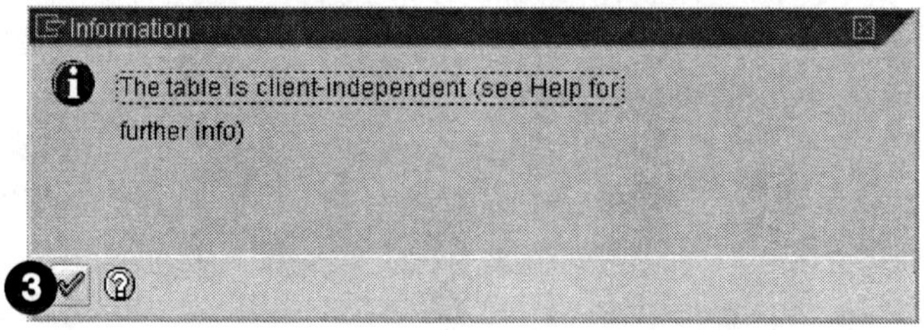

A list of available clients in this R/3 System appears.

4. Select the client to which you want to assign a logical system name and integrate into the ALE environment.
5. Choose .

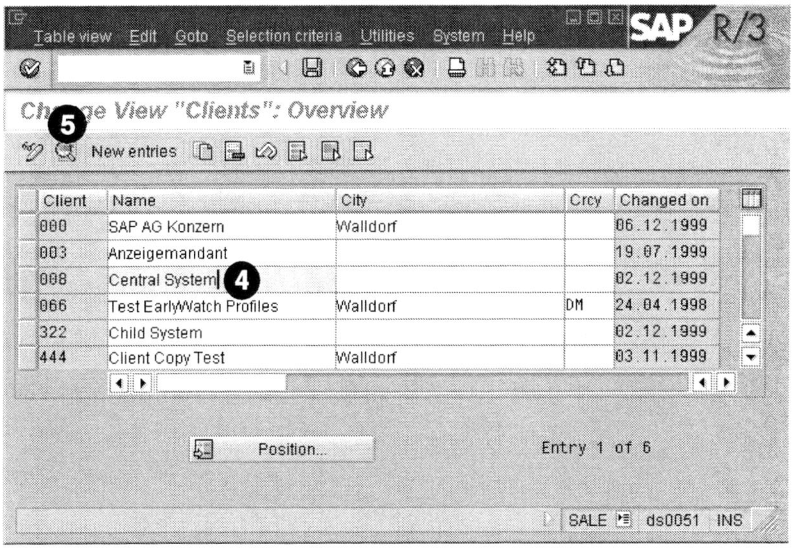


6. Enter a description for the client, if necessary.
7. To assign a logical system to that client, enter the logical system in **uppercase**.
8. Choose .
9. On the next window, choose  to proceed. You will receive a message that your data has been saved.
10. To assign another logical system to a client, choose  and repeat steps 4–9.

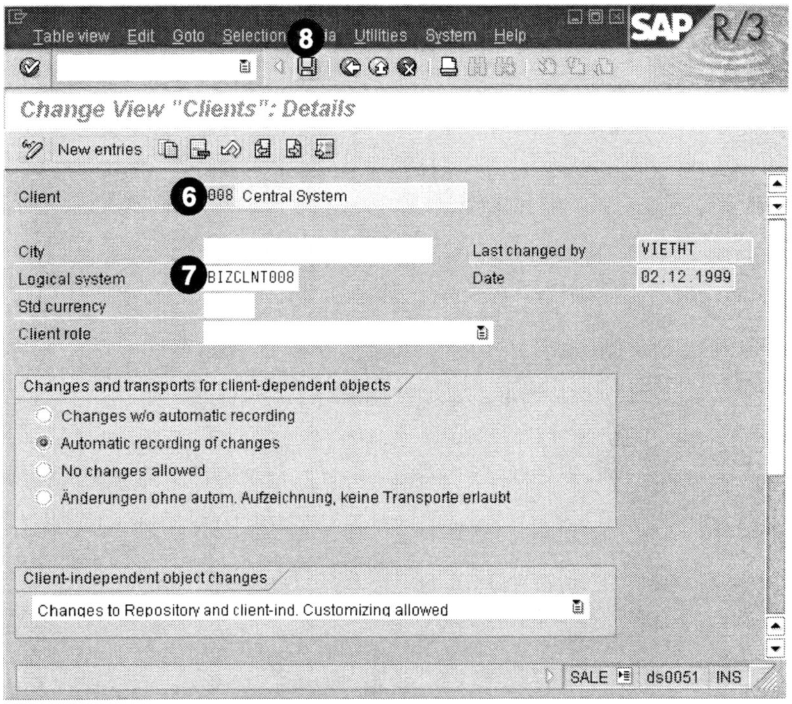

To assign a client of a different R/3 System to a logical system, log on to that R/3 System, start transaction **SALE**, and repeat steps 2–9.

# Defining Target System for RFC Calls

After assigning logical systems to clients, you must define the target system for RFC calls.

1. From the *Change View "Clients": Details* screen, choose twice to return to transaction **SALE**.
2. Under the nodes *Sending and Receiving Systems* and *Systems in Network,* choose next to the IMG activity *Define Target Systems for RFC calls.*

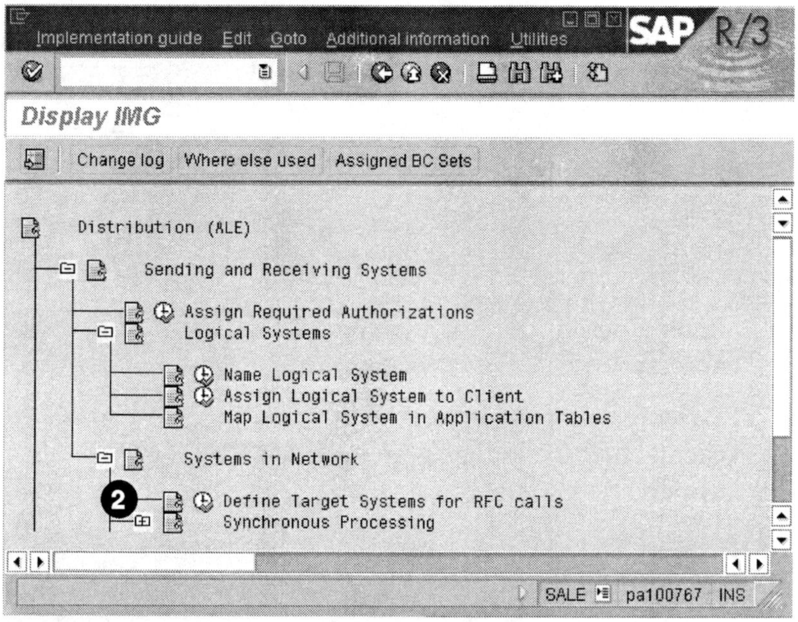


3. Choose *Create.*

Tips & Tricks

An RFC destination is always created from the client where you are currently logged on. To define an RFC connection from client 008 to client 322, you must be logged on to client 008. RFC connections for the Central User Administration always need a back-and-forth connection. To define the RFC connection completely, you also need to be logged on to client 322 and set up client 008 as the RFC connection.

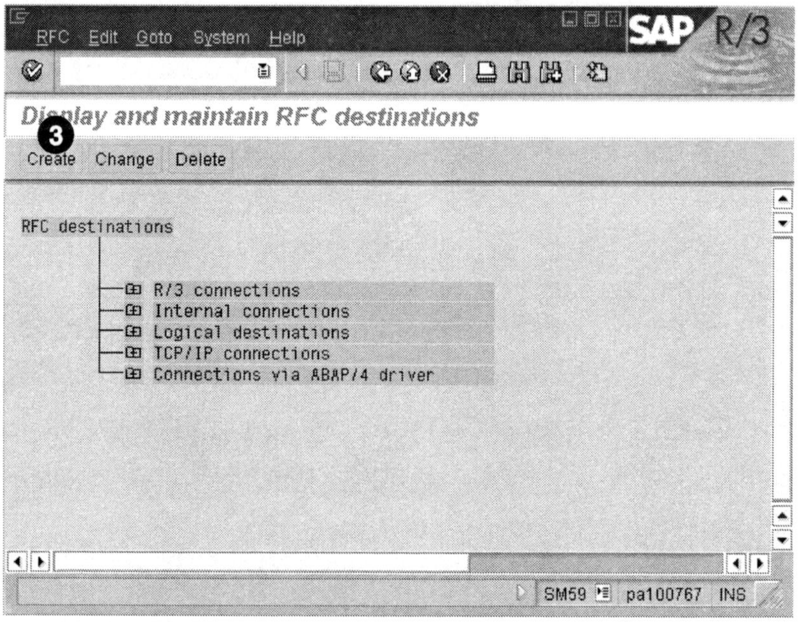

4. In *RFC destination*, enter the name of the logical sytem to which you want to define a RFC connection from your current system. Remember to use **uppercase**.
5. In *Connection type*, enter **3** (default value), if it is a connection to another R/3 System.
6. Under *Description*, enter a detailed description for the RFC destination.
7. In *Client*, enter the number of the target client.
8. In the *User* and *Password* field, enter the user and the corresponding password you specified for the internal communication of the systems in the ALE environment.
9. To save your data, choose 💾.

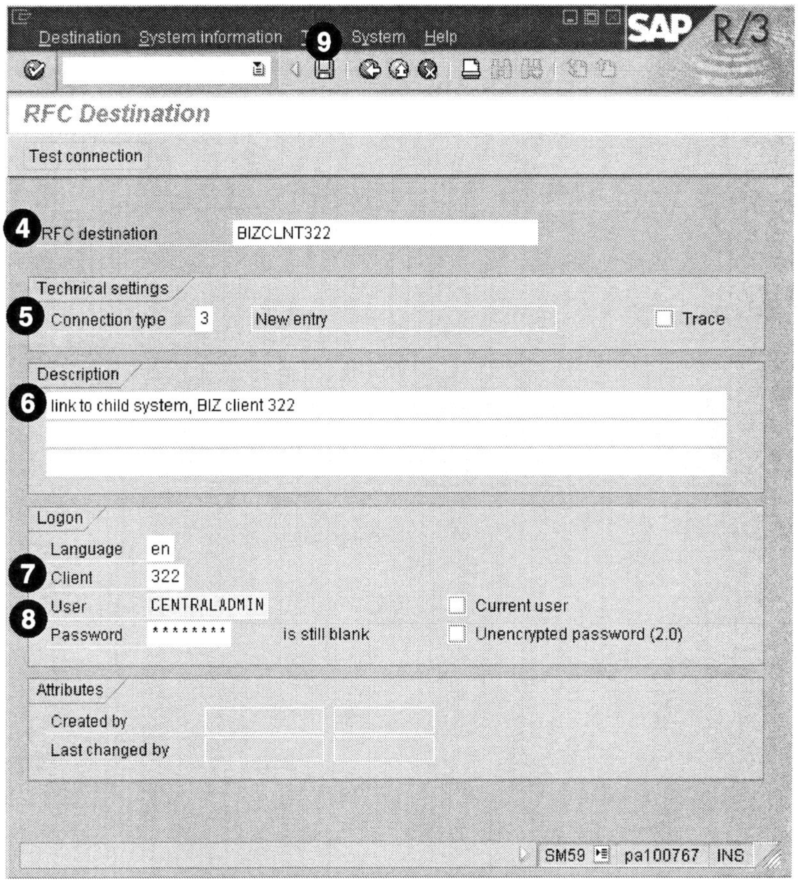

The message *Destination XXXX saved* appears.

New options appear on screen. You can now choose to use a load distribution (recommended). If you do not want to use the load distribution, skip ahead to step 14.

10. Select *Yes* for *Load distrib.*
11. In *Target host,* enter the number of the message server. See the *Tips & Tricks* below.
12. In *System number,* enter the system number of the message server. See the *Tips & Tricks* below.

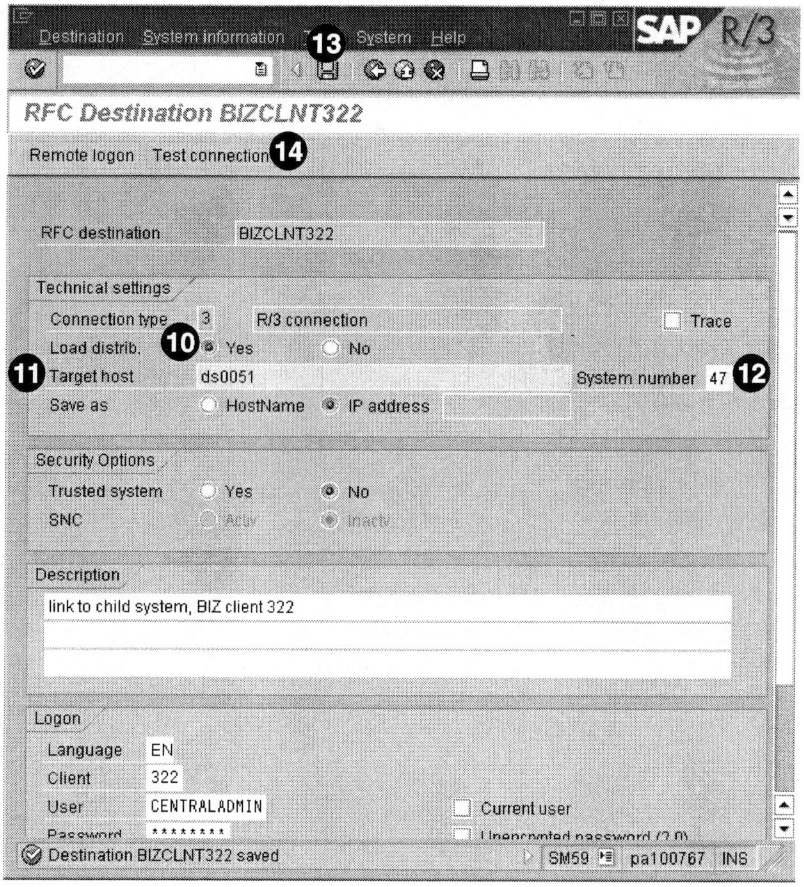


Tips & Tricks

To find the name of the message server of the target host, go to the target system and start transaction **RZ03**. Usually you will see a list with several server names. The correct message server is the one that has an *M* listed in the *Services* column. The name of the message server appears as the first part of the *Server name,* in front of the underscore. The last two digits of the *Server name* represent the system number.

13. To save your data, choose .

    A status message appears saying: *Destination XXXX saved.*

14. Choose *Test connection* to test if the connection works correctly.

A correct connection test looks like the screen to the right.

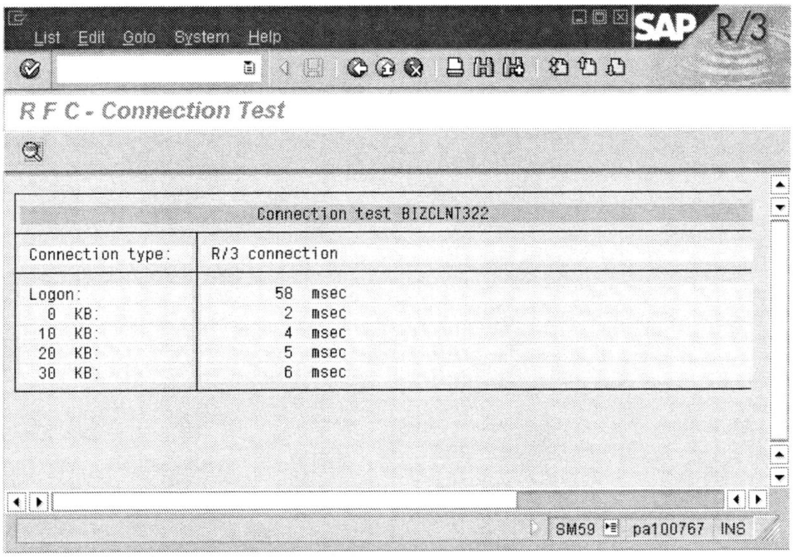


Tips & Tricks

A test with *Remote login* would not work if you used the *System user* (CPIC) for the connection. If you used a *Dialog user*, you can use *Remote Login* for an additional test connection.

To enter another RFC destination in the same R/3 System, choose twice and repeat steps 3–14.

To enter another RFC destination in a different R/3 System, log on to that system, start transaction **SALE**, and repeat steps 3–14.

# Distribution Model

The distribution model describes the ALE message flow between logical systems.

1. Log on to the central system of the ALE environment.
2. In the *Command* field, enter transaction **BD64** and choose *Enter*.
3. Choose to switch between display and edit mode.

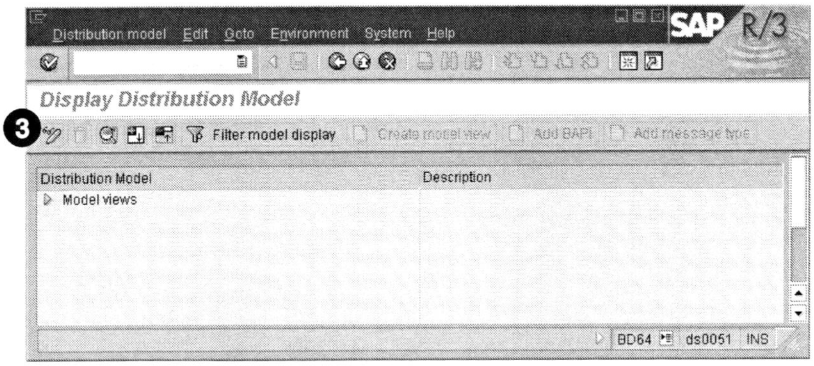

4. Choose *Create model view*.

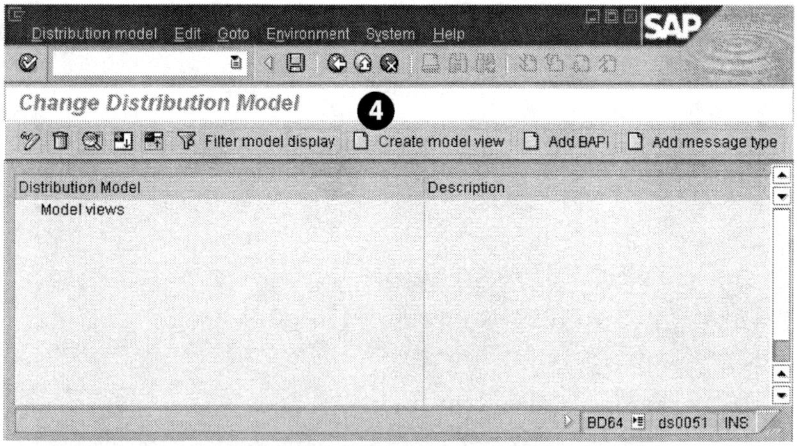


5. In *Short text*, enter a short description.
6. In *Technical name*, enter a technical name for the model view.
7. Choose ✔.

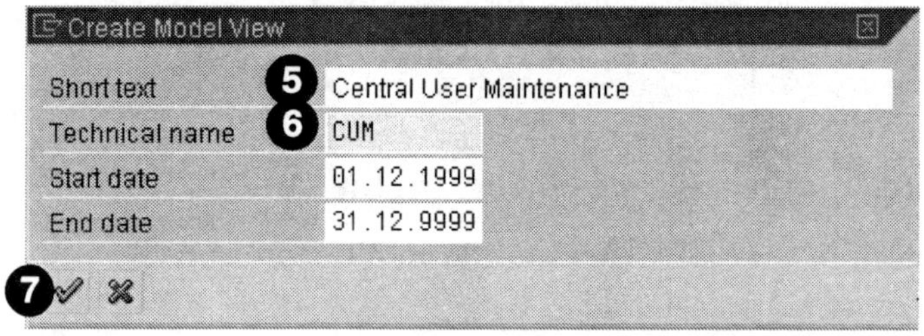


8. Choose ▷ in front of *Model views* to receive a list of all model views, including the one you just created.

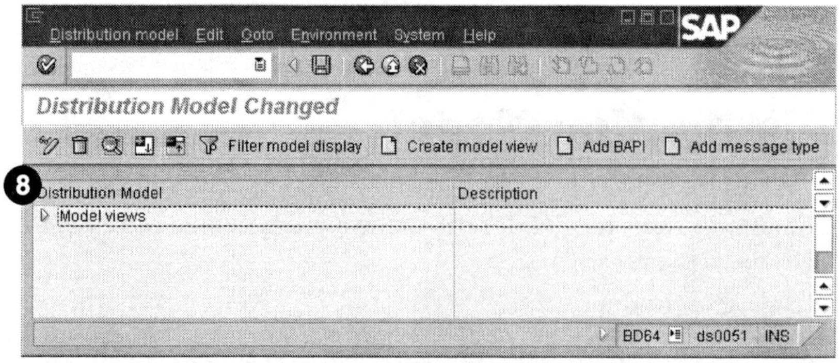


9. Select the just created model view. The entry will be highlighted.
10. Choose *Add BAPI*.

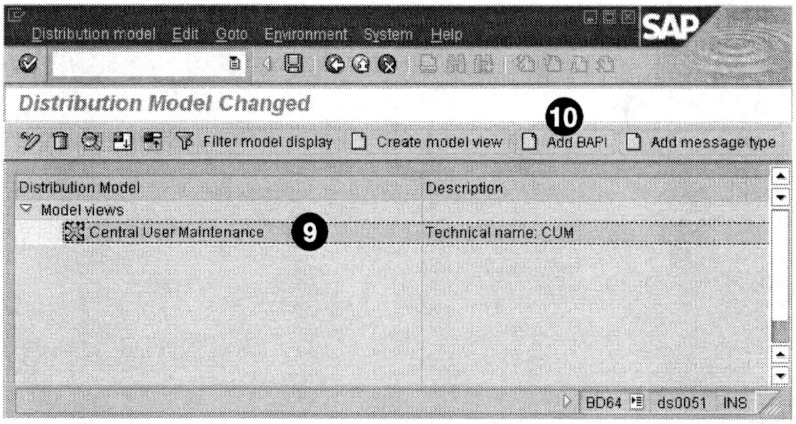


Tips & Tricks

To distribute the data, you have to define two methods for the newly created distribution model. Within Central User Administration one of the methods is for the distribution of the user, and one for the company. These methods are realized through BAPIs (Business Application Programming Interface).

11. In *Model view,* enter the technical name of the newly created distribution model.
12. In *Sender/client,* enter the logical system name of the central system.
13. In *Receiver/server,* enter the the logical system name of the client system.
14. In *Obj.name/interface,* enter the object **USER** (note that this entry is case-sensitive).
15. In *Method,* enter **Clone** (note that this entry is case-sensitive).
16. Choose ✔.

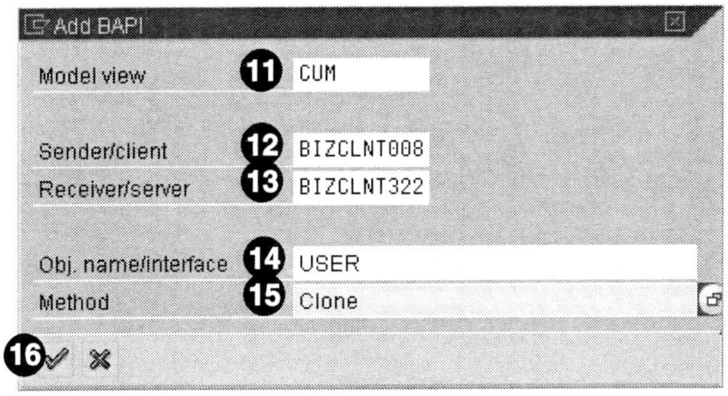


17. Repeat step 10–16 to add a method for the company address. Enter **UserCompany** in step 14 instead of **USER** (note that the entry is case-sensitive).
18. Choose ✔.

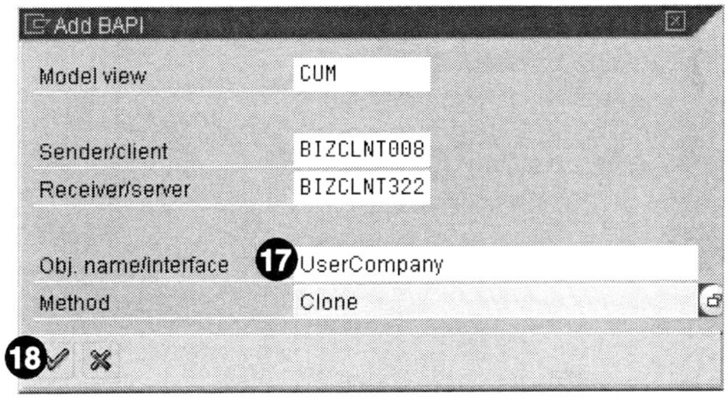

If there are more than two systems in your planned ALE environment, repeat 10–16 for all other client systems.

19. To save the data, choose 💾.

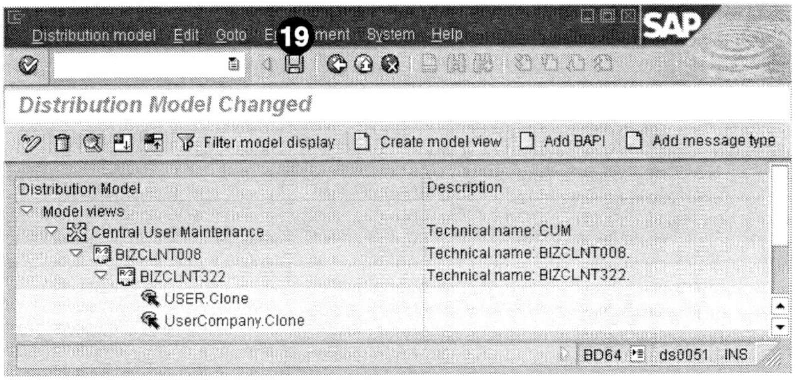


If you expand the model view completely using ▷, your model view for a two-system ALE environment should look like the screen to the right.

# Generating Partner Profiles in the Central System

Prior to the generation of the partner profiles, which sets the conditions for the electronic data exchange in the ALE environment, you first choose the parameters in the current model view as described below.

1. On the *Distribution Model Changed* screen, choose *Environment* → *Generate Partner Profiles.*

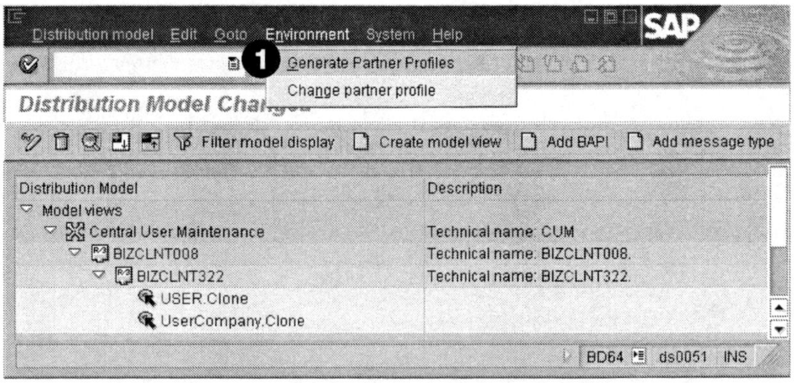


2. In *Model view*, enter the technical name of the newly created model view. Use uppercase letters.
3. In *Partner system*, enter the logical system name of the client system.

Tips & Tricks

If there are more client systems in your ALE environment, select those logical systems using [button].

4. Choose [icon].

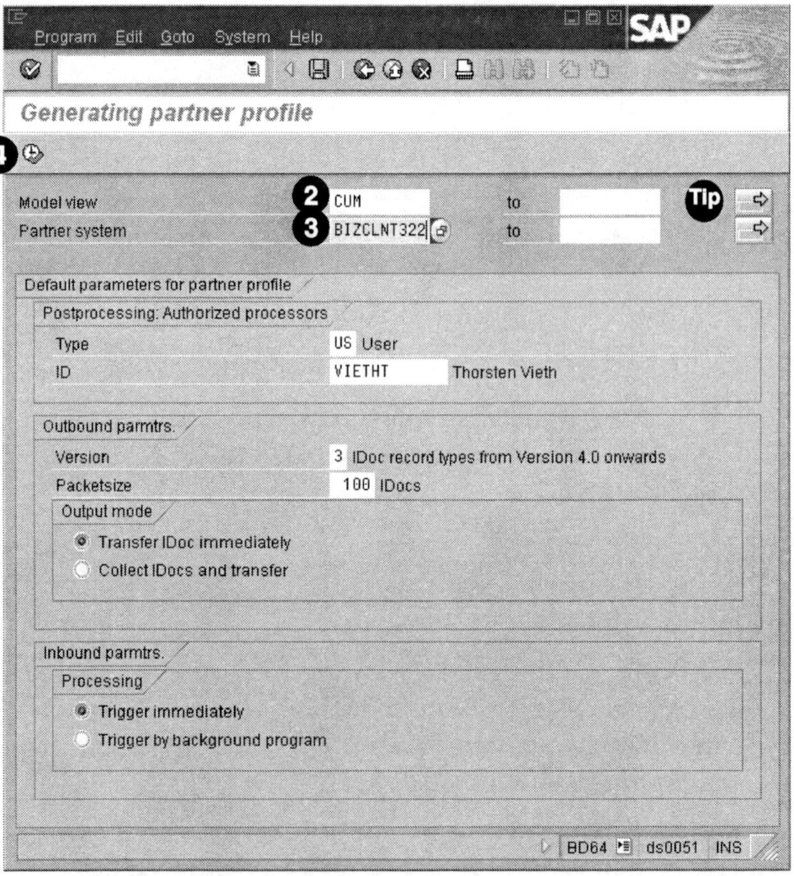


Tips & Tricks

To improve performance, you can select under *Packetsize* how many IDocs (data container exchange between R/3 Systems) will be sent for each RFC process. The suggested value of 100 IDocs is a compromise to keep the number of dialog processes down and at the same time, quickly process changes. To increase the performance, choose a smaller number of IDocs to be sent for every RFC process.

5. You receive the *Protocol for generating partner profile*. Check if the partner profiles have been created successfully.
6. Choose twice to return to the start screen in *BD64*.

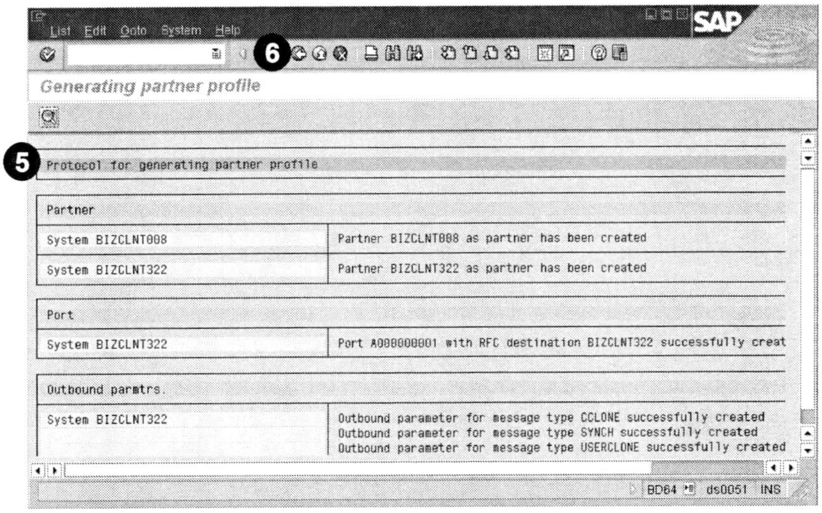


# Distributing Model View

1. Select the model view created earlier. The entry will be highlighted.
2. Choose *Edit → Model view → Distribute*.

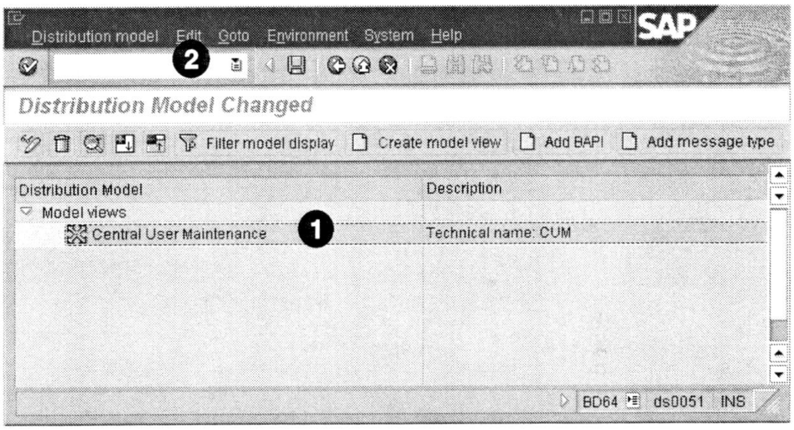


A list appears with all existing client systems in the ALE environment to which the model view needs to be distributed.

3. Select the desired system.
4. Choose .

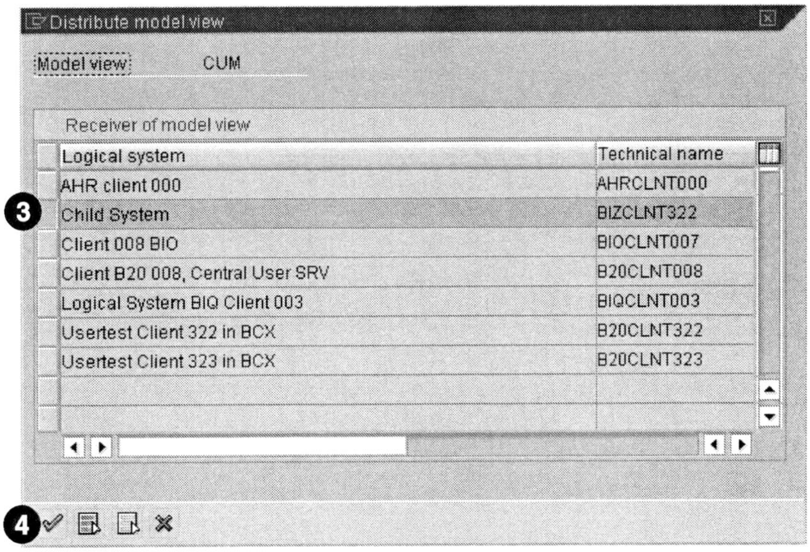

You receive a log if the model view has been created in the client system.

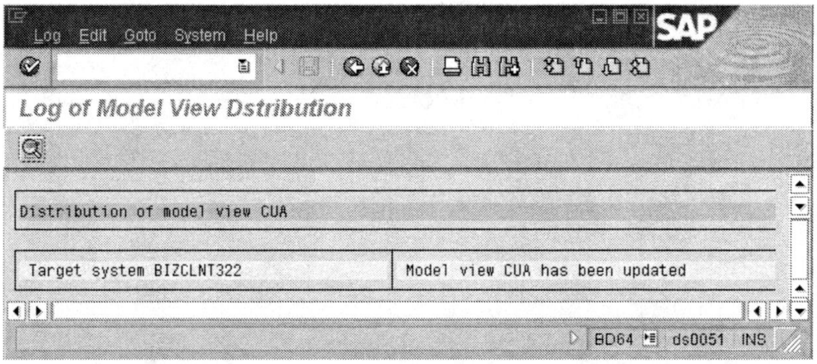

To check if the model view has been established for the client system, perform the following steps:

1. Log on to the desired client system.
2. Start transaction **SCUA**.
3. Enter the technical name of the model view.
4. Choose *Distribution model → Display structure.*

# Generating Partner Profiles in the Client System

1. Log on to the client system.
2. In the *Command* field, enter transaction **BD64** and choose *Enter*.
3. Select the model view created earlier. The entry will be highlighted.
4. Choose *Environment → Generate Partner Profiles.*

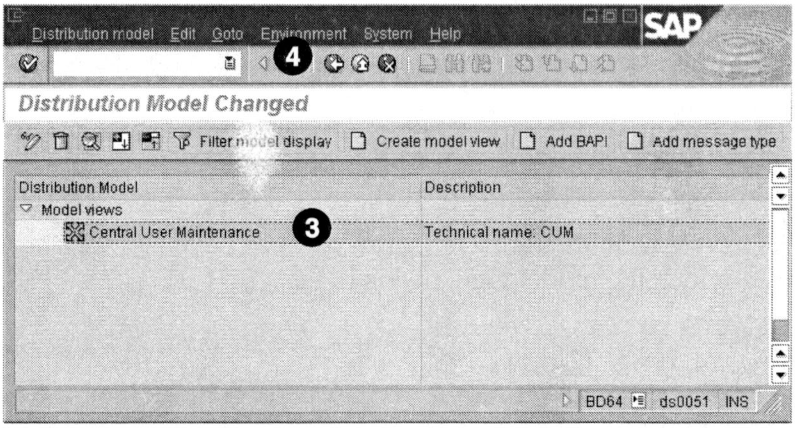

5. In *Model view*, enter the technical name of the newly created model view. Use uppercase.
6. In *Partner system*, enter the logical system name of the central system.

   With this entry, you establish the partner profile for the return conection from the client system to the central system.
7. Choose .

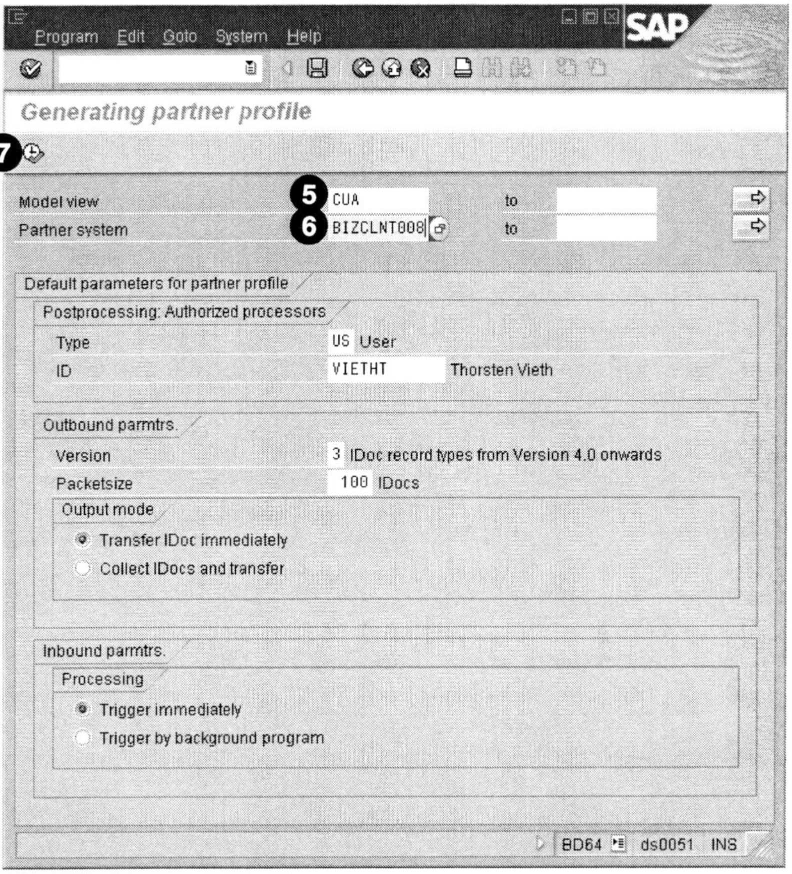


You receive the *Protocol for generating partner profile*. Check if the partner profiles have been created successfully.

Repeat steps 1–7 for all client systems, if neccessary.

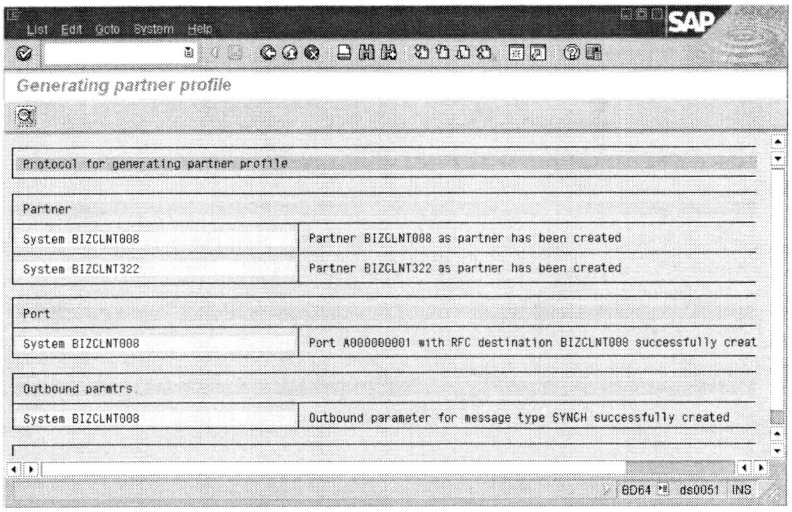


You have now set up the complete ALE environment.

# Chapter 11: Setting Up Central User Administration

## Contents

# Overview

With Central User Administration you can reduce the system administrator's effort to maintain users in the R/3 environment. Central User Administration allows you to maintain the users centrally in one system. The information is then automatically distributed to the dependent systems.

To set up Central User Administration, we assume that you use one user account that has system administrator authorizations for the complete system environment.

> **Tips & Tricks**
> To set up the Central User Administration for your R/3 System group, you need to set up the ALE environment (as described in chapter 10, *Setting Up the ALE Environment for Central User Administration)* for your central system. This central system must now be set up for the user maintenance.

# Assigning the Central User Administration Distribution Model

1. Log on to your central system.
2. In the *Command* field, enter transaction **SCUA** and choose *Enter*.
3. In *Model view*, enter the technical name of the distribution model as created for the ALE environment.

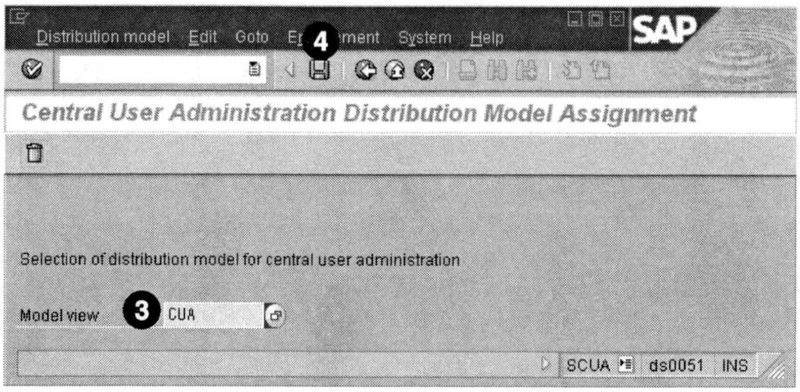


> **Tips & Tricks**
> The model you choose here is the basis for the distribution of user data in your ALE environment.

4. Choose [Save icon].

> **TechTalk**
> Saving the model assignment for the Central User Administration distributes the complete distribution model to all client systems. After the distribution, you can no longer create a user in the client system. From this point forward, a system is defined as the central system and the other systems as client systems of Central User Administration.

Check if the model has been assigned as the client system:

5. Log on to the client system.
6. In the *Command* field, enter transaction **SCUA** and choose *Enter*. The distribution model is entered automatically.
7. Choose D*istribution model* → *Display structure*.

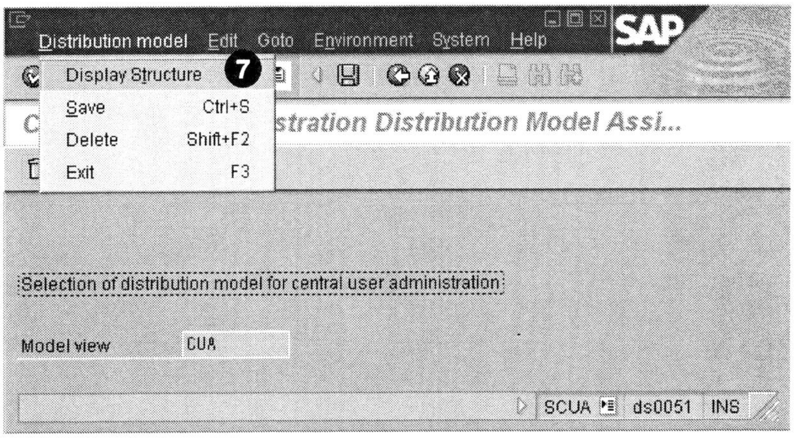


A complete view of the model structure appears.

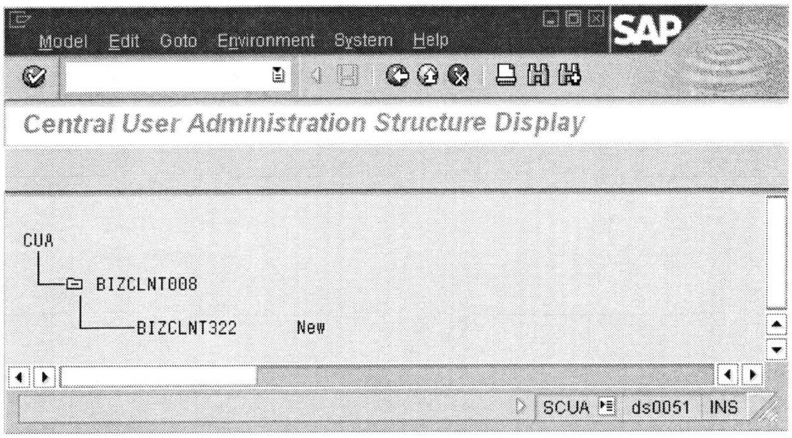

If you do not see any structure, it could be because the data has been distributed asynchronously. If this is the case, go back to the start screen of transaction **SCUA**, wait for two minutes, and repeat step 7.

# Testing Central User Administration

1. In the *Command* field of the central system, enter transaction **SU01** and choose *Enter*.
2. In *User*, enter a user name for the test user.
3. Choose 🗋.

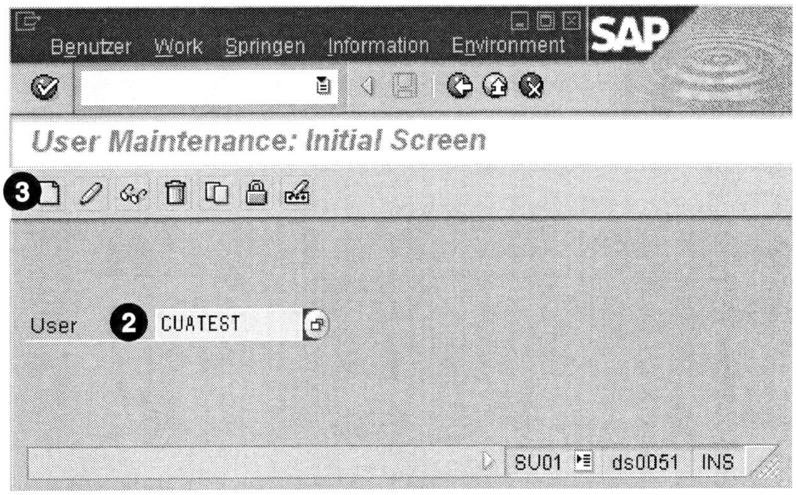

4. On the *Address* tab, enter at least a last name.
5. Choose the *Logon data* tab.

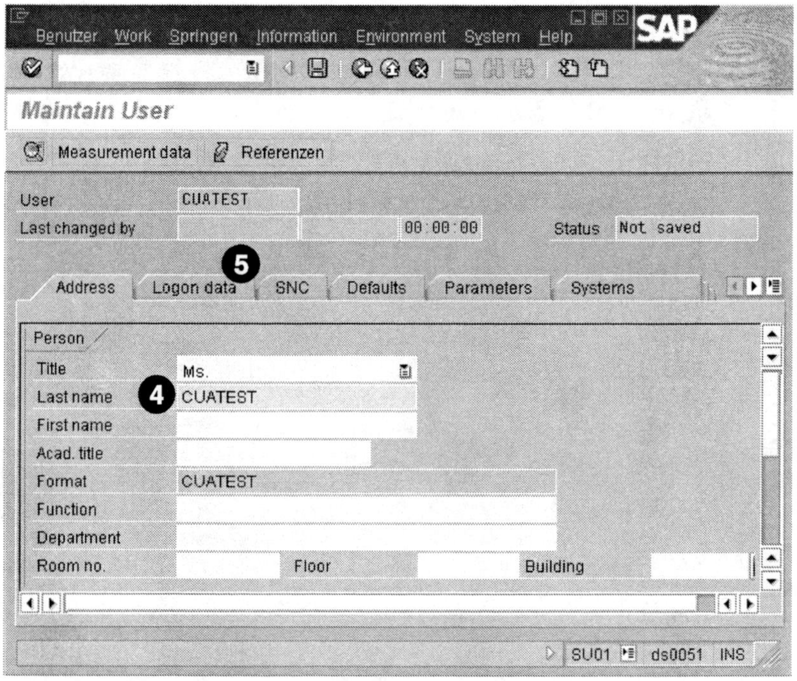


6. Enter an *Initial password* for the test user. You must change the initial password at first logon to the R/3 System.
7. Reenter the initial password.
8. Choose the *Systems* tab.

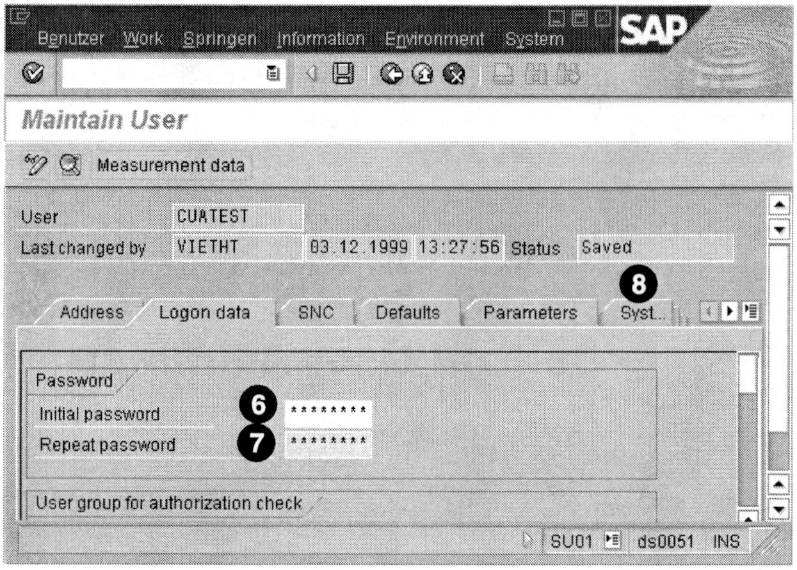

9. In the *System* column, enter the logical names of the central system and of all the client systems in the systems table.
10. Choose the *Activity groups* tab.

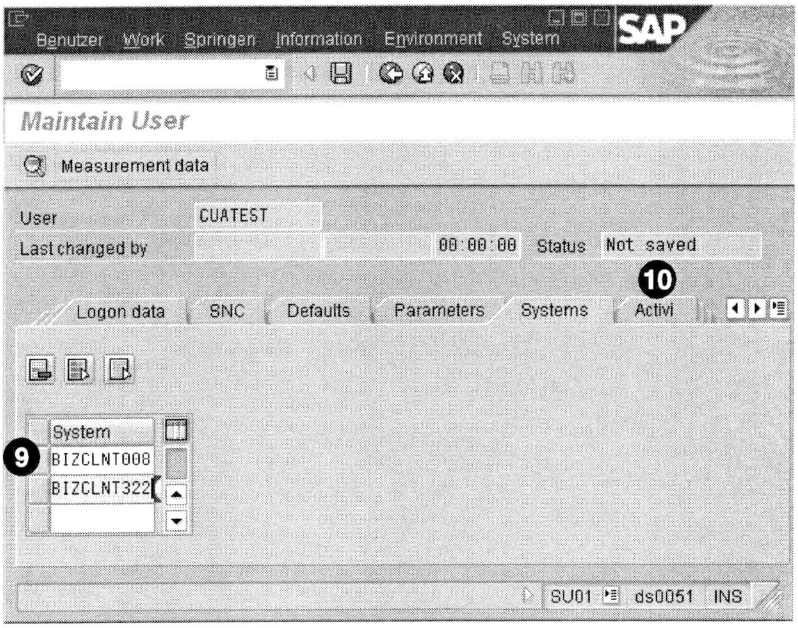


11. Choose *Text comparison from child sys.*

Tips & Tricks

A text comparison is needed to provide the central system with available activity groups from the client system. Only if this step has been performed can activity groups of the client systems be displayed and selected in the central system using *possible entries*. It is also possible to assign activity groups manually from the client system without the text comparison.

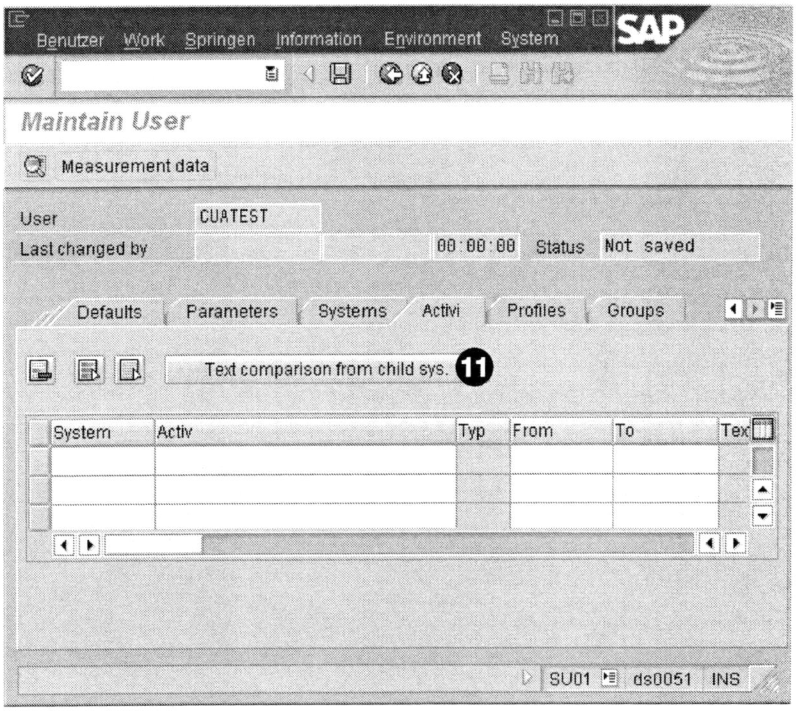


12. Read the dialog window and choose ✔ to continue.

Assign an activity group to the test user in every logical system of the system group:

13. In the *System* column, enter all the logical systems.
14. In the *Activ* column, enter the activity group you want to assign to the test user in the corresponding system (for test purposes, it is enough to assign one activity group per system).
15. Choose [save icon].

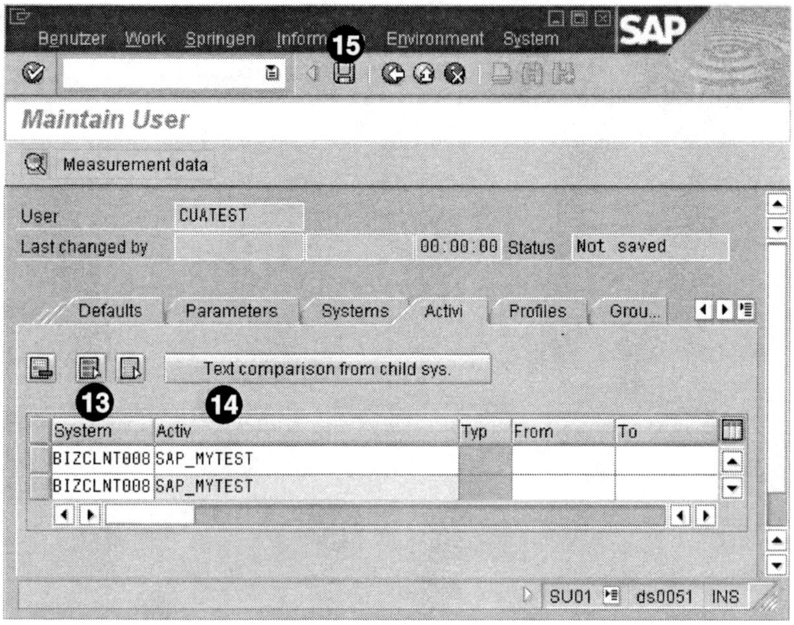


TechTalk

Saving starts the distribution process automatically. The user is created with the activity group assignment in every defined system.

The user maintenance jumps back to the start screen of *SU01*.

You receive the message *User … was saved.* You can now check if the user data has been distributed correctly.

16. Choose *Environment → Distribution log* (transaction **SCUL**).

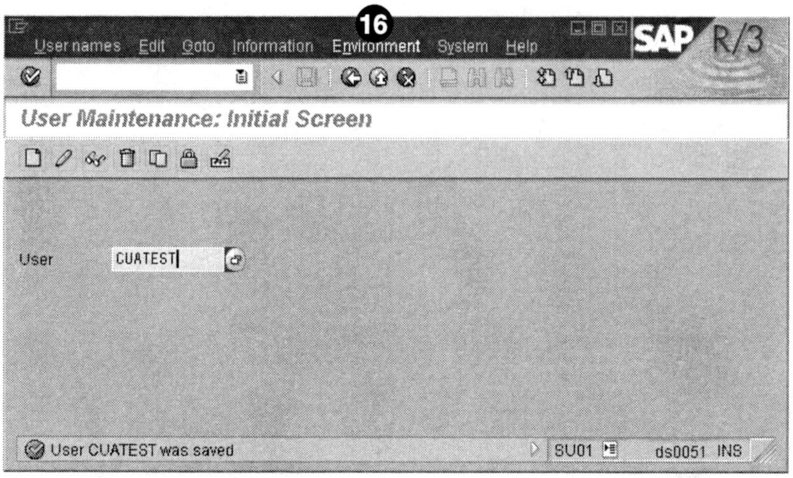

A series of buttons provides access to different log displays.

If you choose *System reports*, you receive the user status sorted by client systems. If you expand the tree, you receive the users of the client systems.

An overview about *Errors, Warnings, Successful,* and *New/unconfirmed* distributions is displayed. Unconfirmed distributions could result from a faulty RFC connection.

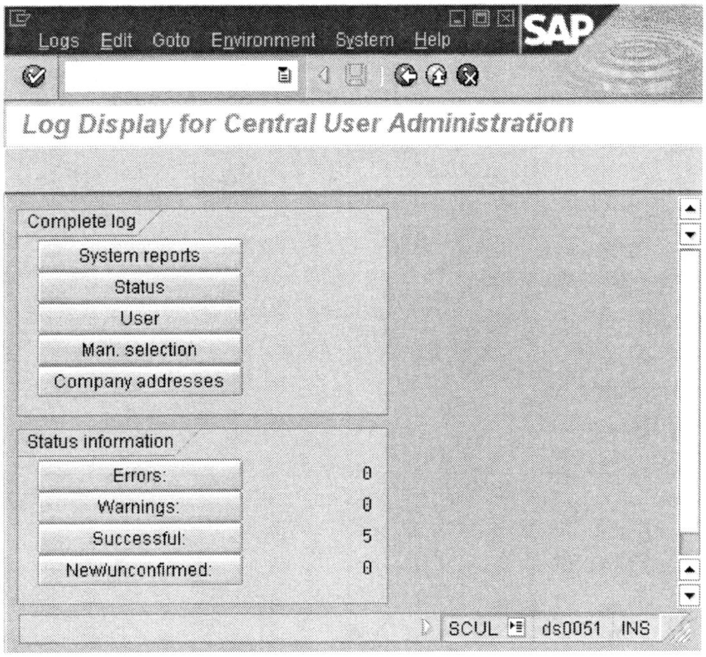


# Migrating Existing Users to the Central System

If you already set up user accounts in the client systems, these users need to be migrated to the central system. If this action has already been performed, you can maintain the user data centrally.

1. In the *Command* field of the central system, enter transaction **SCUG** and choose *Enter*.
2. Select the client system from where you would like to migrate the user data.
3. Choose *Transfer users*.

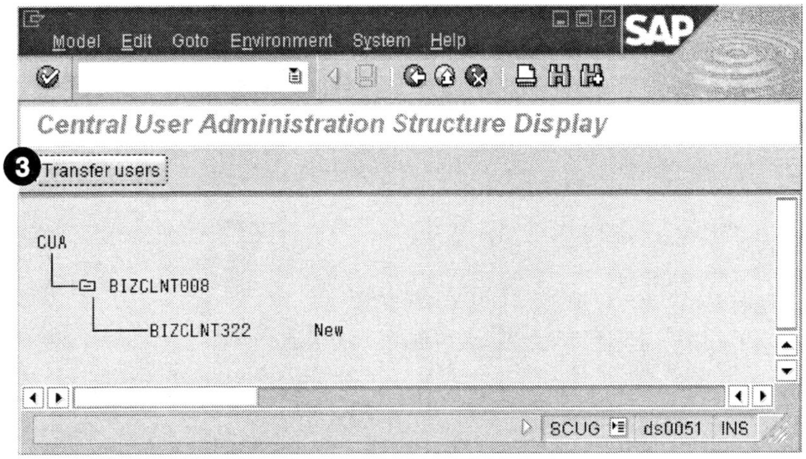

On the *New users* tab, you can see all user accounts available in the client system, but **not** in the central system. You can migrate all these users into the Central User Administration.

4. To select all, choose .
5. Choose  *Transfer users.*
6. Choose the *Identical users* tab.

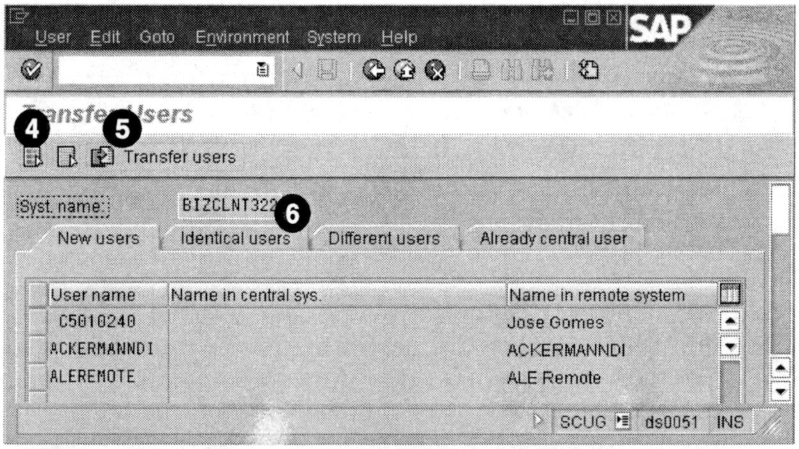


On the *Identical users* tab, all user accounts with identical first and last names in the client and central system are displayed. All of these users can be migrated to Central User Administration. They will also get the client system assigned in Central User Administration.

7. To select all, choose .
8. Choose  *Transfer users.*
9. Choose the *Different users* tab.

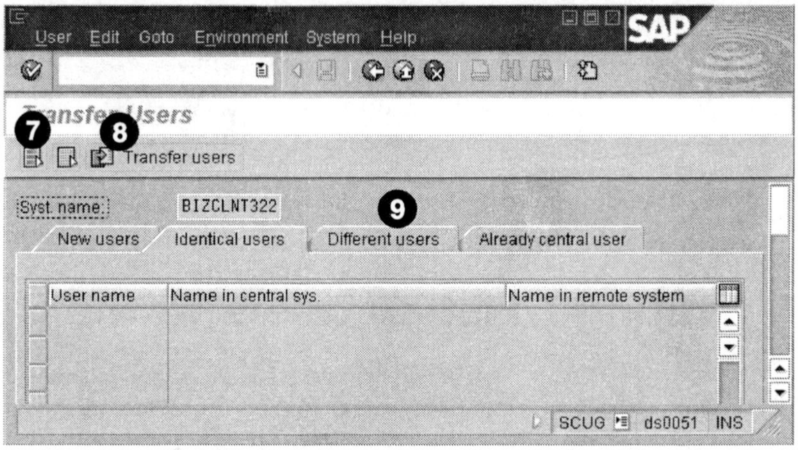


On the *Different users* tab, all user accounts with the same user ID (but with names that are different in the client or central system) are displayed.

10. If the user is correct in the central system, proceed with the following:
    a. Select the desired entry.
    b. Choose  *Transfer users.*
11. If the user is correct in the client system, proceed with the following:
    a. Enter the same name in the central system as it is displayed in the client system. The user is now displayed under the *Identical users* tab.
    b. Select the desired entry.
    c. Choose  *Transfer users.*

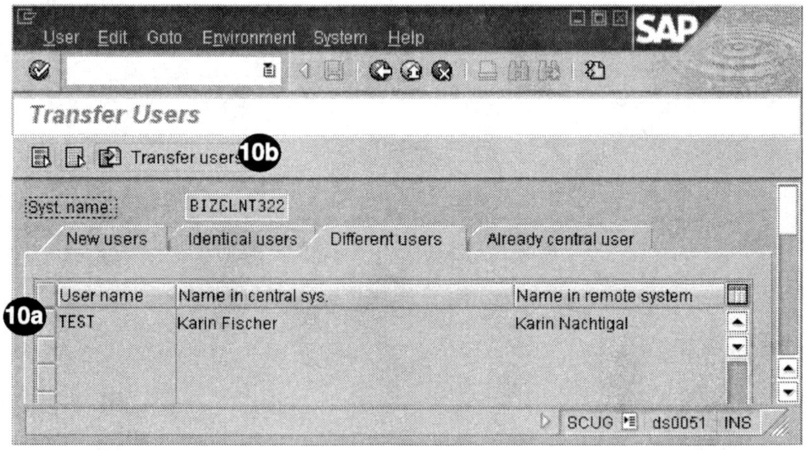

If the different names result from dealing with two different persons, you have to change the user names using **SU01** either in the central or client system. The user name of the client system can be found on the *New users* tab afterwards.

On the *Already central user* tab, all user accounts are displayed that have been migrated using one of the above steps, or have been created in the central system of Central User Administration.

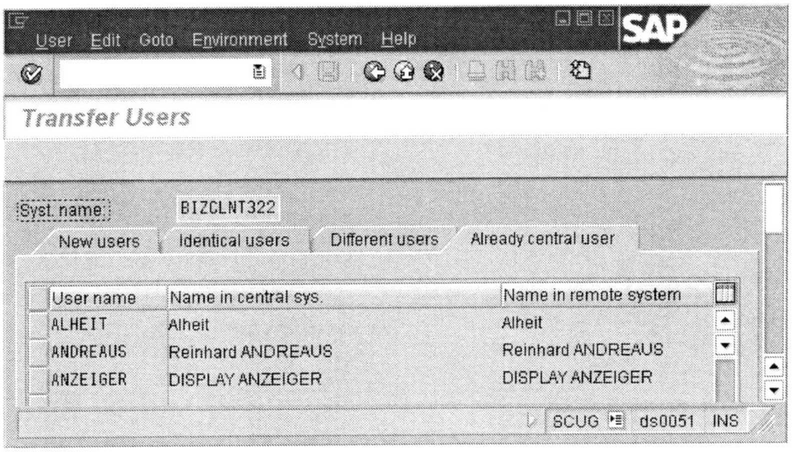


## Defining Field Attributes for User Maintenance

Although it is no longer possible to create users in the client system, you can maintain already existing user data in the client system. Therefore, it is useful to define (at the field level) if and how this data should be maintained. In the following procedure, we demonstrate how to define field attributes:

1. In the *Command* field, enter transaction **SCUM** and choose *Enter*.
2. Allocate on all tabs for each field the attributes described in the table below. Not all attributes can be selected for every field.
3. Choose [Save icon].

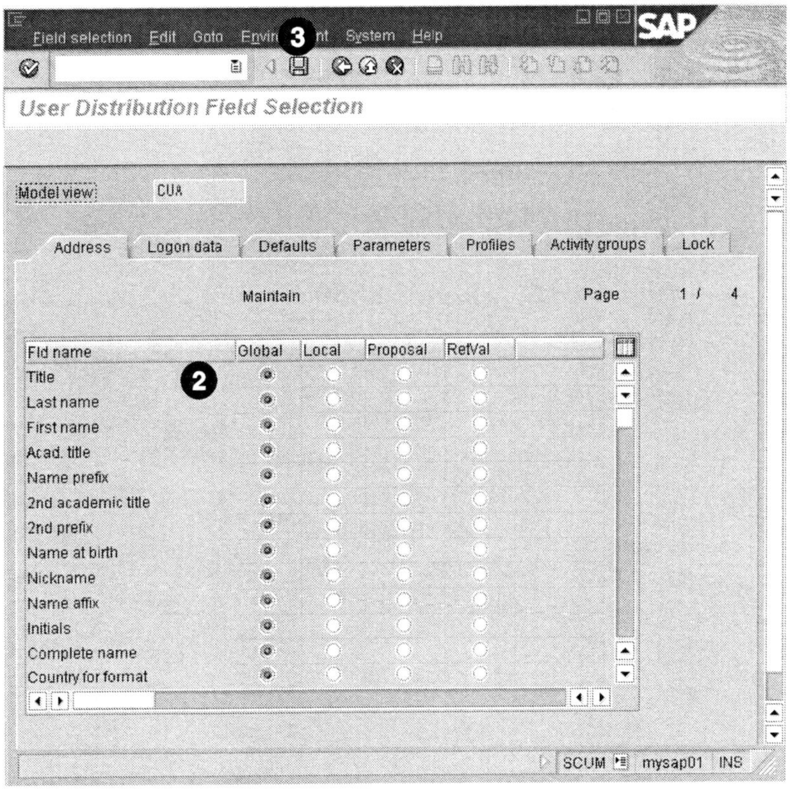

| Attribute | Description |
| --- | --- |
| Global | The data can only be maintained in the central system and is distributed from there into the client systems. |
| Local | The data can only be maintained in the client system and is not distributed. |
| Proposal | During the creation of a user, the suggested value is maintained and then distributed to the client systems. After the distribution, the data is maintained only locally. If a new client system is connected to Central User Administration, the proposed value is distributed to this system. If the proposed value is changed in the central system, it is only distributed to the new systems. Already existing systems are not affected. |
| RetVal | The user data can be maintained in the central system as well as the client system. The changes made in the client system are redistributed to the central system. From there, the data is distributed to all other client systems. |
| Everywhere | The user data can be maintained in the central system and the client system. The changes in the client system are not distributed anywhere. The changes affect only this client system. |

The installation of the Central User Administration is now complete.

# Global User Manager

The **Global User Manager** is an optional tool that simplifies your work with Central User Administration. You can still use the user maintenance transaction and the Profile Generator (PG) to assign users and activity groups.

You now have the option to use different grouping types on the user and system level with the Global User Manager. The grouping is carried out through user groups on the user level and through system types for the system.

These maintenance options are combined in the Global User Manager since there are usually no changes to other data in the user master data after the creation of the user. However, system and authorization assignments are an ongoing process.

Caution

If you are not completely finished with setting up the user data, do not distribute the user data using the Global User Manager. Everything that is not defined in the Global User Manager will be deleted in the target system.

Tips & Tricks

It is not possible to assign authorization profiles directly to users or user groups with the Global User Manager. The authorizations are assigned through activity groups. If you want to create an activity group automatically from an existing authorization profile, use transaction **SU25**, step 6. *Copy data from old profiles.*

The main advantage of the Global User Manager is that you never have to view the complete system landscape to assign authorizations. In every task, you only look at a small part of the complete landscape. The diagram below shows that you only look at two sides of the assignment triangle.

| Source | Target |
|---|---|
| User/User group | System/System type |
| System/System type | Activity group/Composite activity group |
| Activity group/Composite activity group | User/User group |

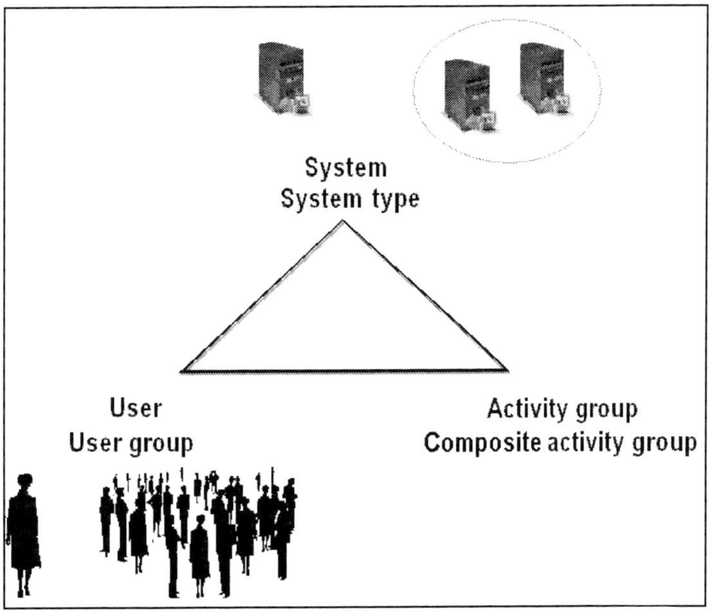


Caution

To model a complete assignment for distribution in the target systems you need to create a closed triangle for that assignment as shown in the graphic above. To reduce the complexity of this process, the Global User Manager is set up in such a way that you only have to assign the other two angles. Once you have completed each of the three angles, the assignments are complete.

# Structure of the Global User Manager

Tips & Tricks

The Global User Manager can only be used in the central system of Central User Administration.

To start the Global User Manager, enter transaction **SUUM** in the *Command* field and choose *Enter*.

On the left tile, all users and user groups in the system environment are displayed.

In the middle tile, all the systems and system groups are displayed.

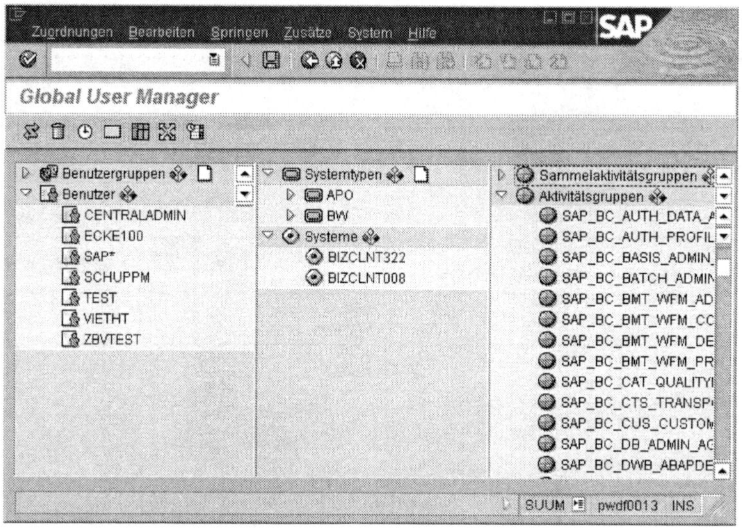


On the right tile, all activity groups and composite activity groups in the system environment are displayed.

Caution

To display the activity groups and composite activity groups of the client system, in the *Global User Manager* choose *Extras → System comparison*. Alternatively, you can perform the *Text comparison for child sys.* on the *Activity groups* tab in user maintenance transaction **SU01** (as described earlier). Note that it may take some time for the data to become available since it is distributed asynchronously.

# Using the Global User Manager

The use of the Global User Manager depends on whether or not there were users in your system landscape before the installation of central user management.

If users already exist, it is advisable to migrate that user master data into the Global User Manager. This ensures that the user data will not be deleted with the first distribution.

## System Landscape with Existing Users

If you want to use the Global User Manager in a system landscape with an existing and productive user, proceed as described below:

1. In the *Command* field, enter transaction **SUUM** and choose *Enter*.
2. From the standard menu bar:

- Choose *Extras → Migration → User* to display the current status of user master records in all systems in the Global User Manager.
- Choose *Extras → Migration → Activity groups* to assign activity groups automatically in the valid systems in the Global User Manager.

Caution

The data is only updated on the single user level with the current status in the Global User Manager after the migration. Do not start with the creation of user groups and system types if you are not completely finished with the migration.

Tips & Tricks

Activity groups should be named clearly in the system landscape. The system landscape acts like a single system. Therefore an activity group should only exist once in this system. If an activity group with the same name exists in multiple systems in the system landscape, it will appear multiple times in the activity group list in the Global User Manager.

Caution

In the Global User Manager you can create assignments on the single user level, as well as on the user group level. This ability may lead to unwanted effects after a user migration.

For example, you migrated all developers in your system into the Global User Manager as described above. Then you defined a user group for all developers that contains the same authorizations that you defined earlier on the single user level. If you assign all developers to that user group, it would lead to a double assignment of the same authorizations. If you deleted the assignment of one user to this user group, this user would still have the authorizations on the single user level. Therefore, you must delete the assignment to the single user level as soon as you assign the user to a user group after the migration. The single user assignment should be used to give a user additional authorizations that deviate from the standard.

## System Landscape Without Existing Users

If you have no existing users in your system landscape, the migration of the user master data does not apply. You can immediately start with the creation of users in the user maintenance transaction `SU01` and create the authorization assignments in the system landscape through the Global User Manager. Every user only needs to be created once in the central system, and might get assigned to other systems with the help of the Global User Manager. The creation of that user in the other systems, and the assignment to the activity groups takes place automatically through the Global User Manager.

### User Creation

1. Create a user in transaction *SU01* as usual (see chapter 9 for detailed information).
2. Enter a *User group* on the *Groups* tab for the current user (if this user group has already been created in the Global User Manager). You will not need to make that assignment in the Global User Manager anymore.

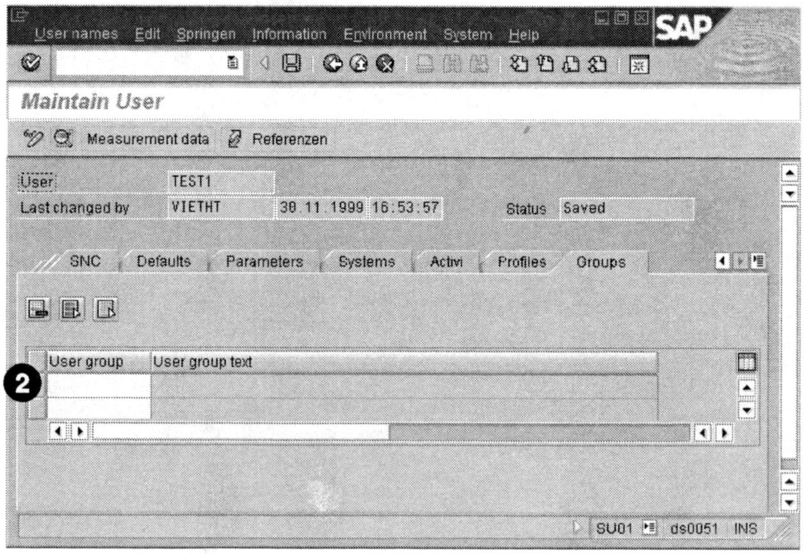

You should only create assignments on the *Systems* and *Activi* (activity groups) tabs if you are certain this assignment is only valid for the single user. Otherwise, create the assignments for user groups in the Global User Manager.

All data entered in transaction *SU01* is also available in the Global User Manager. All assignments created in the Global User Manager are also available in transaction `SU01`.

## Defining System Types and User Groups

We now demonstrate how to group multiple systems into a system group.

1. Choose 🗋 next to *System Types* to create a system type.

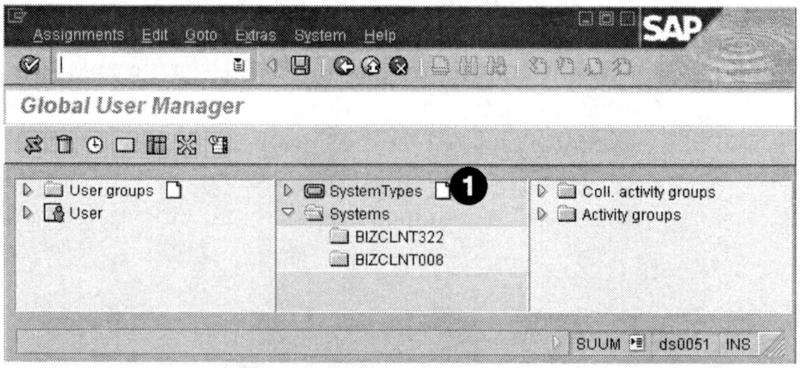


2. In *System type*, enter a name for the system type.
3. In *Short text*, enter the short text for that system type.
4. Choose 🗋 to create the system type.

5. The new system type appears in the list.
6. To assign a system to the just created system type, select the desired system from the *Systems* list. Move it using drag and drop into the new system type (in our example *DEVEL).*
7. Repeat this procedure for every system you would like to assign to a system type.

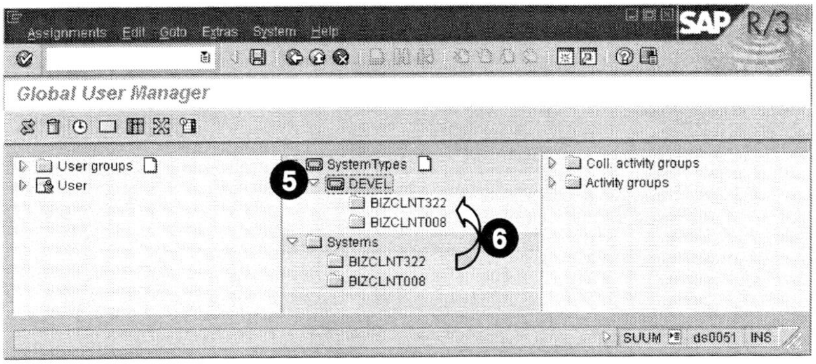


TechTalk

One system can be assigned to only one system group. A user can be assigned to different user groups.

In the following steps, we demonstrate how to define a user group.

1. Choose 🗋 next to *User groups*.

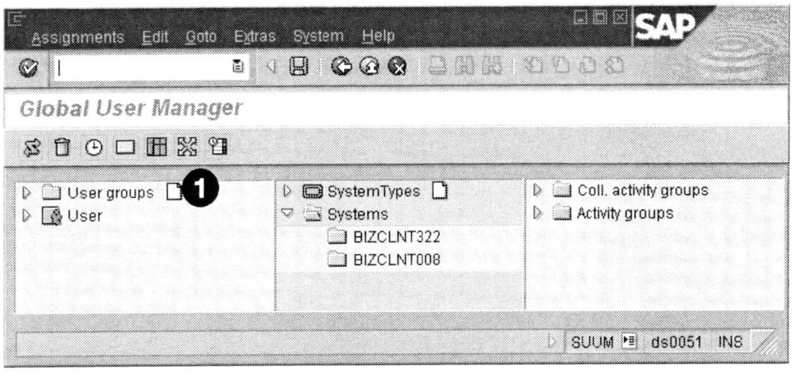


2. In *User group,* enter a name for the *User group.*
3. In *Short text*, enter the short text for that user group.
4. Choose 🗋 to create the user group.

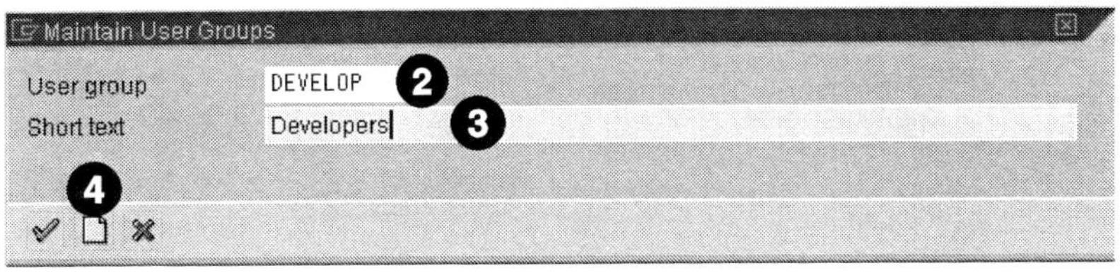

5. The new user group appears in the list.
6. To assign a user to the just created user group, select the desired user from the *Users* list. Move it using drag and drop into the new user group (in our example, *DEVELOP*).
7. Repeat this procedure for every user that you would like to assign to a user group.

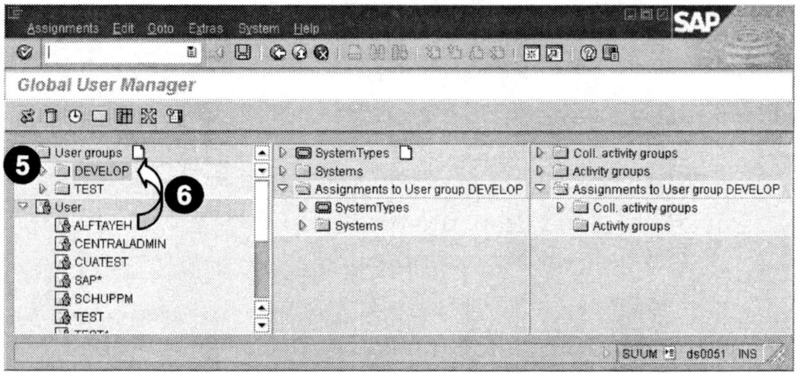


## Modeling with the Global User Manager

In the following procedure we demonstrate how to assign the correct systems and activity groups to a user group.

1. Select the just created user group.
2. Choose to display the assignments.

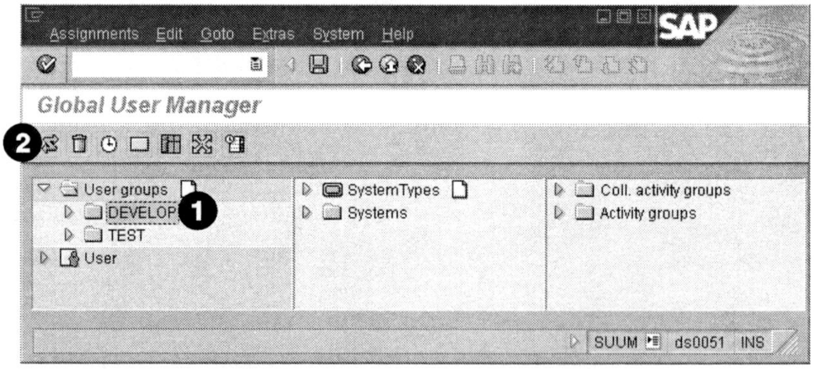


3. You receive the current status of the system/system type and activity group assignments for the selected user group. In our example, we have made no assignments for the user group *DEVELOP*. Therefore, no assignments appear, just the folders.

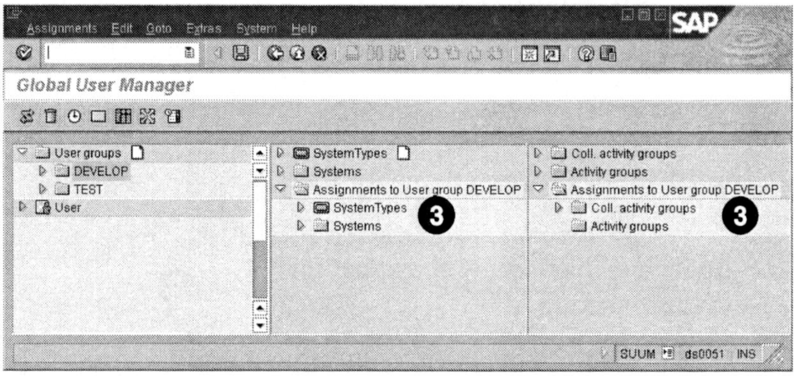

4. To assign a system or system type to a user group, select the desired system or system type from the *Systems* or *System types* list and move it using drag and drop into the desired folder (for example, a folder belonging to *Assignment to User group DEVELOP*).

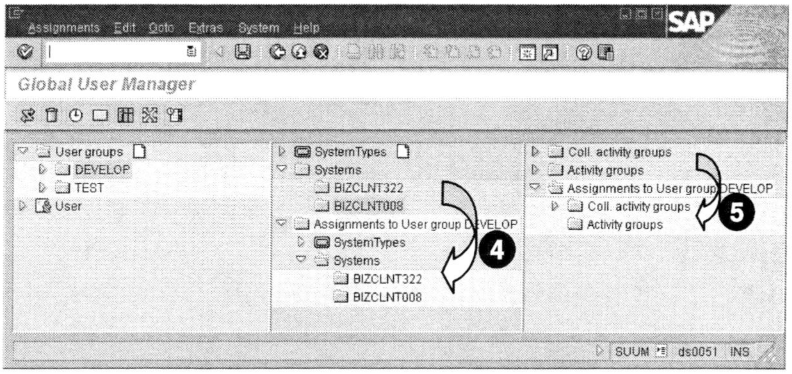


5. To assign activity groups or composite activity groups to the user group, proceed with the same procedure.

Tips & Tricks

To reduce the number of displayed entries in a list (for the user, activity group, etc.), choose the selection icon next to the desired entry.

Tips & Tricks

Remember that according to the assignment triangle shown earlier, you have only defined two of the three angles so far. In the example above, we focused on the user group to assign systems and activity groups. What is missing is the assignment between activity groups and systems. If you migrated the activity groups, the assignment has been performed automatically and the triangle is complete. If not, you have to define the assignment for every activity group.

Tips & Tricks

You have the option to display and maintain assignments from every corner of the triangle. If you display the assignments of an activity group, then you can maintain the system and user groups for that activity group. If you display the assignment of a system type, then you can define the user and activity groups that are valid for this system type.

## Authorization for the Global User Manager

With the Global User Manger, you have the option to maintain users and all their authorizations in every system from the central system of the system landscape. This option can be very useful, but also very problematic if used incorrectly. For example, all users in a system type could be deleted very easily. Therefore, it is very important to pay careful attention to the authorizations of the modeler and administrator of the Global User Manager.

We recommend you use the four-eye principle, where one administrator models the assignments and another checks those assignments before the data is distributed. The modeling is the uncritical part, because no data is being changed in the client systems. This happens only during the distribution.

The distribution only takes place on those issues for which the administrator has the distribution rights. In this way, it is possible to have different administrators for selected systems in the system landscape. These administrators can then only distribute the data for which they are authorized.

The following table displays the relevant authorization objects for the Global User Manager:

| Task | Object | Activity | S_USER_GRP | S_USER_SYS | S_USR_AGR |
|---|---|---|---|---|---|
| Display/ create/ delete assignment | User<br>User group<br>System<br>System type<br>activ. group | Model (68), Display (03) | User group of the user<br>User group | System<br>System type | Activ. group |
| User in user groups | | Assign (78) | User group of the user<br>User group | | |
| Change System type | | Assign (78) | | System<br>System type | |
| Create user group | | Create (01) | User group | | |
| Migrate | | Migrate (90) | | * Comment: entering of single system not possible | |

## Distributing Data in the Global User Manager

Before the distribution, you should always display the data and check it. In the following steps, we demonstrate how to check the data.

1. Inside the Global User Manager, choose ▦ to display the distribution data.
2. Check if the data for the users is set correctly for the distribution.

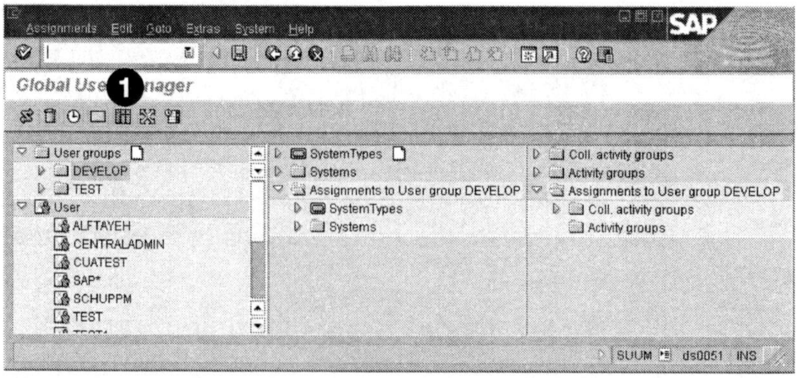


Caution

Only distribute the data after you have randomly checked the user data.

You can distribute the data from the Global User Manager manually immediately or create a background job to distribute the data.

### Immediate Distribution

1. To trigger the distribution immediately, choose .

   The data is distributed right away. Remember that it can take a while until all data is available in every client system, since the distribution happens asynchronously.

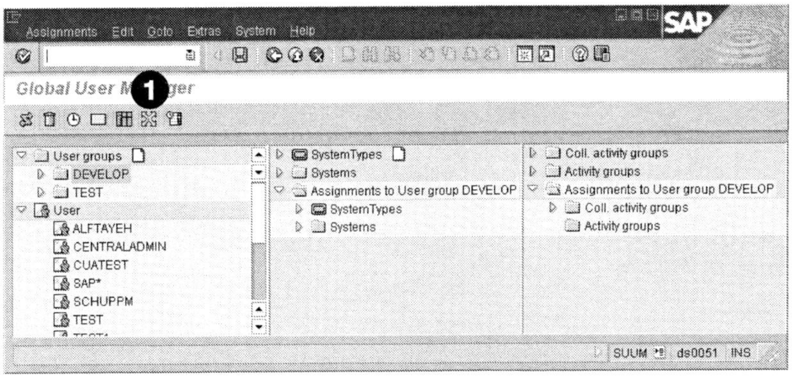


Immediate distribution can cause a lot of network traffic in your system landscape and slow down the performance of systems. If you want to avoid this slowdown, you should schedule a regular background job to run at night.

During the distribution, the data is entered into transaction *SU01* according to the modeling in the Global User Manger, and from there distributed to the client systems. In the client system, only the users are created and the activity groups assigned. Other data is not distributed, but kept in the central system. Therefore, in transaction *SCUL* you can expect to find only some logs, namely those for the distribution of the activity group assignment and for users created or deleted.

To reduce the data flow that occurs during the distribution, only data that has changed since the last distribution is distributed.

### Scheduling Background Distribution

1. To schedule a background job for the data distribution, choose *Extras → Schedule distribution.*

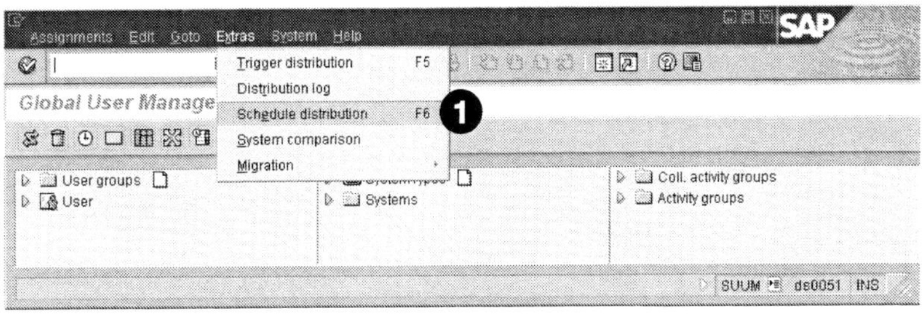

2. Choose ✔.

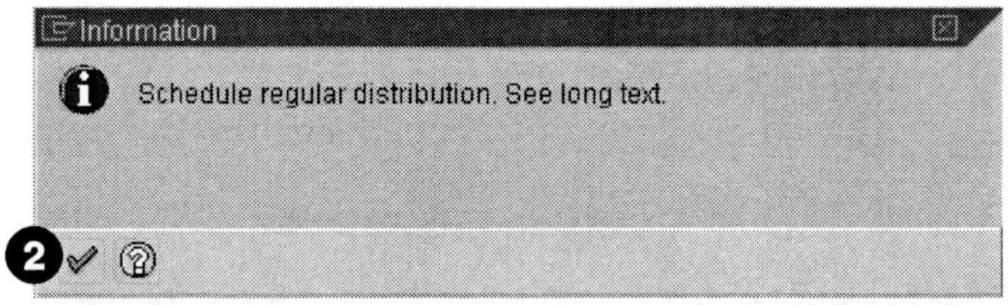


3. In *Job name*, enter a job name.
4. In *Job class*, enter a priority for the job class.
5. In *Target server*, select the central system as the target system.
6. Choose *Step* to plan the ABAP program *RSUSR500*.
7. Choose *Start condition* to schedule the time for your job.
8. Choose 💾.

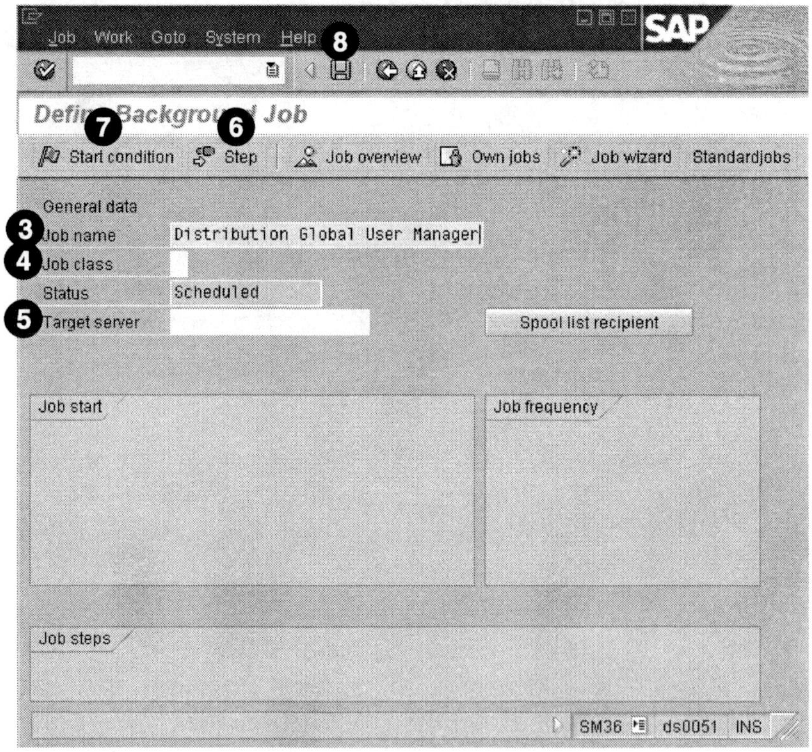


If you process the administration of user data in the Global User Manager with the four-eye principle, you should be aware that there might be conflict, as you cannot check the data before the automatic distribution.

# Chapter 12: Tips and Troubleshooting

## Contents

# Overview

When users execute a transaction or report that is not included in their user menu, they may see the system message similar to: *You have no authorization for Transaction….* This message means that either their current authorization profile does not contain the required authorization to execute the transaction, or the values maintained for the profile's authorization are insufficient. The missing authorizations can be determined either by tracing authorizations with transaction *SU53 (Display check values of authorization checks if: not authorized)* or with the system trace transaction *ST01*.

Transaction *SU53* is included in the activity group *SAP_BC_ENDUSER_AG,* which is included in the user role template *SAP_EVERY_EMPLOYEE.*

It is also accessible using the menu path *System → Utilities → Display Authorization Check* from the main menu.

# Tracing Authorizations with Transaction SU53

By executing transaction *SU53 - Display check values of authorization checks if: not authorized* from the user menu or by entering **SU53** in the *Command* field, you can at any time analyze an authorization-denied error in your session. Transaction *SU53* can be accessed from any of your sessions, not just the one where the error occurred. You cannot, however, analyze an authorization error from your own session in another user's logon session.

Tips & Tricks

At the transaction start, transaction *SU53* is protected by authorization object *S_TCODE.* You should give all users access rights to transaction *SU53.* Thus, in case of a problem, your help desk can easily analyze problems that use transaction *SU53.* Transaction *SU53* is included in the activity group *SAP_BC_ENDUSER_AG* which is included in the user role template *SAP_EVERY_EMPLOYEE.*

Caution

If you are using structural authorizations, *SU53* is not very useful if the transaction where you are receiving messages *You have no authorization for…* is an HR transaction or a transaction that calls HR objects. *SU53* only reveals the last authorization check failure based on the ABAP code statement *Authorization-Check.* However, structural authorizations do not always use the *Authorization-Check* statement in determining accesses. Therefore, if extensive structural authorizations are used, the *System Trace* (transaction *ST01*) will be of more benefit than *SU53.*

**Example:**

In the following example, we demonstrate how a user, who has the user role template *DATA_ENTRY_CLERK* (we created this activity group earlier in the book), tries to run *transaction FB04 - Document changes*. Since this user has no authorization for this transaction, the error message *You have no authorization for Transaction FB04* is received. The user has to use *SU53 - Display check values of authorization checks if: not authorized* to find out what authorization is missing.

We start where the user has attempted to run transaction *FB04* and receives the error message: *You have no authorization for Transaction FB04.*

1. Start transaction *SU53 – Display check values of authorization checks if: not authorized* from the user menu, or enter **SU53** in the *Command* field.

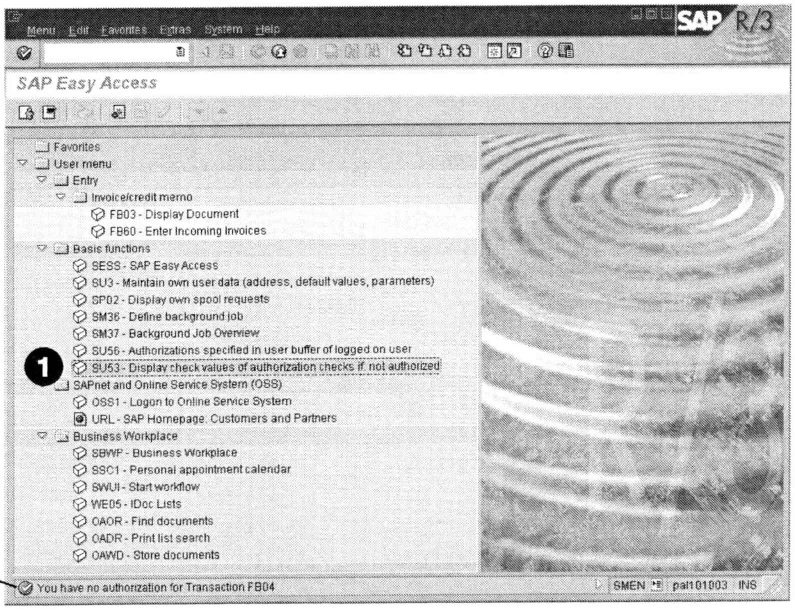


2. The system displays the checked authorization object that caused the error message with the corresponding field values.
3. Also displayed are:
   a. The current authorization in the users assigned authorization profile.
   b. The authorization field values for this authorization.
4. To print this information, choose *Values → Print.*

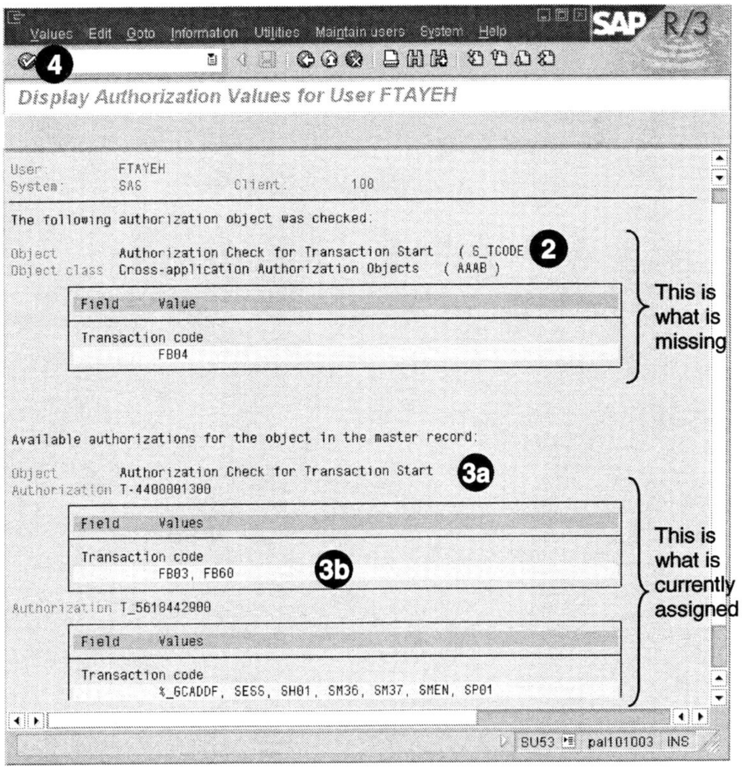

Tips & Tricks

To add the missing authorization to the user's current authorization profile using the Profile Generator (PG), see chapter 8, *Inserting Missing Authorizations*. Also refer to the SAPNet – R/3 Frontend note numbers *23342* and *18529* (formerly OSS notes).

# System Trace Using Transaction ST01

You can use the **system trace** to record authorization checks in your own session and other users' sessions. Start transaction *ST01* (system trace) and run the transaction the user is having authorization problems with. As soon as you get stuck, stop your trace. We use the trace for authorization checks though it is capable of tracing much more. Everything you have done in the R/3 System that requires authority checks is recorded in the trace with the object's fields and the tested values.

Caution

Using *ST01* (system trace) severely affects system performance!

**Example:**

In the following example, we demonstrate how the administrator can create a system trace of another user's session. User *FTAYEH,* who has been assigned the user role *DATA_ENTRY_CLERK,* is trying to run a transaction *(FB03)* for which he has authorization and one transaction *(FB04)* for which he has no authorization. At the same time, the administrator uses transaction *ST01* to create a system trace for the attempts of user *FTAYEH.*

To set up the system trace transaction:

1. Start the transaction *ST01* – *System Trace.*

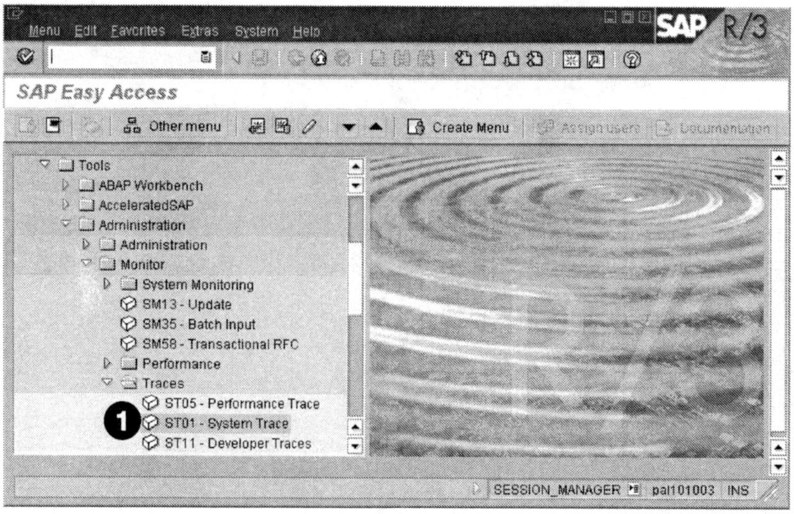

Tips & Tricks

Check the *Trace status* before using the system trace. If the trace is active, do not interfere, because there is only one trace system for each R/3 instance.

2. You can see if another user has used the system trace and when it has been activated.
3. Many different *Trace components* exist and each can be switched on with its own flag (and filter).
4. Some selections are directly visible in the checkboxes. Ensure that only the *Authorization check* checkbox is selected.
5. Other trace component selections are grouped and might contain only partial selections. Check all icons to ensure that nothing is selected.
6. To restrict the trace to a specific user or session, choose *Edit → Filter → Shared*.

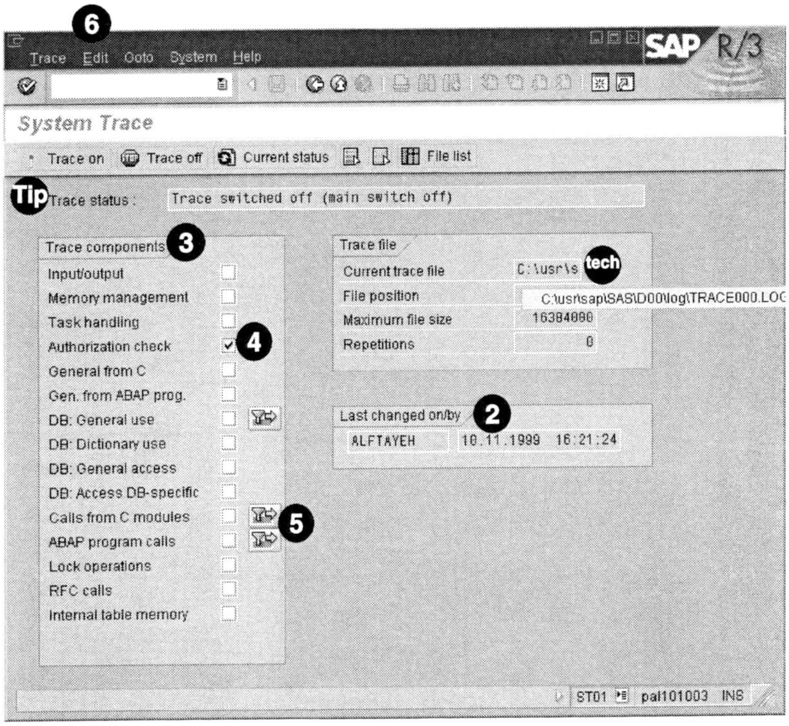


TechTalk

The trace file's name and storage location is shown in the field *Current trace file*. The trace is added to the existing file until the maximum file size is reached. Then a new file needs to be created (see later in this section).

7. Enter the name of the user for which you would like to run the trace. In our example we want to trace user *FTAYEH's* transactions.
8. Choose *Back*.

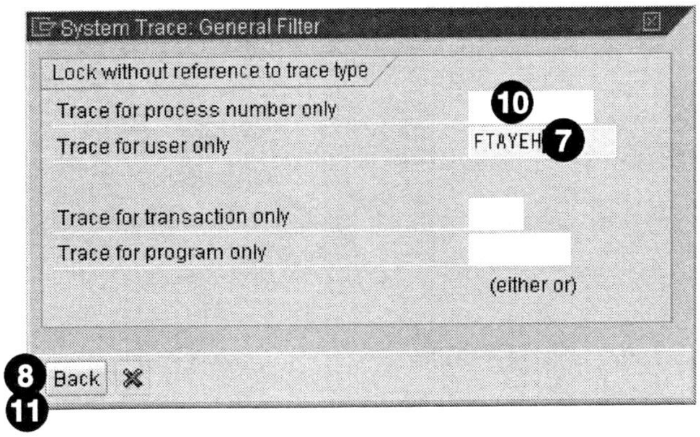


Tips & Tricks

You also have the option to filter the data for either a certain transaction or program.

9. On the *System Trace* screen, choose *Edit → Write options*.

10. To save your trace on the hard drive, select *Trace: Write to disk.*
11. Choose *Back.*

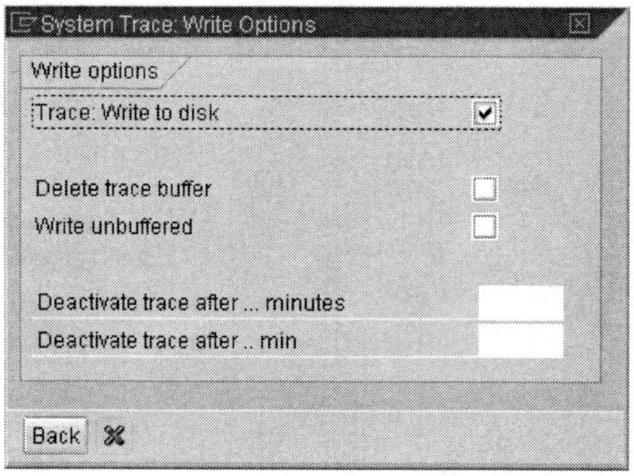


Tips & Tricks

You also have the option to either define a time frame for the trace to run or to use the buffer.

12. To save your settings for the next time you use the trace, choose *Edit → Settings → Write to database.*
13. Your data is saved with the following settings: *Client, username, default.*

    The system is now ready to begin the trace. At this time, we recommend that you have the user's session you would like to trace ready (or open another session to trace your own transaction).
14. Choose *Trace on.*

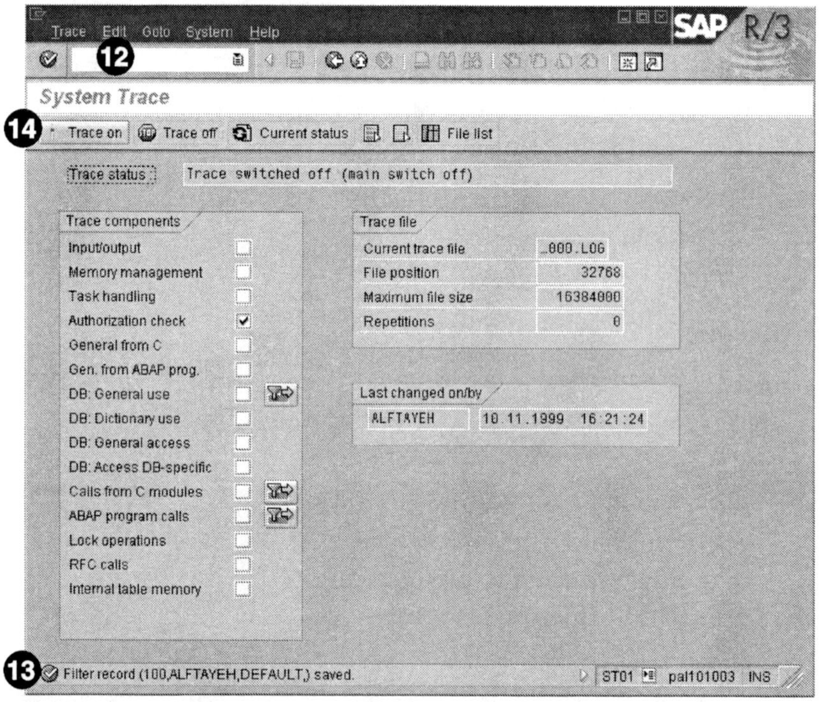


Tips & Tricks

To use your individual settings the next time you start the trace, choose *Edit → Settings → Read from database*. All the checkmarks you set will appear in the corresponding checkboxes.

15. Choose *Yes.*

    From now on every action that user *FTAYEH* performs is recorded in the trace.

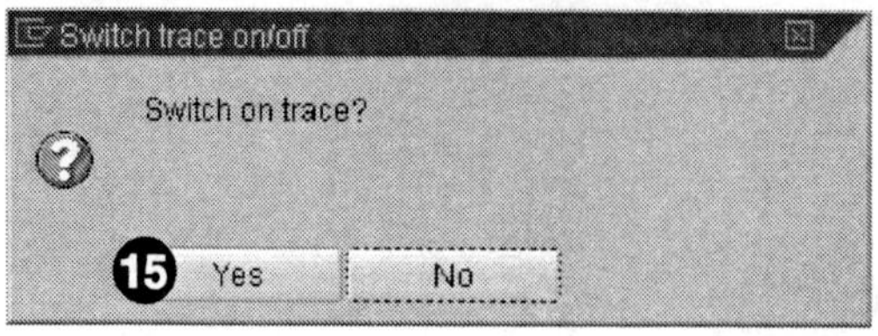

16. Change to the user's session you want to trace.

    The user should now run the transactions you would like to investigate. In our example, we first start transaction *FB03*, then *FB04*.

17. Begin the transaction (for example, *FB03 – Display documents*).

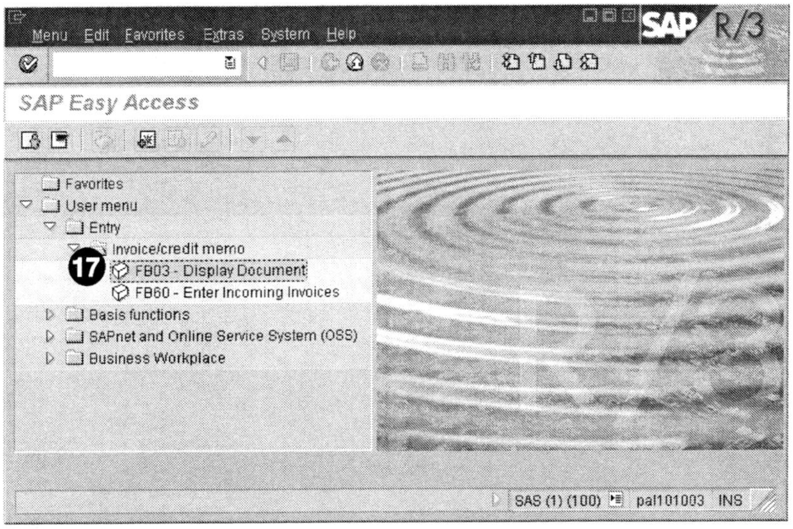


The transaction starts because user *FTAYEH* is authorized to perform it.

18. Begin another transaction (for example, **FB04**).

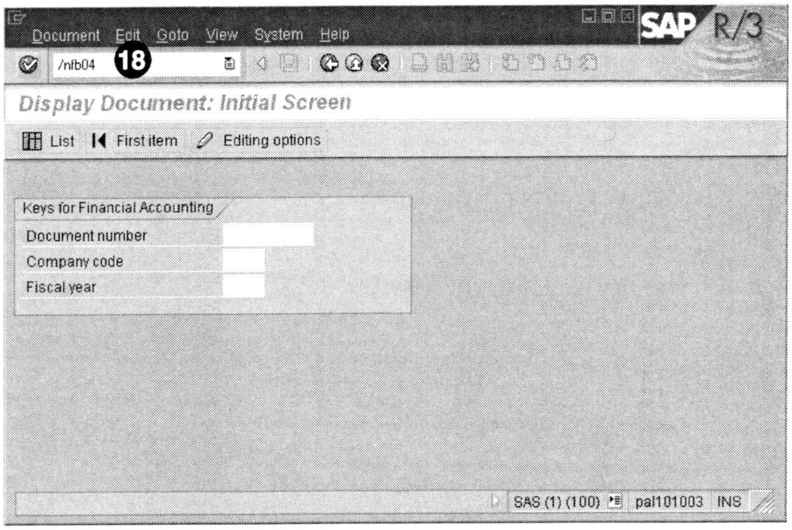


Since user *FTAYEH* is not authorized to perform FB04, he received the error message: *You are not authorized to use transaction FB04.*

The system also jumps back to the user menu.

Error message

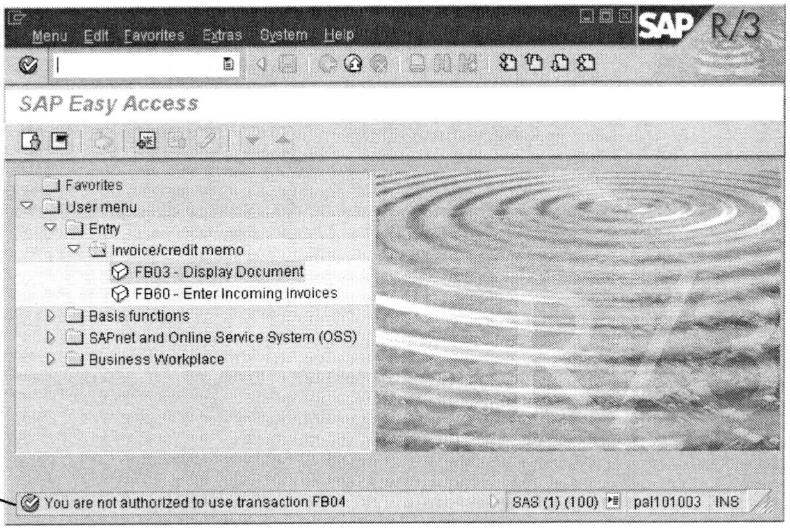

19. After completing your system trace, switch back to the other session, the trace session.
20. Choose *Trace off*.

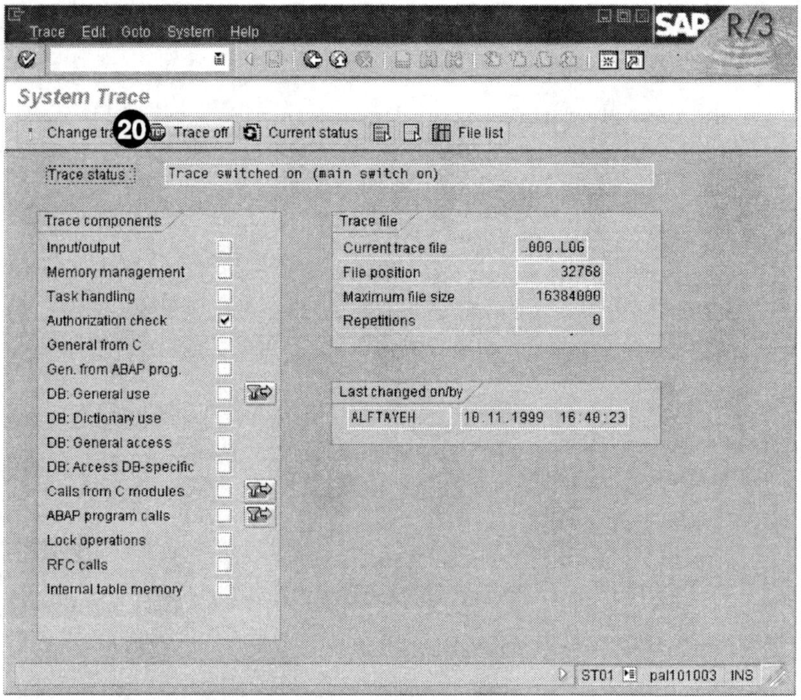


21. Choose *Yes* to stop tracing.

    The trace is now ready to analyze. See the next section on how to analyze a trace.

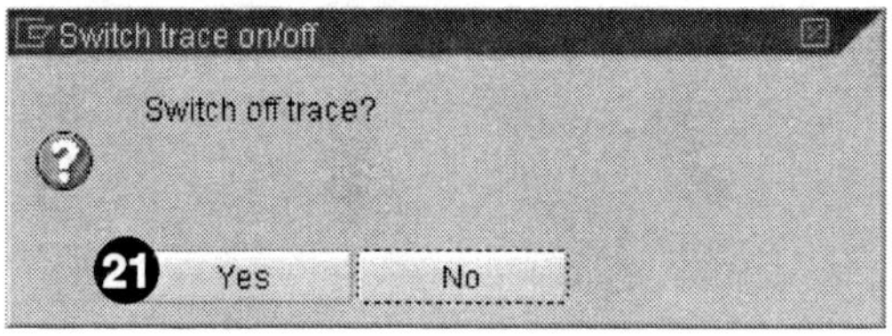

# Analyzing a Written Trace File

1. To display the trace results, from the *System Trace* window, choose *File list*.

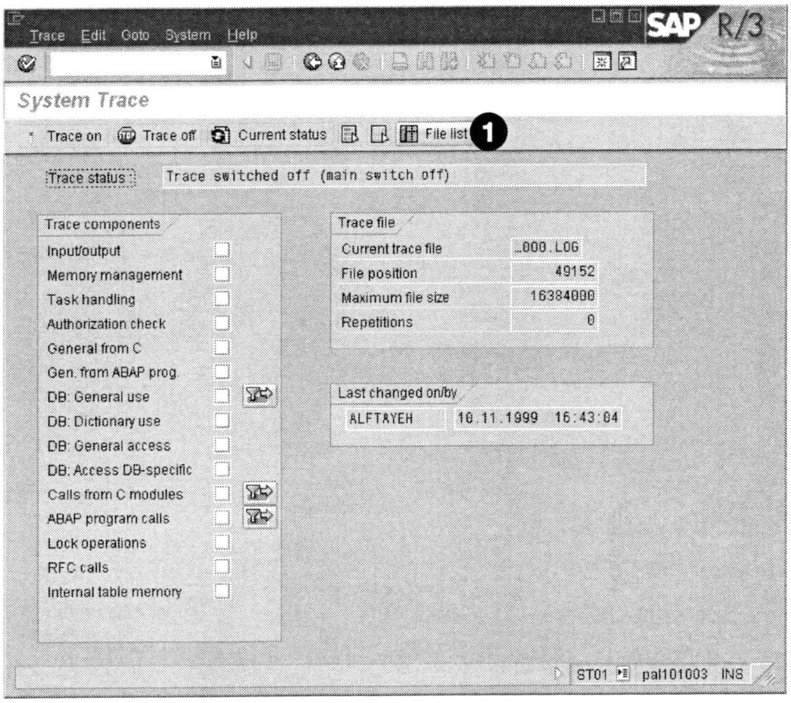


2. Select your trace.

Tips & Tricks

If you see more than one trace, select the correct one. To determine the trace name, see the *TechTalk* on page 12–5).

3. Choose *Analyze*.

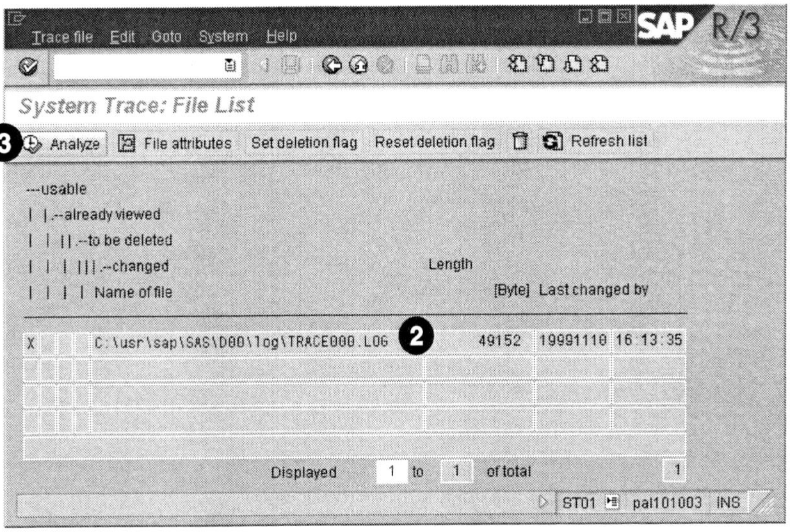


Caution

Be aware that the trace file can be extremely large. Be patient because it may take some time to display it.

4. Select all the options you want to consider in your analysis (for example, *Trace for authorization checks*).

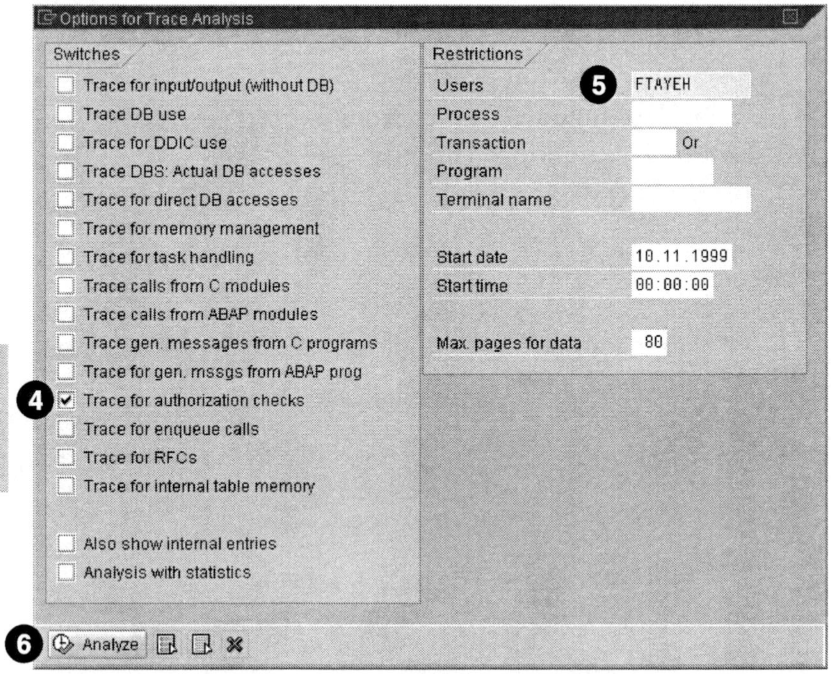


**Tips & Tricks**

If everything is selected, it might be easier to choose [icon] to deselect all first and then reselect one or more checkboxes.

5. Under *Restrictions*, enter the desired user.
6. Choose *Analyze*.
7. The first page of the trace file appears. By default, *With authority check* should be selected.
8. Scroll down until you see the transactions that were used by the user.

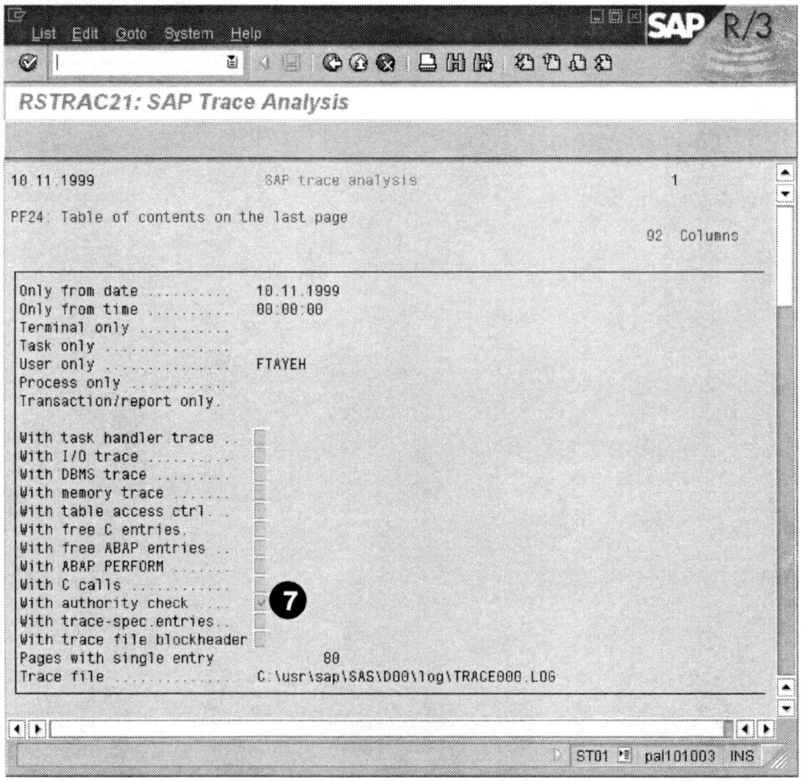

9. Since the trace lists can be very large, the output is compressed. The *Number of records printed* is the number of lines currently displayed.
10. These lines appear in the box(es) above the *Number of records printed*. In our example, all the authorizations checked with the required field values have appeared. This is the information you are looking for!
11. The return code for each of these authorization checks also appears.
    - The return code for FB03 is *0* which means it is okay.
    - The return code for FB04 is *1* which means the check has failed.
12. The text shows the object that was checked.
13. The last item on the line is the transaction code that was checked.

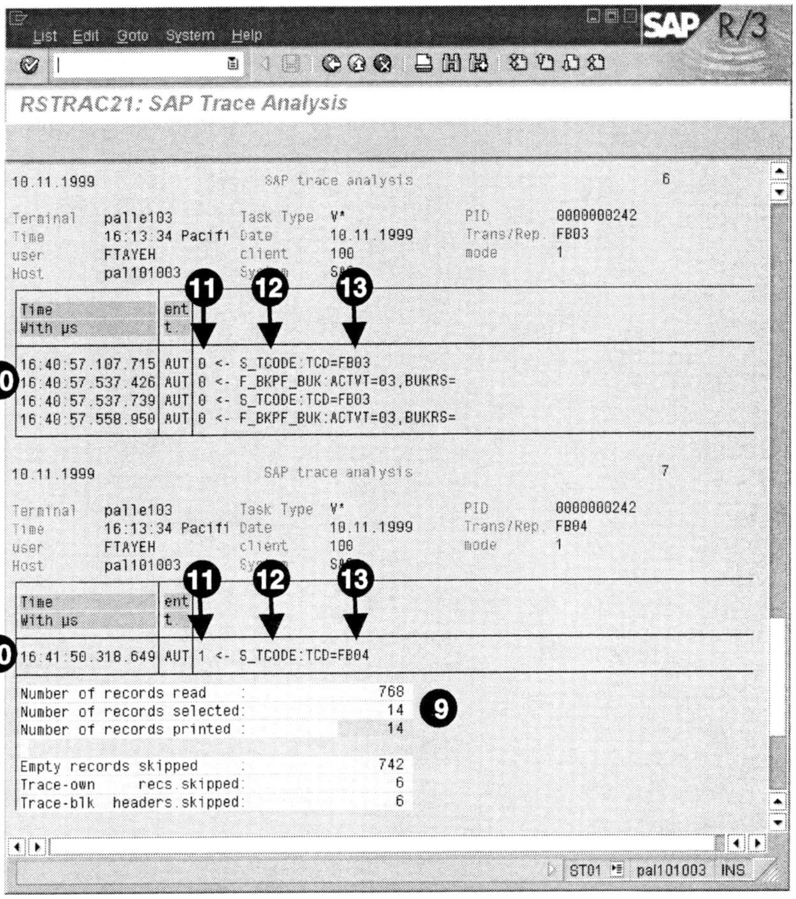


Tips & Tricks

If the return code is:

- Equal to *0*, the authorization check is okay
- Greater than *0*, the authorization check is **not** okay

# Reducing the Scope of Authorization Checks

## Overview

The basis for all switches is the activation of the PG. You can also switch the RFC, S_TCODE, and global deactivation switches. Based on these, you can deactivate authorization checks using *SU24*. Inside the activity groups you can inactivate authorization objects and set the activity group and user assignment validity period.

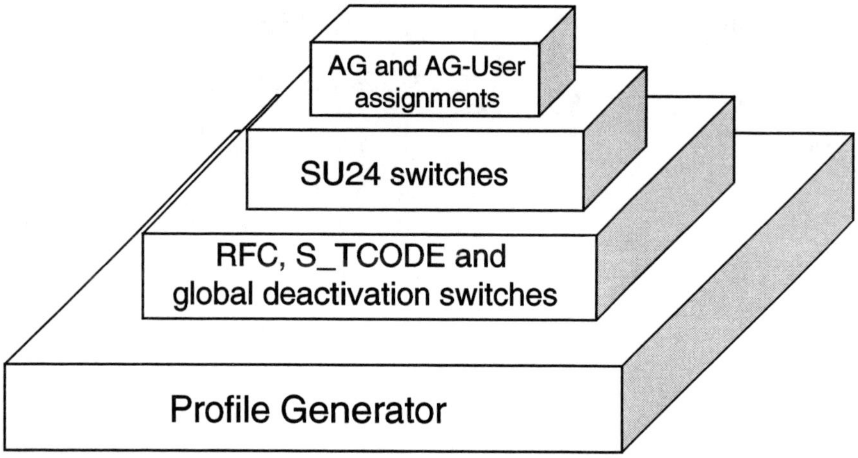


In the following sections, we describe the single layers in more details.

## Enabling the Profile Generator

Before continuing with this section, you need to have at least set and activated the system parameter *auth/no_check_in_some_cases* = *Y* (default value), and run *SU25* which copies the SAP check indicator defaults and field values from table *USOBT* and *USOBX* into the customer tables.

## Enabling/Disabling Other System-wide Checks

### Enabling auth/tcodes_not_checked

R/3 is not fully a transaction-based authorization system. It is also an object-oriented authorization system. A business process in R/3 can be accessed by several mechanisms (for example, transaction code, BAPI, etc.), but transactions are most common. R/3 protects particular objects or pieces of the business process within the transaction. R/3 defines which objects are "securable" in the standard system, and one business process or transaction code may require access to a varying number of predefined objects. However, R/3 also uses the transaction code as the "first line of defense" to prevent someone from accessing parts of the system. In the event that a user enters a transaction code to perform a task, the system checks the user's authorization object *S_TCODE* to ensure they have the correct *S_TCODE* transaction code before continuing. In certain cases, you may wish to eliminate this "first line of defense" if you find it cumbersome to protect each and every transaction code in the system. As such, you can disable the check for *S_TCODE* using the system-wide profile parameter *auth/tcodes_not_checked*. In the system, *S_TCODE* is active by default.

## Enabling auth/rfc_authority_check

SAP has vastly enhanced its use of the RFC (remote function call) functionality in recent releases of the R/3 System. RFCs are used throughout the system so that one portion of the R/3 System can "communicate" with another part of R/3 (for example, creating a sales order via workflow may invoke an RFC to communicate the information that is being passed into the sales order create function in workflow processing). RFC's are also critical in permitting systems and applications external to R/3 (for example, a web page) to communicate with R/3 with BAPIs. As BAPIs utilize RFC functionality, authorization checks are performed based on the BAPI used. One of R/3's core approaches to securing the RFC functionality is to introduce another new authorization object called *S_RFC* which gives people access to particular groups of RFCs. In particular, every RFC belongs to a function group. Many RFCs can belong to one function group (for example, the function group for MM Purchase Order Processing). The authorization object *S_RFC* can be restricted to give users access to particular function groups. However, the tremendous amount of RFCs in 4.6 complicates which function groups you should give people access to. Therefore, R/3 provides a mechanism to disable the check against the *S_RFC* authorization object at a system-wide level. The system-wide profile parameter *auth/rfc_authority_check* can be changed from its blank default to one of the following:

- 0 = No authorization check
- 1 = Authorization check active (no check for same user, no check for same user context and SRFC-FUGR)
- 2 = Authorization check active (no check for SRFC-FUGR)
- 9 = Authorization check active (SRFC-FUGR also checked)

## Globally Deactivating or Activating Authorization Checks

You can also globally deactivate or activate authorization checks with transaction *AUTH_SWITCH_OBJECTS*. The system does not execute any authorization checks for deactivated authorization objects. You have several options to reach transaction *AUTH_SWITCH_OBJECTS*. You can use the IMG (see step 1), transaction **SU25** (see step 2) or use transaction **auth_switch_objects** directly.

1. Choose next to *Switch off authorization checks globally (optional)* and continue with step 3 (or enter **su25** and continue with step 2).

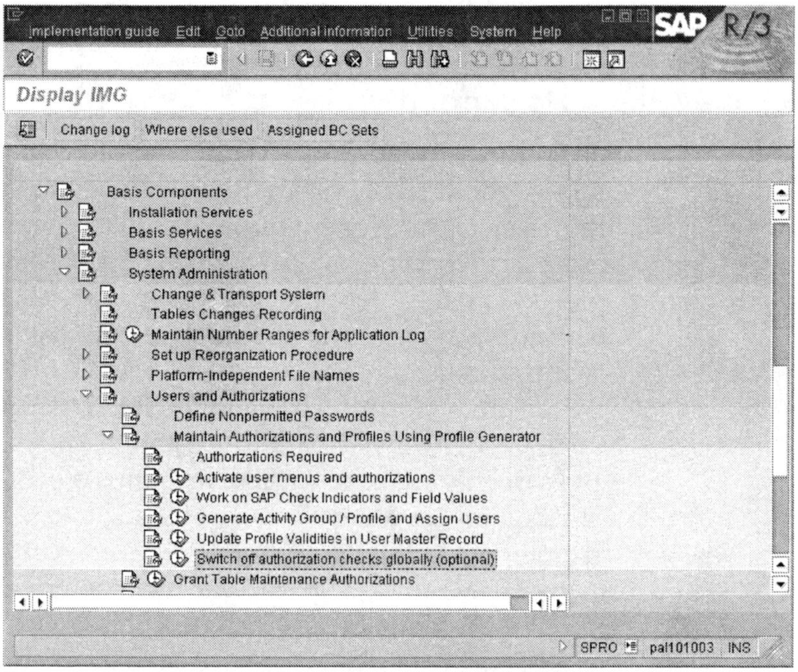

2. In transaction *SU25*, choose 5. *Deactivate authorization object globally*.

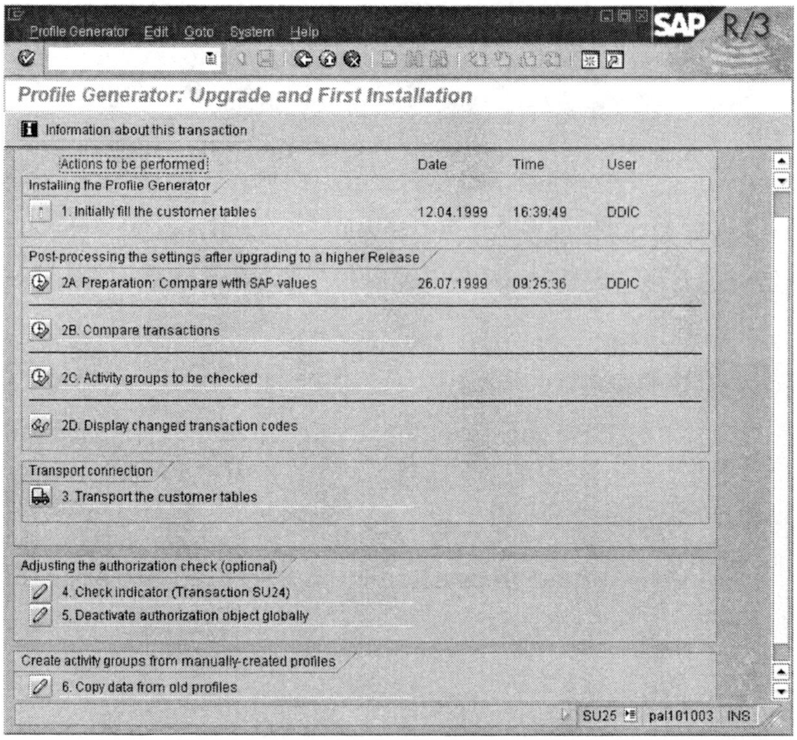

3. Read the information carefully and choose .

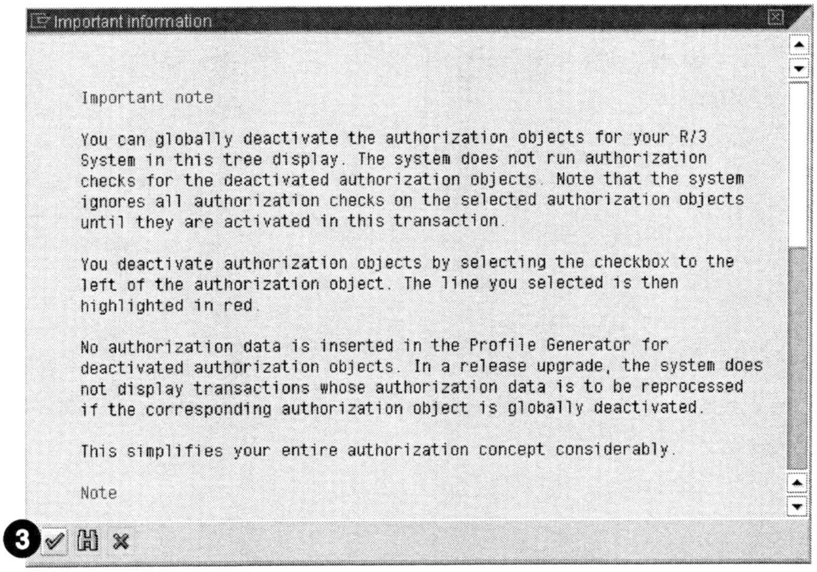


4. Deactivate an authorization object by deselecting the checkbox next to it. The deselected line is highlighted in red.
5. Choose .
6. To activate your data, choose .
7. For a detailed explanation about the authorization object, choose  next to the authorization object.

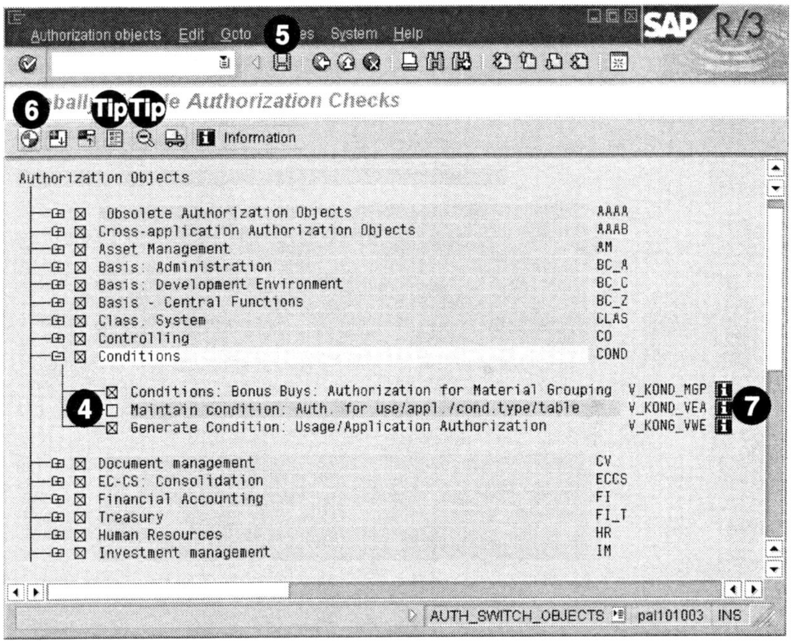


Tips & Tricks

Choose  to switch the technical names on and  to switch the technical names off. To view the color legend, choose .

8. You receive detailed information about the selected authorization object.
9. Close the window to return.

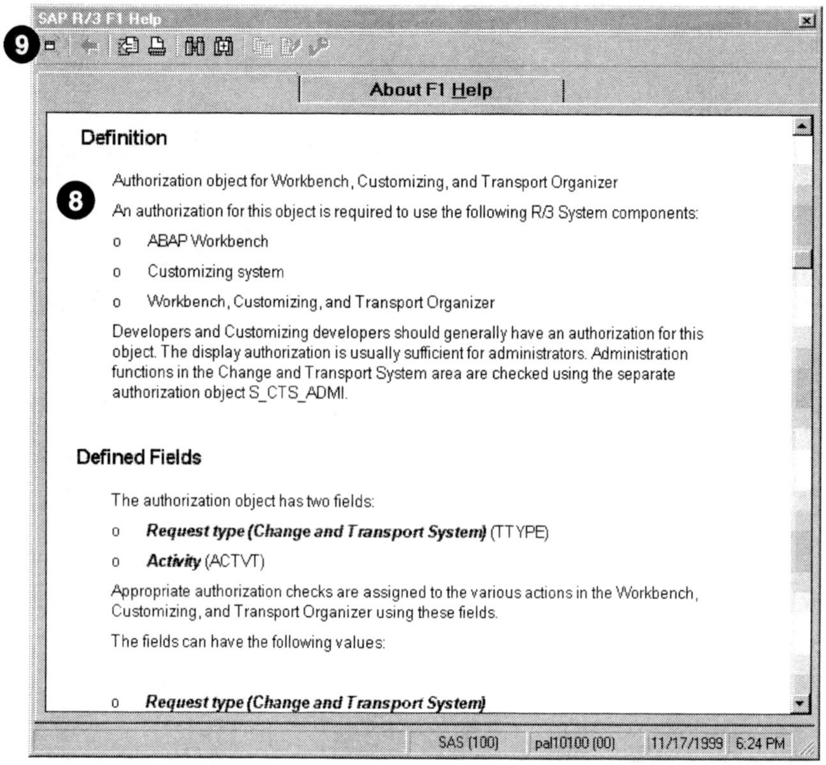


TechTalk

When you save and activate your data, the system also checks the authorization object *S_USER_OBJ*.

The values for the system parameter *auth/object_disabling_active* can be an *X* or blank. The *X* indicates that the parameter is active and the blank indicates that it is not. If it is not active, with *SU24* got switched off, your changes will not affect anything. However, the default value is set to active.

10. Authorization objects beginning with *S_* or *P_* cannot be switched off.

    If you try to switch those objects off and save them, you will receive a warning message.

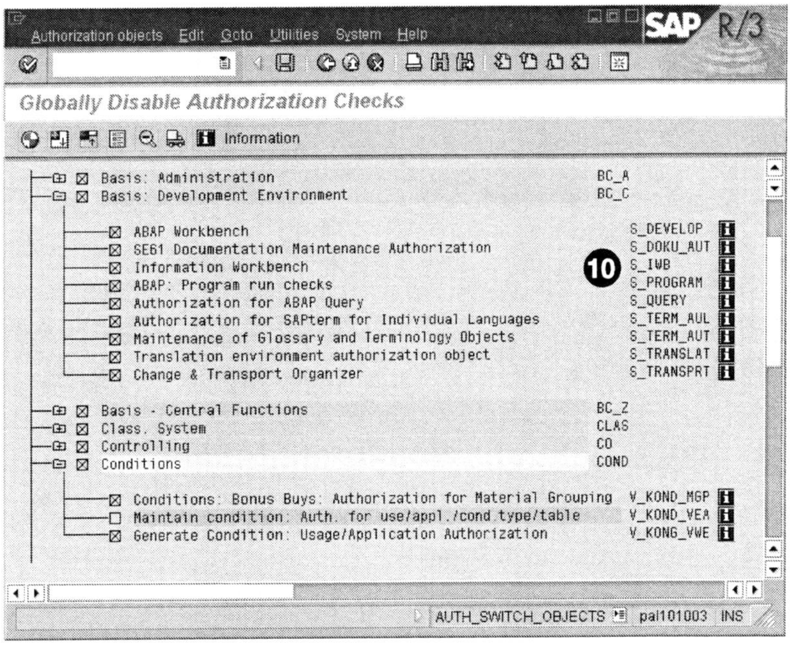


11. The system ignores that you have switched off those authorization objects.
12. Choose ✔.

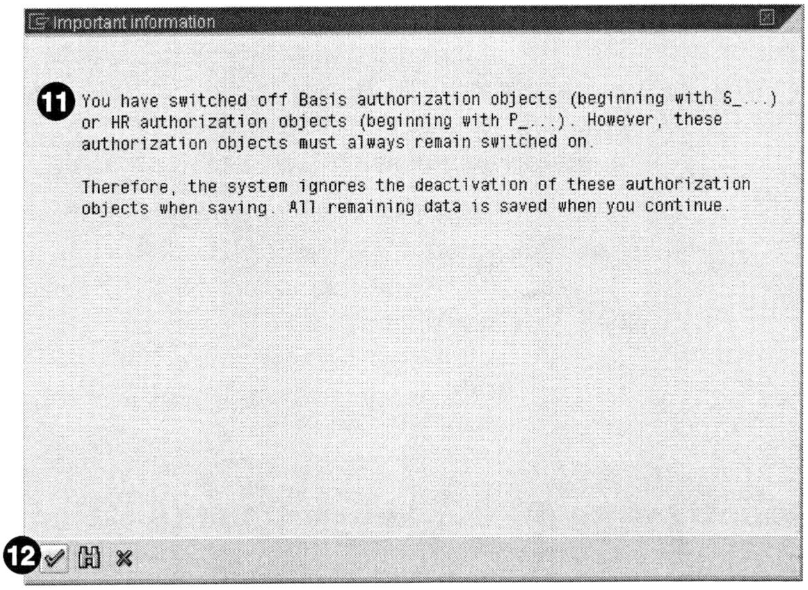


**Caution**

You cannot globally deactivate authorization objects beginning with *S_* (Basis) or *P_* (HR) in transaction *AUTH_SWITCH_OBJECTS*.

**TechTalk**

No authorization data is inserted in the PG for deactivated authorization objects. In a release upgrade, the system does not display the transactions where authorization data will be reprocessed if the corresponding authorization object is globally deactivated.

When you activate previously deactivated authorization objects, you may have to maintain the authorization data for many activity groups.

If you activate previously deactivated authorization objects, these objects are not contained in any activity groups. In this case, in the transaction *PFCG* on the

*Authorizations* tab, choose *Expert mode for profile generation* to generate profiles and the option *Read old status and merge with the new data*. Maintain any missing authorization values and regenerate the profile.

### Parameter Transactions

The parameter transactions are an exception to other transactions. These transactions work with a powerful core transaction, which is restricted by the fact that the initial screen of the core transaction is filled and skipped in the parameter transaction.

You cannot exclude authorization objects from direct use in parameter transactions, but only with the corresponding core transaction.

**Example:**

Parameter transaction = *F48V* (Management of Document Archives)

Core transaction = *SARA* (Archive Management)

To set the check indicator of transaction *F48V* to *N* (no check), you need to change the check indicator of the core transaction *SARA*. You can find the name of this transaction in the right-hand column *TCode* overview in transaction *SU24*. If you double-click on the parameter transaction code in field *TCode*, the system branches directly into the check indicator maintenance of the core transaction.

If the authorization object for parameter transaction *F48V* is set to *C* (check), but under the core transaction it is set to *CM* (check/maintain), the field values for *SARA* will be suggested as defaults in the PG. If the authorization object is also set to *CM* in *F48V*, the field values maintained for *F48V* will be recommended as defaults in the PG, and the entries for *SARA* will be overwritten. You can maintain or overwrite the field values of the core transaction for parameter transactions in *SU24*.

## Deactivating Authorization Checks Using SU24

Caution

Optional: Normally you do not have to make any changes in transaction *SU24*.

However, if you do make changes in *SU24*, the changes must be made in the DEV system and transported to other systems. Never make changes in any other system.

In the PG, you have the option to deactivate and activate authorization checks against different authorization objects.

Whenever you perform R/3 transactions, many authorization objects are checked that arise through work areas called in the background. For the authorization checks to be successful, the user must have the appropriate authorizations. For this reason, most users receive more authorizations than necessary, leading to an increased maintenance load. But the core transaction is always protected by object *S_TCODE*, and authorization checks that belong to pure background functions are deactivated. (This has nothing to do with background processing).

In R/3, many authorization objects go unused by most customers. You can deactivate the authorization check against the objects using transaction *SU24 - Maintain check indicators for transaction codes*. This deactivation results in clear authorization profiles and better performance.

You can deactivate authorization checks for any of the following reasons:

- Not all authorization objects are used (for instance: *F_LFA1_BEK*)
- Many authorization fields have been maintained with an asterisk (*)
- Authorization profiles are too large
- Each transaction is checked by *S_TCODE*
- Needless authorization checks reduce the transaction performance

The following examples illustrate when to use *SU24*:

- If a warehouse worker removes goods from the warehouse, and the remaining stock falls short of a critical limit, the system triggers either a purchasing order, a production order, or both. These operations are carried out because of the system settings and therefore require no further actions by warehouse workers. Accordingly, these workers should not have authorizations for purchase or production orders, so the check against this object should be deactivated.
- Authorization object *F_LFA1_BEK* (Vendor: Account authorization) protects the vendor master records at account level. That is, with this object, it is possible to divide the vendors into groups and only assign the accounting clerk the maintenance authorization for vendors from a certain group. If you do not want to make any authorizations at this level and allow all accounting clerks to maintain all vendors, it is best to deactivate this object.

  Only if you have set the check indicator to *CM* (*Check/Maintain*), will the authorization and predefined authorization field values be displayed for changing.

## Reducing the Scope of Authorization Checks

Authorization checks are carried out wherever they are specifically written into the source code of a transaction. However, with transaction *SU24* you can set check indicators to exclude certain authorization objects from authorization checks. You can exclude particular authorization checks either in specific transactions or R/3 System-wide, without changing the program code.

Before the authorization profile is automatically generated, use the check indicators to control which objects appear in the PG and which field values display.

## Maintaining Check Indicators for Transaction Codes

To access the transaction for maintaining check indicators, enter transaction **SU24** in the *Command* field, or navigate using the IMG. In the following procedure, we show you how to get to *Maintain check indicator* transaction using the IMG (transaction code **SPRO**). If you enter **SU24** directly, start with **step 4.**

1. In the IMG follow the menu path *Basis Components → System Administration → Users and Authorizations → Maintain Authorizations and Profiles Using the Profile Generator → Work on SAP Check Indicators and Field Values* and choose next to that line.

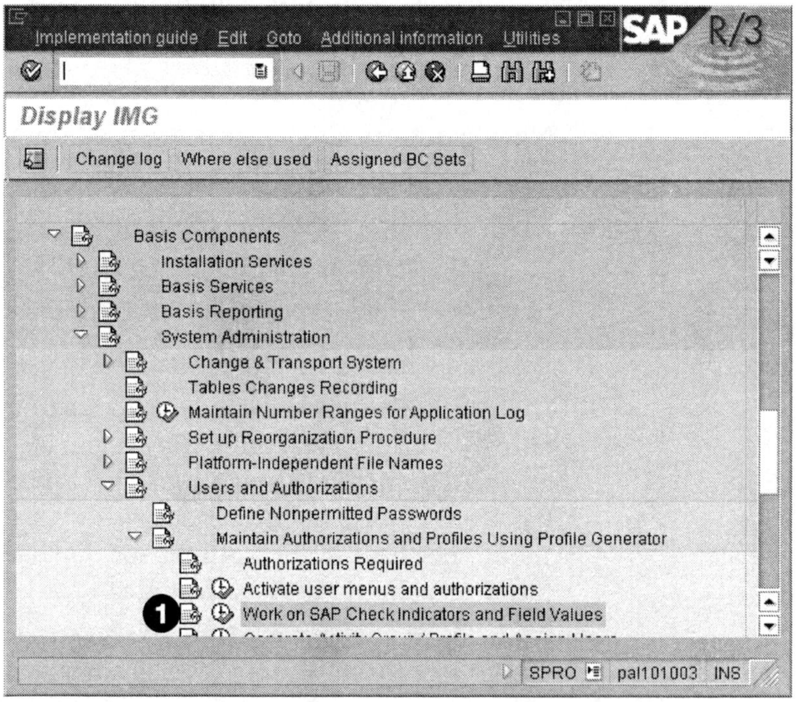


2. Select *Change test status* (this translation is incorrect; the text should read *Change check indicator*).
3. Choose *Choose.*

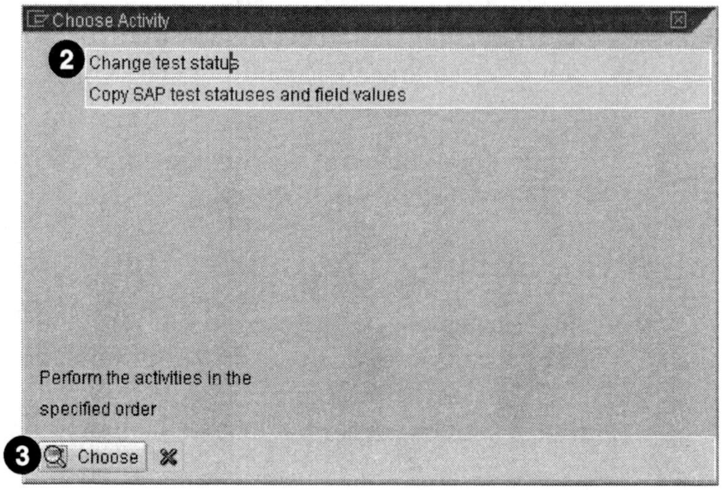

4. Select *Maintain check indicators for transaction codes.*
5. Enter either a single transaction code (for example **MK01**) or a range of codes for which you want to list the check indicators.
6. Choose [execute icon] to execute.

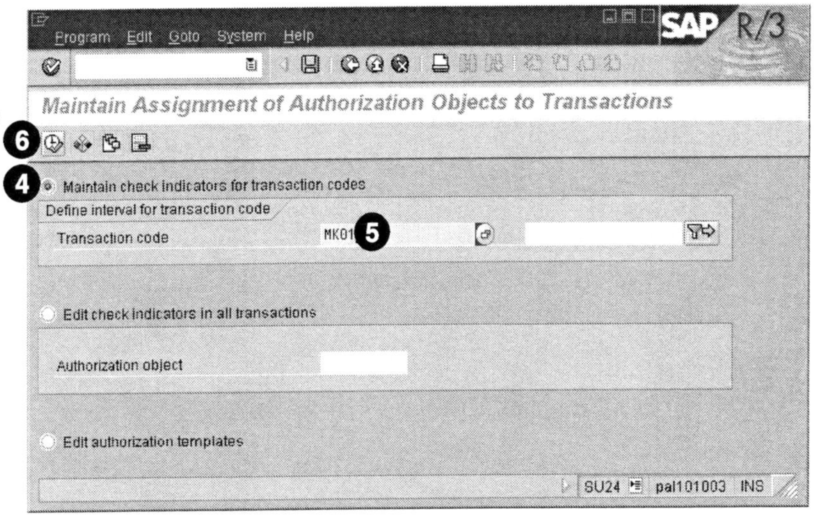


7. Select the appropriate transaction (in our example, only one is shown, but more than one could appear).
8. Choose *Check indicator* to display the current active check indicators for authorization objects in the selected transactions.

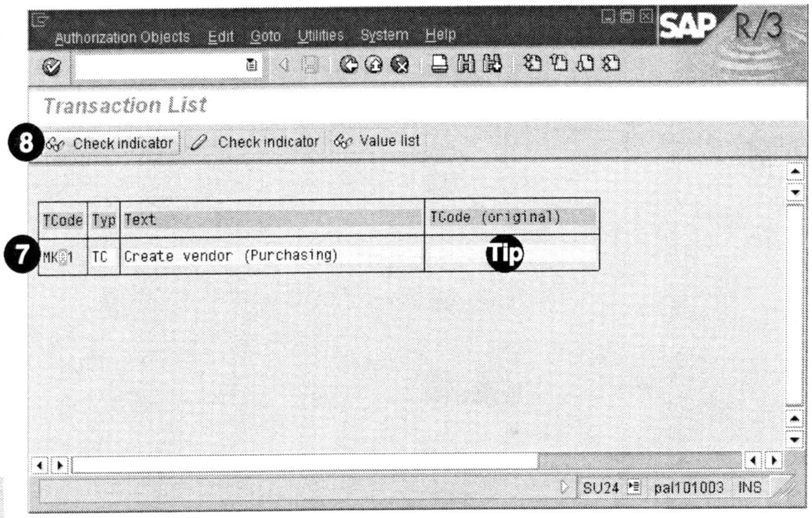


Tips & Tricks

If you are dealing with a parameter transaction, the core transaction appears in the *Tcode (original)* column. For more information, see *Parameter Transactions* on page 12–18.

A list of authorization objects appears in the *Object* column for the selected transaction involved with the check.

9. Choose *Field values*.

**Note**: There are three objects that have the check indicator set to *CM*.

TechTalk

The table displayed on the right is table *USOBX_C*.

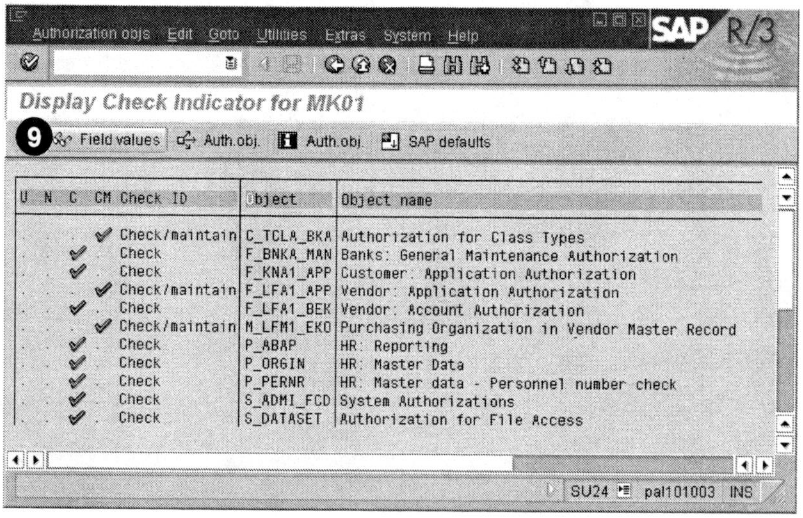


Tips & Tricks

**Explanation of Check Indicators**

*CM = Check/Maintain*

- An authorization check is carried out against this object.
- The PG creates an authorization for this object, and field values are displayed for changing.
- Default values for this authorization can be maintained.

*C = Check*

- An authorization check is carried out against this object.
- The PG does not create an authorization for this object, so field values are not displayed.
- No default values can be maintained for this authorization.

*N = No check*

- The authorization check against this object is disabled.
- The PG does not create an authorization for this object, so field values are not displayed.
- No default values can be maintained for this authorization.

*U = Unmaintained*

- No check indicator is set.
- An authorization check is always carried out against this object.
- The PG does not create an authorization for this object, therefore field values are not displayed.

Caution

The check indicator of an authorization object is important for the PG. The PG only creates an authorization for an authorization object if the check indicator is set to *Check/Maintain (CM)*. Predefined values for this authorization are already maintained in the authorization overview. You can only predefine authorization values for an object if the check indicator is set to *Check/Maintain (CM)*.

10. Three objects get displayed with predefined values, since only three objects had the check indicator set to *Check/Maintain*.
11. To change a check indicator, choose [icon] to toggle between display and change mode.

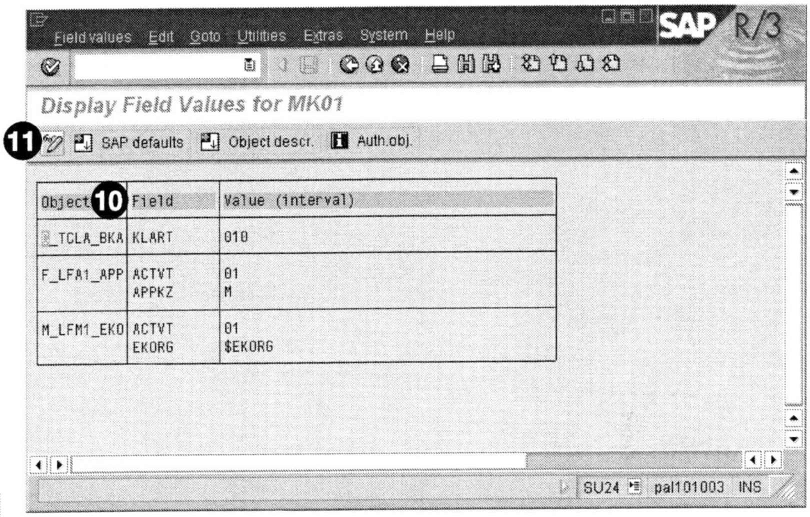


TechTalk

The table displayed on the right is table *USOT_C*.

12. Enter a transportable change request number, or use [icon] to create a new one.
13. Choose [icon].

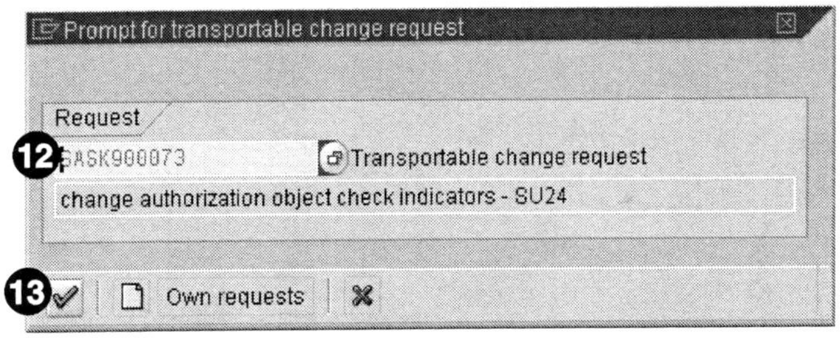


14. To change the authorization field values for one of the objects, choose [icon] next to the object's field name (for example, the object *F_LFA1_APP* and the field *APPKZ*).

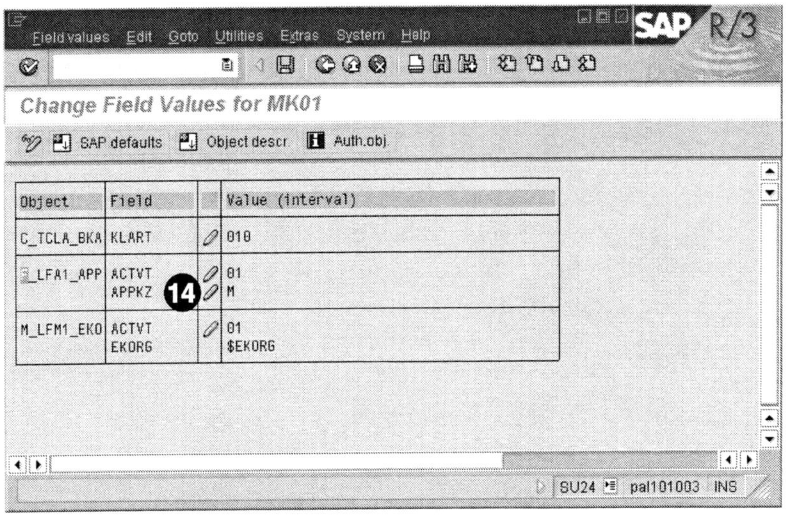

15. Select the desired value (for example, we added *F Financial Accounting*).
16. Choose .

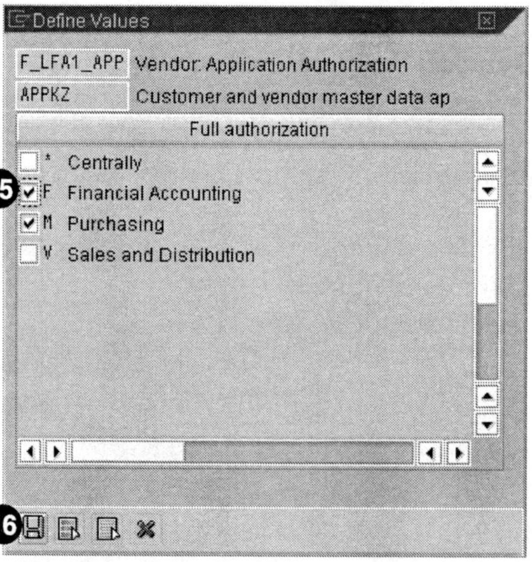


17. The value was added.
18. Choose  *SAP defaults* to compare any changes you might have made.

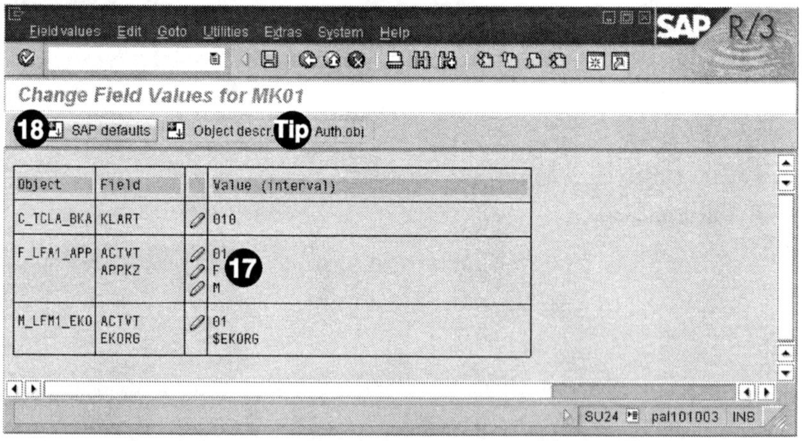


Tips & Tricks

To display the long text for the authorization object, choose  *Object descr.*

19. In the *Value (interval)* column, review your changes (this is table *USOBT_C*, which represents customer settings).
20. In the *SAP value (interval)* column, notice the originally delivered SAP default values (this is table *USOBT*, which represents SAP defaults). Values that have changed from the SAP defaults are in color.
21. To save your changes, choose .
22. Choose  or  *SAP defaults* to hide the SAP default values.

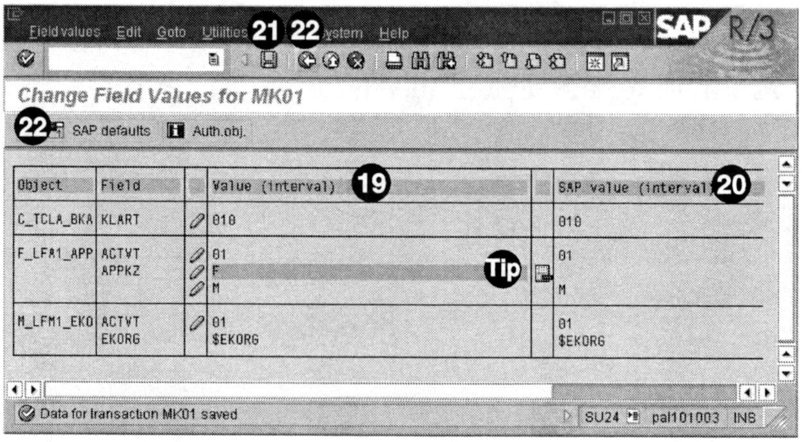


Tips & Tricks

To skip your changes, choose  for the appropriate value you changed.

23. Choose to switch to change mode for the check indicators.
24. To change a check indicator for an object, click in the appropiate column (*U, N, C, CM*).

    Notice how the cursor changes to an iconized hand as you move over the check indicators.

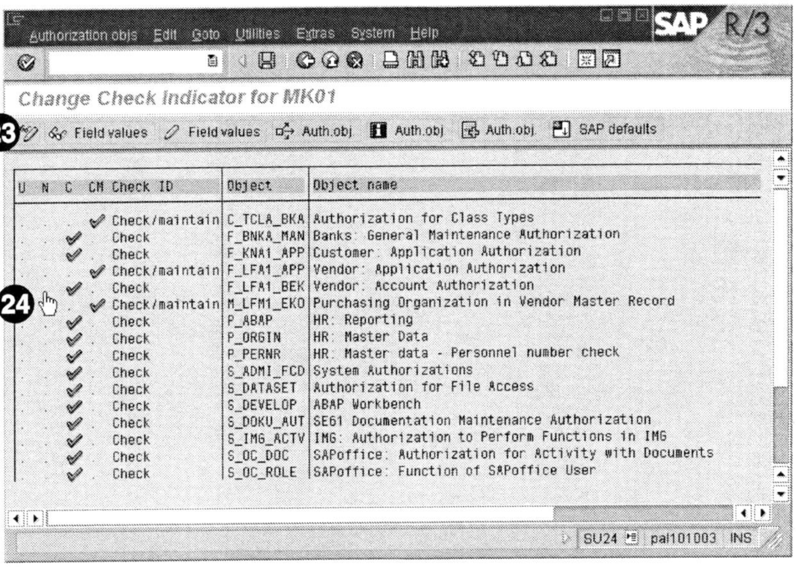


In this example, we clicked in the *N* column to set the check indicator for object *F_LFA1_BEK* to *No check.*

25. The check indicator has successfully been changed to *N*. Therefore, *F_LFA1_BEK* will no longer be checked in transaction *MK01*.
26. Select an object and choose *Auth. obj.* to view a where-used list.

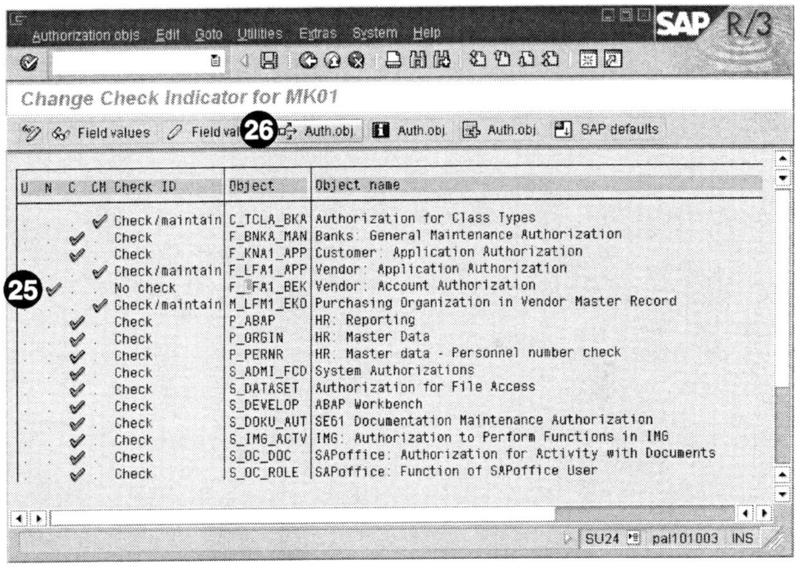


27. You have to determine a specific transaction code range. To search through all existing transaction codes, enter an asterisk (*).
28. Choose .

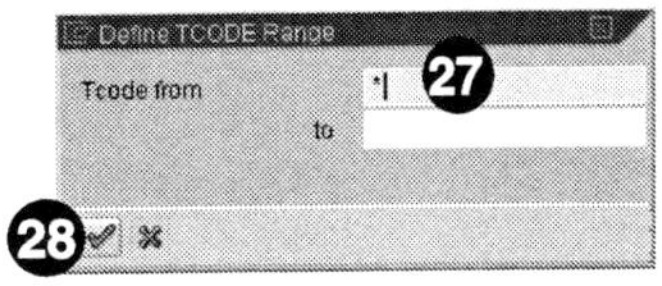

29. The generated list shows all transactions where the selected authorization object is used.
30. Choose ⟲.

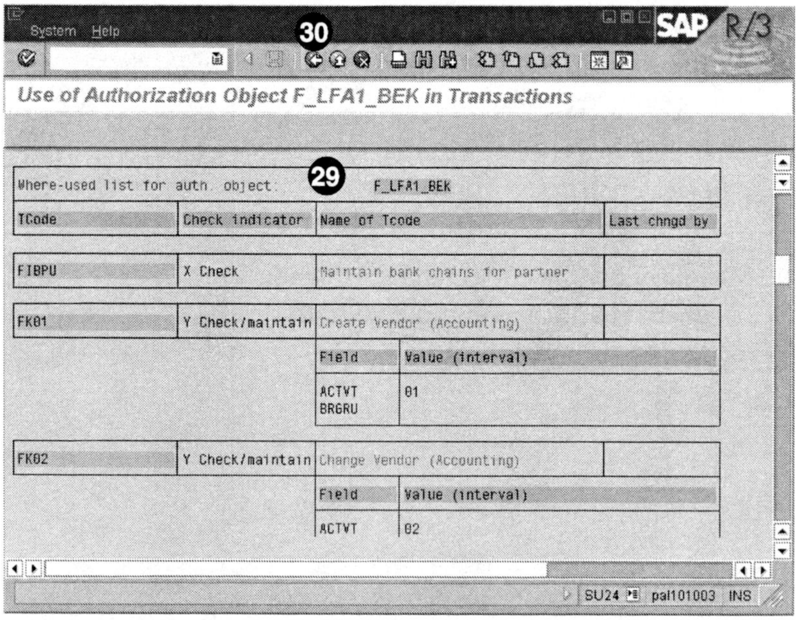

31. Choose *SAP defaults* to display the SAP check indicator defaults in the same list.

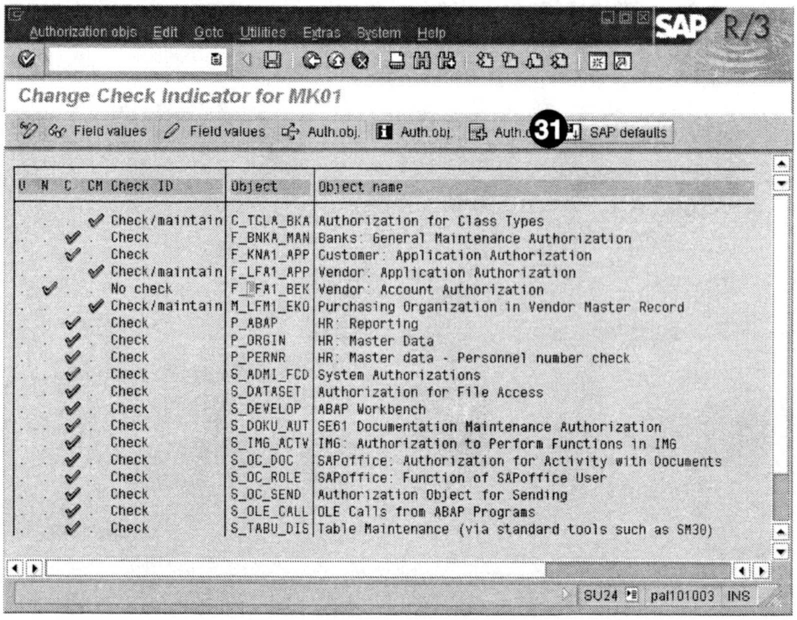

Both table entries in tables *USOBX* and *USOBX_C* now appear for the selected transaction (in this example, *MK01*).

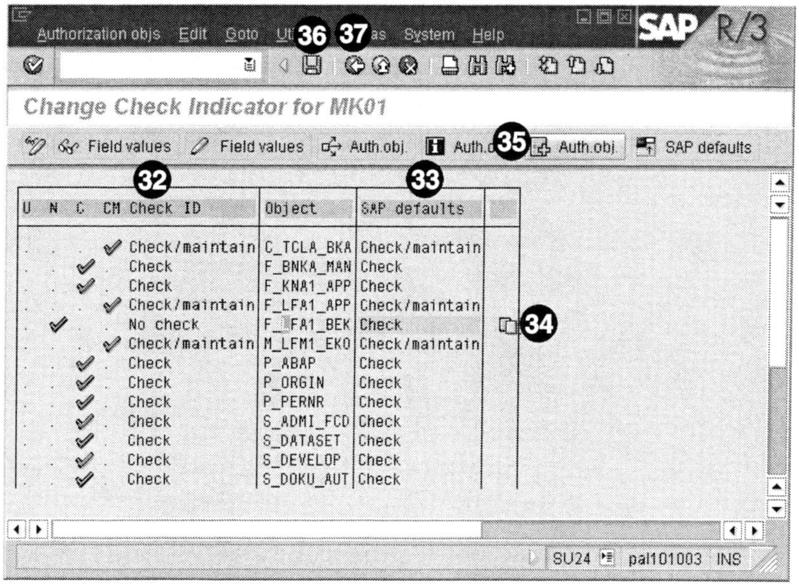


32. In the *Check ID* column, review the current active check indicators for this transaction (entries in table *USOBX_C*).
33. In the *SAP defaults* column, review the SAP check indicators default values (entries in table *USOBX*).
34. To skip your changes, choose to reset to the SAP check indicator default value for this authorization object. Settings that differ from SAP defaults appear in color.
35. Choose *Auth. obj.* to add a new object for checking. There must also be an *AUTHORITY_CHECK* call in this program for the new object.
36. Choose .
37. Choose .

Caution

**Exceptions**

Authorization objects from the Basis (S*) and Human Resources Management applications (P_*, PLOG) cannot be excluded from checking, because the field values for these objects must always get checked. Transactions whose check indicator cannot be changed because of a local lock (ENQUEUE) or a lock in the correction and transport system (for object catalog entry *R3TR SUSK <Tcode>*) are also shown in color. A short error message appears in the description field.

Caution

**Important Information Concerning Profile Matchup After Changes in SU24**

If you generated authorization profiles with the PG, after making changes to check indicators in transactions, a profile matchup is required (even if the PG does not indicate this need for the appropriate authorization profiles).

1. After making changes to check indicators with *SU24*, remember the transactions that are affected by the change.
2. Find out in which activity groups these transactions have been selected. To help identify the appropriate activity groups, choose *Tools → Administration → User maintenance → Information System → Activity Groups → List of Activity Groups According to Complex Selection Criteria*.

3. In transaction *PFCG* select the activity group to be regenerated. You cannot select more than one activity group at a time. When maintaining the authorization data, be sure to select *Expert mode for profile generation* and then *Read old status and merge with new data.*
4. Regenerate the profile.
5. No user master comparison is required. Remember, changes become active with the next system logon.

## Mass Change of Check Indicators

You can also globally change authorization checks for an authorization object in transactions where the authorization object occurs. You can also specifically exclude individual transactions from the global change.

To access the transaction to *Edit check indicators in all transactions,* enter the transaction **SU24** in the *Command* field, or navigate using the IMG as described in the section before. In the following procedure, we show how to get to *Edit check indicators in all transactions* by entering **SU24** directly.

1. In the *Command* field, enter transaction **SU24** and choose *Enter*.
2. Select *Edit check indicators in all transactions*.
3. Enter the desired *Authorization object* (for example, *F_LFA_BEK*.
4. Choose .

   A list of transactions is displayed on the next screen. The entered authorization object appears with the appropriate check indicator per transaction.

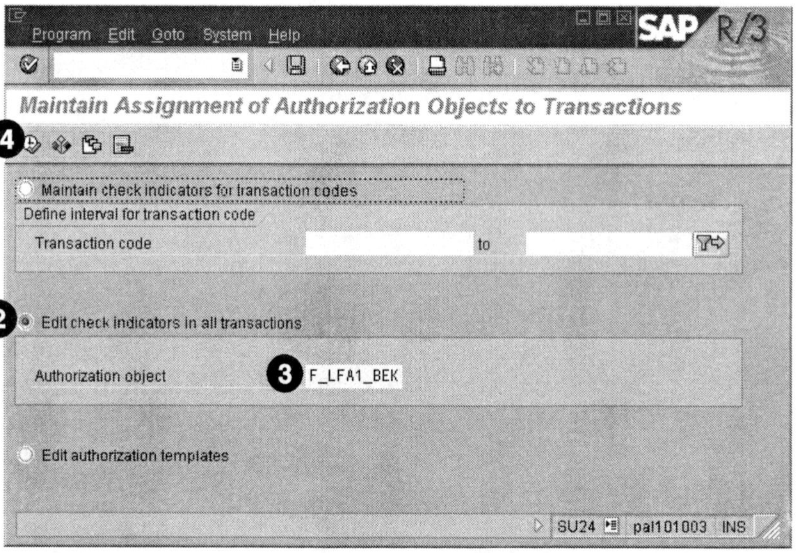

5. To alter the check indicator either for selected transactions or globally, choose one of the following options:

   a. Select the transactions for which you wish to change the check indicator.

   b. Choose [icon] to select all transactions first and then deselect individual transactions as necessary.

   To ensure that the PG actually creates an authorization, we need to change the check indicator for the appropriate authorization object from *C* (*Check*) to *CM* (*Check/Maintain*).

6. To simultaneously change the check indicators for the selected transactions, change the check indicator in the first line, which contains the name of the authorization object, by clicking in the column for the new check indicator below (*U, N, C, CM*). We chose *CM*.

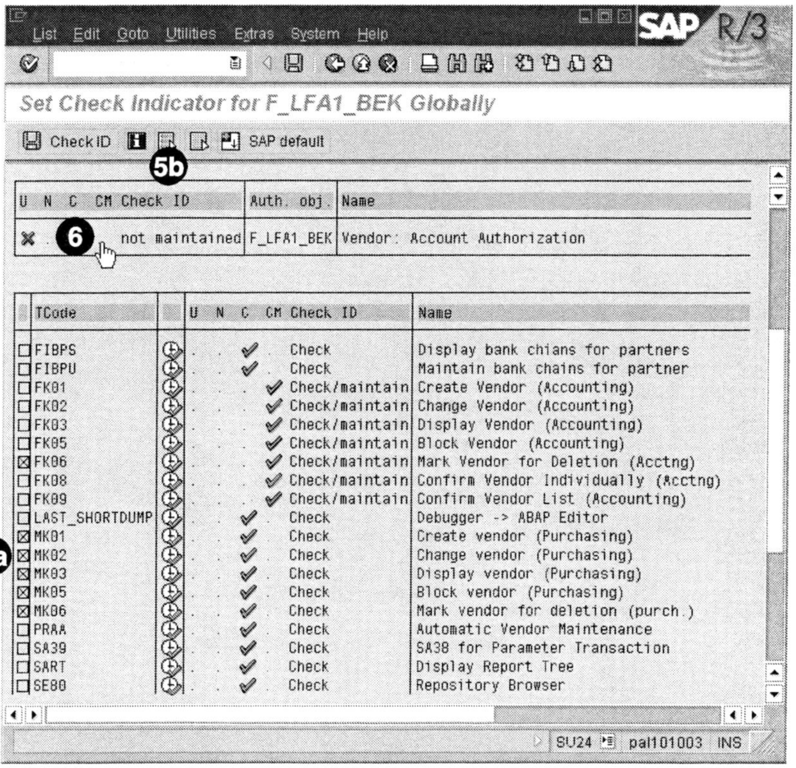


Tips & Tricks

To check the transaction executed by the transaction code displayed in column *Tcode*, you can choose [icon] next to the transaction and it will be executed.

Tips & Tricks

**Explanation of Check Indicators**

*CM = Check/Maintain*

- An authorization check is carried out against this object.
- The PG creates an authorization for this object, and field values are displayed for changing.
- Default values for this authorization can be maintained.

*C = Check*

- An authorization check is carried out against this object.
- The PG does not create an authorization for this object, so field values are not displayed.
- No default values can be maintained for this authorization.

*N = No check*

- The authorization check against this object is disabled.
- The PG does not create an authorization for this object, so field values are not displayed.
- No default values can be maintained for this authorization.

*U = Unmaintained*

- No check indicator is set.
- An authorization check is always carried out against this object.
- The PG does not create an authorization for this object, therefore field values are not displayed.

Caution

The check indicator of an authorization object is important for the PG. The PG only creates an authorization for an authorization object if the check indicator is set to *Check/Maintain (CM)*. Predefined values for this authorization are already maintained in the authorization overview. You can only predefine authorization values for an object if the check indicator is set to *Check/Maintain (CM)*.

7. Only the check indicator for the transactions you selected have changed.
8. Once a check indicator in the list is set to *CM (Check/Maintain)*, the *Fld values* button appears. By clicking this button, you can maintain the authorization field values of the selected authorization object for all transactions whose check indicator has been set.
9. Choose *SAP defaults* to compare the current settings with the SAP defaults.

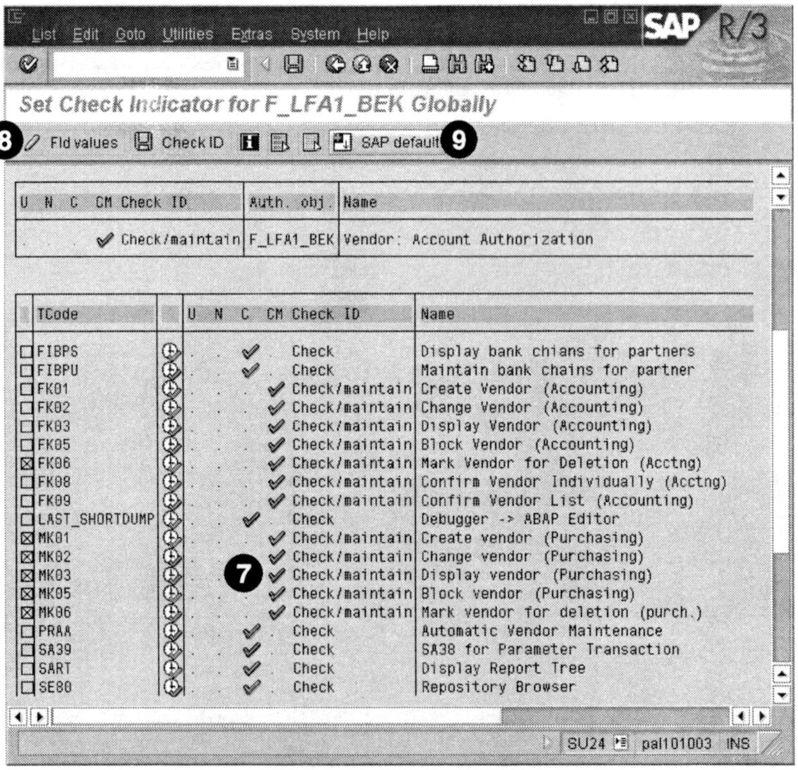

10. The changes of the check indicator are shown in red.

    To highlight all transaction codes that have changed, choose *Edit → Changes → Display in color*.

11. In the *Check ID* column, notice the changes you made (entries in table *USOBX_C*),

12. In the *SAP defaults* column, notice the SAP check indicator default values (entries in *USOBX*).

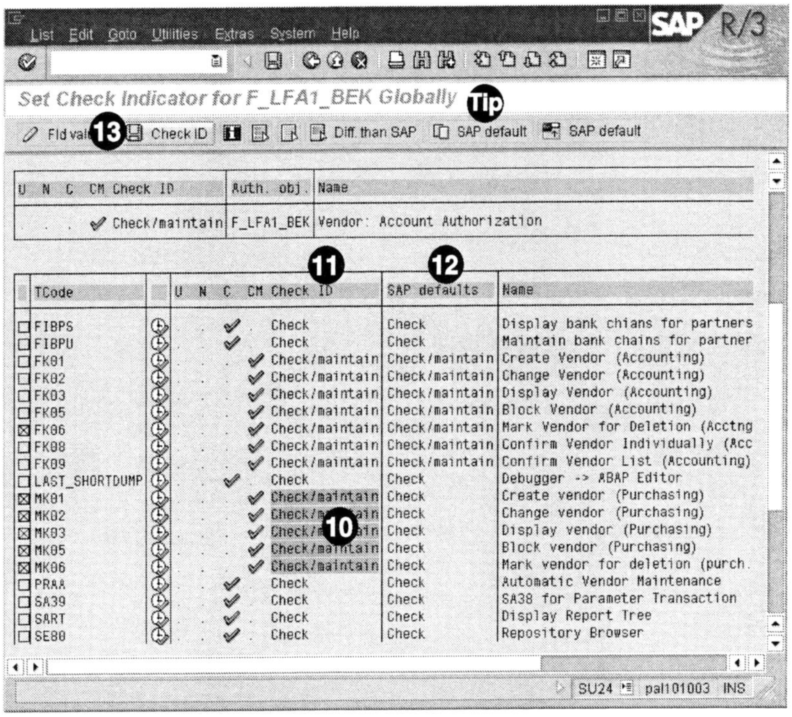


Choose *SAP default* if you want to restore the selected transactions to their original delivery status set by SAP. During installation, this step restores the check indicators and field values to the setting in the R/3 System.

13. Choose *Check ID*.

14. Choose *Yes*.

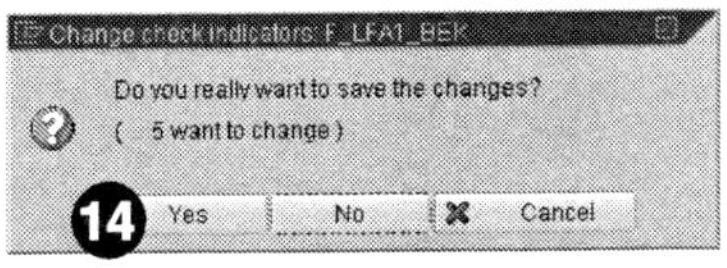


**Exceptions**

Authorization objects from the Basis (S*) and Human Resources Management applications (P_*, PLOG) cannot be excluded from checking, because the field values for these objects must always get checked.

Caution

**Important Information Concerning Profile Matchup After Changes in *SU24***

If you generated authorization profiles with the PG, after making changes to check indicators in transactions, a profile matchup is required (even if the PG does not indicate this need for the appropriate authorization profiles).

1. After making changes to check indicators with *SU24*, remember the transactions that are affected by the change.
2. Find out in which activity groups these transactions have been selected. To help identify the appropriate activity groups, choose *Tools → Administration → User maintenance → Information System → Activity Groups → List of Activity Groups According to Complex Selection Criteria.*
3. In transaction *PFCG,* select the activity group to be regenerated. You cannot select more than one activity group at a time. When maintaining the authorization data, be sure to select *Expert mode for profile generation* and then *Read old status and merge with new data.*
4. Regenerate the profile.
5. No user master comparison is required. Remember that changes become active with the next system logon.

## Maintaining Authorizations in the Activity Groups

Please see chapter 6, *Advanced Profile Generator Functionality,* since we described this topic there in detail.

# Chapter 13: SAP Security Audit and Logging

## Contents

# Overview

The purpose of this chapter is to make you aware of your responsibilities as the R/3 System administrator(s) for security, which includes:

- Protecting the R/3 System
- Preparing you for a computer security audit

Generally, the system administrator is responsible for responding to the findings of an R/3 System audit.

In this chapter, you learn how to analyze authorization logging from a security perspective. You learn how to prepare for a typical system audit.

**Refer to *System Administration Made Easy*, Release 4.6A/B, chapter 11, the section *Security Administration*, which served as the basis for this chapter.**

This chapter is only intended to serve as an introduction to computer security. Considering the growing importance of security, we advise you to work with your auditors, finance department, legal department, and others who might be affected by system security.

# Audit Tools (SM20, SM19, SECR)

## Security Audit Log (SM20)

### What

The Security Audit Log records the security-related activities of users in the system. These activities include successful and failed:

- Dialog logon attempts
- Report and transaction starts
- RFC/CPIC logons

Other events written to the log are:

- Locked transactions or users
- Changed or deleted:
  - Authorizations
  - Authorization profiles
  - User master records
- Changes to the audit configuration

The log is created each day, and previous logs are not deleted or overwritten. The log files can become numerous and large, so we recommend that the logs be periodically archived before being manually purged.

> **Note:** The log files are operating system log files. Transaction *SM18* (*Security Audit: Delete Old Audit Logs*) is one mechanism to purge these files. Other operating system archiving techniques may also be used.

An audit analysis report can be generated from the audit logs. You can analyze a local server, a remote server, or all the servers in an R/3 System.

### Why

The information in the security audit files can be manipulated to tailor the audit analysis report based on certain criteria. The report assists the administrator to:

- Reconstruct or analyze incidents
- Improve security by recognizing inadequate measures
- Trace unusual user activities
- Understand the impact of changes to transactions or users

### How

To start a security audit, you can do one of the following:

- Set the profile parameter *rsau/enable* to 1
- Dynamically start it using transaction *SM19* (See the section *Setting Security Audit Log Parameters* on page 13–5).

The number of audit logs created by the system depends on the following:

- You may choose to set the maximum space for the security audit file in parameter *rsau/max_diskspace/local*.

  At this point, when the limit has been reached, logging will end.
- You can define the size of an individual security log file to fit the chosen archiving media.

  This definition means that the system produces several log files each day, and these files can be, for example, archived periodically onto CDs. The profile parameter is *rsau/max_diskspace/per_file* and the maximum size per file is 2 GB.

Caution

> You cannot set both parameters. You have to choose the method by which the audit files are created.

## Running the Audit Log

This procedure assumes that the audit has been running for some time and that audit logs have been created.

1. In the *Command* field, enter transaction **SM20** and choose *Enter* (or from the *SAP standard menu*, choose *Tools → Administration → Monitor → Security Audit log → SM20-Analysis*).
2. On the System Audit Log screen, complete the steps below:
   a. In *From date/time*, enter for example, **13:00**
   b. Under *Audit classes*, select:
      - *Dialog logon*
      - *Transaction start*
      - *Report start*
3. Choose *Re-read audit log.*

   This button is used to read a log for the first time.

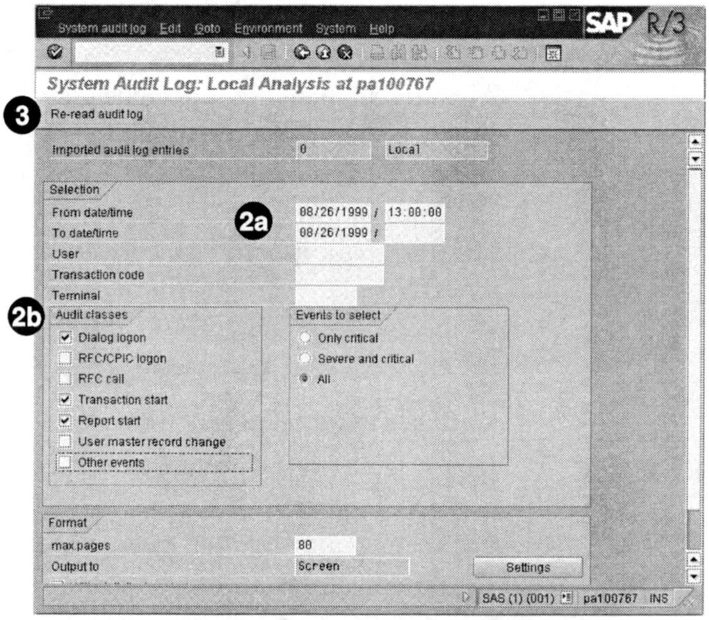


   The security report is displayed.

4. To review the details of an audit message, select a line and choose [icon].

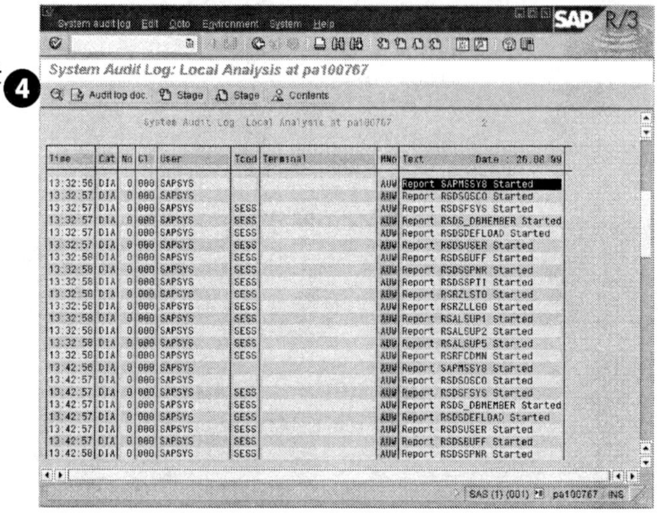

Documentation for the message and technical details appears. This display is most useful when displaying negative messages such as failed logins or locked transactions.

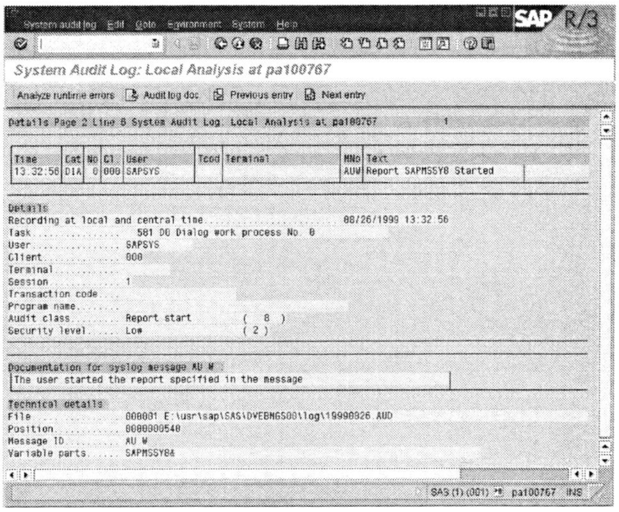

## Setting Security Audit Log Parameters (SM19)

### What

The audit log parameters are the criteria used to write the types of audit messages into the audit log file. The parameters are grouped into audit profiles that can be activated at the next system startup (configuration status) or applied "on the fly" (dynamic configuration).

### Why

Audit profiles need to be created first before audit logs can be written. These profiles limit the amount and type of data written into the security audit files, making the subsequent security reports more meaningful to the administrator.

### How

Decide what to audit and set selection criteria either at the database level or dynamically at the application server level:

- If the audit configuration is permanently stored at the database level, all application servers use the identical criteria to save events in the audit log. The settings take effect at the next application server start.
- At the application server level, however, dynamic changes can be set to individual application servers and distributed to the entire system.

  The new criteria remains in effect until the server is brought down.

You can define up to five sets of selection criteria or filters. The system parameter, *rsau/selection_slots*, that defines the number of filters has a default value of 2. You can activate an audit in the dynamic configuration using transaction *SM19*.

1. In the *Command* field, enter transaction **SM19** and choose *Enter* (or from the *SAP standard menu*, choose *Tools → Administration → Monitor → Security Audit log → SM19-Configuration*).

   Configuration status refers to the storage of the parameters in the database.

2. Choose .

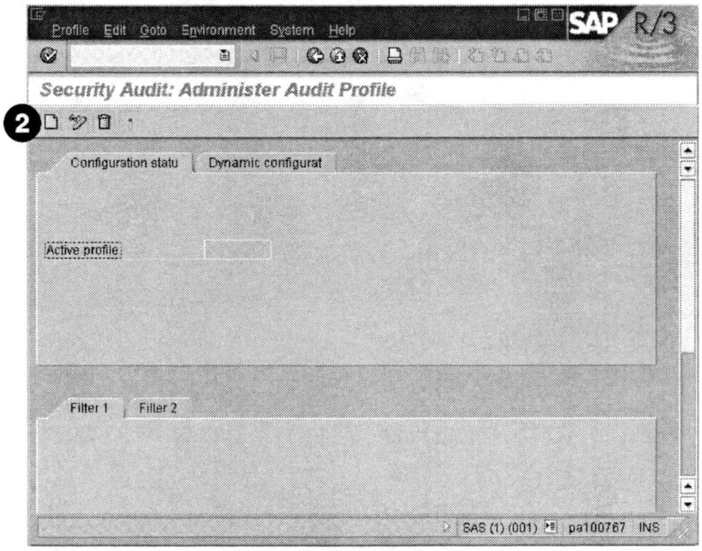


3. Enter a profile name (for example, **AUDPROF1**).
4. Choose .

5. In this screen, you may specify two filter groups and define the types of audit messages that will be written into the log.

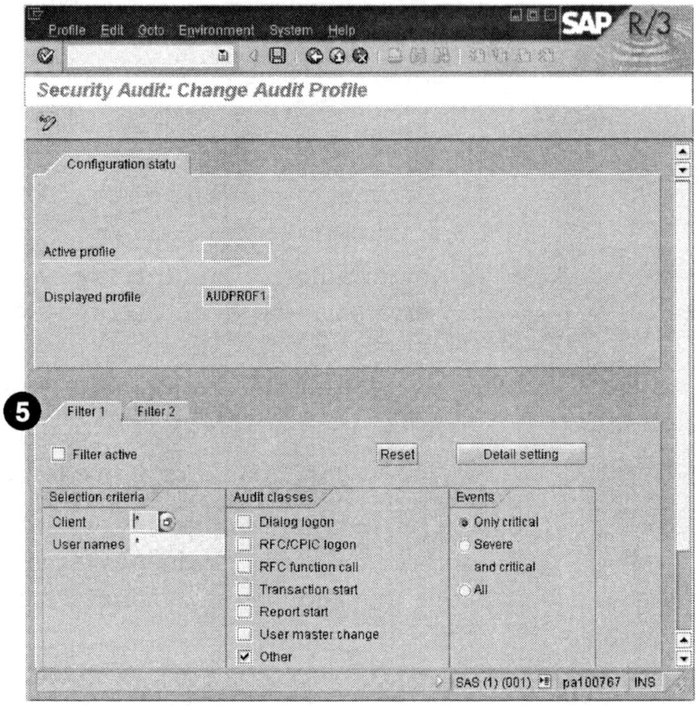

### Defining Filter Group 1

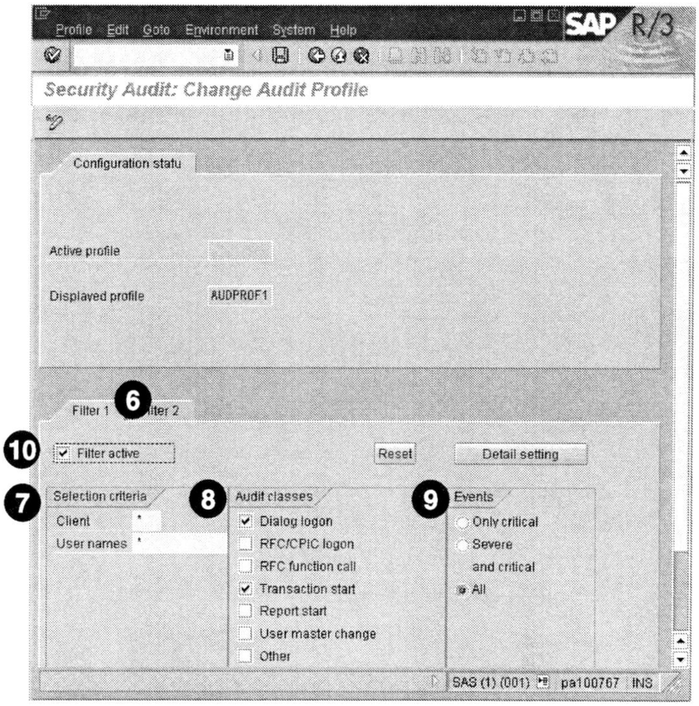


6. Choose the *Filter 1* tab.
7. Under *Selection criteria*:
   - Enter * in *Client.*
   - Enter * in *User Names.*
8. In *Audit Classes*, select:
   - *Dialog Logon*
   - *Transaction Start*
9. Under *Events*, select *All.*
10. Select *Filter Active.*

### Defining Filter Group 2

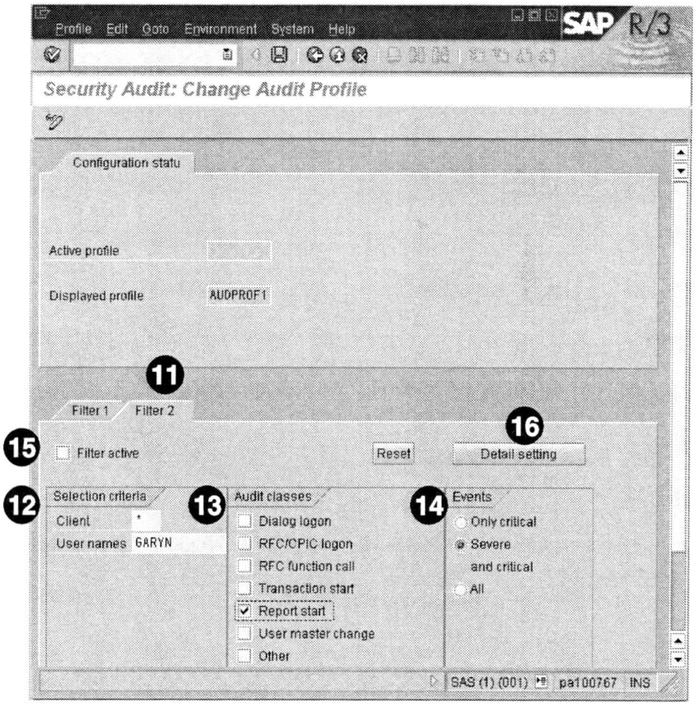


11. Choose the *Filter 2* tab.

    This filter traces the reports started by one user.
12. Under *Selection criteria*:
    - Enter * in *Client*.
    - Enter a user ID in *User Names* (for example, **GARYN**).
13. In *Audit Classes*, select *Report start.*
14. Under *Events*, select *Severe and critical.*
15. Deselect *Filter Active.*

    This setting allows you to save the filter settings, but does not activate them.
16. Choose *Detail setting* to drill down to the audit class and event class categories.

17. Scroll down to *Report start*.

    Notice that the category is automatically chosen based on the earlier selection of event type and audit class type.

18. Choose ✓.

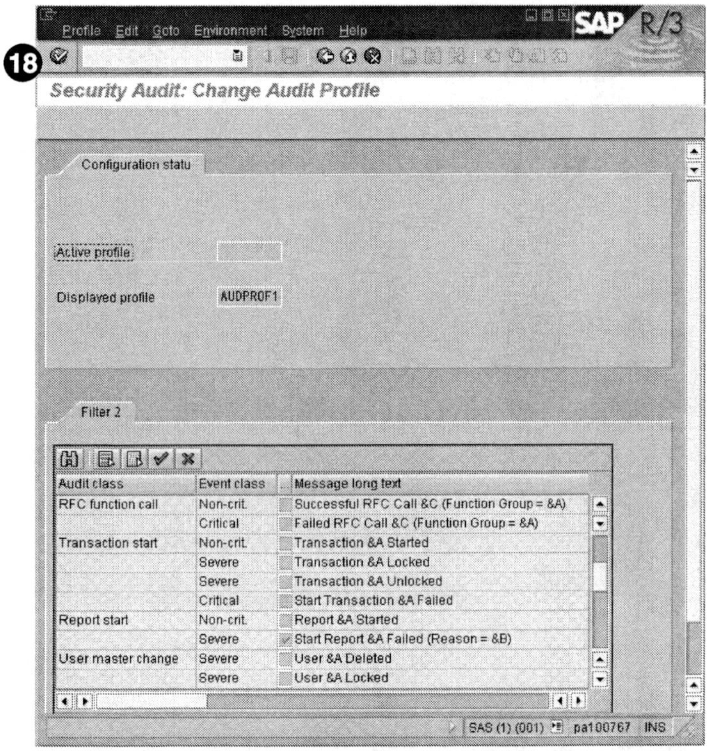


19. The general categories are cleared indicating that settings were browsed or defined at the detail level.

20. Choose 💾.

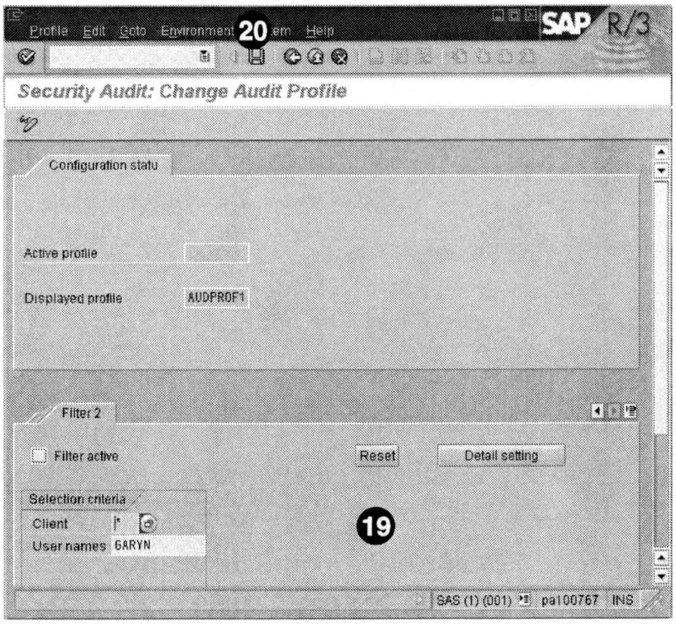

21. A system message notifies the user that the profile was saved successfully.
22. To activate the profile, select .

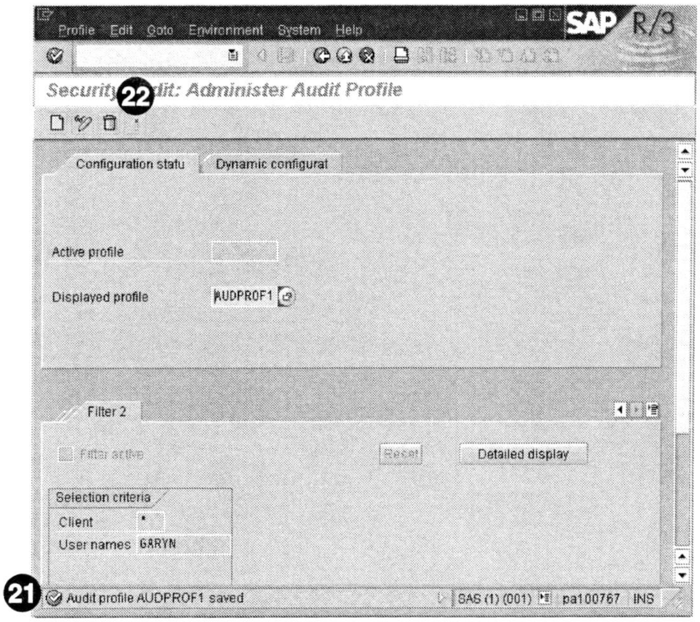


23. The profile name now appears in the *Active profile* field.
24. A system message indicates that the profile will be activated when the application server is restarted.
25. To dynamically change the selection criteria for one or more application servers in a running system, choose the *Dynamic configurat (Dynamic configuration)* tab.

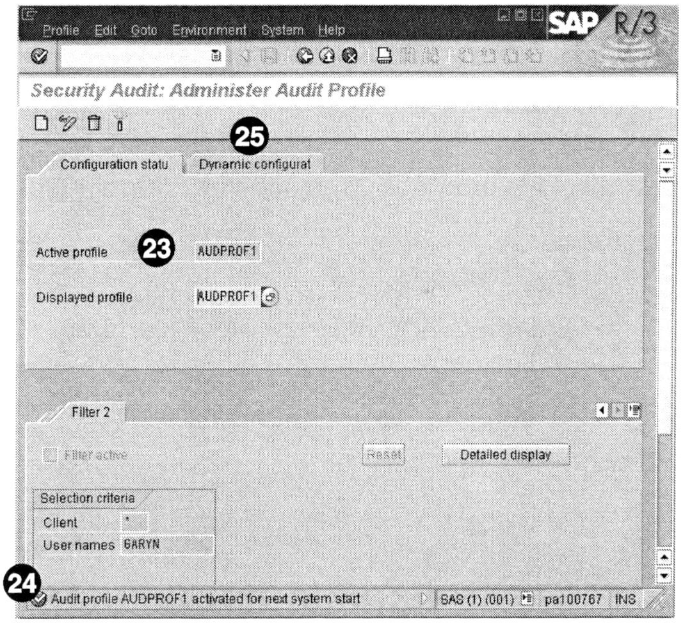

26. In this example, the audit has been running for some time (indicated by the current file size greater than zero) before being stopped briefly. The red ■ in the *Stat.* (Status) column indicates that the audit is inactive.
27. Choose .

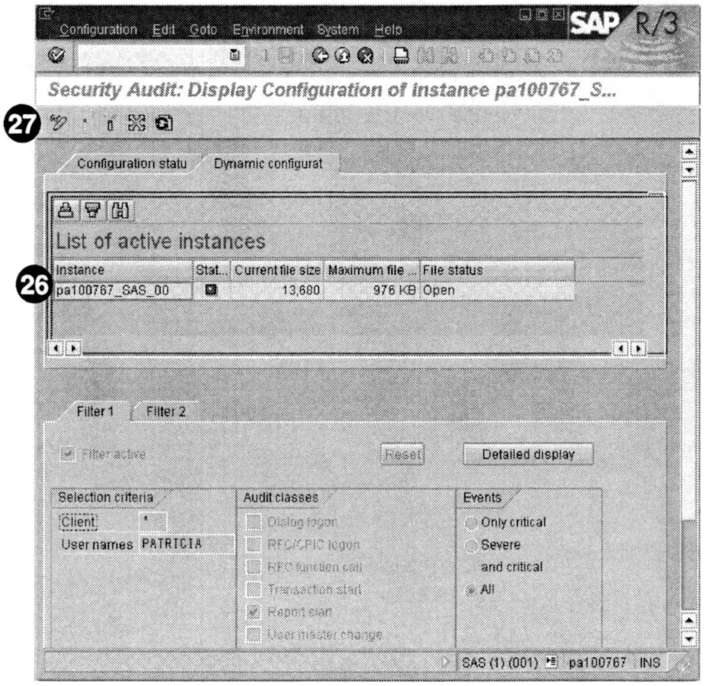


### Running an Audit on a Different User

In this procedure, we run an audit on a different user and check all the reports that were started.

1. On the *Filter* tab, enter *Selection criteria:*
   - Enter * in *Client*.
   - Enter a user ID in *User names* (for example, **Patricia**).
2. Under *Audit classes*, select *Report start*.
3. Under *Events*, select *All*.
4. Under *Filter 1*, select *Filter active*.
5. To activate, choose .

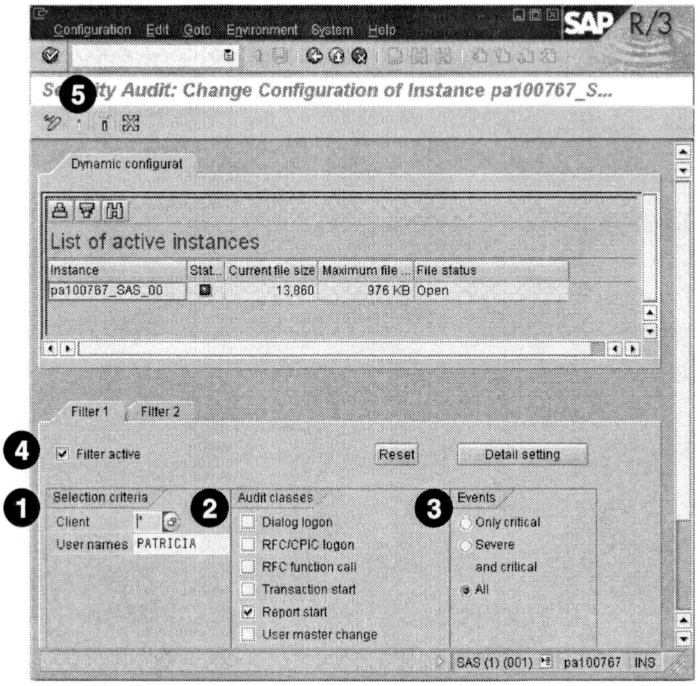

6. Choose *Yes*.

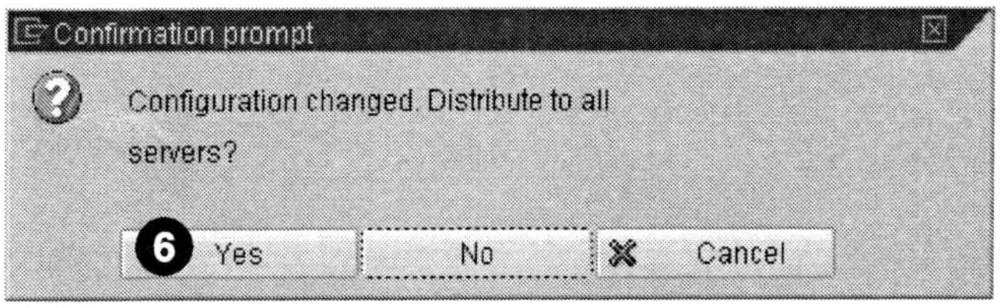


7. A green appears in the *Stat.* (Status) column and a system message indicates that the configuration was activated.

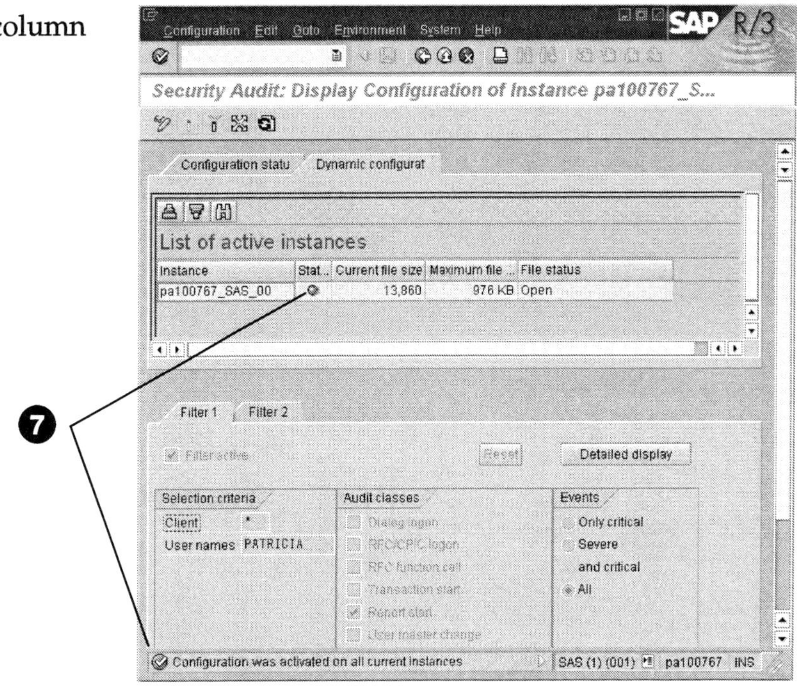


## Audit Information System (SECR)

### What

The Audit Information System (AIS) is designed for system and business audits and will likely be run by internal or external auditors. It puts in one place many of the R/3 security tools. The center of the AIS is the audit report tree, structured around a range of auditing functions and default configurations including:

- Auditing procedures and documentation
- Auditing evaluations
- Downloading of audit data

AIS can be effectively positioned as the SAP tool for internal auditing and data protection, external auditing, ongoing security control checks, interim audits, preparation of year-end closing statements, year-end audits, etc.

AIS uses standard R/3 reports and transactions to conduct the review and is a standard component in Release 4.6A. However, you can import the AIS into your system back to Release 3.0D or higher. For more information on AIS and its availability, please refer to

SAPNet – R/3 Frontend notes *77503* and *100609*. AIS also provides an interface to export data to an external auditing system that analyzes financial statements.

#### Why

Auditors examine the results of automated and manual financial and system procedures to ensure that there is a checks-and-balances infrastructure to prevent fraud and other problems. AIS enables the auditors to test transactions and run reports during the inspection.

#### How

To start AIS, call transaction **SECR**. There are two ways to conduct an audit:

- Complete
- User-defined

## Complete Audit

While it is not possible to show all the functionality of the AIS here, we provide the following scenario of investigation:

In the *Command* field, enter transaction **SECR** and choose *Enter* (or from the *SAP standard menu,* choose *Information Systems → SECR-Audit Info System*).

1. Under *Choose view*, select *Complete audit*.
2. Choose the execute icon.

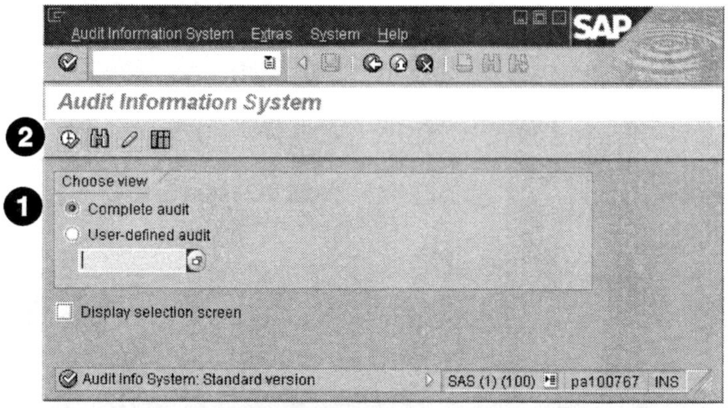


A complete audit consists of a system audit and business audit. The structure on this screen is *Audit_All* with a standard view.

3. Click the nodes (+) to expand the following:
   - *System Audit*
   - *Business Audit*

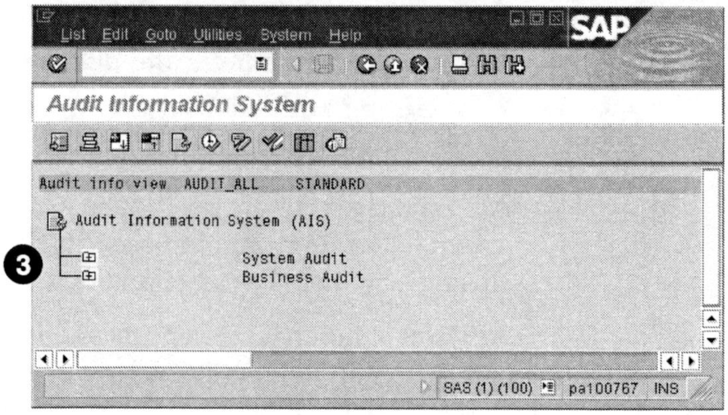

**System Audit**

The following example shows how to use the AIS.

1. Under *System Audit*, click the node (+) next to *Repository / Tables*.

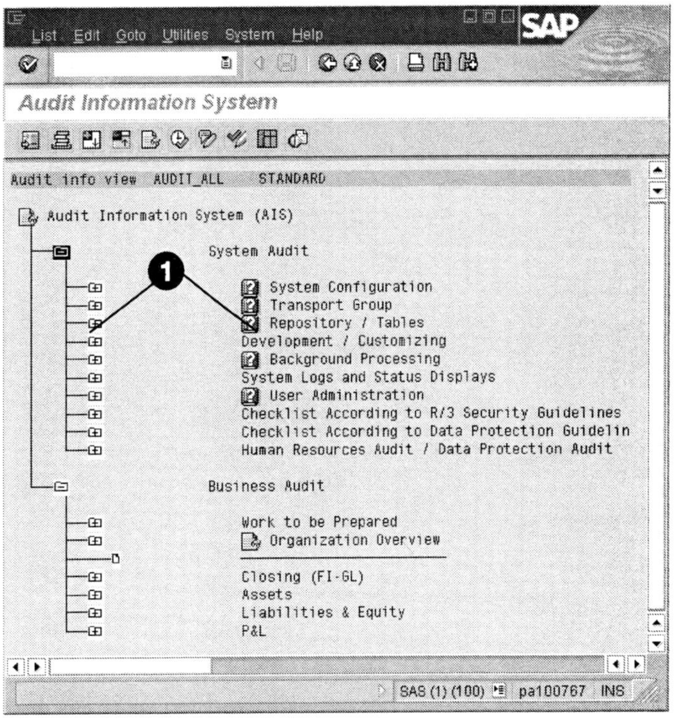


2. Click the node (+) next to *Table Information*.
3. Choose [icon] next to *Data Dictionary display*.

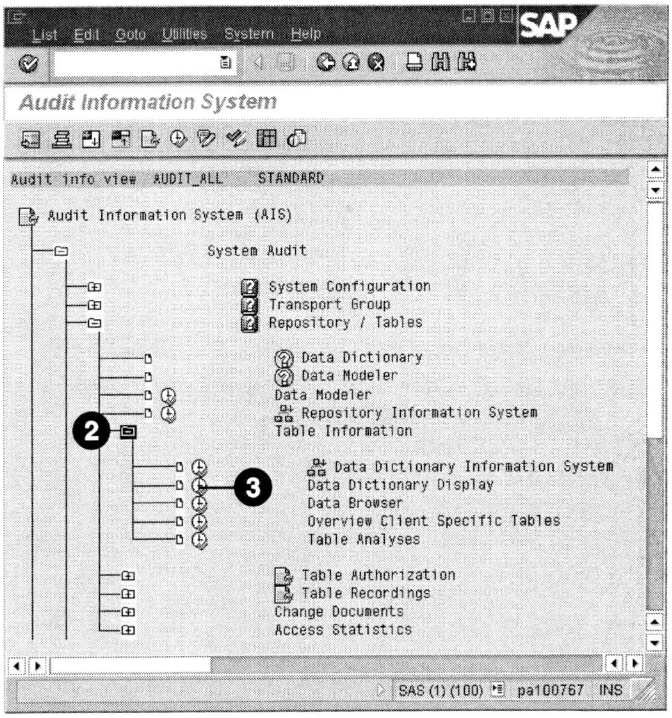

The transaction is executed and you are brought to this screen.

4. Choose [icon].

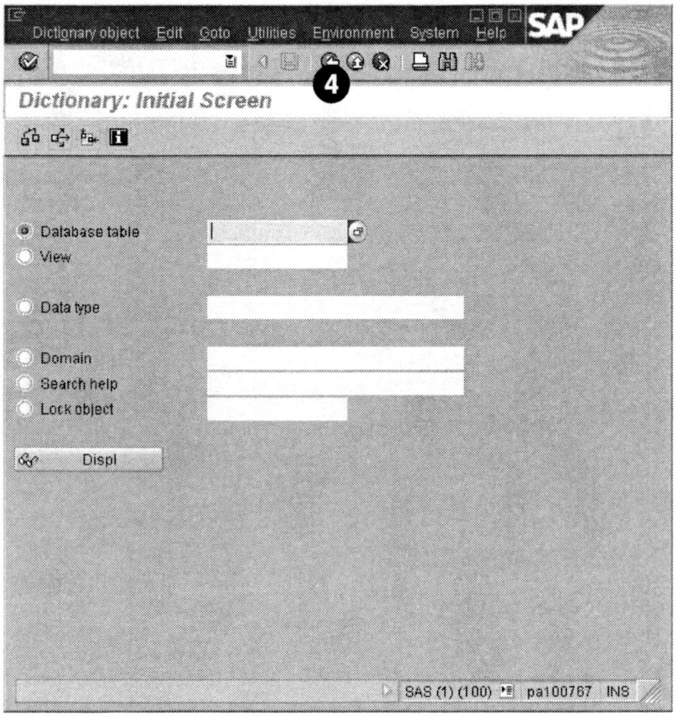


**Business Audit**

1. Under *Business Audit*, click the node (+) next to *Closing (FI-GL)*.
2. Click the node (+) next to *Balance Sheet/ P&L/ Balances*.
3. Click the node (+) next to *Balance Sheet/ P&L*. You can execute different reports to inspect the financial balances.
4. Choose [icon] next to *Profit and Loss Projection*.

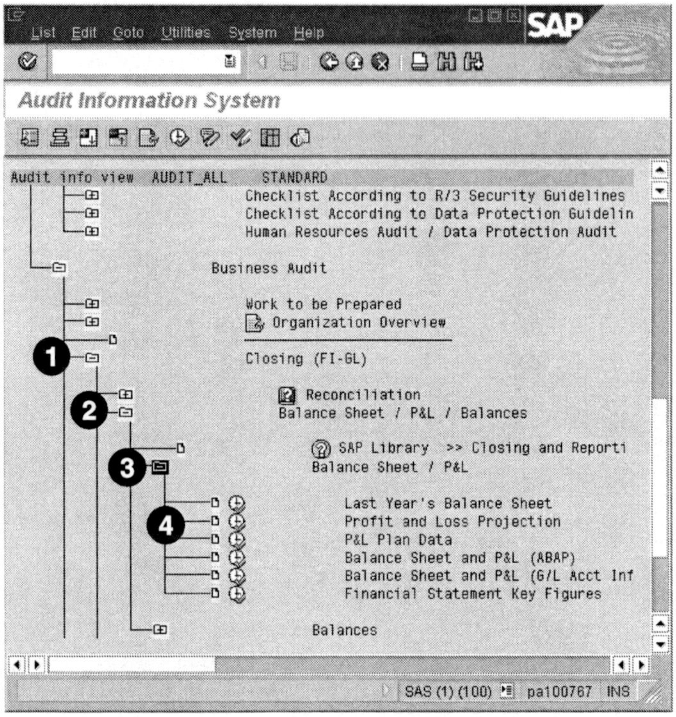

5. On this screen, you can enter criteria for your report, then choose .
6. Choose .

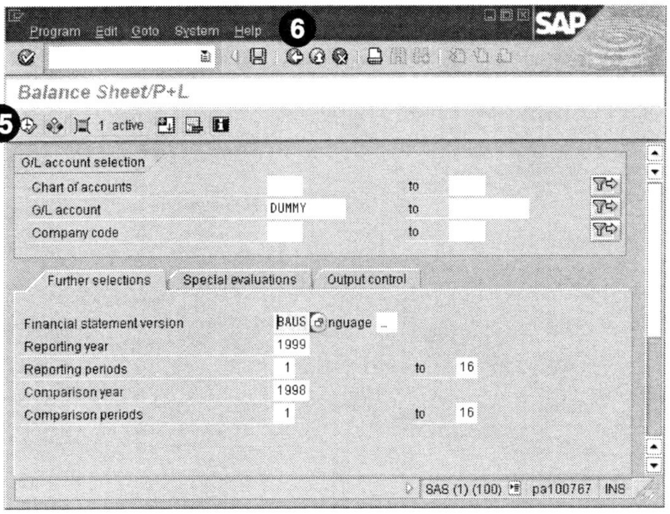


## User-Defined Audit

You can also conduct a user-defined audit by creating a view or subset of a complete audit.

In the *Command* field, enter transaction **SECR** and choose *Enter* (or from the *SAP standard menu*, choose *Information Systems→ SECR-Audit Info System*).

1. Select *User-defined audit*.
2. Under *User-defined audit*, enter a view name (for example, enter **ZVUE**).
3. Choose .

View names should start with *Y* or *Z*.

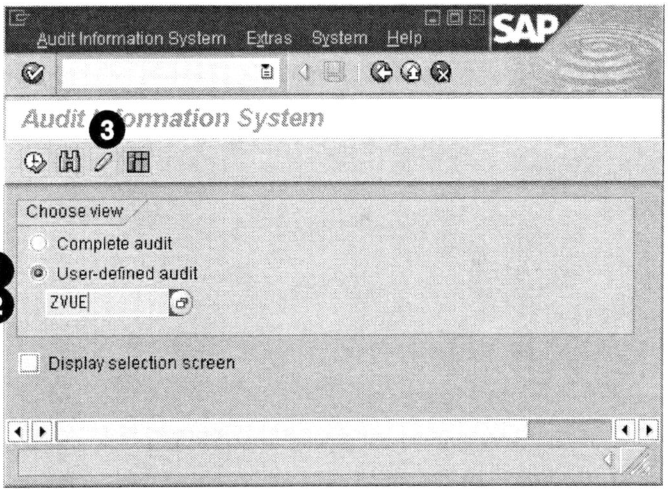

4. Under *New view*, in *Name*, enter the name of the view (for example, **ZVUE**).
5. Under *Select using*, select *Manual Selection*. You will select the procedures that will be included in the view.
6. Choose ✔.

   When you create a view and enter a different name in *Name*, the name of the view is what was entered in the main screen.

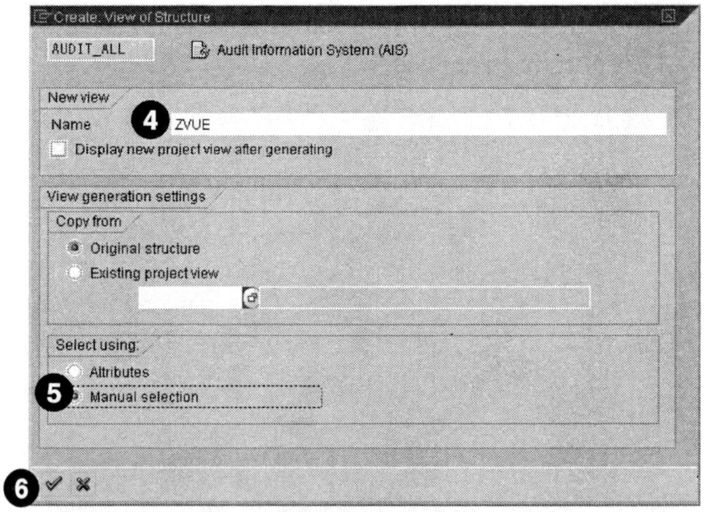


We want to include all the procedures for a system audit in this view.

7. Select *System Audit*.
8. Choose .
9. To generate, choose .

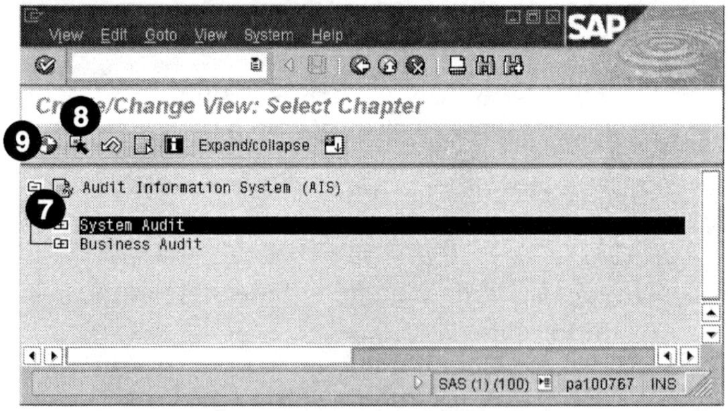


A message indicates that the generation was successful.

10. Choose .

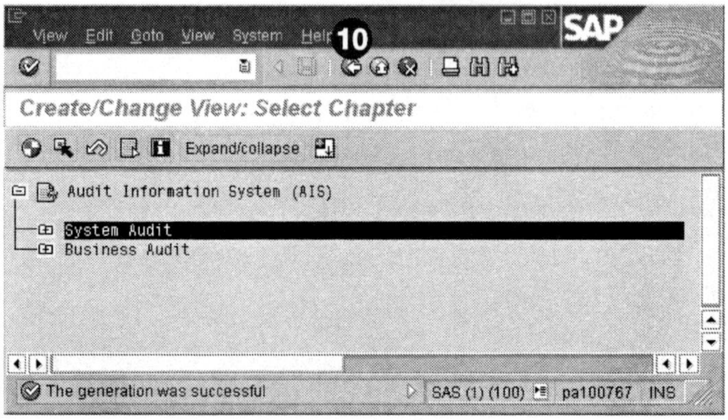

11. Choose *Display* to check the view of this structure.

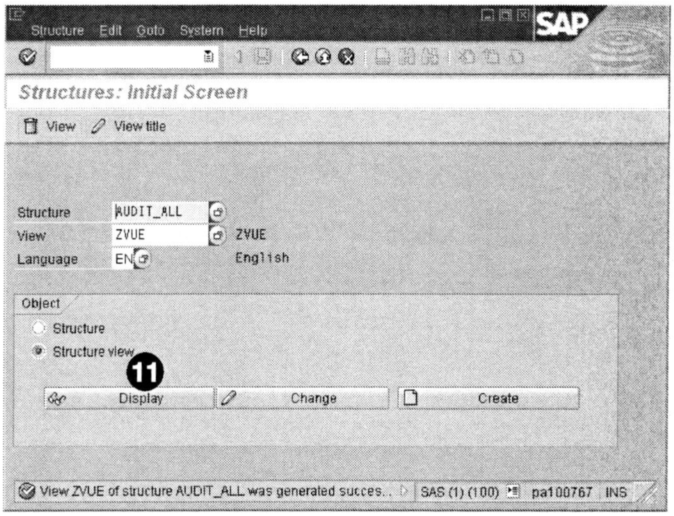


12. Click on the *System Audit* node (+) to expand it.

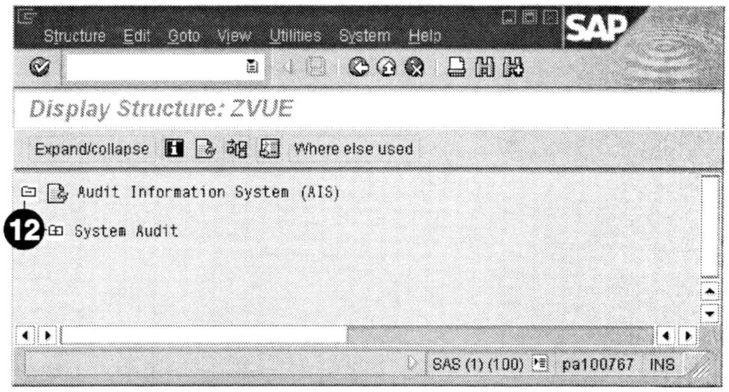


The screen on the right shows all the procedures for the *Audit_All* structure with a *ZVUE* view.

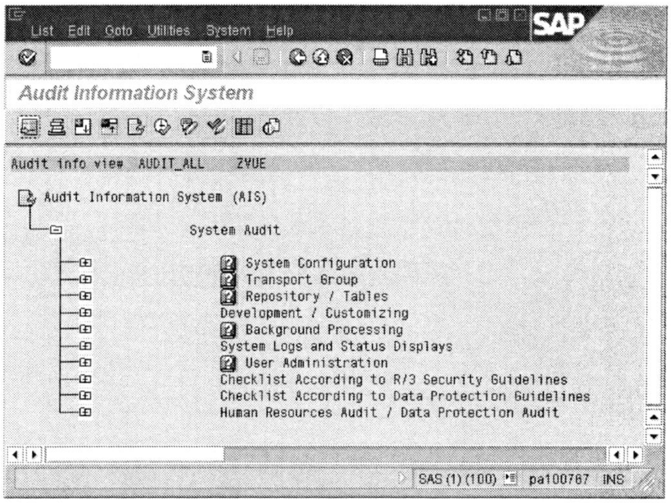

## User Security Audit Jobs

Many of the user security audit jobs/programs are included as part of the AIS, as well in the standard R/3 System.

#### What

There are several predefined SAP security reports, including:

- *RSUSR003* Check for default password on user IDs *SAP** and *DDIC*
- *RSUSR005* Lists users with critical authorizations
- *RSUSR006* Lists users who are locked due to incorrect logon
  This report should be scheduled to run each day, just before midnight.
- *RSUSR007* Lists users with incomplete address data
- *RSUSR008* Lists users with critical combinations of authorizations or transactions
- *RSUSR009* Lists users with critical authorizations, with the option to select the critical authorizations
- *RSUSR100* Lists change documents for users and shows changes made to a user's security
- *RSUSR101* Lists change documents for profiles and shows changes made to security profiles
- *RSUSR102* Lists change documents for authorizations and shows changes made to security authorizations

Some of these reports have parameter tables that need to be properly maintained for best use. Review and analyze these reports based on your knowledge of the company. However, be aware that security issues may exist. If you have a small company, these issues cannot be avoided because one person often must wear many different hats.

#### Why

Tips & Tricks

Your external auditors may require some of these reports to be executed as part of the annual financial audit.

#### How

You can use one of the following transactions or manners:

- *SA38* (ABAP: Execute Program)
  This transaction only allows the program to be executed.
- *SE80 (The object navigator)*
- The User Information System.

Only the *SA38* manner is described below.

**SA38 – ABAP: Execute Program**

1. In the *Command* field, enter transaction **SA38** and choose *Enter.*
2. In *Program,* enter the report name.
3. Choose ✅.

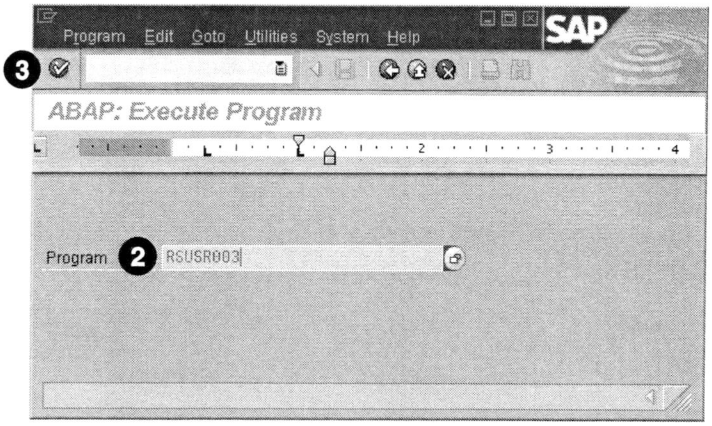


**Notes for Specific Reports**

*RSUSR008* (lists critical combinations of authorizations or transactions):

- These combinations are maintained on table *SUKRI.*
- Dangerous combinations include the following transactions:
  - *RZ02* (with anything)
  - *RZ03* (with anything)
  - *SE14* (with anything)
  - *SU01* (with security, users, and profiles)
  - *SU02* (with security, users, and profiles)

# Audit Tasks (SM21, STAT, ST03)

## Reviewing Validity of Named Users

**What**

All users who have left the company should have their R/3 access terminated immediately. By locking or deleting these user IDs, you limit access to only those users who should have access to R/3. Periodic review assures that the task of locking or deleting has been completed.

> **Note:** If the HR module is implemented, there **are** mechanisms that integrate with the authorization system to have such changes in user accesses occur automatically.

**Why**

Proper audit control requires that a user who no longer has a valid business need to access R/3 should not be allowed to do so.

Deleting or locking these user IDs also prevents anyone who had been using the terminated user ID from accessing the system with that ID.

Tips & Tricks

One of the audit procedures that your external auditors will use is to test whether a person who does not need to access R/3 has a live user ID.

**How**

1. In the *Command* field, enter transaction **SU01** and choose *Enter* (or from the *SAP standard menu*, choose *Tools* → *Administration* → *User maintenance* → *SU01-Users*).
2. Choose *possible entries*.

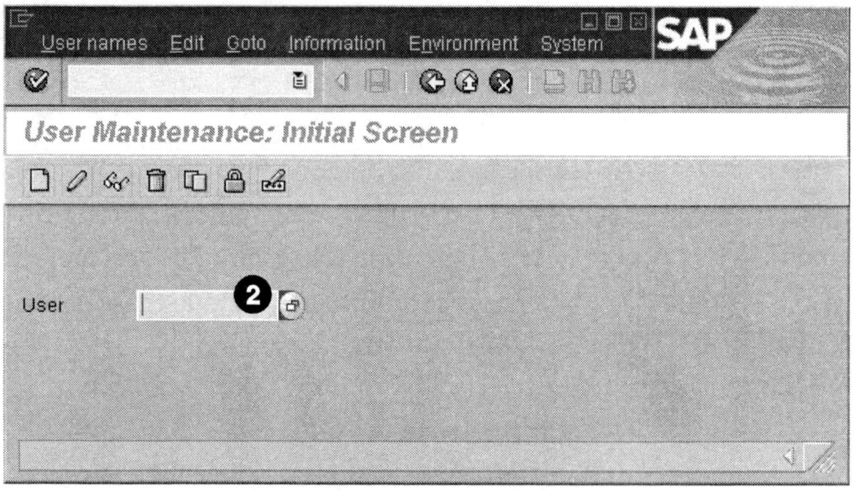


3. Review the active users.

   Verify that these users are indeed valid users.

Tips & Tricks

In a large company, you should do a random audit on **at least** twenty users. The minimum number should be determined by your auditors.

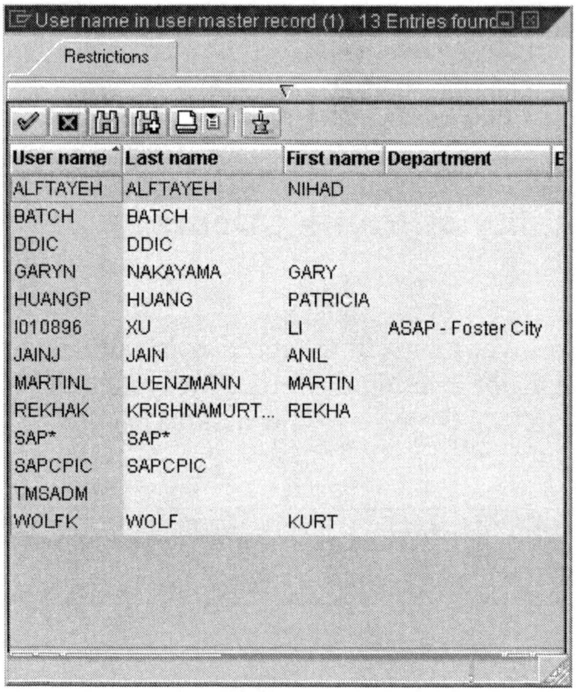

## Reviewing Profiles for Accuracy and Permission Creep

#### What

A **permission creep** is an incremental increase in permissions given to a user over time. If left unchecked, increased permissions may grant a user more authority in the system than is required or intended.

#### Why

Users may have undesirable authorization(s) or combinations.

Tips & Tricks

Your external auditors may have an audit step to check for permission creep.

#### How

You can conduct a spot audit of:

- Individuals
  - Review the security forms for a user, compare these forms to the *activity groups* and *profiles* assigned to that user, and investigate inconsistencies.
  - Review the *activity groups* and *profiles* assigned to the individual for reasonableness.
  - Review the individual profiles assigned for content and check to see if the profile has been recently changed.
- Profiles (transaction *SU02)* and authorizations (transaction *SU03*)
  Check to see if the change date is recent.

You can also execute the following audit reports:

- *RSUSR100* (user changes)
- *RSUSR101* (profile changes)
- *RSUSR102* (authorization changes)

For additional information on these reports, see the *User Security Audit* section on page 13–18.

## System Log (SM21)

The R/3 System logs all system errors, warnings, process messages in the system log (SysLog), and user locks due to failed log-on attempts from known users. The SysLog writes to two different types of logs:

- Local Logs
- Central Logs

Use the transaction *SM21* to access the system log output screen. With this transaction, you can read any of the messages that are contained in the system logs. You can modify the view to meet your needs. A wide range of selection criteria is available to analyze the system.

The following example shows how to use the system log for monitoring security issues such as failed logon attempts:

1. In the *Command* field, enter transaction **SM21** and choose *Enter* (or choose *Tools→ Administration → Monitoring → System Log*).
2. Specify the selection criteria for your system log analysis report (for example, *From date/time, To date/time, User, Transaction code, Process, Problem class, etc.*
3. (Optional) You may enter the message numbers (for example, **US-3**) for failed logon attempts for locked users, and choose ✔ *Use*.
4. Choose ✔ to display the system log report.

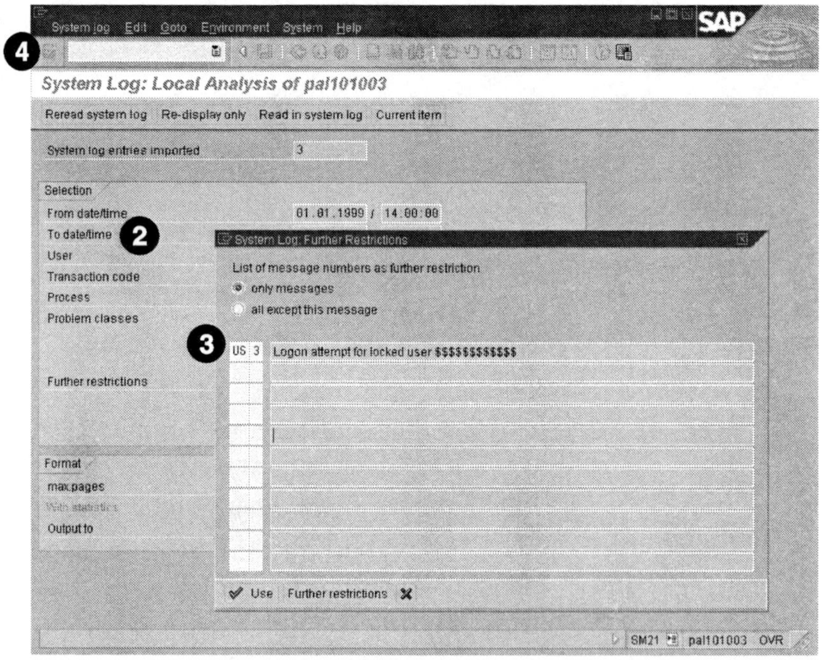


5. On the *System log: Local Analysis* screen, you can view the system log analysis report and drill down each item for detail (if necessary).
6. Choose ⊙.

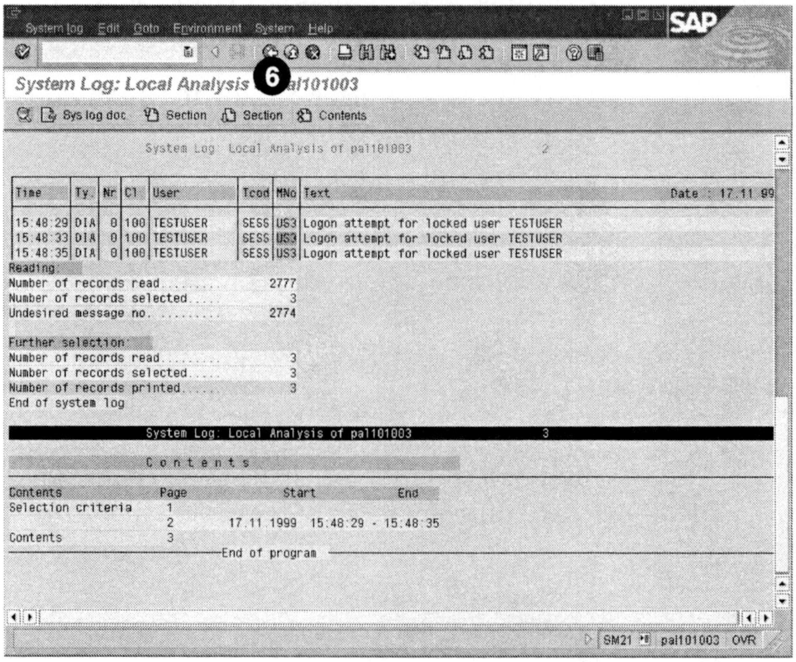

### Local Logs

Each R/3 Application Server has a local log that receives all the messages output by this server. SysLog records these messages in a circular file on the server. (This means that when this log file reaches the maximum permissible length, SysLog overwrites it, starting over from the beginning).

### Central Logs

We recommend that you also maintain a central log file on a selected application server. Each individual application server then sends its local log messages to this server. The server that you designate to maintain the central log collects the messages from the other application servers and writes these messages to the central log.

The central log consists of two files: the active file and the old file (the location of the active file is specified in the *rslg/central/file* profile parameter; the location of the old file is specified in the *rslg/central/old_file*).

The active file contains the current log. When it reaches the maximum size, the system writes to the old log file, makes the previously active file the old file, and creates a new active file. The switch occurs when the size of the active log file is half the value as specified in the *rslg/max_diskspace/central* parameter.

## Statistic Records in CCMS (STAT)

The Computer Center Monitoring System (CCMS) performance analysis tools within R/3 logs all R/3 activities categorized by transaction and user in statistical records that can be useful for audit-trail purposes. You can access these records with the transaction *STAT* or from the *SAP standard menu*. This transaction provides you with the detailed statistical records (including user statistics).

1. In the *Command* field, enter transaction **STAT** and choose *Enter* (or from the *SAP standard menu*, choose *Tools* → *Administration Monitor* → *Performance* → *Workload* → *Statistics records*.)
2. Provide the desired selection criteria (for example, by entering criteria for user, transaction, program, task type, work process number, start-time, etc.).
3. Choose ✔ to display the statistic records.

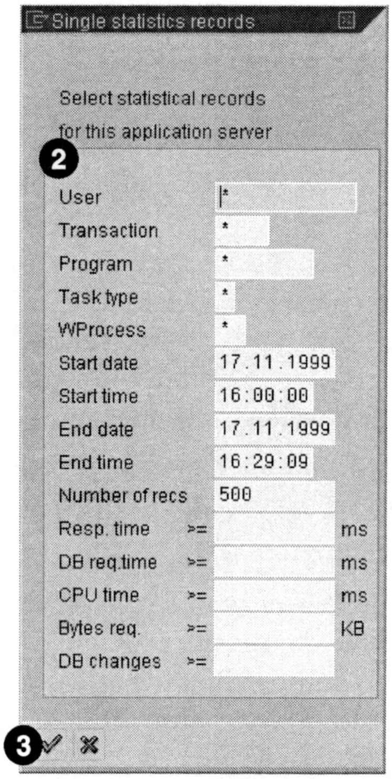


The *Workload: Display Statistical Records* screen appears.

4. Place the cursor in the user-information and double-click for further detailed information.
5. Choose ⟲.

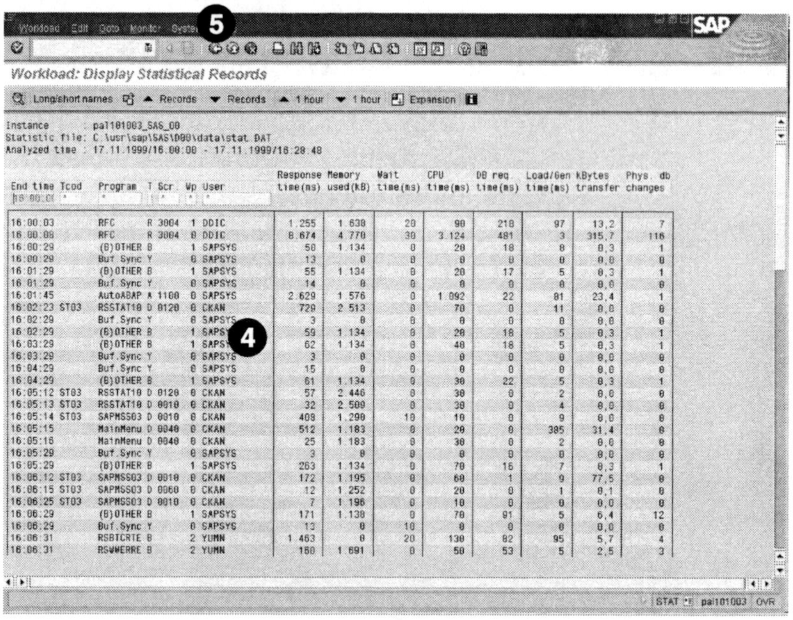

## ST03 – User Profile

The Computer Center Monitoring System (CCMS), transaction *ST03 – User Profile*, can be used to collect information about:

- The servers and logged on users
- User and servers in use

The user profile list provides you with an overview of the logged on users and their accumulated response times. The detail screen shows the list of users together with their dialog steps activity and response times.

1. In the *Command* field, enter transaction **ST03** and choose *Enter* (or from the *SAP standard menu*, choose *Administration → Monitor → Performance → Workload → ST03 – Analysis*).
2. Choose *Performance database*.
3. Choose one of the following when the dialog box appears:
   - Single stat. records
   - Today's workload
   - Last minute workload
   - Local alert monitor

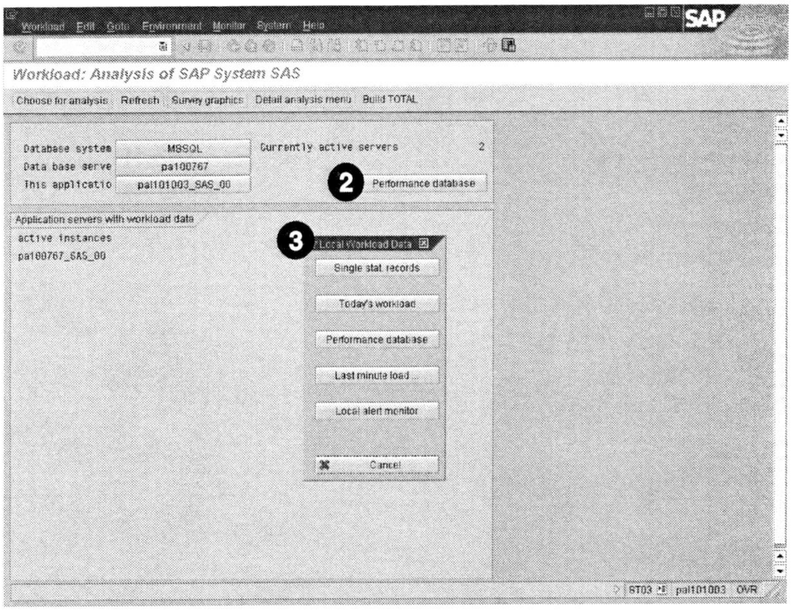


4. Choose *Goto → User Profile* to obtain the *Workload: User Profile Report*.

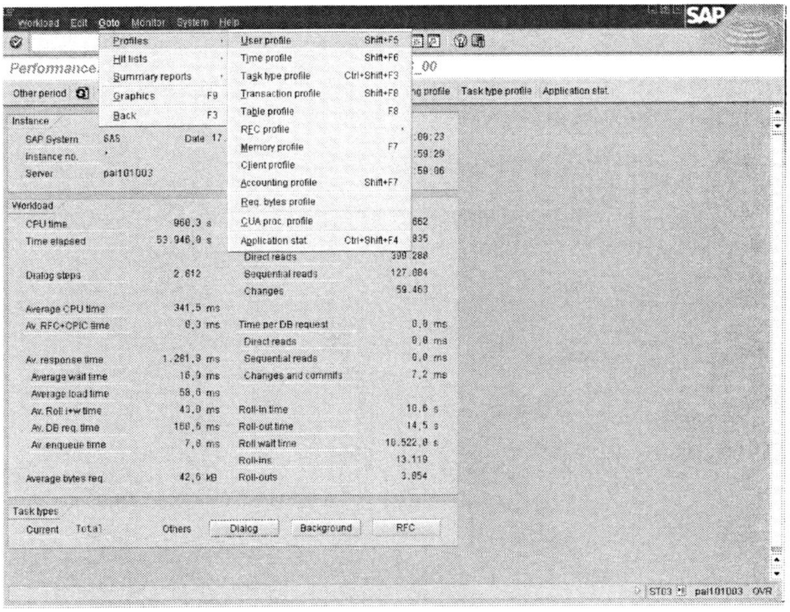

5. The *Workload: User Profile Report* screen appears.
6. Double-click on the user name in the *User* column to obtain additional detailed information regarding the transaction activity by user in a list format.

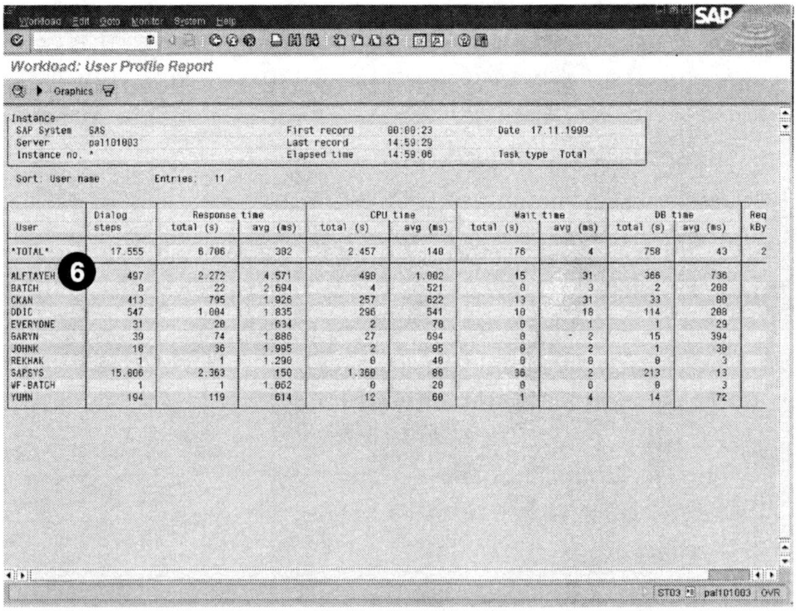


The detailed transaction information appears for the chosen user.

7. Choose ⊗.

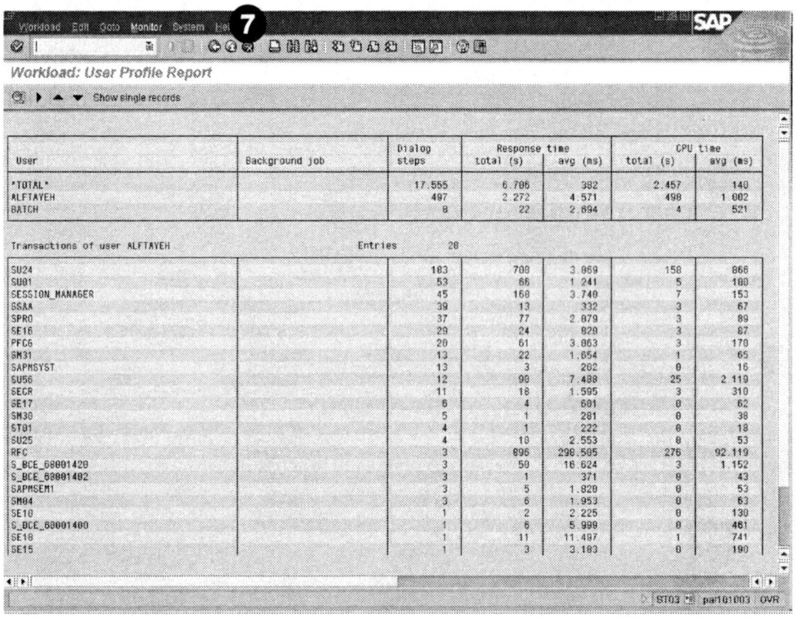

# Logging of Specific Activities

R/3 logs other specific activities in various logs. We discuss the following specific logs below:

## Logging Changes to Table Data

We recommend that you activate the logging of table data for those tables that are critical or susceptible to audits. Again, you must explicitly activate this logging. Note the following:

- You must start the R/3 System with the *rec/client* profile parameter set. This parameter specifies R/3 logs for all clients or only specific clients. We recommend setting this parameter to log all clients in your productive system.
- Set the *Log data changes* flag for those tables that you want to have logged. If both of these conditions are met, the database logs table changes in the table *DBTABPRT*. (Setting the *Log data changes* flag only does not suffice in recording table changes; you must also set the *rec/client* parameter.) You can view these logs with the transaction *SCU3*. Within R/3 Release 4.6A or greater, you may call report *RSVTPROT* for the evaluation of the both:
  - The customizing object and table-log database
  - Report *RSTBHIST* for table analysis with history

Caution

If a standard-delivered SAP table is not set up to permit logging of changes and you wish to change it, then this action is considered a modification to the R/3 System. To see if a table permits logging of changes, go to transaction *SE80* or *SE11* and look at the database table's technical settings (this is a button inside of the screen where the table is defined) at the field called *Log data changes*.

1. In the *Command* field, enter transaction **SCU3** and choose *Enter*.
2. Select *List of change docs*.
3. Choose [icon] to obtain the analysis of the change documents list for both customizing objects and tables.

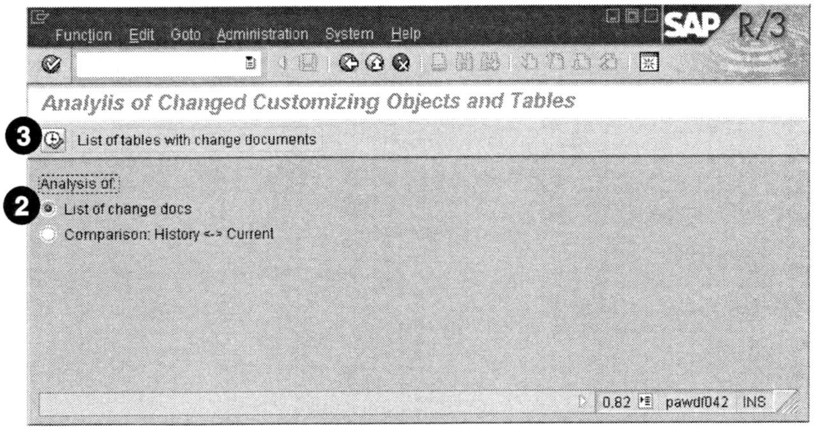

4. Run the *Evaluation of change logs* program (*RSVTPROT* for the evaluation of both the customizing object and table-log database) with the appropriate selection criteria.
5. Choose to the display the records.

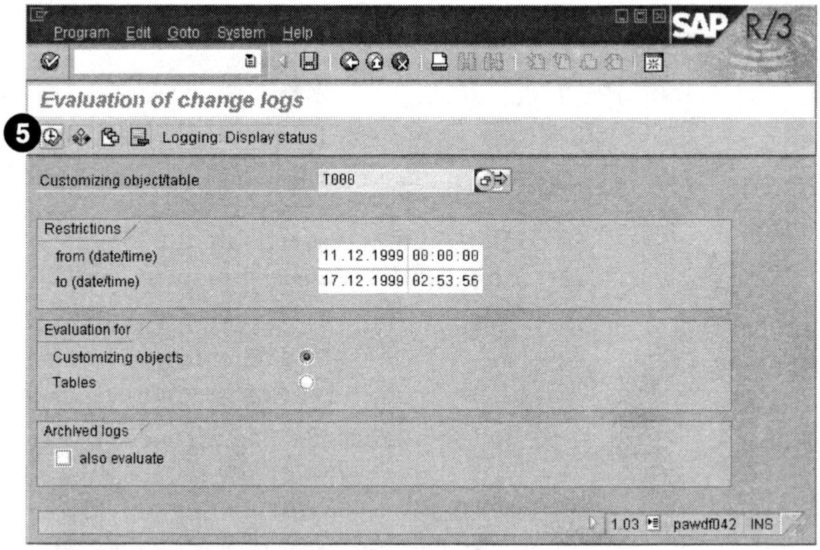


The transaction is executed and you are brought to the *Evaluation of change logs* screen.

6. Choose .

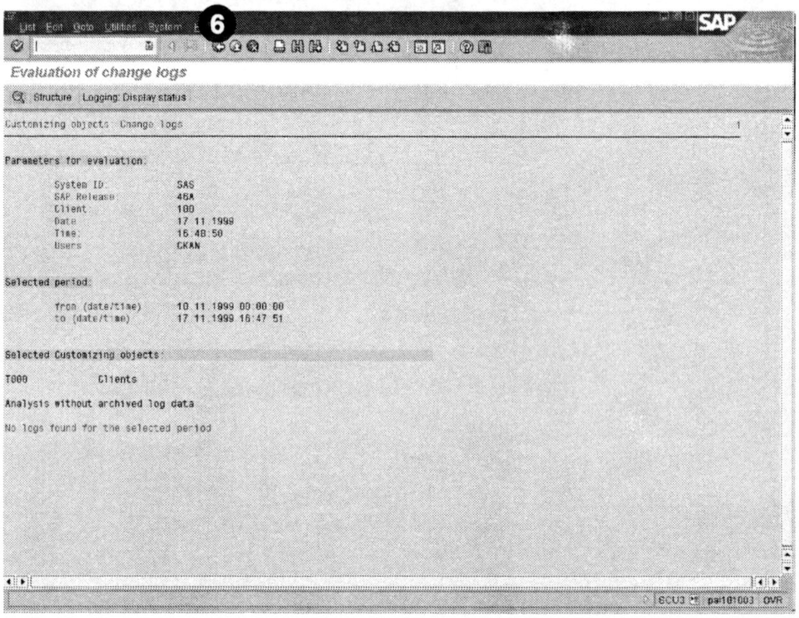

# Logging Changes to User Master Records, Profiles, and Authorizations

R/3 logs changes made by a user administrator in nontransparent tables in the database. Access to these tables is protected by the R/3 authorization concept. Once these logs have been archived, they are deleted. Depending on your release, use either the authorization infosystem or transaction *SU01* to access these logs. You can view the following changes:

- Changes made directly to a user's authorization

  These are changes made to the profile list in the user's master record. This does not include indirect changes that occur when authorizations or profiles are changed. View the change documents for the profiles and authorizations to check those changes.

- Changes to the:
  - User password (hashed representation only)
  - User type
  - User group
  - Validity period
  - Account number
- Changes made directly to profiles or authorizations.

For more information, see *BC Users and Authorizations → Creating and Maintaining User Master Records → Displaying Change Documents.*

# Chapter 14: Upgrade

## Contents

# Before Doing Any Upgrade

Before doing any upgrade, you should:

1. Review the SAPNet – R/3 Frontend notes for the version you are upgrading to. When searching R/3 SAPNet – R/3 Frontend notes, perform several searches. For example, first search on the component *BC-CCM-US**. Then search on the key words `authorization`, `security`, and `user master` for the release you are planning to work on.

2. Review release notes related to authorizations for **all** versions between the version you are currently using and the version you will be implementing. For example, if you are upgrading from 3.1H to 4.6B, read the release notes for versions 3.1I, 4.0A, 4.0B, 4.5A, 4.5B, 4.6A, and 4.6B. To review the release notes, choose *Help → Release notes* on your system. Select the *Complete list Rel. 4.0* and then choose the specific release you want to get information on. In the tree structure that appears, use the search function and perform a search on the words `authorization`, `checks`, and `security`. Also, you will want to read the section on the tree beneath *Basis → Computer Center Management System → Users and Authorizations*. Review the release notes because they tell you what new functionality is now available, as well as changes to existing functionality that you may need to consider in the new upgraded environment.

Tips & Tricks

Be aware that the above mentioned release notes only tell you what is new for the tool itself. It does **not** tell you about new authorizations and the purpose of new authorizations in applications. For information about new authorization functionality available within a particular application, you must read the release notes for that particular application.

3. Devise a backup and disaster recovery plan for authorizations. Be realistic. If you have done extensive modifications or changes to standard SAP R/3 logic, these changes may cause problems after the upgrade. You may want to create a temporary group of activity groups that can be used in the interim so operations can continue. Discuss your backup plan with the project management or system administrators. A good idea is to create these temporary activity groups immediately when you get access to the new system.

4. Make certain that the Basis team recognizes and appropriately allocates in the upgrade timeline that the authorization person is an **integral** part of the upgrade procedure, and that the upgrade, from a technical perspective, is not complete until the authorizations portion is also complete.

5. If you have made **any** changes with *SU24*, then it is highly advisable that you download to a local file (and save outside of the R/3 System) the contents of the two tables *USOBT_C* and *USOBX_C* from the version you are upgrading. These tables may be needed in the event that a disaster recovery needs to be performed.

In this chapter, we show you the steps required after an R/3 System upgrade. This information is advantageous immediately after your upgrade. Be sure to read this chapter before continuing your work with the Profile Generator (PG) in a new release.

The specific steps involved after the upgrade depend on the source and target release you are coming from.

## Validation Steps After Upgrading Is Completed

1. Install add-on components to the upgraded system, if any (along with whatever authorizations come with that add-on component, for example deduction management components, Audit Information system).
2. Upgrade the report tree migration:

   The data structure of the report trees changes. To continue using your self-created report trees, they must be adjusted to the changed data structures. The SAP-provided report trees generate into area menus automatically. The migration is performed using the transaction *RTTREE_MIGRATION*. The transaction is executed in the client containing the production versions of the report trees. During the migration, transaction codes are automatically assigned for all reports in a tree. This makes it possible to add reports to the user menu in activity group maintenance. If you want to create transaction codes with a company-specific prefix, you can set this by going to the SAP Reference IMG and choosing *Basis Components → System Administration → Users and Authorizations → Set namespace for report tree migration and specific IMG activities.*
3. Validate the user master records for new fields with new values, if needed *(SU01).*
4. Ensure that the PG and other system parameters are selected as required (see chapter 3, *Setting Up the Profile Generator*).
5. Upgrade the activity groups with transaction *SU25* and perform steps *2A* to *2D.*
6. Use user master reconciliation (transaction *PFUD*), if needed

Make certain that your report trees have upgraded properly. If upgrading from Release 3.1x or below to 4.6, some core changes have been made to the functionality and presentation of report trees.

If upgrading from 3.1x or below to 4.6, be aware that there you are now involved in a system that has a lot more functionality to deal with the world "outside" of R/3. These calls that work outside of R/3 are commonly handled through very special types of function module. A function module belongs to a function group. The *S_RFC* authorization object is critical in systems more recent than 3.1x. This authorization object may be totally "shut off" via a *RSPARAM* parameter value, but we do **not** suggest shutting it off. As such, you will need to deal with *S_RFC* after the upgrade.

First upgrade your DEV system. Perform all the steps in DEV. Determine what is and what is not transportable to the QAS system and PRD system. Almost nothing needs to be done directly in PRD as you should be able to transport almost everything from DEV. No one should ever attempt to update authorizations in solely PRD.

The user master record has remained relatively the same throughout the releases. However, there are two things that should be noted in transaction *SU01*.

- On the *Defaults* tab, there are two new fields:
  - *Personal time zone* – This field should be filled in after the upgrade. A small conversion program can be written to fill this field.
  - *Date format* – This new field permits you to use the date format *YYYY-MM-DD* (be aware that some places in R/3 have not been coded yet to recognize this new format).
- On the *Address* tab, there is address information about the user. This address information is linked to the 4.0-introduced functionality for the central address management component of R/3.

# Converting Previously Created SU02 Profiles to Activity Groups

## Creating an Activity Group from Manually Maintained Profiles

If you created profiles manually using transaction *SU02,* you can create an activity group from these profiles. The profiles can be single, as well as composite. Use transaction *SU25* (Upgrade and first installation).

1. In the *Command* field, enter transaction **SU25** and choose *Enter*.
2. Choose step *6. Copy data from old profiles.*

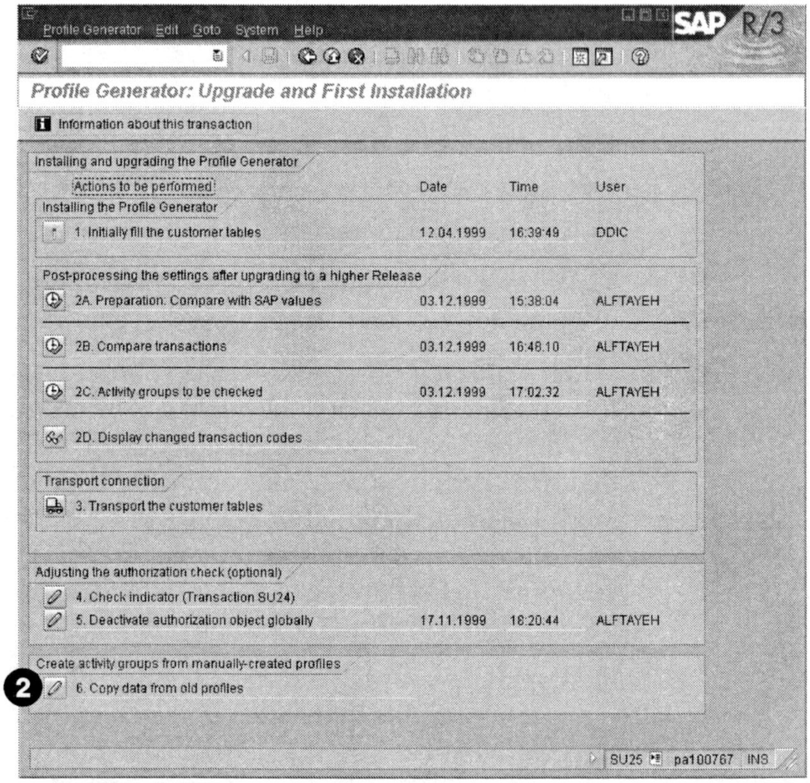

3. Read the *Important information* window.
4. Choose ✔.

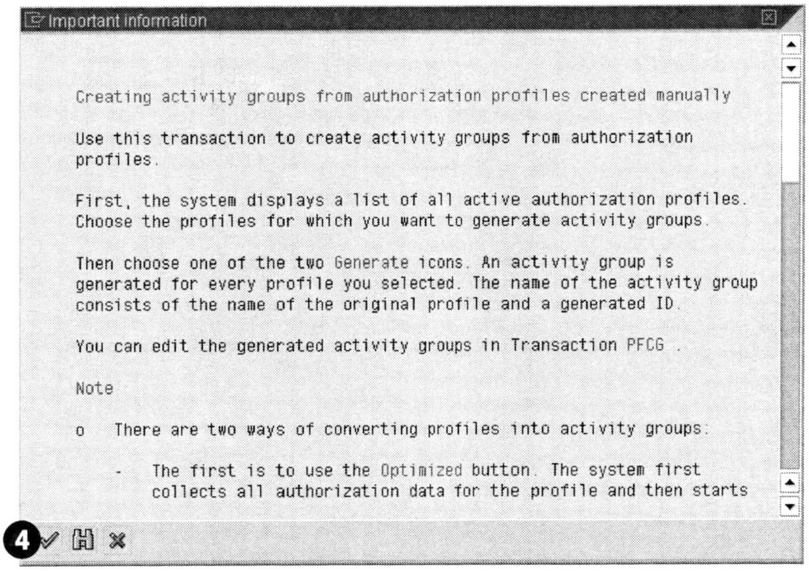


The system proposes all the manually created profiles.

5. Select the profile you want to convert to an activity group (for example, *NAF:PG:01*).
6. Choose *Optimized*.

See the documentation from the *Important information* window above for the benefits of this option.

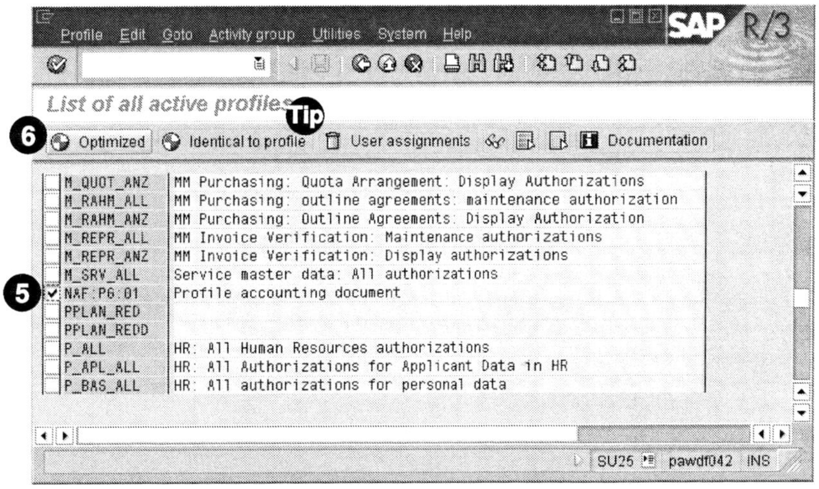


Tips & Tricks

You also have the option to use *Identical to profile* if you would like to have the authorizations data converted identically in the activity group. The *Menu* tab would remain empty though. The *Menu* tab also remains empty if you choose *Optimized*, unless you have discrete values for *S_TCODE* in your profile. Generic values such as *SE** or ranges from *S–P* are ignored.

7. Choose *Yes*.

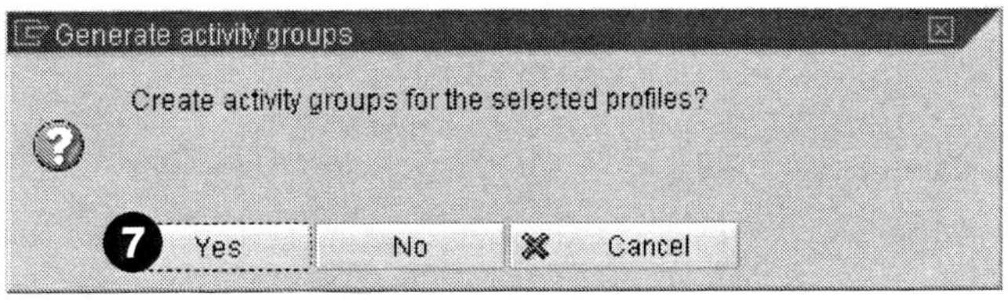

The *List of activity group created* screen appears.

8. Double-click on the activity group.

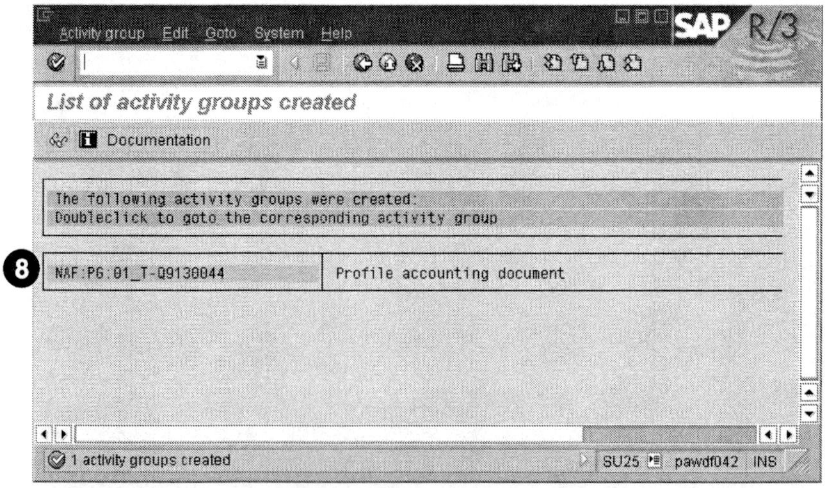


The *Change Activity Groups* screen appears. To maintain the activity group, perform the following steps.

9. In *Description*, the description that existed for the SU02-created profile will default into this field.

At the time of this writing, the SU02-created long description text was **not** copied into the newly created activity group.

10. On the *Description* tab, provide a detailed description under *Activity group description*.

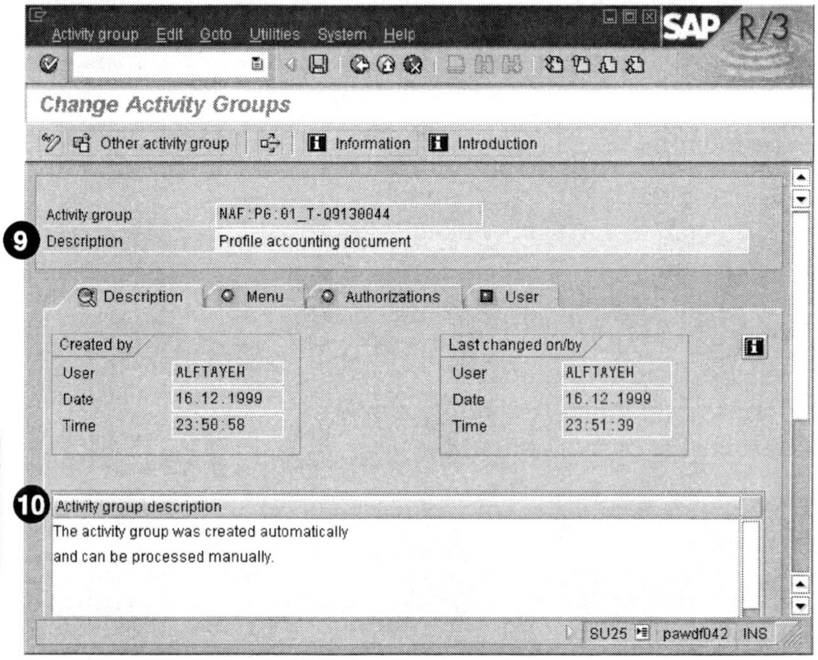

Tips & Tricks

On the *Menu* tab, you can add other transactions, or web addresses. If in the manually created profile you had a value in the authorization object *S_TCODE*, the system creates a menu. This menu will be the launch pad for the user for the Easy Access menu.

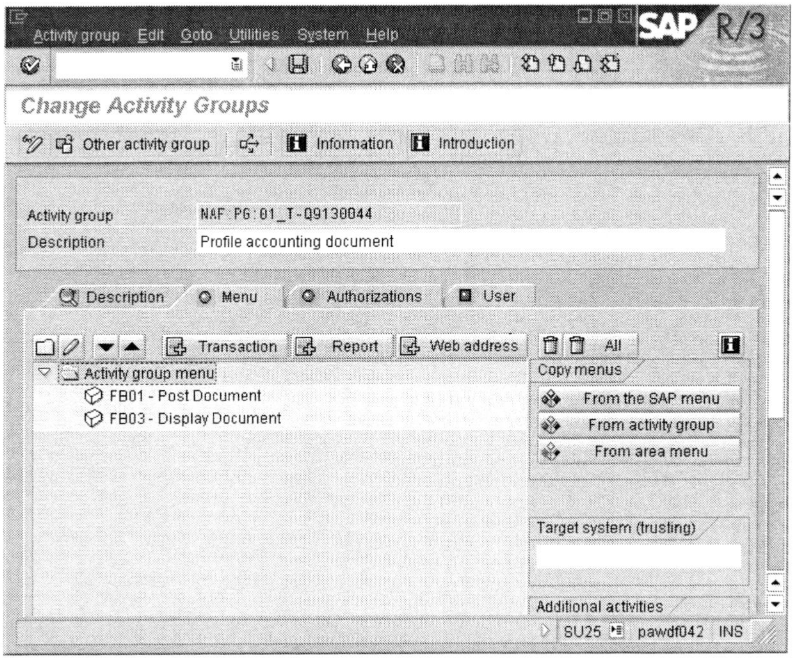


11. On the *Authorizations* tab, choose *Change authorization data.*

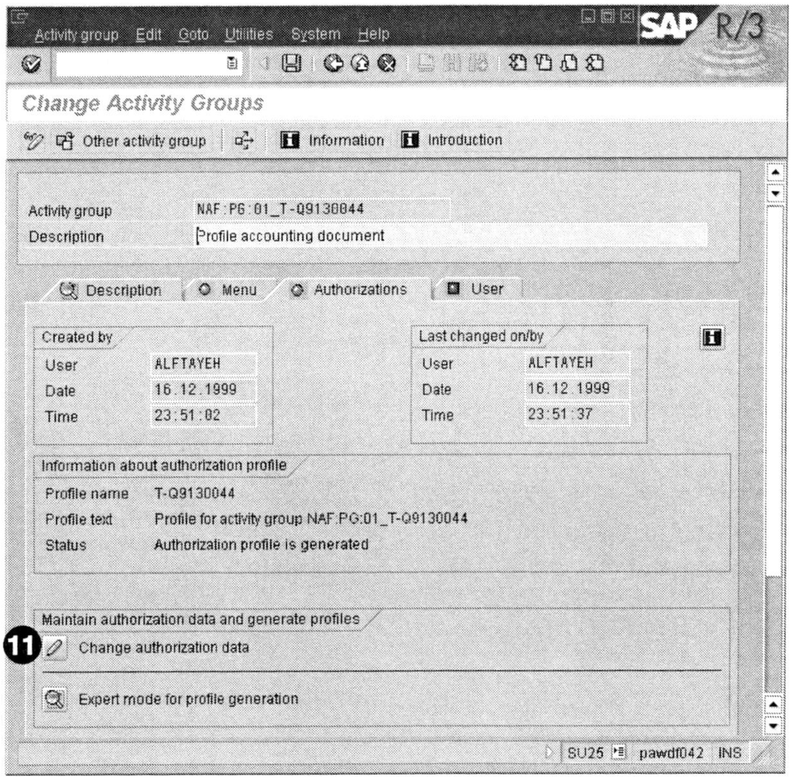

12. Review all traffic lights that are not green and click on the pencil icon to place values in the field (or click on the asterisk to allow all values in this field).

    When all values are complete, the traffic lights turn green.

13. Choose the Save icon.
14. To create the profile, choose the Generate icon.
15. Choose the Back icon.

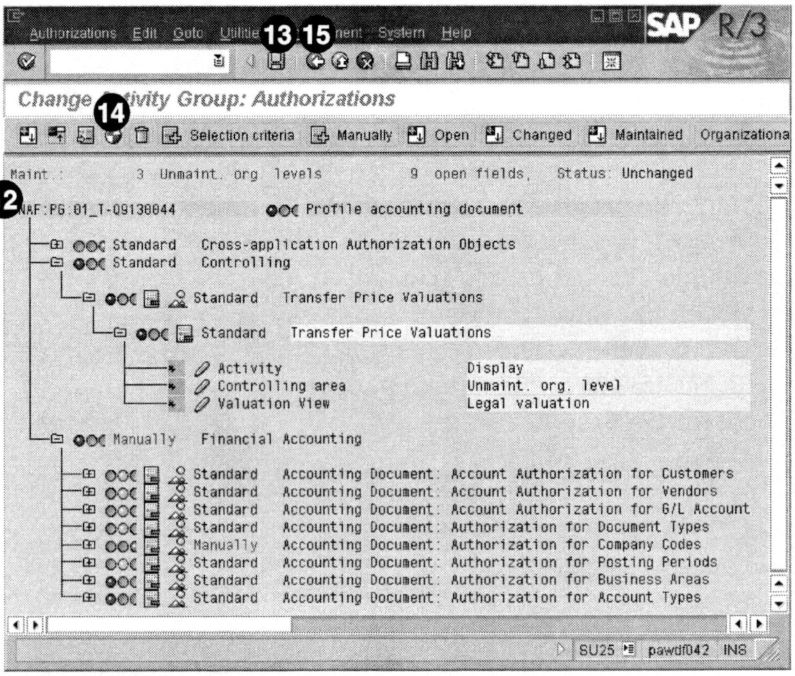


16. On the *User* tab, choose *User compare*. Compare the user master record to transfer the generated profile values to the user master. This record may differ from the original, depending on the adjustments that were made.

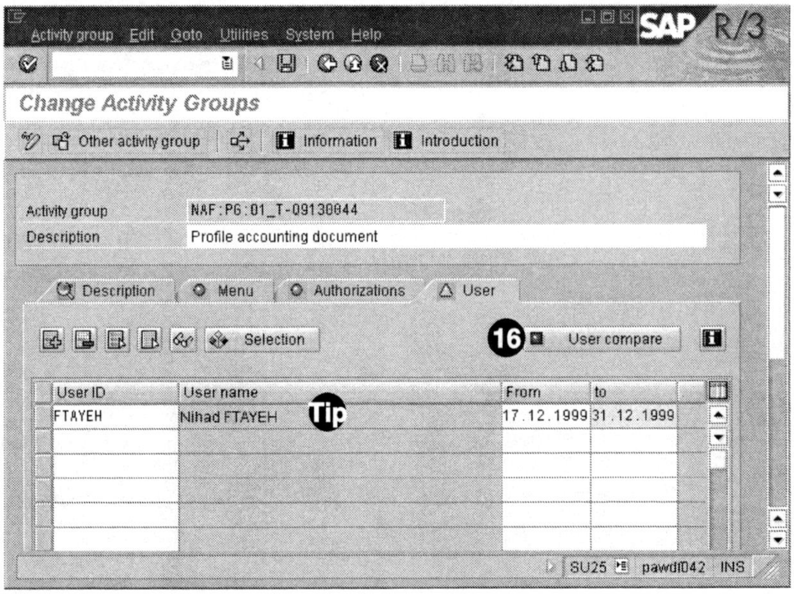


**Tips & Tricks**

If a user was assigned to a profile, then the user is automatically assigned to the just created activity group.

## Removing User Assignments from the Original SU02 Profile

You can remove the user assignment from a profile with *SU25* or *SU01*. In the following procedure, we demonstrate how to remove a user assignment from a profile that has been created without the PG.

1. In the *Command* field, enter transaction **SU25** and choose *Enter*.
2. Choose step *6. Copy data from old profiles.*

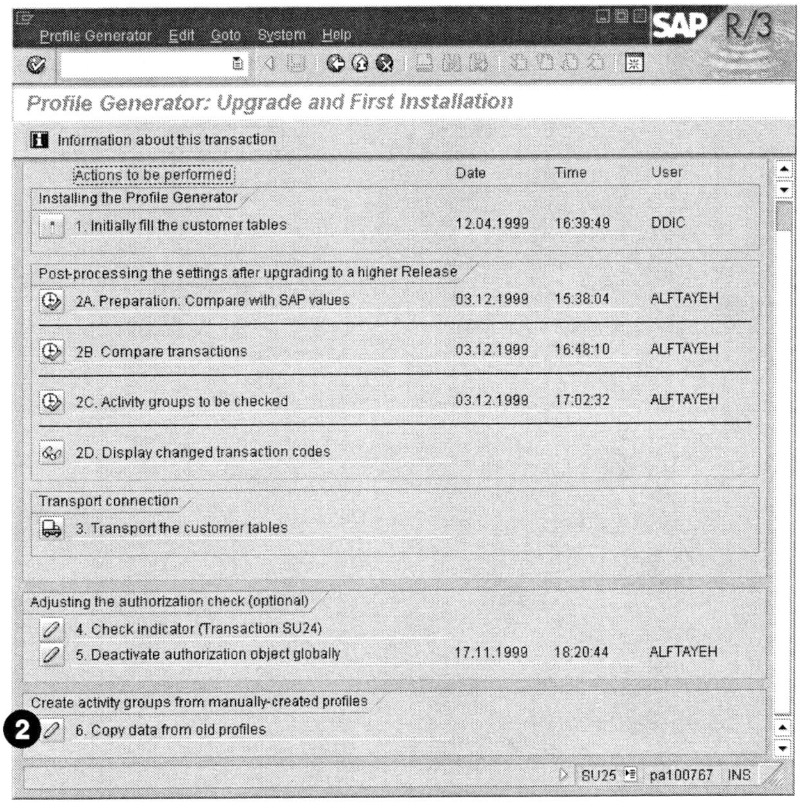


3. To continue, choose ✔.

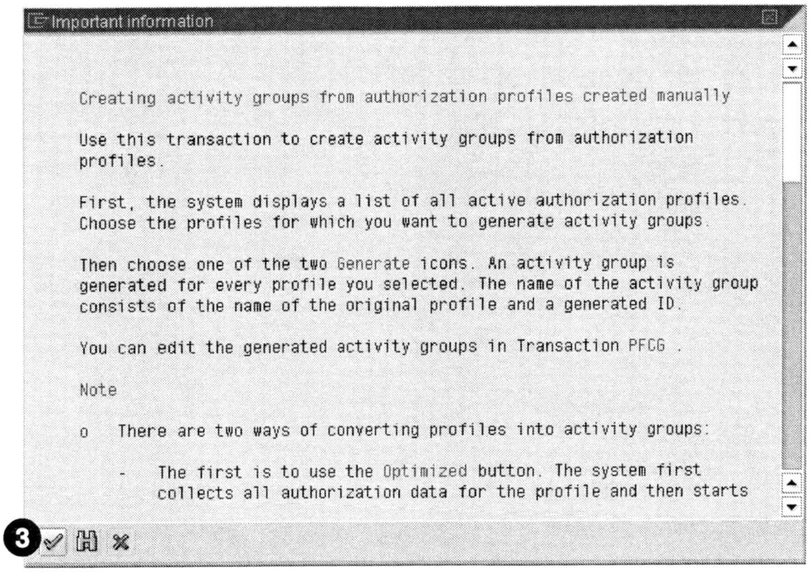

A list with all active profile appears.

4. Select the profile(s) from which you would like to remove the user assignment (for example, *NAF_003*).
5. To delete the assignment, choose 🗑 *User assignments*.

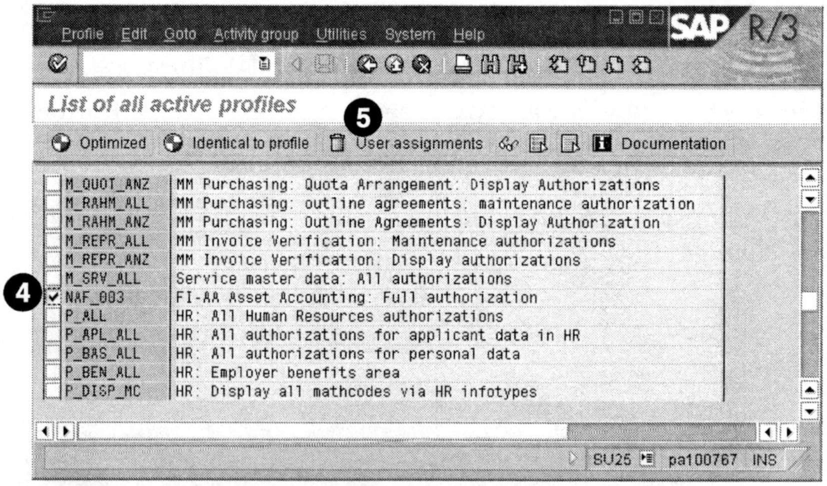

6. Choose *Yes*.

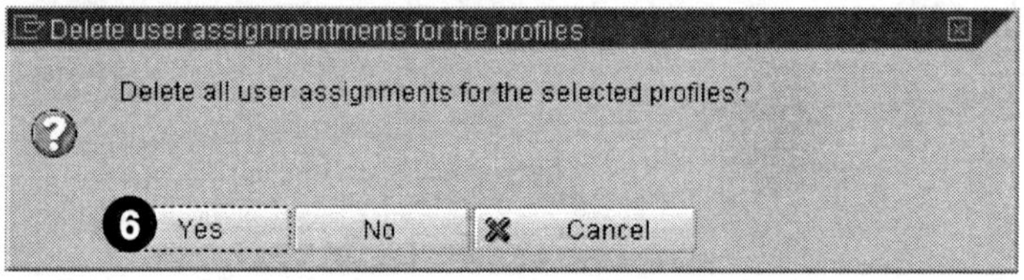

7. The system returns the affected users and removed profiles that were removed from the user master records.

   If no users were assigned, you receive no message.

8. You can now check the selected user master record to see that the assignments to the manually created profiles were removed.
9. Choose ⟲ to return.

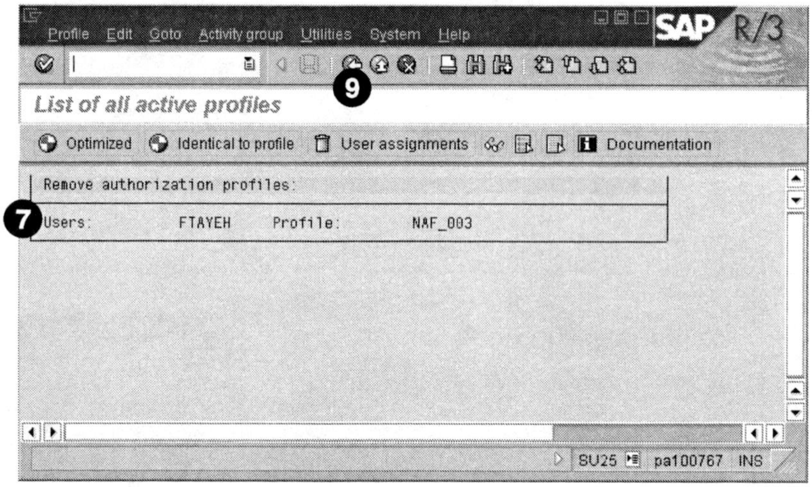

# Upgrading from a Release Prior to 3.1x to 4.6 A/B

Read chapter 3, *Setting up the Profile Generator* and chapter 10, *Tips & Troubleshooting* if:

- You are upgrading from a release prior to 3.1G
- In the release prior to 3.1G, you could not or did not use the PG
- You want to work with the PG now

You face two main questions:

- Do you convert the authorization profiles created with transactions *SU02* and *SU03* into profiles that can be maintained by the PG?
- Do you re-create the authorization profiles from scratch using the PG?

The following sections provide some hints to answering these questions.

## Converting Existing Authorization Profiles for the Profile Generator

First, create and save a new activity group for each job. Rather than selecting business transactions from the company menu tree, choose the *Authorizations* tab in the *Change Activity Groups* screen. Then follow the steps described in chapter 6, *Inserting Authorizations from a Profile.*

The advantage to this method is that you can work with existing, well-tested profiles. If object *S_TCODE* does not have an authorization, manually insert one. Maintain the permitted transaction for each activity group as authorization values for object *S_TCODE* in the profile you will generate for this activity group. You can, of course, maintain an asterisk (*), but this is a disadvantage, because users would receive more access than you want to give them. The other disadvantage is that since the user-specific menu is missing, you cannot re-create the information saved in an activity group. You may convert your old profiles and work with them until you need to re-create and delete them.

See also *Converting Previously Created SU02 Profiles to Activity Groups* on page 14–4.

## Re-creating the Authorization Profiles from Scratch Using the Profile Generator

Follow the instructions in chapter *5 User Role Templates*, chapter 6 *Advanced Profile Generator Functionality*, and chapter 8 *Missing Authorizations.*

# Upgrading from Release 3.0F to 4.6 A/B

An upgrade from Release 3.0F to 4.6A is not possible if you use R/3 HR Support Packages. Further information is available in SAPNet - R/3 Frontend note *128454.*

After your 4.6 upgrade, if you create activity groups and generate profiles in Release 3.0F with the preliminary version of the PG, then:

1. Make sure that the instance profile parameter *auth/no_check_in_some_cases* is still active.

   Follow the instructions in chapter 3, the section *Checking the Required Instance Profile Parameter*. If the parameter is inactive, it needs to be activated.

   The PG is already active in Release 4.6 though.

   Apply the appropriate advance corrections for Release 4.6 or any available Hot Package by referring to chapter 3, the section *Applying Advance Corrections to your R/3 System.*

2. Because the customer tables *USOBX_C* and *USOBT_C* were not a part of the Release 3.0F version of the PG, copy the SAP defaults in these customer tables.

   To copy these defaults, run transaction *SU25* and perform the steps in chapter 3, the section *Loading the USOBX_C and USOBT_C Tables.* In transaction *SU25,* perform the first step called *Initially fill the customer tables.*

   Also read chapter 12, the section *Reducing the Scope of Authorization Checks* to learn more about the new functionality. Then decide whether you need to perform additional steps on the check indicator settings for the transactions you are using.

3. After the upgrade to Release 4.6x, a profile matchup is required for all profiles generated in Release 3.0F. After the upgrade, the PG does not automatically inform you that a comparison is necessary for these profiles (in transaction *PFCG,* the light on the *Authorizations* tab remains green for the profiles created in Release 3.0F, and transaction *SUPC* does not indicate whether a matchup is actually required). Nevertheless, the SAP default data for check indicators and field values in the new release has been improved, so that a profile matchup is essential to ensure proper working profiles after the upgrade.

To perform a profile matchup:

1. Access the PG (transaction **`PFCG`**).
2. Select an activity group created in Release 3.0. You can only select one activity group at a time (see the following *Tips & Tricks*).

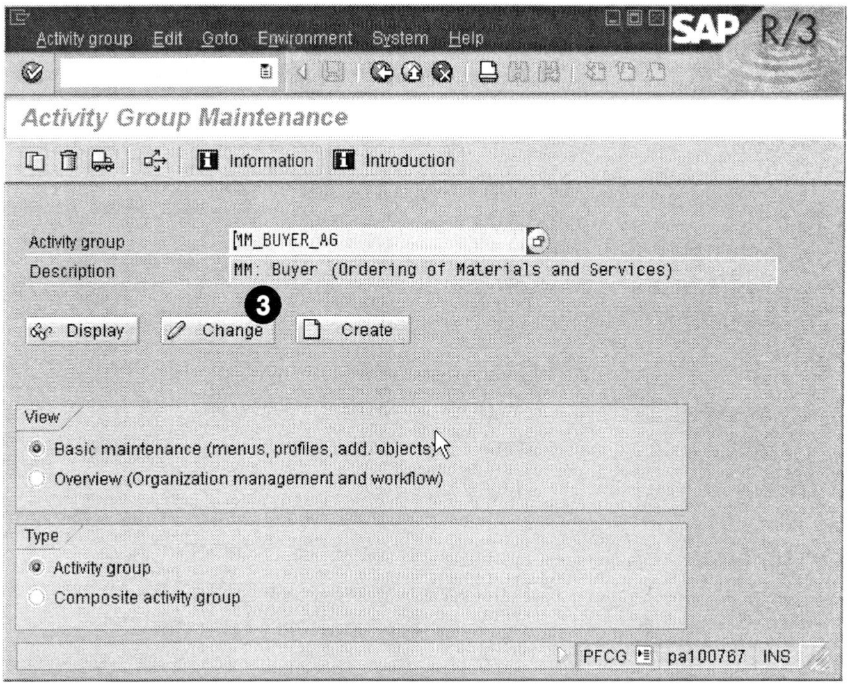


**Tips & Tricks**

This procedure has to be performed for each activity group separately. To speed up the process, use transaction *SUPC* where you get a list of all activity groups. Select the activity group that needs to be maintained by double-clicking on it.

3. Choose *Change.*
4. Choose the *Authorizations* tab.
5. Choose *Expert mode for profile generation.*

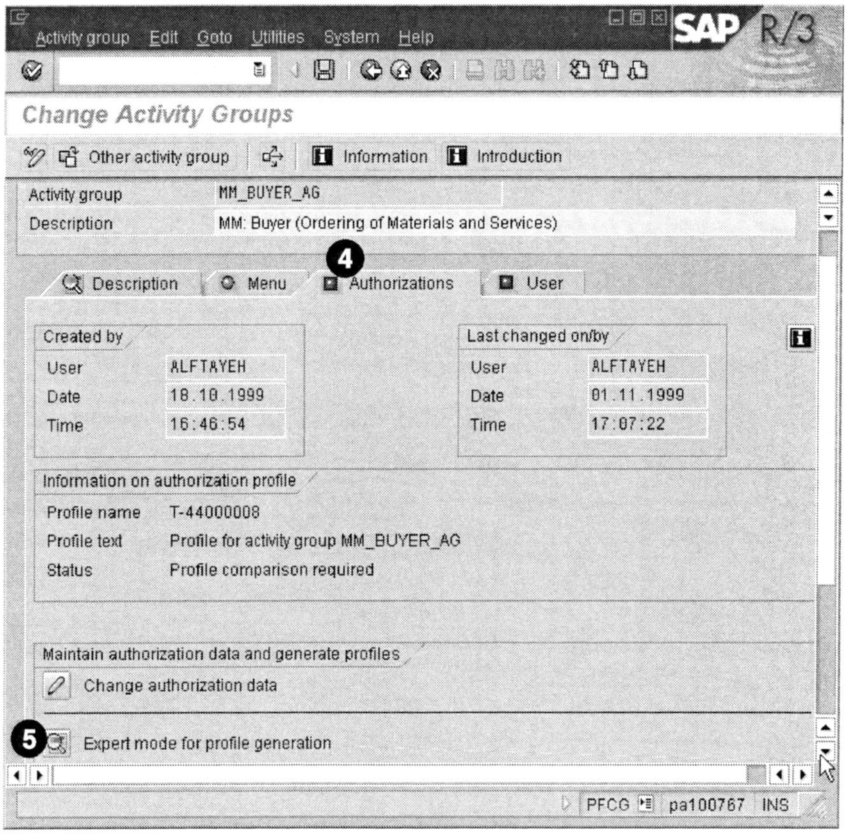

6. Select *Read old status and merge with new data* as the correct maintenance type.
7. Choose ✔ and postmaintain any open authorization fields on the next screen, if required.

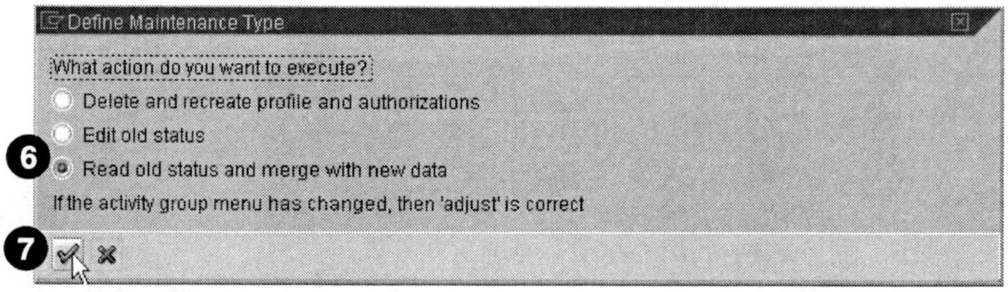


Due to changes in the SAP defaults for check indicators and field values in Release 4.6x, the PG may create some new authorizations. If you see new authorizations created where you have already maintained authorizations, deactivate or delete them.

The system includes the new required authorizations without checking for existing ones. This feature may sound unusual but offers improved system performance. To postmaintain all open authorization fields, follow the instructions in chapter 6, *Regenerating the Authorization Profiles after Making Changes*.

8. After regenerating all the profiles, you have completed the upgrade steps for authorization profiles created in Release 3.0F.

No user master comparison is required for profiles already assigned to users, but remember that changes become active with the next system logon.

# Upgrade from Releases 3.1G, 3.1H, 3.1I to 4.6 A/B

After creating activity groups and generating profiles in Releases 3.1G, 3.1H, 3.1I, 4.0A or 4.0B, 4.5x with the PG, when you upgrade to Release 4.6x:

1. Make sure that the instance profile parameter *auth/no_check_in_some_cases* is still active.

   To do so, follow the instructions in chapter 3, the section *Checking the Required Instance Profile Parameter*. If the parameter is not active, it needs to be activated. The PG is set to active in Release 4.6.

   Apply the appropriate advance corrections for Release 4.6 or any available Hot Package by referring to chapter 3, *Applying Advance Corrections to your R/3 System*.

2. In the *Command* field, enter transaction **SU25** and choose *Enter*.

3. Choose step *2A. Preparation: Compare with SAP values*. This step is used to prepare for steps *2B* and *2C*.

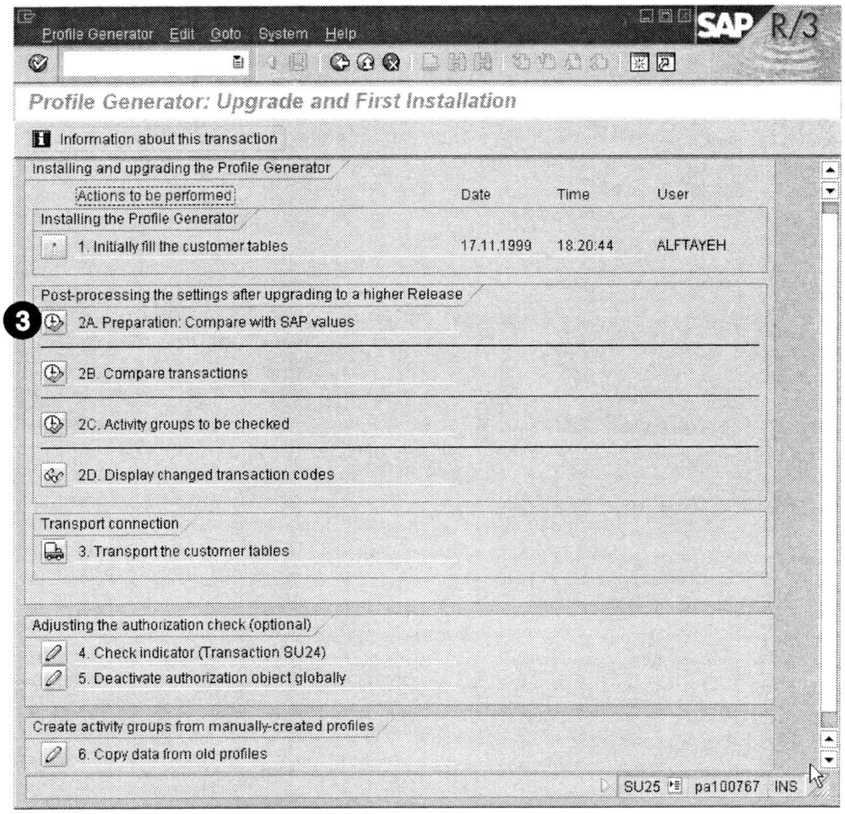


4. Choose ✔.

Tips & Tricks

This step might take several minutes.

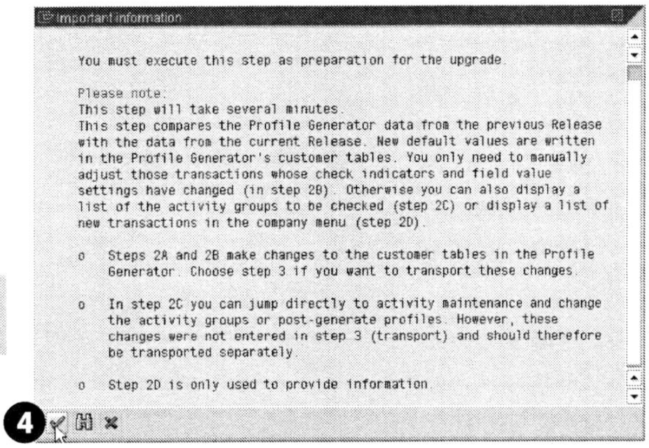

5. Choose *2B. Compare transactions.*

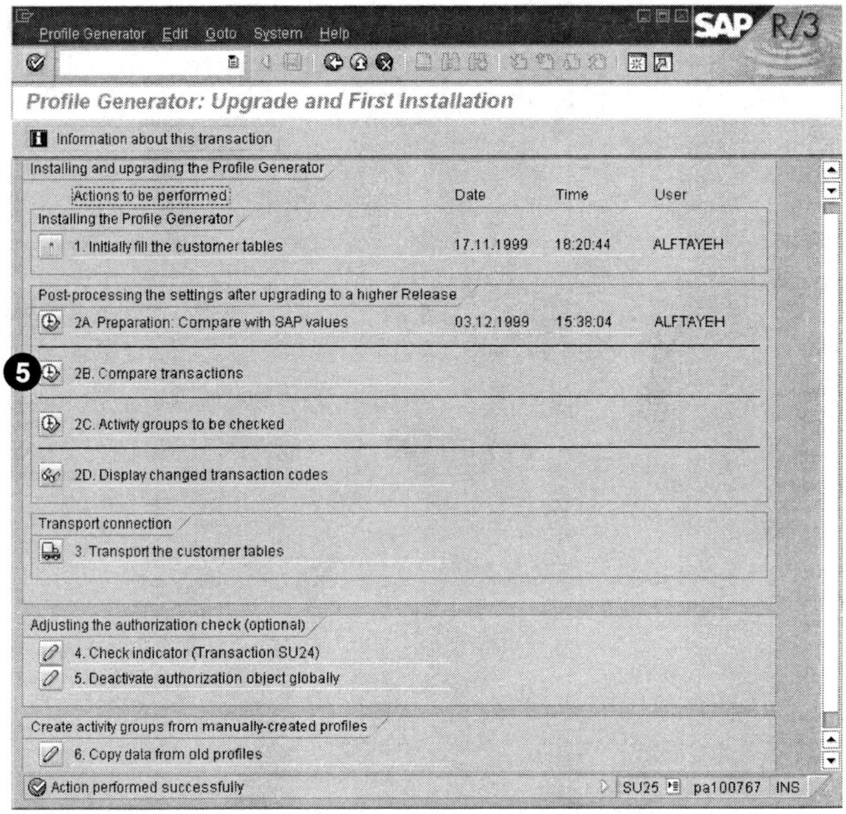


6. Choose ✔.

   The upgrade report you started in step *2A.* updates customer tables *USOBX_C* and *USOBT_C,* but does not overwrite the entries you changed in releases before 4.6x.

   If you have not changed check indicators and field values with transaction *SU24* in releases before 4.6x, you will see the following status message:

   *You do not need to maintain the transaction.*

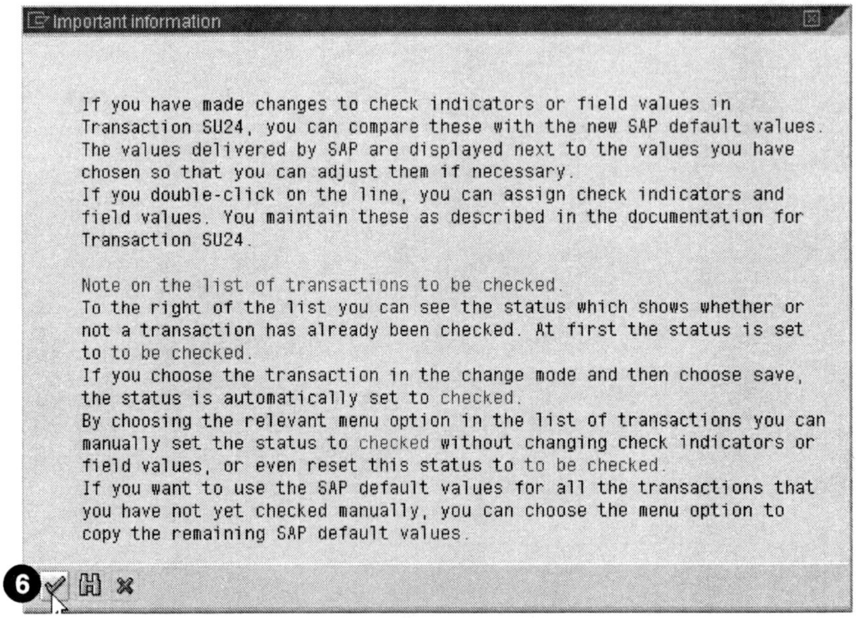

7. If you made changes, these changes will still be active after the upgrade. The output will be a list of affected transactions (in our case it is *MK01*).
8. In the output list of transactions, you can see the *Status* which shows whether a transaction has already been checked.

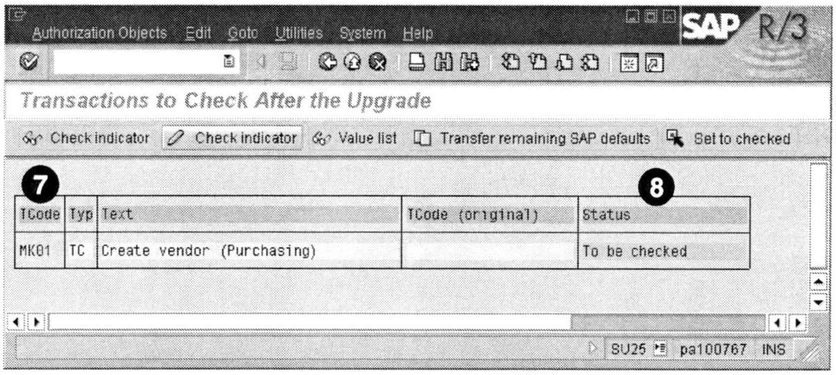


9. Select a transaction where the current status is *To be checked*.
10. Choose *Set to checked* to set the status to *checked* without changing any check indicator settings for this transaction.
11. Choose the *Transfer remaining SAP defaults* button to change the current active check ID setting to the SAP default value and the status to *checked*.
12. Choose *Check indicator*.
13. Choose .

    If you save without making any changes, the status is automatically set to *checked*, and the changes remain.
14. Choose any other menu option to make additional changes to this transaction and its settings for check indicators and field values.
15. Once finished, choose .

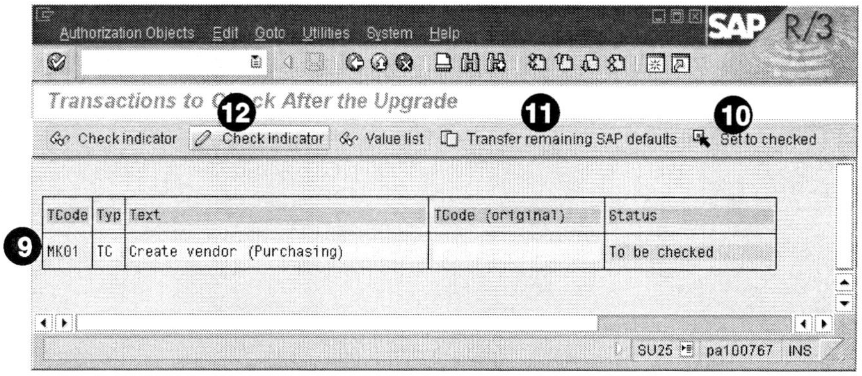


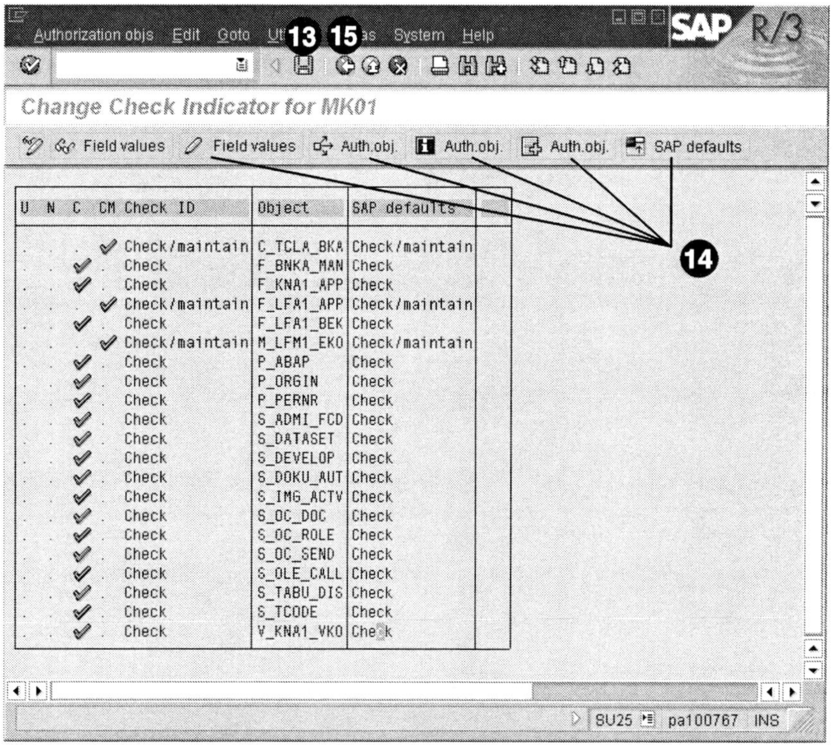

16. The status has changed to *checked*.

17. To use the SAP default values for all the transactions that you have not yet manually checked, choose the *Transfer remaining SAP defaults* button to copy any remaining SAP default values (in our case, we do not have any further transactions).

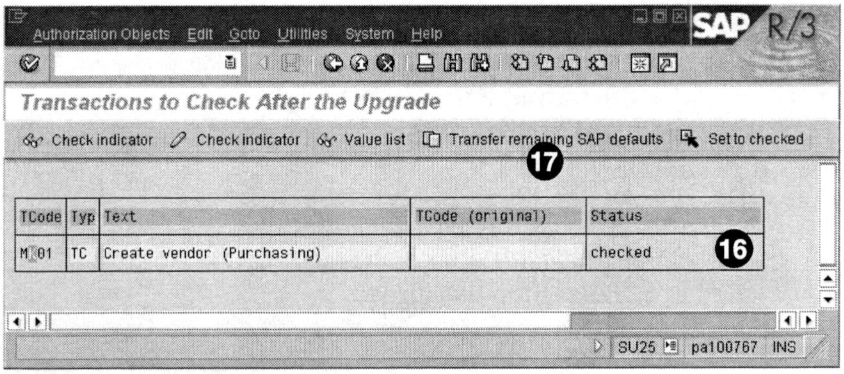


18. Choose ✔.

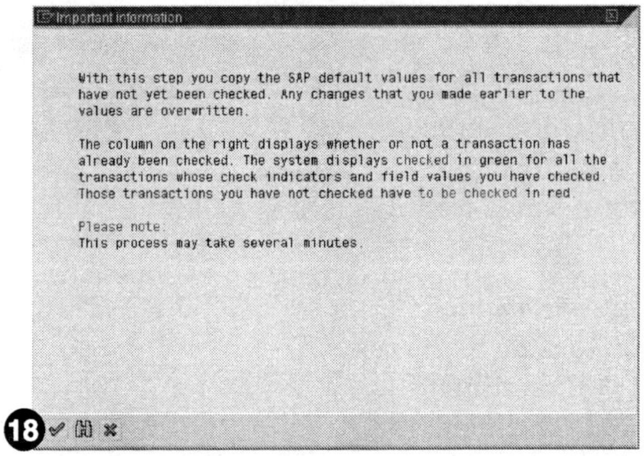


19. If you had other transactions all their statuses would have been set to *checked*.

20. Choose the back icon.

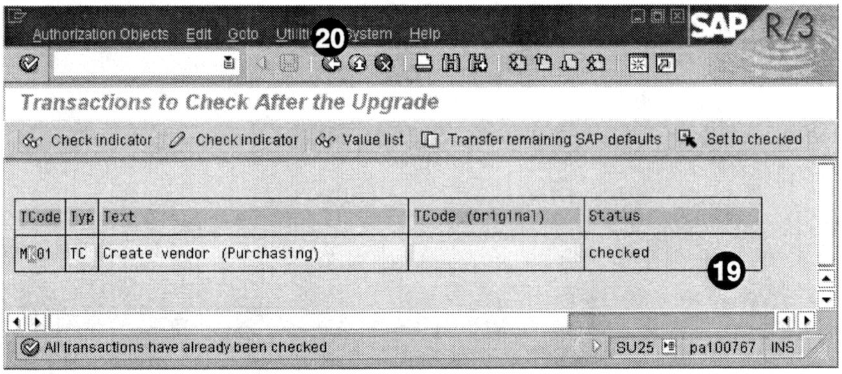

21. Choose 2C. *Activity groups to be checked.*

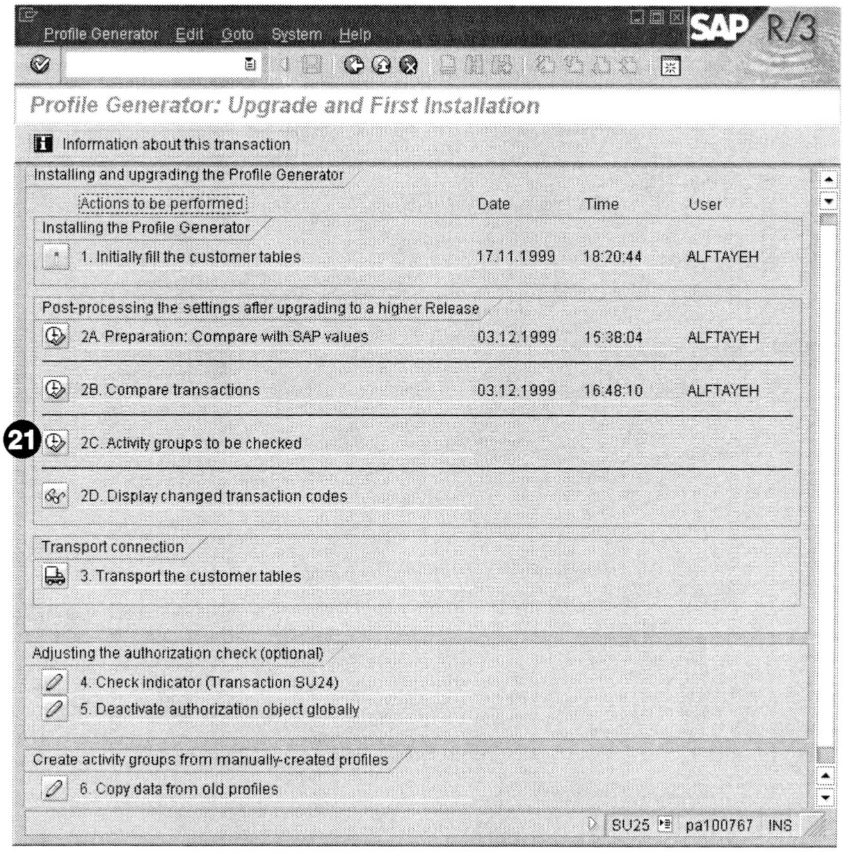


22. Choose ✔.

The output is a list of activity groups that are affected by either changes you made or by changes from our improved default data.

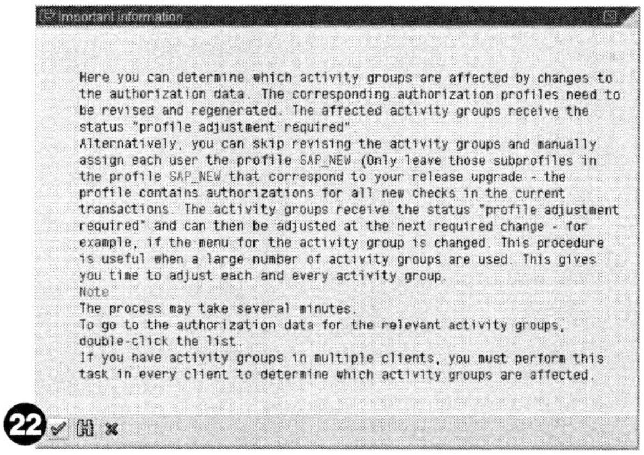

23. For the listed activity groups, changes have been made to check indicators or default transaction values. Therefore, the corresponding authorization profiles need to be adjusted.

    Make sure you select each entry in this list.

24. Double-click on the activity group you would like to adjust.

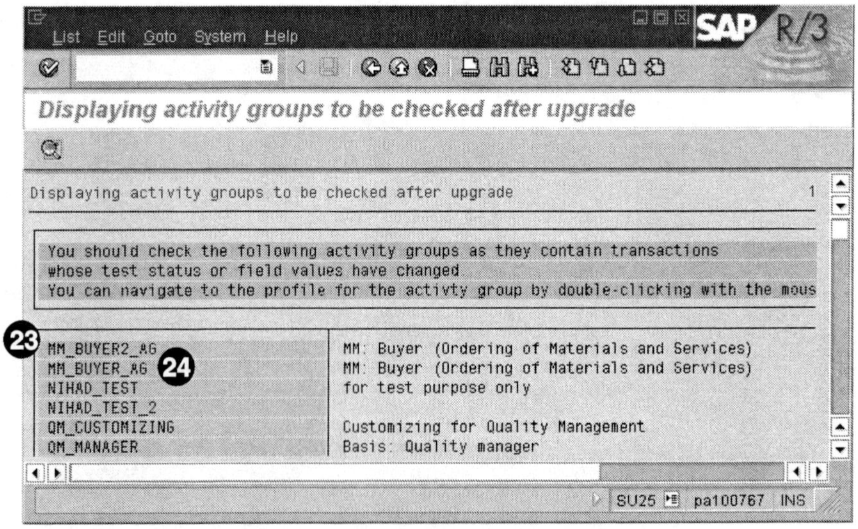


25. Depending on the changes, you might have to maintain the correct organizational level.

26. Postmaintain any open authorization fields, if required (yellow or red lights).

    Due to changes in the SAP defaults for check indicators and field values, the PG may create some new authorizations in Release 4.6x. You will see new authorizations created where you have already maintained authorizations (these are identified by the ones that say *New*). Just activate, or delete, the new authorizations. The system includes the new required authorizations without checking for existing ones for the same authorization object. This feature may sound unusual, but has more advantages than disadvantages and also improves PG performance.

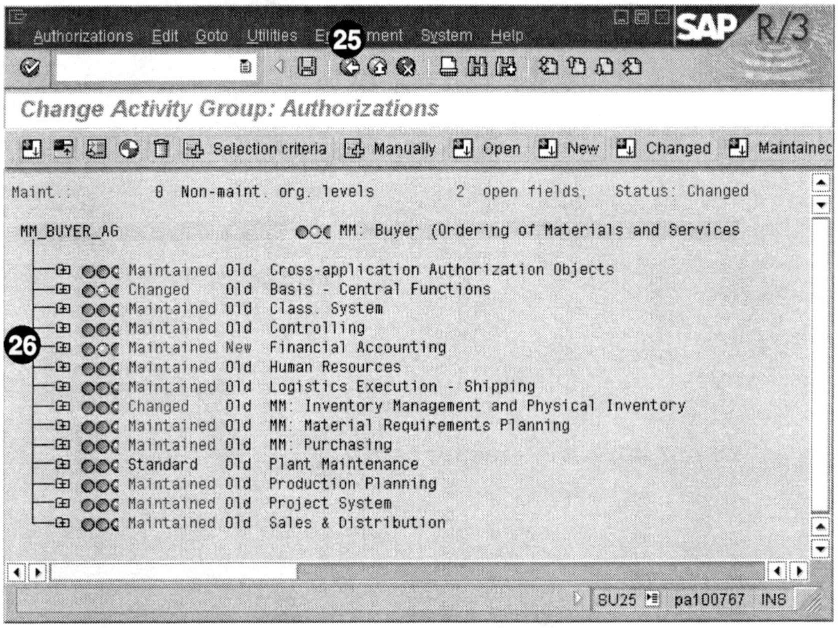


To postmaintain all open authorization fields, follow the instructions in chapter 6, the section *Regenerating the Authorization Profiles After Making Changes*.

27. After regenerating, choose ⊖.

28. Continue with the next entry in the list of activity groups with this same procedure until you have adjusted all activity groups.

Caution

> After completing steps *2A*, *2B*, and *2C*, you have performed the most important steps after your Release 4.6 A/B upgrade.
>
> You still need to perform step *3. Transport the customer tables*, and transport the changes you made in steps 1 and 2 to your other R/3 systems. All systems must have the same settings for check indicators and field values.

29. Choose *2D. Display changed transaction codes.*

    This report lists all activity groups where transactions have been replaced by other transactions. The old and new transactions are also displayed. You can change the transaction code in the corresponding activity group by double-clicking on the entry in the list.

    You have completed the upgrade steps for authorization profiles created in releases prior to 4.6x.

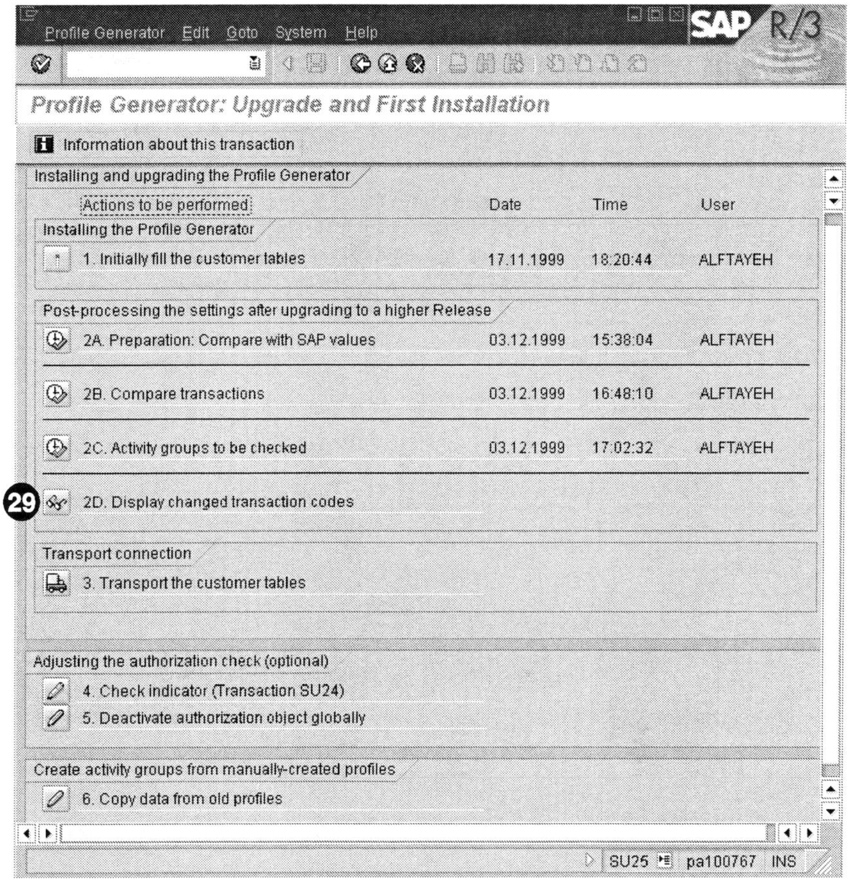

# Upgrade from Releases 4.0x or 4.5x to 4.6 A/B

If you are upgrading from 4.0x or 4.5x to 4.6 A/B, you should proceed from steps *2A* to *2D* in the same way as in the section before.

**In 4.6, responsibilities no longer exist**

If you worked with the R/3 System in Release 4.0x or read the 4.0B *Authorizations Made Easy* guidebook, then you may have wondered what happened to the functionality called "responsibilities." In Release 4.5 and 4.6, responsibilities were replaced by a concept called "derived activity groups" and these derived activity groups function slightly different from the 4.0 responsibilities. If you used responsibilities in 4.0 and upgrade to 4.6, your responsibilities are converted automatically into derived activity groups.

For detailed information on derived activity groups, see the corresponding section in chapter 6, *Copying and Deriving Activity Groups*.

# Appendix A: SAPNet – R/3 Frontend Notes

## Contents

# Overview

SAPNet – R/3 Frontend notes, formerly known as Online Service Support (OSS), contains information regarding known errors (and subsequent means of addressing such errors), some advice, and general information related to the R/3 System. It also serves as one of the core means of communicating problems with your R/3 System to the SAP R/3 support services portion of the SAP worldwide organization. The support system, maintained entirely by SAP, contains hundreds of thousands of "notes" that address topics ranging from R/2 systems, R/3 systems , and many of the add-on components to these systems. For more information about what the SAPNet – R/3 Frontend system is, please refer to *www.sap.com* and go to the SAPNet section.

The note numbers provided in this appendix represent only a fraction of all the notes related to authorizations. As hundreds of notes for the various SAP products are created every day, this listing of notes represents "a snapshot in time" of those that existed at the time this writing and were selectively included here. It is by no means a comprehensive list.

Notes in SAPNet – R/3 Frontend are separated in many ways. One of the most common ways is by the "Component" or "Application Area" in the system that was affected. The following table describes some of the most common application areas where notes may be found. These areas can be used to search the SAPNet – R/3 Frontend notes database for additional security administrator information

| Application Area | Description |
|---|---|
| BC-CCM | Computing Center Management System |
| BC-CCM-USR | Users and Authorizations |
| BC-CCM-USR-ADM | Users and Authorizations Maintenance |
| BC-CCM-USR-KRN | Users and Authorizations Kernel Functions |
| BC-CCM-USR-PFC | Profile Generator |
| BC-CTS-ORG | Workbench/Customizer Organizer |
| BC-FES-SEM | Session Manager |
| BC-SRV-REP | Reporting |
| BC-BMT-OM | Organizational Management |
| BC-BMT-OM-OM | Organizational Plan |
| FI-AP-AP-B | Payment Program/Payment Transfer |
| MM-IM-GF-REP | IM Reporting (no LIS) |
| PA-PA-XX | All Countries (Personnel Administration) |

Each application area can also be searched using a keyword such as *profile generator, PFCG, activity group, predefined activity groups, authorization, profile, user, SU53, security* and so on.

## SAPNet – R/3 Frontend Notes

**(As of December 1999)**

Legend:

- RI = Release independent
- * = 4.6A , 4.6B
- OR = older release, but still valuable information

| Subject | Release | Note | Title |
|---|---|---|---|
| Authorization Check | RI | **18529** | Which authorization objects are checked |
| Authorization | RI | **20643** | Naming conventions for authorizations |
| Authorization Check | RI | **20534** | Authorization check - a short introduction |
| Authorization Concept | RI | **28175** | Questions regarding the authorization concept |
| Authorizations, Reporting Tree | RI | **7642** | Authorization protection of ABAP/4 programs |
| Authorizations, Trace | RI | **65054** | Trace function: multiple users |
| Documentation, Basis Knowledgeware Products | OR | **61675** | Info for customer - Basis Knowledge Products |
| Hot Packages | OR | **33525** | Important Information about Hot Packages |
| Hot Packages | * | **53902** | Conflicts between Support Packages/LCPs & Add-ons |
| Hot Packages | * | **97612** | New Hot Packages for Profile Generator |
| Knowledgeware Products | OR | **52286** | Questions and answers on the R/3 Basis Knowledge Product CDs |
| Naming Conventions | * | **16466** | Customer name range for SAP objects |
| Organizational Management | * | **31621** | PD and Workflow application do not run correctly |
| OSS | RI | **26740** | OSS Registration Form (for North America) |
| OSS | RI | **28750** | Documentation on training info in the OSS |
| OSS | RI | **29501** | Search procedure for notes and messages in OSS |
| OSS | RI | **30068** | SAP America's Production Registration Form |

| Subject | Release | Note | Title |
|---|---|---|---|
| OSS | RI | **33246** | SAPLOGON for OSS |
| OSS | OR | **35010** | Service connections: Composite note (overview) |
| OSS | RI | **36677** | Structure of application areas in OSS |
| OSS | RI | **45027** | User maintenance and creation in OSS for customer |
| OSS | OR | **50464** | FLCS Feedback for the Notes within the OSS System |
| OSS | RI | **64417** | OSS corporate group functionality: Collective note |
| OSS | RI | **75002** | Confirmation of OSS Registration |
| OSS and OSS1 | RI | **17285** | Log on to OSS (Transaction OSS1) |
| OSS and OSS1 | RI | **22235** | OSS1: What to do if R/3 will not run |
| OSS and OSS1 | RI | **33135** | Guidelines for OSS1 (Version for SAPSERV3) |
| OSS and OSS1 | RI | **33221** | Easy-to-use guide for Transaction OSS1 |
| OSS and Printing | RI | **15641** | Print / Download in OSS |
| OSS and Printing | RI | **26746** | Downloading – Printing notes in OSS |
| Passwords in R/3 | RI | **2467** | Answers on "Security" |
| Patch download from SAPSERVx | RI | **13719** | Advance transports to customers |
| Profile Generator | * | **76802** | Problems with table SMEN_DATES |
| Profile Generator | * | **85234** | Missing authorization when using the Profile Generator |
| Profile Generator | * | **90770** | *0 problem for the PG |
| Profile Generator | RI | **144034** | Regeneration of activity groups-authorization loss |
| Profile Generator | RI | **113290** | Merg. Process with authorization data: Explanation |
| Profile Generator, Transport PD objects (activity groups) | OR | **77607** | Transporting PD objects by client copy |
| Report RHAUTUP1 | OR | **82145** | Activity group maint., user master data comparison |
| SAP Software Change Registration | OR | **27532** | SAP Software Change Registration (SSCR) |
| SAP_NEW | RI | **28186** | What does the profile SAP_NEW do? |
| SAPNet | RI | **69224** | Access to the SAPNet server with OSS User ID |
| SAPSERVx | OR | **40024** | Transferring customer files to sapserv# with ftp |
| Security in R/3 | RI | **27928** | Consequences in transport during password change |

| Subject | Release | Note | Title |
|---|---|---|---|
| Security in R/3 | RI | **30724** | Data protection and security in R/3 |
| Security in R/3 | RI | **35493** | Secrecy and Data Security Obligations |
| Security in R/3, ABAP | RI | **13202** | Security aspects in ABAP/4 programming |
| Security in R/3, CPI-C | RI | **29276** | SAPCPIC: Where are passwords visible? |
| Security in R/3, Customer Exit | * | **37724** | Customer exits in SAP log on |
| Session Manager | OR | **74089** | Generation of Session Manager menus takes too long |
| SU53 | RI | **23342** | You are not authorized to ... > Analysis |
| SU53 | OR | **78106** | *SU53*: Authorization value contains special chars |
| SU53 | OR | **87926** | *SU53*: Object name overwrites object text |
| System Profile Parameters | RI | **31395** | System parameters: Defined where? Displayed how? |
| Transporting | RI | **11013** | Transporting profiles and authorizations |
| Transport | OR | **86544** | Transport profiles, author., in logon language |
| Transport, User Buffer | RI | **84209** | Authorizations not current after profile transport |
| Transporting, AS/400 | * | **37987** | AS/400: Importing transports |
| User administration | RI | **10187** | Users with large master rec. missing authorizations |
| User administration | * | **144194** | Central user distribution: too many ALE processes |
| User administration | * | **143999** | Cen. User adm.: SU01 Last change not always dspled. |
| User administration | * | **136647** | Use of wildcard '*' in authorizations |
| User Information System (SUIM) | OR | **40689** | New reports for the user information system |
| User Information System (SUIM) | OR | **85158** | Where-used list: Surnames missing in user list |
| User SAP* | RI | **4108** | How to assign an identifier to SAP* |
| User SAP* | RI | **4326** | How do I delete the user SAP*? |
| Users and Authorizations Kernel Functions | * | **171191** | Authorization Buffer is filled during each logon |
| Workbench/Customizer Organizer | * | **167393** | Development Class Change only with admin. Authorization |

| Subject | Release | Note | Title |
|---|---|---|---|
| Payment Program/Payment Transfer | * | **182120** | Incorrect authorization check for check management |
| IM Reporting (no LIS) | * | **183847** | MB51, MB5, MB5S: PO/sched. Agreement displays |
| All Countries (Personnel Administration) | * | **161191** | Auth. Check of not integrated personnel numbers |
| All Countries (Personnel Administration) | * | **171580** | Authorization level M is handled incorrectly |

# Appendix B: Frequently Asked Questions

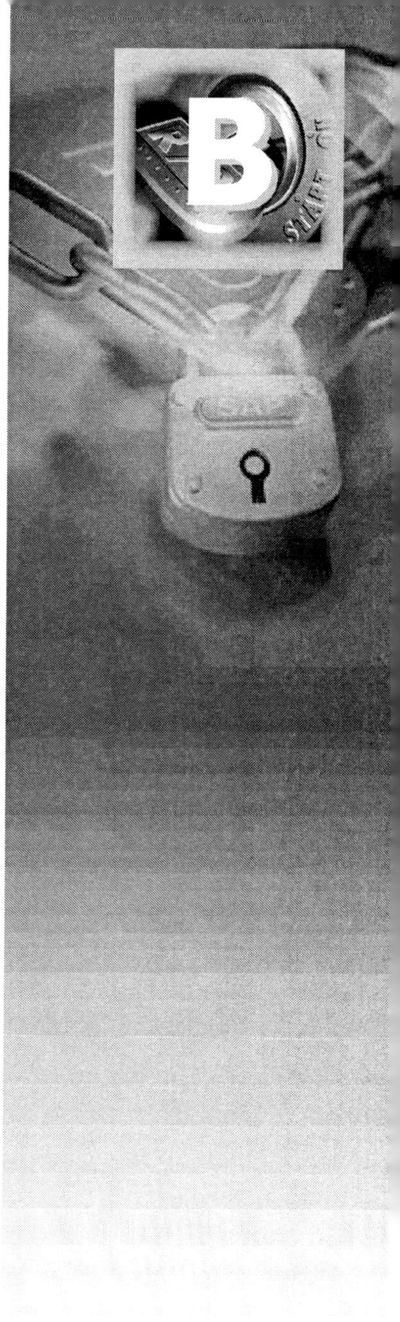


## Contents

# Overview

This appendix contains some of the most frequently asked questions about R/3 and the Profile Generator (PG). We hope the answers:

- Help you to better understand the system
- Facilitate your implementation
- Resolve basic system issues

# R/3 Initial Screen (SAP Easy Access Menu) and Favorites

### If a user has several activity groups assigned to them with the same transaction code, will the transaction code appear multiple times on the SAP Easy Access Menu? Is there a way to "merge" the repeated transaction codes?

The transaction code will indeed appear multiple times. At present, there are no merge capabilities to eliminate repeated transaction codes.

### If a user has many activity groups or many transaction codes, is there an effect on performance (for example, the time for the first screen to be processed)?

Each "branch" or "node" on the SAP Easy Access menu represents items that a user has access to. Performance does go down with a large number of nodes, but from preliminary testing by SAP development groups, the system can handle an extensive number with a reasonable response times (more than a user can handle in a reasonable lifetime). The testing of a menu/branch/node structure of 20,000 nodes has been shown to provide good response times.

### What happened to the Report Trees in 4.6 and are they in the SAP Easy Access screen?

Report Trees in 4.6 are now client-independent. They exist in the SAP Easy Access menu. Reporting trees and area menus have been merged in functionality and in one tool. Please see the release notes related to this topic.

### Will one user (for example, the Authorizations Administrator) be able to view the Favorites of another user? Will a user be able to add any transaction code to their favorites?

At present, one user cannot view the favorites of another user. A user can add any transaction code to their favorites. However, a user cannot execute the transaction code unless they have appropriate authorizations (S_TCODE) to do so. Favorites, at present, are not viewed by SAP development, as "security relevant."

If a user copies some transactions from their menu to their favorites and later on these transactions are taken out of their activity group, the transactions still remain in the user's favorites. The user will not have authorizations for these transactions anymore. Manual maintenance of the favorites is needed.

# Profile Generator Setup

### How does the AUTHORITY-CHECK work with the Profile Generator?

When AUTHORITY-CHECK is called, the system checks whether the system parameter, *auth/no_check_in_some_cases* is set to *Y*. If the parameter is not set to *Y*, the normal AUTHORITY-CHECK is conducted. If the parameter is set to *Y*, it searches for an entry in table *USOBX_C* (refer to structure *USOBX_C*) with the current transaction code and authorization object. If nothing is found, the normal AUTHORITY-CHECK is conducted. If an entry is found (and *USOBX_C-OKFLAG* is set to *N*), no check is performed, regardless of the actual user profile. In all other cases, the regular authorization check is conducted and succeeds when the user profile contains an authorization with the corresponding expressions for the current object.

In a new installation the parameter is set to *Y*, since the PG is already activated. For more information, see chapter 3 *Setting up the Profile Generator*.

### Do I need to shut down and restart the instance after I changed the system profile parameter?

Yes, you must restart the instance after adding the instance profile parameter. For further information on how the PG is set up and what settings need to be performed, see chapter 3, *Setting up the Profile Generator.*

# Working with the PG and Profiles

### Can I include an existing profile in an activity group?

Yes, you can include an existing profiles (single and composite) into an activity group. Please refer to chapter 8, the section *Manually Postmaintaining Authorizations.*

### Why is only one profile sometimes generated?

Technically, only 150 authorizations can fit into one profile, so several profiles are created for large activity groups. Since the last two digits are required for the internal numerator, only 10 digits are available for the profile name.

### Can I manually change generated profiles from PFCG in SU02?

You can only change generated profiles with transaction *PFCG*, where you have all the same options as in transaction *SU02*. To block generated profiles for maintenance, use *SU02*. In other words, if the profile was created as a result of *PFCG*, you cannot change it with *SU02*.

### Can I include manual profiles in the Profile Generator?

In the PG, choosing *Edit → Insert auth. → from profile* includes all authorizations from a manually created profile in a generated profile. These authorizations remain in manual status and, if the activity group changes, the authorizations remain unchanged when you compare the profile. However, you can only insert authorizations from a single profile.

### Can I manually enter generated profiles in the user master record?

Yes, but we do not recommend it for the following reasons:

- If the activity group is extremely large (or is increased by a later change), the PG generates more than one authorization profile and automatically updates the affected user masters, which have to be manually inserted.
- When assigning with the PG, you can include time dependencies and assign the profile for a limited time period.

### Is it possible to change the profile name later?

Yes, only the long text (descriptive text) to a profile can be changed with the PG, which does not affect the authorizations used in this profile. It is not possible to manually change the technical profile name of a generated profile with the PG.

### Can I copy an activity group, and will this procedure also copy the profile?

Yes, you can copy activity groups, but while copying, choose a different name for the new activity group. The activity group, the activities, and the profile data are then copied. See chapter 6, the section *Copying and Deriving Activity Groups* for detailed information.

### If I generate a profile that may use a previously built authorization, will the system create a new one or use the existing one?

Every time you generate a new profile for an activity group, new authorizations are created. It takes longer to search for existing authorizations with the same values than to create new ones. Each authorization can only be used in one activity group.

### How do I restrict activities by specific time periods?

Even if you do not use BC-Org, you can still choose to assign activity groups to users for a limited time. This action makes sense, for example, when your company enters a new fiscal year. Physical inventory activities should only be allowed for a limited period of time. For further information on setting time limits, refer to chapter 9, *Assigning activity groups*.

### Which transactions are used by the PG to maintain a specific authorization?

On the *Change Activity Group: Authorizations* screen, choose *Utilities → Settings → For Overview of Authorization Object Use,* to import an icon into your profile tree. This icon, which looks like a mountain, displays the transactions for which the *Check/maintain* flag is set for the object.

## Authorization Checks (SU24)

### What do the different check flags stand for?

*CM (Check/Maintain)*

- An authority check is carried out against this object.
- The PG creates an authorization for this object and field values are displayed for changing.
- Default values for this authorization can be maintained.

*C (Check)*

- An authority check is carried out against this object.
- The PG does not create an authorization for this object, so field values are not displayed.
- No default values can be maintained for this authorization.

*N (No check)*

- The authority check against this object is disabled.
- The PG does not create an authorization for this object, so field values are not displayed.
- No default values can be maintained for this authorization.

*U (Unmaintained)*

- No check indicator is set.
- An authority check is always carried out against this object.
- The PG does not create an authorization for this object, so field values are not displayed.
- No default values can be maintained for this authorization.

To learn more about transaction *SU24,* please see chapter 12, the section *Reducing the Scope of Authorization Checks.*

### Why Does the Profile Generator Maintain Authorizations for More Objects Than You Can See?

With transaction *SU24* you can browse the entries of tables *USOBX_C* and *USOBT_C*. The PG uses table *USOBX_C* to check for transactions in the corresponding activity groups where the authorization object's authorizations are to be maintained. The corresponding values are stored in table *USOBT_C*. But, the parameter transactions are an exception. These transactions work with a powerful core transaction, restricted by the initial screen of the core transaction that is filled and skipped in the parameter transaction.

The authorization checks are coded exclusively in the core transaction. However, the authorization field values can be specified more precisely in the parameter transaction than in the core transaction. The PG first maintains the authorizations in *USOBX_C* and *USOBT_C* under the parameter transaction, and then lists authorizations for all authorization objects in the core transaction as *to be maintained.* As a result, for the parameter transaction, more authorizations are maintained than can be seen in *SU24.*

For example, transaction *OC41* (which maintains exchange rates) uses the general table maintenance transaction *(SM30).* On the initial screen for *SM30,* enter the view name **V_TCURR** and choose *Maintain.* The PG reads *SU24* for *OC41* and maintains an authorization for the object *S_TABU_DIS* with the *Change* and *Display* values for the activity and the *FC32* value for the authorization group. The PG also reads *SU24* for the core transaction *SM30* and maintains an authorization for *S_TABU_CLI* with a *BLANK* value, because this object is not listed in *SU24* under *OC41.*

### How Do I Reduce the Scope of Authority Checks in R/3?

See chapter 12, the section *Reducing the Scope of Authorization Checks* in this guide.

### How Can a Customer Include Individual Authorization Checks in a Transaction?

For individual authorization checks, there are the so-called field exits. These are enhancements that you can create for any data element, and where you can implement your checks. Field exits are always run if a field was selected on a screen for this data element. When you create the field exit, you can determine whether this check should be carried out:

- Always
- Only on certain screens
- Only in certain transactions

For more information on field exits, see the online documentation for transaction *CMOD.*

### When Starting Transactions, What Should I Know About the New Authorization Check?

Each time a new transaction is called (*MM01,* for example), the system checks whether the user is authorized to start that transaction. (No check takes place for the ABAP command *CALL TRANSACTION.*) If you use the PG and its menus to form activity groups, an authorization for object *S_TCODE* is automatically defined for each activity group. It contains the exact transactions that you selected for the activity group.

If you want to allow transactions that you did not assign using the activity group menu, manually add an authorization for object *S_TCODE,* and enter the missing transactions. You can now avoid problems when you compare the authorization data.

*S_TCODE* is found in the object class *Nonapplication-specific Authorization objects.* The *S_TCD_ALL* authorization is delivered with the profile *SAP_NEW_30E,* which allows you to execute all transactions. By giving restricted authorizations for *S_TCODE,* the user administrator can restrict individual users or user groups to remain within the transactions they require. The authorization checks defined by the developer with transaction *SE93* (transaction maintenance), or in the ABAP source code, continue to be performed.

These are the advantages of the new authorization check:

- A guarantee that each transaction performs at least one authorization check
- An easy way to determine which transactions a user can execute

## Upgrade Procedure (SU25)

### Is there a way to run the SU25 steps in "simulation" or "test" mode?

At present, it is not possible to run a simulation or test mode.

## Including Transactions or Reports

### How can I include individual authorization checks in transactions?

For individual authorization checks, there are the so-called field exits. These are enhancements that you can create for any data element, and where you can implement your checks. Field exits are always run if a field was selected on a screen for this data element. When you create the field exit, you can determine whether this check should always be carried out only on certain screens or in certain transactions. Further details on field exits can be found in the online documentation for transaction *CMOD*. NOTE: Field exits get invoked *after* the user attempts to process a particular screen. Field exits do not prevent users from entering a screen which contains the field. As field exits can be made to be screen and program specific, it is possible that SAP can define new screens and programs which will (e.g. after an upgrade) render the field exit as non-functional. Field exits of such sort must always be considered after an upgrade.

## Missing Authorizations

### What if an authorization is still missing for the generated profile, and the user gets a "No authorization..." message?

Remember that if implementing any portion of the HR component of the R/3 System, there is a possibility to enable certain parts of the authorization system that are NOT related to the profile generator (example: Implementing HR structural authorizations). As such, the "No authorization...." message would be correct and the system is not in error. If convinced that there is an error in the system, create an SAPNet – R/3 Frontend note to specify the transaction and the precise error message (preferably a copy of the output from transaction *SU53*) that you included in the activity group. To correct the error in your system, see chapter 8, the section *Manually Postmaintaining Authorizations*.

# User Administration

### How can the work involved in maintaining/setting up authorizations be divided up amongst multiple people?

Since the PG selects the authorization objects, it is no longer necessary to decide who maintains authorizations for an object. The check against the object *S_USER_AUT* is carried out only if the administrator manually inserts an authorization. With authorization object *S_USER_AGR*, a check is possible at the activity group level to see who is allowed to select which transaction for this activity group. For a further classification into authorization and activation administrator, see *Administration When Using the Profile Generator* in the online documentation.

# Transporting

### Do the USOBX_C and USOBT_C need to be transported between clients?

No. These tables are client independent. They only need to be transported between systems.

### Is there a way to transport activity groups?

Yes, you can either use the standard transport connection in transaction *PFCG* or use mass-transport activity groups inside the PG.

### Does the transport of activity groups between two clients, in the same system, work with transaction *SCC1*?

Yes, after being imported to the target client, the transported activity groups are now active and do appear in transaction *PFCG*. This step was not possible in releases before 4.0B.

### What if the generated profile only has authorizations for object S_TCODE?

The SAP default tables may not have been copied into the customer tables. If you get a *No organizational data available* message, run transaction *SU25*. See chapter 3 in this guide for more information on transaction *SU25*.

# Tables

### How do I display the transaction codes that are included in an activity group?

Run transaction **SE16** *(Tools → ABAP Workbench → Overview → Data Browser).*

1. Enter **AGR_TCODES** in the *Table name* field.
2. Display the table contents (*Table → table contents*).
3. In the selection screen, enter the activity group name in the field *AGR_NAME*.

4. Choose *Execute* (or choose *Program → Execute).*
5. You will receive a list with all transaction codes in that activity group name.

### How do I display in which activity group a certain transaction code is being used?

Run transaction **SE16** *(Tools → ABAP Workbench → Overview → Data Browser).*

1. Enter **AGR_TCODES** in the *Table name* field.
2. Display the table contents (*Table → table contents*).
3. In the selection screen, enter the transaction code in the field *TCODE.*
4. Choose *Execute* (or choose *Program → Execute).*
5. You will receive a list with all activity groups name where that transaction code is being used.

### How do I display which activity group is used by which user?

Run transaction **SE16** *(Tools → ABAP Workbench → Overview → Data Browser).*

1. Enter **AGR_USERS** in the *Table name* field.
2. Display the table contents (*Table → table contents*).
3. In the selection screen, enter the activity group name in the field *TAGR_NAME.*
4. Choose *Execute* (or choose *Program → Execute).*
5. You will receive a list with the names of all users that are assigned to that activity group.

### How do I display which user is assigned to which activity group?

Run transaction **SE16** *(Tools → ABAP Workbench → Overview → Data Browser).*

1. Enter **AGR_USERS** in the *Table name* field.
2. Display the table contents (*Table → table contents*).
3. In the selection screen, enter the name of the user in the field *UNAME.*
4. Choose *Execute* (or choose *Program → Execute).*
5. You will receive a list with the all activity groups this user is assigned to.

### Does the authorization object allow activities not maintained in table *TACTZ?*

Table *TACTZ* contains allowable activities for an authorization object. If you find a transaction looking for an authorization object with an activity that is not maintained or offered by PG, maintain the missing activity for the appropriate authorization object in table *TACTZ* with transaction *SM30.* The PG then offers this value.

### What is the structure of table USOBX_C?

| Field name | Key | Description |
|---|---|---|
| NAME | X | Program/transaction/function module name |
| TYPE | X | Type of report |
| OBJECT | X | User master maintenance: authorization object |
| MODIFIER | | Last changed by |
| MODDATE | | Date of change |
| MODTIME | | Time of change |
| OKFLAG | | N = No authorization checks<br>X = Authorization checks take place<br>Y = Authorization checks take place; default values in USOBT_C<br>U = Not maintained |

The *NAME* and *TYPE* fields identify a transaction, and *OBJECT* identifies the authorization object. *MODIFIER, MODDATE, MODTIME* contain administrative information about the most recent changes. *OKFLAG* is important because when it contains the value *N*, no authorization check is performed for the transaction and authorization object.

#### Examples

Enter *NAME* = **VA01**, *TYPE* = **TR**, *OBJECT* = **C_STUE_BER**, *OKFLAG* = **N**. Every authorization check, AUTHORITY-CHECK OBJECT C_STUE_BER ID... will succeed, regardless of the user's authorization profile.

Enter *NAME* = **VA01**, *TYPE* = **TR**, *OBJECT* = **C_DRAW_TCD**, *OKFLAG* = **X** or another value <> **N**. An authorization check, AUTHORITY-CHECK OBJECT C_DRAW_TCD ID... will succeed only when the user's authorization profile contains the combination of fields or field contents, under ID.

# Appendix C: Important System Profile Parameters

## Contents

# Incorrect Logons, Default Clients, and Default Start Menu

Use the following system profile parameters to set incorrect logon limits and the default client:

- **Login/fails_to_session_end**

  This parameter defines the number of times a user can enter an incorrect password before the system terminates the logon attempt. The default is three characters, but this value can be set to any number between 1–99.

- **Login/fails_to_user_lock**

  This parameter defines the number of times a user can enter an incorrect password before the system locks the user from making additional logon attempts. If the system locks, an entry is written to the system log, and the lock is released at midnight. The default is 12 times, but this value can be set to any value between 1–99.

- **Login/failed_user_auto_unlock**

  This parameter unlocks users who got locked out by logging on incorrectly. If the parameter is set to *1* (the default), due to a previous incorrect logon attempt, the system does not consider users locked. The locks remain if the parameter value is *0*.

- **Login/system_client**

  This parameter specifies the default client. This client is automatically filled in on the system logon screen. Users can enter a different client.

- **Login/ext_security**

  Since Release 3.0E, external security tools such as Kerberos or Secude have managed R/3 System access. If this parameter is set, an additional identification can be specified for each user (in user maintenance) where users log on to their security system. To activate, set the value to X.

- **Start_menu**

  This parameter specifies the default start menu for all users and can be overwritten with the user-specific start menu (transaction *SU50*). The default is *S000*, and this value can be set to any other area menu code.

# Setting Password Length and Expiration

Use the following system profile parameters to specify the minimum length of a password and the frequency with which users must change passwords.

- **Login/min_password_lng**

  This parameter defines the minimum password length. The default is three characters, but this value can be set from three to eight characters.

- **Login/password_expiration_time**

  This parameter defines the number of days after which a password must be changed. The parameter allows users to keep their passwords without time limit and leaves the value set to the default, 0.

To make the parameters globally effective in an R/3 System, set them in the default profile, *DEFAULT.PFL*. To make them instance-specific, you must set them in the profiles of each application server in your R/3 System.

## Specifying Impermissible Passwords

To forbid use of a certain password, enter it in table *USR40*. You can maintain this table with transaction *SM30*. In *USR40*, you may also generically specify prohibited passwords.

There are two wild-card characters:

- A question mark (?) means a single character.
- An asterisk (*) means a sequence of any combination characters of any length.

Examples:

- *123** in table *USR40* prohibits any password that begins with the sequence 123.
- **123** prohibits any password that contains the sequence 123.
- *AB?* prohibits passwords that begin with AB and have an additional character, such as ABA, ABB, and ABC.

## Securing SAP* Against Misuse

**Login/no_automatic_user_sap***

If the parameter is set to *1*, then *SAP** has no special default properties. Resetting the parameter to *0* allows logins with `SAP*`, password `PASS`, and unrestricted system access privileges. Even if you set the parameter, ensure that there is a user master record for *SAP**. If a user master record for *SAP** exists, it behaves like a normal user, is subject to authorization checks, and its password can be changed.

## Tracing Authorizations

**Auth/check_value_write_on**

By entering transaction `SU53` in the *Command* field, you can analyze an authorization-denied error that has just occurred in your session. This function is active only if you have set the system profile parameter to a value greater than *0*. By default, the function is inactive, and the parameter value is *0*.

## Profile Generator and Transaction SU24

**Auth/no_check_in_some_cases**

By using transaction `SU24`, you can activate or deactivate authorization checks for transactions. This function is active only if you set the system profile parameter to *Y*. By default, the function is inactive, and the parameter value is *N*. To activate the parameter, set the value to *Y*. If you want to work with the PG, the parameter must be set.

## User Buffer

**Auth/auth_number_in_userbuffer**

To have a good performance in the system, the names of all the authorizations included in a user master for a user are buffered in a table. In the standard, this buffer can deal with up to 1,000 authorizations. If a user has more than 1,000 authorizations the value can be set to *2000*. The default value is *800*, but this default value can be set to between 1–2000. If for any reason you have to reset the user buffer, see Online Service System note *84209* and *75908* for detailed information.

## No Check on Object S_TCODE

**Auth/no_check_on_tcode**

From Release 3.0E, the system checks on object *S_TCODE*. In specific instances, you can turn this check off, but this step results in a big security risk for your system. By default, the function is inactive, and the parameter value is *N*. To switch the check off set the value to *Y*.

## No Check on Certain ABAP Objects

**Auth/system_access_check_off**

Use this parameter to turn off the automatic authorization check for particular ABAP language elements (file operations, CPIC calls, and calls to kernel functions). This parameter ensures the downward compatibility of the R/3 kernel. By default, the function is inactive (value = *0* and check remains active). To turn the check off, set the value to *1*.

# RFC Authority Check

### Auth/rfc_authority_check

You can use this parameter to determine whether object *S_RFC* is checked during RFC calls.

- Value = *0,* no check against *S_RFC*
- Value = *1,* check active but no check for *SRFC-FUGR*
- Value = *2,* check active and check against *SRFC-FUGR*

# Glossary

| Term | Definition |
|---|---|
| **ABAP** | ABAP is an interpretative, platform-independent, fourth-generation language tailored to develop business applications. The language supports structured programming and contains elements necessary to call external relational databases through open SQL calls or database-specific native SQL calls. The developer is not required to know the underlying infrastructure. |
| **ABAP Development Workbench** | The ABAP Development Workbench provides a complete client/server runtime environment and extensive management and tuning tools. The Workbench is SAP's integrated tool set to develop enterprise-wide client/server applications. This toolset is particularly suited to R/3 customers who want to enhance standard R/3 business applications with customized, add-on functionality.<br><br>The major components of the ABAP Development Workbench include:<br>▸ ABAP Programming Language<br>▸ ABAP Dictionary<br>▸ ABAP Editor<br>▸ ABAP Function Library<br>▸ Data Modeler<br>▸ R/3 Repository<br>▸ Test Tools, Screen Painter<br>▸ Menu Painter, Workbench Organizer/Transport System<br>▸ R/3 Repository Information System<br>The workbench is also available to companies who are not R/3 users, but want the benefits of SAP's proven development environment for their software projects. |
| **ABAP Dictionary** | The ABAP Dictionary, a component of the Development Workbench, is a central information base for application and system data. The Dictionary describes this data from a logical point of view and stores information about how the data is reproduced in the underlying relational database. The ABAP Dictionary is active and fully integrated with the other Development Workbench tools. Any changes to the Dictionary are automatically and immediately updated throughout the system. |

| Term | Definition |
|---|---|
| **ABAP Editor** | The ABAP Editor, a component of the Development Workbench, provides the following functions to support the application developer:<br>▸ Syntax check with automatic correction of errors<br>▸ Insertion of coding patterns for frequently used instructions<br>▸ Navigation into other workbench tools<br>▸ Generation of where-used lists for all data objects<br>▸ Split-screen editor with program comparison |
| **Activation administrator** | An activation administrator activates authorization profiles and authorizations, making them effective in the system. These administrators can only change or delete the profiles and authorizations specified in their authorization profile. |
| **Active plan version** | This is the plan version that the R/3 System recognizes as valid and currently in operation. The information in the active plan version is used to perform all day-to-day processing and cross-application maintenance.<br><br>You must designate one plan version active if:<br>▸ You are a SAP Business Workflow user<br>▸ Integration is active between PD and other R/3 business applications, such as the PG<br><br>Your selected plan should reflect the actual state of operations at your firm. Any other plan versions your company maintains can be used to experiment with different organizational scenarios. |
| **Activity group** | An activity group is a collection of individual activities that are routinely performed together or are affiliated in some way. For example, the translation tasks activity group could include all tasks, reports, and transactions associated with translation. You set up activity groups by linking single activities under an activity group name. A single activity may be included in more than one activity group. |
| **Application server** | A computer where the application logic and application control services of the R/3 System run. |
| **Authorization** | An authorization is the authority to perform a particular action in the R/3 System. Each authorization refers to one authorization object and defines one or more possible values for each authorization field listed for that authorization object. A user's authorizations are combined in a profile that is entered in the user's master record. |
| **Authorization administrator** | The user responsible for maintaining authorizations and authorization profiles is the authorization administrator. For security reasons, this user should not be authorized to activate authorizations and profiles or to maintain user master records. Otherwise, one user would single-handedly define, activate, and assign system access authorizations. |

| Term | Definition |
| --- | --- |
| **Authorization check** | This check decides whether a user is authorized to execute a particular function. Processes, functions, and data accesses in the R/3 System can only be performed when user authorizations have been checked in the respective system and application programs. |
| **Authorization concept** | General access to a standard database for different applications requires reliable mechanisms designed to ensure the confidentiality of personal information. A multilevel, graded authorization concept has been set up to regulate data access. Only those people with active user master records can access the system. The authorization concept covers the structure and functionality of authorization assignment and checking in the R/3 System. Authorizations protect the system from unauthorized access. |
| **Authorization field** | One element of an authorization object is the authorization field. In authorization objects, these fields represent values for individual system elements, which undergo authorization checking to verify a user's authorization. |
| **Authorization group** | An authorization group is the combined fields of the authorization objects *S_DEVELOP* (program development and program execution) and *S_PROGRAM* (program maintenance). The authorization group field contains the name of a program group that allows users to perform the following operations:<br>▸ Execute programs<br>▸ Schedule jobs for background processing<br>▸ Maintain programs<br>▸ Maintain variants<br><br>When creating a program, you can specify an authorization group as one of the program attributes. This step allows you to group programs for authorization checking. |
| **Authorization object** | Another element of the authorization concept is the authorization object that allows you to define complex authorizations. An authorization object groups up to 10 authorization fields in an "AND" relationship to check whether a user is allowed to perform a certain action. To pass an authorization test for an object, the user must satisfy the authorization check for each field in that object. |
| **Authorization profile** | The authorization profile is another element of the authorization concept that gives users access to the system. The profiles contain authorizations identified by the authorization object and the authorization name. If a profile is specified in a user master record, the user has all the authorizations defined in that profile. |
| **Authorization trace** | This is a transaction that records all the required authorization objects in a processing step. |
| **Background process** | The background process is the noninteractive execution of programs, which in the R/3 System, are handled like online operations. Background processes often use the same programs that control the dialogs. |

| Term | Definition |
|---|---|
| **Business process** | Business processes group tasks made across cost centers in your company. This process enables you to structure your company's processes by function.<br><br>Examples include:<br>▸ Developing a product<br>▸ Drawing up a quotation<br>▸ Purchasing a material<br>▸ Processing an order |
| **Business Workflow (SAP)** | This support, provided for by transaction processing in the R/3 System, takes into account the business environments' needs. |
| **Check indicator** | A check indicator is set to determine whether authorization objects are unmaintained, not checked, checked, or checked/maintained. |
| **Client/server architecture, 3-tier** | Owing to the software-oriented client/server architecture of the R/3 System, logic and data of the three implemented levels—database, application, and presentation services—can be distributed among dedicated servers. The individual services can be flexible, either as clients or servers, depending on the tasks to be performed in each case. |
| **Composite activity groups** | A composite activity group is an activity group that contains multiple activity groups. |
| **Customizing & Configuration** | In SAP terminology, customizing is the implementation of configurations within the flexibility of the R/3 System. It is the basis for every R/3 project, whether it is an introduction, subsequent project stage, or process change. The configuration includes:<br><br>▸ R/3 Procedure Model, a procedural guide for structuring a SAP implementation<br>▸ R/3 Reference Model in the Business Navigator, a graphical description of business processes<br>▸ Implementation Guide (IMG), menu-led parameter settings<br>▸ Project management through upload and download facilities and to and from Microsoft Project<br>▸ A model company (IDES), a fully integrated and preconfigured system used for training and testing<br><br>The customizing tools also belong to the Business Engineering Workbench and are provided at no extra charge with the R/3 System. Add-on customizing is discussed in the *ABAP Development Workbench* section. |
| **Database server** | This is the computer where a database is installed. Specially optimized hardware may be used for running databases. |

| Term | Definition |
|---|---|
| **Desktop** | A PC that is used as a workstation is considered to be desktop. Ideally, the desktop has access to all systems and functions needed for a user to manage authorized tasks. |
| **Dynpro** | Short for dynamic program, a dynpro consists of a screen and associated processing logic, such as validation procedures. Each dynpro controls exactly one dialog step. |
| **Easy Access Menu** | The Easy Access menu is SAP's new GUI for working with the R/3 System. The Easy Acces menu is based on the user role template that has been assigned to an user. The menu contains only those transactions and reports that the user got assigned through the activity group assigned to him. Therefore the user will only see those transactions he is allowed to perform.<br><br>A user can choose between two different views of R/3:<br>▸ The complete SAP menu<br>▸ The user-specific menu |
| **Generate** | This function saves and activates an object. Before activating the object, the system automatically performs a consistency check. |
| **GSS-API** | The GSS-API is the standardized Security API with a standard communication model to abstract from the individual products and their characteristics. The Common Authentication Technologies (CAT) work group of the Internet Engineering Task Force (IETF) defines the standardization proposals. The functional specification of GSS-API Version 2, the version supported by R/3, is currently an Internet draft. |
| **Human resources planning** | Personnel planning and development deals with anticipating future personnel needs. Planners should consider short-, medium-, and long-term goals when considering company policy and the costs involved. Good human resources planning ensures that the company has the appropriate number of employees with the required skills in the correct position. |
| **IMG activity** | An Implementation guide (IMG) activity is an explanation of a system-setting activity. Activities in the IMG are linked directly to the corresponding customizing transactions, used to create the appropriate system setting. You can use IMG activities to record the notes that document your system settings. You can also base the recording or status of project management information on IMG activities. |
| **Implementation** | This process involves switching from an existing management system and business practice and having R/3 run part of, or the entire, business. |

| Term | Definition |
|---|---|
| **Implementation Guide** | Also referred to as the IMG, the guide is a tool for configuring the R/3 System to meet customer requirements. For each business application, the implementation guide:<br>▸ Explains all the steps in the implementation process<br>▸ Tells you the SAP standard (factory) settings<br>▸ Describes system configuration work (activities) and interactively opens the activities<br><br>The IMG are structured as hypertext. The hierarchical structure reflects the structure of the R/3 business application components and lists all the documentation related to implementing R/3. The IMG contains active functions with which you can:<br>▸ Open customizing transactions<br>▸ Write project documentation<br>▸ Maintain status information<br>▸ Support your project documentation work and the management of your R/3 System implementation. |
| **Implementation project** | This project relates to the implementation of a specific group of R/3 functions and processes with a common go-live date. |
| **Implementation strategy** | An implementation strategy is an approach to R/3 implementation. The strategy is based on long-term perspectives and includes all steps across the whole enterprise planned in connection with implementing the R/3 System. Establishing this strategy is an essential part of project preparation and impacts the sequence of implementation projects. |
| **Infotype** | Infotypes allow you to describe, or define the different attributes that objects have. Within personnel development (PD) there are many different infotypes, each one describing a specific set of attributes. Some infotypes apply only to certain types of objects, while others can be defined for any type of object. |
| **Instance profile** | The instance profile contains application server-specific configuration parameters, which complete the set values of the default profile. |
| **Job** | A job is a general classification of work duties, such as secretary and manager. Many employees may have the same job classification. That is, there can be 20 secretaries and eight managers. Jobs should not be confused with positions (see below). |
| **Menu** | Menus are control elements, offering the user a range of options which, when chosen, prompts the system to execute an action. The layout of the menu bar has been defined for each R/3 System level. Menu options are selected either with a single mouse click or by positioning the cursor and by pressing *Enter*. |

| Term | Definition |
|---|---|
| **Menu bar** | A menu bar is the bar across the top of the window located just above the standard toolbars. When you choose a menu option from the menu bar, you open a dropdown menu with different choices. The system automatically includes the *System* and *Help* menus. |
| **Name range** | The name range is a key area of a table. It effectively reserves part of the key area only for customers or for SAP. |
| **Network security** | Network security is a network connection configured to protect SAP and its customers from problems, such as unauthorized access inherent to WAN network connections. |
| **Organizational level** | Organizational levels are hierarchical levels where certain data in a material master record is created. Examples of organizational levels are client, plant, and storage location. |
| **Online Service System** | See SAPNet – R/3 Frontend notes |
| **Password** | A password is a user code that comprises the following elements that users need to logon to the system:<br>▸ String of figures<br>▸ Letters<br>▸ Special characters that the user must enter<br>▸ A user ID |
| **Plan version** | A plan version is a designated area where you deposit, or store, sets of information. Whenever you enter any information in PD, you must specify the plan version where the information should be kept. A single plan version could include information from any of the PD modules, such as Organization and Planning, Seminar and Convention, or Shift Planning. You can maintain more than one plan version. This allows you to use different plan versions to represent different scenarios for your firm. However, you must designate one plan version as the active plan if you are a SAP Business Workflow user and if integration is active between PD and other R/3 business applications. |
| **Position** | Positions are the individual employee placements or assignments in a company (for example, secretary of marketing or a sales manager). By creating positions and creating relationships between the positions, you identify the authority structure or chain of command at your firm. Positions should not be confused with jobs (see above). |
| **Presentation server** | A computer, usually a PC or Macintosh, used for presentation in the R/3 System is called a presentation server. |

| Term | Definition |
|---|---|
| **Process flow view** | The process flow view is one of the two navigation paths in the Business Navigator, the other being the component view. The process flow view of the R/3 Reference Model provides process-oriented access to the scenarios and processes in the Model. It is arranged as a structure with the following levels:<br>▸ Enterprise areas<br>▸ Scenario processes<br>▸ Processes |
| **Process selection matrix** | The process selection matrix is a model type in the R/3 Reference Model. The matrix describes the assignment of processes to scenarios, which are the columns in a process selection matrix. Processes belonging to a scenario are listed and assigned under that scenario (column head). Scenario and process icons provide access to corresponding EPCs. |
| **Profile** | A profile is a collection of authorizations for particular user groups, entered in the user master record. The same profile can be assigned to any number of users.<br>There are two types of authorization profiles:<br>▸ Simple, a collection of authorizations for a particular task<br>▸ Composite, a collection of several simple profiles |
| **Profile comparison** | When an activity group is modified using transaction *PFCG*, its associated authorization profile is not automatically updated. The user must carry out a profile comparison to ensure that the authorizations contained in the authorization profile correspond with the new contents of the activity group. |
| **Profile Generator** | The Profile Generator (PG) supports the authorization administrator setting up the authorization concept at the customer site. According to a set of application components chosen by the administrator, the PG automatically creates an authorization profile. The administrator can then easily customize and modify the authorizations in the profile by using special maintenance transactions offered by the PG. |
| **Program attribute** | A property of a program is called a program attribute. The attributes of an ABAP program define its basic characteristics, so that the system can process it correctly. The program attributes include the following elements:<br>▸ Program title<br>▸ Program type<br>▸ Program status<br>▸ Authorization group<br>▸ Development class |

| Term | Definition |
|---|---|
| **Push button** | Push buttons, or buttons, are graphical control elements that you click once to execute the functions linked to them. In the R/3 System, you can also start functions with the keyboard. To do this, place the cursor on the button and press either the *Enter* key or *Enter* button. Push buttons may contain text or graphic symbols. |
| **Radio button** | The radio button is another graphical control element that allows the user to select an item from a list of fields. If the user is allowed to select several fields at once, checkboxes are used. |
| **Release Changes and Upgrades** | You can generate specific IMG for release upgrades or changeovers. These guides contain a specific list of IMG activities, including all changed or new functions in the new R/3 release. This facilitates the implementation of release projects. All release notes can also be immediately accessed from this location. |
| **Report** | A report selects data from a database and displays it in a structured form for analysis. You may print the report results or display them online. The system also provides the option of saving the selected report data, to review without having to re-create it. |
| **Responsibility** | Responsibilities differentiate authority profiles generated from activity groups. Responsibilities are linked to authority profiles and to activity groups. An activity group is an object where you collect a number of system activities. An authority profile is generated using PG, which designates the user's authorities in the system. Responsibilities don't exist in 4.6 any more. |
| **SAP Business Workflow** | SAP Business Workflow 3.0® comprises technologies and tools to automatically control and execute cross-application processes, which primarily involves coordinating the:<br>▸ Persons involved<br>▸ Work steps required<br>▸ Data (business objects) that need to be processed<br><br>Our primary goals with the workflow are to reduce throughput times, to reduce the costs involved in managing business processes, and to increase transparency and quality. |
| **SAPNet - R/3 Frontend notes** | The SAPNet – R/3 Frontend (formerly known as Online Service System) provides a direct communication link to SAP, allowing customers to quickly and efficiently obtain problem-solving information for the R/3 System. |
| **SAP standard menu** | From the SAP standard menu, you can access the full range of SAP functions. |

| Term | Definition |
|---|---|
| **SAP GUI** | SAP GUI is the graphical user interface of the R/3 System. |
| **SAP router** | SAP router is a software module that acts as part of a firewall system. SAP router simplifies the configuration of network security and the routing of traffic to and from R/3. The SAP router establishes an indirect connection between the R/3 network and an outer network. There is restricted access to the application layer between client software and the R/3 application server. |
| **Screen** | A screen is, essentially, the primary window of a session. |
| **Secure Network Communications (SNC)** | Within the framework of the Secure Network Communications project, SAP is implementing the GSS-API in R/3, enabling R/3 to be integrated into company-wide network security systems, such as Kerberos or SecuDE. As the GSS-API is the standard interface in the security area, SAP operates with all GSS-API compliant security systems. |
| **Select** | This function allows you to select an object for further processing by placing the cursor on the object and clicking on the object. |
| **Session** | A session is a window where the user processes a certain task. When you log on to the R/3 System, it automatically opens the first session, but you can simultaneously open up to nine sessions. The number of the current session appears in the status bar. |
| **Session Manager** | The Session Manager does not exist in Release 4.6 anymore. It has been substituted with the Easy Access Menu. |
| **SSCR** | SAP Software Change Registration (SSCR) is a procedure that registers all modifications to R/3 Repository objects and provides an overview of modified R/3 Repository objects. SAP matchcodes and tuning measures, for example, creating database indices and buffers, are not registered by SSCR. |
| **System parameter** | A system parameter is the basic system configuration required to ensure smooth functioning of the software. |
| **Table** | Data can be arranged in table form. A table consists of columns (data values of the same type) and rows (data records). Fields identify a record. |
| **Transaction** | A transaction is a series of related steps required to perform a certain task. |
| **Transaction code** | A sequence of four characters represents a SAP transaction. To call a transaction in the R/3 System, you can follow an IMG path or enter the transaction code in the command field. For example, *SM31* is the code for the table maintenance transaction. |
| **User maintenance** | User maintenance transactions allow the system administrator to create and maintain user master records. This process includes generating and assigning authorizations and their profiles. |

| Term | Definition |
|---|---|
| **User master record** | This record contains important master data for an R/3 System user. Only users with a user master record can logon to the system. A user's authorizations are defined in the user master record. |
| **User role template** | A user role template is an activity group which serves as the basis for the user menu when an end user logs on to R/3. |
| **Validity period** | Validity periods define the life span of an object or infotype record. When creating objects and infotype records, specify a validity period by providing a start and an end date. |
| **Work process** | The application services of the R/3 System perform special work processes, such as for dialog processing, updating of the database as dictated by change documents, background processing, spooling, and lock management. Work processes can be assigned to dedicated application servers. |
| **Workbench Organizer/ Transport system** | The Workbench Organizer is a central management tool for large-scale project management that supports individual developers and large project teams.<br>The Organizer also does the following:<br>1. Organizes related project components into orders<br>2. Locks the components during development<br>3. Stores a version of each project between transports<br>The transport system supports the transfer of development objects between distributed systems by creating an extensive log recording of when and why each transport was executed and who executed it. |
| **Workflow task** | A workflow task is a multistep task defined by the customer, which references a workflow definition. Workflow tasks (organizational management object type WF) are client dependent, have a validity period, and are plan-version specific. |
| **Workplace** | The main right tile on the screen where most work is performed (field entries, selections, etc.). On some windows, the workplace covers the entire screen. |
| **Workplace menu** | The left tile on the *SAP Easy Access* screen where each node represents different levels in the R/3 System. The *User menu* and *SAP standard menu* buttons provide different views of the workplace menu. |
| **Workload monitor** | The workload monitor displays the distribution of the workload across servers and transactions. |

# Index

## A

# B



# C

## P



## Q



## R

## U

## W